Hometown Memories . . .

Hitch Up the Horses We're Going to Town

Tales from the Good Old Days in North Central Michigan

A TREASURY OF 20TH CENTURY MEMORIES

OTHER BOOKS FROM HOMETOWN MEMORIES

Claremont Tales
Taylorsville Tales
Burke County Tales
Catawba County Tales
Cleveland County Tales
Blue Ridge Tales
Foothills-Piedmont Tales
Memorable Tales of the Smokies and Blue Ridge Mountains
Caldwell County Tales
Albemarle Tales
Lincolnton Tales
Montgomery Tales
Lee County Tales
Rowan County Tales
Cold Biscuits and Fatback and other Richmond County Tales
Skinnydipping in the Mule Trough and Other Rockingham County Tales
Lunch in a Lard Bucket and Other Cabarrus County Tales
Rooster in a Milkwell and other Moore County Tales
It Always Rains When Old Folks Die and other Tales from Davidson and Randolph County
A Prayer for a Baby Goat and other Tales from Alamance County
The Mill Village and the Miracle Bicycle and other Tales from Gaston County
Wilmington Tales
Guilford County Tales
Asheville Tales
The Class of '47 Was Me and other Tales along the North Carolina Coast
The Elegant Tarpaper Shack and other Tales from the Heartland of North Carolina
Outhouse Spiders and Tin Tub Baths—Tales from the Blue Ridge Mountains
Wringer Washers and Ration Stamps—Tales from Forsyth County
Front Porch Stories, Back Porch Bathrooms —Tales from Alexander, Davie, Iredell, Rowan, and Yadkin Counties
Crank Victrolas and Wood Cook Stoves —Tales from Green, Lenoir, Pitt, and Wayne Counties
Mules, Mud and Homemade Soap —Tales from Anson, Stanly and Union Counties
Life in the Good Old Days in Alamance, Caswell, and Rockingham Counties
Life in the Good Old Days in Catawba, Lincoln, and Gaston Counties
Life in the Good Old Days in Buncombe and Henderson Counties
Moonshine and Blind Mules and other Western North Carolina Tales
Ain't No Bears Out Tonight and other Cabarrus County Tales
Two Holers and Model T Fords and other Randolph County Tales
Ham Biscuits and Baked Sweet Potatoes and other Montgomery, Richmond , and Scotland County Tales
Possum Hunters, Moonshine and Corn Shuck Dolls and other Tales from Wilkes County
Chasing the Ice Truck and other Tales from New Hanover County and Wilmington
Steam Whistles and Party Line Phones and other Tales from in and around Roanoke
Squirrel Gravy and Feed Sack Underwear—Tales from the Tennessee Mountains
Miners' Lamps and Cold Mountain Winters—Tales from Southwest Virginia
Cold Outhouses and Kerosene Lamps—Tales from Southeastern Ohio
Coal Camps and Castor Oil—Tales from Southern West Virginia
Brush Brooms and Straw Ticks—Tales from Northwest Georgia
Dust Storms and Half Dugouts—Tales from the Upper Panhandle of Texas
Lessons by Lamplight—Tales from Southeastern Kentucky
Frozen Laundry and Depression Soup—Tales from Upstate New York
Paper Dolls and Homemade Comforts—Tales from Northwestern Virginia
One-Room Schoolin'—Tales from Central West Virginia

Cow Chips in the Cook Stove—Tales from the Lower Panhandle of Texas
Moonshine and Mountaintops—Tales from Northeast Tennessee
When We Got Electric…—Tales from Northwest West Virginia
Outside Privies and Dinner Pails—Tales from Southwest Iowa
Milking the Kickers—Tales from Southwest Oklahoma
Rolling Stores and Country Cures—Tales from Northeast Alabama
Penny Candy and Grandma's Porch Swing—Tales from North Central Pennsylvania
Rumble Seats and Lumber Camps—Tales from Northern Michigan
Lye Soap and Sad Irons—Tales from Northwest Missouri
Almost Heaven—Tales from Western West Virginia
Hobos and Swimming Holes—Tales from Northern Wisconsin
Saturday Night Baths and Sunday Dinners—Tales from Northwest Iowa
Sod Houses and The Dirty Thirties—Tales from Northwest and North Central Kansas
Coal Oil Lamps and Cattle in the Crops— Tales from Northern and Mountain West Idaho
Morning Chores and Soda Fountains—Tales from The Texas Hill Country
County Schools and Classic Cars—Tales from Northeast Iowa
Dust Storm Days and Two-Holers—Tales from Southwest and South Central Kansas
Wood Fire Saunas and Iron Mines—Tales from Michigan's Upper Peninsula
Kerosene Lamps and Grandma's Washboard—Tales from Northeastern Missouri
Picture Shows and Five Cent Moon Pies—Tales from North Carolina's Blue Ridge Mountains
        and Foothills
Corncob Fuel and Cold Prairie Winters—Tales from Eastern and Northeastern South Dakota
Filling Stations, Shine, and Sorghum Molasses—Tales from The Tennessee West Highland Rim
Down in the Holler—Tales from Southwestern Virginia
Monday Washdays and Outhouse Roosters—Tales from West Virginia's Eastern Panhandle
        and also Northwestern Maryland
Party Line "Rubberneckers"—Tales from Southwest and South Central Wisconsin
Tumbleweed Feed and Gopher Trapping for Pocket Money—Tales from Southeast
        and South Central North Dakota
Willow Whistles and Barefoot Summer Days—Tales from Southeast Kansas
Pie Suppers and Wind Up Record Players—Tales from Southwest Missouri
Victory Gardens and Long Handled Dippers—Tales from Southwest Minnesota
Wind Chargers and Syrup Dinner Pails—Tales from Southern South Dakota
Swimming Pits and Tire Tube Sledding—Tales from Southeastern Ohio
Iron Wash Kettles and Peddling Wagons—Tales from Southwest Kentucky
Company Script Cards and Battery Radios—Tales from Southern West Virginia
Threshing Rings and Chalkboard Lessons—Tales from Central Wisconsin
Rabbit Tobacco and Mountain Farms—Tales from The Tennessee Mountains
Field Mules and Buttermilk Cornbread—Tales from Northeast Georgia

At Hometown Memories, our mission is to save and share the memories of days gone by...before they are lost forever. As of this publication, we have created 92 books of memories, and saved and shared over 23,000 stories and 12,000 pictures. We hope you enjoy them!

Hometown Memories . . .

Hitch Up the Horses We're Going to Town

Tales from the Good Old Days in North Central Michigan

A TREASURY OF 20TH CENTURY MEMORIES

Compiled and edited by Todd Blair and Karen Garvey

HOMETOWN MEMORIES, LLC
Hickory, North Carolina

Hitch Up the Horses We're Going to Town

Publisher: Todd Blair
Lead Editor: Karen Garvey
Design and Graphic Arts Editor: Karen Garvey and Laura Montgomery
Marketing Research Director: Laura Montgomery
Office Services Assistants: Lisa Hollar and Tim Bekemeier
Warehouse Manager: Tim Bekemeier
Assistant Editors: Monica Black, Lisa Hollar, Danis Allison, Greg Rutz, Amanda Jenkins, Aubrey Rogers, Reashea Montgomery, Sandy Mathewson, Stephanie Hicks, Cathy Elrod, Pamela Beard, Sherry Calhoun, Lindsey Riley, Sabrina Rankin, Wendi Byas, Phil Gnadt, and Tiffany Canaday

ISBN 978-1-940376-20-2
Copyright © 2015

Published by

Hometown Memories, LLC
2359 Highway 70 SE, Suite 112
Hickory, N. C. 28602
(877) 491-8802

Printed in the United States of America

Acknowledgements

To those North Central Michigan folks (and to those few who "ain't from around here") who took the trouble to write down your memories and send them to us, we offer our heartfelt thanks. And we're sure you're grateful to each other because, together, you have created a wonderful book.

To encourage participation, the publisher offered cash awards to the contributors of the most appealing stories. These awards were not based upon writing ability or historical knowledge, but rather upon subject matter and interest. The winners were: Lorraine I. Bull of Bailey, MI; Wayne E. Diveley of Sanford, MI; and Donna Carpenter of Newaygo, MI. We would also like to give honorable mention to the contributions from Michael O. Patterson of St. Louis, MI and Laura Sue Piechowiak of Saginaw, MI. The cash prizewinner for the book's cover photo goes to Darrell Towersey of Alma, MI (you'll find their names and page numbers in the table of contents). Congratulations! It was extremely difficult to choose these winners because every story and picture in this book had its own special appeal.

Associate Editors

Wayne George Aebig
Barbara Ann Bell
Tom Boursisseau
Lorraine I. Bull
Mildred Cline
Betty E. Crawford
Mabel B. Crooks
Joanne Lee Durham
Mary Lou Ely
Elizabeth J. Gardner
Norma Aebig Halverson
Dave R. Jones
Carol Jurek
Frederick J. Karns
Diane Kern
Sally L. Kioski
Marsha A. Klein
Michael O. Patterson
Alta C. Reed
Karen Rolley
Sharon Kathleen Smith
Reva Swanson
Alan Van Duinen
Shirley A. Weber
William J. White
Marilyn Witting
Gloria Woodbury

INTRODUCTION

We know that most folks don't bother to read introductions. But we do hope you (at least eventually) get around to reading this one. Here's why:

First, the creation of these books is in its sixth generation after we took over the responsibilities of Hometown Memories Publishing from its founders, Bob Lasley and Sallie Holt. After forty nine books, they said goodbye to enjoy retirement, and each other. Bob and Sallie had a passion for saving these wonderful old tales from the good old days that we can only hope to match. We would love to hear your thoughts on how we are doing.

Second—and far more important—is the who, what, where, when, why and how of this book. Until you're aware of these, you won't fully enjoy and appreciate it.

This is a very unusual kind of history book. It was actually written by 309 Michigan old-timers and not-so-old-timers who remember what life was really like back in the earlier years of the 20th century in North Central Michigan. These folks come from all walks of life, and by voluntarily sharing their memories (which often include their emotions, as well), they have captured the spirit and character of a time that will never be seen again.

Unlike most history books, this one was written from the viewpoint of people who actually experienced history. They're familiar with the tribulations of the Great Depression; the horrible taste of castor oil; "outdoor" plumbing; party line phones; and countless other experiences unknown to today's generation.

We advertised all over North Central Michigan to obtain these stories. We sought everyday folks, not experienced authors, and we asked them to simply jot down their memories. Our intention was by no means literary perfection. Most of these folks wrote the way they spoke, and that's exactly what we wanted. To preserve story authenticity, we tried to make only minimal changes to written contributions. We believe that an attempt at correction would damage the book's integrity.

We need to include a few disclaimers: first, we asked for names because we think names make stories better. However, important names are missing in some stories. Several folks revealed the names of their teachers, neighbors, friends—even their pets and livestock—but left out the names of some important characters. Second, many contributors did not identify dates or names in pictures or make corrections to their first draft copies. We're sure this resulted in many errors, but we did the best we could. Third, each contributor accepts full responsibility for his or her submission and for our interpretation of requested changes. Fourth, because some of the submitted photographs were photocopied or "computer printed," their quality may be very poor. And finally, because there was never a charge, "fee," or any other obligation to contributors to have their material included in this book, we do not accept responsibility for any story or other material that was left out, either intentionally or accidentally.

We hope you enjoy this unique book as much as we enjoyed putting it together.

The Hometown Memories Team
August 2015

TABLE OF CONTENTS

The Table of Contents is listed in alphabetical order by the story contributor's last name.

To search for stories by the contributor's hometown, see index beginning on page 347.

Melvin J. Gay	311	Dave R. Jones	310
Verla Germain	82	Dorothy E. Jones	244
Laurence Gibson	316	William A. Jones	176
Robert Gofton	83	Carol Jurek	31
Frank J. Gotts	273	Susan Cunningham Kane	280
Genevieve Morell Gracey	337	Kay Kantola	205
Kent Graf	204	Frederick J. Karnes	169
Susan Granger	204	Richard K. Karns	60
Pauline Grant	331	Bernie Kelsch	107
Nicholas S. Green	23	Diane Kern	141
Rich Greenfelder	234	Sally L. Kioski	327
Velma Grey	178	Ruby Klanecky	88
Marge Griebel	225	Karl H. Klein	57
Joyce Griffin	73	Marsha A. Klein	198
Antonette Groulx	304	Erma Ott Kleinhardt	277
Donna Gunderson	59	Betty Konesko	225
Patti Gustin	74	Jerry J. Konopnicki	137
Richard "Dick" Guttowsky	49	Rula Koutras	256
Mary Ann Hale	254	Edwin M. Koziol	156
Norma Aebig Halverson	52	Paul Kruska	215
Thomas Haradine	94	Evald Kruut	73
Keith Hardy	112	Irene Lange	337
Patricia A. Haring	163	Richard Langin	23
Margaret Harris	240	Barbara J. Langley	69
Donna Hart	80	Charlene Laper	76
Richard E. Hartlep	91	Lois Laplow	176
Sandra L. Hecht	165	Donna LaRoche	70
Robert Gregor Hegler	217	Shirley Larson	26
Mary J. Heiskala	213	Louraine T. Latty	126
Elizabeth Hepworth	187	Judy Laux	44
Joanne Hetherington	73	Carolyn Lawmaster	103
Sharon Hilyard	111	Melvin R. Lefevre	67
Jack Hitchcock	124	Oliver "Ollie" Leigeb	120
Linda Hodges	336	Alberta Leiner	334
Margaret M. Holey	197	Bruce Kenneth Lennox	46
Lynn Holmquist	46	Marian Lewandowski	146
Ronald Hoodak	122	Diane Lintemuth	334
Creal Hoover	119	Jack L. Long	47
Dolores Howell	309	Cora Longstreet	110
Patricia Hubbert	303	Richard Lound	89
Dorothy I. Hulliberger	145	Patricia Love	289
Keith A. Humbert	137	Clara B. Lozen	323
Edwin W. Iles	192	Luann L. Ludwick	131
Edwin W. Jablonski	113	Richard Floyd Lumbert	333
Betty Jacobus	270	Esther A. Mack	136
Agnes Jason	207	Hayes J. Mack	135
Robert Jennings	38	Jack J. Mahar	321
Bille D. Jex	23	Barbara Green Martin	297
Helen Johnson	194	Florence M. Martin	24
Jeannette Johnson	271	Jean S. Mathieu	25
Merrily Ann Johnson	231	Julia M. Mazurowski	319
Michael E. Johnson	321	Joy McCrory	275
Mable Johnston	241	Dennette McDermott	40
Betty-Ann Jolin	293	Dorothy Clark McKandes	48

John McMillan	227	Jerry Schmolitz	73
Gerald Meade	35	Karen Schoeppach	184
Loretta R. Merritt	67	Martha Schoolcraft	129
Mary Jane Michael	333	Linda Benedict Schultz	343
Michael R. Miller	258	Joyce Abler Schumacher	229
Debby Mitteer	77	John Schwarz	305
Rita Morgan	56	Norma Seelye	183
Mary Morningstar	82	Clyde Shaffner	52
DeVere Mosher	44	Grover Shaw	306
Alma Moyes	36	Viola Shephard	230
Joan L. Mulder	212	Phyllis Jean Short	193
Patricia Murphy	138	James M. Shoup	267
Doris Murray	266	Virginia Showalter	134
Marian (Fabera) Neely	295	Emily Slivinski	325
Pamela Lillie Newman	250	Jerry Slivinski	325
Wanda Ogg	41	Katherine Smekar	35
Eugene Olivares	104	Sharon Kathleen Smith	159
Elaine L. Onan	245	Lillian M. Smokoska	24
Barbara L. Orlando	43	Reneé Sova	77
Tresa Pangborn	287	Violet Stachowiak	113
Betty J. Parker	155	Dolores Stack	179
Jean Parkinson	100	Lola Wright Steele	147
Carl Patterson	22	Shirley E. Stoddard	340
Michael O. Patterson	18	Robert R. Stroope	174
Joan S. Pavlick	271	Ann M. Stueber	34
Florence Pemberton	37	Tuesday Summers	257
Timothy L. Perry	84	Reva Swanson	128
Mildred Peterson	174	Marion Tedhams	253
Alice Piechotte	50	Donna R. Thiedman	284
Laura Sue Piechowiak	20	Ilene R. Thomsen	148
Lillian F. Pieniozek	248	Jack Thornton	273
Jerry Pietrzak	233	Marion Frahm Tincknell	152
Judy Pranger	54	Ann K. Tomcho	285
Mirdza S. Randall	53	Darrell Towersey	21
Joan Ransom	322	Curtis H. Truemner	38
Madeleine J. Reagan	323	Nellie Mae Everett Turner	301
Sharon Reavis	88	Evelyn Genson Urban	291
Richard Redifer	79	Betty J. Van Alstine	175
Alta Reed	117	Helen Van Andel	270
Janet M. Reis	177	Alan Van Duinen	324
Helen Rice	142	Keith Van Sickle	186
Laurel Richert	320	Bob Walker	222
Sharon Ritter	97	Kenneth Warner, Sr.	190
Robert K. Robart	314	Alma Elizabeth Watton	95
Charles Robinson	123	Shirley A. Weber	61
Marian K. Rodriquez	110	James H. Wetters	78
Karen Rolley	175	William J. White	200
Marlene Rood	339	Awilda Whitehill	256
Venessa I. Rosenfield	252	Louis H. Witting	259
Sylvia G. Rouech	120	Marilyn Witting	98
Carol L. Salgat	210	Janet J. Witucki	305
Ronald Sampson	40	Dorothy Baer Wolf	72
Floyd W. Schmid	238	Glori Woodbury	190
Delores F. Schmidt	147	Nancy Wrathell	53

The Tales...

True stories intentionally left just as the contributor wrote them.

Mother Saves the Day
By Lorraine I. Bull of Bailey, Michigan
Born 1933

This is my true story:

By the light of the kerosene lamp and with a cold, wet wind whipping around our old house, we children played school – always school – always on rainy evenings – and always big sister Evelyn, the only one of us kids who could read very well, was teacher.

My younger sister and brother, Joan and Johnny, known as "the twins," and I were lined up on the old brown imitation leather couch, along with my rag dolls, Joan's teddy bears, and Johnny's little toy black Scotty dog. Joan would only play school if her bears were counted as students. And Johnny followed suit with his toy dog. Poor Evelyn put up with this ragtag collection, as she wanted all the pupils she could get. She'd grit her teeth and hold the <u>Elson Basic Primer</u> in front of us and each bear and the dog in turn and read aloud, all the while pretending we were doing the reading.

Meanwhile, out in the kitchen our mother made supper on the old wood range. As she worked, she often sang bits of favorite hymns and songs from World War I. Many times Evelyn taught school to the background strains of *K-K-K-Katy*, *Till We Meet Again*, and *Let the Lower Lights Be Burning*.

On pleasant evenings, we all went down to the barn with Dad, and Mother would help with the milking. This was a fun time, as the barn cats would line up by our three cows, Lucy, Nellie, and Fanny, and sit there with their mouths open. Waiting. Every so often Dad would aim a teat at one of the cats and give a big squeeze. We'd giggle like mad, as the cat gulped down the milk!

But on this stormy night, Dad went to the barn alone, and we children played school. After a while Mother called, "Come! Wash your hands. We're about to eat. I see your daddy's lantern coming."

Then Dad, all dripping wet, entered the kitchen. As he set the milk pails beside the milk separator, he announced, "Old sow had her litter tonight. Only three of them. Then she stepped on one. Made a huge cut in its back."

"Oh dear!" cried Mother. "I'd better go see what I can do for it."

"No use," said Dad. "The gash is so deep that pig's probably dead by now."

Few people nowadays know how important one little pig was to our family's financial picture back then.

"We shall see," said Mother and promptly lined us children up by the kitchen window. "Don't you dare move!" she said. "If you kids get to 'mukin' around and tip over the lamp, you'll burn the house down!"

There we stood; our noses pressed to the cold glass, with tears streaming down our

Lorraine Slott Bull, Johnny Slott, Poochie (the dog), Lorraine's mother, Alice Slott, Evelyn Slott, and Joan Slott Ransom in 1940

15

Lorraine's parents, John and Alice Slott in 1952

cheeks as we watched the lantern light grow smaller and smaller and at last disappear inside the barn. It was the first time we'd ever been left alone, and we were scared to death!

Soon, although it seemed like forever, Mother and Dad were back in the kitchen. "John, get the Aladdin lamp going. I'll need the brighter light. Evelyn, get my sewing basket. Lorraine, Lorraine, where are you?"

I'd taken one look at that bloodied mound Mother was just removing from her clutched apron, and I had crawled behind the wood box. With her free hand, Mother was clearing a spot on the table. With no nurses training and only an eighth grade education, Mother proceeded to sew up the gigantic gash. I poked my fingers into my ears, but nothing would drown out the pig's screams or the twins' excited comments, for while I hid behind the wood box they had climbed up on chairs for a better look.

"Hurry, Lorraine, Mama's sticking the needle right into the baby piggy! Oh, look! Now she's pulling the thread through it!" Hurry up, Lorraine; you're missing all the best parts!"

I stayed behind the wood box and sobbed.

After a while, Mother was coaxing me out. "Come see the baby piggy now, Lorraine. Look, Sugarnose. He's all better." Tenderly, she led me into the living room where Evelyn sat in a rocking chair holding the baby pig. He was snuggled up in one of the twins' old receiving blankets and nursing from one of their discarded baby bottles.

And Evelyn? Evelyn was all smiles, no doubt visualizing a new pupil for her classroom.

And me? I looked from that little pig to my mom and I beamed. What did I ever have to fear? Wasn't I the luckiest little kid in the whole world? Didn't I have a mother who could do anything?

Lorraine Bull in 1942

The Flats
By Wayne E. Diveley of Sanford, Michigan
Born 1950

It was in June of 1958 when my folks moved from Johns Drive to M-47, or Midland Road in Saginaw Township. I was seven years old and my sisters were nine and twelve. There was a girl living next door that was my age and a boy on the other side who was a couple of years older than myself. We all got along quite well. It was a very nice area, and Dad had an acre of land. We had a lot of lawn that included a hill in the back that was difficult to mow in the summer, but was a winter paradise for us kids for sledding! The back of the lot

16

was lined with elm trees. Past that was acres of flat land, some woods, and the Tittabawssee River. What more could a young boy ask for? It was like having your own park right in your own backyard.

The flats and the woods belonged to a farmer a few houses south of Dads. In the summer, the flats were occupied with a herd of cattle. There was no fence between the woods and the flats and the cattle would wander into the woods, especially on hot days. Now, if you go into the woods and climb a tree, you could drop down on a passing cow and ride her right through the forest. However, if she don't care to be ridden, you'd better be prepared to grab another tree branch and ease yourself down to safety!

Now, this farmer that owned the woods didn't want the woods and he told us boys to cut down any and all the trees we wanted to. So, we chopped down an area of trees and built ourselves a "corral" and fenced in about six or seven cows. That was just for fun. They stayed penned up for a while until they decided to leave and walked right through our fence. Remember, we were just kids.

Anyway, the cows had to stay up by the barn in the winter because the flats always flooded in the winter and spring. In the winter, we had acres of ice, plus you could even skate through the woods, usually. Every kid I ever met, including myself, is an idiot! You put on your clothes, put on your coat, put on your socks, put on your skates, and go out for hours. Hey kid! Ever hear of frostbite? That was more painful than getting your peepee caught in your zipper! Any man that says he never did that as a kid at least once is lying!

Remember: the back of the lot was a row of elm trees. This boy decided to build a tree house. So I did. I climbed up one of these trees as high as I could, about ten feet, and there I began to build my tree house. It turned out to be rather small, rather hard to get up into, and very unsafe. Dad got a real kick out of the construction of what I called a "tree house." The following weekend, Dad started building me a "real" tree house. I overheard Dad tell my mother, "If I don't build that kid a decent tree house, he's gonna kill himself!" Mom said, "Well, you'd better get to it!" so he did, and it was a masterpiece. He built a six foot by six-foot deck at the base of the tree and then added posts on all four corners about four feet high. He then put another deck on top of the first with a ladder reaching to it. Then, on that deck was another ladder going up the tree about 15 feet high. This ladder lead to a trap door that went into my new tree house. It was about six by six, had a tin roof and glass windows that opened and were safe, and was....a masterpiece!

"Hey, wait Dad, there's another tree just down this row where you could build a platform for jumping off and swinging on a rope." He built that, too, about ten feet off the ground. The rope was tied to a limb about 30 feet high. Now, to get to this platform, you had to take hold of the rope on the ground, run, and swing yourself up to the ten-foot high platform. Worked out great!

Well, this story is over. I'm at the end of my rope, and you may be, too! Those really were the "Good Old Days!"

A Home of Love and Peace
By Donna Carpenter of Newaygo, Michigan
Born 1936

On the nights when sleep does not come easily I return to the house at 1915 Ring St. in Saginaw, Michigan. I walk up the steps to the large covered porch and open the door, and there it is. In the autumn of 1944 when I was eight and my sister, Roma, was six years old, we moved there with our mama and daddy. Roma and I shared over four years of our childhood there. While writing this I had an insight that has taken me over sixty-five years to realize. I have tried to share that house with others, and they look at me like they had just heard about a house described on Zillow. Trying to explain the birdseye maple floors and the white organdy crisscross curtains did not impress them at all. But I didn't give up!

They had to hear about the summer Daddy told us he could buy one full size bike and we would have to share until the next summer. We chose a J.C. Higgins with white fenders with blue trim, a passenger seat over back fender, and a fancy light on front fender. We shared the bike, and the next summer Daddy said he was prepared to buy another, but one of us would have to take the old bike. That was fine with me! I think I considered it mine from the beginning. None of my audience seemed overly impressed with that bike of mine. Well then, I would share more.

I never see hollyhock without remembering those in our back alley. We used toothpicks and turned them to dancing girls. Or I would describe the large purple lilacs that grew on the west side of the house. I spoke of taking our Saturday night baths and getting all warm and comfortable listening to Judy Canova's radio show.

And then today it happened! I realized it never was about the house! It was about experiences and relationships that formed our little family. It was about my daddy, after having worked all day, sitting down on that living room couch and trying to teach his little girl how to do long division.

It was about the time my sister and I discovered if you turned this little thing on the valve you could make air come out of our 1936 Ford's tire. One day while happily enjoying our new discovery, we looked up, and there was Daddy smiling at us. He had been bothered with a leak in that tire and had had it in and checked and they could find nothing. Now he had discovered his leak.

Another day, I was busily cleaning Daddy's pipe stand and his pipes. It was the middle of the day, and he generally was at work. He must have come home for lunch. I turned and looked behind me and there he was, smiling. He said, "You know, I wondered what was always stopping up my pipes."

Nothing ever feels any better than being put to bed with a sheet or blanket that has been warming over the stove. Mama would tuck us in by covering us with one of those warm blankets.

There was just something about those two. They loved us, and they loved each other. I recall when he hugged her I tried to wiggle in, too. Our home was one of peace. There was never, no not ever, fighting, or arguing. Roma and I never fought (still don't). Our parents did not fight with each other, and we did not fight or sass our parents. We always knew they were the big people, and they were the boss.

Looking back at the popcorn, and the car rides the four of took in our 1936 Ford, and the shows we went to together, it was peaceful. Our world was at war. I recognized the window stars but wasn't affected, because we knew no one in that terrible war.

It really would have made no difference where the house was; it's where we were together. Both Mama and Daddy are gone now and Roma and I look back on a sweet little house on Ring Street, but what we are really remembering is the love and protection bestowed upon us there!

A Kid's View of the Depression
By Michael O. Patterson of St. Louis, Michigan
Born 1933

It's funny how our mind is able to remember things from so long ago. As I write this, I'm 81 years old and I can still remember back to when I was three or four years old. I remember going to visit my grandfather Swank when he was dying of cancer. He was at home in an upstairs bedroom and he was on the bed when I first saw him. He looked frail, gray-haired, and wasn't moving hardly at all. He could hardly talk, but he managed to say, "Hi Michael," to me. It bothered me that he was so sick. My mother asked me to give grandpa a kiss, and it was something I really didn't want to do. They urged me on, so I kissed him on the cheek real fast and then ran for the stairs. He died shortly after that, there in his home. I wish that I would've known him better. I understand that he was a good man and worked hard. He had raised my mother and five other children. That was the first time that I'd come face-to-face with death, but not the last.

Strange, but one of the other things I remember has to do with being disciplined. It happened at about the same age as above. My Grandma and Grandpa Patterson were visiting us. I must've done something wrong because I had been spanked and set on the back porch. I was sitting there feeling sorry for myself, thinking of vengeance, mad, and trying to figure out why this was happening to me. As I sat there, my grandmother came out and sat down beside me. She didn't baby me or comfort me or anything like that. She just started talking to me, she told me she knew how I felt. She said that I was having bad thoughts, mean thoughts, and I needed to stop thinking like that. I thought to myself, how does she know what I'm thinking? She told me to calm down and to tell my brain to stop thinking bad thoughts. She went on to explain

18

that those are the thoughts of the devil. She said to just tell those thoughts to get out of the way. She said to tell the devil to get out of my head. She explained that by doing that we can control our own feelings. Then she simply got up and went back in the house. I tried it, and it worked. I used that advice throughout my life.

Believe it or not, we lived in a Sears Roebuck packaged home. It had been built by some other people and then purchased by my mother and father, with a mortgage to the bank. It had three bedrooms, a living room, and kitchen. It had a porch on the back and a porch on the front. It had a pump in the backyard for water and an outhouse behind the garage. There were just two of us kids at the time, myself and my brother who was 16 months younger. There was a big backyard to play in and we took full advantage of it. We were lucky because there were several other children our age nearby. So we always had someone to play with.

We were fortunate it turns out, because both of our parents worked. Dad was a baker at a local bakery located downtown. It was called the Model Bakery and dad worked long hours there. It was the middle of the Depression and very difficult for people to find work. My mother also worked part-time at the local butter and poultry plant. So, much of the day, we had a lady who came in to look after us boys when mom was at work.

The town we lived in, Alma, located in central Michigan, had many small businesses and manufacturing companies at that time, and many of the people in our end of town worked for these companies. Many, however, did not have jobs. One of my uncles joined the Navy and another became employed with the WPA and helped put in sewers and water lines to the house. I remember it was a big day when we had running water in the kitchen and a toilet and bathtub installed upstairs. We still didn't have hot water however, because the gas lines weren't put in until a couple years later. Mother cooked on an old kerosene range. There probably aren't very many people around who remember this type of range. It had a large glass container that had to be filled with kerosene and turned upside down and placed on the end of the stove. There were four burners that were round wicks that had to be lit with a match and the oven had wicks in the bottom of it that also had to be lit

by hand. The amount of heat that you wanted was controlled by a knob that moved the wick up or down. You have probably figured out already that it wasn't a very safe appliance.

My mother had to take me to school the first day of kindergarten, because I was determined not to go. However, after a few days you couldn't keep me away. After the first day, we made arrangements so that I could walk to school with some of the older kids in our neighborhood. Back then, there seemed to be a lot of childhood illnesses—mumps, measles, scarlet fever, chicken pox, and many more it seemed like—and I had them all. There weren't any cures for these diseases back then and the doctor would just make you go to bed and take some obnoxious-tasting liquid. Then he'd tack a sign on the side of a house, which warned everybody that the house was quarantined, and to stay away. By the way, doctors came to your house in those days. They would expect to get paid, and hoped it was cash, but many times, they would accept homemade bread, chickens, or something else.

It was about this time that something happened to change the way that I looked at my father. Dad always took us boys with him whenever he went to town, and we liked to go with him. He knew everybody it seemed, and everyone spoke to him. We were walking down Superior Street and were in front of the Strand Theatre, when the policeman came down the street and stopped to talk with dad. Dad asked him how things were going and he said, "Fine," and said that he had been taking lessons on ways to subdue criminals. With that, he said, "Here, let me show you," and he reached over, grabbed my father's hand, and began twisting his finger, saying, "See, I can put you right down on the ground." But my father didn't move. Instead, he stood tall, looked down at the policeman, and said, "Go ahead and break it. I'm not going down on my knees here, in front of all these people, on Main Street, and particularly not in front of my two boys." The policeman let go of my dad's finger and stood up with his head down and said he was sorry. Dad wished him well and we went one way and he went another. It wasn't until after we and the policeman had parted that dad rubbed his finger very vigorously. Dad never said anything about it again. But it was something that stuck with me through the years.

It was December 7, 1941. Everything changed that day. The Japanese had bombed Pearl Harbor. The United States was now in two wars, one in Europe and one in the Pacific. My brother Fred had been born earlier that year. My dad felt that he needed to do something. He talked it over with mother and said that he was going down to enlist in the Service. Mother was upset, but she knew that he had to do what he had to do. He was dejected when he returned from the enlistment office. He said that the man in charge told him to go home. He said that he needed to stay home because he was 31 years old and had four children. Well, dad still felt that he should be doing something for the war effort. He heard from his brother-in-law, that Dow Chemical was looking for men to guard their plant. Dad applied for and got the job. He rented a room and went to work in Ludington. It was about two weeks before we would see him again. Dad told my brother and I that we would have to pick up the slack. We would have to look after Mother and do the chores. We had already been carrying coal from the basement for the space heater in the room and then taking the ashes out and dumping them in the driveway. Now, we were going to have to make sure that the stove was stoked for the night. Also, we would have to go to store for mother, shovel the snow from the driveway, and otherwise do whatever mother needed done. It all went pretty well. In the morning, we would get the fire going, take out the ashes, get ourselves ready for school, and mother would have breakfast for us. When we came home after school, we would do it all over again. But we didn't mind, because we knew it had to be done and we knew how hard things were for mother. On July 29, 1942 (I was nine years old) I wrote dad the following letter:

Dear Dad,
Mama went up town Saturday. She bought a new dress and a pair of shoes. Come Back Soon. You know the lamp burned out last night, we put the kitchen light in it and now there isn't a kitchen light. Sharon is jumping on my back so I can't write very good. I will have to quit. Please write to me
With love,

Michael

This little letter was found in mom's things after she died in 2006.

Sixty-Eight Years of True Love
By Laura Sue Piechowiak of Saginaw, Michigan
Born 1931

In early 1945, my family moved from Dawson Springs, Kentucky to Saginaw, Michigan. I was fourteen years old at the time and I cried for days because I hated it here. I started school in the ninth grade and met some very nice girl friends.

We started going to a roller skating rink where you had old fashion skates, and they had skate boys with keys around their necks to fit and tighten the skates to your shoes. The boy that fitted my skates was the cutest boy I ever laid eyes on. We went skating regularly and I always looked for him. I finally got acquainted with him and found out he was eighteen years old, and was going to the army so I lied about my age. I told him I was seventeen. I fell in love with him on sight, and he liked me too.

He would not have given me the time of day if he knew my true age of fourteen. He went to the army for almost two years and we corresponded all while he served in Korea. I have all the letters he wrote to me from 1945-1946. They have yellowed with age.

When he returned home, I was just two months from my sixteenth birthday. Christmas of 1946, he asked me to marry him and because I had lied about my age, I thought it would be over. I had to confess the lie, so we went to the Strand drive-in for a chocolate malt and I had to tell him I was only fifteen. I thought my dream of being with him was over.

After all, he was twenty and I would not be sixteen until January second. He sat silent for what seemed like an eternity. Then he looked at me and said, "I love you and we will work it out." We waited until I turned sixteen and we were married on June 21, 1947. My dad would not sign for me because of my age. I had to have a parent's consent. My mother gave in for she knew if she did not, we would

20

find a way. We have three daughters. Cathryn was born May 16, 1948, eleven months after we were married. Shellie was born November 5, 1952, and Terry on February 3, 1961. We also have eight grandchildren, seventeen great grandchildren. We will be celebrating our 68 anniversary this June 21, 2015.

This is my true story of how I met and married the man I loved when everyone said it would not last. My husband turned 88 in November 2014. I turned 84 in January 2, 2015. Wow, where did all those years go?

Finis and Laura Sue Piechowiak and their family

Adventures in Scouting
By Darrell Towersey of Alma, Michigan
Born 1930

Scouting has been around for over one hundred years. Scouts have taught the importance of community service and discipline. Some of my fondest memories are the adventures my twin brother and I found ourselves on while we were growing up in the 1940s. Our dad was the Scoutmaster of Troop 110 at the Alma United Methodist Church. My twin brother and I were too young at the time to be in the Boy Scouts (you had to be twelve years old). Of course, when your dad is the scout leader, there are some benefits.

My dad was always looking to find a way to fund activities for his troop. Fundraising looked a lot different in the 1940s. Pizza kits, cookie dough, and selling candles were no sure fire way to make money. The Depression was wearing on everyone's purse strings so the Scouts had to be creative. The United States was in the middle of World War II and everyone was asked to do their part. There as a great need for newspapers, magazines, rags,

and cardboard. Collecting these items was a good way to make money for an organization and help with the war effort. On Saturday mornings my dad would hook up his trailer to his 1937 Ford, throw my brother Delbert and I in the car, pick up some Scouts, and drive around two to pick up newspapers.

A year later, the city was having a scrap rubber drive. The government needed all the old rubber that could be collect, old rubber tires, etc., for the war effort. The city parked a big semi-trailer in front of City Hall to fill with rubber. Even though my brother and I were still too young to be in Boy Scouts, we still wanted to be part of the effort. Our dad had us hook up Bonnie, our pony, to an old trailer. Then we picked up a couple of Scouts and headed out to collect rubber. One of our first stops was at a man's house who happened to write for the *State Journal*. He told us that we should have signs on the cart so people knew what we were doing. We went on but eventually the newspaperman caught up with us. He had made signs and put them on our cart for us. He also insisted we meet him later that afternoon at City Hall. All day we traveled around town collecting old tires and anything else made of rubber. As we made our way to City Hall, we were met by the newspaper writer, along with other city leaders. There in front of the semi-trailer, we posed for our picture that would be in the *State Journal*. My brother, Delbert, held on to Bonnie's neck while I help onto the reins with the other two Scouts in the cart. Much to our surprise, not only did our picture appear in the newspaper, but it also flashed on the screen of the Strand Theater prior to the movie for an entire week.

The Scouts continued to collect newspapers and other items needed for the war. Delbert and I finally were old enough to be actual Scouts. Our dad would drive the Ford and with no safety restrictions back then, everyone would just pile on. A couple of guys would sit on the fenders in the front of the car and hold onto the headlights. Two other guys stood on the running boards holding onto the doors and the rest would jump onto the trailer. War supply collection was a Saturday tradition. There were contests amongst school grades and any team with the Towersey Twins on it would always win.

One day Delbert and I traveled between to local junk dealers trying to get the best price on cardboard. The first offer was fifty cents a pound but by the time we were done, we had negotiated our way up to eighty cents a pound. During World War II, the government offered a General Dwight D. Eisenhower medal to any child that could collect 1,000 pounds of newspaper. Delbert and I both received one and mine is still pinned to my Boy Scout shirt.

One of my most memorable Scouting events occurred in the winter of 1942. It was around this time that someone in President Roosevelt's cabinet sent a small group of Navy men to study at Alma College. Alma College was small, and with most of the college age men in the service, the college was having financial trouble because of low attendance. So this helped both the Navy and the college.

One of the professors at Alma College was a young German man. His name, I believe, was Hans Ricker. The Navy students tormented him continually, making remarks about him being German and a Nazi. The professor came up missing, and all kinds of rumors spread around Alma. Most of the rumors surrounded the premise that the professor was a Nazi spy. The Alma police began to look for him. My dad went to the police and volunteered the Boy Scouts to help look for the missing man. The police declined the offer, alluding to the thought that kids would simply be in their way. Weeks went on with no clue as to his whereabouts.

It was a cold winter and the Pine River had frozen over. My dad organized a hike across the river. Using a hundred foot rope for safety, the boys all took hold as they crossed the frozen water to get to the Conservation Club cabin. If I remember correctly, the door was locked and my dad had left the key in his car. After instructing the older Boy Scouts to hold down the fort, my dad headed to the car to get the key.

While he was gone, we started walking around the park. We ended up on the south side of the park by the softball field. The equipment storage building that was attached to the press box sat next to the field. We were looking around and tried to open the door but it was locked. The window to the press box was open, and one of the Scouts crawled through the window and came out with a scarf and a hat on and glasses in his hand. Being inquisitive, the others started looking around to see if they could get into the equipment

room. One of the boys looked through a knothole and started yelling, "There's a dead man hanging in there!" All of the Scouts had to look in the knothole. We all stood around chattering and making up stories about who it might be until my dad came back from the car. When my dad finally returned we could not get the story out fast enough. My dad sent us promptly to the cabin to eat our lunches as he went to contact the police.

If you haven't yet guessed, it was the German professor hanging in the equipment building. It was a long time before any of us could shut our eyes and not see that man hanging. When the weekly paper came out, there was just a small article reporting that the professor had been found. No mention of the Boy Scouts and no mention of any kind of investigation.

Not many Boy Scouts can share a memory like that. Growing up I may not have had the technology that the kids have today. We were not entertained by computers and video games. The activities we engaged in would probably not interest many kids today, but we had fun helping out our community and the war effort. We did not have to go to movies to experience suspense and excitement. We created it for ourselves.

Lost Clothes
By Carl Patterson of Marion, Michigan
Born 1928

I was six years old in the summer of 1934. Our family of ten lived on a farm in Osceola County, Michigan. I had three older brothers. The four of us were within five years of age.

The Middle Branch River flowed across this farm. It was a nice warm day, a good day to go swimming. We got permission from our mother and walked back to the river where we stripped our clothes and hung them on some brush. We did not have bathing suits; never heard of them! So, we swam Nature's way.

As we stepped into the river, a huge whirlwind came along and swept away all our clothes. We tried to find them, but they were never seen since. As my brothers were all older and bigger, they chose me to go to the house for clothes and to explain to our mother what became of the ones we wore to the river.

I took my time!

Summer Vacation
By Nicholas S. Green of Stanwood,
Michigan
Born 1938

At the end of my sixth grade, my parents sent me to summer camp. I really had a ball at camp. We really got in touch with nature, like turtles, baby ducks, snakes, etc. On the camp property, there were the remnants of a rock walled basement. The boys at the camp found that the basement harbored hundreds of baby garden snakes. At the end of my vacation, I decided to catch a couple of dozen garden snakes, take them home, and hand them out to some of my friends. I put the two dozen snakes in a large brown grocery sack.

I didn't realize that my step-father was deathly scared of snakes. I brought the snakes in the house and set them down at the end of the couch. My parents worked the night shift at Kellogg's. Well the snakes somehow got out of the grocery sack and when my parents came home from work and turned the lights on, the snakes were crawling all over the front room floor. The night air was filled with screams and "#%)(&#$%.

Phone Memories
By Billie D. Jex of Saginaw, Michigan
Born 1931

When I watch my grandchildren using their cell phones to call and text their friends, I am reminded of my own telephone experiences many years ago.

Growing up on the east side of Detroit, Michigan in the 1930s and 40s, my family and many other families were unable to afford telephone service. Emergency and important phone calls were made at the local drugstore on a pay phone for five cents a call.

Finally, in December of 1946, my parents made arrangements to have a telephone installed. I was fifteen years old and could hardly wait to be able to talk to girlfriends and boyfriends on the new phone. At this time, the telephone number consisted of four digits preceded by an exchange. Our new number was Hickory 1947. The first two letters of the exchange were dialed followed by the number.

On New Year's Eve of 1946, we received many calls. The callers dialed Hi-1947. Some callers hung up when we answered and others wished us a Happy New Year!

Upon graduating from high school in 1948, my first full time job was with Michigan Bell Telephone Company as a long distance operator. My desire to talk on a phone came true again and this time I was paid to do so!

Reminisce
By Richard Langin of Sheridan, Michigan
Born 1958

Do you remember things when you were a kid? I do so let me share a few with you.

After the first moon landing I bought a plastic replica of the Apollo craft and its pad. One day the neighbor boy came over to play and went upstairs to my bedroom to play with the spacecraft. Shortly after the neighbor boy arrived, my parents could smell smoke upstairs. When my parents and I went upstairs, we found a pile of melted plastic on top of my dresser. The neighbor boy had lit a match under the spacecraft trying to send it back to earth!

During the 1970s disco was big, long hair and afros. One day after coming home from high school, I convinced my mother to put a perm in my hair. After my mother applied the perm, my hair rubbed out along the sides but my hair in the middle was flat! I looked like Bozo the clown! The only alternative was, yes you guessed it, to shave my head! The next day at school, the school kids thought it was a new fad and baldheads and Mohawk haircuts developed! Who would have thought a bad perm would lead to a new fad!

Some kids when they were younger swiped pumpkins. My friend and I swiped Christmas trees. One year after being chased by the farmer, we took the tree home to his mother and decorated it. After decorating my friend's mother said "Boy that's a beautiful tree." My friend said "Not bad for a swiped tree." My friend's mother was a minister and she said, "Boys undecorated that tree and take it back to that man!" As my friend and I walked up to that man's porch with that tree, he had a large grin on his face. The man said, "Boys you won't do this again will you?" My friend and I said "No sir!" A lesson learned.

The Cousins' Visit
By Lillian M. Smokoska of Saginaw,
Michigan
Born 1921

In the year of 1926 on an old farm in Reese, Michigan, a little five-year-old girl named Lilly was playing with her brother, sister, and several visiting cousins from Saginaw. The kids liked to go in the old barn and see the cows and pigs. It was stinky but they didn't mind the smell.

Lilly, the five year old had on her "Sunday Best" dress because her favorite Aunt, Aunt Anna, and her five children were visiting all day Sunday.

The "Old Folks" were all inside the house so the kids were all left on their own to do whatever mischief they could find. For instance one Sunday earlier, Paul, the oldest, buried our favorite cat alive. Thank God, Paul's little brother told on him and we drug our pretty black cat out alive but very groggy, just in time. We told our folks but he didn't get the "lickin" we had hoped for. He was a troublemaker.

Today, this Sunday, we all stood around the enclosure, which kept the pigs in the barn. The older kids were whispering and laughing to each other but Lilly didn't catch on. Her sister, Leona, nine years old, asked Lilly would she like a ride on the pig's back. In fact, they held the pig in place so Lilly could crawl on its back. They promised faithfully that she wouldn't fall off into the pig mess, and there was a double layer of it. So she let them help her onto the pig's back and she anticipated a nice smooth ride around the pen. But instead, the cousin whacked the pig on the butt and poor Lilly flew up in the air and down into the pig mess. And boy did she stink! As the other kids were laughing their heads off, Lilly ran crying into the house to her mother to be cleaned up. As usual, no one got punished. Lilly was sure glad when the cousins went home! Lilly was of course me!

Thieves and Liars
By Florence M. Martin of Gowen, Michigan
Born 1922

The story I am about to tell you goes a long way back. I grew up in Greenville. I was the fourth and first girl out of seven brothers. And then, the five sisters came along. We did not have it easy growing up. But, my father was strict when he was home after work. The one thing he was very strict about was thieves and liars. When I was around 15 years old, I went to Clay Street School. We lived at the end of South Webster Street. We always came home at noon for lunch. Well, I had the notion to stop at the dime store, which is still there. There was a balcony at the east end. I walked in to go to the school supplies, which was toward the front of the store on the north side. Well, I saw some nice shiny notebook paper. I always had to use Big Chief Tablet paper.

I looked around, and no one was in sight, so I slipped the notebook paper inside my jacket and slowly walked to the next aisle and out the door to school. I got on the corner of South Lafayette and crossed over on the other side. I don't know why I did that. Then, about four stores down, someone tapped me on the shoulder and asked, "What have you got there?"

"Nothing," I said.

"Under your jacket," he said.

So, I pulled it out and said, "Oh, you mean this?"

He took it and said, "Come with me." Well, I was scared to death. I was crying and begged him not to tell my dad. He would beat me or kill me because he hated thieves and liars. He took me up the back stairs where the

Stanley, Florence, and Ernie

24

Florence in 1936

offices are all open. To this day, I don't know what they said to me. Then, they let me go.

I was late for school, and the teacher never asked me why nor did my dad ever say anything. I think they knew that they put the fear of God in me…a lesson I'll never forget.

I helped bring up my five younger sisters and my own two sons. This is one thing I made sure they knew…that stealing and lying is a no-no. Then, I tell my story. Thank God, I learned a good lesson. So, that is my story, the God's truth.

The Cabin at Grass Lake
By Jean S. Mathieu of Midland, Michigan
Born 1963

My dad's cabin was an island of refugee away from the city and the sharks. Every weekend in the summer, my sisters, brothers, and I would load up the station wagon and head for the woods and a cute little swamp called Grass Lake. I would spend the hours gunning down frogs and snakes with a worn out BB gun. After that got old, Dad would pack everyone up, go to either Trout Lake or Hoister Lake, and swim for hours. The camp fires at night made everyone warm and cozy inside and then Sunday morning would come and hit like a brick wall. Back to the sharks.

We had an old BB gun lying around collecting dust, but when boredom settled in like rigor mortis, I would take it down and go hunting; small game at first, like leaves. Then I would move to bigger prey like frogs. I plugged a frog once and it made me sick, so I just stuck with non-living things. Although snakes were awfully tempting.

When Dad said lets go swimming, everyone would grab their pants running for bathing suits and something to float on. Either Trout or Hoister, it didn't matter. Trout Lake sported a rope swing and an old dam to jump off of. Hoister had a timber log that jettisoned over the lagoon, which was its jeweled attraction. Swimming across the lagoon to the other side, without getting a leach on you was monumental and considered highly respected.

The fire at night was the last hoorah before the end. All the people from the neighboring cabins would gather around the ritual pit. There was adult talk and kid talk, with the occasional, "Stop playing with the fire Phillip!" from a grown up. We always had an abundance of sparklers too. I don't understand the fascination, they lasted thirty seconds, and causes pain if you step on them, like an idiot.

I will always cherish my memories of Grass Lake. Mom and Dad are gone now. My sisters and brothers have cabins of their own. Oh, they invite me up and everything, but I feel like I am intruding on their memory building times. I will always cry for the cabin and my goodbyes will be written on these pages. Giving me the opportunity to think about those times gives me a sense of a time when I was free.

I wonder if the cabin cries for me?

War Years in Detroit
By D. L. Farnham of Big Rapids, Michigan
Born 1928

I was born in 1928 in Detroit. (The Depression started in □29. Recovery started with Defense work as preparation against Japan. Fortune Magazine warned to "get ready" as early as 1937!) The Draft caused labor shortages in all Detroit and we kids spent our allowances on war stamps out of patriotism towards the coming war. Help so scarce, my summers at 13 and 14 were in the Merchant Marines, restricted to the Great Lakes on the S.S. Columbia Steam.

Entering high school all boys were enrolled in R.O.T.C. and in three years, I rose to Captain with awards in Rifle Firing. With my uniform and saber, plus my target rifle, I rode the bus in public. (There was no bullying in school then!)

I finished college prep program in three years and finally got my parents' permission to "join-up." (I'd seen a Colliers Magazine ad saying if I was 16 and 17 in six months I could join the Coast Guard. At the Recruiter's, with my mother in tow, he foxily said, "Oh, that quota's full." But the same deal applied for the Paratroopers. My mother was horrified! (She had shielded me from sports to protect my hands as a budding artist. I taught Technical Illustration at Ferris State University for 28 years…I also had a fear of heights after seeing my dad fall.) So I enlisted, went to the 82nd Airborne Reserve and, after the war, served in the 84 Airborne called back to Korea and enrolled in college at Wayne University (later a State school) in Art of course. In six years of service, I made 32 jumps and joined our local Civil Air Smoke Jumpers and taught observation as I tested and passed flight tests. (The Air Force had taken over the Civil Air Patrol by then.) Got my wings!

Meanwhile, Detroit racial relationships had deteriorated from a great influx of families from the South. There was mass exits of whites to the suburbs like Warren, where we went so I could work in "War-Work" at the Chrysler "Missile Plant" prepping for war, this time with Russia. When they launched their first satellite, President Eisenhower then ordered seven-day and -night shifts to get ours up…I worked 4 p.m. to 4 a.m., seven days at a time! (I worked five years there.)

By the late □50s long-time (former) residents, who had flown from the city, could see disaster coming from the corrupt administrations and I moved my family and me to Big Rapids (50 miles north of Grand Rapids) to the bourgeoning town, as the Ferris campus grew exponentially.

Horse Rides
By Shirley Larson of Midland, Michigan
Born 1931

It was back between 1944 and 1945, my folks decided to move to a small farm on Merdian Road, toward Edenville from Sanford. There were three of us kids. My brother, who was sixteen months older than me, and my sister was three years younger. I was between thirteen and fourteen years old.

This farm consisted of a cow, two old workhorses, a goat, and a few chickens. It was always mine and my brother's job to milk the cow. Instead of taking turns, we each had a stool and got on each side of the cow and milked at the same time. There was no arguing over turns and saved a lot of time.

Now, I do not know what made us do it, but one day when the folks were working, we decided to surprise them and butchered the goat. I do not remember how we did it, but we had it all done, cleaned, and ready for our mother to cook. We must have heard them talking about it, as I do not remember getting into any trouble over it.

I can also remember about being bored on a Sunday afternoon when I was about fifteen years old. I decided to put the harness (all by myself) on one of those horses and hitched it to a buggy we had. I went down the road about a mile and a half to a girl friend's (Loretta Hyatt) house to see if she wanted to go for a ride. We had so much fun. We could not stop laughing as we rode down Flanders Beach Road on a hot summer day. I have never gotten over all the attention we got. The trip was about five or six miles. The beach was loaded with swimmers.

There was a neighbor kid (Willie Thomas) that lived down the road, and one day he and my brother had a bet of which horse would win in a race. Down the road they went, of course, my brother won the race, but as they returned, our horse began to stumble while going up our long driveway. Then he began to cough up blood and actually his lungs. He managed to walk out and lay down behind the barn and died right there. That is what my folks came home to. The consequences have long been forgotten.

This is only a few of the things I remember about this place, as we only lived there about four years. I married shortly after that, and then the childhood days are over fast. Now I am eighty-three years old, a mother of four, a grandmother of seven grandsons, a great grandmother of nine, and a great, great grandmother of seven.

You Will Go Places
By Wayne George Aebig of Rothbury,
Michigan
Born 1926

When I was seven years old, my dad asked me to help with the farm work. If I needed something, my dad was always there to help. He had fifteen cows, so he milked eight of the hardest ones, and I did the seven easy ones. I fed and grained the cows, and he did the horses, pigs, and chickens. When the weather was cold, I would get my chores done and run over to Carpenter School, build a fire, and run back home. Then I would take a bath, change clothes, and run back to school.

We had a very bad winter in 1936. The snow in our front yard was about twenty feet deep. When we ran low on supplies, Dad would hitch up the horse to a sleigh and head cross-country. He did business with the Franklin Grocery Store. He took eggs and milk and traded them for flour, sugar, spices, etc. In order to get to town, he would get a pair of pliers, wire cutters, and some baling wire. When he came to a fence, he cut the wires and drove the horse through, then repaired the fence before leaving.

Dad got sick one time. He called Dr. Peetz, who came out on a Model T snowmobile. It had runners on the front and tracks on the back. He checked Dad over and gave him enough pills for one week. The charge was one dollar.

There was a man named Ed and he hated kids, so we waited until he went to his outhouse and tipped it over on the door with him in it. Later we had a big storm and there were limbs and other stuff, so we boys cleaned up his yard. He saw us do it, and he turned out to be our friend.

Dad always said apple pie without the cheese is like a kiss without a squeeze. On holidays, the girls asked what kind of pie he wanted. His answer was always yes, so they each brought him a different piece of pie each.

George Aebig during WWI

Dad bought a small farm north of Shelby, and all of us kids went to Shelby School. I had a teacher named Annie Dickey, which I hated. If your work wasn't done and done right, you would report to her room and do your work until she Okayed it. She told me, "If you do your work now and do it right, you will go places." I will never forget Annie or the inspiration of my life.

After high school, I joined the Navy during World War II. I took my training and was assigned as a coxswain on a Higgins boat.

George Aebig with one of the first cars in Shelby

My job was to land Marines on Iwo Jima shore safely. When the famous flag was raised on Iwo Jima, I had the honor of saluting it being raised.

After the war was over, I came back to Shelby. I got a job working for Westing and Swanson Lumber and Construction Company. After several small jobs, I worked for Hooker Chemical Company. I bought a farm east of Shelby and built a new house, and there is where I raised my family. After a divorce, I bought a farm east of Rothbury. I now live alone and do all my own housework and farm my forty acres. I am now 88 years old and am thinking of retiring.

Wayne Aebig in 1944

Pepe
By Linda Collins of Greenville, Michigan
Born 1948

Nobody had a better childhood than I did. Animals played a really big part in all that we did as kids. Fortunately, I had parents that usually welcome any stray cat or dog into the family. Our house was always full of strays or unusual creatures.

For my twelfth birthday, I begged mom and dad for a monkey. As usual, my parents went to great lengths to fulfill my request. We named him Pepe; he was immediately adopted into our family of animals. Pepe was hard to manage and extremely unpredictable. Just when you thought you knew how he would react to a certain situation, he surprised us and did just the opposite. Life with Pepe was challenging to say the least. Pepe brought many lively and wondrous experiences into our lives.

When he arrived, our lives were changed forever. He was very shy, scared, and demanding with a voracious appetite for exotic treats such as coconut milk, along with ordinary delights like eggs, bacon, and toast with grape jelly. He immediately became like another child in our family. He sat at the table and helped himself to whatever he wanted from our plates. He ran around the house sometimes knocking things over causing general havoc on a daily basis. There was never a dull moment when Pepe was on the prowl. Rarely did we watch television; we had all the entertainment anyone could ask for.

He hated the feared, the dreaded broom, which my mother used to discipline the little renegade. He would jump into the cage and slam the door behind him, acting very repentive for smashing a vase or lamp, or smearing food all over the kitchen table and floor.

Christmastime brought many opportunities for him to touch and scrutinize the decorations around the house. He couldn't help himself from flying into the tree sending it crashing to the floor. All the lovely glass ornaments we had were no longer. Dad finally wired the tree to the door and the ceiling to prevent him from smashing all of our antique decorations.

In the summertime, Pepe became public enemy number one to the many birds in our backyard. He would climb up the old maple tree and gently reach into the bird's nest filled with little, blue eggs. He would delicately pick up the egg and carefully watch as he tipped his hand sending it crashing to the sidewalk below. The robins got wise to his lethal tricks and began to peck him, viciously plucking all the fur from his head and tail as they chased him back into the house. In fact, the birds would line up on the porch banisters to prevent him from coming out of the house by swooping and pecking at him. Pepe got the message, which ended his short career as a nest robber.

When Pepe could no longer climb in the trees without being harassed, he took up the art of running on the telephone wires, which required great skill and balance. He traveled several miles away from home teasing the birds and irritating the dogs below as he went along his merry way. The neighbors would call our house to say, "Mrs. Collins, your monkey is up here on some dog's back." My mother would reply, "Don't worry, he rode up there, he can ride him back. He'll be home before dark." Pepe was deathly afraid of the dark. This fear guaranteed that he would return home before sundown.

On Sundays we took rides in the mountains or went to visit friends. In our absence, Pepe, who could not be kept in his cage, took this opportunity to roam around the house getting into all sorts of trouble. On one occasion, he raced upstairs to find something interesting to destroy. He happened upon my mother's precious mink stole hanging on the back of the bedroom door. We arrived home to find that he had chewed off all the little mink feet and tails on her stole, depositing them in a nice little pile on the floor. Oddly enough, neither mom nor dad said much about it. "Such is life when you have a monkey around the house!"

One Sunday afternoon, Pepe decided to go upstairs again. This time, into the bathroom he scurried and shinned up the pole to the cupboard door and pushed a large jar of Pond's Cold Cream off the shelf and into the toilet bowl below, smashing it, causing water to gush out all over the floor and onto the furniture in the living room below, soaking mom's new red couch and chair.

Pepe played with the cats and teased the dog until it would lose all patience with the little pest. He would stick his finger in the dog's ears and eyes and run up and down his back. Pepe would then scamper off and shinny up the drapes or run to higher places to escape the dog's wrath. There was never a scarcity of laughter in our house.

After dinner one Sunday afternoon, we went for a ride in the country. While we were gone, Pepe must have been bored, so he climbed onto the kitchen table, spying a bowl of mashed potatoes and a small bowl of grape jelly. He made little round missiles out of the potatoes and jelly smacking them on the sides of the cabinets, walls, and the curtains. We arrived home to find little; hard balls of paste stuck everywhere. We all laughed heartily as we scraped off the little, sticky balls.

Pepe was extremely intuitive. Once while we were picnicking, a little boy came over to see the monkey. Pepe wasn't happy being constrained by a leash and collar, so I didn't know how he would react to a stranger touching him. Sensing there was something different about this little boy, he laid flat on the table and let the boy stroke him from head to tail. We were amazed, as the little blind boy calmly talked to him and felt his sombrero and vest. He wanted to know what color he was and what his clothes looked like; I was at a loss for words. How do you explain color to a blind person? Pepe somehow knew this little boy was special, because he normally would have bitten a stranger, especially a child.

That wasn't the only time he astounded us with his sensitivity. Pepe witnessed our cat getting hit by a car in front of our house. He ran out to the cat and sat down beside him, refusing to leave. He screamed and cried, realizing the cat was dead. He had an acute sense of death. When mom would thaw out a piece of meat or a chicken for dinner, he would go berserk, screaming, and jumping up and down.

Like a crow, anything shiny or glittering would attract his attention. He carried off dad's cufflinks, mom's earrings and watches, or anything that reflected the light. He had secret caches all over the house. When mom couldn't find the matching earring, she had to conduct a search of all the corners and hidden places in the house hoping to find the lost treasure.

One night, he was prowling around the bathroom and found a box of Ex-Lax in the medicine cabinet. Even though he never cared for chocolate candy, he gobbled the whole box, dropping the wrapper and box on the floor. Dad came home from work to find the empty box on the floor. He came in the bedroom to tell me that Pepe would probably die, and not to feel bad if we found him dead. Surprisingly, the next morning he was sitting up on the perch in his cage waiting for breakfast.

The mentally ill lady next door could see

something swinging in the windows from a distance and saw a line full of diapers with holes in them. Her curiosity got the best of her and she couldn't help herself any longer. Having never been to our house before, she opened the door and walked in unannounced. Pepe was sleeping in the transom above the door. When he saw her come in, he swooped down on her, knocking her to the floor. She screamed and ran out, never to return. She called one day to ask why our diapers had holes in the middle. I said, "The hole is for his tail." Failing to explain that it was for a monkey and not a baby, I'm sure she wondered what kind of a baby we had over there, and just couldn't stand not knowing what it was.

As Pepe traveled around the neighborhood on the telephone lines or on a dog's back he would stop to peer into someone's window. He managed to frighten many little old ladies who were cooking in their kitchens, never expecting to see a monkey staring at them or sampling their baked goods. Most of the neighbors knew about him so they would hand him a cookie and he would be on his way to the next stop. When night approached, he would scurry along the telephone lines to reach safety before dark.

I wouldn't recommend having a monkey as a pet, but it was a good experience for us as a family. We enjoyed him and loved him dearly. He died of a heart attack—it must have been high cholesterol from all the eggs, bacon, and toast with butter—at the ripe old age of six, a respectable age for a squirrel monkey. We have many fond memories of our little, long-tailed fellow. I remember him strutting around in his little cowboy outfit or in the Mexican outfit with the brightly colored vest complete with diapers.

Son of the Sixties
By Lloyd David Ball of Morley, Michigan
Born 1953

My son of the sixties might have been named Scott, Mike, Dave, Dan, or Tim, but I'll choose Jeff. Jeff freely rode his bike along the county roads of Pine Township of Montcalm County. He would have known the many pleasures and joys of a blue-skied endless summer day. Jeff rose to the aroma of homemade bread being toasted, the sizzle of bacon and eggs in a black cast-iron frying pan and the tangy taste of fresh orange juice. He eagerly spread tart strawberry jam on his toast, which his grandmother had preserved a summer ago. What an incredible way to start the day of a happy, healthy, carefree ten-year-old boy.

Jeff grabbed his fishing pole and tackle box and zoomed out the screen door to meet his lake friend, Ron. Ron and his family lived most of the year at their home in Lansing. Ten years ago, Ron's father had purchased several lake lots at Rainbow Lake and had built a summer cottage with the help of his two brothers and his father. This cottage and its surrounding property had become a favorite welcome haven to the children of the lake community. Ron's mother was well known for her warm, friendly smile and bountiful supply of chocolate chip cookies and cherry or grape Kool-Aid. When very hot summer days did not motivate oven baking, she would treat the lake kids to graham crackers with vanilla frosting.

June would bring the summer residents to the lake. Much fun and many adventures needed to be crammed into this two and a half months' time frame; there was never any time to waste as swimming, boating, backyard baseball, bike riding, and baseball card trading beckoned. Jeff and Ron would fish the early morning hours until the rising summer sun demand their presence in the blue waters of a lake most welcome. Swimming produced hunger, which was as easy to satisfy as the opening of a jar of Jif peanut butter. More swimming and bike riding were to follow only to be interrupted by the ice cream truck. Its bells would ring, its horn would toot, and its back doors would open. Such choices for a summer boy in the endless sun-drenched days of the sixties. Jeff knew the days and the times this treasure truck would make its journey down Johnson Road en route to Langston from Trufant.

Some early evening television nestled with family in the living room with summer breezes drifting though open windows. A sleepy dad snoozing and snoring in his big chair careworn after a hard day's work. A lovely mother with a tender heart and nurturing manner gently doing supper dishes as to not

30

disturb him. Jeff and his two older brothers slipping out the door running down west bank to the lake beach for an evening swim; soap and towels with them; bathing in nature's beautifully warm and mild bathtub. Off to bed as the critters of the night orchestrated them into gentle sound sleep. Another day would soon emerge.

The summer lake gang would always eagerly await and anticipated two special summer events the Fourth of July and the start of the Ionia Free Fair. Fireworks displayed against a July night sky softly pelted into the blanket of deep purple lake water, no early bedtime this night. Attending the fair was the summer's biggest event full of rides, games, and sleepy-headed boys who could not keep their eyes open beyond Sheridan or Stanton on the way home.

The August water looked and felt different than June and July water. Mother Lake was changing telling Jeff and his buddies a change of season was not too far away. The summer kids and their families would soon return to their city homes. School clothes and school supplies would be purchased soon heralding the start of a new school year at Lakeview. Why do summer months fly by so quickly when you're ten?

Nature's cycles and seasons would come and go. Jeff and Ron would graduate from separate high schools; attend different colleges and choose different careers. They will forever share in the memories of carefree summer days spent in an environment of nature at its best. No cell phones, personal computers, DVDs, VCRs, electronic games, nor CD players. A 45rpm record of a favorite singer played over and over again, a television which offered programs from three networks, walkie-talkies, scooters, red wagons, balsa wood airplanes, trips to town to shop, the dime store with countless toys, the corner drug store with a soda fountain. These things I'm sure Jeff would remember and Ron and all the other summer lake kids! It's their duty to pass onto the next generations to come the magic of these days, of that time, of that era.

Could even I go back just one more summer day to see Jeff and Ron and the others? Will you come with me?

Founding of the Kawkawlin Fire Department
By Carol Jurek of Hemlock, Michigan
Born 1940

I would like to tell you about my dad, Patrick H. Confer, who was the founder of the Kawkawlin Township fire department. He was its chief from its inception until his death from a heart attack at age 54 in 1969.

In the mid-1940s, the only fire trucks in the area were in Bay City. Once there was a fire in the township and by the time fire trucks arrived from the city, a little boy died. My dad said, "This will never happen again." He went to the township board and petitioned them to buy a fire truck, which they did.

In 1948, Pat got on a train and went to Pennsylvania to pick up the 1947 International fire truck. Since he owned and operated a service garage and 24/7 hour AAA wrecker service, which was right across the driveway from the house, it was a perfect place for a fire department.

One of the problems was the service garage only had two stalls and he needed both of them for his business. So using his own funds, he had another stall added to the garage in which to house the fire truck.

Problem number two was that they had a truck but no one knew how to operate it. Jake Homan, a retired fire chief from Bay City, was pressed into service to train the volunteers. He remained their mentor for many years.

Problem number three was in 1948 the only phones available out in the country were party lines. It was bad enough that the business was on a party line but now the fire department was on the same line. Can you imagine calling the fire department and continually getting a busy signal? This was also our personal phone line. After some long discussions with the phone company and sometime later, they finally ran a private line for the fire department. Also, since there were no cell phones, pagers, etc., someone had to be in the house or garage at all times to her the phone. So my dad had a very large bell put on the garage and the back of the house so that we could go outside. When the phone rang, someone would make a mad dash to answer it.

There were no fire hydrants at that time so the fire truck had to carry its own water supply which they got by pumping water out of the Kawkawlin River. One time they had a house fire almost out when they ran out of water. By the time they got to the river, filled up the truck and got back to the house it had burned to the ground. So my dad said, "This will never happen again." Shortly after this happened Dad bought a military surplus fuel truck that had been converted to a water truck. The township never reimbursed him for this. He never ran out of water again.

Now this truck created another problem. Where were they going to keep it? So Dad built a separate building next to the service garage to house both trucks.

Since he could not run the 24/7 wrecker service, the fire department, and the service garage by himself, he hired a man to help him. Since this person had to be close and also available 24 hours, he built the "little house" right behind the main house. The hired man, assistant chief, lived there rent-free with his family.

Patrick H. Confer

My mom also played a major role in the running of the fire department. Since there were no cell phones, pagers, etc., the only way to get the firemen to the fire was to call them. She had a list of all the men (there were no women firemen at this time) and knew what their work schedules were and when they were available. She also did all the paperwork involved in the records for the State of Michigan, what firemen went to what fire, where the fire was, estimated damage loss, etc. She also always had coffee and cookies or sandwiches, etc. ready when the guys got back from a run and were done cleaning up the trucks and hoses.

One summer night a fire call came and my dad took the truck and headed for the fire and mom jumped out of bed in her nightgown and started to call the volunteers. Well, before the trucks got back, another fire call came. Now remember there were no two-way radios, cell phones, etc. Even though she was barefoot and in her nightgown, she jumped in the car and rushed to the fire scene only to find that the trucks were gone. She figured they were at the river filling up so she gets back in the car, drove at a high rate of speed to the river where she found the trucks, and got them to the other fire in time to save the building. After she got home she thought oh my gosh if the police had stopped this woman who was racing around the countryside in the middle of the night in her nightgown and asked her what she was doing and she said she was looking for a fire truck, they probably would have locked her up.

This fire department was ahead of its time. Long before Toys for Tots, these firemen were delivering toys, fruits, and candy to under privileged families on Christmas Eve. My mom would have the school give her a list of names and ages of these children. The firemen would go to stores in Bay City and get their broken toys, which they fixed. Mom would sometimes be up late at night sewing doll clothes. I know that some of our Christmas presents ended up in a box for a needy child if the firemen didn't happen to have an age appropriate toy for them.

So this is the way it remained until October 5, 1969 when Dad died very suddenly. They soon built a new fire station on Parrish Road and named it the Patrick H. Confer Fire Station.

Deer Hunting
By Bruce A. Beckert of Saginaw, Michigan
Born 1924

Suddenly, I realize with a great deal of alarm, that the deer hunting season is almost upon us again. November 15th in the state of Michigan, possibly in other places as well, marks the start of the gun season for deer. On this day, all things in Michigan stop. There are ten million or so people in this state, but less than five percent take to the woods with a gun. The other 95 percent breath a big sigh of relief, knowing that on this day, and possibly for several days onward, nothing need be done. One can simply say that it can't be done due to deer hunting.

In my day, and that must take us back to about the 1940s and ☐50s, we shot at only the male of the species. In fact, the horns had to be three inches long, and that necessitates careful identification, saving many human lives in the process. Nowadays, the ladies, wanting equal rights, have caused a major change. Hunters can shoot at any kind they see, often even at each other. Indeed, the woods was a much safer place in my hunting days.

Up to this point, I have not mentioned bow hunting, which goes on interminably from October into January. Bow hunters ask no quarter and are given none. Bow hunters also shoot both doe and bucks. Uncle John hated doe deer while gun hunting because they would walk right up to him and spoil his concentration while he was looking for a buck to come by. When bow hunting began to become popular, Uncle John could hardly wait to learn all about it and get out there and get even with all of those doe. The very first season that Uncle John bought a bow license, the same old doe that had tortured him so often, came right up to him. Point blank range. He drew the string taut and let one of those Fred Bear Archery razor-tipped arrows fly right in her face. The old girl ducked just in time and the arrow grazed her ear ever so slightly, just bringing forth a very small bit of blood. Nevertheless, Uncle John suddenly felt very bad about it all and he immediately went back to his cabin and burned up the bow and all his arrows in the wood stove.

Fast forward to November 15th and now Uncle John is out there at his favorite spot, sitting on his favorite stump, with his favorite rifle all loaded and ready. Up comes the old doe. She looked at Uncle John accusingly and wiggled her wounded ear at him. Who knows what might have happened if there had been open gun season on doe in those days?

We never had those kind of problems within my little family deer hunting group. In fact, we never shot a deer at all. But we sure put forth our best efforts. My mother was paranoid about my sister and I getting lost in the woods. She insisted that all of us have matches, a compass, and a police whistle. This last item was really why we never saw a buck.

Mother had a code of whistle blows. Four blows was for, "I got a buck." Understand? Four syllables, four blows on the whistle. More important though was the next coded message. Three blows, "Where are you?" Mandatory answering message, two blows. "I'm here." One long blow was for "lost."

As soon as we had parked the car and all the guns were loaded, we all trouped off to find a good spot to see a buck. Daddy led the way, me next, then my sister, and finally mother. Soon mother would see some Michigan Holly and get out her deer skinning knife to cut down a sprig or two to decorate our home for Christmas.

I would lag back a little and sister would catch up and hiss in my ear, "Let's go find someplace else, this spot is absolutely devoid of deer." Dad didn't care that we did this because he knew my sister and I had spent lots of time in the woods over the summer and never got lost. Mother was not too sure. Especially about me, being only ten. Sister, on the other hand, being 14 could always be found anywhere, anytime, by anybody, once informed there was a damsel in distress.

Well, all this aside, sister and I would soon be off into the swamp, grazing on the wintergreen berries. Then would come the whistle. "Where-are-you?" Oh rats. Ok, she won't give up and if she keeps on with the three blasts, there won't be a deer within three counties.

So we would answer with our two blasts, and mother would soon be on our trail, toting her sprigs of Michigan Holly. Daddy, on the other hand, would be far ahead and find himself solitude and usually see lots of doe. Never any bucks.

I didn't mention the clothing we wore up

till now because I wanted you to worry for a bit that we might get cold. Mother always did. So we had to wear lots and lots of very warm clothes. For starters there was the thermal union suit underwear. You could absolutely go out in the woods with this only and stay warm. Nothing more would be required. However, on top of the union suit, we had regular pants and shirts, then a quilted vest. Over this came a Soo Wool shirt, Soo Wool pants, and finally a bulky Soo Wool coat.

On our feet were wool socks, covered by another pair of standard socks, then some dark grey shoes of heavy wool called "felts," and finally very clumsy overshoes with rubber bottoms and leather tops.

Now factor in that opening day in Michigan is always balmy, about 70 degrees is normal for November 15th. You can imagine how miserable we were.

We also wore an ammunition belt around our waist. My sister and I used mother's and dad's shotguns with slug loads. These were their pheasant and duck guns. For deer, mother had a 30-30 lever action Savage and dad had a Remington automatic.

Because we were expected to become so lost that the whistles would be out of earshot and we would have to signal with our guns, we had to carry at least 50 rounds. Fifty shotgun slug cartridges weigh a whole lot. Seeing a little guy like me so loaded down, they finally allowed me to carry a 22-pump, making my load much lighter.

Once, while I was busy answering a call to nature, a rabbit cam by—they were in season all fall and winter and made reasonable good eating in the absence of venison—so I took aim with the 22 and fired off all 15 shots with my pants zipped down. Not the best situation. Indeed, that would spoil anybody's aim.

As far as I know, I never even grazed him. My sister, hearing the commotion, and then seeing my rabbit, took aim with her 20-gauge shotgun. The slug blew him away, with not enough left to skin out for dinner. I was sorry then that I had given up the shotgun and slugs. But I was sorry for the rabbit too and never tried to shoot one again.

Anyway, finally the morning hunt would be over and we would all go back to the car and have a big lunch. Then dad would allow that we all take up stations some distance apart. He would place us so he knew right

where we all were and caution us not to shoot each other. He also cautioned mother that now that everyone knew where everyone else was, please no more with the whistle.

Dad would then trudge off to make a big circle and drive the deer back to us. And he would have said to stay alert. Sure thing dad. Full of lunch, warm as toast in my three layers of clothing, propped up against a nice comfortable stump. Dad wasn't gone more than a few minutes and I would be out like a light. In those days I didn't snore yet, so no one knew I was asleep. Mother and sister were already snoring candidates, so they couldn't chance any rest.

I secretly thought that dad favored me and would herd any deer he found in my direction, but I just couldn't help it. So I am sure lots and lots of big bucks with huge racks ran right by me. But they would be for some other lucky hunter. Of course, dad was always peeved when he finally completed his big circle and found me snoozing, but that was part of growing up—having your dad get peeved at you.

You know, a lot of people count sheep when they can't sleep. Not me. I think of Soo Wool clothing, warm, fuzzy shoes, and a comfortable stump. Bang. I'm gone.

Following the Snow Plow
By Ann M. Stueber of Saginaw, Michigan
Born 1924

It is January! It is Michigan! And again, the snow is falling. Any amount of snow that falls in my neighborhood, I immediately think of my kindergarten days (I will be 91 in February 2015). We lived about two blocks from Houghton Grade School, so that meant walking to school and home again. I was a small girl about three feet tall and most snowbanks were over my head.

After a heavy snowfall one day, my dad walked me to school. I could not see over the banks of snow. Now, here's the memory I have of that morning. Our sidewalks were being plowed by a man holding a very heavy wooden □-shaped plough while holding the reins of a horse pulling the plough. We followed the man, plough, and horse to the corner where he turned the corner to continue ploughing another side of our block.

Many changes in my lifetime, but this is one moment I will never forget.

The Red Snowsuit
By Gerald Meade of Greenville, Michigan
Born 1932

You can't go home again. In a world of rapid advances in technology, our culture is mutating at a dizzying rate.

For those of us who have never been inoculated for homesickness, the past improves like good wine with age. The simplest insignificant memory grows more precious for the fact that it is the currency of a world that no longer exists; and is likely never to return.

I remain part of that world: a homing pigeon, unable to escape the magnetic field surrounding central Michigan.

I couldn't have been more than five years old when I got a red snowsuit for Christmas. Couldn't wait to step out in the bitter cold and knee-deep snow to share my pride and excitement with my best pal—the neighbor's dog.

The magic of that moment faded in a flash when he apparently mistook me for a fire hydrant!

We remained friends, but until spring came and I could shed that prized snowsuit, I kept a comfortable distance between us so he couldn't make that mistake again. (Man's best friend, indeed!)

Saginaw in the '50s
By Katherine Smekar of Saginaw, Michigan
Born 1947

I lived in the city of Saginaw on N 11th Street. Our family lived one block from Houghton School. I went to Houghton School only for kindergarten and then walked to a Catholic School called Sacred Heart that now the church is torn down.

I can remember the milk truck that delivered us milk in a small insulated box on our front porch. I also remember a horse-drawn wagon that came down our street selling vegetables. And don't we all, that's around my age, remember the boys who pushed the ice cream carts with the bells ringing to alert us he was near.

How many of us remember going to the movies back then? I remember 50 cents for the adults and 25 cents for us kids. Do you also remember double features and ten cartoons? We sat there so long out legs would fall asleep!

We also went to Hoyte Park ice skating, sledding, and the toboggan run on weekends with the heated warming house.

When I was a kid I can remember going on Porter Street and getting a live chicken and my dad telling us to pray for the chicken before he chopped off his head for supper.

I remember the shoemaker who was a few blocks from our house who fixed the soles of our shoes and sold kids ice skates and you could trade them in as you grew to get the next size.

Also, a few blocks away was a meat market we went to and the meat man gave us a piece of bologna as our mom purchased our fresh meat. Also across the street was a bakery where we got bread and buns. Now there are not very many bakeries or meat markets.

Up in the middle of Saginaw in the main part of the town, Genessee Street was our trip to shop on Saturdays. Woolworth's and Kreskies was the five-and-dime the old location of Sears and other stores and they were not that far from the Hoyte Library and now the Castle Museum that was, back then, the main Post Office, two big banks, Ace Hardware, and a shoe store.

But the best was the city busses that took you uptown. Where we lived the bus stop we had to wait at to get us home was in front of the Planter Peanut store and, boy, was that good smelling the fresh cooked peanuts as you waited to get on the bus!

What good memories it was to live in Saginaw during the '50s until we moved to Bridgeport in 1960. I'm sure a lot of others who lived in Saginaw City during the '50s and would hope all those good times would come back again. Love those memories and wish that it was nicer and simpler not to have all those electronic gadgets we have today, that complicates our cities these days.

Now I live in Saginaw Township and

when we drive through that part of Saginaw City, it brings back all these memories when I was a kid.

My Brother's Keeper
By Alma Moyes of St. Louis, Michigan
Born 1929

When I was small, I remember walking to country school, Baily School in all kinds of weather. We went across a neighbor's (Hazel Ebright) yard to make it a little shorter. Once I was chased by a bull. I climbed a fence to get away from him. We were all in one room at school. When it was nice out we'd eat our lunch outside. I remember sitting on a stile over a fence and ate my lunch. We played games after we ate, usually hide and seek or tag. We didn't have any swings or merry-go-round and we had lots of snow back then. One day we went to city school and we were separated and I cried for my brothers and sisters. We still lived in the country. One day I lost one of my mittens and mom made me walk two miles to find it. I found it back at the schoolyard. After that, mom pinned them to my sleeve of my coat. One day I was in a swing and a boy stood up and pumped me to see how high we could go and we went way over the swing set and I landed in a sand box and I was unconscious. I woke up in the teachers' lounge, but wasn't hurt too bad. One day I was sitting on the merry-go-round and a boy pushed it so fast I fell off. I was

Alma with her sisters, daughter, and son

unconscious again.

I was a middle child of ten. My brother was three years older than me and he was born with Polio so he and I was in the same class at school so I could watch him. Many thought we was twins. When I was seven and he was ten we had a paper route. I pulled him in a wagon in the summer and we had a box on a sled in the winter. One day I was pulling him on the sled and I hit a dry spot and he fell out and hit his head. Boy, was he mad at me, but he got over it. We were always together. I was like a mother looking after him. One night we slept outside in a homemade tent made out of blankets tied to a tree and he walked in his sleep and one night I woke up and he was walking down the middle of the road. I ran out there and brought him back to the tent.

When we had measles or mumps, we were quarantined. Daddy had to find room somewhere so he could go to work. We couldn't go anywhere and no one could come until we were over whatever we had. We always had a garden and I helped daddy. My brother and I was digging potatoes and I had a hoe and he reached for the potatoes and I came down with the hoe and hit him on the head and he was bleeding and he got mad at me again. He chased me and I ran in the house to mom and I hid under her apron.

My brother and I would put garden stuff in a wagon and we'd go to the neighbors and sell it. We collected newspapers and we'd take them to town and sell them. We needed

Alma with her sisters

money for food. One summer we worked in the pickle field and the sugar beets. We were always busy, it kept us out of trouble. We had fun doing it. When I was nine years old, I babysat for a family close by. As I got older, I'd stay with different families and babysit and also go to school. I'd come home on weekends unless they needed me to take care of the children.

I remembered so many events that occurred: First World War; Second World War; Roosevelt's death and when was President. And many others, first man on the moon, the polio epidemic. Many things that happened in our world, too many to write about. We worked together as a family. We never went hungry but we loved each other. I'm so glad I grew up when I did no TV, no computers, and no phones. Mom made our clothes or we were helped out by some richer people. That's what people did back then. It taught me to do the same today.

Alma's second grade class

My Victrola
By Florence Pemberton of Big Rapids, Michigan
Born 1929

Born and raised on a farm in the late ☐20s, outhouses and chamber pots were a necessary part of life, along with Sears & Roebuck and Wards catalogs. City folk had to put up with castor oil to get things moving, but country folk could use safrass tea to take care of consumption. Our home was heat by wood. Dad would chop and split the wood and I was to load it on my sled to haul it to the kitchen where it was piled for mom to cook with. Sometimes, if I was not as quick as pops thought, I got a helping hand in the right place to get my attention.

Party lines usually took care of important news in the neighborhood or world affairs. In winter, those wind-up record players whiled away the hours. (I have one yet.) My Victrola has the original needles yet also. Those wringer washers took a lot of hard work away from the weekly washings, but watch your fingers, they could get pinched easy. One washer sprang a leak while washing, so it was lifted outside quickly, and then mopped up the kitchen.

My homemade clothes were mainly pajamas; toys were strap-on roller skates and blankets thrown over a clothesline (when not in use for hanging clothes at washing time). I was the leading lady and could outride, outshoot, and knew where the bad guys were.

Teachers were not usually my thing, but my third-grade teacher had my number. She knew before I did what I would do. Never quite figured her out, but I loved her. She taught in a one-room school, taught all (kindergarten thru eighth grade) every class, every day; school plays on Mother's Day, Valentine's Day, Thanksgiving, and Christmas programs. The whole school would go for a Christmas tree. The boys would assemble a stage for the program. In my later years, if school was closed, I'd put on my skis and ski the seven miles to school, even if it was closed because of bad weather. I have over seven years of certificates that I received in grade school of neither being late or tardy. The one-room school I attended was heat by wood. The boys had to remove the ashes and haul in wood for the next day and the girls had to clean the blackboards.

Rumble seats were great. Don't forget to close them before the rain. Snowstorms were not as bad as I see them now, but of course, I didn't have to shovel or plow. Just put on a snowsuit, grab the skis, and take off for the closest hill.

"Many hands make light work" was my dad's favorite rule, so watch out cows. Hand milking a.m. and p.m. was part of my chores, along with running the milk thru the separator. Mom would keep the cream to make butter; whole milk was used on the table and for the many cats around the barn and the pigs.

Haying was a wild time in the summer. The hotter it got the better the haying. Sometimes hay was brought to the barn loose, later years we got a bailer.

A stream ran thru part of the farm, so my dog and I would go swimming. I learned to swim by watching the dog "dog-paddle." Being an only child, my dog was my constant companion. There were not as many cars back then, so my dog ran loose. One time he got caught in a pen where pigs were waiting to be butchered. Dad heard him and called me so I ran to the place, climbed the fence, grabbed a large branch, beat the hogs on the snout, grabbed my dog, climbed over the fence and walked home. One time in the creek where we swam, I got caught in swift water and my dog jumped in to save me.

Going to town was special for me. We had a buggy and drove a single mare. Sometimes the train would be going thru and would scare the horse, so we had to stay well back from the tracks. There was a sidetrack, so sometimes the train would switch off a car or two to be left. The train would then make several trips forward and backward, till it had what would go to the next stop. I enjoyed watching the switchovers.

At one time, our town had a freezer where people could butcher a cow, pig, or whatever, and put the meat in the freezer. The worst part of that seemed to be at mealtime, the meat was in the freezer and we were at the table.

Our town has river running thru it. It used to be floating logs to the mill, but is now just for tubing, swimming, or fishing. There are two bridges crossing it. When I was younger, I'd walk across the bridge on the underside, not realizing the dangers. It was quite a drop from the girders to the water. But I was young, what could possibly happen?

Kids today have no idea about the "old days," and most of them don't have time to sit and listen. My husband's son saw my wind-up Victrola and was fascinated for half-hour (he's 50).

Air Craft Spotting
By Curtis H. Truemner of Bay City,
Michigan
Born 1934

The last few years there has been a resurgent of interest in World War II and all though I was seven when the war started it was the biggest thing in our lives and occupied most conversations at family gatherings. The question at our house was would my dad be drafted. He was 38 at the time. The Army drafted the young guys first, starting at 19 or 20, and, as the war dragged on into 1944, older fellows were called up, but by that time my father was past the age and had four dependents so he was not affected. He did volunteer for the civilian defense core and did his time as an air craft spotter in our town at a small building that was installed on top of a store in downtown Sebewaing. I went with him one evening and with great anticipation climbed the stairs to that lofty perch to see if we could spot any incoming enemy planes. I assured my dad that I was confident that I could tell the difference between a Messerschmitt and one of our planes. As it turned out all we had to do was count the sea gulls that passed over. So much for our war effort.

Each December many of us pause to remember the attack by the Japanese on Pearl Harbor, Hawaii. On that day in 1941, mom, dad, and we kids had made a visit to mom's grandparents in Clare, Michigan. As I remember, it was Sunday evening when we arrived back in Sebewaing and heard the news about the attack. I can remember lying on the floor in front of the radio and hearing the sketchy reports. At that time, I had no idea where Hawaii was or the great significance of this event. The immediate impact on our lives was very little except for the speculation as to what was to come and would we be attacked here at home, very little happened for the first few months in Sebewaing, Michigan.

Growing Up In Au Gres
By Robert Jennings of Au Gres, Michigan
Born 1950

The weather has been getting colder. This morning the weatherman said that a polar vortex will bring much colder temperatures to us tonight, just in time for deer season!

Deer hunting now, at least for me, has much more to do with tradition and camaraderie than the actual hunting, especially now that my brother, Dick, is sick with leukemia. He and I started hunting with my dad and uncles when we were 14 years old so this will be my 50th year of hunting with Dick. I am just happy that we have another year to carry on this special tradition.

Both of my parents were born here in Michigan. My father was born here in Au Gres and my mother, Baga, was born just north of Au Gres in Alabaster, Michigan. Baga's parents were both of Irish heritage and born here in America. My grandfather was English and born in England. My grandmother was of German heritage and born here. Even though she was born here, German was spoken when she was growing up.

When I was 11 years old we lived on the Au Gres River so we spent a lot of time fishing for perch, bass, pike, or whatever we could catch. Baga's parents would often come down to visit and fish with us on Sundays. We didn't have poles with reels, so we used long poles to push ourselves up and down the river. We also built rafts from cedar logs and used long poles to push ourselves up and down the river. Later on, when we were a little older, we had a small aluminum boat and motor and did a lot more exploring up and down the river.

We did a lot of the same things that kids do today, including a lot of baseball, both as an organized little league and almost daily neighborhood games. We also played basketball, but football was not something that was played and we didn't really know much about it. Football did not come to our school until I was a senior in high school in 1968.

I think the biggest change from my generation to that of today is electronics. There were not any computers, cell phones, iPad, play stations, etc. when I was 11 years old. Heck, we didn't get our first black-and-white television set until 1957 when I was seven years old. We did play some of the same board games that are played today, including Monopoly and checkers.

Work took up a significant amount of our time. I started my first paper route when I was ten years old and delivered *The Bay City Times* after school and in the summer on my bicycle. My mother would sometimes take me on my route by car when the weather was really bad. I remember that I could usually coax her into it if I wanted.

I think I was about 12 years old when I began working several weeks each summer in local farm fields. Several of my friends and I supplemented a workforce composed of families of Mexican migrant workers. We hand weeded and hoed farm crops, including navy beans, lettuce, and carrots at 50 cents an hour. I considered it decent money in those days, eventually working my way up to $1.00 per hour as a teenager. It was hard work, but we played music on our transistor radios and had fun.

One winter, when I was about 13 or 14 years old, I also worked for a relatively short time at the local bowling alley setting pins. After someone bowled, we would pick up their bowling ball and put it on the chute to send it back to the bowler. We were paid ten cents a game and would usually sit up on a small seat between two alleys and set pins for two different lanes. I was hit many times with flying pins, usually on the legs. It was a dangerous job and I eventually ended up with eight stitches under my eye. I still have then scar. That ended my pin setting job. Looking back, I can't believe that kids were allowed to do such a job.

I still live in the same small town of Au Gres where I grew up. I visit Baga, who is now 96 years old, almost every day in the same house where I was raised, and where

Deer hunting

39

she has lived now for over 70 years. My two brothers and I shared one bedroom and my two sisters shared another. It was a very small house by today's standards.

The City of Au Gres has changed through the years with many buildings and businesses coming and going, but the one constant being that it has remained as a small resort town on Saginaw Bay.

My grandpa, along with my dad and uncle ran a local grocery store, Charles Jennings & Sons. It was less than a block from the school so I would stop in every day on my way home, to read comic books and maybe get a piece of candy or ice cream. My father ran the meat department. Like most everyone in town, we were relatively poor, but always had plenty of food to eat. In fact, we led such sheltered lives in a small town, that I did not even realize that we were poor until years later.

School was basically the center of our universe and life revolved around it. We started school at 9 a.m. and were released at 3:40 p.m. I started elementary school in a building that was torn down long ago. When I was in the fifth grade, we moved to a new elementary school, which is the same building still in use today. We did not have a hot lunch program until the new school was built and it cost 20 cents a day. There was a set schedule for the same basic menu every week, with little variation and no choices. Wednesdays was chili day and one of my favorites. Grilled cheese and tomato soup were also a favorite, but I can't remember if we had it on Mondays or Tuesdays!

A Letter From a Great-Great Grandmother
By Dennette McDermott of Natchitoches, Louisiana
Born 1962

This is a letter from Carrie Stearns Brewer, who was my great-great grandmother, to her niece Nellie Brewer, dated September 11, 1887 from Clare, Michigan. These are passages and quotes from the letter that I own now.

Carrie was a widow as of 1881 and had three children, and eighty acres of land in Clare. She decided to return to teach school in Clare, Michigan.

"I have stood morning examination and school teaching remarkably. I could not get the rooms I wanted 'til Friday, and so that was examination day. So, I could not move that day…I took the regular examination without favor. I did not expect to, but Mr. Doherty was away and one of the other members of the board conducted the examination alone, and entire stranger to me. I did not study up as well as I would if I had expected to go through the whole, but I felt pretty well that I got through without favor. Our new professor assisted in looking over the paper and he told the assembled company at his table at the restaurant (Mr. Elden's family and… take their meals at the restaurant and have a private table all to themselves) that my paper on arithmetic was very good indeed, the best there was then. I only missed on out of thirteen and that was one that had no place on that list of questions, so the examiner said. It was about the columns of a pyramid…We moved Saturday. I did not get settled as much as I wanted to…I commenced school with eighty-eight scholars, one thirteen years old, the other from eleven to five ages. I have ninety-three on the roll and more to come. I have eighty-seven and eight every day. Three in a seat, and twelve or fifteen in chairs. It was hard work to learn so many names and faces, but I have nearly learned them now. It took quite a while to get them in running order, but I am succeeding finally. I was very tired and sleepy all night after the first two or three days, but I am getting use to it and like it. I have to be jack-of-all-trades: nurse, surgeon, hairdresser, etc…I have second grade A + B. First grade A + B and chart, second grade reader. Spelling and arithmetic into multiplication table is what second grade "A" studies."

Picking Fruit
By Ronald Sampson of Pigeon, Michigan
Born 1932

My memories go back to the early years of my youth. I was somewhere between eight and nine years old and lived in a neighborhood rich with other kids my age. We had about the same number of boys and girls, and we all joined in playing together. There were some

40

Ronald A. Sampson

things the boys got into that were just a little bit much for the girls.

One of our favorite things to get into was when the fruit trees would ripen. Our groups of boys knew where every apple, peach, pear tree, and grape vine grew in our neighborhood. The best way to pick the fruit from the trees was to climb a utility pole that was next to the garage. This offered an easy step to the lower branches loaded with fruit and offered very good cover from being seem by the owners. We could not pick many because our pockets were not very deep. Sometimes we were spotted and had to jump off the garage and make our get-away down the alley. We were all so fast that no one ever got caught.

Grape vines were a little different. There may have been dogs in the yard so we had to sneak in and quickly grab a bunch, and make a fast get-away. We never destroyed anything or broke any branches on the trees. I guess we were just young boys doing what boys do.

Today's young people sure miss out on having fun outside. We also entertained ourselves playing games like baseball, football, tag, Kick the Can, and other games we could think of. Now kids seem to sit in the house and play with their computers, video games, and cell phones and let the world pass by.

Snowstorms and Harvesting
By Wanda Ogg of Gladwin, Michigan
Born 1930

When I was five years old, I started school. The school was one and a half miles away so I had a long way to walk, the closest, other pupil lived three quarters of a mile away. This was a county school grades kindergarten through eight.

My parents spoke German at home and I could not speak English. My teacher could not understand me, so she told my parents that they would have to speak English.

The first winter, we had a huge snowstorm and the road drifted shut. We had no school for a week 'til the road could be plowed. There were very tall snow banks on the side of the road.

My parents told me if I got into trouble at school, I would get a spanking when I got home. The only spanking I got was for loitering too long on my way home.

We had no plumbing in the school, so water was carried in by the bucket for drinking. We also had an outhouse. This was no fun in the wintertime, and it was very cold. At least we did not stay there very long. In summer, there were always bees in there also.

We did not have any plumbing at home, so we had to carry water to the house. It was heated on a wood stove. We also did all the cooking and baking there. Needless to say, we had to also carry in wood every day to keep the stove going.

I slept upstairs, above the kitchen. The only heat was a register in the floor, so the room was quite chilly. The stove fire usually went out overnight, and when it was real cold there was ice on our water in the morning.

We heated the water for baths and washing clothes in a boiler on the stove. We took turns washing. The water was poured in a tub. Everyone used the same water. We would pour more hot water in as needed.

The first wash machine had a wooden tub and scrub board. The wringer was pulled back and forth by hand. Our second wash machine was a gasoline Maytag washer. The clothes were hung on outside lines in summer and in winter we had a clothes bar set up behind a stove to dry them on. Our soap was homemade. I had the croup several times and my parents gave me a big spoon of kerosene to break the cough. It was nasty.

My mother sewed all my clothes except my snowsuit and jackets that I wore. When I was in eighth grade, we had a blizzard and the teacher dismissed school early. We had to walk home. About a half mile from the school, it was so deep that I could not go any further, so I stopped at a neighbor's house (whom I knew) and they let me stay all night. The next day the plow came through and I walked home.

I had a sled in winter and used it for hauling wood to the house. In summer, I had a red wagon to get the wood to the house. We did not have air conditioning.

We used horses for the farm work, as we had no tractors. When it was harvest time, a big thrash machine would go from farm to farm. My mother would do a lot of cooking as all the neighbors would come and help and they were good eaters. The man who owned the thrash machine was a big man. My mother set her pies on a windowsill to cool and when it came mealtime, one pie was missing. Guess who ate it? The men washed their hands in a tub under a tree.

Our meat was preserved by canning and smoking. We had a cellar under our house that kept things quite cool. We stored apples, potatoes, carrots, and onions there. We made sauerkraut and either canned it or put it in crocks. We butchered our own pigs and beef. This was always done in winter.

We raised our own vegetables and fruit, and canned a lot. We had shelves in the basement, and these were always filled. We had no pressure canners so all canning was done by hot water bath.

In the winter months we use a chamber pot. This had to be emptied each morning. Those were the good old days. I really do not miss them.

Coal Cellar
By William Denzer of Saginaw, Michigan

I think about my childhood years, often. Most of the thoughts center around being thankful I grew up when I did, feeling safe and secure in a family with traditional beliefs and values, and a world that did not seem to be too threatening or complicated. My childhood was a world of simple toys, outside activities, family vacations, dedicated teachers, and caring, responsible parents (who I frequently pushed to the limits). My grandparents and other family all lived in state. We had no cell phones, no computers, no internet, no cable, and no technology overload. I was born during World War II, so I grew up during the rebuilding events following that war.

The first real outside play activity was in the neighborhoods I lived in. In the early years, I played Hide and Seek, King on the Mountain, and later in my middle years I played Capture the Flag. As I grew older, I did organized recreational sports such as basketball and football. Basketball opened up new friendships and distances. My town was divided by a river to an east/west side situation. At ten to twelve years of age, I rode my bike across the bridge to the baseball diamonds to play ball.

A few years later, I rode to friends' homes on the other side of town, something parents do not allow today. My school years were filled with teachers focused not just on subject matter, but student potential. Maturity has taught me that my toughest and strictest teachers pushed me reach my potential even though I did not like them at the time. Homework came first at home, followed by chores, then play, and meals were timed to daily activities.

Dinner was on dad's return from work. Our chores consisted of dishwashing in the kitchen sink, lawn mowing initially with a reel type mower, hanging up clothes on the lines strung in the basement or outside. Mom washed clothes with a machine that had a hand ringer to squeeze the water out of the clothes. We also hoed and weeded the garden.

We did not have a lot of free time. Since we grew older, our responsibilities increased. Our entertainment was black and white TV with access to about five stations, radio, and our parents' record player. We occasionally played board games like Monopoly, and Ping Pong on our ping-pong table when I was about ten years old.

Our vacations were always by car. Many vacations traveled out of state to New York City, Washington DC, Virginia, and Florida in my teens when my grandma moved there. She moved to a place that was busy, but understandable. Today seems more pressure laden and less focused on face-to-face human connections.

The best way to follow my childhood chronologically is an age-by-age memory trip. At two years old, I came to Saginaw, Michigan living next door to a house with a coal cellar that a truck filled periodically. At five years old, I played King on the Mountain with older kids in the neighborhood. At eight years old, we moved to our second house with a new school, TV, and new neighbors. We began TV watching. Generally, our parents' choices were *Ed Sullivan*, *Amos and Andy*, and *Boston Blackie*.

At age eleven, we moved to a new home built by grandpa. It was a house away from my second school parking lot, and behind the high school football stadium of the public school I would eventually attend. That home was my first memory of a party line phone. You would pick it up and sometimes other people would be talking, or you were talking to a friend and you would hear a click and some adult would ask if you would get off since they had to make a call. We lived there all the way through high school.

At thirteen years old and through high school, my focus was mostly sports, academics, and summer vacations. We spent many weekends at our grandparents' cottages, outhouse, and all which was not my sweetest smelling event with flies and no comfort. Girls were not a priority for me, as there always seemed to be too much drama attached. I was friends with different girls, but dating was out 'til college time, which was probably my first kiss.

I am seventy-two years old now and thankful I grew up when I did. I know many generations might say that, but I feel ours was the best of times, historically. The world is moving at an increasingly frantic pace. Our security, privacy, and freedoms are much more at risk. Traditional beliefs and values are being set aside to self-service. Technology is advancing at break neck speed with more focus on economic value, than value to society. Just try to fix problems with your own computer, automobile, etc.; or resolve issues over the phone with any supplier of products or services if you can get to a person.

Childhood was fun. Eleven years old - water balloons on Halloween, twelve years old – baseball recreational league state championship, fourteen years old – ride ejection off a friend's motorbike, and seventeen years old – graduation and nineteenth in my class of 700 plus at a three-year high school versus a traditional four year high school today. I do not regret the time at all, I preferred it. By the way, I do not own any kind of phone you can carry outside of the home. Text, Twitter, Toot, or Twiddle on.

Penelope in the Outhouse
By Barbara L. Orlando of Rothbury,
Michigan
Born 1932

This is the story of a little girl who was five years old back in 1937. We had an outhouse my dad built, and he moved it every year after Halloween, because the local boys always tipped it over on that night. Anyway, the outhouse had regular toilet seats in it and old catalogs for paper. I would always wrinkle the paper to make it softer.

My pet hen called Penelope would come to the door and want to set on the catalogs and lay an egg. I never knew laying an egg was such a struggle, but she sure made a load of noise. Penelope would let us pick her up and carry her around. She was a very special hen.

What Red Light?
By Carolyn Fleming of Saginaw, Michigan
Born 1938

After asking my dad's permission to drive his '55 Chevy, off I went to pick up my friends on a very rainy night. At seventeen and just out of Driver's Ed, I had a lot to learn.

My friends were squirming, because they knew I had a hard time seeing the road, as the rain was blinding. I could no longer see the centerline, so I pulled and pushed every lever and knob I could reach. My friends sat speechless as they watched other cars pulling off the road as we drove by.

Out of nowhere, a police officer turned on his "bubble machine" and pulled up behind me. He seemed upset as he asked, "What's the red light for?"

My answer aggravated him further when I replied, "What red light?"

He scared me by saying, "Get out of the car!" He guided me to the front of the car and quickly pointed to a red light.

Quickly I explained, "My dad is a volunteer fireman in Auburn."

Without another word, he headed back to his police car. I can still remember his body was shaking with laughter. This adventure made me a celebrity at Handy High for quite some time!

A Wonderful Town
By Judy Laux of Greenville, Michigan
Born 1934

I was born at Belding City Hospital on Sunday, July 22, 1934. Dr. Hollard delivered me. My parents were Edward and Dorothy Engemann. I was their first child.

Belding was a wonderful town to grow up in. We had a wonderful library that still stands today. Main Street stretched for four blocks. We had a movie theater and a ballroom above it. Young people from all over came to visit the Rose Ballroom.

Belding was a thriving community. We had several grocery stores, small local stores and big ones like Kroger and A&P. We had three car dealers and several clothing stores. We had a weekly newspaper, *The Belding Banner News*. The owner and publisher was my grandfather, Edward Engemann, Sr.

Many of the local businessmen gave tickets for the items purchased in their stores, and on Saturday nights around 7:00 p.m., a drawing was held, and money and/or prizes were given out.

The advent of World War II was a difficult time for Belding. Many of our young men joined the service or were drafted. Their departure created a real void. Many foods were rationed. Butter, milk, eggs, cheese, and especially meat were often hard to obtain. You not only had to have the money but the proper coupon to go with it. Nothing with "Made in Japan" was allowed in our house.

The war finally came to an end. The soldiers returned home. The soldiers and sailors were met with a warm reunion, hugs, handshakes, and kisses. Now they faced the task of picking up the pieces and going on with their lives.

My Years as a Kid
By James Albertson of Bay City, Michigan
Born 1935

As you are interested in people's years as a kid, these are some of mine.

As there wasn't any television, I would listen to the radio to programs such as *Dick Tracy* and *The Lone Ranger*.

There were three party phone lines. It seemed that someone always was on it when you wanted to make a call. The phones were dial rotary phones. There were only five numbers. You would dial 0 to get the operator to make a long distance call. There were also phones that were cranked, and you asked Central to make contact to where you were calling.

I have been through some home remedies. They worked out better than what is in the drug stores today.

I had a memorable teacher in the eighth grade, as he was always there to be helpful.

I have been in winters when we shoveled two and three foot snowbanks. Snow blowers weren't around then.

As there was a lot of kids throughout the neighborhood blocks, we always had some kind of game going.

We had milk delivery, and it always came in quart glass bottles. The cream was at the top.

We have had family reunions once a year for many years.

Thanks for the consideration.

Paper Routes and Daydreams
By DeVere Mosher of Saginaw, Michigan
Born 1937

Where do I begin?

Let's start with discipline coming from my mother. She was not one to say, "Wait until your father comes home." Oh, no, she would take care of what I had coming right then and there. I do remember that Father always said, "There are two things that I will not tolerate: a

DeVere Mosher with Dad and Grandpa

liar and a thief."

Growing up in the forties and fifties, we were a long way from the first moon landing. However, I do remember a character by the name of Flash Gordon. The story was a fantasy about space travel starring Flash Gordon. How we would daydream about how neat it would be to have space adventures like Flash Gordon! But this could never be (or could it?).

I, as a young boy, loved to listen to the radio and enjoyed such programs as *The Lone Ranger*, *The Shadow*, *Terry and the Pirates*, and of course, *Jack Armstrong, the All-American Boy*.

Mother was always busy. Let's see, it seems like Monday was when Mom would do the family clothes washing. And to make that chore easier, she was lucky enough to have a wringer washer and of course twin tubs. I loved those wonderful smells from Mother's kitchen.

I also remember the milkman who delivered fresh milk to our outdoor milk box. You see, in those days milk was delivered by horse and wagon.

Growing up I guess life was pretty good. As a youngster, my main jobs were cutting grass in the summer and cleaning my room almost every day. For a few years, a paper route kept me busy.

I would have to go to town to pay my newspaper bill. I would either walk to town or ride the bus. Going to town was a big deal.

Usually a friend joined me. It was a nice town with many stores to visit: dime stores, clothing stores, restaurants, and oh yeah, my favorite, the Planters Peanut Store, with the yummy smell of fresh roasted peanuts.

Summer time was great. I loved to play ball. I knew that I would be chosen to play. After all, it was my ball and bat.

School was okay, too. I mean, the teachers were dedicated, and they really cared about you if you gave them half a chance.

Now that I am grown up, I'd like to say thank you, teachers and parents. God bless you all.

Blue Racer Snakes in the Pines
By Mabel B. Crooks of Edmore, Michigan
Born 1921

I was brought up in the country on an eighty-acre farm a mile and a half near a village on a crossroad called Entrican. My address, however, was Stanton. There were five children in our family: my brother, my twin sister, and me. Then seven years later, my red haired sister was born and then seven years later my youngest sister was born.

We attended a country school two miles away. At this time, I was six years old. The school was named Clifford Lake School, as it was near to Clifford Lake. After we left our house, a girl from the neighbor house joined us. Then there was no more houses until we came to the schoolhouse a one-half of a mile later. We walked on a narrow dirt road through the wood, by a gravel pit, and a river and swamp. In the spring we would pick trillium, jack in the pulpit, and violets.

One day walking home by the gravel pit, a blue racer snake stretched out across the road, so we did not dare to go any farther. Finally, it slithered away in the ditch. By that time, our teacher came along in her coupe. No doubt, she thought we were playing. She took my twin sister and me in her car and dropped us off. At our home blue racer snakes were known to lie among the pine trees. The road is still there as a dirt road. It is now known as Lover's Lane.

Those were fun times in the good old days. I am now 93 years old and my twin sister and I celebrated our 90th birthday three years ago.

On Top of the World in Reed City
By Lynn Holmquist of Reed City, Michigan
Born 1946

I am a 68 year old woman who was born and raised, and still resides in a small town in central Lower Michigan called Reed City. I lived on the "other side of the tracks," referred to as Irish Town.

What fun my friends and I would have in that close-knit neighborhood. We would put pennies on the railroad tracks that ran through our town and wait for the train to run over the coins. I would hate to have to count the number of flat pennies we all collected over the years.

The lumberyard was right across the street from my home at 408 South Morse Street. I loved to climb to the top of the lumber piles. Once on top, I would lie on my back, look up at the sky, and think I was "on top of the world."

My friends and I would walk to the Dairy Queen just blocks from where we lived. There we would enjoy a Dilly Bar. Then we would jump on a huge trampoline that was located behind the Dairy Queen.

As a girl growing up, I remember so many "hot spots," including a bowling alley, a theater, a roller rink, and an ice skating pond. There was also a gathering spot called Mikes; inside you found a soda fountain, a jukebox, a dance floor, and a pool table. Wow, we had it all!

Today however, so much has changed. No longer do we have any of the above mentioned places. The last original business, Wrights Bakery, located on Upton Avenue, closed its doors in the winter of 2014. I am glad to say that the new owner has bought the site and opened its doors shortly after Wrights closed. The new business is called Stone House Bread.

As I look back I have so many fond memories of growing up here, and I wouldn't have wanted to be born or raised anywhere else. I loved that feel of a small town community, where you knew and played with all the neighborhood kids, just waiting for that dreaded nine o'clock whistle, which meant get home now! I miss that whistle, even after all these years. It was a good childhood, and I'm proud to say that my home is and always will be Reed City, Michigan.

Adventures on Ojibway Island
By Bruce Kenneth Lennox of Saginaw,
Michigan
Born 1937

My grandparents raised me. I loved and still love them. My parents separated when I was about six. Nana and Bobba took me in, and the adventure started.

We never locked our doors. We knew our neighbors, especially the kids. Bobba, my grandfather, had a barn in the backyard with all kinds of tools and wonders. Our house was a meeting place. We made toy guns, swords, and skateboards with old roller skates.

I traded an electric train at Butch's Swap Shop on Hamilton Street for an old girl's bike, age nine (me, not the bike). Bo Dore, Larry Acker, Larry Gosen, and I and more kids rode to Anderson Pool and the Saginaw River, where I fell in. I learned to swim that day, only about six strokes, but I learned.

We fished off Ojibway Island. It was all trees and bushes then. We took our fish to the Saginaw Zoo and tossed them over the fence into the bears' pool. What fun it was to watch them.

The five and dime burned down; I don't remember the year, but we went through the rubble. We found toys and all kinds of wonderful things, especially the old metal squirt guns.

When we got twenty-five or fifty cents, we went to Kresge's Basement. It was downtown on Genese Street.

We went to the Wolveren Theater and the Court for the Saturday matinees. That cost nine cents. We went to Farnum's or Chambelin's Drug Stores for Lemon or Cherry Cokes. They were six cents each. Both of those stores were on Court Street.

I got my haircuts for twenty-five cents at the shop on Court Street. It was in a block of wooden buildings, three steps up from the sidewalk.

I belonged to Scout Troop 39 at the First Methodist Church for six years. We went to Jamboree on Ojibway Island, tents and all, like scouts. The church was on Michigan near the courthouse. It has moved since then.

The library was another hangout. We spent a lot of time at church for Sunday school, Methodist Youth Fellowship (MYF), and Bible class.

I did not see a television until I was fifteen. Saturday was the radio day. There were kids' programs in the morning, like *Big John and Sparky*. In the evening, *The Shadow Knows* and *Gang Busters* were on.

Crime, we never heard of it. The school I went to, North Intermediate, is gone now.

This does not do justice to my childhood, over sixty years ago.

bugs and had never seen any, coming from downtown Detroit. Myron and I just laughed.

I sure miss Anna, Albert, and Myron! They are fine memories. They are all deceased, along with the farm home and buildings. No one would even know of their existence or of them every living by me. My home is gone, just like the memories of them, and now I am the only person to tell the history. I sure loved them and am happy to know they did exist.

Memories of Anna
By Clayton Brauher of Vestaburg, Michigan
Born 1951

My name is Clayton Brauher, and I was born November 19, 1951 in Gratiot County, Michigan. Gratiot County is located in the geographical center of Michigan. I was raised and lived near Riverdale, Michigan, over on the west side of Gratiot County. Many things have come and gone in the sixty or so years, such as building sites and the people who once lived and thrived there.

One of the near neighbor families I had were African Americans. They once lived in South Carolina and moved to Detroit, Michigan in 1910. Later, around 1945 they relocated to central Michigan. Anna was the oldest, and she told me her father was a freed slave. She had other siblings, but I never was acquainted to any of them. She was the youngest of them, and she was born in May of 1891 and she died in 1994, just after celebrating her 103rd birthday.

Her only son, Albert, lived with her. I worked for him. He had a gardening business, raising collard, mustard, and turnip greens. He and his mother, Anna, raised the finest watermelons you could ever eat. She brought with her to Michigan her secret of raising them from the southeastern state. Anna had a grandson, Myron, who lived with her and Albert. He was a very good friend of mine. Myron and I worked with Albert raising vegetables and various fruits.

They would occasionally have company to come and visit from Detroit. One time there were two brothers, Sputnick and Bunkey Johnson, who came to stay, and one night Myron and I caught them hiding up in an apple tree. They were afraid of the lightning

The Hideaway
By Jack L. Long of Saginaw, Michigan
Born 1937

Shortly after World War II, my parents bought this house with a side yard. I was about eight years old. Dad and Mom were both working. Mom worked the second shift, and Dad worked the day shift. My two brothers and I had to be in the yard during the time Mom left for work and Dad came home.

Those were the days before television, and my two brothers and I had to find something to do with each other during the time we were stuck in our own yard. As most siblings, we were always fighting and arguing. When I got tired of all the noise, I would go to my secret hideaway.

My hideaway was a tree in the back corner of our yard. It was a maple tree with heavy foliage. I remember when someone told me it was a maple I attempted to get some maple syrup from it, and then I was told it was the wrong kind of maple.

I would climb about fifteen feet up in the tree and would be in a totally different world, a world where a ten year old could use his imagination and be anything his mind wanted him to be. I can remember flying P-40s over Germany, blowing up German planes and railroads to bits. I also flew B-24s over the Japanese held islands and bombed them into submission. It also was my treehouse when I wanted to be Tarzan. I also shot many Indians and outlaws from those lofty heights.

It was my refuge when I was sad and disappointed. It was a place a boy could go just to get away from the problems of being a boy. I would sit up there for hours just watching the world go by. If I was extra quiet and sat very still, hardly breathing, the birds would come by and land only an arm length away and go about their business.

The nicest thing was I could climb that tree and my brothers would never find me unless they stood under the tree and looked straight up. To this day, I don't think anyone knew where my hideaway was.

A couple of years ago I drove past the old place. The house is gone and a new one is in its place, and the vacant lot has a house on it. But the tree is still there and is giving shade for two families. But somehow it doesn't look that high anymore. The tree, I believe, is about 75 years old, and I wonder how many boys and girls have found that old tree to be the comfortable hideaway that I did fifty years ago.

Dorothy Clark in 1948/49

A Flashback on the Good Old Days
By Dorothy Clark McKandes of Saginaw, Michigan
Born 1937

Your request for people telling a "downhome" story about their childhood years is perfect timing, especially since I am approaching my 60th high school class reunion to be held September 18, 2015.

I immediately started reflecting on my past. I have so many fond memories, and it seems the good outweighs the bad. I am a native of Saginaw, attended the public schools, graduated from the newly built Saginaw High in 1955, and pursued a college career all the way to a Master of Arts (M.A.) degree with honors from Central Michigan University.

In my earlier childhood days, I attended Houghton Elementary and lived at 1310 Carlisle Street. In a class of around twenty-seven students in the fifth grade, there were three African American students.

We rarely had a substitute. I really can't recall the teachers not being in attendance on a daily basis. During those days, we had respect for our teachers and parents, which is lacking with many of the youth of today.

My junior high school days were spent at Central Junior High, located at the time at 900 South Weadock. The building was vacated after sixty years of service. My father and two aunts who arrived in Saginaw in 1928 were products of the junior high school and were identified as a three-generation Central Junior High School African American family.

I had wonderful memories of seventh through ninth grades. My favorite subjects were English, Typing, and Music. The students elected me president of the Acapella Choir in the ninth grade. My favorite teacher was Ms. Dorothy Lumbum, who taught gym.

The first couple of years of college was a learning experience, getting acquainted with new friends and learning new surroundings. However, things began to get better. My roommates were super and my grades improved, which made it worthwhile attending college.

While attending college, during the summer months I worked for the Parks and Recreation Department in Saginaw as a playground leader, cashier, and pool attendant. In 1957, I was the first African American female candidate for Ms. Anderson Pool Queen.

During my first year in 1956 at the college, the girls in the dormitory would come to our room, especially on the weekends. We'd turn on the record player, enjoying newcomer none other than Elvis Presley. On the radio from Nashville, Tennessee, the sounds of Bo

Diddley and Little Richard were heard. Those were good times and a break from our lessons.

My roommates were two Caucasian women and one African American woman. We were very close and got along very well. My African American roommate Miss Climetene "Clim" McClain and I remained friends for many years, and she passed away in 2010. She was a classy lady who served as secretary to the Board of Governors at Wayne State University in Detroit, MI for many years.

I have dedicated my life to education, community service, church, and volunteer work. I retired as an educator in 2003 after twenty-five years of service. When I think of any of my successes in life I am thankful to God from whom all blessings flow; my wonderful parents, who were excellent role models; and my friends, who have had the same values, goals, interests, etc. *All* have enriched my life.

Thank you for the opportunity to 'flashback' on the good old days. Much success with your history book. I enjoyed sharing.

You Can't Beat the Good Old Days!
By Richard "Dick" Guttowsky of Freeland,
Michigan
Born 1946

I was born in November 1946 to a very loving set of parents. I was the last of four children. I had two older brothers and an older sister. My sister was the third born, and I was nine years younger than her, so I'm not sure I was planned. I used to kid my mom a lot about that, and she never did give me a straight answer. My dad was sick a lot, so he would struggle with two or three jobs to try to make ends meet. He was a very hard worker and did a lot of janitorial jobs and was very proud of his work. You could see your face in his floors that he would take care of in the schools and offices he cleaned.

Back in the '50s and '60s as I was being raised up, in Carrollton, MI many things were different. It was a wonderful era. Kids played ball at the local ball field or in an empty lot till the street lights came on and the parents never had to worry about them. There were

no drive-by shootings or a lot of bullying back then. Most people never even had to lock their house when they went away. Those were the good old days!

I can remember many times when my mom would send me to the corner store, Klink's Market to get a few things, like bread and milk, and I would sign for them. My dad would pay them on Friday when he got paid. If they ran short, the storeowner knew us all by name and trusted his customers, as the customer trusted them.

I would come home from school, Bethlehem Lutheran School and Mom would have fresh baked bread, cinnamon rolls, coffee cakes, or cookies on the table. On Sundays, we would come home from church, Bethlehem Lutheran Church and the windows in the house were all steamed up from the Sunday dinner cooking in the pressure cooker. I still remember the sound of that. Ha ha, the good old days, indeed!

My dad's family was very musical, playing almost any instrument you put in their hands, and they sang too. Most of the time that was our family's entertainment on the weekends. Dad and his brothers and sisters would play music, and as kids, if we didn't join in, we would be off playing in a ballgame. They even played in some blind pigs during Prohibition. I ran into a former policeman who told me he used to go into the blind pig and listen to them because they "could really play some music."

I have memories of laying on the bed with my dad on Friday and Saturday nights, listening to *The Grand Ole Opry* on the old Silvertone radio. Back then, we didn't have a TV. My sister and I used to play marbles a lot on an oval rug Mom had. That was our entertainment. Also back then we didn't have computers, tablets, and all the technology around today, so we made our own entertainment and did many things as a family. Once again, those were the good old days!

When TV came out, the shows were outstanding. I remember watching *My Friend Flicka*, *The Roy Rogers Show*, *Howdy Doody*, and the list goes on. In the evening there was *Little House on the Prairie*, *Bonanza*, Art Linkletter, Red Skelton, and again, the list goes on. It is hard to beat them good old days!

I followed in my dad's footsteps as far as music goes. When I was four or five, I remember the neighbors coming over and asking me if I would come and sing for their company. I grew up playing music and singing. It was what I did and still do. I have sung in many establishments around our area, and presently I sing in several nursing homes and assisted living places and love it. I always tell people there is no better medicine than music and laughter, and I strongly believe that. It does my heart good to see them old people tapping their toes to the music and sometimes singing along with me. I am often asked how I got into music, and I tell them the story. I also tell them I have always loved old people, and now I am one. How time flies by when you are having fun in the good old days!

Back in the day, the music was great. There was Elvis, Motown, and all the doo-wop stuff and nothing better than country music. When a car came down the road, most of us could tell you what type of car it was and what year it was. If you was really good and into cars, you could even say what size motor it had in it, the cubic inches, and the horsepower. The cars today look a lot alike. Don't get me wrong, they have come a long ways, but they still don't have the style of the '50s and '60s cars. Those were the good old days!

I always had a job as a kid, shoveling snow, cutting grass, working at the corner grocery store, or whatever. That would put a little money in my pocket. When Mom would buy my school clothes each year, if there was something a little special I wanted she would say, "I was going to buy these at this price, but if you want those, you can pay the difference and get them." I had one bike as a kid, and it was an old used one. It pedaled so hard I would usually walk it home, because I was too tired from pedaling it.

Even though we didn't have much my dad would say, "You have the rest of your life to work, so if you want to play sports, you do it. We will figure it out somehow." And I did. I loved sports almost as much as music and still do. I went to a brand new high school, Carrollton High School, so we usually played against kids that were older than us and more experienced, so the first couple of years we kind of took it on the chin, but I would not have it any other way. This past summer we had our 50th class reunion, and oh, how great it was to see some of the old friends. Oh, the good old days!

When I graduated from high school, I was still only seventeen. My dad was disabled with no money coming in yet, so as soon as I was old enough, at eighteen, I got a job working for General Motors in a foundry. Until my dad got his Social Security, which took much longer than it should have, I paid their bills and had no problem with that. They were outstanding parents, and it was the least I could do. Back then, if you were not cut out for college or could not afford it, there were good paying jobs in the auto plants. Another sign of the good old days!

My dad passed away at 59 with emphysema. This terrible disease eventually got my sister too at an early age. If there is one thing that is better today, in my opinion, it is the amount of people who quit smoking and smoking not being allowed in many public places. My mom passed away at 94 with Alzheimer's, which is another terrible sickness. It took two of her sisters, one of their sons, and now my oldest brother has it pretty bad. It is very hard to watch them fade away and not even know you. It's very hard to see anyone go through that, but especially a close loved one.

I feel I was very fortunate and lived through an outstanding era. When you grow up with loving parents and good times, there is no way you can beat the Good Old Days!

The Lady of the House
By Alice Piechotte of Saginaw, Michigan
Born 1926

I grew up in a small town. I was the lady of the house at twelve years old. I walked to school because there were no buses. High school was a mile away.

We lived in a rental apartment with no bathroom. It did have strange wallpaper. We had an outhouse and the chamber pot upstairs. We had no car, phone, or running water. The town pump was a block away. We did have a cistern. Cars did have rumble seats. Gas was eleven cents a gallon.

On laundry day, we had a pail with a rope tied to the handle. We pulled enough pails of water to fill a boiler on the stove. When it got hot, we dumped it into the wringer washer. We did a batch of white clothes first and then

Alice and her friend Pat

graduation, I got a job at the same post office. We had to hand stamp every letter. It was a one-room post office with no restroom.

We took turns on Saturday night for our weekly bath. We had a galvanized washtub in the kitchen. During the week, we washed in a washbasin. For drinking water, we had a pail of water on the cupboard with a dipper hanging on it. Everyone drank from it.

We had an icebox, which was four feet tall with two doors. There was a bucket in the bottom to catch the water. We had two signs for twenty-five or fifty pounds of ice. We put the sign in the window so the iceman knew which one we wanted.

My brother had a paper route. I would help him deliver papers, and he paid me twenty-five cents. On Sunday, my friends and I took the bus downtown for a nickel to the movies, which was ten cents and bought a candy bar for five cents.

We did have one radio. It was on the table by my father's favorite chair. We had to listen to his programs. My aunt gave me a wind-up record player. My father wouldn't listen to my country music, and I couldn't listen to his symphony music.

My mother did take us to a swimming hole down to the river when we were young. By the time we walked home, we were hotter than when we went. It was called B.A.B.

My mother had died when I was young. Women gave birth to babies at home. She died in the next bedroom giving birth to my brother, George.

Those were the "good old days."

the dark clothes. In the summer, we hung the clothes outside. In the winter, we put nails on top of doorframes in the living room and strung rope back and forth. We had to duck under the clothes.

There was no television, so we played outside a lot. We played baseball, jacks, jump rope, marbles, and hopscotch. After dark, we played hide and seek. We bought our first television in 1949. It was black and white.

To keep us well in the winter my father lined us kids up to get our weekly teaspoon of fish oil. When we caught a cold, my grandmother would mix up our cough medicine with whiskey in it.

Being lady of the house, I had to shop for groceries. My father gave me twenty dollars. I rode the bus for a nickel downtown to the A&P Grocery Store. I bought a week's groceries and rode a cab home. At that time, hamburger was nineteen cents a pound.

There was no mail delivery. My daily job was to go to the post office for our mail. Later on after

Carrollton, Michigan Post Office where Alice worked in 1944

51

The Boys' Idea
By Clyde Shaffner of Freeland, Michigan
Born 1940

The early 1950s lent itself too many good memories at the Phetteplace Country School. One of which was the day we 7th and 8th grade boys found the clean out door in the bottom of the furnace chimney. This set the idea that behind the door had to be some good up draft and along with that came the thought that this might unroll some toilet paper. We had several rolls at hand in the nearby storeroom. We let the draft take several rolls up and out to "teepee" the trees in the whole area. That was how a few 7th and 8th grade boys could "teepee" about 80 or 90 trees at one time.

I don't think the teacher ever had a clue how this happened. I was one of those 7th grade boys at Phetteplace School.

Shelby Public Schools
By Norma Aebig Halverson of Muskegon, Michigan
Born 1931

In 1936 my parents bought a house north of Shelby. It had a long woodshed with an outhouse at the end. My dad removed the woodshed and the outhouse and built a bathroom inside the house. We used chamber pots in the upstairs bedrooms. We called them commonets.

We were still feeling the effects of the Depression of 1929 and could not afford much. Therefore, my mother used home remedies for our ear aches and other illnesses.

We all huddled around the radio to listen to the Lone Ranger. No televisions back then.

Yes, we had party line phones. When the phone rang, everybody picked up their phones. If school was cancelled because of weather, one long ring was given and everybody picked up the phone so the message was given, "There will be no school today in Shelby."

My brother, Wayne, used to race in the Jalopy Races. My mother would never go and watch him, as she didn't want to see him get hurt.

When we took our Saturday night baths, we all used the same bath water. There were 6 children. We always had to conserve water.

My mother took feed bags and washed them up to make clothes for us. The bags came in prints and designs.

My mother was scared of storms so when the thunder and lightning started, she took us to a room and closed all the curtains.

My sister and I had pet rabbits. We raised quite a few and named them after our friends. One night, dogs got into our pens and killed most of our rabbits.

My dad had a workshop where he kept his carpenter supplies. After he left for work, we took out his boards, tools and nails, and made cages, tracks, and houses. When he came home, he took everything apart and put it back in the shed. He never got mad at us, but did lock the door.

During recess, we would pick sides and play hide and seek. It was war time so we had Americans against the Germans.

We took field trips to Pipers Creek, Claey's Orchard, and the sugar bush shack. They tapped the maple trees and gathered pails of sap, which was boiled down into maple syrup. When we visited them, they gave us samples of maple syrup.

Every Saturday night, they had outside movies, which we liked to go to.

In 1941, when I was in the 4th grade, we wrote 'A History of Shelby Public Schools.' We gathered information from our local

Peggy, Diane, Patricia, Marcia, Jean, and Karen

people. We are very proud of our story, as it shows how Shelby Schools have improved. This was a school project and was never published.

The Nifty Fifties
By Mirdza S. Randall of Big Rapids, Michigan
Born 1942

In the early '50s, my family lived in Grand Rapids, Michigan on Howland Street off lower Monroe, one block from the Grand River. We had just arrived from Europe, 5 or 6 years before, as refugees. I was the oldest, then my brother, and little sister. We had all kinds of "adventures."

Once the boys on the black caught some nasty water snakes and chased us girls with them. Ugh! My older cousin actually built a raft on the riverbank and used a pole to maneuver it. I wanted to get on too, but he said no.

One interesting thing we did was to put good sized rocks on the railroad tracks because we thought we could derail the train. We never did.

A quart of milk was delivered every day and put in the insulated box on the porch and the empty one picked up. There was always two inches of cream on top. Yum!

One summer there was a tornado. The skies turned pink and pea green. The wind and rain arose and blew metal garbage can lids around. We kids got into bathing suits. Our parents were upstairs with our dying grandfather. With our limited English, we thought somebody said it was a "tomato." I saw the tornado, or tomato, go up and down across the river. No one knew to be afraid and run to the basement. The next day, we heard what all happened where it actually hit. It had ended at Comstock Park. Also, Allendale. This might have been 1954. Cows were driven feet first into the ground. A few people died, and we kids on the block, unknowingly, had fun.

In winter, we sledded down the steep end of the street joyfully avoiding the parked cars.

One summer while I was at camp, one of the newer boys on our block dared to walk on the elevated Leonard Street railroad bridge over the river. A train came and everyone survived, but him. He froze and was hit and died.

We often went to the movies. One evening a friend and I saw a scary movie. While walking home in the dark, suddenly Gilbert, my neighbor, jumped our screaming from the bushes. We were scared to death.

In summer, we put on roller skates onto our shoes using a metal key and skated on the cement sidewalks. The sound alone was mesmerizing from metal to cement. We also played a lot of jump rope at which I excelled. Then there was marbles using a cigar box with a hole in it. Certain marbles were prized, like a cat's eye.

We had a couple of old spinster sisters next door. One day, I was on their porch and soon was surrounded by angry yellow jackets. I got stung so badly.

We also had a crabby old couple on the other side. They loved their flowers and built a tall fence around their property. What they didn't know was that Gilbert and friends built a "clubhouse" right up against their fence. I wanted to be a part of whatever was going on there, but they kept me out. It was probably for my own good. However, Mary Anne Borkowski was allowed in.

Another thing about Mary Anne- she and I went to the 5 and 10 store. When we came out, she grinned and opened her coat. To my horror, she had all kinds of merchandise stashed in it!

Such was life on Howland Street. My parents soon decided to move across town for a safer environment for their children. Boy, was I sad and miserable to be parted from my friends. I'm sure that all across America, much of the same scenario played out but we kids thought we were in Shangri-La on Howland Street. And for a while, we were.

The Rooster at the Outhouse
By Nancy Wrathell of Sanford, Michigan

I remember when I was about 3 or 4 and had to use our outhouse. When I went outside, my mother heard me screaming and found our bantam rooster on my head pecking me! From that day on, I disliked chickens and when I got older and was sent out to get the eggs, I took a stick with me to chase the hens off their nests to get the eggs.

I remember one year when we got a lot of snow and it drifted so high it reached the top of the fence where the chickens were. I had to walk up over the fence to get into the pen.

Once, my sister, two neighbor girls, and myself smoked a whole pack of unfiltered Lucky Strike cigarettes when I was about 13 or 14. I never got sick but I never became a smoker! Our parents never found out we did that. We lived in Midland, Michigan at the time.

My Father's Rifle
By George Fabera of Hale, Michigan
Born 1941

I was born March 18, 1941. The fifth of a six child family. We lived in rural Prescott, Michigan. The day before I was born, the road commission plowed the road to my family's house with a bulldozer because the snow was so deep, so the doctor could get there for my delivery.

When I was 5 years old and walking 2 1/5 miles to Nester School, we had to cross a creek on an iron bridge with iron guard rails. It was a daily thing to watch the creek flow for a little while. I learned don't put your tongue on an iron rail when it is extremely cold. I left some "skin" off my tongue there when I jerked it loose. I cried for ½ mile before I told my older sister what happened.

It was not an unusual winter to walk on snow banks beside the road and be higher than the telephone wires.

It was interesting to go to a one-room school with 8 grades. We had a music teacher come once a month to teach singing and a nurse would come once in a while to check the health of pupils.

After my older brother and sister started high school, the bus driver would let us younger kids ride the bus and drop us off when we got to our country school. He would pick us up when we were walking home also. I hated it when there was a substitute bus driver because the regular driver gave us rides on his own.

My mother got the responsibility of raising us six children when I was 8 years old. We had some cows and she worked out to make ends meet. Most of her jobs were physically demanding, like peeling the bark off pulpwood with a draw knife. She would come home tired and sore. She had a bad leg, which she broke as a youngster in Indiana when she was playing with her cousin's (Wendell Willkie) motorcycle, and it tipped over on her and broke her leg. The doctor who set the leg had bones overlapped and they healed that way.

An uncle from Indiana traded a Winchester 4590 rifle for a 30-30 rifle my father had. The 4590 was a beautiful rifle. It was nickel plated (shiny) with a gold seal on it. The only thing is if you didn't scare the deer away with the shiny rifle, it didn't shoot straight enough to hit one. Venison was a large part of our diet.

My mother eventually sold this rifle for $40.00. The man who bought it, later sold it for $200.00. It was then sold to someone in California for thousands of dollars and then donated to someone in Arizona and then financed the building of a library. Back then antiques had little value to a fairly large family trying to survive.

This rifle was researched back to being a part of the Chicago 1904 World's Fair. I would sure like to know where the rifle is now.

When I was a young teenager in high school, I used to work for a man in my spare time and summers, cutting wood and putting up hay. One of my memories is when he stopped at the high school I was in and got permission from the principal for me to go to the woods when he had a tractor to take home. I took his brand new Nash Rambler back to school and after school was out, I drove it to his place. The highlight of this is I drove it over 15 miles without a driver's license. I was too young to get one.

I graduated from high school at age 17, then joined the Army.

My graduating class has a reunion every year (57 years this year) and out of the 30 graduates, there are still 26 alive.

The Family Farm
By Judy Pranger of New Era, Michigan
Born 1944

The farm that I grew up on was 60 acres with 20 of that in the woods. "A wonderful place for children," my parents thought when

Ken Huston and Judy's dad, Loren in 1952

they bought the place, the summer I turned 8. The 2-story farmhouse had a large attic for storage and 2 bedrooms upstairs and a dirt floor cellar. A big oil stove that sat off to the side of our dining room heated the kitchen, dining room, living room, and one bedroom that was on the main level. There was also one bathroom that was an add-on and some heat went up the stairs to our two bedrooms. In the winter, if it got in the single digits outside, we would close off the living room where the TV was, but we didn't watch it all that much. We would heat our blankets before taking them upstairs to our rooms. Us 2 girls would often see snow on our window sills as we were on the east side of the upstairs and it sure didn't take us long to dress in the mornings.

Girls wore skirts and petticoats with snow-pants under them for our mile walk across fields to school. I was the oldest so I made the path for the younger ones. It was my responsibility to see that my 2 brothers and young sister got to school and home again, as our one car was used to get our dad to work. When the wind would blow the snow so our gravel road was closed, Dad would stop on his way home, once a week, to get the groceries and we would bring our sleds the quarter mile to the nearest plowed road to help Dad haul the groceries home. It could be several days that Dad would park the car in a friend's driveway on that main road, and would walk home, and then walk to the car the next morning to shovel it out before going to work.

Our school had a playroom with a ping-pong table and basketball hoop for inside play on rainy days; or the room could be used for potlucks. We would have social events like a play we would put on for a community gathering. What fun it was, as we could pretend to be someone in the play and dress up and sing crazy songs. Everyone would have a part. The 7th and 8th graders would put up the stage in front of our classroom and help the younger ones learn their lines. We still had our classes of reading, spelling, writing, arithmetic, and geography. It was the 8th graders that got the Christmas tree from a farmer nearby, and organized the playground games. I could hardly wait to be an 8th grader. We enjoyed sliding, building forts, and making snowmen in the winter, and as soon as the snow was off the fields, it was tag, hide and seek, and baseball season. The little ones ran bases, and the teacher was the umpire. Parents would drive us to other schools for an after school game.

Besides baseball, there was asparagus to pick. Sometimes, we had breakfast before Dad fed the calf and chickens, to get an hour or two on the job before school. A quick hand washing so we were ready to say the Pledge of Allegiance to our flag, as this was important to each of us. Then after school, we hurried home and to the field to finish picking the green vegetable. If we were finished before the canning factory closed, the farmer would give us a ride home on the tailgate of his truck, usually just in time to set the table for supper. After supper, it was chore time; gathering eggs, feeding livestock, or planting or weeding a row in the garden. Dad raised

Fae planting her garden in 1952

55

a two-acre garden of every kind of vegetable to feed a family of six. We even had our own popcorn that we dried by our oil stove in the fall.

Sunday mornings, it was hurry to get the animals fed, have a family breakfast, and then pile into our station wagon to get to church before the 9:30 bell. Sunday after dinner, it was family time. Dad would read a long story to us. We would have popcorn and make fudge. In the summer, we would take long walks in the woods to look for mushrooms and wild flowers, or to see where the deer slept, or to count squirrel nests.

Summer was also a time for picking what was ripe in the garden so Mom would can or freeze it for winter. I trained the calf for the Hart Fair, which was also our winter meat, along with our chickens and rabbits, and sometimes a couple squirrels that my brothers would hunt. Grandpa and Grandma would often come and help prepare the chickens and rabbits for the freezer, and spend the day with us.

Fun family time was year 'round on the farm.

Judy's farmhouse in 1952

Snow Jell-O and Swallowing Bees
By Rita Morgan of St. Louis, Michigan
Born 1950

I grew up in a small town in northern Michigan. We had a very large family; 20 children, nine boys and eleven girls, one boy was still born.

When I was in high school, Mom had twins! There was one more baby after the twins. Most of us were born at home, assisted by the preacher's wife, until the doctor could get there. We did not have a phone, at that time, so someone had to run to a neighbor's to call. If someone was on the party line, you had to wait.

I was number eight; everyone knew their number. Dad had a nickname for each of us. Not to be used by others.

My dad built our house from used lumber he got from tearing down old homes. We lived in the basement for a few years. We didn't have electricity until we moved upstairs. I was six then. When living in the basement, Mom cooked on a large woodstove. She made several loaves of bread weekly. We ate a lot of pancakes, potatoes, beans, and macaroni. (Government surplus). We also ate wild game.

In winter, Mom made Jell-O in a large, metal pan. She would sit it out in the snow and we would watch out the window to guard it until it was done.

We picked wild blueberries, and blackberries. Mom canned them, and we ate them in the winter.

We ironed our clothes with flat irons, heated on the stove. We had a wringer washer that would have to manually turn the wringer. Later, we had one that plugged in. Lots of diapers to wash and hang on the line outside to dry. One time, when using the wringer washer, I got my long hair caught in it. I did remember to hit the top of it to get my hair out.

We listened to a radio that was hooked to a car battery. The Grand Ole Opry was a favorite. My dad played a violin and we sat around on the floor listening.

Our uncle lived next door and he and my dad drilled a well, which we shared until they got in an argument. No more water for us. We had to haul it from other neighbors, or from a spring down by the lake.

We also had an outhouse. It had two adult holes and a small one for babies. We can laugh about that now.

We lived close to the one-room school. We did very well, as we listened to the teacher teach the older kids. We took wax paper to sit on when playing on the slide. Parents did not know about that. It went really fast. But was not very safe.

My dad worked in the woods cutting trees. He used a horse to pull them when I was a kid. It was very hard work in the winter.

We lived close to Mullett Lake. It was fun in the summer. We learned to swim at an early age.

We also lived close to the church and were involved in several activities there. We joined 4-H and learned to cook, sew and knit. I learned how to sew on a treadle sewing machine.

Winters were long and cold. We played outside by sledding, skating, making forts, and snowmen. It was fun to play in but we hated to shovel it.

My brother made maple syrup from gathering sap from the trees.

I went fishing with Dad. He let me row the boat. He got tired of baiting my hook because I was just feeding the fish. I had to sit still and watch.

Water was heated in a washtub for bathing. Babies first.

My dad smoked a pipe, and my sister got in trouble for washing them. She said they stunk.

When I was 8 years old, my friend and I used to get a drink of water from an outside faucet near her house. One day, I got there first, put my mouth on it, and turned it on. I swallowed several bees. Her mom put her finger in my throat to make me vomit. The bees came back up, still alive.

We had no medical or dental insurance so we would have to suffer with a toothache. When I was in 5th grade, my teacher took me to get a tooth pulled. Mom would mix turpentine and lard, and put it on us when we were sick.

I slept with my sister, and I had a very bad cold. We were teenagers at the time. She told me to go put Vicks on my chest. I didn't want to wake up anyone, so I didn't turn on a light. I reached the jar up on a shelf, and put it on my chest. I could not smell because of my cold. Back in bed, she said I smelled like Noxzema. I turned on the light. She was right.

We played '45' records. My dad said if he heard "Wooly Bully" one more time, he would get rid of them. My brothers used them for Frisbees.

The only time all of us kids were together is when Mom died. We have a family reunion every summer, but someone is always missing.

City Boy to Country Boy
By Karl H. Klein of Saginaw, Michigan
Born 1933

I was born in Saginaw, Michigan during the Depression to hard working immigrant parents from Hungary. I was one of six children and didn't speak English until starting school. We had no indoor plumbing until much later when we moved to a better house. In winter we'd go down to the Saginaw River with our sleighs and cut ice for our icebox and get drinking water from a pump on our city street corner. Things were tough but we all worked hard to be a family. I even remember digging a spot in our backyard with a spade for a small garden. My mother worked for many years at Daily Pickle and so did my two sisters. She cooked the old fashioned way, making noodles, buba spatzles, strudels, knodels, and lots of soups. Once in a while, we'd get a dime to see a show.

As a boy, we'd travel to the Adam Nauman farm in Spaulding Township, where we worked picking up potatoes. They were unearthed by a team of horses pulling a shovel-like device to bring them out of the ground. We picked fruits, vegetables in season, and made sauerkraut from the cabbage. I even got head butted by their Billy goat. You didn't bend over in front of him; he saw an excuse to ram you. We did the haying by piling the hay in small piles, then forking them onto a wagon pulled by horses, and unloading it in the barn by hand to the loft. The modern machinery came later.

I joined the US Navy at seventeen, and was half way around the world by my eighteenth

Karl Klein, Lance, Kraig, little Marcie, and Karl's wife, Marsha in 1969

birthday. I encountered the Korean War, which was very difficult, but it made a man out of a boy. The military experience was a look at a new world and then coming home. I met the right people and secured a job at General Motors. I loved to dance and frequented The Revena Gardens quite often. I met a nice girl at a local B&G Drive-In restaurant in Spaulding Township and was introduced by my friend and coworker, Al Simko. The township had teen dances occasionally and this is where we met our friends and danced the night away to the music of one man, namely Alvin Sawatzki and his concertina.

Well, the friendship turned into love and marriage. My wife worked at the Michigan Bell Telephone Co. and was making a whopping ninety cents an hour. Shortly after our marriage, I got laid off from G.M. but I got a job working on a stone crusher at a gravel pit for fifty cents an hour. I made enough to pay the rent and shortly, got a call back from G.M. Things were looking better. We got a loan from my wife's grandfather and a lot from her parents, and we were in business building our own home. We cleaned cement blocks obtained from an old house and laid our foundation from plans we drew up ourselves. I'd go down to the lumber company and describe what I was doing and they would laugh at my descriptions and get me what I needed with instructions. We learned as we worked, and even dug our own space for our septic tank with a shovel. It's surprising what you can do when you put your mind to it. We planted a garden, canned vegetables and added to our small home, and I got a call back from my G.M. plant. Things were looking better.

We had three children in later years and all loved sports as I did. They all bowled in youth leagues at Candlelight Bowl, belonged to a 4-H club, and learned to sew, cook and can, as well as, making many collectable crafts from traveling vacations. We won many awards at the Saginaw Fair. Their mom was a bowling coach, 4-H leader, and I spent many years umpiring their ball games. One incident in particular comes to mind.

Little Bobby Dey was called "OUT" by me and he stood there a minute and turned around and said, "Mr. Klein, if you weren't so big, I'd wrap this bat around your head." Well, I was a fair umpire and had to call my own kids out. They didn't appreciate it either.

We took our kids on vacations every year. They saw 47 states during their childhood. We never had a chance to go on vacations in the early days, and after fifteen years, we really enjoyed seeing our kids have the opportunity to see things they will remember all their lives.

Looking back, it was a hard life but you learn from hardships. In my youth, I had fun roller skating, ice skating at Hoyt Park, watching fireworks, seeing horses pulling the milk wagon down our unpaved city streets. We played "kick the can" and riding a bike that I made myself. The city dump had a collection of scrap parts and I wasn't ashamed to assemble the parts that were needed, and was thrilled and proud of myself for putting a bike together. It wasn't pretty but it got me where I wanted to go.

Things have changes so drastically for our kids now, but in a good way. Just think of what they will be writing about in the next 50 years. Keep up your religious beliefs, see the good in others, and always know, "What goes around, comes around," and set a good example. I learned that there is a light at the end of the tunnel, which I found through dedication. I climbed up the ladder at G.M. and retired from management. Always have goals in life.

Bob's Puppy
By Janet Coleman of Evart, Michigan
Born 1957

As I stepped outside, I couldn't help but notice an animal eating out of our Bob's dish. It was very early in the morning, with the dew still on the grass and the fresh promise of another beautiful summer's day. No one was in sight. My dad and grandpa must have been down at the barn milking the cows. Mom, my brother, and sisters were still asleep. We'll soon find out that Grandma was not far away. The only one out and about on that front stoop was a little girl watching, what in her young mind, was Bob's puppy eating some breakfast.

We all lived together in a big farmhouse just a few miles from town. There was my dad and mom, my older brother and two younger sisters. Grandpa and Grandma lived in the other side of the house. My Uncle Merlin and Aunt Helen lived on their side as well, until they found their own wife and husband.

Who is Bob you might ask? Bob was the name my grandparents gave all the collie dogs we had to help out on our farm. I think this was Bob number 3. He was the one we always watched out for as we scooted out the door with one of Grandma's big, soft molasses cookies. We had to hold the cookie over our head or else Bob would take it from us, or at least take a bite! If we were in the barnyard and yelled, "Sick 'em, Bob. Sick 'em," he would run over and bite the nearest cow's ankle. Or if you "sicked" him on a snake he would kill that for you. The only time we saw him in the house was during thunderstorms. Then he would creep in, just inside the door until it was over.

Bob was nowhere in sight this morning. The only animal was a medium sized creature, white in color with a long, hairless tail. Of course, it was an opossum. As I reached out to pet this "puppy," he hissed. I was eminently alarmed and reached for the doorknob behind me, but he hissed again. I, taking the only course of action I knew, gave a scream, which made him hiss at me again. So there we were, me screaming, him hissing.

At last, Grandma heard me outside screaming and came out to see what all the ruckus was about. I told her I was trying to pet Bob's puppy but he kept hissing at me. Of course, this made her laugh. "Bob's puppy? Bob doesn't have a puppy! You get in here!" Grandma to the rescue.

My Hero
By Donna Gunderson of Belding, Michigan
Born 1950

My name is Donna Jean Abbott Gunderson. I was born in Sheridan, Michigan on April 11, 1950 at about 11:00am. I have a twin cousin born the same day and I was a twin.

My Grandmother, Dad's mom, would cook hominy. It smelled her whole house and I don't like the smell. She would also make homemade red and white peppermint candy. It was always on the table car for us kids to have. She passed away when I was four years old.

My dad built a house for us when I was older. We lived between Belding and Greenville, Michigan, on the outskirts of the woods. We had both a chamber pot for nighttime and an outhouse for daytime. It seemed like miles away when you had to go bad! We lived on Jenks Road but seems to me it was called Stakes Road then. We were the only house then back by the edge of the woods. We saw wolves out there. There were seven of us, Daddy, Mama and five girls! If we had earaches, daddy would light a cigarette and blow smoke in our ear and it seemed to work. If we had a sore throat, Daddy would put a tie around our throat and that worked too. We had a rotary phone, which was also on a party line. Sometimes we would listen in on other calls.

Saturdays were long days for me. I would get up before daybreak and make a peanut butter and jelly sandwich for me and Daddy to take when we went fishing. Sometimes it was scary on the lake. It was by a cemetery and when it started to get light, you could see the outlines of the gravestones! Then we would go home and then all of us would go to town to get groceries. Then on the way back home, we'd stop at a little store called Dakins and get ice cream cones! Later when we got home we would all take baths one at a time. Us girls in a round tub with water heated on the stove in pails. We didn't have water in the house then. We pumped water in pails from the well and took up to the house.

Sundays was just play day and wash day. I made a car and it was really a piece of wood. I made a bridge in the dirt with holes underneath for the water. Like a lake going under the bridge to drive my car over. Late on Sundays, we would do wash in an old wringer washer. We sometimes used a scrub board and hung them on the line outside. Then before bedtime, we got castor oil to get cleaned out and ready for school on Mondays. Yuk!

One day we had a blizzard with a huge hail stones. We all went to a country school called Forest Grove. It was a one-room schoolhouse, grades one through twelve. My favorite teacher was my music teacher, Mrs. Bird. I really loved to sing and still do. I thought I was a star singer. One day in junior high, some boys dangled another boy out a second story window and we all got spanked for that with a big board! It really hurt. One day at home, I was to get spanked for something so I put a book in my pants. Daddy hurt his hand when he hit the book! So I got sent to the corner which hurt me more because my Dad's hand was hurt which then made me cry.

Sometimes when we went to my grandparent's house, I would help with chores. Like milking cows by hand, feeding the chickens, and slopping the hogs. My favorite pet was a Siamese cat. One day I was sitting outside on a log with my two younger sisters, April and Debbie. A blue racer snake crawled up my leg! I screamed, my older sister Bonnie came and grabbed the snake and threw it across the road. She was the bravest ever! She was also good at getting rid of spiders and bees.

I remember school sock hops and listening to Elvis. Wow! Bo Diddley and Little Richard and a favorite song was Donna, of course, sang by Richie Valence. One day at school, Bobby Goldsboro came and sang Honey. I also got to meet Bobby Vincent at the Ionia Free Fair. One day I got in trouble by melting some of my sister Ruth's 45 records on the heating stove to make bowls. Oops! She was not happy.

Our milkman would leave three bottle of white milk and three bottles of chocolate milk on our front porch. My first kiss was by a neighbor kid. Yuk. But my first real love was a classmate. We grew up together and rode the same bus to school. Talk about moonstruck. So handsome! I got to see him every day, wow! What could be better, right? Well lucky for me it did get better. We are now very happily married. My Hero!

My Remembrance of Reed City
By Richard K. Karns of Reed City, Michigan
Born 1944

My brother Fred wrote an article for the "good old days" book, where he described the town in which we live. Reed City, Michigan from my brother's view is quite different from mine. I am the youngest of a family of twelve, and the sixth boy; our folks liked even numbers. I don't remember the three older siblings at home. The only point of reference I have, of them being home the same time I was, are the stories they told me. My oldest brother is twenty-two years older than me and

was in the Navy during WWII when I was born. Growing up in such a large family had its difficulties, but a lot of fun and adventure too.

In the thirteen years that separated my brother and I, there were some similarities and differences. We lived on the edge of town, so we could have a small farm, which consisted of three cows, pigs, rabbits, and once in awhile chickens. With a large family to feed, there were chores to be done. My chores, although I wasn't big enough as to taking the cow to pasture, or throw the loose hay into the hay loft, we didn't use bails that I remember. I was however big enough to help clean the gutters in the barn, help feeding the pigs, and feed the rabbits, and push the loose hay back into the hayloft so there was room for the rest of the hay. My parents stopped farming in our little farm in 1951.

There was always the garden and that continued way past 1951. With a family our size you can imagine it wasn't a small one. The garden always needed attention and the weeds always needed to be pulled. My two older brothers would use the hoe, my sisters and I would weed on hands and knees. We usually had quite a few of the neighbor kids helping too, because when we were finished, we would go to the lake or the river to swim. Lawn mowing was another chore; it was important to our father that the lawn was kept short. I can't remember just how old I was when Dad brought home a used power lawn mower and none of us boys cared how new it was, it certainly made mowing the lawn easier. Mowing the lawn in our house meant doing the front, side, and back of the lawn.

Like my brother stated in his article, we always had a yard full of neighbor kids. We played all kinds of games and played in the same old deserted mill my brother spoke about. It could be one day a pirate ship, on another day a castle, or a dozen other things we would think about when we were playing. There was a gas reserve station across from our house and they had replaced the three cement slabs in front of the fueling station and just piled them on top of each other on the edge of their property. We called them simply "The Rock." I can tell you the good times we had playing there.

There was an oil refinery across the field from where we lived. There were several

60

large holding tanks there too, about a quarter mile from our house. The dirt that was left over was just piled up and we would close our eyes and run off, landing in the loosed sand below. We called this pile of dirt "Old Suicide." It was considered a rite of passage for our neighborhood to see if you could walk on wooden stilts from our house to "Old Suicide" without falling.

The oldest sister I remember being home is ten years older than me. She had a wonderful imagination, She would make up plays that we would perform and create games we could play after dark. One of the best games was "murder by slips." We would play this on our front porch, which had a light so we could still see. Murder by slips consisted of a designated detective, usually one of the older kids, the murderer, the victim, and the rest of us would be a suspect that the detective would question, trying to find who the murderer was. Everyone who was playing would draw a slip of paper, all would be blank except for the murderer, theirs would have an M on the slip. The porch light would be turned off and the murderer would touch one of those playing. They would yell out and the lights would be turned on and the detective did their thing trying to figure out who the culprit was.

Our family was always playing cards or singing. At one time there were six of us in the choir of the Methodist Church we attended. Our mother often stated she would put her choir up against any ones. It wasn't uncommon to have the neighbors come out to listen to us. Our father was a great one for quoting poetry like "Uncle Josh," "The Wooden Wedding," "The Old Violin," and "The Sword of Bunker Hill."

Reed City in the 40s, 50s, and 60s was a great place to grow up. We had our own bowling alley, a theater, roller skating rink, and so many other things the kids today need to go elsewhere for. In these past decades, the skyline of Reed City looks very different than it did growing up. There aren't the stories or the industry we use to have, but what we do still have is worth having. We have great schools, a state of the art hospital, Susan F Wheatlake Regional Cancer Center, The Old Rugged Cross Historical Society Museum, and we still are a great church community; there are eleven churches.

I am three score and eleven and it is good to remember the old days, but it is even cooler to think of the possibilities that lie ahead and the good things that are yet to come.

A Great Childhood
By Shirley A. Weber of Richville, Michigan
Born 1935

I was born and raised at Weber Lumber (1935) about one mile east of Richville on M-46. Mother, Agnes had five children (Don, Ruth, Shirley, Marie, and Eugene) in six years, all born at home. Need I tell you how close in age we are? When my parents got married, my dad, Elmer Richville took over the business from my grandfather, Matthew Weber. Grandpa had a small office off the kitchen in the house. Every Friday the workers would come in to get their pay. Mom did not know how to drive a car (later she did) so there was no shopping. When she needed things, she would order them from the Penny's catalog and Grandpa would write out a check for the order. My dad would buy the groceries at Kern's store in town. After mom's sister died, who had two sons, they spent many summers with us. There was a huge garden and orchard, strawberry and raspberry patch. Mom canned everything and of course the girls had to help. We even had heifers, goats, chickens, dogs, and cats. There was butchering every year and sausage was made. Mom even rendered the lard and made her own soap. As soon as the girls were old enough and able to help, we were put to work. Cleaning house and hanging up the laundry outside in summer. In the winter, we hung it up in the attic or the basement. There were always lots of dishes to wash, no dishwasher, because Mom made everything from scratch. I, to this day, still love to cook and bake. The children all slept upstairs, we had a big house. There was only one radiator in the hallway for heat, two small closets, and get this, one bathroom downstairs. Sometimes you had to take a number and stand in line. In case of an emergency, there was an outhouse by the wood shed, which got used quite often. When we were little, all five kids, including the boys, would take a bath at one time. There was more water on the floor than in the tub by the time we all got out of there.

My dad employed about 15-20 men at the

Shirley's mother, Agnes Weber and her five children in 1946

business. There was a railroad track that ran behind the lumberyard. The train would drop off boxcars of lumber and pick up the empty ones. When we would hear the train coming, sometimes we would put a penny on the tracks so it would get flattened out. The conductor of the train and the man in the caboose always waved to us kids. Sometimes the younger kids would be hoisted up into the top of the boxcar, after it was opened (narrow opening) and help unload the wood flooring bundles or lumber. We also would have to help pile lumber. Many times hobos would come to the house (they would walk the tracks) asking for something to eat. Mom would make them do some chore before she fed them. As little kids we were so fascinated and felt sorry for them, this was way before welfare, food stamps, or government handouts. There were wild strawberries growing along the railroad tracks, which we

Marvin Bierlein and Shirley Weber in the early 1940s

had to pick and clean. Mom made them into the best jam! There was also a sawmill. Lots of woods in those days, trees were cut down and hauled to the lumber yard to be cut into lumber. As kids, we had to throw slab-wood, outer bark from the logs. We also had to bag the sawdust in burlap bags for the farmers who used it for the chicken coops. As if we didn't have enough to do, Dad would have us help some of the farmers in the area thin and hoe sugar beets, hoe corn and beans. When we were older and could drive the car, we would wear our swimsuits under our shorts. After we were done hoeing for the day, we would go swimming at the gravel pit in Juniata. Talk about being kept busy. I can never remember a time when I was bored! We got our first TV in 1948. Other than all the work, we did have

Shirely Weber hanging up clothes

a fun, loving childhood. There was a ditch running in front of the house. We would build bridges with old lumber that we confiscated. We also built waterfalls and go spearing fish in the spring. All five kids had to take piano lessons. The teacher, Mr. Eggert came to the house. My oldest brother, Don would hide in the sawdust shed and the girls or Mom would have to find him. His lessons were short lived. We also had a big pond at the lumberyard, in case of fire. So in the winter we would go ice skating and sledding. Mowing the lawn was different. Mom would tie a rope in front of the push mower. One kid would pull and the other one pushed the mower. In the fall, we would gather hickory nuts. Before Christmas we would sit around the big kitchen table and remove the nutmeat from the shells. They had to be cracked with a vice first. Mom made some delicious cookies with hickory nuts.

My ancestors came from Germany in

1845. We talked German till we went to school and learned English. During WWII we were not allowed to talk German at the office. Every Sunday we went to church, St. Michaels Lutheran in Richville. We also attended the parochial school and walked one ½ miles one-way everyday unless it rained or snowed too hard. Then we would get a ride. I could write another whole chapter just on the one-room schoolhouse we all attended for six years and the outdoor toilet!

I was blessed to have had a great childhood, loving, kind parents, and a Christian upbringing. I can remember only one time that I got a spanking from my dad. My Mom even had to tell him to do it. And I know it hurt him more than me! And that's another story.

On The Farm
By Mary L. Cotton of White Cloud, Michigan
Born 1934

In 1941, property was cheap and our Malcomnson family found a good deal on a 180-acre farm in Gladwin County, four miles east of Beaverton. It had a large, run-down house, a barn that needed work, and 100 acres of woods. The land was mostly sandy loom, and our neighbors told us it might not grow good crops. There was no running water and no electricity. But just like me at seven years old, it had lots of potential.

We had a strange pattern of moving twice a year. In the summer, we moved to the farm and tilled the land, growing a garden that fed us vegetables all year, because we preserved them in jars. When it was time for school to begin in the fall, we moved to wherever my father was teaching school that year. Mom taught piano to nearly all the little musicians where we were, since she had majored in music at Central Michigan College. Daddy taught elementary and secondary classes and later counseled and taught agriculture. He also trained at Central and then at Michigan State College.

There was my older brother Robert, then me (Mary), next my brother John, and youngest was Ruth. We got quite used to making new friends quickly in new schools. Each time we moved our animals went along. Our cow Suzy soon would walk right up into the trailer without coaxing. She gave us our fresh milk and our chickens kept us in fresh eggs. Grandma Molly Malcomnson also lived with us after Grandpa died.

Some places we lived we added more cows and we kids learned to milk by hand morning and night. My job was also to gather eggs and feed chickens. Some hens didn't want to give up anything, even though I cooed to them as I reached under them. And the rooster was awful; often he would attack me as if he was defending the flock. That's when he got a big kick that sent him flying. Maybe that's how I learned to defend myself.

Milking cows had its own dangers. Their tails were often manurey and wet and they switched them in my face! Some cows moved around a lot, even stepping into the pail of milk. Then we had to feed that dirty pail full to the animals instead of drinking ourselves. It didn't take long to feel familiar with the herd, though, and I would walk among them in the pasture before chasing them to the barn at milking time.

Our food on the farm was cooked on a wood range, and our heating stove was also fueled with wood. We cut trees from our own woods, sawed them up by hand, and hauled them to the yard.

Flushing was unknown at the farm, so we wore a path in the backyard to the outhouse. Inside was a bench big enough for two people, with two round holes cut into the bench. My job was to sweep it once a week and clean all the bugs out. Robert was to regularly put lime down the holes to sweeten the odors. Daddy whitewashed the outhouse inside and outside as needed. In winter, we were allowed to use a "slop jar" at night, as long as we emptied it the next morning and rinsed it out. If we ran out of toilet tissue, we kept an old Sears catalog there for emergencies.

The well was about 50 yards from the house. It wasn't long until a man came to dig a well closer to the house. First he wanted to "witch" a well; using a Y-shaped willow branch. He gripped the Y and walked around until the pointed end forced its way down to point straight to the ground to a water vein. But Daddy insisted the well man should dig right by the house anyway.

For laundry days, we carried extra water for Mom to heat in her large boiler on the kitchen range. She dipped hot water into her wringer Maytag, run by a gasoline engine, and placed the exhaust pipe out the kitchen door. She had a tub of cold water, where she dipped the clothes up and down until they were rinsed and ready to squeeze dry by running each garment through the wringer rollers. Then they were hung on the wire clothesline with clothespins in the backyard. In cold weather, the garments froze dry, going from stiff to flexible as they dried.

Working in the fields, weeding, or hoeing under the hot sun for hours in the corn or potatoes, was boring and back breaking. The whole family started out right after a big breakfast and worked until time for Mom and me to fix a big noon dinner. For once, I was glad I was a girl. The boys kept working with Dad until they heard the dinner bell ring.

In spite of all the work a farm demands, I sometimes had time to lie on the summer grass and watch the clouds change shapes, while my dreams took shape. At night, I might look at stars and moon and wonder at a God who could make beautiful things. At times, I became a glamorous actress and singer on my stage, a hay wagon. Because I was gifted to remember song lyrics, even now I can sing those same songs, at eighty years of age.

Mary Story

My dreams only went as far as finishing high school. I couldn't imagine anything beyond being a teenager. Oh, maybe someday I'd get married to a handsome man with dark hair and a big smile. Like the photos of movie stars that covered the walls of my bedroom.

Barryton ninth grade boys were so immature. Some were cute, all right, and we wanted them to admire us. But they were awkward about approaching girls; they never knew what to say. It's like they waited for us girls to make the first move if we wanted anything to happen at all. And any boys who had a crush on one of us girls just passed notes in class, risking getting caught, or they told their friends to tell us they like us. Cowards!

For now, I would just stick to basketball, singing in the choir, playing my clarinet in the band, and going to church. At least I could count on God to continue caring about me and treating me fairly. He promised that in the Bible, which I enjoyed reading often.

I remember the first time I took God seriously, I was four years old, and I was in Sunday school. We sang about Jesus as a baby, then as a man who did miracles like healing people. He loved the sinful ones who did awful things to him, even killing him after torturing him. How could he forgive them? I wouldn't have. Our teacher, Miss Elma Rau, told us we could be made different and new if we believed in Jesus. I knew in my heart then that it was all true, that Jesus was real and not just a story.

This first year in high school, I was busy enough without worrying about boys, especially adding my morning and evening chores. Saturdays were usually busy with family events, either work projects or rare times of fun. There was my older brother Robert and my younger brother John, besides me. My younger sister Ruth had died when a car hit her as she walked home from Vacation Bible School. My family was never the same again after that happened.

On hot summer days, we would finish our work in the cornfield or in the garden, and then beg for one of our parents to drive us in our 1940 Plymouth to a nearby lake or the Tobacco River to swim. Usually Mom and Dad were too tired or had other plans. When we could go, we had a great time in the water! I never wanted to get dry.

Another recreation our family enjoyed was visiting other families. In the summer we were close to relatives, so we got together often with them to sing around the piano for hours. That's where I learned the words to hymns and folk songs, as well as some popular songs from the thirties and forties.

My mom usually was the pianist for gatherings. She also sang solos and directed church choirs. She got me started singing in public when I was three years old. I still sing occasionally, especially in groups, as an alto. I prefer singing gospel songs.

My cousin Laveria Mishler, Ann Berman, and I formed a trio and sang in churches. We also signed up for a talent show and won a chance to sing on the Midland radio station. We chose "Harbor Lights" because it had such a good three-part harmony. But we were too nervous to do a good job the day we sang on the radio.

In the eighth grade, I was asked to play basketball on the varsity team for the Barryton

Bulldogs. I was never a star, though, and sometimes fouled out because I was not very coordinated. In academics, I studied hard and did well. Two of my classmates and I vied for the top spot in all our classes. Billy and Loren were really smart for being boys. Sometimes I see Loren, a successful attorney in Mt. Pleasant.

In Barryton, I joined the Girl Scouts, too. We did lots of fun things, like swimming, camping, and sliding down the giant hills around the area. We even invited the Boy Scouts once to join us for an unforgettable evening of sliding downhill during a blizzard. There were big bonfires built along the sliding trail. We all brought our sleds and toboggans. Afterwards we met at one of the leader's house for cocoa and chili to warm us up.

A high point of my freshman year was the operetta. I was chosen for the lead in "Sunbonnet Sue." My co-star was Mark, a handsome junior. I sang songs about a poor, ragged girl who was loved and helped to become a beautiful, confident woman. It was a Cinderella story and I got to wear both ragged and elegant costumes.

One older boy, Jack, admired me, maybe because he was in my father's class. He asked me out, but I was too young to date, according to my parents. We did meet several times at events at school, though. I never really fell for him but my dad approved of him. Then there was Zack, from Beaverton. When we lived there in the summer, I saw a lot of him. He even let me ride his horse, Maizie. One moonlit night he left our house, riding Maizie home, lustily singing "Full Moon and Empty Arms." I sighed, watching him from my bedroom window. The next fall when we moved back to Barryton, he continued to come and visit us on weekends. Once he brought me a box of candy and once he gave me a gold heart shaped locket. The last time I saw Zack he had dementia and remembered nothing.

In the spring of 1949, I met Dale. He was different. He could talk to me; he was a good student, and a Christian like I was. We were in the same youth group at the Methodist church. When the teens went roller-skating at Chippewa Lake, we skated together. I was sad when he moved away just as school ended.

But, so did our family have to move, back again to the farm for the summer. I didn't know then that I would never be back to Barryton High School. And I did not know that my life was about to be changed forever by a wonderful male person.

Years later, I did teach English and Reading to seventh graders in Grant, Michigan.

Measure Size Versus Taste
By Valerie Gale of Bay City, Michigan
Born 1949

Going to Aunt Mimi's house was one of the best things in the world. She and Uncle Buddy Martek lived with my great grandfather Louis Tasiemski in the back apartment of a store on the corner of Cass Avenue and Michigan. My sister, Margie, and I spent many weekends there. The store had been Tasiemski's Market in the 1940s and 1950s.

The magical part of the visit was being able to choose candy that was in a huge display case inside the market.

Looking through the glass and seeing black licorice, chocolate bars, golden butterscotch and lemon drops was like being Willie Wonka getting the gob stoppers and chocolate from the chocolate river.

Of course, we were allowed only a piece or two, so we carefully contemplated the size versus taste and carried the "treasures" back into the apartment to savor.

My aunt always left an IOU for the candy. She'd tuck a paper with the amount and price into the cup that sat on a top shelf.

As I remember, we only went once each

Val and Aunt Mimi in 1970

weekend we stayed there.

I suppose it doesn't seem like a big deal today, but for us, it was like tasting happiness and we savored every sweet swallow.

Seeing "vintage" candy at stores still makes me happy and I look for favorites, always careful to measure size versus taste.

Sand Hill Rats
By Lois Doran of Saginaw, Michigan
Born 1925

I was born the middle child of eleven, to good, hardworking, Christian, parents. We were all very close.

We lived on the "Sand Hill." There was a glass factory in the area before I was born, and in manufacturing, they made hills and holes all over the area.

We, the whole neighborhood, were very clannish because our area was just west of the city line, and all the city kids called us sand hill rats.

We were brought up with a very strong work ethic. Before I went to school, I learned to pick potato bugs, and tomato worms, and weed pickling onions.

All the kids in the area were friends and we played kick the can and Go-Sheepy-Go, and the most fun we had was Halloween, before Trick or Treat. One year we went around and collected all the clotheslines and one boy climbed to the top of the school and tied the rope to the bell, then we strung the rope to an area we called the old mine. By all of us getting on the line and working together, we could pull and ring the bell. And we did until the janitor came and saw the bell rope going up and down and no one there.

Another year we pulled Mr. Averill's buggy up on top of the barn and it stayed there until the barn was torn down.

Another year we put Mr. Averill's horse in Mrs. Zignachek's cow shed, and Mrs. Zignachek's cow in Mr. Averill's barn. We all got a big group balling out as we were told Mrs. Zignachek almost had a heart attack.

Our mother was one of the founders of the PTA at our school (it's gone now). We kidded her having fifty years in the PTA.

These were depression years and we all cared about each other and have many wonderful memories.

The Day I Faced Death Twice
By William Fleming of Saginaw, Michigan
Born 1939

When I was fourteen years old, my parents went on our annual vacation from Michigan to Kentucky. Once upon arrival every relative from miles around would gather for a family reunion, there were great grandparents, grandparents, great aunts and uncles, aunts and uncles, and cousins that I never knew about. Food! Wow! Whatever you wanted to eat was there. Needless to say, I ate my share and then some. After the big wonderful meal, everyone was sitting outside enjoying the day and each other talking about news of the day and recalling the past.

My great uncle Weaver chewed tobacco, the hard kind called plug tobacco, the kind you take your knife and cut off a slice. Being a smart fourteen year old, I just knew I wanted a slice of that tobacco. So I asked Uncle Weaver for a slice. In his southern drawl he said, "Y—shhoor" the more I chewed the tobacco the juice started to trickle down my throat, burning; I didn't know you were supposed to spit out the juice. Pretty soon, I was spinning but not moving, I was sick. With a belly full of food and topped off with tobacco juice, my belly felt like a boiler. I went and laid down on the porch, turning all colors of green. My Aunt Mavis just in time finished up in the kitchen and saw me laying on the porch and ask me if I was having fun, and I told her Uncle Weaver gave me a slice of his tobacco. She had a fit, I mean she had a hissy fit. She said get off the porch and go and have some fun. Like a good nephew, I got up and when I did, so did everything in my belly. After that, I enjoyed playing with cousins and had fun. I was told later if I hadn't gotten off the porch, I could have died. I sure learned a lesson that day, never chew tobacco.

As the day turned into evening all the kinfolks started to leave to return to their home to do their evening chores. My savior Aunt Mavis asked me to go home with them, which in a way I felt obligated to, after all, she saved my life. On the way to their home, Uncle JB said there might be a new calf just waiting for us. When we got to their home, we went out into the pasture to see if there was a new calf. When we got to a top of a hill, we spotted mama cow with her baby.

66

Being a stranger mama charged at me with her head down. The only thing I could do was to grab hold and hang on to her head for the ride, somehow Uncle JB got between me and mama cow. To add insult to near death Uncle JB named that calf Larry. Would you believe a fourteen year old would see his life pass by?

Do-Do Trouble
By Loretta R. Merritt of Greenville, Michigan
Born 1938

When I was eight years old, my four sisters and I and our four-year-old nephew Chuck loved playing Hide and Go Seek. My nephew followed me every place I'd go, non-stop. I finally broke away from him. As we were playing hide and seek. I ran into our outhouse closed the door to hide. I didn't know Chuck had seen me go in. He started banging and kicking on the door. I told him "Go away" and he said "No." "I want in." I opened the door pulled him in and stood him on top of the toilet seat. He fell in up to his waist. I then pulled him out. He stunk. I sure did get in do-do trouble. Then I had to bathe him. He never played that game again and I got a break from him. Paybacks are not nice.

My singing partner and I were on our way to Morley, Michigan to do some music. I said to my partner please find a place I have to go to the rest room. He spotted an outhouse by the riverside park. He pulled in. He took a walk to the riverside while I went in the outhouse. Oh my, I heard the most awful noise, I thought was going to drop on the roof. I jumped up then heard my singing partner holler out "What you doing buddy?" The truck driver hollered back "I'm getting ready to remove the outhouse to dump it." My so-called friend said, "I'll give you ten dollars if you'll hurry up." I jumped out of that outhouse in a big hurry. The young man said "Oh my God!" So as you see, paybacks can be a dirty mess, right?

In 1949, I was eleven years old, mom passed away when I was eight. Daddy taught us all right from wrong. One of the most important things is not to take anything you can't pay for. My dad asked one of my sisters to go to Irish Grocery Store and pick up something he needed. I asked if I could go, and he answered yes. Us girls walked to the store as soon as we got in there I spotted my favorite penny candy. I asked my sister if I could have one, quickly answered no. Daddy didn't ok it, or give us extra money. So I did a no-no, I stole two pieces of penny candy. On the way back home I showed my sister what I did, and one for her. She went "crazy." When we got home "ouch," my dad marched me right back to Irish's Grocery store. He told me to stand outside the door. Then he came back out and marched me right back in. I had to face the owner Mr. Irish. Daddy said, "Tell the man what you did." So I did. The owner picked up the phone and told me he was going to call the police. I pleaded please forgive me. He said I was forgiven if I learned that was wrong. Theft is not the answer. My dad was right. Don't take anything you can't pay for.

Doodlebug Tractors
By Melvin R. Lefevre of Bay City, Michigan
Born 1934

It was probably around 1946 when I was twelve years old as my oldest brother was home from the war and my father was not yet bedridden (he died early in my 14th year in 1948) that I took a phone call from my dad. He and my oldest brother were using one of our two doodlebug tractors to tow our one and a half ton Dodge truck trying to get it started, a doodlebug is a car chassis, a seat, and large truck tires on the rear, no body.

At about three quarters of the way around a one-mile square, they pulled into a gas station to get advice or help. The tractor they were using developed problems of its own and they wanted another of my older brothers to bring the Dodge doodlebug tractor. Neither of those brothers were home so dad reluctantly told me to take it to him when I assured him I could start it. It had to be started with a hand crank.

Pleased to be given this responsibility and adventure, and maybe a little bit cocky, I went out, turned on the key, set the choke and went around, one pulled the crank and the engine came to life with the tractor moving forward as it started while in gear. I sidestepped,

67

climbed aboard the moving tractor, and drove it uneventfully to the station about a mile away. I did not bother to tell them these details.

Another brother and I would park that same Dodge truck near the road at the end of the driveway. With a noisemaker car bomb wired in place, we would wait for an old car to come by. At the appropriate time, we would hit the starter setting off the "bomb." More than one car stopped and the driver getting out to walk around his car to assess the damage. Finding nothing wrong with their car they drove away perplexed.

I also attached one of those noisemaker "bombs" to the same brother's car under the hood, while he was no more than twenty feet away, and didn't know until he started his car. I should mention that he was talking, or flirting, with his young girlfriend at the time.

Most of my escapades concern horses. I cared for another older brother's horses while he served in Korea.

I was retrieving a horse from the pasture across the road, riding bareback with only a lead rope for control. This horse was difficult to control using the proper bridle and reins, he was headed home, and I couldn't stop him. He was headed for the gate, which was only a movable section of the barbed wire fence. When we arrived at the gate the horse stopped, I didn't, at least not until I was into the barbed wire.

Another time, another horse, bareback, lead rope only and on an icy road. I took the horse out for water at the hand pump but my brother was watering the milk cows and said they came first, so I took a ride to see a neighbor friend. On the return trip, the horse wanted water and galloped full out. When he tried to turn into the driveway, he slid instead into the ditch and fell sideways onto the frozen rock culvert and my left leg. I got the horse water then went to school with a very swollen knee.

My dad also had me "drive" the plow horse while he handled the one horse plow. That didn't work out very well. I think he did better doing both alone.

Then there were the rides in the woods in which the horse goes under a low branch in an attempt to brush me off. But there were also many good rides. Horses are a sure draw to the pretty girls.

Shop Lifting at Ten Years Old
By Thomas M. Evon of Saginaw, Michigan
Born 1931

I was born on December 5, 1931 in Saginaw Michigan. At four and a half years old, I attended kindergarten at Webber school near by our apartment. For five cents, we got a small milk and graham crackers each day and we each had our own rug to take a nap on at school. We had a coal stove in the front room and little heat.

We had a milkman, junk man on a horse, ice man for the ice box, we had no running water and an outhouse, dirt road and a wooden sidewalk right in the city, took a bath once a week in zinc tub, played sports in school and in ninth grade we won city champs in soccer. Parents were divorced when I was seven years old and just my mother raised me and my brother.

Every Saturday the guys I hung with walked four miles downtown to the movies and after the show we went to a dime store and stole cheap junk and me and a buddy were caught, and the rest got away. This ended my crime spree.

I went to high school and played sports; was on the State Champion track team for 3 years as a shot putter and later inducted in the Saginaw Sports Hall of Fame with our team.

As a child, we were dirt poor. My mother worked in local bars to keep us going. We got help from my Italian grandparents. I was so lacking of the right food, they thought I had tuberculosis. There was little or no help from the government except for surplus food once in a while. No meat, just oatmeal, prunes, pasta, and flour.

I was shy and afraid of girls although in the 12th grade I took a girl to the prom. A buddy got his dad's car after graduation. I had no money, clothes, no transportation so my buddy and I joined the army in 1949 at seventeen years old.

As a kid, us boys in the neighborhood played games in a field and picked junk during World War II. I joined the boy scouts at a catholic school. All us kids had was a Philco radio to listen to Captain Midnight, The Mummers.

While in the Army, I was terrified at getting yelled at but finally got over it. I went to a school after basic and assigned to the

Some of Tom's Korean vet buddies at a party

Engineers. The Korean War started while we were shipping out to England to build bomber bases for the US Air Force new jet bombers. I was there two years. I got out in 1952 as well as all my buddies in my neighborhood and we had a ball for three or four years. We went to dance halls and learned to Polka all the guys were Polish and we joined a Polish club and the American Legion in our neighborhood. A few of us met our wives at the dance halls that played Polish music.

At Saginaw High School, I was president of the Junior and Senior Class and belonged to the National Honor Society by getting good marks. I volunteered at the Legion and we won the Legion honors as the best Post in the state, Post 439, Saginaw 1970 for Americanism.

I joined the Saginaw Police Department in 1955 and stayed nine years, a lot of my police buddies quit the department. Low morale, nobody seemed to back us. I got married and had seven kids. I took too many chances on the police force but I won the meritorious achievement award for good police work. It was given to me by the mayor of Saginaw.

I finally got fed up as many of us did and went to General Motors (GM) as security officer and others went to other police departments. I stayed at General Motors and retired after twenty-seven years, and got

asbestos in my lungs from the GM foundry I was in. We had a lot of fires and explosions in the plant but I'm still here. All my kids are grown up and I talked to four boys to join the service because I couldn't afford college. They made out ok; one spent twenty-three years in the Air Force.

Most of my old buddies are gone now and I am still left. I got a million stories about my life, jobs, and lucky to be alive. I took my brother's advice and he told me to pick a school in the Army and stay out of the infantry. My training outfit went to Korea after basic and I went to England.

Police softball team

I am eighty-three now, when I joined the police department they still had my record of shoplifting at ten years old but they laughed at that and said it was ok.

The Brunt of Many Creative Ideas
By Barbara J. Langley of Gladwin, Michigan
Born 1935

Back in the "Good Old Days," my dad was unable to find employment in the small town of Hale, Michigan that was his hometown. So, we lived in Flint, Michigan where he could earn enough to support his large family. However, his heart was in Hale. So, he moved us back and forth between the two places.

Finally, my poor mother told dad on our last move to Hale that we would be staying there. So, dad worked in the city of Flint on the weekdays and came home on the weekends.

This arrangement was mother's best "weapon." "Just wait until your dad gets home," she'd say over every little infraction.

We were certain she was keeping a master list. It made no difference that my mild mannered, quiet dad never laid a hand on any of us. When dad had to reprimand one of us, it was done privately in his normal quiet voice without threats.

As I think back over the years, many of my thoughts center around my sister Ginger. Since I, Barb, was the eldest of nine children, six girls, and three boys. It was no easy task being the eldest. This put me in the position of second mother. My parents reminded me "You're the oldest. You should know better." The problem was I didn't always know better. The other advice I got was "You're too young to do that." Their advice was confusing to say the least.

My sister Ginger was the second girl born in our group of nine with a brother in between. Unfortunately, for her she became the brunt of many creative ideas thought up by me, and my brother Mel.

One of the first creative ideas Mel and I had for Ginger was when we lived in Flint in an apartment. Dad was at work and mom left us alone while she walked to the corner store. While she was gone, we played Hide and Seek. Mel and I discovered that Ginger fit in a dresser drawer. She went in just fine but every time we tried to get her out, she raised her head a little and we couldn't open the drawer. Mom was really upset when she came home and threatened to tell dad.

Not long after this incident, we moved back to Hale to an old farm with a dilapidated barn and a house too small for our family. It was here our second creative idea came to Mel and me. In the barn, there were wide rafters that ran the length of the barn. Some of the upper sides of the barn were missing. We decided Ginger would enjoy having a rope tied around her belly and let down over the side. Things went quite well until the rope got caught in a crack. We couldn't pull her up or down. Ginger was yelling and floundering quite a few feet above the ground. Unfortunately, we had to get help from mom. Once again, she didn't appreciate our efforts.

Ginger's next unfortunate experience wasn't our idea. Ginger was running through the yard barefoot. She was carrying a switch pretending she was riding a horse. She stepped on an upturned pitchfork and one of the tines ran through her foot and came out the top.

Once again, mom was called into action. Mom talked to Ginger in a quiet voice. She tried to reassure her she would be ok. Ginger had the switch she had been using on her pretend horse. As mom removed the tine, Ginger switched mom on the head. Mel and I couldn't believe our eyes. We knew Ginger would be killed for doing this to mom. However, mom didn't flinch, nor quit the removal process. She completed the task, and picked Ginger up, and carried her into the house. Mom washed Ginger's foot, put turpentine on it, tied a clean white rag around it and she was finished.

Our mom, whose husband worked in Flint didn't have a car, no insurance, or money, had just completed one of many such days in her life with nine children.

The Hicks from the Sticks
By Donna LaRoche of Bay City, Michigan
Born 1929

Could 1929 be the worse year you could be born in? One January 14th I was born in Flint with my twin sister, Della, to a mother and father who had four grown children and a six year old. My dad worked at Buick and was soon laid off. My widowed Gramma owned a farm near Deford. In 1933, we moved there. We had no electricity, no running water, but we did have an outhouse, to a little girl it seemed a mile away. We did enjoy the shadows the kerosene lamps made on the walls. We always had relatives living with us. We ate a lot of potatoes and my mother baked lots of bread every Saturday.

My brother Lloyd became the farmer and bought cows so we could have a milk route in Deford. Gramma was Scotch and always seemed to have a little cash, she had a milk house built and Lloyd milked the cows, sister, Marion, drove the car and I had the honor of delivering the milk. I made a quarter a week. Lloyd had mules and on the farm, we grew sugar beets, corn, and lots of potatoes and other vegetables. My mother would can fruits and vegetables for winter. We had an apple orchard.

Our life revolved around relatives, church, and school. My teachers name was Irma. We had five grades downstairs and four grades upstairs. We had the same six students in our class for the seven years we were there. Rumor had it that my brother, Lloyd, was dating the teacher. We said "no way" and the little sisters confronted their brother who admitted the deed. They were married a year later.

All we had to heat our big ole house was two pot- bellied stoves. They would go out by morning, Lloyd would build fires, and we would run downstairs to the stove as fast as we could to get dressed. Mother had to wash clothes on a scrub board and we would get a bath every Saturday night to be clean for church the next morning. Every winter morning someone would have to prime the water pump before we had water. Most of the kids at school had to walk a long way.

Christmas was fun on the farm. We usually got one gift if we were lucky. My brother, Neil, who is 99 years old now, got a job in the factory and bought us twins Shirley Temple dolls. Oh, we were so proud of those dolls, we received blue plaid snowsuits I was so proud of. Lloyd would cut a tree down and we decorated with popcorn. There were programs at church and school. Della and I sang duets at school. We would sing Jolly Old St. Nick to Santa when he came in.

When we had a telephone installed on the wall, we had to listen to the rings we had six long and six short rings. There were lots of people on our party line. After a few years, we were able to get electricity and an indoor bathroom. What luxuries! Oh how we enjoyed our radio. We listened to Orson Welles broadcast that the Martians landed in New Jersey. Everyone in Deford was talking about it. My wise Gramma said, "It's only a program."

Gramma gathered all kinds of plants out in the fields to use as medicine. She always cured us. She made a cough medicine that was so delicious. She was deaf and slept downstairs and one of us sleeping upstairs would cough. Pretty soon, she would come upstairs with steaming hot onions wrapped in a flannel cloth. Wow when she slapped that on your chest, you yelled, but it cured you.

Gramma told many interesting stories. Her father and his three brothers were in the same regiment during the civil war. One day she was walking down the road and could see a man coming down the road and it was her father coming home safely from the war. How happy she was. She saw General Custer in a parade on his horse. He had long blond hair and he was so handsome.

We had free outdoor movies in the summer every Friday night if it didn't rain. We watched the sky every Friday and we were usually lucky. I had my first kiss at one of those shows. Unfortunately, my brother saw it and I got in trouble. On Labor Day weekend, we had the Deford homecoming with rides and games. My sister, Marion, won a dollar for eating a blueberry pie without her hands. She was a mess, but it was worth it.

The bank was robbed and the bank bags left on a line in back of our house. That was scary as Dillinger, Baby Face Nelson, and those criminals were on the loose.

We were big Detroit Tiger fans (still am) and in the summer, I listened to the radio and run down to the fields where Lloyd worked and would give him the details of the game. I was just a little girl but I became quite an expert on the Tigers.

One of the happiest times on the farm was on Sunday nights when mother played the piano and we gathered around and sang our favorite hymns. When Mother said, "That's all," we said "Play *Pretty Red Wing*," that was the finale.

My brother, Neil, had a little coupe with a rumble seat. One Sunday night he was leaving for Flint for work and I hid in the rumble seat. We got to the other side of Caro and I yelled, "Let me out," he was pretty mad at me.

There were happy times growing up in the thirties. There was also some tragedies in our little town. One friend from school accidentally shot another boy. Another little girl was killed when her drunken father crashed the family car. A bride was on her way to get married and was killed. Of course, we all went to the funerals and the townspeople gave love and support to the families.

My paternal grandfather was W.B. Hicks and he was among other things, the health inspector. When we came down with the measles, Gramps came to our house and nailed a quarantine sign on the front door telling all would be visitors not to enter.

After Gramma died, we moved back to Flint in 1940. Lloyd stayed on the farm, but gave up farming. He sold mules to a farmer ten miles away. The mules broke down the farmer's barn door and came back to Lloyd. When he went out to the barn there they were in their stalls waiting for him.

The kids in Flint called us the Hicks from the Sticks. I was so proud of that name. My mother said to me many years later "We would never have made it through the depression without you." That was quite a compliment for a little girl who was only between 3 and 11 years old during the depression.

Our Little School
By Barbara Boyer of Midland, Michigan
Born 1938

I am writing about the things I remember about the one-room school. I am not a good writer, but here it goes…

Our school was in the Beaverton, Michigan area, out in the country. The name was Billings. We had about 25 students and one teacher.

Sometimes, we walked to school and sometimes my mother would take us.

I had two in my grade; Marie and I. We were there until the ninth grade, and then we went to the city in the ninth grade and completed high school.

We had a woodstove. We had inside toilets. I think they were chemical ones.

I can remember the pump house. In the winter, we would bring pints of milk with vanilla in them, and at lunchtime, we would have ice milk that tasted like ice cream.

About once a week, one of the mothers would bring soup for the school

On all recessed, we would play scrub ball.

On the last day of school, we would have a picnic.

My mother would make me flannel

The students of the one-room school

bloomers to wear to school to keep warm.

All my uncles, cousins, and neighbors went to this school.

In 1953, I went to Beaverton High School and graduated in 1956. The school still stands. A farmer bought the land for farming. It looks like it's still in good shape.

A Practical Joker Revealed
By Dorothy Baer Wolf of Lapeer, Michigan
Born 1924

I owned a drive-in theatre in the '60s and '70s. We had a cook out before the theatre opened. My son sat down in a chair to eat his food, and a firecracker was tossed under his chair. His drink and food went straight up in the air. My older brother was accused of it, and he denied it.

Fast-forward to the '90s. My husband died. At the funeral, members of the family were telling stories about things that happened with my husband. My younger brother got up and was telling the story, and he said he had seen the whole thing. He said it was the incident that my older brother got blamed for. It was actually my husband, his brother-in-law, who tossed the firecracker under the chair. So, his older brother was innocent.

My whole family is known as practical jokers. So this was nothing new.

A Man in the Storm
By Joshua Clark of Reed City, Michigan
Born 1922

In February 1931, in the middle of Michigan, we were a few days into a severe winter storm. There was high winds, drifting snow, road impassable, zero temperatures.

In rural areas in the 1930s, electricity was miles away, and phones were scarce. There were no cell phones, and only a few party lines.

A neighbor of ours lived over a mile away from us. This man smoked a pipe, as did my dad. The man was out of tobacco; Dad lived close. Neighbors shared when possible.

The man dressed for the storm, filled his pipe with the last of his tobacco, lit it, and headed for our home.

He faced into the storm, drifts, blinding snow, zero temperatures. About 300 feet from our home, he had a pain in his chest. The burning tobacco from his pipe blew onto his overcoat burning a funnel shaped hole through all of his garments until, OUCH!

Growth and Opportunity
By Evald Kruut of Mount Pleasant, Michigan
Born 1927

We are not natives of Mt. Pleasant. We moved here in the summer of 1973. Both the University and the town were much smaller then. Our only son, Tom, took advantage of the good schools—as a first grader—that the community had. He also took piano lessons from a professor and won monetary awards at local competitions. He became an Eagle Scout and eventually graduated magna cum laude in mechanical engineering from Michigan Technological University.

In the meantime, the Central Michigan University has grown larger—a physician's assistant program, a medical school, and an engineering department were established. Significant improvements in the city have also occurred—an adequate storm sewer system and a beautiful, new public library! In addition, the local American Indian tribe constructed a four-star hotel and a gambling casino—a negative development in my opinion.

Country School Days
By Joyce Griffin of Shelby, Michigan
Born 1925

I went to a country school. I was lucky enough to live only 1/4 mile from school. So many had to walk at least a mile or so. We never had school closed because the teacher stayed at my parents' home.

My father got up early and went to the school and fired the furnace so it would be warm when the kids got there. When the weather wasn't too bad we took our sleds to school and slid down the hill at noon.

I remember it very clearly, as it was one day at noontime and we went out to play. One of the older kids told me to put my tongue on the pump handle—I did—but couldn't get it off. I didn't know better but I yanked it off. It bled so much the teacher sent me home. There was a trail of blood all the way home. I missed a few days of school. I am now 89 years old but sure remember that day. We never got a car out for six weeks that year.

My Dog Curly
By Jerry Schmolitz of Saginaw, Michigan
Born 1931

Growing up in Saginaw in the 1940s, I lived on the east side near Carroll Street and the 9th and 15th Street area. My friends and I would swim off the railroad bridge off Washington at the end of Potter Street. We would walk in the woods north of the bridge and fish off the drain for perch. Then, we would sell them on the way home.

One winter, we were north of the bridge and ice had formed across the river. So Bill Richter, Russel and Bill Jurek, Jim LaDrig, and I, along with my dog, Curly, decided to walk across the river on the ice. We got almost halfway across when Curly, a Chesapeake Bay retriever, leading the way, fell through the ice. We stopped in our tracks. I had to get my dog out so I decided to crawl out to get him. One of us decided to form a chain. We grabbed each other's legs and stretched out. I reached for Curly, grabbed him by his leg, and pulled him out.

Needless, to say, we followed our tracks back to safety. What could have been a disastrous day turned out to be a very happy memory for all of us and for our families in the future. Thank you Curly.

1945
By Joanne Hetherington of Mt. Pleasant, Michigan
Born 1939

We lived on a farm. At the back of the property was a river. Snapping turtles would lay eggs in the sand. In the summer, we would fine some in our yard.

One year, the river flooded. When the water went down, there were fish trapped in

73

little pockets of water.

We had a lot of snakes in our yard, milk snakes. One day, we found one in the front yard. We took an old tire and rolled it over the snake to make it mad. It didn't hurt the snake but it sure got mad and struck at us. We were around 5 years old or younger.

When I was around 5 years old, my dad was going to town. I was in the yard playing but I wanted to go with him. I was running to get in the car, and ran a pitchfork tine between my toes. The pitchfork was from the cow barn. Well, we went to town but to the doctor. He ran a q-tip with nitro on it into the wound. It burnt all the way in and out.

My mother went to the barn to feed the team of workhorses. One bit her arm. Good thing she had a heavy coat on. It only bruised her arm really bad.

Patty's Story
By Patti Gustin of Green Valley, Arizona
Born 1937

Growing up in White Cloud, Michigan, as a 2nd grader, I remember walking a mile out of town to Louise Johnsons' to pick the milkweed pods; filling gunny sacks from the milkweed that surrounded her dad's farm. I probably got 10cents a bag, but just doing it was passion enough for this kid. These were used for replacing kapok, as a filling for life vests to be used by our soldiers.

My given name was Patty. I changed the spelling to Patti after the 6th grade and Patti Page appeared. My best friend was Kaye. She lived directly across the street. I could close my eyes and walk from my front door to hers. We moved there when I was 5 years old.

Kaye and I could travel through our town peeking in on mysteries and checking hidden places others probably never noticed. We would walk through the downtown back alley, behind local businesses, and would arrive at our favorite spot, the trash burning area behind Lemire's drugstore, waiting for a windless time of day. It was a treasure for us. Those old magazines lay tossed in a heap with covers removed so the store got their credits from the publishers. Movie magazines were our favorites, and Esquire had the best jokes. After a quick read, these were tossed back on the burn pile and we headed off to the courthouse for all the free brochures. We looked for anything to read, as there was no library in our town. When school closed for the summer, our availability of books was lost.

We spent hours in the co-op, darting from feed sack to feed sack pretending we were taking the colorful bags home for our mothers to make us a new garment. The workers let us play until we tried to bring guests into our adventures.

Those were the war years. Many of the young men in town were off serving our country. Wells Branch, the town mayor, and his wife, Margie, lived next door to Kaye. The Branch's had the best front porch to play jacks on. The cement was so smooth we never scraped our knuckles.

Of course, we remember the food stamps and the white oleo with that bubble of coloring to be broken to make it look more like butter. We never did much traveling. Our dad needed the car to go to work and gas was scarce and rationed.

I remember Mother making eggless chocolate cake. Eggs were scarce, also because they were being used for the powdered eggs sent to the soldiers. Everyone had a victory garden. Ours had a rock at the edge where we hid our most precious jewels; a broken locket, pretty marbles, and broken jewelry. Currant bushes lined the garden.

Anything became a fort. The trees in back, with a few well-placed boards, became lookouts. We played with dolls, and dressed up cats or dogs if we could catch them. Even the grass in the alley by the railroad tracks was a place to play. One day while we were working to pack down the grass for a floor, Kaye cut her hand on a broken pop bottle; the blood spurted up like a fountain! Mother had to drive her to Dr. Douglas' office with her arm hanging out of the window because the blood kept squirting out. Kaye was screaming. She had cut an artery. Scary!

We wondered about the history of the mysterious band shell that stood deteriorating in one corner of the park. We could imagine a band playing there in another era. Now, about the park. This held the best and highest slide, teeter-totters, and swings. On the 4th of July, it held the biggest carnival, and the farmers came from all over the county for the ox-pulling contest. There was always an independent baseball game and after dark, we would spread out blankets on the baseball field and watch the fireworks. We were forbidden to venture past the rail fence in the late summer when the gypsies were in town. We were told they might steal us and take us away.

George Decker, the Justice of the Peace, lived across the highway from us. He could ride a bike with one leg, since that was all he had. Every 4th of July, he dragged his cannon out in the middle of the road and shot it off. We always woke to that big boom and knew what day it was.

The store buildings across Main Street, other than Pettit's, didn't hold much for our curiosity. There was Dr. Saxon's office, closed now, as he went to war. He must have chosen someplace else to practice when it was over as it never reopened. Pettit's, SK Riblet's Abstract office. Riblet's adopted a girl, Mary. Joe's wife, Erma, worked there and she typed with two index fingers.

The Post Office had a wall of code locked boxes. We always checked inside in the spring when the boxes of baby chicks arrived, probably headed for the co-op. The chirping could be heard by all who entered. Dutch Bowman was the postmaster. His daughters, Catherine and Shirley, were friends of ours. The owners of Rosenberg's Hardware owned the whole building, which included the post office and their home upstairs. Their son, George, was in the service.

Next-door was Bird's Meat Market on the corner. The bank was across the street. Henry Gustin, a lot of men called him Hank, was head cashier. We heard they adopted a boy and girl. We didn't know them until we were in school, because they were Catholic.

Bonnie Fuller lived in the back of the next store building. She taught piano lessons in the front. Some of her students must have given her poinsettias for Christmas. She kept those tall, spindly things in her front window for years. I never did like poinsettias after seeing those. I didn't have a piano but I sure wanted one, badly. Graves had a piano in the living room, and Kaye took lessons. I'd practice her lesson until someone got tired of my banging on the piano and shut the piano key lid.

There was a fancy tile slab where some said a bakery stood. Walt Graves worked there when he was young. It must have burned down.

Across the alley was Branch's Music Store. He didn't have much to sell, just a few old reeds, and mouthpieces. I heard he also sold real estate, and they lived in the back of their store building, as well. I bought my reeds there when I took up clarinet in the second grade. I took lessons from a one armed band teacher, but I think the only reason he let me be in the band at that age was so I could support the big bass drum on my back when we marched across the football field.

The grassy lot divided this and Cooper Press, owned by CE Cooper, who lived across the street from Jean, and was at the time, our State Representative. His son, Jack, was publisher and editor. Bob Auw ran the printing presses and the linotype machine. When we curious kids showed up to check things out, we would talk him unto printing our names backwards on one of those slugs made by molten lead.

Friday night was my mother's grocery shopping night. The stores stayed open so people could spend their paychecks. We loved those open doored boxes of cookies in Carl Anderson's store. He would use a long stick with a grabber device on the end to get the boxes of cornflakes or some canned good off the top shelves. "Tink" (Ingeborg Brandt, an old maid who lived next door to us) checked out our groceries. People would come in from the country and just mill around the town. Mother would get free gifts in boxes; dishes, etc. One time, there was a washcloth in a box of soap. Once a month, Mother would stop at the window of the "show," to give Mrs. Beach a payment on our mortgage, then stop in Adams Hardware or Rosenberg's across the street. Adams Hardware was fun to wander through. The porcelain toilets sat lined up in the middle of the room. This brought out our worse imaginary deeds. We whispered about just how funny it would be if someone "pooped" in them. With gales of laughter, we would giggle and use this imaginary happening whenever we thought we could make someone laugh with us.

Late in the summer, Branches would have a Red Wing shoe frozen solid in a block of ice for people to guess the date and time it would all be melted. From there, we would make a trip to Pettit's dime store across the street.

Under the very watchful eye of Ginny or Ike Pettit, we would spend a nickel on the penny candy we chose.

Usually Kaye and I would have money to go to the "show," almost always a double feature. Westerns, and those war commentaries. Abbot and Costello was one of our favorites. We weren't allowed to sit near the back. This was reserved for grownups. Mrs. Breach would send us back to the front if she caught us, or come down the aisle to check to see who might be making any disturbing noises. We never got kicked out, even if Clint may have caused us to giggle about some crazy thing. The movies brought us cartoons, comics, and best of all, musicals.

Kaye and I would sing and dance all the way home. When we walked past the Big Chief Tavern, we always had to be on the lookout for drunks. Then we passed two houses; one belonged to the Gannon sisters. Our path home took us past Andy Burkes Station, past Tiny Johnson's house. He was the handyman at the Big Chief.

Clint, Clinton Earl as his mother called him when she was mad at him, spent most of his days down at the Mill Pond over by the dam with his dog, Pal, and his fishing pole. Sometimes Kaye and I would help him dig worms in the muck below our house. He was always bringing a big snapping turtle home for Emma to cook up. Of course, he often had a catch of fish for their supper, too. Emma was a cook at the school, and she also worked as a midwife, helping Doc Douglas with home deliveries. Emma also took on wallpaper jobs, and even took in some kids who needed a place to board. They always had a huge garden, as they had nine in their family. The older three girls were married and gone. Graves still had an outhouse behind the garage. Kaye fell in once. Ugh!

If Kaye wasn't available, I would spend time two blocks away, hanging upside down on the rings and trapeze of the "little" school. I imagined myself in a circus someday. Roller-skating everywhere I went, I carried a key on a shoestring around my neck.

Summers were spent at the millpond down at the end of our road. After the war, Joe got Daddy and other men from town to tear down the old icehouse and the town built us docks and two diving boards. Every afternoon was spent at the pond.

Summer was also the time for the big Methodist Church picnic. It was an all-day event. First was a water toboggan slide then a lunch with every picnic food imaginable furnished by the Methodist ladies. After lunch, we headed to the skating rink. Backwards, forwards, trying all kinds of tricks. Dancing with Kaye, round and round we would flee.

I have no regrets. I loved my life, and growing up in that small town where everyone knew who I was. I wish all children could have had an idyllic childhood like I did.

The Well in the Pond
By Charlene Laper of Lakeview, Michigan
Born 1932

Surprisingly, considering our quite strict mother, my sister and I were allowed to roam freely through the woods and the fields on our farm. We were often accompanied by Leah, a rather slow-thinking woman, whose husband paid his rent on a ramshackle house on the back of our land by working in the fields for my father. Leah rarely did any housework and enjoyed joining us on our adventures. Another companion was Catherine, a twelve-year-old neighbor girl, who was a few years older than my "big" sister, Carol.

One day, the four of us wandered into a neighbor's field and discovered a shimmering, shallow pool of water that spread out over the grass. It was not the usual muddy, swampy ponds we had explored on other occasions but it looked clear and clean. We splashed tentatively about its perimeters and then were drawn to a curious, square, wooden box-like structure in the center. My companions each perched on a side, facing inward, while I stood on the rather unsteady floorboards, which entranced me by tilting back and forth, as I stepped from side to side.

Suddenly, the entire floor tipped into a vertical position and I plunged down.

Leah, uncharacteristically quicker thinking than usual, grabbed my hand and pulled me to safety. We beat a hasty retreat from what we now realized was a well.

Since returning home with me completely drenched would arouse some suspicion, I was stripped of my little dress and panties, which

Charlene and her "big sister," Carol

were hung on a nearby tree to dry. Leah lay down on the ground on her side, and I settled into the grass and leaned against her broad back.

When I was, again, dry and dressed, we walked home with Leah. No one said much. I'm not sure I realized that a tragedy had been averted but I think the others did.

As we reached our driveway, and as Catherine ran across the road to her house, my sister cautioned, "We won't tell Mama and Daddy." I nodded in agreement, trusting the wisdom of her decision.

After we were grown, we sometimes amused our parents with recitals of our childish exploits but this incident was never mentioned. So they, now long passed, never heard the story of the well in the pond.

Shelby Center School
By Debby Mitteer of Shelby, Michigan
Born 1952

Shelby Center School was a small one-room country schoolhouse located on Shelby Road in Shelby, Michigan. It housed grades kindergarten through eighth grades. It was a small building with small classes but held so many memories for me as a school.

When I was in the sixth grade, I attended Shelby Center School. The whole school consisted of about forty students and two teachers. There was one main room, and a curtain was pulled to divide grades kindergarten through fourth grade students from the grades fourth through eighth grade students. The classes of older students were as such: three boys in fifth grade and no girls, four girls and one boy in sixth grade, three boys and one girl in seventh grade, and three boys and three girls in eighth grade.

Each grade/class was called to the front of the rooms for lessons. The lesson was taught, and we were sent back to our seats to work on an assignment. We had a small library just off our classroom (about 6 feet by 8 feet). Since there were often distractions in the classroom, we were sometimes allowed to go to the library to study. There was only room for two or three students at a time. There was a door in the library that led to the outside, and sometimes we would leave the library and get some fresh air. We had to make sure the door between the classroom and library was closed so we did not get caught.

The curtain remained closed every day except Friday, when we would have music. On Friday, they would open the curtain, and we would have music for the day. One of the teachers played the piano, and everyone had to sing. We would often get to choose a song to sing. Knowing that the teacher who played the piano did not like one of the songs in the songbook, we would inevitably choose that song every time. To this day, I still remember the song; "There's a Tavern in the Town."

Some Wild Country Living
By Reneé Sova of Beaverton, Michigan
Born 1961

There are many memorable moments I experienced over the years while living in the back woods of Gladwin County. I was blessed with an animal sanctuary. There were many wild pets that had an abundance to eat. They didn't always get along and they didn't always like to share. I was there five long years and each year the sanctuary grew. The raccoon and deer came first and the raccoon families always became larger. There were skunks, possums, porcupines, badgers, coyotes, squirrels, chipmunks and birds—many varieties of birds. There were also bear all around the property. The raccoons and chipmunks would let me pet them—just some of them.

I don't ever recommend anyone trying to catch or corner any wild animal. I've had the raccoons come to me and they loved me. I am very thankful for the memories that I have shared with you. I truly miss the animals as I have moved on from them these days.

There were years before all the wild pets when I use to take care of my mother in her home. She enjoyed the Canadian geese and the deer and the fish in the pond. I had the pleasure of feeding the geese, deer, and fish for over ten years. I spent time floating on a mat in the pond in the summer months. I would place a saltine cracker in my mouth and the fish would come up and jump to get a bite. Yes, I am brave!

I love animals so very much. I'd love to add that anyone who loves animals should be careful. Animals can sense your feelings. They may be afraid of you! Don't always expect love at first sight. Children should always be with a parent when they're near wild animals. Don't rush a friendship with the wild.

Life on a Michigan Dairy Farm
By James H. Wetters of Beaverton, Michigan
Born 1935

I grew up on a dairy farm near Saginaw Bay. My life changed forever on December 7, 1941. I was 6 years and 41 days old. During 1942, Uncle Howard, my youngest uncle and partner on the farm with my dad, was drafted into the US Navy. I believe he was a cook on one of the small Navy ships protecting cargo ships taking supplies from New York harbor to the Panama Canal. His being drafted left a gap in the farm work force. It was common for farm boys to start out early on helping on the family farm and I was no exception. I started working in 1942. Picking up eggs and feeding my two rabbits were my first jobs. I failed at both! If I did not pick up the eggs after school in the winter, they would freeze where they were laid. Finally, my dad let my rabbits go free because I did not feed them every night

after school.

Then I started feeding cows, calves, and the very ornery bull. The base feed was corn silage, grain mix of corn, oats, soybean meal, plus minerals, and vitamins mixed together. On Saturdays, we would clean calf and bull pens. Cleaning the cow gutters was a morning job, every day except Sundays.

During the war, my younger brother and I made spending money by picking milkweed pods. These were dried in onion sacks. We received 50cents per bag. The dried fluff was placed in flotation devices such as life jackets called Mae Wests. The Navy used them for their pilots since the materials used today were not available in those days. At one time, we were having a hard time finding new patches of milkweed. Finally, we spied a big plot of them. The trouble was, though, there were cattle in the area and a big bull. We decided 50cents wasn't enough reason to confront el torro.

I started driving tractors when I was 7 or 8. These tractors were used to pull two men, Case wire tied balers for hay and straw. My dad was baling hay and straw around the country with that rig. When one field was finished, I drove the tractor and baler down the highway, US 23, to the next job while Dad got gasoline and wire for the next job. The baler had a Wisconsin air-cooled motor and required two men on back to operate. It was hot, dusty work. I was afraid of hay fields with deep ditches. If the tires of the baler went into the ditch, it put a very heavy pull on the little tractor causing the front wheels of the tractor to go up in the air, and that was scary.

I went on to drive tractors for most uses. My dad even let me plow with our bigger tractors although my brother never did. Our tractors were an Oliver 60, 2 70s, and a 77, which was underpowered. One of our Olivers had 40" by 9" back tires. My dad and Uncle Howard were also in partnership with the Parson brothers who lived just south of Linwood Corners. We had a two-row corn cultivator on the Oliver 70 and a four-row sugar beet cultivator on the Oliver 60. I cultivated corn and sugar beets for us, and then the Parson brothers' crops. The Parsons had John Deere models A, M and R. The model R had a diesel motor that had to be started with a small gas motor. It looked like the whole field was turning behind that big model R when I plowed.

A rough ride was guaranteed when I had to pull a spike-toothed drag over freshly plowed ground. The drag was in need of welding regularly and had to be pulled to the Stone garage for repair. New farm equipment was hard to get because steel was diverted to the war effort.

Only once did my Dad let me down. I was dragging a field before planting with a new four-section drag with chains on each end of the drag. At the end of the field, there was a very short turn, which had to be taken with great care. The right back tire of the tractor caught the chain and the chain came up on the tire against the fender. I couldn't get the chain off the tire and walked back home for help. Pa would not come to help. I walked back determined to solve the problem, which I did by brute force. Next time it happened, I knew what to do. Maybe that was the lesson Dad wanted me to learn.

Uncle Howard taught me to milk cows when I was in junior high school. Some cows I could milk well, and others, not so much. We had five milk routes, picking up 10-gallon cans until the mid-fifties when we switched to a bulk truck. Milk was checked before being accepted at the dairy. There was a thorough inspection before the dairy would accept milk from a new farm and then there were occasional checks after that. Mastitis was a big problem on a dairy farm rendering milk from that cow unfit for humans. There were always a number of cats waiting to drink up that milk. We used sulfa pills, penicillin, and terramycin to treat the infections, which were persistent and usually came back. Getting kicked by a cow or chased by the bull were hazards of the dairy farmer's job.

I was driving cars and trucks two or three years before I turned 16 and got my driver's license. My dad tried to get me an early Michigan driver's license but I never got one for farm use. I was one of the few high school students with my own car. In 1953, I got a 1950 Chevy, two-tone hardtop. Wow! It really was a time saver to get back and forth from Handy High School. Working on the farm didn't leave a lot of extra time so having my own car was almost a necessity.

My Sunday school teacher was a master carpenter, and started making church pews. He also was building race boats with World War II fighter aircraft motors. The Canadians could use Spit-fire motors, which were Rolls-Royce Merlin engines in their racing boats. We were limited to the Allison motors, which gave the Canadians an unfair advantage we thought. So, a major part of our Sunday school lesson was about race boats. For teenage boys, this was an excellent Sunday school lesson from a great teacher.

My dad was quite the entrepreneur. If it were about new, improved farming methods, he was doing it. Dairy cows, dairy feed, sugar beets, peas, lima beans, squash, sweet corn, and certified seeds for oats were his areas of interest. He sold Dekalb hybrid corn seed and fertilizers. One Sunday morning after milking cows and washing the milking machines, it was my "day off." At breakfast, Dad said, "You can spend the day with your city girlfriend after you have helped unload the 20 tons of fertilizer coming down the road." I was not too happy but the truck got unloaded.

The sign at the end of our road was the Virg Bes How Farm, for Virgil, Bessie, and Howard. I spent my first 22 years there, leaving after graduating from Michigan State University. It was hard work, and much different from today's farming in terms of the equipment and methods used. The land today is still farmed in part by family descendants.

First Kiss
By Richard Redifer of Freeland, Michigan
Born 1933

These two memories take place in a small town called Kingston, which is located about 25 miles east of Saginaw on M-46. The size of this village is very similar to many of the towns in the thumb area of Michigan.

I entered the Kingston school system in 1946, having moved from Prudenville-Houghton Lake, Michigan.

The main building was a typical red brick, two story building housing grades seven through twelve. Grades seven and eight had self-contained rooms with the high school students moving on a bell. Student enrollment limited the curriculum and activities to the basics. There was a study hall/library room, which doubled as a lunchroom for the students.

With only one stairwell to the second story in the rear, a metal tunnel fire escape was attached on the outside, descending

The school Richard attended in Kingston, MI

downward to the ground level. Usually, two boys were responsible to open the door and assist at ground level. Fire drills were periodically held which was a fun activity.

During the late forties, the area township schools were consolidating with larger town schools. School enrollments gradually increased their enrollment. My class had fourteen students in our 1951 graduating class.

Everybody knew most of the kids who attended. Very few students had cars so most rode a red, white, and blue school bus. With K-12 on the busses, there was always teasing, whining, and noise.

When I was in the eighth grade, I had a girlfriend who I really liked. I believe it was mutual.

Every spring, the school would have an annual carnival-fun night where parents would drop off and pick up their kids, usually around 10:00 pm.

I decided I wanted to kiss my girlfriend, so I prepared myself for this event. I had gone to the Strand Theater in Caro, and observed actors kissing. I thought to myself, "I would sure like to do this with my girlfriend." I didn't know how experienced she was, but I went about preparing myself. I practiced kissing my wrist, hugging my pillow, and rehearsing what to say and do. The annual carnival was going to be my opportunity for this mission.

That night, this girl and I hung out together. In the past weeks, I had practiced diligently preparing for this event. Part way through the evening, I finally went into action.

The spring weather outside was a typical windy, snowy evening. So we put our coats on, and went outside. I knew where I wanted to go, which was underneath the fire escape slide where it was dark. I maneuvered her in front of me, and got face to face. I believed she knew what was about to happen. She had on a long, heavy, wool, winter coat.

I puckered up, eyes closed, going for her lips, and low and behold, a gust of wind came up blowing her wooly collar over her face and lips.

I was committed and continued with the embrace for what seemed like forever, and finally broke it off. This was not my practicing attempt, so we went back into the carnival.

Needless to say, this ended my romance with her, as she dropped me for the school trombone player. Note: because of this occasion, it wasn't until my sophomore year that I kissed again and that was when a freshman kissed me.

Rat Clubbing

Us older boys had an activity called "Rat Clubbing." We would go to various township dumps at night, usually a couple of cars with 3-5 clubbers in each. Armed with flashlights, lanterns, and wooden clubs, we tied our pant legs so the rats couldn't crawl up our legs. Remember, there weren't any plastic bags to put the garbage in, only raw garbage; obviously a lot of slipping and sliding, along with the smell.

You can't believe the number of rats living in a dump. At night, you would see their little beady eyes glowing in the flashlight, along with hearing them squeaking. After a couple of trips through the dump, we would move on to another one. This wasn't a regular activity but was limited to about once or twice a month.

It was always nice to go home and clean up. We always left lots of rats for another outing. As far as I remember, there wasn't any alcohol involved, and we don't know how many rats we clubbed.

Heavenly China
By Donna Hart of Stanton, Michigan
Born 1923

I arrived on the scene in 1923- Stanton, Michigan to Zoreta and Frederick Pakes at the farm home of my grandparents, Mr. and Mrs. George Hillis, and am recalling that era and recent happenings. I graduated from a local high school in 1941. Sunday, December 7th, the radio reported the bombing of Pearl Harbor. We all rushed outside asking the neighbors, "Can this be true?" Sadly, it was.

The Great Depression (1929) sent many into near panic with banks closing. Soon, men were happy to do long, hard work for $1.00 per day. The WPA and CCC camps provided assistance to families, plus local buildings as school gyms (ours included), as well as many state park welcome centers and outbuildings.

Yes, school discipline was followed at home- people respected teachers. Mostly sassing teachers or nasty pranks happened; nothing like the violence of today.

In 1933, via B&O railroad, we moved to Virginia when my father worked as a chemist creating dyes for bone buttons before zippers and plastics. The government called for all businesses to pay a fee and display a card, "We belong to the NRA" (National Recovery Act) - later declared unconstitutional. Dad's employers refused to pay and the plant shut down. Back to Michigan we came that fall.

Recalling the blizzard of 1936. Drifts up to 10 and 15 feet. Dad cut several steps in the snow banks to get out of our yard to the barn.

It took the State Highway rotary plows to open many rural roads. I missed nearly a month of school, as the school in town never closed in all that time.

My grandparents had a wall phone. The line was owned and maintained by the farmers locally, as many as 10 on the line. A crank of the phone called "central," and she would plug in the appropriate line. Of course, all on the line could listen in. One note- the town operator could start the fire whistle and then with a pulley send a note out the window informing the firemen of the location. Some ingenuity, right?

Great-grandfather Pakes came from England and started a meat market here in the late 1800s. It lasted for 3 generations of sons, grandsons, etc. until arrival of the super markets.

Our laundry was done, in early days, on a Florian Washer. A long day's work, I might add. A ribbed rocker rubbed the clothes and a hand wringer removed all the water. Earlier, it was done on a washboard. What a thrill to get a gas motor driven washer, then finally an electric one. The tubs were also used for weekly baths. What fun.

Mom made all of my clothes, dresses, and coats. She would send us to Sears or Alden's for material. No slacks back then. Only snow pants for outdoor activities. My first jeans were to wear to pick up potatoes at 2cents per bushel. Back then, schools closed for 2 weeks for potato harvest in the area.

We enjoyed battery radio and programs such as Amos and Andy, Mr. Perkins, The Shadow, and always the Lux Radio Theater on Sunday night. Several batteries were needed, and costly, so we were selective on use of the radio. Batteries cost $8-$10 each, approximately a week's wages. Dad worked for 10-12 hours per day and wages were $10.00 per week. However, a week's groceries would cost about $2 or $3 per week in the 1930s.

We, as most rural people, had an outhouse and wow, they were cold on a zero temperature night with the cold wind at your backside.

My first date, at the age of 16, was at the county track meet when a handsome student jogged up to me and asked for a date for a church youth group party. That was after he had just finished a 60-yard dash. That handsome student was Thayer Hart. Many dates later, we married and enjoyed 63 years together before he passed away in 2004. We had three great kids, grands, and great-grands. I'm still living on Pakes Road near Stanton where I've lived most of my life.

Finally a family humorous story. Granddad Pakes took many carloads of cattle to sell at the Detroit Stockyard, approximately 150 miles via railroad boxcars. He rode in the boxcars to keep the stock watered and fed. After selling the cattle and receiving a large roll of cash, he proceeded up Woodward Ave. to a prestigious jewelry store there, stating he wished to buy a set of "heavenly China" service for 12. (Havilland, of course). The young clerk just walked away, rolling his eyes. You can imagine how Grandad looked and smelled after riding with cattle. An older clerk walked up and dutifully took his order, and Granddad pulled out a roll of bills large enough to "choke an ox," as they say. This clerk received a nice commission, as that was the practice for clerks in the 30s. The China was service for twelve but had all the serving dishes of all sizes included. Grandad had quite a chuckle to see out of the corner of his eye, the young clerk gasping at the big commission he

81

missed. That "heavenly China" filled a 5-foot China cabinet but all are lost into segments with family members here and there.

Ice Cutting Day
By Mary Morningstar of Shelby, Michigan
Born 1923

In 1936, my family moved from the little town of Shelby, Michigan, population about 1200, to Stony Lake, 10 miles west of Shelby. My father had purchased the little resort store with an attached dance hall, which later had roller skating twice a week and dancing on Saturday nights during the summer.

Before and during that early time, most of the cottages around the lake were equipped with insulated iceboxes, which is what refrigerators were called that kept our foods cold and edible.

In the winter, when the ice on Stony Lake became a certain thickness, the folks living at the lake and the surrounding area, would gather with their ice cutting tool and long poles tipped with hooks, and trucks and wagons for hauling the ice. A channel was cut toward the middle of the lake to a larger square of ice, which was cleaned of snow, and cut into squares the size that would fit into most of the iceboxes. The squares were then guided into the channel up toward shore, and loaded into the trucks or wagons to be transported to the icehouses of various places and farms. My dad's ice was placed in a large wooden building with a thick layer of sawdust covering the floor. Each layer of ice was covered with a thick layer of sawdust to

Cutting ice for refrigerators

Cutting ice from Stony Lake

keep the layers of ice from sticking together, and then a thick layer of sawdust covered the topmost layer. The building was then sealed up, tightly, until summer when the ice was delivered to the various cottages, as needed.

One particular day after school, we youngsters were standing around watching the process when my dad asked me to grab a pole and pull the row of ice back, as there was an uneven square in the channel. He kept telling me to back up, but forgot the ice had been cut behind me. I backed onto the cut ice and, promptly, fell through the ice. The heavy, wool, snow pants and jacket didn't help me to stay afloat. My dad rushed to help, but was unable to find a place to grab, finally having to grab a handful of my hair to hold me up until some of the other men could help pull me out.

Brrrr, was that water ever cold!

My Happiest and Saddest Memories
By Verla Germain of Beaverton, Michigan
Born 1939

I was born in Midland, Michigan in 1939. My first memory, that means the world to me, is when I was seven years old. We lived on Deering Road—at the very end.

The day was January 30, 1947. There was a horrible blizzard going on and my mother went into labor. The snow was at least two feet deep. There was no way out and no one nearby who knew how to deliver babies. Someone called for a snowplow to come. Soon it arrived. It plowed one lane and plowed clear up to our doorway. The plow driver helped load my mother, Marguerite, onto the plow and away they went. Neighbors who lived across the road, Mary and Orlin Johnston, saw the commotion and came over to walk my brother, Karl, (11) and my sister, Marie, (4) and me through the high open tunnel the plow made. It was so high that none of us could see over it.

I remember we weren't afraid. The awesome neighbors fed us something and soon it was time for bed. We were all tucked into nice clean beds. I remember one thing that was funny to us kids but I'm not sure it was funny to our neighbors. The beds were on casters and we found out that if you pushed your hand against the wall the beds would scoot around the room. We had fun with that for a while until we went to sleep. We woke up and were taken home to find out we had a brand new sister, Donna, whom we fell in love with and I still adore her to this day.

The blizzard and the mom being taken to the hospital on the snowplow made the headlines in the Midland Daily newspaper. My tiny sister was dubbed "Little Miss Snow Blizzard." The story was repeated in the paper after five years and again after ten years. By then, I was grown. I don't know when they quit printing the story. I had the newspaper, with my help; write the story again when my sister turned 50.

Now, my next story is the saddest memory I have. We moved to the town of Coleman in 1949 where we lived a busy life on a farm. When I was 15, a lot of us friends would go to the movies once a week. We had our boyfriends and you just sat together—we did not even hold hands. We were just dear friends. One day, I caught my ride into town. It was part way through the movies and my four friends, Wallace Graham and Vernon, Joyce and Connie West, had not arrived. I guess what worried me the most was wondering if my boyfriend, Richard Graham, and his friends had decided not to come and had forgotten to call me. I was there about a half hour when the theater lights came on and, of course, a hush came over the theater. My name was called, as well as the names of four other kids. I remember wondering what the heck was going on but do not remember having any fear. When we got to the area where they sell tickets, there was my mom and the four other moms. I do not remember who gave us the horrible news but each of us was a basket case

and crying tears that would not stop.

The news was that five kids had left North Bradley, a small town just a few miles away, and as the car crossed the railroad tracks, a fast moving train had hit the car killing all five. On the way home, I said to my mom, "My heart breaks for everyone but I know my boyfriend was not killed. I just know that in my heart."

As we were arriving home, our phone rang. It was my boyfriend. He had walked across the tracks to buy a pack of cigarettes. He was walking out of the store in time to see the train hit and kill his brother and his three friends.

The date was January 30, 1955. The saddest part of the awful tragedy was that the other three teens, the Wests, were the only children in their family. With time, our hearts would mend and I would have another boyfriend whom I married and I'm still married to him after all these years.

So ends two memories that stand out in my earlier years. Now, I am a mother, a grandmother and a great grandmother. If I continued with those wonderful and sad stories from my life, I would be here writing for at least one hundred years.

My Memories from Childhood
By Robert Gofton of Midland, Michigan
Born 1927

One for the money, two for the show, three to get ready, four, here I go. To start off, my dad was born in Applegate, Michigan and graduated from Michigan Agriculture College with degrees in Agriculture. My mother, Lois L. Leland was born in California and moved to Michigan when she was 13 years old. My parents were married in Flushing, Michigan where my dad was an agriculture teacher and continued his education at MCC during the summers to get his degree to be a superintendent.

We moved to McBain, Michigan for one year and then to Thompsonville, Michigan where we stayed for four years. That is where my story really starts. I was in the third grade in the fall of 1932. Thompsonville was a town of about 400 people then. They had a sawmill that cut wood for railroad ties. I remember my dad wanting to raise some chickens. He bought 500 chicks, that was before they sexed them, and about half of them turned out to be roosters. So what did we have every Sunday for dinner? You guessed it - CHICKEN!

We lived on the Little Betsie River. My brother, Dick and I went fishing a lot. He is 14 months younger than me. We caught a lot of brook trout. We were always scrapping over something, mostly about who was supposed to split the wood or who was to stake it. So much for us. My dad would go fishing the last Saturday in April and my mother would take my brother and me mushrooming every spring in the North Hills. There were a bunch of hills to the west of Thompsonville that we called the West Hills, which is now called Crystal Mountain.

There were a ton of apple and cherry orchards. They were called Thorn Hill Orchards. My brother worked for them one year.

While we were in Thompsonville, my dad, Claude R. Gofton, was superintendent and also taught agriculture. He remarked to his class one day that the only good crop they could grow in that country was sand burs. Ha Ha. My mother would mix honey and lemon with a shot of whiskey when we would get a cold. My sister, Ann was born December 29, 1934 and my brother and I thought we would get out of doing dishes. WRONG.

We moved to Brethern from Thompsonville, which was about 20 miles south. We spent three years there. There was a small lake about two blocks from our house. We were about 11 or 12 years old when we moved there. We learned to swim in a hurry. In 1935 or 1936, it was turned into a CCC Camp and is now a City Park.

It seems like we moved a lot. From Brethren, we moved in the fall of 1936 to Copemish. We lived there three years and then moved to Hemlock, which was west of Saginaw. In the summer of 1944, we moved to Hemlock where my dad was superintendent. I graduated from Hemlock High School in a class of 21 students—10 boys and 11 girls. When I was a senior in high school, all the boys played all sports. No football. When it was time for basketball tournaments, we played Reese. Coach Burns started the subs first because they had won many games all year. We got 10 points behind, then Coach Burns put in the first string and we never caught up. The next day, The Saginaw News caption read, "Coach Burns sent in the Shock Troops." That was in the fall of 1944.

I joined the Navy in February of 1945. I was on the USS Sturgis. AP 126. I spent two years, ten months and seven days in the service. I was discharged in March of 1948. The Sturgis was converted from a Liberty ship to a troop ship. We took the second wave of troops into Yokohama, Japan in 1945. The Japanese were scared to death of us sailors or any US serviceman. During our next trip to Japan, they welcomed us with open arms and wanted to sell us everything they had including, "Take my daughter back to the United States."

The Value of a Two-Dollar Bill
By Timothy L. Perry of Grand Ledge,
Michigan
Born 1953

What is a collection of two-dollar bills worth? If given as a gift, is it worth more to the giver or the receiver? To some the response is easy: "Tis better to give than to receive." But what if a lifelong loved one offers to pay a debt to you with this prized collection he had accumulated over a lifetime? Sometimes money carries a different kind of value than just monetary value. Sometimes it carries memories of hard times, good times, pain and suffering, mistakes, triumphs, gratefulness, thankfulness, and even love. In the story you are about to read, a collection of two dollar bills becomes a symbol of love which spans the generations.

The values we have as adults are formed, to a large extent, in our childhood. The way we think about possessions, family, and life in general is influenced by the conditions and people we experience as we grow up. Clarence and Mart, two brothers in a family of eight, grew up poor on a rental farm in Big Prairie Township during the Depression. The family struggled to meet their basic needs, as did so many during the Depression Era. Money represented more than material possessions to them. It represented long, hard, backbreaking toil behind the horse drawn plow or at the end

Two dollar bill

of a bucksaw. As important as money was in those days, the value of a hard day's work and the love of family and friends was even more important. Because money was so short, many times the only way they could show their love was to do something for someone. Payment for work done for family and friends was always turned down. So the brothers grew up together learning how to farm, the value of work, and the importance of family and friends.

Clarence and Mart carried their love of farming into their adult years. Both owned farms and farmed part-time during a large part of their adult working lives. Clarence loved working in the fields in the warmth of the summer season. Rising early each day to hear the songs of the birds, the chirping of the squirrels, and the croaking of the frogs was like therapy to him. He shared this love of the land and animals with brother Mart. But as both grew older, they found they had less energy for farming. The cows were sold and the land rented to neighbor farmers, but their desire to work on the land with the animals did not die.

The Livestock Auction

Livestock auctions were an adventure for Clarence and Mart. The steady yell of the auctioneer was almost like music. It was easy to get caught up in the bidding, especially for Mart. Sometimes the prices seemed too good to be true. Sometimes prices were especially good for the sellers and sometimes they were exceptionally good for the buyers.

On this particular day, the bids on the cattle were unusually low, and Mart could not resist. He planned to bid only a few times at the lower price level and then pull out in time so as not to get the winning bid. It was fun for him to raise his finger or nod to the auctioneer and receive immediate recognition as his bid was announced to the crowd. But to Mart's surprise, the bidding stopped well before he expected, and he was recognized as the winning bidder. He was the proud owner of some nice looking cattle. He was elated, but also concerned, for he did not have the money to pay for them.

Clarence had his checkbook along and agreed to loan Mart the money. Mart completed the purchase. The cost of the cattle was approximately $300.00. Mart promised to pay the loan back as soon as possible. Clarence, in the spirit of Perry values, told Mart not to worry about it. He did not want Mart to feel like payment was expected right away. After all, Mart's lifestyle showed the effects of living through the Depression. He was very frugal but had little money to spare. "Pay it whenever you get some extra money, Mart," Clarence said. Mart and Clarence left the auction with the feeling that they had regained the farming spirit, if only for an evening. Of course, Mart was leaving with much more; some cattle to feed.

Much More than Money

Time passed and nothing was said between them about the loan. Whenever it was mentioned, Clarence would tell Mart not to worry and pay it whenever he had some extra money but there was no rush. Of course, things like this between family members can

Fred and Marie (Bartosh) Perry's sons in 1941
Ralph, Mart, Fred, Art, and Clarence

be bothersome to both parties. After all, they had been brothers for over 50 years. Mart began to feel he needed to pay the loan back. He knew that Clarence was never going to pressure him. Mart was putting the pressure on himself. He had very little in his savings account, and what regular income he did have was used for family expenses. The cows had made him very little after he paid expenses to feed and truck them back to market.

What Mart did have was a collection of two-dollar bills he had saved over the years. It amounted to about $270.00. He planned on saving them for a very long time since he felt they would become more valuable as time went on. The two-dollar bill was the only bill with a picture of the signers of the Declaration of Independence on the back. But this was the only money Mart had to pay his dear brother back. Mart offered the collection to Clarence in payment for the loan. Clarence was not sure what to say. This was a collection that Mart had spent years accumulating. How could he accept it as repayment of the loan? This collection meant a lot more to Mart than just money. Clarence gave the collection back to Mart saying he could not take such a prized collection from his dear brother.

"Don't worry about paying me right now," said Clarence. "Wait until you have some extra money. There's no rush." Clarence thought about making the loan a gift to Mart, but that much money would be too great a gift and would either anger Mart or make him feel ashamed that he could not pay it back.

As time passed, things did not get better for Mart; instead, they got worse. He still had the two-dollar bill collection. It was still the only thing he had to pay back the loan to Clarence. Again, he offered the collection to Clarence. This time Clarence agreed to take the collection. He realized that Mart would probably never have the additional money to pay the loan. This was the only way Mart could pay the loan back. By accepting the collection, Clarence realized that Mart valued keeping the agreement with him over this collection that had taken Mart years to collect. Their relationship would remain intact. Clarence accepted the payment but also acknowledged that it was, in a way, a gift from his brother.

A Gift for the Generations

Clarence was not sure what to do with the collection Mart had given him in payment for the loan. He felt a collection of this size should be kept and treasured rather than spent or sold. But what is the appropriate way to preserve and pass along this collection and, more importantly, the meaning of the collection? Clarence struggled for years deciding how to deal with the collection. Then, as he was reaching the twilight of his life, the answer came. He would keep the story about the two-dollar bills secret and reveal his plans for the collection at the appropriate time.

Not long after, Clarence, who had been fighting cancer for several years, learned that the treatments he had been suffering through every two weeks were no longer fighting the cancer but only prolonging his pain. Clarence decided to stop treatment. His life was nearly over. Now was the time to reveal the secret. One afternoon not long before his death, Clarence relayed the story and his wishes to his wife, Martha. As he told the story, his wishes became clear. Pass the bills on to the next generation, to our grandchildren, but not just the bills, also the story. The bills carry the story, which is really the important part. The story is one of a love between brothers and the love a man extends to his grandchildren and the grandchildren of his grandchildren for all generations.

We Raised Good Watermelons
By Waneta Bender of Ithaca, Michigan
Born 1927

I was born at home on Alger Road in 1927. I lived during the Depression but was too young to realize it. I remember hearing Mom feel sorry that she couldn't feed us better, but we never went hungry.

We lived on Alger Road, one half mile south of Washington Road, on a farm called The Sand. We raised good watermelons. Dad worked out as a carpenter, mason, and construction. He built that stone wall west of Ithaca, and he built some houses. He built the first ranch style home in Ithaca.

Mom had a garden and raised and sold strawberries, and raspberries. Us children would pick them for ¼ cent a quart. Mom sorted and sold them. She got 8cents a quart. I remember one summer that she sold 80 quarts.

We got our water at a well south of the

house. We had to pump it.

Dad went to town for groceries on Saturday nights. You took your list in, handed it to the grocer, and we went back in the store, got what was on the list, and brought it up front, then you paid. He usually brought home some candy.

Sometimes, if we ran out of bread, the bread truck stopped at our neighbor, Harry Hart's. Mom would send us down there to get some.

We usually had some cows and did some farming. The older brothers helped with that. The cows were all milked by hand. Mom had chickens too. She sold the eggs to buy other groceries. She raised turkeys to sell but would save those eggs. When a hen turkey got ready to set, she fixed them up a place, and watched until they settled down. In the fall, we had a nice little flock to sell.

Then in 1936, we went to Alabama for the winter. Some of our relatives moved down there to Foley, Alabama. We went three winters until World War II started. Then one didn't travel anymore.

We moved to a farm 1 ½ miles south of Ithaca when we came back the last time. It was on Jerome Road.

One couldn't buy new cars until after the War and lots of things were rationed.

While living on Alger Road, we had a real snowstorm. We were snowed in for a week. No school. One boy, Fred Guild Jr., walked to school anyway. He had his picture in the Gratiot County Herald. He never missed a day of school thru the 8th grade.

Our first washing machine had a gas motor you had to start with a foot pedal. Our dryer was some lines fastened to posts. Our first electric one was about 1943. My brother wired our house on Jerome Road. A bare bulb hung from the ceiling.

Our clothes were all homemade except for shoes and socks. Some were made out of feed sacks.

Nothing was thrown away. Old dresses were made into rugs, or handed down. Old skirts were used for dishtowels to wipe the cooking dishes.

All dresses were starched, sprinkled, and ironed, folded and put in drawers. Left over cloth from dresses was made into quilts.

We had a windmill close to the house when we moved to Jerome Road and soon after, we put in a bathroom.

We didn't have a telephone until I was 16. The line that was in, called the Farmer line, was too full. Later, they put in a new one, and then we got one.

I went to school the first three years at Lewis School on Alger Road. Then went to Wheeler School on Jerome Road. I had good teachers; Alvera Teachman at Lewis School, and Margaret Douglas at Wheeler. Everyone liked her.

When we lived on Alger Road, or The Sand, my oldest brother built our first tractor out of an old car, but it worked. He called it a Doodle Bug.

While living on The Sand one year, we had a hurricane. It took our brooder house across the road. My mom had some chickens, about a month old in it. They were running around. She went out after the storm and rescued what she could. The outdoor toilet was lifted up and sat over a stump in the yard. Some trees were blown over; one on a car. Some other families came and stayed until it was over.

A lady who lived south of us, used to drive y our place often in a Model T Ford. They called her Lady Drayton.

I remember Mom cleaning the lamps and wick on the old Aladdin lamp.

The first time I went to town, I was 16 and went along on Saturday night with my Dad. I did a little shopping in Gays Dime Store.

At Christmastime, the stores were only open nights, 2 weeks before Christmas.

I worked in the glove factory and the shoe factory. I learned to know and love the Leon and Mabel Dilts, Woody Johnson, and Randall Johnson. I worked for them before the shoe factory and for a family north of Alma before it was all built into stores and eateries.

I remember the first moon landing. We lived in Wisconsin and had company for supper. All were out in the yard talking about it with leery feelings. What if they can't get off the moon?

The first car I bought was a 1938 Ford from my brother-in-law's uncle. They used to put it up on blocks for the winter. I paid $200.00 for it. The next one was a 1950 Ford.

Ithaca used to be a nice, little town, until they put the freeway in.

I have been gone from Michigan for over 60 years, so there have been lots of changes.

On the Cedar River
By Sharon Reavis of St. Louis, Michigan
Born 1953

My childhood memories rotated between summer neighborhood play, trips to our cabin on the Cedar River in Harrison, Michigan, and my father's one week per year vacation from work at Paul Cameron Dodge. Our vacations were always spent at Houghton Lake, where Mom and Dad both loved to fish at Palmer's Resort and Cabins.

I always loved playing dress up as a little girl in our neighborhood. My world then was our street only, as I wasn't allowed further. I got a lot of fun clothes and high heels (high for me, that is) from my aunt who was little, and I was big, so they nearly fit me.

Our cabin up north was built in 1966 by my dad and uncle, and money you could call "extra," which Mom had earned babysitting. It was very small and simple, with an outhouse used for a few years until Dad was able to get a real bathroom inside.

"Up north," though only about 65 miles from us, was a whole different world, where I could explore or just lie in the hammock and read. Birds, which Mom loved, were all around. Boys, which I loved, not so much.

My dad would go trout fishing in the Cedar every spring when season opened. I loved hearing the whippoorwills calling up there and we also had a lot of frisky, black squirrels.

During the school year, I walked several blocks to school or even rode my bike. I loved school and Mom liked being homeroom mother, and furnishing creative treats for our room.

One Christmas, she made a popcorn Christmas tree and had a small present wrapped for each child around it. The presents were little animal shaped pencil sharpeners. Mom made everything special in my world, while Dad worked every day, very hard, as a mechanic.

We had a black and white TV all my life at home, usually one that was very "light." We would cover the windows in order to enjoy our favorite parades: Macy's Thanksgiving Day Parade and The Rose Parade. My brother was older by eleven years, so he was working and bought us our first new television, still a black and white, but great to us.

Sharon Reavis in 1953

Our laundry was done in a wringer washer and two tubs for rinsing the clothes thoroughly. As a little girl, I loved helping Mother by using her "wash stick" to bring the clothes out of the water. Later, I was big enough to feed them through the wringer. Occasionally, the stick would go through too, but no finger! I still have the "wash stick," just an old piece of driftwood, but full of memories for me.

It was a wonderful time to grow up and not easily found in our busy world today. By the way, Mom was home until I was in high school, before she did the babysitting job for extra money. Presumably, I was more important.

Gone With the Wind, Remembered
By Ruby Klanecky of Lansing, Michigan
Born 1927

For me, the movie that made a strong impression was *Gone with the Wind*. It presented the Civil War, covering actual facts through fictional characters. At that time, the movie industry was in the early stages of our entertainment world. 15cents bought us a ticket and it only cost another dime for a freshly popped box of popcorn. Most of the children in our Michigan farming community attended a little one-room school. We usually walked the long gravel road leading to the school. Sometimes, a neighbor drove us if the weather was bad. Our teacher and some of the parents organized transportation for taking the children to the small local theater for a viewing of this movie. We were so excited. It was an unusually long showing and in color, but no one complained.

To me and others, it was the most wonderful movie ever made. At the same time, it brought history to life, and our understanding of those historical facts that no reading of any book could convey. After being ushered to our seats, the lights dimmed and a huge screen appeared from behind thick draperies that were drawn open. Music greeted us as we were seated, so the movie could begin. Because the movie was so long, as intermission was presented after two hours so we could use the bathrooms or get a drink before the show continued.

It took Margaret Mitchell, the author, ten years to research, rewrite, and finish this novel. Metro-Goldwyn-Mayer opted to produce this epic story. The owners of these large cotton producing plantations bought African American slaves at auction to work in the fields and to carry out and maintain the household chores. The slaves became their private property and the owners were responsible for their livelihood. It was the most pressing issue of concern for our young country at this time. It divided the country into two separate sections: the North wanted the slaves to be freed, while the Old South needed to keep slavery functional; thus, families were torn apart and the Civil War took place. Many war stories evolved, some true and others fictional.

Many fell in love with Rhett Butler, and others named their babies after Scarlett O'Hara, the two most important characters, and love interests featured in this saga of the Civil War. Rhett Butler spoke one of the most memorable phrases at the conclusion of this story when Scarlett O'Hara asked him, "What am I going to do?" Rhett replied, "My dear, I don't give a damn!" Rhett Butler walked away as she muttered to herself, "I'll get him back."

This film has been shown for generations and will be of interest for generations to come. Making note of the fact this was written as movies and books were under strict censorship for language used, the big argument of the day concerned whether the word *damn* had to be changed because it was too sacrilegious. In the end, all who were concerned agreed it should not be changed.

Later, I sent for, and received, the second edition from Montgomery ward, the mail order business.

Two Runners
By Richard Lound of Shelby, Michigan
Born 1944

Two runner sleds and to think most people under 30 would have no idea what you were talking about, let alone what to do with one if they got a "two runner" for Christmas. And we did, get one for Christmas that is. And we used it pretty much on a daily basis for as long as there was snow on the ground each winter.

I believe a popular one back in their heyday of the 1940s, '50s, and early '60s was the Radio Flyer, but I could be wrong about that name, it has been so long since I saw one, other than in someone's barn up high in the rafters, or a lone one in an antique store with the paint all worn off and the steel runners pretty rusty.

We, as kids growing up in the 1950s and going to a two-room country school, not only took them to school and used them during recess and the noon hour, but we used them on the roads when conditions were good or in the nearby fields when necessary.

Or better yet, at night, after supper, when several youngsters in the neighborhood would get together for a sliding party of a nearby hill, or the roadway where the hill was steep, and the snow packed down for maximum speed.

I was one of eleven children of the Paul and Katherine Lound family who lived on a farm on Woodrow Road, so getting enough kids for an afternoon or nightly sliding party was no problem. One could generally find two, three, or four of my sisters willing to join in some sliding fun somewhere in the area, if not on our own hills on the "back 40."

Our neighborhood was commonly known as Blooming Valley after the name of the K-8 school district and Cobrin Hill was the premier hill. That was not only for its length, over a quarter mile long, but also for its steepness and for the speeds we could reach on the downhill stretch. The road generally was only used by vehicle traffic on the downhill side, because there were no front wheel drive vehicles and hardly any 4-wheel drive trucks, which kept most vehicles off the hill, so there was little danger of ever meeting someone, other than a "two runner" going the same way you were going.

A big bonfire would generally mark the top of the hill and was used for warming and some light to see by, but once you started down, you were on your own as far as seeing where the sides of the road were and one just hoped to keep the sled between the banks.

The two runners were not the only things we used to slide on way back then, but they were the most common snow vehicle for most kids. There were no plastic contraptions, but there were bobsleds, a long narrow 4-runner sled that could hold 6 or 7 or more, depending on the length. Most were homemade, had steering for the guy in front, and could get up some pretty good speeds when the conditions were right.

A few families had toboggans and some even had "Norge Tin," which was a poor kid's toboggan and was really the side of a Norge refrigerator with a curved up front and curved up side. They would go quite well, hold several kids at a time, but one of the real drawbacks of the "tins" was no way to steer, so open hills with as few trees and brush as possible were the ideal locations to use one.

I think television pretty much brought the golden age of the "two runner" to its knees. And later, snowmobiles became very popular in the mid-1960s, which not only gave one the speed over the snow, but eliminated the need to walk back up the hill for another run. Also, the increase of car/truck traffic on the roads and the use of sand and salt on the roadways helped the popular after supper sliding parties slowly disappeared from the small community America.

Fried Fish and Blueberry Pie
By Rosalie Bierlein of Saginaw, Michigan

When we were young, we had a milkman and his horse. We would try to get the horse to follow us and move the wagon ahead of the milkmen by enticing him with treats, but it never worked to our liking since that animal knew his route and only moved an inch or two. We kept on trying, but that horse was smarted then we were.

Every summer our folks took us up north to Elk Lake for 2 weeks. As soon as we reached Clements Dump (my dad's name was Clement), we knew we were only two blocks from the cabin. My dad would laugh since he knew how excited we were. We picked berries, caught pollywogs, and fished. All we ate was fried fish and potatoes and blueberry pie. Our poor mom… all she did was fry fish and bake pies for us, but what a time we had. When we grew up and went back to see the cottage, everything had changed. Somebody bought the cottage, enclosed the porch we used all the time, and knocked down the little house. It just wasn't our cottage anymore.

One afternoon on my way to the beach, I thought I'd be smart and run down the dock to jump in but I didn't see the hole in the dock. One leg fell into the hole and the other leg was laid flat, right in front of me. I couldn't move and was in such pain. I began screaming. Luckily, my brother, Stan Wesolek, came to my rescue, lifted me up from the hole, and put me in the water to cool my legs. I never ran on the dock again.

One of my most embarrassing moments was in the movie theater. My husband said, "Go sit wherever you want," so I headed down the aisle to find a good seat. For some reason, when I found the seat I wanted, I knelt down, made the sign of the cross, and then walked to our seats. My husband was shocked and asked what I was doing. Everybody was laughing. Only then did I realize what I had done.

On a sleepover to my cousin's house, I had an embarrassing moment. We were in Karin's backyard and swinging higher and higher and then we would jump off to see who could jump the farthest. My dress got caught somehow on the chains and as I jumped, it ripped the whole skirt from my dress. When I hit the ground, all I had left on my body was the top of my dress and my ruffled underwear. I screamed and started bawling like a baby and ran inside the house to my cousin's mother, who spent the rest of the afternoon sewing my dress back together.

In the '70s, my brother, Stan, came with his family to visit. They drove in from New York. We had a terrible snowstorm. I think we were dumped with over a foot of snow. They had a Siberian husky so my brother harnessed Kai to the sled and he pulled our children all around the block. We had such great memories of the weekend and our kids were thrilled.

As teenagers, my sister, Barb Konieczka, her friend, Mary Clare Thumme, and I would watch Dick Clark's American Bandstand every day after school. We would dance around the house and sing all the pop songs. When it was time for Mary Clare to go home, I'd walk her halfway home but we were dancing and singing all the way down the street. We always wondered what the neighbors thought, but nobody ever said a word to us.

As kids, we would put on plays in the garage and have haunted houses in our basement. We'd hide in the fruit cellar and rattle the jars, scaring the kids. It would cost 5cents and there were lots of kids coming. Then, we'd sell sandwiches and lemonade. My dad was very shy. He'd always yell when he came home because all the kids were in the yard and he said we were messing up everything, but he never really stopped us. What a fun time.

My brother, Stan, and his pal, Jack Strudgeon, went up north fishing. In the evening, on the 2nd day, it was dark, and a huge sphere or disk, as large as a football field, came down right over them with lights flashing. Then a big light came down on them. They were horrified. After a while, the jets flew over and suddenly the disk, or whatever it was, went up and flew away. They came ashore, shaken to the core, started a fire, and sat up all night. In the morning, when all the people came out, the news reporters came out to interview everybody. They said the time was 12:58, and it was then my brother realized they had lost 17 minutes; their watches had stopped! Of course, it was reported to be testing in the area, but my brother knew differently.

Oldies Dot.ME.
By Richard E. Hartlep of Mt. Pleasant, Michigan
Born 1950

One of the many perks of working with my dad at his corner Sinclair gas station in the town of Mecosta, which straddles east-west state route M-20 in mid-Michigan, was that he had put me in charge of radio listening, an envied position if you ask me seeing as how other '60s teenagers were also enamored with the era's top-40 type radio. For instance, one popular, nationally known station was WLS-Chicago. Providing us kids with a steady earful of Motown ('Come See About Me' by the Supremes) and the British Invasion beat ('Shape of Things' by the Yardbirds) its promo

Richard and his parents, Ed and Betty in 1968

line, or handle, was "W-L-S in Chicago" was like an iconic battle cry for us, as in, it was time to listen up and get down even if it was in front of a bedroom mirror. That must have been me.

But I –we- were blessed with our own local area stations. When Dad and I opened up the doors for business every morning, a slender, mild mannered guy, he would be decked out in Sinclair khaki dark green, whereas I was allowed to wear worn, but still decent, polo shirts, and blue jeans. The first chore I happily performed was to reach up to the Zenith plug-in radio perched above the metal cabinet, which houses the spark plugs and condensers, and turn on either WWAM-Cadillac, WSGW-Saginaw, or WCEN-Mt. Pleasant, and

Richard's dad, Ed, Richard, and Uncle Tony

Richard Hartlep

commenced listening to the sounds. While I worked that is. You know, being a gas station attendant in the age of full service and full service only, I'd be out at the gas pump island pumping that 36.9 Ethyl and 32.9 Regular into the now classic gas-guzzlers, the Olds 4-4-2s and the Buick Wildcats, and while the nozzle was on automatic, I'd clean the windshields. A popular line of an attendant was "It's a good thing cows don't fly." I would also lift the heavy hoods to check the oil and maybe sell a can of Sinclair Extra Duty 30 weight oil. But, I could still hear the music.

Once my town pals, Tony, Mike, and Dixie, sauntered into the office of the quaint, brick building, which was painted white and trimmed in Sinclair red, and green, to basically just hang out and chat while buying 10-cent Cokes. Dixie, relaxing on an old school bus seat, commented to Dad and another customer, "Dick sure knows all the good stations." The expression on Dad's and the adult customer's face was like, "Uh… okay."

Dixie was referring to WZZM-Grand Rapids, a tad more 'rockish' than the other stations. It's where you were most likely to hear Led Zeppelin's 'A Whole Lot of Love,' and the Guess Who's 'American Woman,' and 'No Time.' I think the adults may have considered these hits a tad too kinky and loud to begin with. Dad never said anything, but I bet he thought likewise. Plus, these songs dragged on and on at the end, a feature that annoyed me and still does. Simon and Garfunkel's 'The Boxer,' if you notice, drags on too but it is a more mellow song and you can make out the words better so as to sing along with it. During the summer of '69, ZZM played Johnny Cash's 'A Boy Named Sue' and the Grass Roots 'I'd Cry a Million Tears' a lot. How about twice each hour? Or so it seemed. Funny thing, those two hits always remind me of busy Friday afternoons in summer, when the tourists from downstate motored into town on the way to their cottages at the nearby lakes, and while families piled their way out of a '70 Ford Country Squire station wagons at the gas pumps to go shopping at Uhlrich's IGA and Ray's Party Store. Dad and I would service the car, and maybe I'd repair a spare 8-50-14 size Goodyear tire that had to be used at maybe a rest area over on freeway US 131 or 127, both north-south thoroughfares stretching from Indian to northern Michigan towards the Upper Peninsula. So the two-stall garage, connected to the little office building by a breezeway. When all of the doors were open, it was known as one of the cooler spots in town, and was a busy area. Depending on the chatter and the activity- a zip gun used to cut away rusted out exhaust systems would not only drown out the best of Led Zeppelin but cause neighborhood dogs to bark, oh yeah- one could still hear the radio.

I listened to sports too on the radio, notably baseball. The Cubs on WGN-Chicago, and the Tigers, of course, which were carried on all of those local stations except WZZM. Funny thing, many a pop song brings back memories. Sergio Mendez and Brazil 66s 'Fool of the Hill' takes me back straight away to the World Series of '68 between the Tigers and Cardinals, particularly game 5, an elimination affair played, of course, at the old Tiger Stadium and easily the most nerve wracking game I've even listened to. The Tigers and Mickey Lolich, the starting pitcher won, but it was cold, rainy, and overcast that October day in Mecosta; weather hardly conducive to the nerves. Guess who the Cowsills song 'Hair' makes me think of? No, not the Broadway musical of the same name, but Tigers pitcher

Denny McLain, who won 31 games that year, plus game six of the Series. He was the Man at the time.

As you can guess from the title of this narrative, Oldies on the radio, pleasantly cause me to flashback, reflect on a particular time, and place in that era of top-40 radio.

My First Love
By Edward Breitkreitz of Saginaw, Michigan
Born 1925

It all started when I was 16 years old and in my junior year of high school at Saginaw High. My instructress was my geography teacher, who was a beautiful woman. She was very intelligent and shall remain nameless. The first thing she told me was that I had above average potential and imagination and that if I would invest enough time and energy the sky would be the limit. She also told me that writing short stories is difficult, to say the least—the same thing that the Editor-in-Chief of Guideposts, Edward Grinnen, has told me recently.

I was so enthralled with my teacher, I was sure I was in love with her. Not knowing what the word "love" meant, I wanted to spend as much time with her as possible—even though I knew she was fifty-five years old and I was a sweet 16. This class started at 3 o'clock in the afternoon and ended at 4 o'clock. The first half hour of the class was used for regular geography and the second half was used for our personal project. The second half of the class was the most popular.

With one week left in the school year, my teacher asked me if I could remain after class for a few minutes. She said she had something to tell me. I sat in my seat until the class was gone and then she asked me to come up to her desk. By this time, my thoughts were running crazy, wondering what the good news was about. In the next few minutes, my life ended. She told me she was retiring from teaching and, along with her husband, she was moving to Florida. I was completely devastated. Not only did I love her completely, she was my closest friend and advisor. I'm sure I had a few tears in my eyes. Then she told me to come back behind her desk and she got up from

her chair and gave me a great big hug and a kiss on the cheek. She told me that she loved me like a member of her family, put her arm around me, and walked me to the door. She told me to keep in touch with her about my writing, which I never did. I was completely in shock.

I never heard from her again and never wrote to her about my writing, which in my opinion and to her credit was mildly successful. To this day, I'm so grateful that she was a big part of my life. All my thoughts, memories and love are directed to the finest person I ever met.

Life was Good for a Boy in the 1940s
By Donald Brady of Saginaw, Michigan
Born 1935

When I grew up in Saginaw, Michigan during the '40s and '50s it was the best of times for a 10 to 12 year old boy. We were free to come and go (almost) as we pleased as long as you were home at 5:30 for dinner. Very few harsh questions were asked—only, "Where did you go, who did you go with and did you have a good time?"

There were nice woods at the end of the street and a large field adjoined them. The field and woods lay between Arthur Hill High School and Handley School and they were always beckoning us to come on in. During the week, we were in school but the weekends belonged to us for war games. On Saturday mornings, we would take the bus downtown to see the war movies such as Iwo Jima, Siapan, Wings of Burma with the great warriors like John Wayne, Richard Widmark, Gabby Hayes, William Powell and many more. Well, we watched our heroes win over the Nazis and Japs who everyone hated and booed. We would come home for lunch and then head off to Handley woods to refight the battles. Our weapons were all woodcut out from odd pieces of lumber or a fallen tree limb but we could still shoot and have hand-to-hand combat. We were good soldiers who returned home at 5:30. Life was good.

During WWII, many people grew victory gardens to help the war effort such as many of our neighbors. When fall came and

J F Lady 15th and Donnie Brady

Carson City Memories
By Thomas Haradine of Carson City,
Michigan
Born 1941

gardening was through, we would get Jay Cushman's motor scooter and one by one take turns driving as fast as we could down the street while all the other boys would pick up the rotten vegetables and throw them at the rider. Also, for the war effort, the city pool (Anderson Pool) served what were called Victory burgers that contained pickles, relish, mustard, catsup and onions but NO meat. We loved the food and life was good.

Many of my buddies were Boy Scouts from Troop 66 at the First Presbyterian Church and we would meet weekly to earn badges for good deeds of learning. Then, during the summer, we spent two weeks at Camp O-Ge-Maw-Ke in Mio, Michigan. There, we learned survival skills, woodworking, swimming, crafts, archery, canoeing and fire building (from very little materials). In the evening, we would sit around a big campfire and the counselors would try to scare us with stories about "in the woods not far from here lives a Buffin Wiggle" but they could never tell what it looked like so life was good.

When we all grew up and went our separate ways, these good kids became pharmacists, doctors, dentists, lawyers, teachers, ministers, policemen, auto industry professionals, and the list goes on. I guess I can say life was good in the '40s and '50s for kids to grow up.

In December 1949, my folks, Hersh and Dorothy Haradine bought Harvey Milling Company from Harvey and Gladys Waldron. Harvey's had been a water powered flourmill when the Waldrons purchased the business in about 1945 and converted it to a grist mill. In those past years as a flour mill, their premium product was a flour sold and labeled as "Morning Rose," with a slogan, "The dawn of a better bread." After the conversion, Harvey and Gladys' best known product was their custom manufactured H&G Laying Mash. When Hersh and Dorothy took the business over, only a portion of the mill was still water-powered. There was a dam on Fish Creek north of M-57 that created the millpond with a millrace and flowing south under M-57 and through the east end of the mill. This waterwheel laid horizontally in the millrace and was used until 1953. When ear corn was shelled off the cob, the cobs were blown out into the millrace and floated off to Hubbardston via Fish Creek. At the midpoint of the 20th century, these are my nine-year-old memories of this village:

Our two largest employers were probably Dairyland Creamery and Crystal Refinery. The creamery was in its prime and sponsored the "Dairyland Picnic" every summer which featured a livestock show, talent show, kids games and a picnic lunch (with free milk, ice cream and orange drink for all). A very festive occasion! The refinery processed crude oil via a pipeline from the Crystal oilfields 8 miles north of Carson.

We had two K-12 schools, Carson City Public and St. Mary's Academy. I attended St. Mary's. When I was in third grade, I was taught by Sister Rosarita. She also taught first and second grade, all in one room with probably 50 kids. Father Leo Whalen was Pastor then and there were six Dominican nuns, five teachers and one housekeeper. The sisters lived in the school building. Their residence and chapel were on one side of the building and all 12 grades were on the other side. Johnny Mesco was the school janitor who was constantly tinkering with a coal-fired temperamental boiler to heat that building.

I graduated from St. Mary's in 1960 in the upper half of the bottom third!

We had one hospital, a three-bed unit in Dr. Binkerts' home on Elm Street. Our dentist was Dr. Boonstra and our drugstore was owned and operated by Carl Farwell. Clare Harden was president of the Carson City Bank and Louis Hogan was the teller. There were two barbershops, Kelly's and Fry's. There was one hotel and a pool hall. There were five taverns and five churches. There were six service stations, three car dealers, two farm implement dealers, two restaurants, one lumber business and two more grain and feed mills. We had five grocery stores, a poultry hatchery, a slaughterhouse, and a livestock sale barn. There was a volunteer fire department and a constable/night watchman. Michigan Produce was a successful vendor of beer and groceries to stores all over Central Michigan.

One fellow that left an impression on me was a character known only as "Cannonball." He lived in a shack where Harvey's office is in 2015 and eked out a living salvaging scrap from the city dump. There also were two brothers who had a shop on Elm Street where they repaired clocks and firearms. They were known locally as "Tic-Toc" and "Bang-Bang!"

Every March, there was a maple syrup festival and a three-ring circus came to town every summer. The Grand Trunk Railroad came through Carson every day, running from Durand to Greenville. On one occasion, there was a special excursion train that stopped in Carson and picked up mostly fathers and sons for a trip to Detroit to see the Tigers baseball team.

The Carson City Gazette kept all of us informed of local happenings and the telephone party lines spread the gossip! The telephone number at Harvey's was "4." How simple is that!

A Child of the Depression and WWII Era
By Alma Elizabeth Watton of Bay City,
Michigan
Born 1927

I was born in Bad Axe, Michigan on November 27, 1927, the second oldest in a family of six. We were all born at home. My

At Grandma's

grandmother Apley was an RN and midwife. She saved my life as she delivered me. She loosened the umbilical cord that was wrapped around my neck. My father changed jobs from Armstead Trucking in Bad Axe to Blair Transit in Saginaw. We moved to Bay City on King Street in spring of 1935. My brother, Elmer, (8) and I (7), went to Corbin School. We walked. It was scary, as we didn't know the area. We were the new kids on the block.

We were lucky that our dad always had work during the Depression. My sister, Eunice, was born June 15, 1935 on King Street. That fall, we moved to a bigger house on the corner of Alp and White Streets. My dad was killed in a car-train accident—icy roads at the Michigan Central Railroad Crossing—on January 9, 1936 in Saginaw. My mother was left a widow at 27 with six children, ages 6 months to 9 years. I was 8 and had to grow up in a hurry. We had no family here. We were in a new neighborhood, with no insurance yet from my dad's job, no car, and only a rental house. There was no widow's pension back then. The welfare people wanted her to put us in foster homes. My mother said, "No." She had my 18-year-old cousin from Detroit come stay with us and she went to work at Auto-Lite.

Alma's family reunion in 1935

Us kids all bonded together. Once a month, the welfare woman came to check on us. We would hide in a shed. We had hard times. My two brothers had to have tonsillectomies in February. Mom had to hire a taxi to take them. Then, my brother, Elmer (9), had to have a 9 1/2 hour mastoid operation. We were going to Kolb School then. Kids picked on my brother, Dale, in kindergarten—he was the new kid. I always went to his rescue on the playground—like a mother tiger.

My mom had to give up her job at Auto-Lite because of her nerves. I used to hear her crying and praying at night. She became a waitress at the beautiful Arlington Hotel on Linn Street. It was run by the Hammerbacher family—wonderful people. They took us under their wing. Mom met Carl Reinhardt there 3 1/2 years after our dad died. They were married. He was our guardian angel from heaven. He'd never had any children of his own and took on our family of six kids. He worshipped the ground mom walked on. We were a family again and mom was a stay home mom.

We lived on 34th Street in a beautiful stucco house. We went to Fremont School and were the new kids on the block again. We went to Fremont Methodist Church. Carl was a butcher by trade so we had good meat on the table. He was a super step dad—played baseball with us and took us fishing, skating and on Sunday rides to Bad Axe to visit relatives. He had a short wave radio that we would sit and listen to—there was no TV or phone. Once he made us a batch of root beer pop in bottles. Every one of those bottles blew the caps off - he had capped it too soon.

A beautiful 11-acre farm on Lincoln Road just north of Cass Avenue came up for sale. So, we moved there, went to Bullock one room

school and walked 3 1/2 miles each way—rain—shine —or snow. Then, snow could be up to the top of fence posts. Sometimes we walked in the old railroad bed. We had outside toilets, our teacher built a fire for us, and we had no running water. We had a pail and dipper in the hallway that everyone drank from. We carried sack lunches and we tried to trade our homemade bread sandwiches for store bought bread.

We loved it on the farm. We all had our chores— gardening, working in the 100-tree fruit orchard, picking fruit, Elmer milked cows (I tried - no luck) or feeding the pigs. Carl and the boys built a doodle buggy out of an old tractor. We played kick the can, "eenie-aye-over garage", rode bicycles, tormented bee hives—then ran for the house—and rode our neighbor's old white horse he kept in our barn. Elmer liked to show off riding his bike with no hands—once he couldn't stop and took the garden gate off the hinges.

Grandpa Reinhardt took sick—liver cancer—so we gave up our beloved farm and moved into Grandpa's. Mom took care of him. He had a chicken coop, a big garden, and an outside toilet with three seats. Mom, my sister Joanne and I had our evening stroll out to it to sit and visit. It had a half moon hole in the door and we'd peek out. The house was a big, two-story white one with a big front porch. It had lilac trees across the front and a grape arbor. There was no running water—we had a well and pump and a cistern for rainwater in the basement for laundry. We had a coal bin in the basement. It was on the corner of

Carl and Alma in 1941

612 Woodbridge Avenue and Fisher Avenue. The Consumers Power Tower was across the street. In a severe electrical storm, lightning would strike that tower. Sometimes it would lightning while us kids were sound asleep and Mom would make us come downstairs until the storm was over. To this day, I'm scared to death of storms.

On July 13, 1941, Mom and Carl had my brother, Vern. So, we were then a family of seven kids. We went to Edison School on Midland Road where I graduated from 8th grade and then went on to Handy Junior High for 9th grade. Handy didn't become a high school until 1951. Then, I went to Central High School on Columbus Avenue (east side) and graduated in June of 1946. I had to walk to city bus lines at the corner of Alp and Thomas to ride a Balcer bus—there was no school bus.

I was first to meet the milkman who delivered six quarts of milk in a wire basket on the front porch. It wasn't pasteurized so the cream on top froze. It raised the cardboard cap up and was like an ice cream cone. All of us kids tried to get it first.

I met Annabelle, my future sister-in-law on my first day at Handy. We were both from one room, rural schools and were lost in the city. She lived on the west side of Saginaw Road and walked to Handy. I walked home with her one Wednesday afternoon. (I worked at Fred Arnold's grocery store on the corner of Euclid and John Streets and Wednesday was my day off). I met her brother, Lewis (my future husband). He was working in a co-op from Central High at National Electric. I was 14 and he was 16. We double dated with my brother, Elmer, and his sister Anabelle. We could cruise around for 25 cents worth of gas. We went to Wenonah Beach Amusement Park, which had a ferris wheel, jackrabbit, loop plane, bumper cars, and what was then, LaLonde's Dance Hall on Center Road (we went there on Saturday nights).

Lewis graduated from Central at 17 in 1943. He enlisted in the Navy in August and left for 6 weeks of boot camp in Great Lakes, Chicago. Then, he was home for 7 days and went to the Pacific area. He was in Admiral Halsey's 3rd Fleet on John D. Henley's Destroyer against Japan. Pearl Harbor was already on—December 7, 1941. I remember my neighbor girl and I walked to the Sage Library on that Sunday. When we returned,

my folks were sitting on the front porch all upset. They told us the Japanese had bombed Pearl Harbor. Being a kid, I thought, "So what? That's way across the ocean. What's that got to do with us?" Believe me, I soon knew. All the fellas were leaving for service.

Rationing was on—meat, butter, sugar, bread, cigarettes, nylons, gas—our customers at Arnold's store had to have book stamps to purchase items. Some people were good—some nasty. I told Lewis I'd wait for him—wrote him every day after schoolwork. He said that brought him through. He was in Iwo Jima and seven major battles.

He came home May 7, 1946. I graduated from Central and we were married at Westminster Church on Midland Street by Reverend Donald Lomas. We lived in an apartment on Center Avenue while Lewis and his dad built us a house. Lewis worked at R.W.C. in Salzburg.

We raised two great kids—our son, Bob, and our daughter, Sue. We have four wonderful grandkids now who are all college graduates. Our oldest grandson, Andy, dedicated two years with the Peace Corps in Africa after graduating from the University of Michigan.

Lewis died with lung cancer on May 2nd 1989. We had 43 years of "happy marriage" and he had 43 years with R.W.C. He was such a good man and a wonderful husband, father and grandfather. Now, we have five beautiful great grandkids who he never saw. After he died, I devoted my time to being a companion to my granddaughter, Ashley, who was born special with Downs Syndrome. My daughter (her mom) works ten-hour days in surgery at Bay Medical. Ashley was my salvation who helped me through my grieving period—knowing someone needed me. I am 87 now and count my blessings—good parents and siblings (all gone now except Vern) and a good marriage. Thank you Lord.

Oh, the One-Room School
By Sharon Ritter of Stanton, Michigan
Born 1937

Oh, the one-room school. What memories! When I started kindergarten in the early 40s at the Forest Grove School, an older girl walked me to and from school. Until I was in the 5th grade, I was the only one in my grade so I was put into the middle of 6th grade. I was very happy since that was with my special friend.

Most schools had outhouses but our school had chemical toilets. It was so scary for the little girls to sit above that deep, dark hole.

Water was carried from the well for washing and drinking. Everyone had their own glass in the small cupboard by the washstand.

Recess was such a fun time; tag, softball, pom-pom-pull-away, Annie-I-over, and fox and geese in the snow in the winter. My special friend and I had our own game in one corner of the playground. With a big stick, we would draw a house and use different size sticks for the people. We also loved to swing double; one would sit on the swing, and the other sat on her lap, facing each other, and we would both pump.

We always looked forward to Uncle Charles. He would tell us a Bible story using the flannel board. That made the story seem to come to life.

On Valentine's Day, we all made a beautiful Valentine box (mailbox) and we made everyone a Valentine. My parents owned a wallpaper store and brought home the old sample books for us kids to use. This made our Valentines really special.

During the War, our bright colored pencils became brown ones with a tiny bit of eraser stuck in one end.

We collected milkweeds. The puffy seeds were used in the life rafts for the Navy.

During that time, mothers would take turns making hot oatmeal for our lunch once a week.

There was no elastic for girls' undies. We just had a button and loop on the side to hold them up.

The highlight of the year was the Christmas program. The schoolboard members would come build a stage and put up the curtain. We would practice for weeks. The night finally came with the school filled with parents, relatives, and neighbors.

After the program, Santa arrived, ringing his bells. He would pass out the gifts we had drawn names for, and the teachers' gifts. Last, were the 3x6, colorful boxes filled with Christmas candy and peanuts in the shell.

Sunday school was held at the school with the mothers doing the lessons. Especially during the summer, that was the day we would plan our get-togethers, going to each other's houses, riding bikes, playing dolls, etc. No one had telephones to make any plans. Often in winter, all ages would meet at "Pike's Peak" behind the school for a Sunday afternoon of sledding.

The last day of school was our big school picnic. Tables were put together in the schoolyard, and again, the whole neighborhood would join in with their food. Later, we would get our report cards to see if we had "passed."

I am certain I have forgotten many things about that school, but I made more memories as I taught in a one-room school until they all closed in the county.

I taught for 15 years during the three-day local Heritage Village Festival. I guess it was "borned" in me.

Don't Laugh at Grandma
By Marilyn Witting of Saginaw, Michigan
Born 1930

I remember:

During the 2nd World War, sometimes after dark sirens would go off, my brother, sister, and any other kids in the area would gather on our front lawn knowing the enemy planes would be here and our men would chase them away with our planes. During the day, we would see the farmers go by in trucks taking the prisoners out to work the fields.

Eagle School, the one-room schoolhouse my sister and I attended, had no running

Marilyn's Grandma and mother, Florence VanEaton

Marilyn, her father, Clyde and brother, Cliff

water, but every morning a pail of water was brought in for drinking. Mom, who was born and raised in Detroit, found out that we drank out of the dipper… Next thing for us was a cup with our name on it. Of course, my friends could use our cups. Just don't tell Mom.

Coming to Marlette from down state was so much like Little House on the Prairie. I learned to milk cows, ride the workhorses, and handle them on the wagon for haying. Dad did wonder though, why when he cultivated with them they would stop each time after going down and back. I said I thought they should have a short rest in the shade because it was a big field.

Going to a small high school, everyone was needed for sports, band, etc. I was a majorette, and the first time on the field, the three of us threw up our batons, but mine came down hitting me in the eye and I ended up with a black eye.

During pheasant season, police friends would come up from Detroit for "clay pigeon practice." My grandma informed Mom and Dad she would not be cooking that kind of bird. Mom could do it, but not her. You did not laugh at Grandma.

How I picked out my Own Dad
By Betty Gaffee of Midland, Michigan
Born 1943

My mother was a 21-year-old war widow. My birth father was killed in the Battle of the Bulge in World War II, on February 3, 1945. I was 1 year and 3 months old, and my brother was 3 years and 1 month old, so we do not remember our birth father.

A Western Union person came to our front door to deliver the life altering news to my mother that her husband had been killed. The only thing she asked my mother is, "Are you home alone?" My mother replied that her children and sister-in-law were there. She said, "Ok," and handed my mother a telegram informing her that her husband had been killed in action. No one came until later to explain what would happen and what help she would get. My father had told my mother if he was killed while fighting the War that he did not want to be brought back. He told her he did not want her crying over someone else's bones. She was so young and did not have much family support, so she just did what he had told her to do. So, she did not have a funeral or a memorial, because she did not think she had that option. It was not a good decision because Mom always felt there was no closure, and she thought she had let his family and herself down. Money was a deciding factor because she was very broke and was not sure what kind of pension she would receive. She did not know how she would support herself and her children; she had never had a job, except for babysitting

Betty's mother, Betty Wagner

Betty's dad, Donald Wagner

when she was in high school.

My mom had boarders living with her to help with the expenses. That made for difficulties because the boarders were her sister-in-law and her husband who came back from the War and was a drunk. Lots of fighting over the drinking and the shortage of food. My mom had to ask them to leave in spite of the fact that she needed the money from their rent. She felt that it was a bad environment to raise her children in.

I wanted to be outside all of the time, but as I was only 2 ½ I could not be left alone. But Mom would let me go out if I stayed on the front porch. While I was out there, I liked to talk to anyone going past our house. So, when a handsome Marine just came back from war came by, I asked him if he would come play with me on my porch. I explained that my mom would not let me go off the porch. He came on the porch and was talking to me. My mom comes right out to see who was on our porch. She sees this handsome guy and they start having a conversation. He had just got back from the war and was staying with his sister and brother-in-law across the street. He liked me so much that he came over every day and helped my mom with all the jobs that needed done at our house, and he stayed for dinner, and bought groceries.

I picked out the best man ever to be my new dad. About 6 months later, they decided to get married, and were married for 65 years. I have two more brothers, and we all had a wonderful family life. My dad died in 2012, and they were still very much in love. My mom misses him so much. She is 91.

4th Ward Memories
By Jean Parkinson of Midland, Michigan
Born 1924

The 4th Ward neighborhood was across the railroad tracks and across the Benson Street Bridge in Midland. As kids, we thought we lived in the best part of town. How could any ward compete with what was offered across the Tittabawasee River in the good old summertime! There was a small neighborhood grocery store near a large, open field. As summer approached, the kids waited anxiously for posters to appear in Smith's Grocery Store windows. Guess who came to town to occupy the field? A circus, a tent show, and a carnival!

The circus meant a parade on Main Street, clowns, animals, music, performers, and other events that were part of a circus. I remember a clown on stilts coming over to me at a parade and teasing me about my red hair. I always hated my red hair. A huge tent was put up in the field where we watched people and animals perform.

The tent show had different stage plays each evening, and a matinee on Saturday. That meant coaxing parents to let you attend as many plays as possible during the week the tent show was in town. This inspired us to do extra chores to earn spending money. There was a large tent where the plays were presented. Candy was sold with prizes in some of the boxes. A comedian named Toby entertained and also was featured in one of the plays.

The carnival had a midway, rides, sideshows, fortuneteller, and food. So many exciting things to see and do. I still have two carnival glass goblets I won playing a midway game.

The circus, tent show, and carnival no

Carnival glass goblets won at a midway game

longer come to town. The railroad is gone. The neighborhood has been replaced with softball diamonds. And the bridge I walked across four times a day when attending school has been removed. Oh, the memories.

Our One-Room School

Our one-room school was not in the country, but in Midland's 4th Ward. Each Ward had its own school, but ours was the only one-room school in town.

My first four years of school from 1929-1932 were spent in one room with one teacher. Imagine the work she had to do for lesson plans. Mrs. Walker, the teacher, lived on one side of the school, and Mrs. Brown, the janitress, lived on the other side. How convenient- one to teach and the other to keep the school clean, and start a fire on cold winter mornings so we would have a warm school. Mrs. Walker did a great job teaching us the 3 R's in that one-room school.

Recess was spent playing ball in the open area behind the school- no playground equipment. Everyone went home for lunch since we all lived near the school.

One year, I was given a long story to memorize for the Christmas program. I worked hard and did memorize it, but the program day arrived, and I was home sick. We had made clay bowls for Christmas gifts and the varnish odors made me ill. I missed the program, but I still have that bowl.

Outhouses

Outhouses, sometimes called privies, were becoming obsolete when we were born in 1924. I say "we" because I have a twin sister. I think we were the only twins in town at that time. Our home had a bathroom addition, but the outhouse was still in the backyard. Occasionally, it was more convenient to use the outhouse when we were outside playing. We were small and had to be careful balancing ourselves while sitting in this building. Weather played a prominent part in the use of an outhouse. Imagine not having an indoor bathroom and having to go outside in rainy, cold, snowy weather to use outside facilities. In winter, a path had to be kept cleared for access. The outhouse is not considered part of "good" when you talk about "the good old days."

An outhouse was a common target for mischief. Our neighborhood playmates were together one evening when someone suggested tipping over another neighbor's outhouse. Everyone was agreeable except me. I was scared to death to be involved in anything like that. I stayed on another neighbor's porch while the others left to carry out their plans. While trying to tip the outhouse, they heard someone running across the yard so they had to leave before they finished their prank. The next day, Mother got a phone call asking if we were involved in the previous evening's adventure. She asked me if I was there and I said no. I did not think I was guilty since I had not participated; I did not want to squeal on my friends.

Flooding

I grew up in the flood area of Midland. Flooding was almost an annual event. Most homes were built high enough above ground so floodwaters did not reach the main floor.

Near our property, there was a low spot on Poseyville Road (now St. Charles Street) where floodwater first came across. We kept a close watch and when we saw water coming over the road, we had to move fast to take care of last minute preparations. The car had to be moved to higher ground, either at the neighbors or by the Benson Street Bridge. One time, the water came into the yard before the car was moved. It got stuck in the driveway and a group of neighbors came wearing boots and pushed it onto Benson Street in front of our house so it could be driven to a higher level. The wringer washer machine and tubs had to be disconnected and had to be moved from the basement. Then, we had to catch our chickens and put them in crates to take to our older sister's house along with our dog. The furnace could not be used, so the only heat we had was the kitchen stove. Fortunately, the kitchen was quite large so we shut off the other rooms and stayed in the kitchen. Sometimes the water was almost high enough to get in the house. We were lucky it never got in on the main floor. We did have some scary moments during floods!

Most people in the neighborhood had a rowboat for transportation. Our boat was used to get Dad out to go to work and to get us kids out for school. When I was older, my future husband ferried me out for dates.

All homes in the neighborhood had been removed before the "big" flood in the 1980s. This flood would have been devastating if homes were still there then. The area now has softball diamonds, and when the old neighborhood has floods now, they only create canceled softball games and detours.

Robbery!

My grandchildren's favorite tale is about the attempted robbery of the Chemical State Savings Bank in Midland, Michigan, September 29, 1937, two days after my 13th birthday.

There were many bank robberies during the Great Depression and two armed robbers came to Midland to rob the Chemical State Savings Bank. The robbers fled after shooting the president and vice president of the bank- both survived. The robbers also shot a bystander who later died. My dentist, Dr. Hardy, had a rifle in his office above the bank for just such an occasion. From his window, he shot and killed one robber and wounded the other one, who was soon captured.

We were home from school for lunch and on our way back, we walked through the area where all the action had just taken place; across the bridge, across the railroad tracks, up the hill to Main Street where the bank was located. There was blood on the approach to the Benson Street Bridge where the robbers had been shot. We were so excited about what happened and ran to a street where one of our teachers, Miss Russell, would be on her way back to school. We shouted, "The bank was robbed! The bank was robbed!" and she did not believe us.

A few days later, we and some classmates were walking by Bradley Funeral Home on our way home from school. We knew the deceased robber was there and we went to the door to ask if we could see him. We did get to see him in his casket. The funeral home, now Smith-Miner, is in a new location.

The surviving robber was later tried and convicted of homicide. He was hanged at the Milan Prison with Midland's Sheriff Smith pulling the lever.

In 1992, at our 50th class reunion, I was at a table with Miss Russell (now Mrs. Davis). The bank robbery was discussed and Miss Russell said her first thought was, "What are those kids up to now?"

Miscellaneous Memories

Years ago, some furniture and appliances were much different than today. Before refrigerators, there were iceboxes to keep food cool. Ours was on the screened porch. The iceman would bring blocks of ice varying in weight. We had a sign, and if I remember correctly, the four sides were numbered, 25, 50, 75, 100 pounds. We put a sign in our front window with the weight we wanted pointing up. The iceman would bring that size block and put it in the icebox using his ice tongs. Ice tongs are collectible antiques today. In the summer, Mother would chip ice off the block to put in lemonade.

For music, we had a windup record player (phonograph) in a cabinet with records stored in the bottom section. The top section had a turntable, which played records. A crank rewound the disk when it ran down. Hours of entertainment were provided by this musical device.

Who could forget wringer washers and galvanized tubs? Clothes were washed and put through the wringer and through two tubs of rinse water; they were wrung into a basket and hung out to dry on a clothesline in the backyard.

The milkman delivered our milk with his horse drawn wagon. What a fun memory. The milk was in quart glass bottles. The cream separated and rose to the top of the bottle. Mother poured the cream off to use in coffee. In the summer, the milkman would give us pieces of ice. As kids, we looked forward to petting the horse, and feeding it an apple.

Country and City Memories

By Carolyn Lawmaster of Freeland,
Michigan
Born 1947

I grew up in Windsor, Pennsylvania on the outskirts of the town of Windsor. I was born in 1947, and I don't think there was a better time to grow up than in the '50s and '60s (minus the Vietnam War). Life was simple, happy, and for the most part, safe. We played all day as kids in the summer, whether it be sports, simply reading storybooks, swimming, jump rope, or whatever we could come up with, and we stayed out late at night, sometimes, catching fireflies. Our winter consisted of roller skating, ice skating, and sledding. We also played a lot of board games and cards as a family growing up. We lived in a safe, little neighborhood and our childhood home was only three houses from the elementary school we attended.

We had a fence around our backyard. We had pet rabbits and ducks. They had a nice, warm shed my father built with a door so the ducks could go in and out. We had a male drake duck that only my mother and brother could handle. It would attack my sister and me, including my father. It would take a hold of my father's pants leg, and would not let go. We had a bush in the corner of the fence, near the gate. It would hide behind the bush when my sister and I would be coming home from school, and as soon as we were through the fence, the duck would attack us. Many times, we ended up with a big mark on our leg where Jo-Jo (the duck's name) would bite us. My mother got a female Pekin duck (we named Ko-Ko) in the hopes that it would help Jo-Jo calm down, but nothing ever got Jo-Jo to calm down. We had these ducks until they died.

We had plumbing in our home but my grandparents on my mother's side did not have indoor plumbing. Therefore, if we were visiting or staying overnight, we had to go up the hill to the outhouse or use the chamber pot during the night. The water we drank at my grandparents' home was pumped from a well behind the house, and, of course, everyone drank water from the same ladle in a big pot that held the water. When we were hot outside in the summer, my family and friends all drank out of the water hose when we were playing or working outside. My goodness! How did we ever survive?

My mom had different home remedies she used when we kids got sick (there were three of us). One of the home remedies I remember was lard and molasses together for a cold/cough. There was also something she gave us for sick stomachs but I can't remember what that was.

Of course, Elvis Presley came into our lives on TV, radio, and records in the '50s. My mother and I liked the same singers and records, so we never had a problem listening to the radio or records together, and we definitely both loved Elvis. Later in years, when I got married and moved to Michigan, my husband and I got to see Elvis in person in Saginaw, Michigan. Only a few months later, in August of the same year, he passed away. We still have our ticket stubs and we were so glad that we had gotten to see him in person.

When I was in high school, the federal government provided, to interested students, civil service tests in some of the high schools in our area. If we passed the tests for office work, we were offered a job for the federal government in Washington, D.C. I worked for the Department of Health, Education, and Welfare, specifically for the Office of

Carolyn with her sister, Susan (Sue)

103

Carolyn (Haugh) and Charles Lawmaster in 1969

Education, from August 1965 to August 1969; I started out as a GS-3 rather than a GS-2 simply because I knew shorthand. Shorthand has really been a thing of the past for many years.

President Johnson and, then, President Nixon were in office while I was working in Washington, D.C. The events of the assassination of Martin Luther King, Jr. in Memphis in April of 1968 (there were riots in D.C. among many other big cities in the country) and then the assassination of Senator Robert F. Kennedy in June of 1968 in Los Angeles took place when I was in D.C.

There were military buses that would come to D.C. and pick up girls to go dance at clubs on military bases, and we had to return on those buses as well. I would go dancing three to four nights a week. We, girls, always had a blast. We were young and having the time of our lives. Those bases included Anderson Air Force Base in Maryland, Quantico Marine Base in Virginia, as well as Ft. Belvoir and Ft. Meyer, both located in Virginia. Any military guy I dated for any length of time either ended up going to Vietnam or had already been there. Eventually, I ended up marrying one of those handsome Marines from Quantico, and that's how I ended up in Michigan.

I also got to shake the hands of a couple of astronauts from Apollo 11, the first to land on the moon, July 16, 1969. They were in an elevator in the building I worked in. (Unfortunately, I can't remember which two they were.) I guess I was just excited that I was really shaking their hands.

I often wonder where I may have ended up working in the federal government had I stayed there. When I started working in Washington, D.C., I was only 17 years old. I think I could write a book about my four short years working there. Because I was so young and going to dances, meeting all the military guys and dating, I didn't realize the reality of what Washington, D.C. was really about. I've visited, maybe, three times since I left there and often wonder what happened to all those people I worked with and how things must have changed. As I have grown much older since those early days of my life in D.C., I now understand how I probably should have felt working there; almost like an honor, as well as, the excitement. I guess back then, I didn't realize how important all the things that I got to experience, as well as the events and times of the 1960s, were so important. Years later, I have realized how captivating the 1960s were and the time I spent in Washington, D.C.

In ending, I want to say the 1950s and 1960s were good years to grow up in, when things were more simple as a whole. I was very fortunate to have grown up experiencing what a family really was - a family! Now I am one of the "baby boomers." Sigh. Where has the time gone?

Teenage Memories
By Eugene Olivares of Saginaw, Michigan
Born 1942

We arrived in St. Louis, Michigan on April 11, 1951 as the 11-year-old son of Jose and Alice Olivares. Dad had been hired by G.M. and would be working at the Grey Iron Plant. Our aunt and uncle from Saginaw were our transportation to Saginaw the following day. We moved into my Uncle Eugene Paez rental house in Carrollton. I went to Carrollton Elementary School as a fifth grader with my older brother, Ernie.

We moved to Merrill Street in the city of Saginaw, near the old Central Junior High School. I attended Emerson School. I would learn to play basketball at Central Junior High School with the great Ernie Thompson We watched him play every home game at Saginaw High during the 1961 and 1962 seasons. Saginaw High School won the State of Michigan Class A Basketball Championship title that very year. At the very west end of Merrill Street was where the original Tony Steak Sandwich Restaurant was once located.

Also, remember walking along the railroad tracks that are parallel to Washington Avenue headed towards Hoyt Park for ice-skating every chance we had on Saturday and Sunday afternoons. We would gather at my cousin's house for dinner after church on most Sunday afternoons. Those are great memories.

We moved to Eddy Street on Saginaw's west side the following year where I went to North Intermediate School as a 7th grader and the beginning of the 8th grade. We had to move into Buena Vista School district in the middle of 8th grade because of some of my choices. I got involved in hot-wiring a couple of tractors from the International Tractor dealership that was located where the Saginaw Children's Museum is located today. My friend and I proceeded to drive them down Genesee Street. We were very shortly stopped by the Saginaw Police and were arrested as juveniles and sent to the Juvenile Home out on Tittbawassee Road for two days. Today that building is host to a Hospice organization. My parents decided that it was time for us to move and we relocated in the Buena Vista School district.

I remember the smelliest corner of Buena Vista Township, the corner of Outer Drive and Holland Road. There were many cattle roaming the fields on the west side of Outer Drive, where the old K-Mart store used to be back in the late '80s and '90s. Most mornings when the wind would blow from the west the smell of the cow manure would enter our school bus as we traveled to Ricker Junior High School.

At that time, as 9th graders, we had what we called the King and Queen of our class. I was selected as King of Ricker Junior High as a 9th grader, with my girlfriend, Sandy Owen, as the Queen. It was certainly the highlight of my junior high school days.

Our 9th grade class would become the first class of Buena Vista High as 10th graders to enter the new and most highly anticipated

Eugene and Carol on prom night in 1962

high school in the state of Michigan, at that time. We were the first school in the country that would use TV monitors in our classrooms. The head teacher would deliver his agenda or message for the day from the monitors. In some classes, the entire sophomore classes would be there together in one room. We would have two or three student teachers from the nearby state colleges and universities as assistant teachers.

I also remember the very popular Horseshoe Bar that was located on Outer Drive. There was also the village Pump Bar in the Township of Bridgeport where many up and coming singing groups, such as Bob Seger and his band, the Boss Men with Dick Wagner, would come and sing their new songs. There was also the Keg Bar with the Hawkeye Band, who featured my kid brother as a 20-year-old lead singer, playing with some of the Questionmark and the Mysterians band members. We were too young to visit the establishments as well like the Hidden Hollow in Shields where the group, Count and the Colony, were the house band. Many of these bands would become world famous later on during the '70s and '80s, and some are still famous today, like Bob Seger.

I was working at the A&P Supermarket located at Genesee and Hess Street during my high school years. I was then transferred to the new large A&P store that was built during the early '60s. It was located where the large Kroger store is now at State and Hemmeter Road. I worked on the night crew stocking shelves and later became the dairy and bread manager for about a year, and then was transferred to a store in Flint to be the night crew leader.

I remember, very vividly, one night after leaving the Horseshoe Bar as I approached the stoplight at Outer Drive and Holland when one of my friends pulled up next to me. We turned right (west) on Holland and proceeded to drag race towards the City of Saginaw instead of east and out of town. I was driving my "hot" '58 Chevy Impala 348 cu in, 4-door. We proceeded to reach speeds of at least 90mph and were eventually stopped by the State Police, Saginaw Police and, I believe, even the Sheriff Department as well. We received three tickets each that night for a total of nine points that went on our driving records. The girl in his car later that decade would become my first wife. She was indeed my first love. I remember telling one of my friends in the 8th grade that I was going to marry her. We were married for 24 years, had three wonderful children, but unfortunately I lost her in 1989. I have been married to my second wife, Jean, for 20 years. We have five children, and eight grandchildren combined.

Monday nights were very special for all of us during the '50s and '60s. It was extremely special to be able to walk to downtown Saginaw during that time. We would see most of our friends from other schools there also. Most stores would be open until 9:00pm.

I also remember the Friday night "sock hop" dances that were held at the nearby Saginaw auditorium. There were many other locations for teen dances during that time in Saginaw such as: Daniels Den, the Ace of Club, the Sound Lounge, and the Band Canyon in Bay City. There was also, the Bel Air Roller Rink where they held the "Battle of the Bands" on most weekends. The Beatles from Great Britain were responsible for bringing over the so called "British Invasion" bands during the '60s, '70s, and '80s. I, also, remember the Brockway Roller Rink that we visited during Saturday afternoons.

Also, there were two main drive-in restaurants in Saginaw, Rich's and Raymond's. We would all drive our "muscle cars" from restaurant to restaurant with our friends and girlfriends, on most nights of the week. We would backup our cars so we could see other muscle cars and friends drive by. We would get waited on by waitresses on roller skates. It was the real American Graffiti lifestyles that we lived in. At that time, I drove a '52 Ford, called the "Sniffer." It was about 4 inches high in the front end and about 2 feet high in the rear end and had a puppy painted on the rear bumper. At that time, it was customary that we had names for our hot muscle cars painted on the rear fenders. Later on in high school, I drove a dark blue, white top, 4-door, '58 Chevy. After high school, I also drove a '62 red Chevy convertible with a white top from 1964 until 1970. I wish I still owned those cars today, for they are considered classic cars.

One of the biggest attractions that came to Saginaw during the '70s was when Elvis Presley made an appearance at the Saginaw Civic Center, now known as the Dow Event Center. It was certainly a treat to have had the opportunity to see him perform live here. It was a sad day when he suddenly passed away on August 16, 1977.

I do remember watching on our black and white TV on the horrific day, November 22, 1963 when our President John F. Kennedy was assassinated. Later on that same decade watching Martin L. King, Jr. on April 4, 1968, and John's brother, Robert F. Kennedy on June 6, 1968, being assassinated. These days will never be forgotten by all Americans that were from that era.

I also remember watching our first pictures of the entire Earth from cameras that were mounted on S-11 Second Stage on Apollo 4 and 6 during the Saturn V Launch Vehicle flight. This program was the first US attempt to send astronauts to the moon. It was also an amazing experience to watch Apollo 11 become the first US spaceship to land a man on the lunar moon surface. Neil Armstrong and Buzz Aldrin were the astronauts on that day, July 20, 1969.

I got married, to that girl who was in my '58 Chevy, on February 6, 1966. Her name was Carol Ahrens and her parents owned the

80 acres across the street from the Bel Air drive-in theater on Jane's Street. The farm was a beautiful area to raise a family. In the 1920s, US highway 23 split their property in half. It consisted of 40 acres on each side of the highway. In the 1950s, I-75 highway split their property even more. Finally, in 1969, they started the construction of I-675 on their property and my wife's parents had to relocate. They had to sell their farm land to the State of Michigan so the new bypass highway could be built which exists to this day.

Many weekends were spent going to the Twilight Theater on west State Street. It was one of 2 outside theaters in the Saginaw area, the other was the Bel Air Theater on Jane's Street. Also I remember playing baseball for Buena Vista High School and playing many games at the old Vet's Baseball Stadium on East Holland and Cumberland. The stadium would also host many big time wrestling during the summer months.

I remember the Anderson swimming pool that was located where the new Anderson Enrichment Center is today. It was one of two pools that the city of Saginaw had during the '50s and '60s. The other pool was the old Mershone pool that was located on the west side of the Saginaw River on Johnson Street right across from the current Riverview Plaza. Both were pools that we visited during our teenage years.

I remember the old rotary phones that we had during the '50s and the '60s. I remember one particular time when my father picked up the phone before any of us could pick up and answered for us saying, "I can't stand you," to one of our girlfriends. He meant to say, "I can't understand you," or, "I can't hear you." We had a laugh about that for a long time.

My Story About Growing Up
By Berneta (Bernie) Kelsch of Big Rapids, Michigan
Born 1931

I was born at the home of my paternal grandparents, Amos and Edna Kennedy, in Grand Traverse County, Michigan on September 1, 1931. My grandmother helped my mother through the birth. She went to the courthouse to record my birth, as there was

Bernie with her parents, Leslie and Ila Mackey Kennedy

no doctor present to do so. I have a big sister, Phyllis.

We lived, off and on, with both sets of grandparents: Amos and Edna near Traverse City, and Solomon and Mathilda Mackey near a small town, Copemish, Michigan. Both families were farmers owning their own farms, and by the grace of God, did not lose them in the Depression that enveloped the country.

Both farms had many fields under cultivation, horses, hogs, dairy cows, chickens, vegetable and flower gardens, apple trees, raspberry vines. Everything was preserved by canning, storing, butchering, preserving any way possible.

My father, Leslie Kennedy, was taken out of school after the second grade to help work the farm and was never allowed to go back to school. He became very good with repairs on farm machinery, automobiles, as well as learned the farming business. It was said of him, "He could fix any engine or machine with bailing wire." Later in life, he had a job with a traveling grocery truck going house to house. During World War II, he worked at the Parson's Company making bomb casings for

Berneta and Phyllis

the war effort.

Neither grandparents' homes had water, electricity, or plumbing in their homes. Kerosene or oil lamps were the illumination, water from an outside well, (though the Mackey house had a hand pump at the kitchen sink) and plumbing was an outside "outhouse" with catalogs for paper. I got an anatomy lesson because of the "outhouse." A boy cousin came every summer to help on the farm, and I dearly loved him, followed him mercilessly, even when he did his best to be rid of me. He went into the outhouse; I peeked in through the crack between the door and the wall. What a surprise. I had never even seen a boy baby. I was in shock. I didn't follow him around any longer, and never said a word to him or anyone.

The Mackey house had furnace heat, and a wood stove in the kitchen for cooking, canning, baking, rendering at butchering time, heating volumes of water for washing, bathing, cleaning, etc. The Kennedy home had the kitchen stove and a wood burning stove in the center of the downstairs of the house for heat. The upstairs was heated with registers cut into the floor allowing the heat from below to enter. That was fun for we children because

we could listen in on grownup conversation as voices came through the opening.

Bathrooms had a stand with a large bowl and pitcher for washing up. Chamber pots were to use nights or times during the illness. I don't know where adults bathed, but children bathed in a metal washtub, usually in the kitchen. Bathing was in a Finnish Sauna building at the Mackey home with a huge water tank on rocks where the fire was built. Steam and heat provided by throwing water on the hot stones.

Refrigeration was a wooden cabinet with room for a cake of ice in the top section, covered shelves under that for food storage. At the bottom was a drip pan to catch the melted ice water. Woe, if you didn't empty it timely. A pantry also served, without refrigeration (it depended on a cooling breeze to come through the window).

Ice was harvested from frozen lakes in the winter. Hauled by a team of horses and wagon to the farm to be stored in sawdust in an icehouse, usually a small log building someplace on the farm.

My memories of the icehouse at my grandparent's home was how fun it was to go in it on a hot summer day, especially the day we would be treated with homemade ice cream from a hand-crank ice cream maker. I would beg to turn the crank of the freezer, then quickly beg for someone else to turn the crank as it became harder as the mixture turned to ice cream. Always, there were parents, grandparents, aunties, uncles, cousins, and neighbors for this activity.

Delivering ice became a new business. If you did not have a source of ice, a man would come to your home, deliver the amount of ice you needed for a time you agreed upon for the amount you agreed upon. My sister and I would tease my mom about her iceman "boyfriend." She didn't think it was funny.

Each year, the Public Health Department came to the local schools to give preventative shots to children, I think, at no charge. I don't remember what they were other than diphtheria and whooping cough. There was always a neighbor or family member making ice cream to help children forget the shots.

We did not go to the doctor for periodic checkups. I had many earaches as a child, and the remedy was my dad lighting up his pipe and blowing warm air into the ear(s). One time, I jumped out of a tree in our yard and put a nail into my foot. I did a pretty good job of getting to the house on my backside. Mom washed the wound, comforted me- no doctor's visit, no tetanus shot.

There was lots of music in the Kennedy family. Grandpa Kennedy was a fiddle player. Many times, they rolled up the dining room rugs, entertained friends, and relatives with a concert and dance at their home. They also went to other people's homes for the same parties: Grandpa fiddling, and Grandma playing the piano.

My sister, Phyllis, was, not well, though she did attend kindergarten and part of first grade. It was found that she had tuberculosis and was not permitted to go to school. She was bedridden at home about one to one and a half years before she was sent to a Sanitarium for Tuberculosis in Howell, Michigan. Our mother, Ila, took care of her at home during that time, as no one else could go into her room.

Phyllis was allowed outside if someone carried her. One lovely summer day, she was outside with us as our mom, dad, and I were picking ragweed from the fields. At that time, ragweed was very invasive and the government was paying one cent per hundred plants to help pay people and to help be rid of the ragweed problem.

As we worked, an airplane flew overhead. It was the first one either of us had seen. So, in spite of the hot job of pulling weeds, it was exciting. The only other garden job I had to do was kill the tomato worms on the plants. Ugh, I'd pick ragweed any day. Well, maybe picking cherries is worse. I had to accompany my parents when I was too young to pick and I was hot, dusty, tired, and wasn't patient at all. I had aunties who picked 20 lugs a day. I was asked to leave an orchard in my early teens because I wasn't productive enough. So much for earning money.

There were a few telephones in our neighborhood by this time. They were hung on the wall with a hand crank. You talked with the operator, she rang the number. There were several parties together on one "party line." Sometimes you had to wait. As children, we tried to listen in on conversations, but grandmothers, aunties, and moms watched that that didn't happen often. In an emergency, you would break in and most people were courteous.

Shortly after that, Phyllis did go to the Sanitarium in Howell. Howell was over 200 miles away so we were only able to see her in the summer, usually only once each summer. I went each year but several times, I was not allowed to see her because she was not in a high enough grade. They graded #1 as worst, and #12 as best (cured). Our family did have to have chest x-rays to make sure we had not become infected. She was there between 6 and 7 years. At that time, the treatment was isolation, bedrest, and, if you had only one lung infected, they collapsed the infected lung so it could not travel to the other lung.

When I was old enough to go to school, we moved into Traverse City for the winter. We lived in one-room cabins, occasionally an apartment when money was more plentiful. My father worked at odd jobs and for the WPA, a work program begun by President Roosevelt to give people employment. We were never hungry or homeless, I really didn't know how poor we were because I had many people that loved me, and my mother could fix a wonderful meal from practically nothing.

There were many small grocery stores in neighborhoods in those days. There was a counter with a cash register and the owner or his employee got each item that you wanted to purchase. No cart to push around to fill. When times were tough, some owners allowed you to charge for a few days. It was wartime and many things were rationed or unavailable. Bananas were scarce, so I made it my job to be watchful for them. They didn't require a ration card.

I loved everything about going to school, especially music. I was in choir, a trio, and even some plays. I loved learning. My teachers were wonderful, encouraging and gave me opportunities to grow and become more confident. I also began taking instructions in the Lutheran Church, Missouri Synod and met my Savior.

I walked ten blocks to school, and walked even further to go ice-skating. We walked everywhere, feeling safe, cutting through alleys and fields. Parents weren't really concerned unless we were very late; we knew we had boundaries. The entire neighborhood of kids played baseball, Enie Eine Over, tag, swimming, with only a few windows being hit by an errant baseball. One I had to pay for.

Our parents divorced after Phyllis came home from Howell. It was a tearful time for her because she had not lived through the unhappy part of their marriage. Our mother kept our home together. She had gone to work in a factory and gave us love and encouragement through our growing up years. Again, with the support of so many family and friends.

Like my mother was, my sister is my strength. God is good.

A Rare Surgery
By Cora Longstreet of Fremont, Michigan
Born 1926

The winter of perhaps 1936, we had lots of snow and drifting snow. The roads were blocked until the rotary plow came though. Is that equipment in the Missaukee County building?

In 1941, I spent nine weeks in Cadillac Mercy Hospital. Dr. Alby was my doctor. He knew I needed a rare surgery. There were a lot of prayers for my recovery. The young doctor operated on his dog Inky, so he would be able to operate on me. Sulfa was used. However, penicillin came one year later in 1942. The colostomy surgery was done, and before I left the hospital, Dr. Alby did a reverse colostomy for me.

In 2009, I received a note and a picture of Inky from a classmate, Jack Goodwin from Merritt. His parents were friends of Dr. and Mrs. Alby. When Dr. Alby went to the Navy, they received the two cocker spaniels.

Both Inky and I recovered. I now live in Fremont, Michigan and am blessed beyond expectation!

The Ice Cream Cart
By Marian K. Rodriquez of Saginaw,
Michigan
1950

I am 64 years old. During my pre-teens, I grew up on the east side of Saginaw. I lived on 12th Street between Janes and Lapeer.

A summer memory I miss is the ice cream cart. It was filled with Push-Ups, Fudgsicles,

Eskimo Pies, Popsicles, and ice cream sandwiches. The ice cream cart had bells. The seller, usually a teenage male, would ring the bells while walking down the street.

I remember playing outside and hearing the bells. I would be playing hopscotch with the neighborhood girls. I would run home to get my nickel so I could buy some ice cream. My favorite was the Push-Up!

It is sad that some of our social and societal lifestyles such as a decline and lack of moral values and gang behavior have resulted in the elimination of some priceless events such as the ice cream carts. The sellers became easy targets for fast cash.

An Anchor for Brakes?
By Marcia Collver of Beaverton, Michigan
Born 1922

In 1940, I was a senior at Saginaw High School in Saginaw, Michigan. I was "going steady" with Bob, who was two years older than me. He had a green and yellow convertible with a rumble seat. He paid for it at fifty cents a week. We called it the Green Hornet.

Bob Collver

110

Marcia Collver

We were double dating, and the second couple was in the rumble seat. Bob knew the brakes needed work, so he was driving slowly up to the stop sign.

The cop on the corner was not too friendly to teenagers. So Don, who was in the rumble seat, having found an anchor, threw it out as Bob stood up on the brakes.

The cop was still laughing as we went on our way. The cop suggested we get our brakes fixed.

Civilian Ground Observer Corps.
By Mary Lou Ely of Stanton, Michigan
Born 1932

For me, it was the year I graduated from high school, but for my mom, Genevieve Buckstiegel and her son Dick, it was the start of a very important adventure- a nation adventure!

They were joining the Civilian Ground Observer Corps, of 8000 posts, formed by the Continental Air Command. They were 2% of over 200,000 volunteers participating in nationwide drills, telephoning dozens of coordination centers, which in turn relayed information to the Air Defense Command (ADC) ground control interception centers.

Petoskey, Michigan was an important post since it was about 90 miles from the Sault Saint Marie locks.

The local Petoskey post site was on top of the hill in Petoskey where "The Big Ear" was located, and with the help of a big amplifier, they would listen for airplanes.

Then the binoculars would tell them what kind of plane- Japanese, German, or US, and with a small card held in the hand, they could tell how many miles away and at what altitude the plane was flying.

The post was manned 24 hours a day. My mom would take my little brother, and they would spend 2 hours, once a week, taking their turn defending the USA.

Periodically, the local volunteers would get together for dinner and share information when questions would arise.

Genevieve died a half month before her 100th birthday in 2009. A month later, she received an acknowledgement of her service- stating thanks for her effort in the win of WWII. It was signed: with great respect, Jim Alton, Emmet County Veterans Affairs, and attached was a "pin of wings" from the United States Air Force.

Oh how she would have loved to see that!

Our Christmas Programs
By Sharon Hilyard of Ludington, Michigan
Born 1945

I began my school years in a one-room school that included kindergarten through the eighth grade. I attended that school through the fifth grade. It was called Shore School in Avondale, Michigan. My first teacher was my neighbor, Mabel Collins. The second teacher was Winifred Becker.

Christmas was the one time of year I remember the most. We would prepare for our Christmas program through the whole month of December. One of the men of the community would enlist the help of the older boys at school to bring in a tree that would almost touch the ceiling. The younger children would decorate the bottom part of the tree, and the older children would decorate the top part. We all would make handmade ornaments to put on the tree.

At the front of the classroom, a stage

would be built. Curtains would be hung on wires that would open and close between plays and recitations. We all wanted to be the curtain opener and closer. The curtains would cover the area on both sides of the stage where those who had poems, recitations, or a part in the play would stay until it was their turn.

The whole month of December would be given over to practicing and preparing for the program. I do not remember any of the poems that I said, but I do remember an older girl and boy sitting on a sofa on stage and singing *Winter Wonderland.* I could never figure out why anyone would describe a snowman as parse and brown!

Just before Christmas, the parents would be invited to attend the program that we had worked hard on the whole month. Everyone would be dressed in their best. My mother would make a new dress for me.

At the end of the program, Santa would show up, ringing his sleigh bells. He would pass out candy for everyone.

An Amazing Sight
By Keith Hardy of Kawkawlin, Michigan
Born 1940

This is a true story about the historic Trombly-Bradley House that was constructed sometime between 1835 and 1840. The house stood at the foot of Water Street near the Lafayette Street Bridge in Bay City, Michigan. This bridge crosses the Saginaw River, which flows northward and empties into the Saginaw Bay, located at the south end of Lake Huron.

I was five years old when my family moved into this historic house in the year of 1945. The two-story house had been divided into four apartments, and my family rented one of the lower apartments.

The original former foyer entrance faced the river. It had two full length, narrow windows on each side of the door, and when the new owners split the home into four apartments, these windows were shared by the apartment next to us. One-half of the foyer space was my bedroom, and it was only large enough for a crib, which I slept in at that time.

At night before I went to sleep, I would occasionally watch freighters go through the open Lafayette Street Bridge with all their deck lights on, heading upstream for a delivery somewhere.

One evening, I was staring out the window at the bridge and witnessed an amazing sight that horrified me! All the bridge streetlights were lit, and I witnessed rats and mice numbering in the thousands migrating eastward across the bridge toward the street on which I lived. I was frightened and called for my mother, and she assured me that everything was all right.

As I recall, the dump which was located on the island called the Middle Grounds was infested with rodents. In order to control this infestation, the city announced the closing of the dump to eradicate these pests. The city used fire hoses to saturate this landfill area with fuel oil and had many fire trucks on standby. They closed the bridges and lit the north end of this island, which burned for days. Job well done!

They were Happy, Happy Times
By Thelma Brauher of Vestaburg, Michigan
Born 1928

My name is Thelma Raby Brauher. I was born on the 16th day of August 1928. Myself, along with my three siblings, were all born at the residence of our grandfather's home in Seville Township, Riverdale, Gratiot County, Michigan.

Life has sure changed and is very much different than living in the 1920s and 1930s. My father owned and operated a garage and fueling station in Riverdale where we lived. Growing up, we all helped with work at our grandfather's farm. Grandpa raised chickens and sold eggs to a local business called Rainbow Hatchery, located in the town of St. Louis, Michigan. They would come every other day and gather eggs that the hens would lay. The hatchery would sell the young chicks all across Michigan and the bordering state, Indiana.

I have memories of events held in Riverdale when I was young, such as the free movies that would be shown in Riverdale and sponsored by the local businesses for a nominal fee of twenty-five cents. The movies came to Riverdale on Friday evenings, and they were also shown at other local towns on different days of the weeks. We would bring with us to eat our own popcorn, raised by us on Grandpa's farm while viewing the shows and sometimes sandwiches.

As a child in Riverdale, Michigan from 1936 to 1940, I have fond memories of walking out to Lumber Jack Park two miles north of town on the fourth of July to see what was the entertainment for the day. There was logrolling and rail splitting. It was a joyous time. There was a buffalo there. Mr. Valstine lived there and took care of the animals and other things. Later in the afternoon, there were groups that sang and a large dance hall that drew large groups of couples for happy, happy times. The dance hall is still there, and it had been remodeled. The park is a big attraction yet in 2014. We would walk to and from barefoot out and back and many other children from town. We would stay all day.

Thelma with her aunts in 1983

Feather Ticks on the Porch
By Violet Stachowiak of Bay City, Michigan
Born 1926

Hi! I am Violet Stachowiak. I am 88 years old. I lived in the good old days. We lived on Monroe when I was little, between Kosciuszko and 21st. We had an outhouse, and at night in the house, we had a porcelain pail with a liner.

Everybody had a garden in the summer, and they also had chickens. In the winter when it snowed, Mr. Kaklla had a big plow and a horse and he shoveled the city sidewalks.

Then I had a sister and we moved onto South Sherman. That's where we grew up. We had a space heater for heat. A few years after had an oil furnace. What a relief. We had no refrigerator but we had an icebox and we got ice, 25lbs, 50 to 75.

My uncle Frank had a rumble seat car, and he and his buddy would take me for a ride.

You had to shop for meat every day. The buses were on every day until 12 o'clock. We had a lot of nice stores on Kosciuszko Ave. We had cleaners, meat shops, drug stores, shoe repair, cigar factory, photography, gas station, and a flower shop. You could get an ice cream cone at the city dairy for 3cents. Buses were always full. No one had cars, like now.

You had two pairs of shoes. When it was raining, we ran under the porch. After a nice rain, all the buds came out in the puddles.

Our toys were like stones, and pieces of glass for hopscotch. We didn't even have a bike.

Bath night was Saturday night. The galvanized tub was taken out and we all took turns getting a bath, all in the same water.

If we went to town, we would walk. We could get an ice cream cone for 3cents. We had a vegetable peddler, and milk was delivered every day in glass bottles. The roads, every summer, were tarred and you couldn't go on the street at all for a week. The insurance man collected every month.

In the summer it was so hot after supper dishes, the ladies would sit on the porch and the men would hose the houses down to cool them off. We all had stools and kitchens downstairs; that's where we ate. At night, our mothers would put feather ticks on the porch. That's where we slept all night.

No one had to worry about their kids. It was really a happy life.

A Boy Scout from Taste Rite Bakery
By Edwin W. Jablonski of Prescott, Michigan
Born 1939

A long time ago, 1947 or thereabouts, I belonged to Troop #1 of the Boy Scouts from St. Stanislaus Grade School. We built a sled and had it moved by Balser Bros. Bus from

22nd and Farragut, pulling it behind the bus and spending the day treasure hunting at the Old Boy Scout lodge near the state park.

For some time, my father owned a bakery, "Taste Rite Bakery," across from St. Stanislaus School. I would "cut and wrap" the bread every day before going to church. Dad made sure I was at church on time (8 am). On Friday nights, I would go with Dad to the bakery at 6:30 pm. I would crack eggs by the cases, help load the bread in pans to rise and make donuts by the hundreds. My job was frying, glazing, sugarcoating, frosting, and powder sugaring, starting at 2:30 am until 6 am Saturday morning. This was how I earned my allowance ($5.00 a week). Dad sold the bakery in 1950. I was 10 1/2 years old.

Our playground back then was called, "Murray Bodies," between 24th and 28th Streets between Farragut and Lincoln Streets and the silos, which still stand today for grain storage. We had BB gun fights, climbing the old buildings and shooting at each other until we had an accident. One of the guys was hit in the eye. He was hurt pretty good, but I understand Ken later became captain of the state police post on Euclid.

My Uncle Bob Jablonski was a lifeguard at Bay City State Park, and that is where I first rode in the "rumble seat" with my first cousin, Joe. The water was very clean at the state park, and the lagoon was good fishing during the winter with 15 or 20 ice shanties.

In 1945, The Bay City Times reported that several of us boys ran away from home but were picked up at Clements Airport by my Grandpa Thiesmeyer. As kids, we also had our favorite rock and roll singers. As we played different types of card games, we would call a DJ named "Don Andrews," and he would play our music and use our names on the radio.

I remember in 1947 or 1948, sitting on the railroad tracks behind "Barcraft" on 26th Street, hearing I had lost someone very special: Babe Ruth had died.

I used to ride the same train from behind my dad's house to Kuelman Electric and on to the Sag River and the old Cass Ave Bridge, where we'd swim to the 23rd Bridge. I also rode a bike from 26th Street to the Railroad Bridges off of Old Kawkawlin Road to go swimming.

The Old Wenona Beach was always our favorite. You could see the roller coaster for miles, and we rode the Bullet. I also remember the ghost stories of the Rosenbury building. I worked at the Empire Bowling Alley as a pinsetter for two years (1955-1956).

I met my wife in 1960 at the old YWCA. We were married in 1963. She has now been my best friend for almost 52 years. Thank you for my memories. It's been great.

A Look Back in Time
By Elizabeth L. Berg of Saginaw, Michigan
Born 1938

I once heard a song on the radio, "*I Met a Girl in Saginaw, Michigan,*" which reminded me of how my parents met. Dad had just arrived up from Ohio. He spotted my mother riding a city bus. He decided then and there he would marry her and told her so. They ran into each other again at a weekend street dance. The rest is history. They wed when Ma was 16 and Dad 15, remaining happily so until Dad died. When Dad missed his friends, he hopped a freight train, riding a boxcar back to Ohio with hobos.

Ma told of a prank her brother played on her. Uncle Gene cut a hole in the bottom of a kitchen matchbox stuffed with ketchup-soaked cotton. He stuck his finger up through the hole and ran to Ma crying he had cut his finger off. She screamed, so he revealed the prank.

My brother returned from the Navy with two large canvas duffel bags, which he stored in our attic. My sister and I snuck upstairs to look for sailor hats—all the rage. We happened upon his girlfriend's love letters. Crawling on rafters toward the light to read them, we knelt on a framed charcoal drawing, breaking the glass and ruining Ma's artwork with first place Saginaw County Fair ribbon. Nothing was said. My brother gave us the hats. We returned to the attic to read more letters, which mysteriously disappeared, along with Ma's picture.

We could see passenger and freight trains from our house. Eerie nighttime whistles scared us. We thought someone would jump off and get us. When Ma complained about our fussing, Dad gave us a plate of fudge. We shut right up.

Dad took us to Hoyt Park on a picnic.

A tall wooden slide stood nearby, used as a toboggan run in winter. My sister dared me to slide down it. I did. By the time I reached bottom, my bottom was full of slivers. I ran crying to Dad who pulled my pants down in public and removed them one-by-one.

After attending the Shrine Circus, I attempted to duplicate my favorite act: a lady suspended from a rope by her teeth, twirling around, waving her outstretched arms like a butterfly. I fashioned a large knot on one end of a rope, threw the other end over our peach tree limb, and double tied it. I climbed up, inserted the knot in my mouth, gritted my teeth, then swung down to start twirling—but it was not to be. Excruciating pain forced me to drop to the ground. I thought all my teeth would fall out.

Stores were closed Sundays, reserved for early Mass, the family meal, then visiting relatives. My aunt and uncle's farm on Wadsworth was our favorite. We played outside with ten cousins while our parents visited. Hide-and-seek in the cornfield, running and jumping over bales of hay, and just hanging out in an old school bus parked by field's edge— what fun for a city girl! No indoor plumbing forced us to use their outhouse, which was tipped over every Halloween. Household water was pumped from a small hand pump installed near the coal/wood burning cook stove, where an iron sat ready for pressing clothes.

Family music sessions were held when my brother and family visited, bringing his accordion. Dad played violin. We three sisters played guitar, sometimes mandolin, or ukulele, and sang. During tornado warnings, Dad ran to his bedroom for his violin, and

Elizabeth's parents Harry and Theresa Pahssen in 1928

then to the basement.

A ride in Grandpa's car rumble seat was a surprise. We thought it was a trunk. Our eyes bugged out when Grandpa spat his chewing tobacco clear across the room into his spittoon. Grandma served us coffee, just for grownups, according to Ma.

My brother and his best friend walked me to school. Later, both joined the Navy where his friend was killed in World War II parachuting from a warplane. My brother was still on the ship when the war ended.

First graders were lined up mid-morning on small stools and given a carton of milk. After drinking mine, I needed to use the bathroom. Two nuns were blocking the doorway with arms folded, talking. Too scared to ask permission, I remained seated and wet my pants.

Second grade penmanship loop-to-loop exercises previewed cursive writing. My grandkids cannot read my notes unless printed; they told me teachers no longer teach cursive writing.

We climbed between railroad cars of stopped trains so we wouldn't be late for school. Boys hitched rides on slow moving trains by latching onto boxcar ladders. When we encountered trains on the way home, we yelled out as the caboose passed by "Can we have some chalk?" The man threw out big pieces used for playing hopscotch.

Today's school bullies cannot compete with those of '40s and '50s. When walking to school, boys threw gardener snakes at us, and, if caught, down our uniform blouses. We dodged apples and other projectiles daily.

School closures were unheard of, no matter how deep the snow or frigid the weather. Sometimes sidewalks were so icy we shuffled our feet and slid to school, lest we slip and fall. Public school boys viewed us Catholic girls as fair game in winter. They would lie and wait behind the church on the corner of Elm and Main, armed with a stash of snowballs, pelting us as we walked by, and washed our faces in snow. Bogged down with books and homework, our only defense was scurrying to distance ourselves from their stash.

School playground fights occurred while nuns were in the convent eating lunch. Students picked sides and cheered them on. There were no suspensions, but lots of writer's cramps after written punishments.

While boys fought, we girls traded picture playing cards from our collections. We solicited decks of cards from relatives and neighbors and bought barebacks

Elizabeth and her husband Cecil in 1961

(cards without numbers) at the dime store. A bareback counted as two cards in a trade. Pinups were most coveted, commanding three cards. My collection filled a cigar box, but alas, only nine pinups.

Our school had no parking lot. Everyone walked except those from the country. Our parents paid $50 each per year for us to ride the bus. Only two students drove, parking behind the school. Freshmen were initiated by upperclassmen who ordered us to bow down before them. One boy refused, and therefore he was subject to further initiation. Upperclassmen led him blindfolded to a hallway bathroom, leaving door open for all to see. They ordered him to reach into the toilet and retrieve a peeled banana previously placed there. I can imagine what went through his mind as he attempted to obey their command. He immediately upchucked. Laughing, they removed his blindfold, revealing the banana.

After that, all who witnessed the incident bowed down when asked.

The day of our championship game, the nuns dismissed us during school hours to participate in a snake dance. We formed a human chain and zigzagged through West Side streets, cheering for our team. We were sure to snake by St. Andrew's, our long-standing sports rival. We won the State Championship that year and were proud Midgets.

Science was required for graduation. I picked Biology. However, finding and attaching spiders and bugs to cardboard with stickpins did not appeal to me. One lab experiment counted as half the semester grade. Sister instructed us to kill a frog by inserting and wiggling a needle around in the side of its head. We could then dissect it by cutting capital letter "I" into the front, and creating flaps. When the flaps were folded back, they would reveal intestines and organs. My frog stopped moving, so I proceeded, whereupon it leaped from the table, hopping around with innards hanging out, until it stopped dead in its tracks. Sister told me to pick it up and finish the job, but I was too traumatized to continue. My "A" became a "C."

Typing on old manual typewriters forced us to turn our fingers into hammers, pounding keys down hard enough to make letters visible on paper, hoping our fingers wouldn't get stuck between the keys. Reversing cloth typing ribbons during timed exercises slowed us down.

Dad taught me to drive on back roads with his straight-stick Chevy. No seat belts, no blinkers; Dad stuck his hand out the window, indicating turns. After graduation and a job, I bought an automatic 1957 Chevrolet. I gassed up at full service Seal-co station for ten cents per gallon, including checking oil, washing windshield, even airing tires when requested. Savings stamps given were redeemed towards milk-glass dishes. Hood ornaments adorned cars, rarely seen today unless at a car show. Ma never drove until after Dad died when she took lessons and got her license and bought a car. Uncle Gene bought her a large golden eagle hood ornament, proudly displayed as she drove around town.

We had lots of places to go. Saturday mornings we hopped a city bus downtown for five cents to shop at Woolsworth's dime store or try on penny loafers and saddle shoes at Nobil's. Afternoons found us watching our favorite musicals or westerns for 11 cents admission at Marr or Wolverine Theater. Court St. Theater still stands showing $1 movies. Temple Theater, still the pride of Downtown Saginaw, hosts Russian ballets, symphonies, plays, and other entertainment. Paloma and Franklin theaters closed. Anderson Pool was the summer hot spot. We suffered many a sunburn, aggravated by Saturday night baths, wiping with towels hung out to dry, stiff as a board. Brockway Roller Rink and Hoyt Park provided year-round skating with their welcoming warming house. I first tasted pizza in high school, but preferred Coney dogs at the Old Town Drive-in, served by carhops on roller skates, wearing poodle skirts. It's still there and I still love them.

Strand and White's drive-in restaurants were frequented by teen boys, with collars up and hair greased back, driving souped-up hotrods and convertibles round and round, trying to pick up girls. Golden Glow teen dances attracted crowds from Saginaw and surrounding towns, dancing to live band music, no DJs. It burned to the ground, but was rebuilt for hosts wedding receptions, etc. Ravena Gardens, our hangout after 18, featured the Polka Jacks. Fire destroyed all but the bar; now a party store. I met my husband at Ravena's and we held our wedding reception at Golden Glow. You were an old maid if unmarried by 21. There were lots of shotgun weddings and marriages out of high school, but rarely unwed mothers.

We had public phone booths and party lines—no computers, internet, cell phones, smart phones, iPads, texting, Facebook or Twitter, but we had so much more; we had each other.

Our first TV was 8" which Dad later upgraded to a 12." One night while watching TV, a handsome young man appeared, belting out a song while shimmying, shaking and swiveling his hips. I was mesmerized. His name was Elvis Presley. Years later, I took my teenage son to watch Elvis perform at Saginaw Civic Center, just months before his sudden death. The audience went wild at first sound of introductory drum-roll and appearance of Elvis on stage, wearing his signature flashy cape and bell bottoms. From "You Ain't Nothing But a Hound-dog," to grown women swooning to his mellow "Love Me Tender," or a heartfelt religious song, his energetic performance captivated us all. Security allowed me with others to approach the stage for a close-up look. Over the years, I've listened to Elvis on 78rpm and 45rpm records, 8-track tapes, CDs and DVDs. My daughter gifted me with an Elvis blanket I use when attending my grandson's ballgames. Today, Elvis impersonators perform all over the country, a tribute to Elvis, but none can compare. Elvis will always be the King of Rock and Roll.

The Joe Sanders Story
By Alta Reed of Lansing, Michigan
Born 1922

Every successful, and sometimes not so successful, event, business, invention, plan, or action begins in the mind. An idea, or in today's jargon, a "what if" percolates and one gets involved in bringing that idea to life.

This is the story of Joseph Sanders, who in 1925, newly married, was struggling with his new responsibilities and his future.

Joe's parents, Edward and Emma Sanders, moved to Custer, Michigan when Joe was three. He attended Jenks, Resseguie, and Riverside schools. When he was fourteen, he worked on the Tippy Dam construction project at Wellston.

At sixteen, to seek his fortune, he bicycled to Chicago. He then sold the bicycle and took a train to South Dakota. While there, he worked on a ranch and learned to rope steers. He absorbed all the opportunities that ranch life presented him. He had the misfortune to fall off his horse, breaking his wrist. Unable to work on the ranch, he returned to Custer in 1918. When he was able to, he tried several jobs. He was too young for WWI. In 1925, he met and married Vera Rathburn.

Searching his mind for ideas, he remembered the butchering of cattle at the ranch in South Dakota. This was the answer. He went to the local bank at Custer and requested a $100.00 loan to finance buying a cow to butcher. The banker, John Doe (his real name) said, "No. You have no collateral." Not to be deterred, Joe asked his father-in-law for the money and explained why he needed it. Mr. Rathburn agreed and from this humble beginning came Joe Sanders, Inc. still in business in Custer, Michigan in 2015.

Joe started his business on Conrad Road, south of Custer. He butchered by night and sold his meat door to door by day. In 1930, Joe purchased the bank building on the main street in Custer. As the business grew and prospered, Joe was able to hire many young men who learned their trade from this enterprise.

As the retail stores gradually moved north to US 10 from the main street along the railroad tracks, Joe purchased all the empty buildings to expand and improve his business. He had the first commercial refrigerator unit in the area.

Joe also purchased the pickle vats from Squire Dingee pickle property, had them moved across from the bank building, and then purchased pickles grown by local farmers. He also purchased the animal hides trapped and stretched on wire frames by the trappers in the area.

Joe was very involved in civic matters. He served as village clerk for fourteen years and was a member of the Custer schoolboard for twelve years.

He was also very talented, playing the piano for Saturday night dances at the Odd Fellow's Hall. He also made beautiful music with his violin.

He loved baseball, sponsoring and playing on a local team. My memory here is about one of the games up in the Branch area. Joe was pitching and the opposing team was hitting his balls all over the field. Joe took himself from the mound and Shorty Smith was put in to pitch. Shorty was short, as his nickname suggests, and someone in the crowd yelled, "Mow the grass so he can see over it." Anyway, Shorty was able to strike out the next three batters. But the game was still lost. Those ball games provided much entertainment every summer.

I have many memories of Joe and his family as my home was across the street from their home. Joe and Vera had three children, Leo (1927), Doris Jean (1934), and Carlton (1941).

Leo had a special ability when he was growing up. He could make his chores so interesting and exciting that all the neighborhood children pleaded to do his work for him. And of course, he let them. Joe added to the children's fun by showing off the rope tricks he learned on the ranch in South Dakota.

I was babysitting Doris Jean one day. She was learning to talk and when her daddy left, she said her first sentence. She watched him leave as I held her up to the kitchen window. She looked at me and said, "Daddy car go." Vera put that in her baby book.

My mother told me this story. When Carlton was expected in 1941, the Custer Ladies Aid Society purchased a Bathinette for Vera's baby shower. Vera told the ladies after Carlton arrived, that the Bathinette made it so easy to take care of the baby and how much she really appreciated it. She also said, "But I wouldn't have thought to buy one."

During the Depression years, money was scarce. Joe's meat business was doing quite well, so he was able to pay the teachers at the school partially with meat. I remember having the very best teachers at the time.

Joe and Vera rented out their upstairs rooms to students coming from rural areas to attend Custer High School. In 1935, three boys from Carr Settlement were using this opportunity to graduate. I was tending to Doris Jean when Joe brought the boys in to show them their living quarters. That day I did not know that one of those boys would be my husband for 63 years and six kids later.

The only time one of my own children was called a juvenile delinquent was when my son, Robert, and my brother Vic's son, Ronny, kicked the stopper holding the brine in one of Joe's pickle vats, allowing brine to gush out and the pickles to squash. Joe took the incident in stride, selling the pickles for pickle relish. He scolded the kids, who were about nine at the time, and told them to stay out of mischief. I had the article from the Ludington paper telling of this story on their front page for many years, finally losing it.

Doris Jean married and moved to Connecticut. The last time I saw Leo, he was riding on a Sanders, Inc. float in the Ludington Fourth of July parade.

Joe died after a head on collision on Reek Road, south of Custer in 1966. He was sixty-five years old.

Joe's grandsons and great-grandsons still operate Sanders' Meatpacking business in Custer. Sanders' Meats is best known for its spiral cut hams, which are glazed and sliced in such a way that makes them easy to prepare and enjoy. Some of their specialties are Polish sausage, white and regular brats, Dutch loaf, and salami. They cover a wide range of appetites.

From humble beginnings, a very successful and lucrative business thrived and prospered because of the foresight, hard work, and dedication from one man. Joe Sanders' legacy will live on in the community his business has been so much a part of for many, many years.

How I made my Spending Money
By Creal Hoover of Reed City, Michigan

My name is Creal Hoover. I am 75 years old. I am going to tell you about some of my jobs I had as a boy growing up.

When I was about 12 years old, I got my first job picking strawberries for a farmer. I could pick about 30 to 40 quarts a day. When the whole patch was picked, you went home. You only picked about 6 hours. It was hard on the knees. We got a nickel a quart for picking.

The same farmer liked me and he had me pick pickles later in the season. We got paid 2cents a pound. When you got done in the afternoon, your hands were black and had a lot of pickers on them.

My next job that came along was picking green beans for different farmers. Some paid by the pound, some by the bag, and some by the bushel basket. They would tag the bags and you would get paid at the end of the week. Some kids would steal the tags and put them on their bags. It was mainly one farmer where I would lose my bags. After a while, I didn't pick for him anymore.

My next job was putting up hay for different farmers. I got paid anywhere from 50 cents an hour to $1.50 an hour. The farmers'

Creal's wife with their children Kathy and Sam

wives would always feed you supper. Some would feed you lunch too. Sometimes that was the best part of the job. The farmers wives were really good cooks.

By this time in my life, I turned 15 and I got hired as a pinsetter. This took place in a bowling alley in the days before automatic pinsetters. I started in at 8 and 1/2 cents a line or some people called it a game. You would set pins on two lanes at the same time. You would have to be careful or you could get hit by flying pins once in a while.

I set pins for 4 years through high school. This was how I made my spending money. That is how I supported my girlfriend. I helped get several of my friends' jobs setting pins also. My Dad didn't work during the

Creal with his children Sam and Kathy

119

winter months. This was the only way I had any money.

I usually set pins 3-4 nights a week. I sat pins 31 nights in a row without a night off one time. My report card really suffered. It was a necessity to have a job.

I am just going to list some of the jobs I have had in my life since high school:

Glass company, Fiber Glass factory building pontoon boats and golf carts, I worked on a pipeline and helped harvest Christmas trees, I also worked in a furniture factory covering arms and backs of furniture, a machine shop that I really liked and a door closer plant. Then I built aluminum doors in aluminum plant for 37 years.

I am now retired and enjoying watching my grandchildren grow up. I also have a great granddaughter. My wife and I go for short rides and enjoy watching the Detroit Tiger. If there is anything you want to do, don't wait to do it today. Enjoy your life.

Battery Powered Radios and Saturday Night Baths
By Oliver "Ollie" Leigeb of Sanford, Michigan
Born 1927

Old Radio Programs
We used to listen to Joe Lewis boxing, *Amos and Andy*, and *The Grand Ole Opry*. We had no electricity in our house. We only had an old radio that was DC instead of AC, so my older brothers who had cars and lived at home would park their cars next to the window of our house and run wires into the radio each Saturday night. We would huddle around that old radio to hear through all the static. By the way, there were ten boys and two girls in our happy family. We were poor, to say the least.

Wind Up Record Players
We had an old stand up Philco wind up record player with records about one fourth of an inch thick. It had a needle you had to change when the music got scratchy.

Party Line Phones
We had an old phone that was a wooden box with a crank on the side. To get to talk to someone, you had to spin the crank for maybe two long and one short for your neighbor or whomever you wanted to talk to. I remember

our phone was three short spins or rings. There were no cell phones or iPads.

You first had to pick up the phone receiver and listen to see if anyone was talking on the line, as there were, I believe, six customers on each party line. If someone was on the line and you listened too long, they could tell and would yell at you to get off the phone, because they were using it.

Spankings in School
Yeah, I got a couple of spankings in school, all right. Our teacher would use a one-foot ruler with a brass edge on one side. She would sneak up behind you and grab one of your hands and turn it backwards and hit you with the sharp side of that ruler. That wasn't much fun.

Of course, we wouldn't tell our dad about it. We lived one and a half miles from school, and Dad had no car for a few years. So we were pretty safe by not telling him about it, but you know of all us twelve kids in our family, we cannot remember getting hardly any spankings from Dad. All he had to do was give us a look that told us we knew we had better behave.

Saturday Night Baths
The thing I will never forget was a bath when I was about three or four years old. My mother would put warm water in a washtub and set it next to our wood burning stove. This one time I lost my balance, and the stove was red hot. I reached out to catch myself, and my hand slipped off that stove. But the skin on my right hand stayed there.

We didn't have any storm windows in those days, and it was so cold outside that the frost would build up on the inside. So I put my hand on the ice and melted all the ice from the window. Can you imagine how much infection I could have gotten? My mom got a clean white rag and put a lot of Rawleigh Salve on it, and it was okay.

Water, a Special Gift
By Sylvia G. Rouech of Bay City, Michigan
Born 1937

This is a reflection on water. Most of us take water for granted.

I relax on the deck of our cabin in the peace of early morning and become mesmerized by

Six of Sylvia's seven brothers
Frank, Roy, Ray, Don, Harold, and Rob

the ever-changing lake water.

I sing, "Thank you, Lord; thank you, Lord," for this miracle of water that caresses my body with warmth and healing and complete ecstasy when I shower.

I am small kneeling beside the round, galvanized aluminum tub. Laura is washing my hair, and there is pain, as my older sister's hands are not gentle.

I am a young farm girl walking the lane between the fields of potatoes and wheat that leads to the woods where the cows are loafing in the shade of the trees. They sense my presence and slowly rise, making their way to the water trough, knowing soon I will be at the pump. I pump furiously, trying to out match their thirst and get the water to a level acceptable to my task.

I picture the white, red-rimmed, granite water pail sitting at the corner of the cupboard next to the outside door, easily accessible to whoever needs to quickly quench their thirst. The long handled dipper serves as a common ladle for everyone to drink from. There is no fear of contamination then.

I am in puberty, overly conscious of my body's changes, carefully carrying a basin of water upstairs to my room for the "sponge bath" that was the norm when one got too big for the silver tub and prior to indoor plumbing.

It's a miracle! We get indoor running water, which comes from the cistern in the basement, a high "fortress" of thick cement that requires a ladder to check the level of water. When rain is plentiful, the water from the eaves troughs on the house empties into the cistern, assuring us of enough water to flush and wash. Dry spells require a trip with the farm truck laden with a tank to the small village of Munger, two miles away, to get water to replenish the cistern.

We are conditioned to preserve and use water sparingly. Sometimes this means more than one member of the family must use the bath water, adding hot just enough to make it comfortable. I especially hated bathing after my pa and generally planned my bath earlier on Saturday or escaped to my room for the sponge bath.

I feel the frustration and disappointment when the well driller gets only "salt" when drilling before we build our house – money down the drain. Once again, now in my married life, there is a pail on the cupboard for drinking water. The new house, too, had a cistern and many a laundry day is ruined when the pump gives off its "dry sound" and often there is a wait because of the farming before my husband, Bill, can haul water. Our drinking water comes from a pump in the backyard, just as it did when I was younger. Then we decide to hire Mr. Whipple, a retired farmer who has a business of hauling water, to regularly bring us water.

Sylvia and her brother, Rob

121

Finally, in 1975, we get "city water." Now at last there is plenty of water!

There is so much more I could tell about the water experiences in my life. To me, water is truly a special gift given to us by the Lord. How does one even begin to describe how it feels? How would you?

Grandma Ida
By Doris Barnhard of Fremont, Michigan
Born 1937

I remember the taste of fresh churned butter and the huge round oak table where we gathered to eat. The lane where the cows went to pasture in the morning and lazily returned in the late afternoon. The well-worn path across the field between our house and Grandma's house. I can recall her house better than mine. Every room, every chair, the way it smelled, and the way it was always full of people and good times, but most of all, I remember Grandma.

Grandma Ida was a tall, big-built woman with wisps of gray hair around her face. She wore it in a bun, but some strands always managed to come loose. She was busy, and she was always willing to go anywhere with anyone. It didn't take her long to get ready. Put in her teeth, take off her apron, and she was ready to go.

She had a Model T Ford, and if we were good, she would let us pile in and ride a short ways to the corner where a row of mailboxes held the mail. The best mail was catalogs. We would pour over the pages for hours and dream about the treasures we would buy someday.

Mostly Grandma Ida was busy, but it seemed to me she was not busy at all during strawberry picking time. There was one small, spindly shade tree in the middle of the strawberry patch, and there she would sit in a pretty comfortable looking big wooden chair and wait for us to bring the berries to her. We would start at one end of the row, and when we had picked enough boxes to fill a case we would take them to her. As we lingered in the coolness of the shade tree, she would pick out the biggest and best looking ones and put them on top, making sure the hulls were not showing. Grandma sure made them cases of strawberries look good. I remember thinking her job looked like a lot more fun than mine!

Grandma Ida kept a Mason jar filled with water under the tree. She would give us a long drink and tell us the longer we waited under the tree, the hotter the sun would get to be and the longer it would take to get the berries picked. With a smile and a pat on our behinds, she would send us on our way.

This special woman loved telling stories. One of her favorites was of my birth. Like many in those days, I was born at home, but with a doctor present. There was a problem; I was not breathing and the doctor told Grandma Ida to get two buckets of water ready, one cool and one warm. As she tells it, the doctor dunked me in the cool water and then in the warm water and then back in the cool water. Finally, I took in a breath and opened my mouth and let out a yell, and I have not shut up since. Grandma Ida would always end with laughter, as if it was the first time I had heard this often-told story.

Grandma's joy in life was her family. She raised ten children and probably some grandchildren, too. I hope they have special memories of her, too. Grandma Ida passed away many years ago, and I believe she is in Heaven telling stories and taking care of children and topping off cases of strawberries and making them all look good!

The Day I was Elvis
By Ronald Hoodak of Elmira, New York

Lincoln Elementary Schools holds a special place in my heart and is frozen in my memory. As you young boy, I attended Lincoln School from grades K-6. The school was a two story brick building on a large plot of land located in Elmira Heights, New York. The staff was wonderful. They cared about the students. To this day, I remember the principal and one of the finest people that I have ever known.

In second grade, the faculty decided that the class should put on a talent show for the parents. Some students read speeches. Some danced and some sang songs. I had no idea what I would do until my mother and the teacher had a conversation, which created one of the lasting memories of my life.

It was decided that I would do an

impersonation of Elvis Presley. My mom knew that I had seen Elvis on the Ed Sullivan Show. She mentioned this to my teacher and from that moment on, I was preparing to be Elvis Presley for on afternoon.

On the day of the talent show, our class was placed on the stage, which was located in front of the basketball court in the gym. Fold up chairs where placed on the gym floor for all of the parents to sit on. I remember that the gym was packed with parents. My mother was sitting in the back row and I could see her clearly. She was smiling contently and I was very pleased to see her there.

As the show started, I sat in my seat, waiting for my turn to perform. I remember that I was not nervous. My mother had bought me a toy guitar to use as a prop. I memorized on of Presley's songs and more importantly, I knew how he moved on stage.

My name was called and I went to the front of the stage and started to sing. As I sang, I started to gyrate just like Elvis did on the Ed Sullivan Show. The crowd went wild. People started to clap and cheer. Everyone in the gym was showing their appreciation. As I finished my performance, people kept clapping and cheering. I did not know how to react. I just bowed and got off of the stage.

Weeks later, Lincoln school had an ice cream social. My mom took me and dozens of people came up to us to say how much they enjoyed my Elvis Performance. It still did not hit me how successful I had been on stage. The large crown showed their appreciation by applauding even after I had finished my song. I realize now how Elvis must have felt.

Many months later, my mom showed me a black and white picture that she had taken at the talent show. I was not aware that she had brought a camera to the talent show, but she did. It was a picture of me with my toy guitar on stage impersonating Elvis Presley. I was wearing a cowboy shirt and you could tell that I was right in the middle of the song.

That picture was one of my most prize possessions. It reminded me of how much my mother cared for me. She cared enough to come to the talent show and take a picture of me. Most importantly, I knew she was proud of me and that touched me deeply. My mom passed away three years ago and I think of that day at Lincoln Elementary School often.

I shall always remember Lincoln Elementary School with strong loving emotions.

Lincoln Elementary School is now an apartment complex and my Elvis picture has long since been lost. I regret that deeply. But one memory I will cherish forever—For one afternoon, I was Elvis Presley.

Fire!
By Charles Robinson of Sanford, Michigan
Born 1947

I was puttering in the garden and a couple things happened that I found amusing. One involved alcohol, and the other, fire. By experience, I've found that to be a pretty hazardous combination.

It was Sunday, and I like to do my lawn work and gardening on Sunday. It was a beautiful day and I dutifully mowed the lawn with one hand, and of course, had a glass of wine in the other. The mower kept plugging up with grass so I had to reach under the mower and pull it out. I didn't turn the mower off because it has a clutch on the blade that stops it so it won't cut my finger off.

I remember my dad cutting his fingers badly on a mower blade. He was hard of hearing and couldn't tell if the mower was running so he stuck his fingers under the mower to see if the blade was turning… It was. He told me to always wear my safety glasses when I stick my fingers under the mower. (In case you're wondering where I got my sense of humor.)

Anyway, back to gardening. After I mowed the lawn, I decided to hoe my garden to get the upper hand on the weeds. Things weren't going so well; I was hoeing as many beans as weeds. I figured it had something to do with the wine. I decided to give it up and do something else. I had a pile of sticks and old lumber so I decided to set fire to it and burn it up.

I watched the fire and had another glass of wine while my dog Loco busied himself by digging up a chipmunk. Nothing was sticking out of the ground but the dogs butt and big flag of a tail.

It was now getting dark so I thought I would water what was left of the garden. With sprayer in one hand, and glass of merlot in the other, I was waving the stream of water back and forth when the spray stopped and I heard a hissing sound behind me. I had apparently pulled the hose through the fire and burned it in half.

After I shut the water off, I sat watching the fire die down and recalled several other incidents I've had with fire. One in particular I find amusing, so maybe others will get a kick out of it as well.

When I was eight or nine years old, my dad wanted to build a workshop in the backyard. He bought a barn from a guy to tear down for the lumber.

It was a hard job for me and I suppose it was for Pa as well. The old nails wouldn't pull out and the boards would split, causing a lot of waste.

The waste pile was getting pretty big, so my dad decided to burn it. It was a dry, breezy day but that didn't concern him. Just to be sure, he would post me there with a shovel to keep an eye on it.

There was a big field of dry grass behind the barn and, of course, it wasn't long before it caught fire. I was able to quickly put it out with the shovel. The old dry boards were quickly engulfed in flames that leaped high into the air. I had the challenge of taking care of the flair ups.

As I stood there with my eye on the fire, I suddenly felt heat at my back. I turned around to see the field ablaze. I ran after it with my shovel, and screamed for help from my dad. He climbed off the roof, grabbed my shovel, and started beating the flames. Then he hollered at me to grab a board and help him, which I did.

As my dad would make progress, he would run across the blackened area and help me with my side. Of course, his side would start burning again, so he would have to run back.

After a while, I felt dizzy, as though I was in a dream. My board, however, never stopped going up and down, up and down. I was well out into the field by now, and wondered what had happened to my dad. I hadn't heard from or seen him for quite a while.

All of a sudden, I was nearly knocked off my feet by the blast of a horn. I looked through the smoke to see a big red truck bearing down on me. I scrambled to get out of the way. As it passed, I could see that the driver had a big grin and a cheek full of tobacco. He was laughing as he waved at me.

The truck was from the D.N.R. and had a big plow on the back that was plowing a huge furrow across the field. I later learned that smoke had been spotted by the watchman in the fire tower at Edenville, and they radioed the D.N.R. in Sanford.

After the ordeal was over, everyone was gathered by what was left of the lumber pile and talking. I was fascinated by the tobacco chewing truck driver who could squirt tobacco juice a good twenty feet.

I remember my dad saying that the fire may have been started accidently. Maybe from a cigarette butt. He didn't smoke, and, of course, I didn't either.

After all was calmed down and the truck was leaving, a pickup truck pulled in and drove up to us. A big guy got out and began cussing at my dad. He was the farmer who owned the field we just burned up.

My dad just stood there and took the verbal abuse. He must have thought he had it coming but if I would have still had my board, I would have certainly launched an attack.

It was a quiet ride home with our trailer load of lumber; our faces all blackened, our hair singed, and our clothes scorched, and smelling like beef jerky.

The only words spoken were by my dad as we neared our driveway and they were, "DON'T TELL YER MA." And I never did, at least until now.

Until that day, I wanted to be a fireman. After that, being a cowboy sounded much more appealing. I tried that too, but that's another story.

Canned Venison and Model A's
By Jack Hitchcock of Stoughton, Wisconsin
Born 1932

I was born in August of 1932, in Alma, Michigan. I was fortunate to have great parents and a wonderful family. We were raised to respect others, and to be honest and self-reliant. I was the sixth child of seven kids, so the older brothers and sisters helped to guide our young lives.

When my two older brothers left for the Second World War, this left me with many of their chores. For instance, keeping the fires

Jack and his wife, Grace sitting on the running board of his 1930 Model A Ford

going in the old Holland furnace. I put many tons of coal through that beast. Going down to the basement, poorly lit with a 40-watt light bulb, rather spooked me out for a long time. I did the hoeing of the garden, mowed the lawn with the manual push mower, and learned to earn my own money. I worked at doing janitor jobs like mopping floors in a photo studio on Saturdays. I would sweep the floor at the Greyhound bus station and run various errands to the warehouse for items for the manager who ran the station. His name was Frank Bishop and he had lost a leg in World War I. One day while sweeping the floors, I found a dime. He said if it was on his side of the counter, it was his. If it was on the other side, it was mine. I thought then what a fair and good man he was. I also set pins at the bowling alley and shined shoes at the taxicab station. Sometimes, I was asked to watch the business and sell ice at the icehouse, which was just down the street from us at the Pine River. It was hard lifting the fifty-pound blocks of ice to be placed on the bumpers of Model A Fords and other such cars that had extended bumpers. I often wondered if they made it home without melting most of it. I sold Alma Record newspapers on the streets and in taverns of Alma every Thursday after school. Before the war, my older brother and I gathered scrap metal and newspapers to sell at the scrapyard. We brought along some gunny bags and on the way home, we would fill the bags with corncobs from the mill. We then would sell them in the neighborhood for fire starters. Just another way to earn our spending money.

Thursday nights were quite special. The Masonic Home would allow some of us, if we were well behaved, to see the movie shown for the old folks residents of the Home.

During the Depression, my parents lost the house where I was born, and we always rented after that. We lived in three different houses on the same block. Living only one blocks from the Pine River, it naturally became our playground. We were either in it or on it every chance we had. I can't remember when I first learned to swim so I must have been very young. Life was not all work. We entertained ourselves mostly outdoors. We made our kites out of newspapers and split sticks. We swam in the river, played under the streetlight until we were called in at bedtime. We played kick the can, hide and seek, and made up games without names. We made our toy guns from sticks of wood for playing cowboys and Indians. Our house was next to the lumberyard building and it was fun to sneak in there when they were not working and play on the lumber piles. We did a lot of idiotic and dangerous things but we never got seriously hurt.

In my early childhood, we didn't have a refrigerator but rather an icebox; no telephone; no TV, but a squawky old radio. There was no water heater for bathing so we heated water in a washtub on the kitchen stove. There were no heaters in cars, no automatic transmissions, only clutch shift cars. No fast food shops, no power mowers, only wringer type washing machines, no clothes dryers; clothes were dried on the clothesline outdoors. I saw only steam driven trains until I was sixteen years old. I had not ridden an elevator or even saw one until I was fifteen years old. We didn't have a water heater until I was a teenager. My mother canned about everything we could

Jack's 1929 Model A Cabriolet

grow or buy cheaply in quantity, in glass Mason jars. She canned deer meat that my dad would get during deer season. Many of the factories would shut down for the first week of the deer season. This was a very popular event in those days. Canned venison was very good and we had it often all year long.

During the Second World War, everyone was involved in some way. The government furnished ration stamps to each family. In order to buy most everything, you had to have these stamps. For gasoline, fuel oil, shoes, meat, tires, etc. There was a shortage of many things. I remember I became so hungry for bananas and real ice cream. Everything went for the war effort. Even as a kid, I understood and gladly did what we needed to do.

When the war was finally over, I headed uptown because I knew there would be a celebration. On my way, a man came out of his gas station and said, "Hey kid. I'll give you 25cents if you ring my bell." This bell was about the size of a church bell. I rang that bell for a solid half hour until my ears rang. It was a wonderful celebration all over the town. The main street was packed with people cheering and having a lot of fun. When I got home that evening, I asked my dad what will the newspapers write about now, and will they go out of business. He had a good laugh about that. War news was all I remember hearing about on the radio and read in the papers. My brothers and brothers-in-law and uncles all came home safely. What a wonderful time to be living.

I learned to drive a car at the age of thirteen. I learned on a 1937 Hudson Teraplane that had been hit by a train. My dad made it into a pickup truck. It was probably the ugliest vehicle in town and I was quite ashamed to be seen in it, but it was all we had during the war, as any car was very hard to get. I got my driver's license when I was fourteen years old, which is unheard of today. This came in handy when I helped my dad in his painting and concrete construction business.

On April 12, 1945, I wanted to be the first kid in the neighborhood to go swimming, a bragging right for any kid. Coming back from the river with my hair still wet, I saw my mother running out the back door of our house. I thought she was coming after me to give me a scolding for going in the river so early in the spring. She was so upset over

hearing of President Roosevelt passing away that I guess she wanted to cry to me about it. I didn't like him dying either, but I was glad she hadn't noticed my wet hair.

When I was sixteen years old, I bought a used double-barreled shotgun at the sporting goods store downtown. I walked down the main street without a case for it and I didn't get so much as a raised eyebrow. That's how innocent a time it was in my youth.

In 1950, I got a job at the Ford dealership in their body shop. I was just entering my senior year of high school. My job was sanding cars and prepping before my boss would paint them. I bought my first car there. It was a 1930 Model A Ford, and I paid $63 for it. Model A's have been, and still are, one of my primary interests in life. I have restored many of these cars over my adult life, but I only have one of these cars left to enjoy. I really have used what I learned from my good boss at the body shop.

I left the body shop in October 1951, when I enlisted in the US Air Force. The Air Force put me through aircraft and engine school and then jet engine specialist school. Afterward, I entered a fighter squadron at Truax Field in Madison, Wisconsin. I married Grace, a Madison girl, in 1953, and live in the area to this day, and with the same woman, too.

Green Grass and Blue Skies
By Louraine T. Latty of Saginaw, Michigan
Born 1941

I guess one of my fondest memories is of going out to our garden and picking cucumber, tomato or even pulling a carrot, wiping it on the grass or going to the pump outside and rinsing it off and eating it fresh. The taste was so different back then. We used natural fertilizer, the peels of what we had grown in the garden went right back in.

We rented a house on a farm back in 1956. There was an outdoor toilet, no central heat and a stove that burned coal and wood. A few years later, my dad purchased a kerosene stove, and it had an oven. We bathed in a large galvanized tub, pumping the water in a galvanized pale (no plastic), heating it on the kitchen stove either with wood or corncobs. The kerosene was saved for use in the kerosene stove and only for baking and general cooking. There were five of us kids, and you didn't throw out the water. It went from the oldest to the youngest or the other way around.

We went to a one-room school with only one teacher. It was kindergarten to 12th grade. Also, the school had an outhouse and a pump to wash your hands. It was fun, though the older kids were few, especially the boys because they would quit school at 16 and go to work. Those were the elementary grades. I remember going to a couple of one-room schools from 1946 to about 1952. In middle school, we rode a bus and also in high school. To the fact that we lived outside of a small town, Merrill, Michigan, the bus ride was long. High school did not have a parking lot for students, as only one or two drove a car. We had no vending machines in school. We didn't have a cafeteria; most students would bring their lunch. I worked collecting lunch money from the kids who ate in the cafeteria, so I got a free lunch ticket.

The major difference in school came in 1958, when the school went from manual typewriters to electric. That, at the time, was high technology.

I remember the first time, in 1953, when I went with my mother and dad to a grocery store for the winter months. There wasn't any prepackaged food like meat. You still went to the meat counter to order your meats. We got gingersnaps in a brown bag. I never handled money back then, so I never really paid much attention to the prices. And I was like 12 years old when I went to the grocery store for the first time.

Something that really puts me to thinking is the way we met people back in the good old days. The people you knew were mostly relatives, kids in school and church. When I graduated in 1959, most of the guys and gals knew each other from school and ended up getting married. I met my husband on a blind date through a coworker, but we never would have dreamed of online dating.

In 1960, I applied for a job at our local telephone company. I was interviewed and hired. I was trained as a long-distance operator and ship to shore. Today, I suppose that would be equivalent to an IT person hired for Internet service. We wore headsets with attached mouthpieces. We used cords with a metal attachment to plug into service actions,

so we would connect the caller to the person being called. A director on the job trained us all. We were whom you would get when you dialed "0." At each station, there was a clock. You would stamp the call card; and when they hung up, you'd stamp again. That's what gave you how long the call was. Many people, mostly companies, would have the operator call them and tell them the price of that call. Ship to shore was calls made from a ship bringing cargo deliveries through Lake Huron to companies that could only be reached by a river off the lake.

When you lived in the country, there were no close neighbors. Your playmates were your siblings, and your mom handled any squabbles. Back then, it was rare not to have a mother home all day. Chores first, no backtalk or you got the what fore. That then was told to dad when he got home. And depending on what you did, the what fore could be from extra chores too early to-bed or a spanking, if what you did was really bad. I remember my older brother stole some apples from a farmer's apple tree. The farmer came over to tell dad; when the farmer left, my brother got a spanking. It was a leather strap on a wooden handle. Just looking at it made you scared to do anything wrong.

My younger sister was a grade behind me, but we had study hall together in school. In study hall, the boys seemed to have a harder time paying attention to what they were there for, like getting homework done. A couple of boys started to tease my sister, and my sister having gotten up and moved, decided enough was enough. She then went into the library, got a large thick book and came back to the study hall; she proceeded to smack both of the boys on the head with the book. They all were sent to the principal's office. My sister was sent back to study hall after her explanation of what happened. The two boys had to sit in the office and write, "I will not pester another student."

I never realized, until I started thinking about it now that we were poor growing up. We had no running water, an outhouse, no refrigerator, no phone (until I was 19 years old), one pair of shoes and only three outfits. But, I think we didn't even notice we were poor. So many were in the same position.

Back in my childhood days, I think we seen a lot more green grass and blue skies.

Christmas 1936
By Reva Swanson of Grand Ledge, Michigan
Born 1928

Mama made Christmas out of nothing in 1936. That's what we had…nothing. Daddy was out of work, and we were in the middle of The Depression. He was a furniture upholsterer, and most people were in the same boat…little or no money. Daddy had his own shop in Grand Rapids. But in 1933, he realized that to make a living for his family, he needed something besides his upholstery business. So, we moved to a small town on the west side of Michigan, where he had 40 acres and could raise some potatoes, other vegetables and have a cow and chickens. There were even a few old apple trees.

The house had three bedrooms upstairs and one down. That was enough room for six kids. The only difference between our family and the Dionne quintuplets was that Mama had her kids one at a time. There was a large kitchen with a wood-fueled cook stove and a potbelly stove in the living room. We had no electricity and no running water. All us kids had chores to do, ranging from chopping and carrying in wood for both stoves to carrying water uphill from the well; gathering eggs; milking the cow; making beds; setting the table; doing the dishes; and when we got older, learning to cook and sew.

The living room contained Daddy's workshop tools, his sawhorses, his treadle sewing machine, and a workbench. So, I guess it's good we didn't have much living room furniture.

Mama's boon and blessing was her treadle Singer Sewing Machine, which was in one corner of the kitchen. My aunt, who was Mama's sister, was always on the lookout for something Mama could make over or tear up for carpet rags. We had bare floors, but Mama could work wonders with her crochet book. To get dressed on a chilly morning, we had a rug by the bed we could step on and then over to the register, where the heat was coming up. Daddy had lots of upholstery samples, which she sewed into quilts for

our beds. They weren't filled with down, but they were heavy enough to keep us warm. We never turned over once we got in bed, from the sheer weight of the quilt on top.

Early that winter, we had a fire in the chimney from an overheated stove and daddy spent the last of his money to get the roof fixed after the fire.

Children nowadays see what they want for Christmas by watching the TV ads. We had the Sears catalog, which had every kind of toy and the price. We four girls took turns thumbing through the pages, looking at the beautiful dolls. Mama warned us not to get our hopes up too much because we didn't have much money. And, we knew about Santa Claus because we had listened through the floor register in our bedroom directly over the living room.

Mama was a good cook and always made our own bread; she did a lot of canning and could stretch a meal to feed another mouth if our old friend, Mr. Stubbs, should happen by one evening.

It was after Thanksgiving, and daddy was down to his last $0.50. It was a toss-up whether he filled the car with gas to go looking for work or gave the money to Mama for flour and yeast to make bread. He opted for the gas and set off to Scottville, a town nearby, to ring doorbells and ask for upholstery work. God must have been listening to our prayers. There just happened to be an old lady who had a chair she needed done and wanted to get it fixed as a Christmas present for her husband. Daddy

Reva's parents, Florence and Harry Mearett with their children

128

brought the chair home in his trailer, which advertised "Merritt's Upholstery Shop" on the side. When the chair was done, daddy took it back to Scottville, and mama went with him. We older children babysat the younger ones. Daddy had earned $10 to do their Christmas shopping.

Just before Thanksgiving, all our dolls disappeared. And when we asked Mama as to their whereabouts, she acted mysterious and couldn't give us a straight answer.

The Sunday before Christmas was the kids' program at the little Methodist church in town. My sister, Ruth, and I were chosen with other children our age to sing "Silver Bells" and some others said their pieces. When the program was over, Santa Claus came down the aisle of the church ho ho ho-ing, and passing out little boxes of candy that had handles like little suitcases. Each child had his or her very own box of candy.

Daddy went to the woods and cut down a pine tree to put in the living room. We made paper chains and other ornaments to hang on the tree, along with some icicles mama had saved from previous Christmases. The tree looked great.

Christmas morning, we scurried into our clothes and hurried downstairs as fast as we could. Mama declared we had to eat our breakfast first, so we gobbled it down as fast as possible to get to our presents.

The upholstery shop had been converted to a living room with the tools and sawhorses put away, and the tree stood in the corner with toys and gifts for everyone. There was a pair of skates for brother Bob, who was 13. The skates were not new, but they were in very good condition. Jack, who was four, got a sled that had a shiny new coat of paint. There were dolls for all four girls. Amazing! They looked just like our old dolls, but they had bright, shiny, clean faces and new dresses. There were oranges for each of us, which were a real treat. Mama made us all mittens and hats with her crochet hook. My aunt had sent us all some little gifts. I received a book, "A Child's Garden of Verses and Quotes" by Robert Louis Stevenson. She knew how I love to read.

What a wonderful Christmas! We had food on the table; toys to play with; a roof over our heads; warm beds to sleep in; and the love of our parents. The best part was none of it had to come from the Sears catalog.

Life Was Grand and Simpler
By Martha Schoolcraft of Greenville, Michigan
Born 1937

Have you ever climbed a telephone pole? It is quite an adventure if you keep your eyes on the pole! I don't think the current poles even have the metal "climbers."

We didn't have computers, iPhones, etc., so we played outdoors. After dinner was over, if our parents didn't need anything from us we went out the door. No one told us when we had to be in, as we already knew it was "when the street lights come on." We didn't worry about strangers accosting us; we simply played with our neighbors. We played all sorts of games: tag, hide and go seek, kick the can, and hopscotch, as well as had bike races. Sometimes we even climbed on our garage roofs. Our roof was very close to our neighbor's so we'd jump back and forth between the two.

We didn't have dishwashers, so our stay-at-home mothers were busy with such chores. Dad was probably in the living room reading the paper. Mother also had to deal with a wringer wash machine. Water had to be heated, then a rinse water prepared, all went through the wringer, and then she had to carry the load out to the clothesline to dry. What a chore!

Now and then, we would go down to our nearby elementary school and play on the equipment: teeter-totters, monkey bars, and merry-go-rounds. Fun! A neighborhood boy once gave me his ring. I guess it was supposed to mean we were going steady. I can't remember how old I was, but soon after, I went to the school and hung upside down on the monkey bars. The ring escaped from my pocket, never to be seen again. I guess I was too young for such things.

We had a primitive cottage (more work for Mother). It was on a lake, and we spent the summers there. The only bathroom we had was an outhouse some distance from the house, so during the night we used chamber pots. We had to empty our own, I'm sure! We had no hot running water, so we had to heat the water for dishes, etc. We were in the lake almost every minute of the day and had to pull the bloodsuckers off our legs when we got to the dock. I read a lot that summer in a hammock and remember once having a snake curled happily on my stomach. He was a little one!

The cottage and our house also had iceboxes. We had no refrigerators. The iceman stopped in front of our house with his truckload of ice. The ice was protected by a large rubber curtain hanging over the back opening of the truck. This served to protect the ice from the heat and road dirt. He'd hop out, grab his tongs, and take a block of ice into the house. Maybe you've still heard your grandma or great-grandma call her refrigerator the icebox. They worked well!

Every morning after breakfast, we'd line up so Mother could give us our teaspoon of cod liver oil. It tasted awful, but I imagine it kept away some health problems. Our doctors were good but didn't have all the antibiotics and things that we do now. The doctors then were even known to make house calls! My mother-in-law was at our house once and became very ill. It was two o'clock in the morning, and our doctor had never seen her, but I called him anyway. He came right away in the dark and made sure that she was all right.

We didn't have television either, so we would lie on the floor in front of the radio and color. We listened to *The Shadow*, *Sgt. Preston of the Yukon*, and *The Lone Ranger*, to name a few. If we wanted to see TV, we had to walk into town and watch through the window of the hardware store. My dad soon began to talk about getting a television. The picture was small and black and white. So one day as we walked home from school, we heard the turning of a TV antenna on our roof. Needless to say, we ran the rest of the way. Most of the pictures were test patterns, which came on in the evening. Daytime had very few programs, but we loved it all.

Telephones were hard to use. There were party lines where another family shared your line, and when you picked the receiver up to make a call, you could hear them talking. Some people loved to listen in and others minded their manners and hung up! There was an operator who knew everyone's phone number, and she could put you right through to your party if the line was clear.

Life then was grand and much simpler than now. But today has its fabulous inventions and life-saving miracles. Always enjoy where you are and what you have. Life is short, and you'll want to enjoy every minute.

Growing Up on Peeler Street
By Bertha Cross of Blanchard, Michigan
Born 1938

I was born on Sunday, September 10, 1938. I lived all of my first eighteen years at Peeler Street, which is now gone. We never thought about whether we were rich or poor, because everyone on Peeler Street was about the same.

We had no running water and no electricity. We had an outhouse, as did everyone on our street. As always, the *Sears and Roebuck Catalog* was not very soft. We had a pump in the back room where we would carry water for Mom and fill the reservoir, which was on the old cook stove. That way she always had hot water when needed. Grandpa also used that back room for keeping watermelon and other things cold.

Bertha in the backyard

130

I can still see the beautiful roses that Grandpa raised and the plum tree in the front yard, the hibiscus, the plants, and other flowers. Of course, we cannot forget the catalpa tree outside Grandpa's bedroom.

I remember when Grandpa was going to watch me and my younger brother. Well, my brother wanted to play cowboys and Indians. I was the cowboy. Well, he tied me to the big tree and left me. I guess something else caught his interest, because I had to wake a very unhappy Grandpa to release me.

We had an icebox in the kitchen where Mom would get fifty pounds of ice when the iceman came by. It was our job to empty the pan under the icebox, and if we forgot, well, it wasn't a happy sight.

I remember when Mama was ironing we used to sit in front of the ironing board and listen to her sing. She had a beautiful voice. One particular April Fool's Day we kept trying to catch Mom on a joke, but she was too smart. But then the man way behind us had a cow, and it got loose. So we went to tell Mom. Of course, she did not believe us. It took us about ten minutes to make her come and see. At that time, the man was coming for his cow. Mom had a big smile on her face and said, "You got me after all."

We grew up in a two bedroom house with a grandpa, mom, dad, four girls, and one brother. It never seemed crowded when it came bedtime. Every morning in the winter time, the first thing we did was to take a spoonful of onion syrup, and we never had colds.

The winter time was especially wonderful when all the kids on our street came to the hill across from our house. There was cardboard pieces. No one had a sled; they cost too much money. We made or own fun. After sledding, we would make snow angels and play duck, duck, and goose. After we got tired, we would go home to a big potbelly stove in the living room. Sometimes if Dad put too much coal in it, it would turn red hot. Now that was hot.

In the summer, there was an old man with a horse cart out selling his fresh vegetables. We would beg Mom for a nickel so we could buy a small watermelon, which we shared. It was sweet and delicious.

Mom would go downtown on Fridays and would come back with a bag of popcorn and a big pile of comic books. My favorite was *Archie*. Then she would return them when we were done and get us some more the next week.

I can remember when Dad called us outside to see the big airplanes in formation flying across the sky. Dad said they must be going to Japan. It was a sight that I will never forget.

There are so many great memories I just can't write them down. It would probably take a year.

Chasing Chickens, Cinder Scars, and Teen Slang
By Luann L. Ludwick of Mesa, Arizona
Born 1941

I grew up for the most part in St. Louis, Michigan. My grandparents lived in Mt. Pleasant, Michigan and in St. Louis. I remember visiting my grandparents in Mt. Pleasant in the summers. Grandma had an old wringer washer with a scrub board, and she hung clothes on the line to dry, holding the line up with a stick so the clothes didn't drag the ground. My favorite memories of her were chasing chickens around the barnyard on a Sunday to cook for Sunday dinner. She would wring their necks and then chop them off, and we would dunk them in a bucket of boiling water and pluck the pinfeathers. They were terrible smelling but gosh, those were the best chickens ever.

Luann's Grandma Brondstetter in 1958

Grandpa was crippled and bedridden, so I spent many a day on his bed listening to the Detroit Tigers on the radio with him. That is where I got my love of baseball. He used to tell the best stories. We didn't have television yet, so those times were so precious to me.

Summers there are a special memory for me, because that was where my cousins and I would play in the barn. We would swing on the pulleys from one haymow to the next, fish in the pond, and help Grandma in her garden. The neighbor boy would come over, and he taught me how to ride a horse bareback. What wonderful memories.

My grandfather in St. Louis was a mailman and a wonderful man. He always had candy for the kids on his route and whistled as he walked his route. He truly was the old fashioned mailman who walked the route and knew everyone in town. He loved his flower gardens and had many. I got in trouble when I was four, because I picked my mom a bouquet of tulips; I picked the tops off every one. He was pretty upset. My great-granddad (his father) was a bee keeper. Oh wow, that honey was so good in the comb.

I remember the old candlestick telephone at their house with the ringer on the wall. It was a party line, and the ring at their house was one long and two short. Grandma was a bit nosey and used to listen in on other people's conversations.

When the war broke out, Dad joined the Navy, so my mom and I went to live with my grandparents in Mt. Pleasant. I remember Mom helping my grandparents with cooking,

Luann with her dad, Fred Sigourney in 1946

cleaning, and laundry. When Mom did her ironing, so did I on a little ironing board. I remember clearly "shopping" in the cupboards and my mom and grandma checking me out at the counter.

I remember my great-grandma slept in the bedroom downstairs in the room behind the potbellied stove. Every morning my mom and grandma got her up and ready for the day. She had long white hair that touched the floor, and they would braid her hair in one long braid and then coil it around to make a bun on top of her head.

Grandma had an old cook stove in the kitchen where all the meals were made. That thing was huge, and she baked some of the best baked goods around. There was an old icebox on the back porch that had to have these big chunks of ice put in it to keep the food cold. She had a big garden out back and canned everything she could to keep all of us fed. Grandma had an old treadle sewing machine and made the best clothes ever.

It was nothing for someone to come in the middle of the night to get Grandma to go deliver a baby. She delivered a lot of babies back then. I sometimes think that might be why I had the desire to become a nurse. My grandpa's brother was a doctor and built the first hospital in Mt. Pleasant, which still stands. My grandpa's sister had a son who became a doctor and built a clinic in Mt. Pleasant, which still employs a lot of people today. He was the one who delivered me when

Luann and her mother, Arlene Brondstetter Sigourney in 1946

I was born.

My cousin and I got in all kinds of trouble when we were young. We would fetch Grandma's canned good out of the old cellar. It had those doors that opened outside, and we would sneak down and get what we wanted, eat some, and make mud cakes and pies with the rest. Of course, then we had to go get a switch off the lilac bush to get our switching for getting into things we shouldn't.

We used to help Grandma slop the hogs, milk the cows, clean the rabbit pens, gather eggs, and feed the chickens and the rest of the farm animals. I can remember walking way out behind the barn to the pasture and shooing the cows back up to the barn. Cow pie was warm gushing up between my toes on the way back.

The day Dad came home from the Navy was a wonderful, joyous day. Mom and Dad were so excited that I got crushed between the two of them. Mom was swatting flies, and when she saw Dad she screamed and threw her hands up in the air, and the flyswatter landed behind the stove. We all had a good laugh about that.

We moved back to St. Louis. I started school at Michigan Avenue Elementary School. I couldn't figure out why the kids cried when their moms left them. I thought it was a great adventure. We had a sandbox right in the classroom.

I remember walking to school in snow up to my behind. It was cold, and it seemed like I always had chapped lips. I don't care for cold weather now. We didn't have cafeterias, so we brown bagged our lunches. We had great lunches. I remember an old lady who used to look out for me on my way to and from school (it was a mile from our house to the school), and she would invite me in for cookies and hot chocolate. I remember when they opened the swimming pool in town, and I would spend as much time as allowed there. I had chores and homework that always had to be done before any TV, reading books, swimming playing outside, etc.

I was a good kid; I knew if I got in trouble at school that it would be a whole lot worse when I got home, so I behaved in school. It also helped that I had seen the rubber hose that the principal used on the "bad" kids. I really didn't have a favorite teacher, because I really loved school and I liked all my classes.

I cried when it was time to graduate. I knew that I would miss all my friends and teachers.

Dad built us a house right next to my St. Louis grandparents. I had my own room, finally. I remember the first Christmas there. We were on our way to church for services, and Dad said if I watched the moon, I would see Santa. I watched all the way into town, and I swear to this day that I really saw him. I also remember sitting on Santa's lap and asking why he had pants like my dad and why his ring was the same as my dad's.

I was fascinated with my grandparents' records and record player. They had an old Victrola that you had to wind up with a lever on the side, and it had a big bell speaker on it. Grandma had colored 78 records. I remember one was named *Blue Skies*. I couldn't play it unless they played it for me. Thanksgiving was always fun at their house, because we ate a big turkey dinner with all the trimmings, and then watched the Lions play football. This was, of course, after they got a television.

I grew up with pets. We had almost every kind of dog imaginable, and my mom kept every stray cat that came her way. We raised German shepherds. When I was little, we had an American bulldog named Topsy.

Dad drove a 1950 Ford. I remember that car, because it was the only one we had. I don't remember what he had in the forties. I remember my grandparents had a Studebaker. It was pink and had a split back window, and I really remember the door, because I got my finger caught in the door. They kept yelling for me to come inside, and I told them I couldn't because my finger was in the door. I still have the scar.

Speaking of scars, I still have a cinder scar in my knee from running up the driveway at my other grandparents' house and tripping and falling. They always threw the cinders from the furnace in the driveway. They were called clinkers.

When I was ten, I got a Schwinn bike for my birthday. I rode that bike all over town. On Saturdays and Sundays after church I rode to the Gem Theater and watched movies; westerns on Saturdays and romance movies on Sundays. It was a grand time. I later got a job as the usher and snack girl.

My first job was as a soda jerk at the local drug store counter. That was fun for a while, because the owner let me eat all the ice cream

Bob and Luann Ludwick in 1959

I wanted. To this day, I don't much like ice cream. My second job was as a carhop at the drive-in restaurant in town. The third job was the movie theater job.

We used to listen to *The Shadow* and *Luigi* on the radio. Then after television arrived, it was a little tiny round screen in a big square cabinet that only got three stations on a good day. It came on at daylight and went off at dark. We watched Roy Rogers, Gene Autry, Sky King, *Howdy Doody*, *Leave it to Beaver*, and *Lights Out*.

My first boyfriend let me ask him to the Sadie Hawkins dance. From then on, we went steady. He had a '46 Mercury that was robin egg blue and had glass packs. It was hot. We would go to the drive-in movies, fishing the river by his house, to mixer dances after the games, and hang out at the Conery, the local teen hangout. Elvis was hot then, and we would dance to his music. It was while I was in high school that St. Louis was put on the map! We were named the Middle of the Mitten, and the sign is in the park in front of the high school.

I had a lot of girlfriends; we had parties, mixed when our parents would let us, or just pajama parties. We played 45 records on the record player: Elvis, Rick Nelson, The Big Bopper, Ritchie Valens, and too many more to mention were our choice of music. In the summer time, I would invite one or two friends at a time to go to the cottage at Higgins Lake. My grandparents had a cottage there. That was a fun time, swimming and meeting new friends. Oh my, the movie *Peyton Place* was popular, and parents weren't too keen on us going to see it. Some of our slang was: cool man, keen, guy, boppin' to the tunes, etc.

When I met my future husband, I was introduced to the old outhouse. His parents had a cabin on Rock Lake without indoor plumbing. I learned to water ski out there. We eventually ended up inheriting it along with his sisters and brother. We had some great times there as well.

Well, these are some of my memories about growing up in Michigan. I no longer live there, but I have a lot of wonderful memories.

Snowed In
By Virginia Showalter of Mt. Pleasant,
Michigan
Born 1926

My dad and mom, Oscar and Maye Curtiss, had a farm, which my dad worked on. He had horses, which he used to work the farm. He had cows and sheep and pigs and chickens—just a regular farm. I believe it was about in the fall of 1935 or the spring of 1936 when we had to walk a mile and a quarter to school. It was Gilmore Road that they lived on and we walked a quarter mile on Gilmore Road to Pleasant Valley Road where the Delo School was located one mile away. We walked one mile on Pleasant Valley Road, and I don't remember what the weather was that morning, but during the day it was snowing and the wind blew—a real blizzard. My dad brought one of the horses to school to get us home. My brother Stanley and I and Eugene, Donna, Rich Curtis who lived across the road from us all rode home on the horse's back. What fun we had because we were snowed in for several days! The kids who came from the other way were snowed in at Gerald Fuller's and Len Booth's place. I'm so glad for my dad and his horse. Thinking back, those were the best days of our lives!

Pork Fries
By Hayes J. Mack of Saginaw, Michigan
Born 1933

Bazley's Meat Market was located on Genesee Street in Saginaw. The market was a long, narrow store. The meat counter was also long and narrow and went into an L shape at the back of the store as you went along. When you first walk in, you have your cold cuts, and then it went on from there, the different types and cuts of meat you could get.

One fine Saturday afternoon my wife and I went to do our shopping. She was walking along looking at all the different things that she might want to buy. As she reached the back of the store, she saw something that intrigued her, only she had no idea what it was. I was still at the front of the store looking at the cold cuts. Since we were so far apart, she decided to yell across the store, "Hayes, What are pork fries?" Everyone in the store started laughing. I yelled back to tell her, "I'll tell you later." She was so embarrassed when we got in the car and I told her they were pig testicles.

Hitchhiking Mishap
By Donald E. Elliott of Saginaw, Michigan
Born 1929

I'm in my eighties and I would like to tell you about the incident that happened to me and my pals when we were kids in our teens.

World War II was on and as you would know, there was rationing and scarcity of everything.

I lived and grew up in Bridgeport and when we earned enough we would hitchhike to town to see a movie at The Center or Mecca Theatre.

It cost a dime. You could enjoy two full features, a comedy, and the news and a serial. Then we would walk back to the edge of town to hitchhike back to Bridgeport.

On this particular day we all were standing on the side of the road just pass the fairground entrance hitchhiking when a young woman stopped her car, and we ran and opened the doors and jumped in and the woman started screaming at us and yelling at us to get out. We were all confused and wondering what was going on, then she yelled, "I live here and you kids are blocking my driveway and I just wanted to drive in and couldn't because your blocking the way!"

We all piled out red faced and laughing our heads off. We eventually got a ride back to Bridgeport.

There are hundreds of incidents that have happened in my years growing up, but that incident still brings a smile to my face.

I and one other pal is still around, all my other buddies have passed on. The 1940s will always be in my mind. There was more kindness, and caring then, because we were in a terrible war and everyone helped each other.

I hope my little incident brings a smile to everyone who reads this.

Pay It Forward
By Robert A. Bellomo of Canadian Lakes,
Michigan
Born 1945

We arrived to our winter five-month retreat in Sebring, Florida. When you rent you have to buy and bring everything you will need, clothes, and all your toys. The biggest expense is going to be buying all your groceries. We made our purchases at Waymart's and tried paying for our items with our Visa. Traveling away from our home in Michigan confused our charge in Florida and it got rejected. We tried to call the Visa office but could not get through to clear the issue.

With a $500 bill to pay, we did not have enough cash to cover it. Having some of it plus the ATM machine, for a limit of two hundred dollars still left us short about one hundred and fifty dollars. A young man was standing by the machine, and saw our dilemma and offered to loan us the rest. Our place was too far to go home for the money and the frozen groceries would never survive. So I took his offer. All he asked me for was a phone number. Promising to return in about twenty minutes with his money, he agreed.

Mary Beth and I drove home. I had the cash there so I returned to the store. I met the young man and handed him one hundred and eighty dollars. He tried to refuse the extra twenty dollars but I insisted he take it and thanked him for being so trustful.

The bank manager witnessed the whole

episode and commented what an outstanding young men he was. Since then I have helped a number of elders at the checkout line, who had to return items because they lacked the cash to pay for them. Great feeling to help others in need.

Ice Cream Lard
By Esther A. Mack of Saginaw, Michigan
Born 1937

I was a waitress at Doyles. It was a hamburger joint/car hop type of restaurant on Genesee Street by Niagra in Saginaw along the river. This was the only restaurant around that served a scrambled hamburger. To this day, I don't remember another restaurant that served scrambled hamburgers. They had a lot of truckers that would come in to eat also.

At ten p.m. every night, they had a lady come in to make fresh donuts. I was a second shift worker. One night while I was working, I walked back in her area to get something. I noticed a big medal bowl sitting on the counter full of ice cream. It looked so good. I grabbed a spoon out of the silverware bin, shoved it into the ice cream filling the spoon as full as I could get it all the while thinking how good it was going to taste. My mouth was watering as I shoveled it in. Imagine my surprise when I popped the heaping spoonful into my mouth only to discover it was lard.

I ran to the nearest trashcan gagging all the way and spit it out. All I could taste for the rest of the night was lard. Needless to say, I didn't do any more sampling unless I asked what it was from there on out.

The Snake
By Winnona Evanauski of Holton, Michigan
Born 1943

I was raised in my great grandparent's family home in Holton, Michigan in Muskegon County with my parents, sister, three brothers, and my paternal grandparents. Before my birth, our homestead had been a very productive one hundred sixty acre farm

Winnona (Marvin) Evanauski and her brother, Paul Marvin

for many years.

When I was about twelve years old, nearly sixty years ago, on a bright, sunny, and very warm summer day. I decided to bake a blackberry pie for supper. So I made the short trek, about one eighth of a mile on the well-worn path out to pick the berries, real large "black caps" in our small but abundantly producing berry patch and our dog, Rex came along with me.

When we were almost there I saw a big Blue Racer Snake just up ahead of us. Now I cannot stand snakes, not even to look at them! Before I could take another step that snake stood right up as if it had legs and was really hissing and at its full length looked about four feet long. Well, I screamed and took off running back to the house and Rex took off after the snake.

Of course, there was no pie baked that day and it took me two to three weeks before I ventured out to the berry patch again.

I had some people who would not believe me about the snake "standing up" but I know it did and I have never forgotten the sight of it and the fear I felt. I never did know if Rex got it or if it got away, but I was sure glad to have Rex go with me whenever I made any trips out to the berry patch.

136

Christmastime Excitement
By Jerry J. Konopnicki of Coleman,
Michigan
Born 1946

When I was a young boy, I use to love listening to stories my dad would tell about growing up during the Great Depression. He was one of ten children from a rural family. Back then, there weren't any food stamps or welfare of any kind. Yet, they made it through and did well in life. Here is a Christmas story my dad told that always reminds me of how things have changed and how grateful we should be. This story is branded in my memory and in my dad's own words, the way he told it. Here it is:

In the days before Christmas, we put up a tree. We would decorate it with a few homemade ornaments and popcorn. Mom would yell because we were always eating the popcorn off the tree. The day before Christmas, Paw hitched the horse to the buggy and was going into town. He wouldn't let any of us go with him, and so we all assumed he was going to get us something for Christmas. In anticipation, we all hung up our socks. Now here's something I want you to understand. My paw didn't have a nickel, and when I say he didn't have a nickel, I mean he didn't have a nickel. Back then, there was a lot of bartering going on. You would take produce, eggs, or something of value and trade for something you needed.

Ma had gotten up early Christmas morning and had the woodstove glowing. The old farmhouse was toasty. Us kids all woke up about the same time and rushed downstairs. We didn't expect much, but the excitement was still there. In each of our socks, there were some peppermint candies. We thought we had the world by the ass!

My Dad: An Inspiration
By Keith A. Humbert of Midland, Michigan
Born 1923

I was born on the 17th of January 1923. Good ol' Dad was, and is, my hero! He was lacking in education and only had grade school, but was well read, smart, and loving.

He lived by these rules: You can lose your health or wealth and recover, but once you lose your good name, it is gone! There is no future in unskilled help. As good as you are, and as bad as I am, I'm as good as you are as bad as I am. Bad and good, we're really talking about equality. Like our Constitution, all men are created equal.

He also believed in work. This was during the depression; any legal work was honest work. Dad knew firsthand about unskilled help. He took an honorable job that paid and almost living wage. Not all people should go to college. We need all kinds of skilled professions that give satisfaction while providing a good wage. I have a degree in engineering. Two of my children have master's degrees. The third is a paralegal. They are all happily married and retired. The four grandkids all have degrees and three have children. Quite a legacy for a man with no real education! My two brothers did well also.

Dad was well read, up on current events, had a connoisseurity about the world. My fondest memory was setting on Dad's lap while he read Robin Hood, Kidnapped, Robinson Crusoe, and other children's books. I did the same with my children. Without his guidance, I doubt that I could have earned my degree in engineering (when I met my wonderful wife of 68 years!) When Dad was dying of cancer, I wrote him and thanked him for being the father he was. This world is a better world because of him: a real man with a lowly job as a custodian, but he left a great legacy.

The Good Old Days
By Barbara Ann Bell of Saginaw, Michigan
Born 1930

We had a potbellied stove to heat the house, it was in the dining room of our house, and it was metal and burned wood and coal.

We had no running water in our house, we had a pump in the backyard, and we had to pump water for cooking, drinking, and washing. We also had what we called a cistern in the backyard beside the house on the ground, where rainwater collected, we could use that water to wash clothes, and for our weekly baths. Bath night was Saturday night only. We didn't have a bathtub so we had to take our bath in a round metal tub, we had to heat the water in a pan on the stove and then pour it in the tub, and in the winter, we took our bath by the heating stove to keep warm.

We walked to school, rain, sleet, or snow, there were no rides, the school didn't close for the weather, and there were no snow days.

We didn't have an inside toilet, our toilet was in a phone booth size building we called an outhouse, it was in the backyard of our lot, cold in the winter and smelly in the summer.

We were too poor to have a car so we walked and sometimes took a bus.

We were poor but didn't know it as everyone else was poor where we lived.

Us kids played outside most of the day and what fun we had. We played jacks, marbles, kick the can, hide and seek, and many other games and we were in the house before dark.

At night for entertainment, we listened to the radio. We would turn out the lights, lay in bed, and listen to radio shows like The Green Hornet, The Squeaking Door, and Inner Sanctum, just to name a few. I was too scared to get out of bed to turn off the radio.

Ice Cream Cones
By Marilyn F. Clink of Midland, Michigan
Born 1931

It was a warm, July night at the farm. Supper was over, dishes washed, and put away. We grandchildren were tired having played all day in the barn, sailed high on the rope swing grandfather had hung on a strong branch of the cottonwood tree, and explored the woods behind the barnyard. Grandfather must have noticed how listless we were sitting in the living room and suggested we go for ice cream cones after the *Huntley-Brinkley News Report* was over.

Soon all seven of us piled into the Model T Ford and off we went with grandmother waving to us from the kitchen window. I wondered why she did not come along, but as we neared the tiny town of Onekama, I forgot about her in my anticipation of the chilly sweetness to come. We pulled up in front of the Blue Slipper Saloon, the only place in town

that had ice cream in those days. Grandfather told us to stay in the car and he would bring out the cones. Sure enough, it was not long before he came out, loaded down with seven double dipped vanilla cones. He told us he was going back inside to talk with some friends and would be back soon. Happily, we licked away and when every single bit was gone, grandfather reappeared. He would climb into the car, smiled cheerily at us, and drive back to the farm.

My grandmother was waiting for us, and saw our excited faces. Smiling, she asked if we had a good time and then turned to grandfather. Seeing his cheery grin, she turned to the wood stove and poured him a cup of coffee. It was a long time before I realized why he really had made the trip for the ice cream cones.

Marilyn's grandparents

Toboggan Ride; Fear of Horses; the Milk Man
By Patricia Murphy of Hemlock, Michigan
Born 1916

I would like to tell a few of the experiences I remember from earlier days in my life. One was about the time I said to some friends, "I want to go down this toboggan slide on my skis." They told me not to do it, that it would be too dangerous. I thought that I would like to try it. I climbed up to the top of the toboggan slide with my skis. The toboggan slide is a slide of ice the width of a toboggan, which is about two feet wide. On the sides are two rails made by boards that are about six inches high and run from the top of the slide to the bottom. The purpose of the rails is to keep the toboggan on track. This particular slide went through a forest of big evergreens. At the bottom, the toboggan run went over a creek and out into a field.

As I looked down on the slope, I began to have second thoughts. What I was going to do might have seemed foolish to some, especially facing the toboggan run from the top, but I was thinking about fun. I thought, I can do this; I will just slide down there and it will be fun. I knew that once I started, I would not be able to get off the toboggan run, or stop, or even slow myself down. My friends' warnings did not dampen the excitement I felt, so I put on my skis. The skis were six or more feet long and had a leather strap that held them onto my boots. They were simple skis with about a one- inch strap over my toes to hold them on my feet.

I leaned forward and down I went. I had not taken my poles with me because I knew I would not use them. I tried to keep my skis away from the wooden rails and keep my knees bent. I occasionally looked at the ice of the toboggan run, but most of the time I was looking up ahead on the slide. The trees on each side flew by. Some of the tree trunks were a yard or less away from the edge of the run. I went so fast I hardly knew what I was doing. Before I knew it, the ride was over.

Once at the bottom, I came out onto a flat area and went out into the field until I slowed down and stopped. Whew, I thought, made it! My friends were angry with me, and said, "You do that again, and we will tell your mother!" I was fifteen.

Another early memory in my life involved horses, of which I am deathly afraid. Before beginning, let us set the scene.

I was in my twenties, and had grown up in a small town. I did not know any farmers, had never been on a farm. When I married, we began living on a farm in mid-Michigan, near Hemlock. I had been used to having hot water, an indoor toilet, a bathtub, and I did not have the slightest idea about how to use a coal range for cooking in the kitchen. Because the war was on and some factories were making armaments rather than appliances, we did not have a refrigerator or a washing machine. I used the clothesline out in the back yard to dry the wet clothes. In the winter, I hung the long johns and winter tops on the lines out in back, and I remember that it was difficult to get the

frozen limbs through the door. The outdoor biffy was also a novelty. My life on the farm was very different from what I had been used to.

When farmers put up hay in those days, they would cut, rake, and then fork the hay onto a wagon. The horses pulled the wagon right into the barn, up to the barn floor. My husband would stop the horses under the hayforks next to the haymow. To move the hay from the wagon to the mow required a four-pronged metal fork that stabbed into the hay and locked into position so that it held the hay. The hayfork was attached to a rope on a pulley, and this rope lifted the hay to the peak of the barn. At this point, a series of pulleys on a metal track along the peak of the barn was used to move the hay into the mow. Once the hay was in the desired spot, the forks were tripped and the hay fell into the mow. My husband was remarkably skilled at putting the hay right where he wanted it. On the other end of this arrangement were the horses, which had pulled the wagon into the barn: they were now hooked to the rope that was tied onto the forks.

My job was to drive those horses briskly across the barnyard so as to pull the hay up to the peak of the barn. These were not little ponies, but sturdy workhorses. Their hips were taller than me. They must have weighed more than a thousand pounds, and they were heavy with huge legs and hooves. Once when my husband was away, our horse, Queen, got her feet snarled in the page wire fence and stood there most of the day. Finally, I went down there to see what was wrong and to see if I could get her out of the fence by myself. I got down on my hands and knees by these huge feet, took hold of her foot, and tried to pull it out of the wire. After struggling, she and I pulled her foot out and she walked calmly away. I was shaking. Working with horses was certainly a new and terrifying experience for me. I was afraid to get near them.

When putting up hay, my job involved driving the horses. Once the hay was in the forks, I would start the horses. Marching right along, we would walk across the barnyard and the hay would ride up toward the peak of the barn. In order to get the hay up to the peak so that it could slide down the rail, I had to drive the horses right up to the fence. In fact, the horses had to have their heads over the top of this fence. Fortunately, these workhorses knew what to do, and would walk calmly. I was a nervous wreck.

The only other moment I feared was when I had to bring them back around by the barn door again, and hook them onto the rope once more so that we could take up the next batch of hay. Then I would have to take hold of the chain and hook the chain into the crossbeam, so that we could start all over. To hook on this chain, I would have to get down by their feet and make the connection. Oh, those feet!

Some years later, we acquired a tractor. My husband would milk the cows by hand, put the milk into milk cans, and cool them in the watering trough. A milk can is about two and a half feet tall, metal, with two handles and a cover that fits fairly snuggly. Regularly, the milkman used to come and pick up the full cans and leave off some empty cans.

It was spring and it was raining, and it had rained. The milkman would not drive down our road because there was a deep puddle of water in the gravel road, down near the corner. We had to either get the milk to the corner or else throw it away. My husband loaded the milk cans on the stone boat, a kind of flat, wooden raft that slides over the ground. He hooked the tractor onto the stone boat. He rode the stone boat to steady the cans. My job was to drive the tractor (another new job). The milk truck was waiting at the corner.

I got on the tractor and looked back to see what was happening on the stone boat: all set. We started out slowly down the road. As we neared the mud puddle, I thought I would need more speed, and so I pulled on the gas lever. The tractor jerked and the motor stopped, right in the middle of the puddle, deader than a doornail. Milk cans tipped over, milk poured out and my husband tried to grab the cans and stand them back up again. The tractor was dead, the milk was flowing, the milkman was aghast and the air was blue.

My Busy Childhood
By Joanne Lee Durham of Greenville,
Michigan
Born 1933

I don't remember the years of some of the things that happened while I was a young girl, but we lived with my grandparents and my mom. While we were there, we had chores to do on the farm.

The one chore I remember was that we had to cut some wood for the woodstove. We used a long handsaw, and my mom said, "Don't stand on the cover of the well, or you'll fall." I was the skinny one, so I stood on the well. I was sawing, and yes, I fell in. I hung on to the wall of the well and my sister went and got Mom. Wow! She threw down a rope for me to catch. She said that if I missed it, I'd fall down all the way. Thank the Lord I caught it! I also caught it for being on the well! She said for not doing what I was told, I could go to bed with no supper. And I lost one of my new shoes down the well, also. Mom didn't care.

I remember also of living behind an old couple. After school, I would go to their apartment and sit on the porch and feed the lady's husband crackers while she got supper ready. He was crippled, in a wheelchair, and couldn't talk, just nod his head. I made ten cents a week doing this. I thought I really had a lot of money.

Then Mom and us moved from Belding, Michigan to Greenville, Michigan into a house. A lady who lived next door to us gave me her son's guitar. It was bigger than me. I went to all the old people's homes and made believe I could play it and I sang. I love to sing and still do.

Back in those days, they paid about two cents for newspapers and books. I went and got a lot of papers from the older people and sold them. Sometimes I'd get 25 to 30 cents. We used to have an outhouse to go to the bathroom and an old catalog book to use. You'd have to kind of rub it back and forth to make it a little softer. It didn't always work too good.

One day it was nice and sunny and windy out. While we were playing with some friends, they asked if we had an umbrella. I said, "Yes, we do." I got it and we climbed up onto the outhouse roof and jumped off. The wind blew and we broke my mom's umbrella. We didn't set too good for a couple of days, but never done that again!

One night while Mom was cooking supper, I was watching her make gravy. I thought I could help her while she was mashing potatoes, so I stirred it and got burnt by spilling it on my hand. I still have a scar of it.

Joanne Lee Durham

I remember wanting to go to the movie, but I had a rash on my face, so Mom said that I had better stay home. I asked her to call up a doctor to find out what it was. Before show time, I got to see a doctor. He said it was only heat rash, so Mom let us go. Guess what? When I came out of the movie, I had spots all over me. The heat rash turned out to be the measles. All the kids that went to the show with us got them!

I guess you could say that I had a busy childhood. For some of it I also got spanked, and I guess I had it coming to me.

Sparky's Story
By Diane Kern of Bay City, Michigan
Born 1947

I lived on a forty-acre farm with my dad, mom, and sister. It had a house and barn with a creek that passed between them and a wide shallow drainage ditch on the edge of the lot.

On one side of the barn, dad opened it up so the cows could come and go from the weather. Dad had a herd of Herefords, about twenty or so, so cute little calves with white faces. One day my sister and I walked out to the barn to a spot dad had fixed up for the cows, and on the floor wiggling around were

two things we thought were kittens. It turned out to be little baby raccoons.

I looked around but did not know where they came from. We took them up to the house where mom helped us feed them with a doll's baby bottle. Later I went out to the barn and found another one, but it did not make it. They were so small, no bigger than a woman's hand. With hard work and a lot of care for a few weeks, we gradually started to add cat food to feed them.

When they got big enough, my aunt took the raccoon, Mickey, to take care of. They released him into the grove of trees, letting him live on their land. My sister and I took care of Sparky.

He was gentle like a dog, and it was fun watching him hunt fish and crayfish in the creek or crickets and grasshoppers in the field. Our dog, Jack, and cat, Spot, were good, they even shared food! Dad was working on a new house. He had a basement dug with a ladder sticking up. Sparky would play on the ladder, crawling up and down it. Watching him walk and hanging upside down was so darn cute! When it got into the fall, we would come home from school and find Sparky on top of the chimney on the roof of the house. We had a collar on him. Dad said he did not think they would try to kill him if he was a pet. When he was about one or two years old, we took the collar off, but you could still see where the collar was on his neck. We were worried he would get caught on something. His hair was misplaced for quite some time. Eventually, I think about three years old, he came back once in a while. Then he just quit coming. I will never forget my friend and buddy, Sparky!

Five Cent Candy Bars and Ten-Cent Bread
By Susan Emerson of Auburn, Michigan
Born 1951

I remember when the stores were open to 9:00 PM on Fridays and when banks were open to 8:00 PM so you could get your check cashed. Stores were never open on Sundays.

City kids had to walk to school and only country kids could ride the bus. Girls could not wear pants to school. The school told you how short your skirt could be. You got your yearbook at the end of the year so your friends could sign it. I remember that we had to take coal to school for heat. Sometimes the snow got so high that we had a week off of school.

Gas cost only a quarter a gallon and it was common to shove eight people in a Volkswagen. The gas stations gave you a drinking glass if you bought eight gallons of gas. You could get two cents back if you returned bottles. A&P was the place to go to shop for food. I still remember the smell of fresh ground coffee at that store. Bananas and grapes were eight cents per pound and bread was a dime per loaf.

On Sundays, family always got together and visited each other. We had dancing in the barn. There was roller-skating at the skate park and also there were bands there. At the beach, there was a rollercoaster. We went to penny arcades. Ice skating rinks had a warming house where you could pull off your wet gloves and put them on the heat pot to dry them. There was always a nice man working there. I remember playing in the washtub for a pool. The barn in the hay mound was a nice place to play. Games we played were: Kick the Can and Red Over. We would go to the pond and net the tadpoles so we could watch them turn into frogs. I remember the shows: Captain Kangaroo, The Jetsons, and the Flintstones.

People would babysit for only 25 cents per hour. Candy bars were only a nickel while a bag of penny candy cost only ten cents. I remember shopping downstairs at Kneeps. They would deliver a dress for you. There were birds and toys downstairs at the Woolworth Store. The Event Store was for nylons and sleepwear. The Southend Library was upstairs on Broadway and J.C. Penney was downtown. I remember having lunch at Kresky's. There was the Cunningham's Pharmacy, the Sub Dub Shop, and the Rosenbery Furniture Store.

The doctors would come to your house, and if you needed to go to the hospital, he would even take you there. You could walk home at 2:00 AM and not be afraid. I remember that my aunt lived in the city and she could still have her chickens. Ladies always wore hats to church and would use juice cans for rollers in their hair.

Sugar Beets
By Helen Rice of Pinconning, Michigan
Born 1937

It was a cold day in 1937. I was born in Pinconning on a farm. My parents were farmers.

We had pigs, cows, chickens, and a horse to pull the plow to work the fields. We had to wash clothes by hand. Later we had a wringer washer.

When I was about three or four, I fell in the rinse water tub; they had to pull me out. We had no indoor plumbing. We had to go outside to the outhouse. No running water, we had to take a bath with just a tub of water and a washcloth.

When I was big enough to go to school, I walked one and one half miles to the Indian School, which was a one-room school. We brought our sack lunch; sometimes the teacher would warm up a large can of beans on the wood burning potbelly stove, so we had something hot.

In winter, the snow was very deep and we had to walk on top of it.

When I was about ten or twelve, I had an acre of sugar beets as a 4-H project. I had to care for them myself, weed, pull and top them. But I had to help my folks with their crops first.

I had to milk a cow each evening by hand. My Dad said I should have to cut my nails they were always long. I told him my cow was used to it so it was okay.

I remember the icebox we had and the root cellar, to keep potatoes, cabbage, carrots, and other vegetables in.

In those days, your neighbors helped each other whether it was hauling hay or hoeing the crops, no charge.

You would visit with neighbors. When I got in the ninth grade, I could ride the bus to Pinconning High School.

I started to work out when I was thirteen. I washed dishes at Wilsons Cheese Shop, and then I worked as a waitress for sixty-five cents per hour.

We had gotten a black and white television when I was about fourteen. We thought we had the finer things in life.

Those were the Good Old Days. My dad would take us to the movies on Saturday night, if we had our work done. My favorite was Roy Rogers and Dale. I did like Westerns, still do.

We would catch frogs and sell them. A man would come in from Chicago and buy them.

We didn't have much money for a lot of things, but we all worked together.

My Dad had a bad heart so; he was not able to do the heavy work. He passed away when he was fifty-four years old.

Preferring Modern Conveniences
By Betty E. Crawford of Bay City, Michigan
Born 1928

Before television and personal computers appeared on the market, we used our combined ideas to entertain ourselves.

After school and before doing our homework we'd dash home to listen to Jack Armstrong, the All American Boy on late afternoon radio; it was a walnut dome table top Philco with limited access to stations. When our homework was done and dinner dishes washed, Mom, sister, and I gathered in the living room for our evening entertainment by the Green Hornet, Dr. Kildare, Fibber McGee and Molly, Spike Jones, just to name a few.

Just before bedtime, Mother read a chapter from a Jean Stratton Porter book, The Girl of the Limberlost, or Freckles or from the latest borrowed book. My sister and I learned to love books and reading from those evenings. They opened our imaginations to other worlds.

With lots of time on our young hands on weekends, and no bicycle, roller-skating was fast transportation, especially when the wheels were oiled. We made sure our shoes were tightly laced, then attached our skates to the soles and tightened the front and back clamps with the steel key, and finished with adjusting the leather strap across our ankle. Many of us remember skinned knees from falls when tripping on sidewalk cracks.

Another inventive exercise was using a wooden circular ring from a barrel, rolling it ahead of us down the sidewalks with a T-shaped baton. It was a little tricky keeping it from soaring into the streets, but with practice, we became pretty proficient and raced each other.

Winters were a challenge. First of all, we didn't have central heating. We kept cozy with a Heatrola in the middle of the living room, stoked periodically with coal hauled in with a black coalscuttle, the same oval shaped bucket that we loaded to dispose of the ashes. They were great stoves, stood about four feet high on four molded feet. The cast iron firepot was encased with a multi-brown enameled jacket and sent a glow into the room through the isinglass window centered in the door. The top was grated allowing precious heat to dry our soaked home knitted mittens and socks.

Every morning the milkman would leave two quarts of whole milk in the box on the edge of the porch. If we slept in, they stayed there for a couple of hours in freezing temperatures. We'd find the cardboard cap protruding one to two inches above the glass bottleneck. After they thawed in our wooden icebox and the cap lodged in place, we would shake each bottle. Those were the days before pasteurized milk, so the cream rose to the top and needed to be blended to keep the milk full bodied.

These are fond memories, but I prefer living with our modern conveniences.

The Barn on Christmas Eve of 1944
By Thomas A. Coleman of Ludington, Michigan
Born 1935

It got dark early, just like now, and even with the snow, darkness prevailed. Only four years before had the electric co-op managed to sign up enough subscribers to bring power to the farm, but electricity was expensive, there was a war on, and most everything was rationed. For these reasons, lights were few and used only when needed.

Before supper and before gifts were opened, chores had to be done. The women, Grandma, Mom, Aunt and my sister would be preparing a traditional Swedish Christmas Eve supper of mashed potatoes, fruit soup, lutefisk (a kind of reconstituted dried cod) with white sauce, canned garden vegetables from the garden and a desert of mixed whipped cream, pineapple and rice with a cherry on top. I have no idea of how that got to be a traditional Swedish dish. The men, my great-uncle and I, did barn chores, which included feeding the cows (seven) and draft horses (two) and doing the milking.

The new yard light was a thankful and safer replacement for the kerosene lanterns that had been in use only a few years before. Also, there were the three 60 watt bulbs lighting the cow barn. Swing open the outside door and…it was warm. The body heat of the cows and horses brought it to near shirtsleeve temperature. The two horses on the left would give a greeting rumble and maybe a stomp. The cows would raise their heads and murmur a welcome in anticipation of food and udder relief.

It was brown and gold—old brown wood, brown gold and tan Gurneys, and one little Jersey. We kept those because the butterfat of their milk was higher and we churned butter, which we sold in town. The soft light would flicker on the metal of the neck yoke chains and the links tinkle with their movements. Stalls would have been cleaned earlier and replenished with new straw. That was golden too and still smelled of summer. The barn was clean.

To bring in the hay from last summer meant climbing up into the loft, pitching down the right amount of hay to the big barn floor, and then carrying by the fork full to the mangers.

We fed at that time so the cows would have something to do while we milked. With electricity had come a milker, but before that we milked by hand, head pressed against the warm flank of the cow and milk streams singing into the bucket. The barn cats would come looking for a treat, and we might give them a squirt, but we'd always leave a big sardine tin full of foamy milk as a reward.

The barn on Christmas Eve was a warm, golden place full of shadows and sounds, gifts of food and feed being exchanged between men and animals. A quiet place with the jingles, small sounds of contentment, good smells of the earth's products, and a feeling that things were all right on Christmas Eve.

Jackknives and German Army Camps
By Theodore G. Zoulek of Shelby, Michigan
Born 1937

At the time I was born in 1937, in the same little farm town village there was only around 400 people that lived in the village limits. Some of the memories I have shared with my 12 grandchildren and 13 great-grandchildren. They all live just one hour from where I still live alone since my wife Wanda passed away going on four years ago. I was blessed to grow up in a great farm country community and was able to work on many farms there within my first 18 years. Yes, I cut hay, corn, milked cows, and even castrated pigs at various farms in our county. Just a couple of stories I will share with you, which I know you, will really enjoy.

My mother's dad gave me a double-blade jackknife to show me how to carve many things by the time of my ninth birthday. So, as my 80th birthday is not far away and I still do a lot of carvings, when I was 14 I carved with a chainsaws as well. I was a Cub Scout at the age of seven and continued until I was nine. I then turned into a Boy Scout for three more years. I had planned on continuing as a Boy Scout, but I had new interest by my 13th birthday. Yes, I had to get my mother and father a good reason to stop the scouts. We lived in a small village that had very few things that were entertaining events other than school or working on farms during entire year round. I told my folks that I needed to concentrate more time on my education, special sports, and new entertaining events such as fishing, hunting, riding my bike, and even going to the church and rolling skating about twice a week. This was when I first got concerned about having a girlfriend. Being in the high school level and all these new concerns and events, I had to make these choices on my own.

So I would like to share a couple stories with you that I remember as if it was just yesterday. First of all, when I was only seven during the Second World War. It was a very scary time in my life. The two most important memories during that time was when we had air raids sirens very often. We had special locations to go to for shelter to make sure we would be safe at school, home, or even when we were working and farming in the area.

When I was about seven years old, we had a German prison camp in our small village when I had many bad dreams during that period. I was told that Michigan had about three or four of these camps during a course of about two years. It took some time to get a good feeling. One of those special camps was close to where we lived in the village of

144

Shelby. You probably won't believe it, but all the kids that lived in my area had a small ball field that we played at during the evenings or days off from school. This ball field was just a hundred feet from the German campground. These Germans soldiers all watched us kids every time we played. They yelled and said German words that we could not understand. But then I gave them some hard candy that my mother gave me and they really liked it. So, every time we played at this ball field they were pointing at me. Yes, I knew right away that they wanted some of my hard candy.

Later on in my life, we had a visitor at our church, which we attended every week. The special event was a special men's breakfast that we had visitors come to eat with us. One of our church members came with a German soldier that spent time in the Shelby village camp for over a year. He got up and talked about his stay in America and about when he was at The Shelby camps. He had one story that stayed in his memory and began to tell about a young boy that had given him hard candy at all of the ball games that he had watched at the Shelby, MI camp during that same period. I had to stand up to tell him that the little boy was me with the hard candy. Yes, it's really too bad that many of our young children don't hear these special stories from their grandparents or older friends.

Childhood Happenings
By Dorothy I. Hulliberger of Belding,
Michigan
Born 1935

I was born in a house near Trufant, Michigan. We had an outhouse and a pump outside for water. My dad lost his job and we lost our house, so we moved to another one that we rented. He tried to buy the other house back, but they wouldn't let him.

We had an icebox for our cold things. We had another outhouse and a pump for water again. My mother used a scrub board and tubs. My brother and I had to carry water for the laundry. We had a barn that we played in. One time my sister fell from the floor above from a hole. She wasn't hurt. We played across the road in the sand. One time we buried our toys and later we couldn't find them. One time

Dorothy and her brother, Johnny

my folks were gone and my older sister was watching us younger children and I climbed up on the cupboard to get the butter. The cupboard fell over with me and the glass broke. I cut the back of my head. I have a scar there yet. They caught heck for it. I didn't.

We didn't have any electricity, either. We burned wood for heat and maybe coal. One day the fire was too hot or something and it caught fire from the stovepipe upstairs. We all got out all right and they were able to save some things. We lived in my oldest sister and her husband's house and they moved to Grand Rapids for a while. My dad built a house down the road from there. It was small. Five of us had to share one bedroom. We had a radio. We listened to it and it and also had a wind-up record player they saved from the fire. My dad used to make wine and one time I snuck some and got silly and sick.

I went to a one-room schoolhouse with outhouses. One day I got blamed for a mess in one and the teacher used a ruler on me and it wasn't even my fault. She wasn't my favorite teacher, either. One thing I did do though was put a thumbtack on a boy's chair. Ouch! I got in a fight with a classmate and kept saying, "Come a little closer and I will fight you." I kept walking home. She gave up. We didn't have a telephone or TV for years.

One day I walked home from my friend's house with a pain in my side and was sick. I blamed it on the raw potato I had eaten over there, but it turned out to be my appendix. I had it taken out and my dad saved it in a jar. We used to walk over to the lake and swim in our favorite place. My sister cut her foot once and had to have stitches. Me and my two brothers and some other kids were playing in a tent by the lake one time and my one brother went home and told on us. My dad came after us and we got a spanking.

We used to walk quite a ways to school even in cold weather. We would stop at this one house to get warm because she always gave us homemade cookies. In good weather, we walked for miles to visit a friend. We used to ride with a neighbor to go to the movies on a Saturday night. I used to get it in for the price of "Under 12 years old" because I looked younger. It was cheaper.

One winter the snow was so deep you couldn't get down the road. We made a tunnel in the snow in the road. We used to walk over to where my uncle was working on a farm and I would learn to milk cows by hand. We used to work for our neighbors picking up potatoes at ten cents per crate. We used to take watermelons until we got caught. One time I was picking up potatoes and ripped my pants on purpose so I could go home. I used to have a crush on a schoolboy that I went to school with. We would walk over to their house and play "hide and go seek" and "spin the bottle." The boy I liked kissed me. We would walk home from their house after dark and get scared walking home.

Back in Time
By Marian Lewandowski of Bay City, Michigan
Born 1926

I was born and lived on a farm in Hampton Township for the first twenty-one years. In 1926:

Average Income $1418
New Ford Vehicle $310
Gallon of Gas $.23
Loaf of Bread $.09
Half-Gallon Milk $.56
Double Dip Ice Cream Cone $.05

Farming was the dominate way of life. Anything from a few acres to forty or sixty acres was considered good size; compared to today where hundreds of acres are the norm. It was known as "garden" farming, which provided sufficient edibles for family and others. Biggest crops being produce, sugar beets, chicory, and grains. The land was tilled by horses. Cattle, Chickens, and pigs provided necessary meat.

Wood and coal burning stove were the main source of heat and creating hot water. Laundry was done on scrub boards using homemade soap. Around 1930 electricity, wringer washers, and telephones came into being. Telephones were a rather large gadget on the wall, party lines, and you could "ring" up to six ringy-dingy homes on your half.

We used a churn to make butter. How we would argue over whose turn it was to do the next hundred turns. Brothers in due time fashioned a chain and a motor to manage the task.

Colds were treated with hot lemonade drinks and hot toddies along with lots of Vicks chest rubs.

A piano teacher came to the house at $.50 per half hour.

Outhouse and chamber pots were the norm.

Wedding parties and funerals took place in the home. Somber pictures.

Children played games of their own creation with sticks and stones. Hopscotch and ball and jacks were favorites.

Winters were long, cold, and lots of snow from early November into early April. Two to three foot ice cycles hung from the eaves. Summers were mostly hot with no air conditioning.

Saginaw River was used for some logging but mostly for ice blocks, ice fishing, and regular fishing as a source of food.

Businesses that are gone by the wayside are Bay Osteopathic, General, Mercy and Samaritan hospitals consolidated into McLaren Bay Regional Hospital, Bay City Shovels, Beutel Canning (tomato), Chicory Factory, Defoe Shipyard, Electric Auto-Life, Industrial Brownhoist, Lewis Manufacturing, Self Serve Lumber, Westover Kamm lumber yard, Colonial, Empire, Lafayette, Regent, Washington, and Westtown theatres. The State is the only survivor, which has been restored and updated. It brings in special performers and shows. Other businesses are Batchke, Hazels and Stroemers Greenhouse flower shops, City Dairy, Stevens Creamery, Goddeyne Jennison and Rechlin hardware stores. Clothing and general merchandise stores include Bay City Cash, Czuba', Evenknit, Kresge's, Mill End, Wendland, Yankee, and Sears and Target close the end of January 2015. A&P grocery, Red Lion Hot Dog and neighborhood grocery stores disappearing thanks to Kroger, Meijer, and Wal-Mart.

General Motors and Bay City Chevrolet now GM Powertrain are still with us. Peak employment was nearly 4,000 and now under 400.

We had two-room schoolhouses with two teachers each doing all the subjects for four grades. There were no snow days and we walked or road our bikes to school. Hugo, Jones, Nivens, Nolet, Raby, and Ridge Road Schools joined Essexville and Bay City system and a bus system was initiated.

The Wenonah hotel burned and the Third Street Bridge collapsed into the river.

The Bus Accident
By Lola Wright Steele of Gladwin, Michigan
Born 1941

January 15, 1951 was just a normal day for the Wright family and the community of Gladwin, Michigan. Children had gotten on the old red, white, and blue school bus and went off to school, farmers were tending to their work, and mothers were doing their usual work and all was well. For me after school, I did my weekly piano lesson and walked over a mile to my aunt's home just outside of town. The next morning, I road my cousin's bus to school. That afternoon, I got on my regular bus but never arrived home. Our road commission in Gladwin had gone on strike. The roads were slippery going down Barn Road. We were going north and a cream truck carrying several ten-gallon milk cans was going south. The bus and the milk truck collided on a bridge below a sloping hill, sending a busload of children upside down into a freezing cold river stream. Our bus driver was injured, as were several of the children. One older boy on the bus kicked out the emergency door and the older boys began to help the children out the door. One little girl was caught on something and cried when one of the rescuers wanted to cut her down. She did not want to ruin her new coat. The young man, who enjoyed opening the bus door to let off children, was seriously injured in the back. An older high school girl had bad cuts on her face. Two little boys who were in the front seat behind the bus driver were killed. My best friend and I were sitting in the second seat back from the front on the right hand side and we were both severely injured. Someone took both us girls and had laid us on the riverbank, thinking we were dead. I had always heard that it was my brother Jim but have recently heard differently. One of us made a noise and the bus driver came and gave us CPR. I ended up in the hospital for about six days, four of them I do not remember, as I was unconscious. My best friend ended up with a broken leg and spent a long time in the hospital and at home. For several summers, she had to have surgery on one leg or the other to make them even. Some of the children who were injured were taken to the house above the river and laid on the homeowner's bed. My two older brothers walked home, which was about a mile and three quarters from the accident. Their pant legs were all frozen. They had to tell my parents what had happened and they told them that I was dead. I can only report what I was told later as I do not remember what happened. I do remember the superintendent coming to visit us as I was recovering. It was amazing how all the other kids just went back to school the next day or so. Back then, there was no grief counseling or other pampering; life just went on. Most of those who were on the bus that January 16, 1951 are still alive. For me, I would like to know the rest of the story, not just bits and pieces for lack of memory.

Melted Ice
By Delores F. Schmidt of Saginaw, Michigan
Born 1931

I do not know where to start. I guess it will be about a few things my mother told me when she grew up – it was in Boyne City, Michigan. Her dad, my grandfather, who was in the Bolshevik Army in Russia, died a young man in his early 40s and all his uniforms burnt in a house fire. I never knew him. My mom and family lost everything and they would not have had a Christmas if it was not for the Salvation Army.

She had to walk to school with snow up to her waist. She would come home for lunch, have fresh baked bread with "lard," and then back to school. She eventually moved to

147

Saginaw, Michigan and worked in a match factory where she met my dad, Joe.

They married and had three children, and that is where I came in. I remember going to Hoyt School until the second grade, then on to Holy Family where I grew up and graduated in 1949. I was taught by Dominican Nuns and lived two houses from school. My dad was a chauffeur for twenty years for a very rich family.

We lived behind the big house in an upstairs apartment. I grew up there until I was fifteen years old. We lived in "the Grove," as it was called, across the street from Hoyt Park where I would ice skate every night during the winter months. In the summer, I would fish and play marbles with the boys in the neighborhood. There were no girls to play with.

The Jones' next door had a goat and we played with it. We walked everywhere, to the Court Theater about one mile from home and then down town to the Temple Theater about another mile and a half from home. I remember about half a mile home from town, we went into a store and listened to a radio. We were at war with Japan and they had bombed Pearl Harbor, killing our men and sinking our ships.

I am eighty-three years old now. I have a white rotary phone in my kitchen, an answering phone in the living room, and a push button phone in the bedroom. I have a wringer Maytag washer in the basement and also a tredle sewing machine. My mom used to make all our dresses, pants, etc. We were very poor!

I remember my dad must have made my mom angry about something. She put a plate of scrambled eggs over his head. We also had an icebox and had to make sure we had a "block" of ice from Winkler-Lucas Ice Co. to keep food cold. I remember once, we forgot about the ice. It melted and all that was left was water under the icebox. What a mess with water all over the floor.

We spent three to four weeks in the summer time on the farm in Gaylord, Michigan and did farm chores. We fed the chickens, made butter with a churn, milked cows, and drank warm milk. We went to town and watched outdoor movies on Friday night. We had no running water and had an outhouse. We also had a big garden. Had a wood stove in the kitchen to cook on. Also, we had a "so-called" pantry off from the kitchen.

I also remember being at home and listening to mom's radio on Sunday nights, in bed, to *Inner-Sanctum, the Squeaky Door*, and I think during the week to *the Lone Ranger* (I forget what night).

Come In! Come In!
By Ilene R. Thomsen of Sidney, Michigan
Born 1926

A flyer fell out of my newspaper, as I glanced at the caption, "Help was needed to remember" the Good Old Days. It was like a knock at the door! Come In! Come In!

A long road, we cannot turn every stone, just a pebble here and there!

I was the fifth in the line of seven. Raised on a farm near Amble, Michigan and grew up with no electricity, no inside water, outhouses, and mostly hand-me-down or homemade clothes, toys and automobiles.

The Amble creamery whistle was our time

Ilene Morgan with her brother, Bernard Morgan in 1933

An underground storage cellar
Ilene's grandfather, Elmer Morgan and her father, Victor Morgan

clock in the morning at 7am. The creamery closed and Amble faded!

The water pump with well pit was always home to snakes. The large marsh lake on the farm was a snake haven!

Winter storage was a stone underground cellar and two years ago, it was still intact!

I walked three miles to the one-room school. I usually cut across a neighbor's cow pasture to save time. One time the bull was out and gave me a run for my life. I jumped over the fence one-step ahead of the bull! The neighbor came with a pitchfork just in case!

A snake in the outhouse caused some excitement. A blue racer was in the paper box! No one would go in until the snake was out!

Free shows in Amble were our outings. We sat on blankets on the ground to watch Gene Autry and Champion.

I went wading in the neighbor's creek. I always had to check for bloodsuckers when getting out and often found them between my toes.

A windstorm brought down five huge poplar trees in the yard. They fell like dominoes just as brother and I leaped to the porch.

I collected many Indian arrowheads from the sand blow at the edge of the marsh. It was believed to have been an Indian camp.

I didn't have a sled so we used a board as a toboggan. I had the best sliding hill in the area so others shared sleds for use of the hill!

Too many green apples in the spring usually meant a bellyache with downtime. Pa's home "cure-all" remedy was Epsom salt, called parents "Ma and Pa."

Mischief-makers were brother, just older, and I. Brother built a boat, three sided with a board bottom and a triangle shape. One afternoon after school, we decided to try it out. A neighbor kid went with us. We put it in the marsh lake and brother rowed. The neighbor and I had our school lunch pails. We were just out when water came in so fast and we couldn't bail it out fast enough! Somehow, we got back to shore before the boat went down! Without those lunch pails to bail with we never would have made it back!

Another time, everyone talked of strawberries and cream. We knew of a patch of wild berries, so brother and I went and picked them. After getting the berries, we needed the cream. You see, we thought "cream" not "ice cream." Just over the fence was the neighbors cow and brother milked while I petted the cow to keep her content! We went home so proud but Ma did not appreciate it!

One day we found a hawk's nest with three of the most adorable little ones, so soft like fuzz balls. We took them home thinking surely that the old sitting hen would mother them. As kids, we couldn't understand why she would have no part of them. Ma came out about then seeing what we had and gave orders to march them right back to where we found them! Mother hawk was soon back with the family.

Pa would sometimes tell stories. Seems the outhouses were often the topic. Never did hear much about Grandpa's mail-order-bride. Only that she came, stayed less than a year, and left Grandpa deeply in debt. No one talked about it!

We had our chores, our duties. Always dishes to wash, weeds to pull but somehow there was time. Time!

I married and that began another story, another road in Sidney, Michigan.

Over the years when I would suggest reading a story to my grandsons, I would get the unanimous request, "Don't read Grandma, tell us about the Good Old Days."

Ilene (Morgan) Thomsen

Polish Immigrant
By David J. Banaszek of Saginaw, Michigan
Born 1940

I am of Polish descent. My mother came from a town in Poland somewhere west of Warsaw and about midway to the western border.

My dad was born in Forest City, PA in 1908 and my mom in 1911. She was three when the family came over. Her dad and mom were dirt poor. He had what was considered an okay job tending the landowner's livestock. My mom remembers going with him to a nearby river that ran downstream from a vodka factory. They would go there to snag potatoes out of the river for food, and get coal from along a railway track, to pick and bag coal to heat the home. In the winter, my grandpa tended either the cattle or the sheep, standing in either the cow plops or the sheep crap, to keep his feet warm.

They came over in 1914, the start of World War I. Mom related that on the way over the tramp steamer they were on didn't know the name of it, was fired on by a German U Boat. One of the shells shattered a portion of a wood handrail that ran along the top edge of the ships side rail. As my mom told it, "No more firing from the submarine, everyone was afraid, and very scared and very nervous!

The Germans surfaced, tied on to the side of the ship, now standing dead in the water. The Germans boarded machine guns at ready.

At three years old, mom remembers, the passengers saying the Germans must have had engine problems, they were aboard some length of time, and left, never firing another shot.

They went through Ellis Island, New York, and they were quarantined for at least a week. They all checked out with no communicable diseases. They had to have someone they knew in the United States of America that would vouch for them, and board them, until Grandpa got a job and they could go it alone.

Oh yeah, mom related to us, that as they were entering the main building on Ellis Island, she was sitting on her dad's shoulders. As they passed through a very large door to the main room, where they were separated from the sick, above her on the top of the large doorsill was a canning jar, she reached it, and found it filled with hard candies. She was overjoyed and all the three brothers and the sisters just laughed and filled their faces.

My Grandpa got a job in Saginaw, Michigan shortly after getting the lay of the land. He spoke little English, and that was broken.

He obtained a job working in a rail repair yard about two or three miles from where they had acquired a home. His job was to take off and replace the wheel on the railroad cars of C. and O. Railway Company by himself. The Americans that worked on the same job worked seven men to a wheel. Talk about

150

discrimination!

He was just a dumb "Polock" and they let him know it. But he had the guts to leave the land he was born in and with every bit they owned came over here.

Mom learned English at Holy Rosary Catholic grade school and in her early twenties, got a job at Lufkin Rub Company, and became an inspector of the brass points that make a folding rule fold. Her brother my Uncle Joe, became a Navy flyer out of Pensacola, Florida, flew a P.B.Y., they could land on the water, and later a twin tailed, P40 Reconnaissance plane. He was later after the war hired at a mental institution in Traverse City, Michigan. He stayed in the Navy and retired a Full Commander. Uncle Stan became an engineer.

My brother and I never spoke Polish, we were Americans! Of course, we knew a lot of the bad words!

If Mom and Dad wanted to talk privately, they spoke Polish. Dad's name was Adam. I loved them both.

Alice's Little Lamb
By Alice Jane Vliet Anderson of Big Rapids,
Michigan
Born 1922

I am ninety-two and a half years old, and yes, I certainly do remember the old days. I was born August 28, 1922 in my grandparent's home in Clarkston, Michigan, a small town about ten miles north of Pontiac, Michigan. It was the Great Depression and along with everyone else, my father lost a good job. My grandfather died and my grandmother still owned her farm about seven miles from Big Rapids, Michigan which was home to Ferris Institute, a pharmacy school of about five hundred students and is now Ferris State University.

Grandma Vliet, my mother, my father, my brother of five years old, and I at eleven years old drove to farm. There was a big change, a nice house and out buildings, but no electricity and no running water. There was a windmill and if the wind did not blow to send the water into the house, someone had to pump by hand to make the water come underground by pipe into the house.

Grandma had cataracts in her eyes and it was very hard to see, so she had to get a Delco System, which made electricity. How wonderful. Yes, we had an outhouse and chamber pots we called them vessels and kept them under the beds. Each of us kids was responsible for emptying our own. We were taught to call the outhouse Rodney, as my mother thought it sounded nicer.

Our Aunt Zoe came to visit and was asked if she wanted to go to Rodney with us. Of course she did, so here she came with hat, coat, gloves, and purse. We laughed. She thought it was a small town near us.

We had a party line phone, two long rings and two short rings was ours. As kids, it was fun to listen in but frowned upon if we got caught. Librado was a paste put on a plaster and put on our chest for colds. Vicks was also used. We had a wringer washer with an agitator that swished the clothes around in the water that had been heated in a reservoir on the end of the cooking stove. Clothes were put in the washer and the clothes ran through the wringer twice in both hot and cold water, and then hung on the clothes lines, during both winter and summer.

We went to a one-room schoolhouse through eighth grade. We always had a big Christmas Program and all of the students participated. The night of the program, parents came to watch their children. The kids were allowed to walk home and let off steam. I was about twelve and the kids thought one of the boys should kiss me, and he did. Of course, they all went home and told their parents, who in turn got on the party line and called my mother and guess what. I got a good scolding. We had lots of blizzards and no snow school days. We had to wear the beloved long underwear.

We would go to the town of Big Rapids on Friday nights and again on Saturday afternoons to watch the outdoor movies. It was a big deal. We planted potatoes that had sprouted by putting them in chunks. We had baby lambs, I had a favorite one, and I could bottle-feed it. I liked to gather the eggs that the chickens laid. I also could feed pigs in the pigpen and they gladly came when I called, "Here pig, pig, pig." We had kittens and puppies, cows, and horses. After the cows were milked, the milk was put into a separator. What came out was skim milk and pure cream, which was made into butter.

I learned to iron clothes young and also to dust furniture, ugh! The after war "baby boom" brought us a boy in 1945. As a mother of three children, two boys and one girl, they liked the older days' stories. It was an unbelievable time. My husband and I have been married seventy-three years. We have nine grandchildren and ten great grandchildren.

The Power of Imagination
By Marion Frahm Tincknell of Saginaw, Michigan
Born 1928

He kept his vigil deep inside the cave, watching over his injured companion, tending the wounds, and leaving only under cover of darkness to bring back water and supplies. The faithful white horse grazed the edges of the remote ledge outside the cave, never abandoning his watch while his master lay unconscious. The suspense lasted for weeks, enticing devoted listeners to the radio to discover whether their beloved masked man would survive. Of course, Tonto did save the Lone Ranger, and both continued their sallies against the forces of evil in the Wild West.

"You haven't fooled me with your magical mind games. I have only to shoot above the indentations of your footprints in the carpet to put an end to the Shadow!" I edged closer to the radio absolutely sure that the Shadow was trapped. How could he get out of this unforeseen turn of events? Every Sunday night, I eagerly awaited the unctuously threatening announcer explaining how the Shadow had learned to "cloud men's minds so they could not see him," ending with "The Shadow knows" and a lovely wicked laugh.

I could see everything happening on the radio. I didn't need movies to have the marvelous scenarios playing vividly in my mind. When I finally did see a Lone Ranger movie, I was disappointed that he was not as nobly handsome as the hero in my dreams.

No one had difficulty envisioning the cascade of junk that tumbled regularly out of Fibber McGee's closet, nor any problem witnessing the snippy, smart-alecky Charlie

McCarthy outwitting Edgar Bergen. After torturing myself with two episodes of *Lights Out*, I vowed never again to put myself through such horror. To this day, I vividly remember those stories, one about scientists who threw liquid hormones into the yard and then were crushed by earthworms the size of freight trains, and the other about a couple driving a deserted highway at night and overtaking and passing, over and over, the same driverless truck, ending with their car smashed and truck-tire marks beginning and ending nowhere.

My imagination served me superbly well in creating my own movies of the books that I read, and in the brilliant color that the movies of the forties lacked. My book friends – Heidi, Rebecca of Sunnybrook Farm, Ann of Green Gables, Freckles, Pollyanna, Girl of the Limberlost, Mary who found the Secret Garden, the Five Little Peppers, Little Women, Meg, Jo, Beth, and Amy, Hans Brinker, King Arthur and his noble knights, Mary Poppins – and ever so many more, all, to this day, create images in my mind that I remember clearly from the first time that I met them.

When I wasn't reading or listening, I was imagining, acting out stories in my mind, or dramatizing, alone or with my brothers, around the living room or back yard. I think I did not know how to be lonely. In fact, I often preferred to be alone so that I could construct time to suit my imagination.

Today, children see pictures everywhere and never have to rely on their imaginations for anything. The television is on all day and, failing that, the children turn to their computer games for entertainment, more pictures, and more violence. They don't have any concept of stories without battles, conquests, and property damage. Even if they could comprehend a plot concerning interpersonal conflict or the search for one's mission in life, they would reject it as not exciting enough. When they go outdoors to "play," they don't know what to do. Are there any equivalents today of our "cops and robbers," "cowboys and Indians," or "house" and "school?" We could lose hours of summer evenings in the intricacies of "hide and seek" or any number of games, which had rules made up in the moment of invention.

Children's outdoor time now is organized in structured sports in which parents have more stake than their kids. Kids do not play anything just for fun anymore, just for the thrill of running around with their friends. Could three friends play "football" with a wadded up burlap bag? Could kids "ice skate" on a frozen lake in their winter boots? Would any kid find amusement making clothes and musical instruments for a troll doll? Could a collection of stuffed bears and animals serve as characters in a story, ongoing for a week? Could two boys plan war campaigns with sixty decks of cards?

If children don't learn to use their imaginations, who is going to write tomorrow's stories, movies, and TV plots? Who will invent new machinery, medical equipment, computer software, and games? Will our bodies change to become giant cushions supporting heads designed only to watch pictures?

Sugar Cookies
By Janice Baker of Bay City, Michigan
Born 1947

I remember when my parents bought our first television. I was about five years old. I enjoyed watching *Howdy Doody* on weekday afternoons, Roy Rogers, and *Dale Evans* on Sunday evenings. They sang "Happy Trails to You" after their show.

My mother did our family wash with a Maytag wringer washer. She did not want us near it because she was afraid we would put

Janice's mom walking away, her grandmother, Helen Wejrowski, her brother, John, and her mother's sister, Grance Wejrowski

our fingers in the wringer. We did not have a dryer so mom always hung our clothes on the clothesline outside. I remember her bringing in our jeans and they stood up when she brought them in.

On Sundays, after we went to church, my dad liked to make our breakfast. I remember the sound of crackling eggs. He liked to make sunny side up eggs the best. After breakfast, we would go to Fisherville on Midland Road to visit my maternal grandmother.

Grandma did not have much money. She lived on a farm and her home had no running water or an inside toilet. There was a well outside and she heated her kitchen with a stove that she put coal in. She was a good cook and made her own bread. She made large sugar cookies and always had some for us when we went for our Sunday visit.

My mother would always tell us, "Do not ask grandma for anything." I was the oldest kid and had two sisters and one brother. We would walk into grandma's house and my little brother would ask, "Can I have a cookie?" My sisters and I would just laugh because mom had just told us not to ask for anything. Grandma was so happy to give us each a large cookie. My mom would say, "Mom, do not give them a whole cookie. Break it in half so they will not waste it." My grandma would say, "Evaleana, I made the cookies for them, I want them to have a whole cookie."

Her cookies were really good. I wish I had the recipe, but grandma never wrote anything down. I remember seeing her making a pot of soup and she would spoon some out of the pot and taste it, and then she would add some more salt or another seasoning. We would crack walnuts by putting them under grandma's rocking chair and as she would rock the walnuts would crack. She would always laugh at that.

Grandma did not drive so before Christmas she asked my mom to go to St. Laurent Brothers to buy some candy and nuts for the holidays. When we went to St. Laurent Brothers to buy the candy for grandma, we had to go across the Third Street Bridge. I always was uneasy about going over that bridge. Years later, that bridge collapsed. When we left the St. Laurent Brothers store, we went down Water Street and there was a display in the Rosenburg Furniture store window. It was a Santa sitting in a big green chair. We

Janice's sister, Sandra, her brother, John, Janice, and her sister, Beverly

really liked it. We would ask dad if he would go around the block again so we could see it. He knew we enjoyed seeing it, so he always went around the block again for us.

My mom came from a large family of nine. On Christmas Eve my mom's family would go to grandma's house. On Christmas Eve, we went to grandma's house in the evenings so when we went down Midland Road lots of the houses had Christmas lights. It was a fun ride. My sisters would say, "Look on my side, the house has all different color lights."

When we got to grandma's house, she had all of the candy and nuts set up on the table. As the evening went on, the door would open and we would run to see who came in. It was fun to be with our cousins and to see everyone so happy. My grandmother passed away when I was fifteen so there were no more trips to visit with her, but my parents took us to visit our cousins quite often.

Because my mom and dad were raised on a farm, they did some of the things at our home like they did when they were growing up. We had chickens, and my sister, Sandy, would play with them. We even gave them names and we would make them mud pies.

The neighborhood kids would go down the road where they were working on putting in an overpass over the expressway. We would take our round discs and slide them down the

hills. There was water in the ditch below and we would skate on it in the winter. I remember in the summer, we would walk in the ditch with our bare feet and we would see crayfish.

Farm House
By Helen Eichstaedt of Au Gres, Michigan
Born 1935

My name is Helen Jantzi Eichstaedt. I am married to Rudy Eichstaedt; we have been married for sixty years. We were married July 31, 1954. We were both born and raised in or near Au Gres, Michigan.

I was born in a house in rural Au Gres. My father, Menno Jantzi, went to Turner to get a doctor. My dad said it was so foggy that he had to put his head out the window to see. My parents at that time lived with my father's mother and sister.

I am an only child as my mother could not have any more babies, and this fact made her sad her whole life. I attended a one-room school in a small community up through eighth grade. I walked to school three quarters of a mile in all weather. After eighth grade in Delano School, I rode a bus to Au Gres. I graduated four years later.

Rudy and I were high school lovers and married July 31, 1954. We raised four daughters on a small farm near Au Gres. Outhouse and chamber pot was part of my young life. My parents never had a bathroom until after I was married.

My first baby, Peggy Ann, came exactly nine months after we married. We lived in an old farmhouse that Rudy's parents owned. They said that we could live there free for fixing and repairing the house. The house was full of bed bugs. There was a big black potbelly wood stove. My Father bought sulfur and started a fire with wood and let it burn all night. The smoke killed the bugs and we never had trouble with them ever again. My mother helped me wallpaper the walls and we rented an electric sander, and we sanded the hard wood floors until they were just beautiful. I varnished the floors, painted, and made curtains and we had a nice home.

There was no bathroom, but a room for one. The next year we put in a septic tank, stool, and running water. By May 28th, the next spring we had another baby girl, Catti Jane.

154

The name Jane was for my grandmother Jane Vandeusen. Eighteen months later another baby girl, Pamela Sue, was born. Then by October 30, 1960, another and the last, baby girl Penny Kay was born. Four babies in a little over five years took a toll on my body. I had a large ovarian cyst and had surgery to remove the cyst, and the doctor tied my tubes. There would not be any more babies.

Rudy was born in Au Gres also, in a house with a mid-wife, Mrs. Doan, no doctor. He is the youngest of six siblings. With four babies, Rudy worked at a small shop, Bopp-Busch, for almost twenty years. He still farmed with his father and we had many rough, poor years ahead.

I raised a garden, and canned and froze everything I could. We lived on venison, rabbits, squirrels, geese, and many kinds of wild life Rudy could hunt. He fished in winter on the ice, as he gets sea sick so bad in a boat, so he only fished in winter.

When my baby Pam was three months old, we moved to a new small, small house across from the farm. His brother built the house and the walls were almost ready to be plastered. We borrowed $3,000 to but the house and finish the building. Rudy's father was a carpenter by trade and he helped us build the kitchen cupboards, closets, etc. How I missed my old huge farmhouse. There were two small bedrooms in the new house.

We had three children in one bedroom, and Penny was almost five years old and was still sleeping in a crib in our bedroom. We borrowed another $3,000 to build an addition of two big bedrooms and another bathroom. We had bought used twin beds and had two girls in each bedroom, then turned the small bedroom into a utility room. We tore out a wall in the kitchen where the utility room was and made a larger kitchen. We still live in this house today.

Over the years, we have had bad luck. Rudy got his arm stuck in a corn picker and almost lost his arm. The doctors save his arm, but it was crippled. I have had ten surgeries. The last one was December 2, 2104 for a hip replacement. Rudy has had many strokes, seizures, and has slight dementia today.

Our four girls all got married; they gave us seven grandchildren and nine great grandchildren. We feel truly blessed. Without my faith in God, I could have never lived to be almost eighty. Rudy will be eighty in July 2015. We got married in the Au Gres Methodist Church and had all our babies baptized, and some of them married in the same faith and church.

Respect
By Betty J. Parker of Au Gres, Michigan
Born 1933

I was born in Banks area of Bay City, Michigan on October 14, 1933. I had pneumonia at one year old. The doctor said he could not do anymore for me. A neighbor, Mrs. Letaurnal, did a mustard plaster and onion plaster for my back and chest. It worked and I am in very good health today at eighty-one years old.

At Kolb School, my kindergarten teacher brought her dog to school every day. A blind Collie named Sweetie. I continued on at Park School through sixth grade, and then to Handy High School through eleventh grade.

Growing up, we lived in one house with an outhouse. We lived in only one house that had hot water. So for all my young years, I remember heating water on kerosene stove in galvanized tubs for baths, also for laundry with Fels Naptha Soap melting in one. A washing machine was brought to the kitchen where a chair was sitting with another tub with cold water for rinsing. First whites were washed, and then ran through the wringer to the rinse water. Dad had to put blocks on rollers to keep them tight to wring out dryer. We would hang the clothes on the line outside in summer and upstairs in the winter.

Summer games played were Blind Man's Bluff, Crack the Whip, throwing tennis balls over the roof to another person, walking on stilts we made out of wood, walking on cans we crushed over our shoes, hopscotch, jump rope, and tag. All the free things we had were paper dolls or coloring books on rainy days.

Winter games played were ice skating and shoveling snow. We lived down a long hill by the railroad tracks on North Arbor St. and when we needed coal for heat we had to shovel it all the way down. The plows never came down there. We shoveled snow to get money for Saturday cartoons and chapter play (twelve cents). We had a lot of snowball fights and built forts and snowmen. We made hills of snow and ran down them with our sleds.

In summer, my brother took us to "free shows" in his rumble seat. I remember the car in the winter, never had a heater. He used a "Bull Durham" bag filled with salt and hung it on the mirror to keep the windshield from frosting up. We had iceboxes in those days. You would hang a card in the window for the iceman, and if you got sick in winter, you got a dose of Castor oil or Molasses.

We never had a TV growing up or a record player. We had an old Roller Piano, and a rotary phone with a party line. I used to baby sit for my older brothers and sisters for fifty cents a night. There were no cell phones in those days or electronics, just good old family time.

I remember walking across 3rd Street Bridge; it would swing open to let a boat through. There was a seat to sit on and it swung out over the water. Since then, 3rd Street Bridge fell into the water. Going to the beauty shop for a perm is – those old hot electric rollers all over your head.

My mom, I, and my brother and sister walked one mile to church every Sunday and back. We attended Christian Assembly Tabernacle where Reverend Ross Roeder preached, we had two hours of church and one hour of Sunday school. We walked everywhere we went.

My dad worked for St. Lawrence Brothers' roasting peanuts for peanut butter. He passed away in 1945 from cancer of the blood stream. Five of us kids were still at home and mom had to work at restaurants doing dishes to help feed us. Dad's social security was not enough. I would go help her, so she could get done sooner.

Her legs were starting to swell and so she had a stroke when I was about fourteen. She was paralyzed on her left side. They would not let me stay home from school. I had to go for my four solids – no lunch, study hall, or gym. I had to dress and feed her before I left and get supper when I got home and everything else.

I never had much time for Sock Hops and all the other things that come with being a teenager. I got her back to walking (with God's help), but I would go back to the "good ole days" anytime. Today there is not much "family time." There are too much electronics.

I would not want to raise a family today.

There is no respect. I met the man in my life in 1947 and we got married in 1950. We had seven children and 21 grandchildren and 22 great grandchildren. We were married for 59 years. He passed away six years ago. I never had a TV 'til after we married.

Oh, also, I never had any spankings. There was respect in those days. I remember John F. Kennedy being shot. I was working in the grocery store when the news came on the radio. I felt very horrified that someone would kill our president.

My Dog, My Companion: Peanuts
By Edwin M. Koziol of Scottville, Michigan
Born 1930

In the early 1930s, there were very few cars on the road, and when one did pass our farmhouse in Victory Township, it usually was a Model-A Ford, and on rare occasions, a Model-T. They made a lot of racket and traveled at speeds that dogs could keep up with. Our dog Peanuts wore out a path along the roadside by chasing every car that went by. We lived at the bottom of a river valley and couldn't see an approaching car until it made its appearance on the crest of the hill, but we could hear it coming when it was a half mile or more away.

In my pre-school days, my nephew (who was three months older than I), my brother (who was 16 years older), and I would spend a Sunday afternoon on our front porch waiting for a car to go by. We would try to guess the direction from which the next one would come. The object of our game was to see who could pile up the most correct guesses. Often we would have to wait so long for a car to appear that we became bored and would quit the game.

Our family car was a Hudson sedan. It had a straight eight engine and so much leg space that it came equipped with extra fold down seats attached to the back of the front bench seat. There were no seat belts, and when my nephew and I were alone in the back we seldom sat still, and nobody seemed to care. We often tried to get Peanuts to ride with us, but he always refused to enter the car. He didn't even want to enter our house. When we

Edwin Koziol and Peanuts

once coaxed him to enter, he daintily tiptoed on the linoleum floor as if walking on sacred ground, which he didn't want to defile, and he made a dash out the door at the first chance he got.

When my mother collected enough eggs to sell or if enough money came in from the cream we sold or from some other farm source, we went shopping in Ludington, a town on Lake Michigan about ten miles away. The highlight of the trip for me was our visit to the dime store. My mother would help me mount one of those stools at the soda fountain and treat me to a hot dog, which cost around ten cents at that time, or if I wanted, I could get a hamburger, which cost just a few cents more.

Before we started to go home, we usually stopped at a gas station where an attendant would come to the driver's window and ask how many gallons we wanted. First, he would work the pump handle that was attached to the foot of the gas pump to fill the glass tank at the top of the pump to the proper level of gallons, and then he would unlatch the hose from the side of the pump and empty the glass tank into our car tank. At every stop, the attendant would lift the hood to check the oil level, wash the windshield, and check the air in the tires.

In those days, there were more gas stations in existence than there are today. I remember at least four that were located in Victory Township. Today there aren't any. One was located on Stiles Road two and a half miles from us, and the gas truck that supplied it with fuel would pass by our house. It had a heavy, long chain attached to its rear end, which dragged on the road. I never knew why, but I assume it had something to do with their fear that static electricity could ignite the gasoline.

On our way home from town, everyone in the car would try to be the first to spot our dog Peanuts. Peanuts would hear and recognize the sound of our car long before we reached home and he would run out on the road to greet us as we approached. We would meet usually about a quarter mile from home, and he would then run alongside our car back to the house. If it was night when we returned home, the first thing we spotted of Peanuts was his shining eyes bouncing up and down as he ran toward us in the glow of our headlights.

I really loved Peanuts. He was a very intelligent, kind, and loyal member of our family. I'm not sure of his breed. I think he was a pit bull. Peanuts was my brother's hunting companion. His specialty was treeing squirrels. He would chase one up a tree and keep barking at it until my brother showed up on the scene. Peanuts loved hunting squirrels so much that even in the off season, when our family was out working in the field, we could hear him barking somewhere deep in the woods informing us that he has a squirrel trapped up in a tree.

Unfortunately, we couldn't stop Peanuts from stealing eggs from the chicken coop. Eggs were a major source of the meager amount of money my mother had to buy food. My nephew's dad constructed an elaborate gate to block the chicken coop door. It had holes only large enough for the hens to walk through, yet Peanuts somehow managed to continue stealing eggs. My mother was very concerned about her ability to supply bread for our table. After all, we were in the middle of the Great Depression when money and food was scarce. I knew something was going to be done.

One day while my nephew and I were deep

in the woods fishing from the riverbank at our favorite pool, we heard my brother discharge his shotgun nearby. I knew immediately that it meant the end of Peanuts.

Brady's Flats; Riding Bikes
By Kent Graf of Caro, Michigan
Born 1954

There was a time in the 1960s when young boys spent most all day outside running and riding bikes. There was a magical place, or so it seemed, that was owned by the Loren Brady family. The sixty acres of land in section eight of Columbia Township on the eastern out skirts of Unionville was bordered by the Wiscoggin Drain on the west and Graf Road on the east with the Russell Drain running through it. The drains were surrounded by bottomlands that did not lend themselves to farming.

There was a nice little clearing in this bottomland nestled between a high bank and the creek (Russell Drain) and surrounded by a very nice wooded lot. The Brady Family was nice enough to let the churches and town folks use this area for picnics and general fun, hence it was called Brady's Flats.

I remember attending many church picnics in Brady's Flats. There were bonfires to enjoy and singing plus all the great food. I was a member of the Moravian Church, which was just west of the 'Coggin, so it was easy to organize and go there. We lived about a mile south, and before I could even drive a car, I would take the farm's International Super A down the road to the flats. We had a small homemade two-wheel trailer that my grandfather, Oscar Graf, built. We would use that hitched behind the A to haul picnic supplies and people. The removable sides were used for the seats.

Kids from town would use this area as a big playground. There were a lot of walking trails created throughout this area, so riding bicycles around the trails and up and down the small hills was a lot of a fun. Of course, with the creak drain running through it there would be some swimming when weather was real hot. There was an old sawmill on the east side of the picnic area too. We would play in there and ride the old roll track on a scrap piece of lumber. Sometimes we played hide and seek

or had war games using wooden guns that we made at home. As we got older, we would ride motorcycles around the trails and the hills. We also took the tractors down there and drove around where we could.

It was a great time in life when everyone seemed to be friends and enjoyed getting together. That area seemed really big especially using a child's imagination.

The year was 1967, and living on the farm was a lot of work. It kept us busy and was also a lot of fun at times. I was thirteen years old at the time and dad had retired the 1950 Chevrolet Coupe Deluxe in favor of a new 1968 Chevrolet Impala.

I got to take that 1950 Chevy for farm use. Ha, ha! I made a trail around the outside of our eighty acres and would drive that car around every night after school. I spent hours spinning the wheels and kicking up dust and blasting through mud puddles after it rained.

There was a huge ditch on the south end of the farm called the Bach Drain. My farm trail did an S-curve where this drain went north and then turned to the west. It rained quite a lot one day and Billy Levalley, a friend, was riding along. We hit a huge water puddle near the big ditch, and the muddy spray went everywhere. There was so much spray the windshield wipers could not clear it, so there was no way to see. Billy said, "You better turn, the ditch is ahead." I turned just in time to avoid landing in the bottom. Wow, that was close!

I drove that car around the fields for two more years and had a blast. Some of the neighbor kids ended up with cars too. Buddy Moore had an old Plymouth, Allen Strieter and Billy also had old cars. We got them together one day and we went tearing up the trail around the farm. It was great fun and did the dust roll.

On my fifteenth birthday, I had thirteen other kids over for a party and we all ended up packing into the 1950 Chevy. There was barely room to even steer let alone shift three on the tree. Kids were yelling and screaming as we went along. What a blast.

Billy LeValley, Doug Link, Ryamond Balzer, and I were very lucky to have motorcycles when we turned fifteen. Billy had a Honda 65 while Ray, Doug, and I had Sears 106s. We rode more miles and had more fun, even before we ever got driver license on those little bikes that we did later. We skipped football practice one afternoon to go riding and Ray took a spill on his bike and smashed it up. We got into a lot of trouble for that little episode.

My girlfriend at the time was Dawn Herman, and I would ride the Sears from our farm on Graf Road, going south on Hoppe Road, and then west five miles to Thomas Road, then north again for two miles to Bay Park Road and visit her. I would use all the back roads to get there, avoiding the main highways. Often times we would then ride some more out near Thomas' on Saginaw Bay. We had a great time together and I remember Dawn could do a lot of talking and I would just love to listen.

Doughnuts
By Sharon Kathleen Smith of Rincon, Georgia
Born 1940

My mother's family came down to Alma, Michigan from Onaway, Michigan when she was thirteen years old. They, and many others, relocated with The Lobdell Company after its consuming fire in northern, Lower Michigan in 1926. It became The Lobdell-Emery Company and remained a major part of the Alma economy until its doors closed for good in 2005.

When mom was a teen, she met the man who would become my father. He worked in the bakery in Alma and was the delivery boy who would make the swing in a little van out into the Little Crystal-Half-Moon Lake Area, north and west of Alma, taking baked goods orders to families in the "boondocks."

"Come with me on my run," he said one nice day, and mom, a cute little "flapper" went along. "Now if you want anything to eat, just help yourself and I'll take care of it," he said indicating the trays of boxes behind their seats. "Well, I'm not really hungry," Mom coyly replied as they started out, but at every stop while he delivered, she'd eat a doughnut. They were the newly invented frosting: "glazed doughnuts." She told us later, "I couldn't resist!"

"Last stop," Dad said, "Fancy tea party, special order." When he turned for the order

of "you know what's," all were gone! Mom started to cry, but dad reassured her all was well, (She could do no wrong in his eyes.) He went in with his best substitutes. "Boy! I had to do some fast talking in there!" he said when he came back. He had soothed the lady's ire and convinced her to take something else, the old charmer.

Mom made doughnuts for all of us (Dad and five children) through the years. She made fried dough-puffs from her best homemade bread dough, shaking them in a paper bag with cinnamon and sugar to make them more delicious! But she never turned down one of her favorite things: glazed donuts.

I got into trouble with doughnuts myself, when in the ninth grade at Stillwell Junior High in Alma. We lived about a mile from the school in the east end of town and I was able most days, to walk home for the lunch hour, and back. One day, I came home to find that the "Apple man" had come. In the 1950s, apple-growers would load up bushels and pecks of various kinds of apples and peddle them door to door in all the neighborhoods in town. So we had fresh apples for eating and cooking and mom was making doughnuts! She offered to make soup for me but I said no. My first class after lunch was Home Economics and we were studying nutrition. This day, teacher said, "Now class, I want each of you to tell aloud what you had for lunch."

Clair and Vivian Patterson

159

Uh-oh, I thought. When my turn came, I had decided to speak right up. "I had two apples, six doughnuts, and a glass of milk." Teacher was disgusted, "Well! Sharon!" she said, as the class laughed. I said, lamely, "I couldn't resist!" I can't remember my grade that year for Home Economics; probably just as well.

About the year 1950, when I was ten years old, the city began to sponsor a decorated bicycle parade downtown in the middle of the summer with prizes!

I entered the first year. My younger brother and sister were too young. In those days, crepe paper came in large flat folds like yards of cloth. We cut our own streamers and made special things like rosettes and leaves. My mother was so inventive. She made a kind of raised oval hoop out of clothes hangers fastened to both sides of the rear carrier on my bike. This rose up well above the head of the seated rider, and behind, and could be decorated (in my mind, anyway) as beautifully as the Hanging Gardens of Babylon.

I dressed up in my Halloween, dyed blue curtains fairy costume mom had made the year before, decorated every inch of my bike in blue and white crepe paper, hung flowing streamers and a sign, "Fairy-Land" from the hoop and won first prize! I can't even remember what it was, but it was like fuel to the fire for my mom who was determined that my younger brother could win next year. The next summer came. She hung a "work of art" crepe paper picture of an American eagle from his hoop, helped him decorate his bike in red, white, and blue, dressed him in khaki and an old M. P. helmet. In the meantime, I dressed in my elder brother's Robin Hood costume, decorated with green and streamers with a sign "Sherwood Forest" from my hoop, all the while grumbling that "no one is helping me!"

Then, whatever the reason, judges tired, perhaps, of patriotic themes, my brother didn't win. I did, again. He went with me to the Montgomery Ward Store, the little M.P. and the tall Robin Hood. We chose a small table size, Art Deco Style radio. There was a lot of good stuff to listen to in those days, (our favorite, "Let's Pretend" on Saturday mornings.) None of it politically correct, but all for children, morally perfect. That was my last parade. A neighbor boy called out one day later, "Sharon, are you going to be in the bicycle parade next year?" I told him no,

because I was too big. "Good!" he said. He was relieved. I didn't mind! I was growing up.

Buggies and Lunchtime Syrup Pails
By Joseph H. Fishel of Hart, Michigan
Born 1924

I was born on a small farm in Mason County, Riverton Township, on Hogenson Road, ½ mile north of Sippy Road. I was the seventh of nine children. My father rented our house; us three youngest children were born there. Our only form of transportation was horse and buggy, or a team and hay wagon.

One day my mother decided she would go to Scottville, about seven miles away, and I could go along. So, it was horse and buggy time. We were going east toward Wiley Store when a right side wheel came off. Mom was not able to lift the buggy and I could not replace the wheel since I was only four. Soon a man came and put the wheel back on for us. After we returned home, my Dad examined the buggy. He discovered the axel had been assembled backwards; he knew this because the threads on the ends of the right axel were left-handed threads.

In 1927, my Dad bought a new Model-T Ford truck—a flatbed model with open slat sides. When we would take a ride, seven of us older kids rode in back and two babies rode in the cab on Mom's lap. My Dad always drove.

Then came the Great Depression. In 1929, my dad decided to go back to Brown County, Indiana, where he was from. So on Election Day, we were heading south near South Bend, Indiana. It was dark. Suddenly, we were rammed from behind by a drunken driver. No one was injured, but the truck needed repairs. The other driver's insurance took care of that, but since we had to wait for the truck, his insurance also paid for our hotel rooms. The next morning in the dining room having breakfast, the waitress asked what I would like. Being in a strange place and very bashful, I could not think of anything except "fig bars," which got a laugh. So mom ordered for me.

My dad rented a house for us in Martinsville, Indiana where my grandfather, Jacob Fishel, lived. What I remember about him was that he was a Civil War veteran, was blind, and had a beard. He was in the Regimental Band and played the fife (like a flute) during the war. We stayed the winter there. In the spring, we came back to Mason County where my Dad rented a farm on Hawley Road. Then he rented a farm on Sippy Road across the road at St. Mary's Lake.

In 1931, I went to school for the first time at St. Mary's Lake School, located on Marrison Road, a quarter mile east of Hogenson Road. I carried my lunch in a small tin syrup pail like a lot of the other children. At first recess, most other kids grabbed their lunch pails and ate a sandwich. I ate my whole lunch because I still could not tell time and thought it was lunchtime. At noon, I thought the day was over, so I walked home. Mom was surprised to see me. She said, "It's only noon! Go back to school." That turned out to be a long day. By suppertime, I was very hungry.

Later, Dad rented a farm on Sugar Grove Road, a mile east of Custer Road. Then he bought a 40-acre farm on Stiles Road south of Chauvez Road. We lived there when I was drafted in the U.S. Army in January 1943.

When I turned sixteen, I had learned to drive the car, a 1927 Buick seven-passenger straight eight. The car dealer said that it had been owned by Greyhound Bus Co. as a short-trip bus. The way I learned to drive came about because at haying time, one horse became very lame, so Dad hitched the car to the hay wagon to haul hay. I drove the car while Dad pitched the hay on the wagon and my brother George built the hay load.

It was time for me to get a driver's license, so we went to the Sheriff's Office in Ludington. He needed a birth certificate, so we went to the courthouse. They had no record of my birth. The doctor who had come out when I was three days old had not recorded my birth, as he should have. So we had to go home and get the family Bible and bring it to the courthouse to prove I was really who I claimed to be. Mom had recorded all nine of us children. That family Bible is now in my possession.

The fall I turned 18, World War II had begun. Young men were being drafted. A farmer who had several threshing machines had come to our place to ask if I was available to work, which I was. We went around the county threshing field beans. Most places provided meals for the threshing crews. At one place, as we were eating supper, a young girl was helping her mother serve. I took a look at her, and the idea came to me: This is the woman I'm going to marry. Yeah, right.

About a year later, I was drafted. I spent nearly three years in the Army, serving in China, Burma and India. We were on a troop ship coming back to the U.S. when the war ended. I received a furlough and orders to my next camp.

When I got home to my parents' farm, green beans were being canned at a factory in Scottville. Since they needed help, I got a part-time job there. As I was busy doing my thing, a young lady passed by. Wow! I asked a co-worker, "Who is that?" He said, "That's Mildred Marrison. She lives a mile west of Custer Road on Marrison Road." I knew right away who she was: the young woman I had met three years ago. So, I took it from there. We were married 68 years before she passed away in October 2014.

Jogging the Memory
By Paul R. Desander of Saginaw, Michigan
Born 1947

A look at your memory jogger brings back thoughts of my childhood. I could write on a number of these topics, but will narrow my vision to a few.

One-Room Schools: I was born in Saginaw, Michigan at St. Mary's Hospital in 1947. I was raised in Taymouth Township. I was a single sipping. Therefore, when a youngster, I had to make up games and use my imagination to occupy my time.   I had many childhood friends just a quarter of a mile down the road from my residence. I would spend much time being babysat by a couple of older girls if mother needed to go away shopping.

No one had many toys: What we had we generally made, such items as slingshots and bow and arrows. As we played in the sand, we would make wood soldiers and construct sand castles. We would let our imagination run wild. Some pretty impressive constructions were done that I still remember today.

First days of school: As I turned five years old, I still remember my first days of school. There weren't any busses. So we walked to school. Just like the old saying, "I walked two miles to school each day, uphill both ways in snow this deep." This was a true statement. My one-room school was two miles from my home. All the kids would walk. As kids got to my house, they would take me, care for me, and protect me from harm. Sometimes, if we were lucky, one of the older neighborhood boys would drive a team of horses with a hay wagon and pick me up along with other students along the way. When we got to the school, he would pasture the horses in the schoolyard. When school was done for the day, we all would repeat the process. However, this was a treat. It didn't happen very often.

A typical day of school K-8: One teacher and nine classes. Kindergartners had little curriculum. The program was designed basically to allow the young student the development of being away from mother and home. There was lots of being read to by the older upper grade students. Graham crackers and whole "just milked" cow milk, sleep, and play time recess was the highlight of the day.

Games and Classmates: Back in the day, there were no play scrapes. If there were swings and seesaws, they were homemade by a few concerned parents. Many games were tag, red rover, and pie.

Tag: There were many versions of tag. They all began with someone being "it" and trying to chase someone down and tag them before they got to a safe zone. There was always one less safe zone than player in the game. Therefore, there was always someone without a safe place. There was lots of running.

Red Rover: Choose Sides and form two lines hand in hand. And try to win as many team members as possible from the other side. How this was done was by choosing a member of the other side to try to break your line. If they were not successful in breaking your line, your team got to pick a member of the other team to join their team. If they were successful in breaking your line, the other team got to pick a member from your team. It all started with one team inviting the other team to come over by saying, "Red Rover, Red Rover, let Paul come over." Therefore, Paul would try to break their line. The game went on until recess was over. I don't remember anyone ever winning that game.

Pie: This was a winter tag game. A large circle was made in the snow and divided up like a pie with a free spot "Safe Spot" in the middle. This was the only safe spot. You could only chase a player to tag them by following the lanes of the pie. With one free "safe" spot there were many players running around that could be tagged.

Baseball was King: All students were invited and all would play. Yes, as seen many times on Sandlot fields, sides were chosen by selecting captains. This was usually one of the older students and start by tossing a bat to the other Captain. Alternating Captains would go had over hand to the top of the bat. When the bat runs out of room for another hand, the Captain would choose "Eagle Claw." He would put his/her finger on the top of the bat while the opposing Captain would try to swing the bat out of your hand with only three tries. The winner got to choose the first team member.

Everyone Plays: With a one-room school with around thirty to forty kids, everyone had a place on the team. When it was your turn to bat, an upper classman may help you bat the first time. A new player would start out with grounders. As you improved, you would progress to one in the air and two on the ground until you were getting all three pitches in the air. The game would go from one recess to another, or until one team just got too far ahead on runs and we would start over. Think about it, first graders against eighth graders. The game was about learning the game and not winning the game. Everyone would go home and have a backyard game. Such games as "500" where a fielder would get points if you catch a fly ball, bouncer, or grounder. When a fielder accumulated 500 or more points in the field, they got to bat. If you hit a foul ball, you were out and players would rotate. Indian Ball was where you hit balls to the fielders. You put the bat on the ground facing the fielders and players would roll the ball trying to hit the bat. If they hit the bat, then they could bat. If we had four players, we would have a game.

Schoolroom: I believe I learned more in the schoolroom from the upper class students. As the teacher would be giving instruction to the other grades, upper class students would be helping lower class students with their studies. They would do such things as helping with reading, doing flash cards on Mathematics, Penmanship, Geography, and homework. As assignments were complete, a student would listen quietly as the teacher gave a lesson to the class next to you. Most generally, those students were upper classmen. Therefore, an underclass student received a preview of things to come. I know today that I learned more from my classmates than from the teacher.

Spanking at school: Classroom discipline was never a real issue. As you may have seen on TV shows as *Little House on the Prairie*, sitting in a corner might be seen more often than slaps on the hands or spankings. Missing recess and writing on the blackboard was usually punishment. Although as the memory jogger said, "It wasn't the licking at school you feared but it was what was going to happen at home once Dad and Mom found out." I still remember my mother saying, "Just wait until I tell your dad about this when he gets home."

Patricia Cameron

A Loving Large Family
By Patricia A. Haring of Clare, Michigan
Born 1944

I was born into a very large family of seventeen births. We grew up in rural Gladwin and had fantastic neighbors and friends.

My mother passed young leaving nine of us kids at home. An older sister and her husband lived very close and she cared for us

Patricia's parents, Doc and Vera Cameron in 1924

every day. What an angel uh?

In the winter months, school may be shut down for eight to ten days because of the plugged roads. Us kids would help my sister wash woodwork, the painted white cupboards, and varnish that ever loving scrolled furniture. But then we would play for days.

We built snow forts and the boys partitioned rooms off. We had a kitchen, living room, and a bedroom. We'd steal cookies and fruit from the house "like we had to" and have fun, fun, fun. I remember getting a little set of tin dishes for Christmas and we used these, even a real coffee pot. I'll never forget those cute dishes of mine.

Our brother was the driver on our sled. The hill was very icy and steep. About five of us would lie on top of each other and really go! He happened to hit a fence post and about killed us all. He was knocked out and some of us were kind of bloody. We went to the house for repair and go right back sled riding. I think the saying is "no sense-no feeling."

The corncrib was another playhouse in the summer. After the pig feed was gone, we'd sweep it out and have cement blocks for chairs and a big spool for a table. The cats were our babies and we diapered them with

Pat with her brothers and sisters

old rags and used old towels for their blankets. We received quite a few scratches but Porter's Salve healed us up quickly. We had a large farmhouse so my sister and I swept the downstairs floors. I'd go halfway which was a crack in the flooring and she would continue to other half of the rooms. Sisterly love uh? This chore was done daily. My older sister, the caregiver, baked pies, bread, cookies, and cake about twice a week.

Our meals were five-course every day. We had our own places at the table to sit down. Vegetables and fruits were canned by the hundreds of quarts. Our meats of course were raised on the farm and a big potato bin was also full in the fall. We also had our own apples and onions. Hotdogs and lunchmeat were a real treat for us. My dad sold cream to the Kraft Creamery and of course, the Inspector came often and would give us kids our own little box of Kraft caramels. They were so good! We also had our own milk but we'd get butter and cheese off the Kraft truck.

Our groceries were about $20.00 a week and we'd have a trunkful for that price. Every week we'd get a big bag of candy that we shared equally. See, we were good! We also shared chicken pox, flu, mumps, measles, and whatever else came along.

When us girls had to use the outhouse, the boys would sometimes rock it and tell us girls the rats would bite our butts. We'd soften up the catalog sheets with our hands that was our toilet paper and run to the house to wash our hands. Bath water was also shared by us kids, girls first then the boys. The boys put us in an inch of our life if we peed in the water. "Like we'd tell them, right?"

The laundry was horrific in size and I remember my one brother getting his arm in the wringer. Not good! The clothes for ironing were dampened, starched, and ironed to perfection. Us younger girls got to iron the pillow cases, hankies, and boxer shorts. We were considered growing up with this chore. Another married sister helped iron for hours.

When we were driving age, my dad would let us take the car to town to "drag main." We'd bring the car home pretty empty and sometimes not enough gas left to get back to town. Not good! After a while, he put a gas barrel in the yard, but then our friends would happen to run out in the area and Dad would give them gas. You always "helped thy neighbor" and he wouldn't be angry with them.

Most of us kids graduated high school and could have continue your education if you wanted. I should have because here comes another story. I married a big ol' teddy bear of a man. He was from a family of sixteen, great family. Anyway, he gave me his checkbook and told me I could write the checks from now on. Oh my, my! This I did all over. He didn't tell me I had to write them and subtract them from the ledger so I continued writing, "man all those checks." I was really rich. I didn't take bookkeeping in school; I took home economics. Well the bank called me and

Pat and her husband of 50 years

wanted myself and my husband to come up and talk to them. I said okay and asked him if he was buying a new truck. He said no, so we went up to talk to the officers of the bank. They told my husband I'd overdrawn his account horribly and I told them I had all them checks and I know I had married a rich man. Anyway, after our talk they would take so much a week out of his check. This is where payroll deduction plan came in effect I'm sure. Good thing we were newlyweds. I had my first lesson in bookkeeping that weekend. Actually, I pretty much check my math over and keep a pretty good checkbook today! The ledger I mean!

We always had Friday night date night. We'd go to town and have a couple of toddies and supper out. One Friday night when we came home, my husband decided we should mow the lawn. It was pretty wet that week and the rain was supposed to start again. So we got on our mowers and cut the lawn. Well I got stuck in the lower part of the yard. He saw I was stuck and came over to help me get out. He got off his tractor and gave me a great big push. I got out and continued my job. I looked over the yard and there he laid in the mud, face and belly down. I'm laughing like no other, went over to check him out, and maybe help him. He got up, shook his head, and didn't find it really funny. We both continued our one and a half hour job, me laughing the whole time to myself.

We raised four children and have eleven grandkids. My husband had health issues and passed in 2013. I wouldn't change a thing if I could. Wonderful memories and what a milestone we shared!

PS I don't ever remember myself or my siblings getting a spanking. Go figure, we were loved!

Grandma's Farm
By Sandra L. Hecht of Saginaw, Michigan
Born 1940

We visited Grandma at her dairy farm during the early 1940s up north in Kalkaska, Michigan. The trip from Kawkawlin, Michigan was a long 225 miles. Railroad tracks and telephone poles with aqua-colored glass insulators followed the highway. It seemed to take forever. Dad broke the monotony as he yodeled and sang country songs.

My brother and I volunteered to collect eggs from the hen house; nobody told us hens didn't appreciated that. And the mean gander goose would chase us across the yard all the way back to the house.

Mealtime with Grandma meant, "put only on your plate what you plan to eat, no wasting, otherwise, no leaving the table until your plate is clean" Oh, no! Here comes still warm milk straight from the cow and barn. Good thing she knew I was lactose intolerant.

We were certain to use the outdoor privy before dark when we might hear yelping coyotes in the orchard.

Nobody told us stay away from the spring fed pond where the cows drank and a black moccasin snake swam. We saw it once and that was enough!

Nighttime came and we slept upstairs with no heat, on straw mattresses under cowhide covers.

Think of living in the Snow Belt here during a severe snowstorm. Grandma tied a rope from the house to the barn so she could find her way to hand milk ten cows. Thank goodness, she finally got a milk-pasteurizing machine.

When Grandpa rode his tractor for the first time since horses, he yelled whoa when he stopped at the end of a row. The whole family witnessed that and broke out in laughter.

Life was interesting at Grandma's farm.

When we first visited, we still used hand water pumps inside and out. By the way, only certain individuals were able to use a slingshot shaped willow branch to locate a water source for drilling the well.

A cistern caught and stored water from roof eves after rain. Water was heated a top the large wood burning range where Grandpa cooked pancakes on the iron grill.

A sod floor basement cellar held fresh and canned veggies; outside of dairy products and we excused Limburg cheese, nasty! Grandma had a hand spun butter churn for making butter of which they sold at the farm or in town.

There was a parlor with a player piano and in the corner an old Singer sewing machine with a foot pedal. She sold many quilts as a substitute income. Some were made from floral print seed bag material. Grandma sold many!

A clock had a chime for each hour, hand wound; it rested on a wall shelf next to her chair and footstool. It faced the potbelly wood stove and overhead on the wall a plaque read, "Jesus never Fails." We relocated her woodpile into the addition at the backdoor. Ha Ha Gander Goose

Spring-cleaning meant total house cleaning, dusting and airing out; wood burning isn't clean energy.

I never understood what they did to frozen line-hung laundry. The old wringer washing machine was dangerous. It could catch aprons, fingers, or hair too near the wringer. But it's something how they reused rinse water in a separate tub. Wonderful the phrase, "Waste Not."

Darning socks and patching is now a lost art. Here is my poem: *Darned Socks*

Did you know that Mother "darned" socks
Do you know what that means today
It wasn't that she thought socks were darned
Such as they stunk on sweaty days or got muddy
On muddy days or were misbehaved playing hide-n-seek separated in the washing machine
Think it over now young whipper snapper
Do you know there is a clue because in the old days
They fixed things rather that throw them away
So so sew what do you think, would you know how
Or what darn is

Childhood

Dad built the swing from used telephone poles and it was stronger and taller than usual. It had double seats and we sometimes placed a plank across them to seat a third friend. We lived on sandy soil perfect for contests to see who could swing the highest then jump off the furthest then mark the result in the sand. One time we dug a deep tunnel and nearly got caught in a cave-in. Not a good idea!

Girls made long connecting chains from dandelion stems, jumping rope, played house with dolls, and hide-n-seek. Boys played cops and robbers with cap guns, built forts, played ball, rode bikes, went fishing, played marbles, and tag. The list goes on and on.

The ditch was full of carp and bloodsuckers.

Our little dog Blackie jumped in trying to catch a carp; he was good at this. When he got on land, he was full of green algae and burs.

Dad had a very old Model-T car with a rumble seat. We invited neighborhood kids for a ride to vacation Bible school. Part way there the motor fell out. Dad simply got out, put the motor in, and reattached it. And we were on our way.

The boys always returned to the ditch despite the bloodsuckers; remember how they were used by doctors to pull poisons out of sick people's blood? The ditch was a real draw for muddy shoes and clothing. Mother was noted for hosing them down from head to toe before they entered the house. I wrote a little poem in regards:

Peagreen Dutch Monster
Mother told bedtime stories
This one made us flinch
About a peagreen monster
Who lived down in our ditch
He was the type of monster
Who like to bite your jeans
And if this ever happened
Kids could turn peagreen
Since we felt quite threatened
Imagining those sharp monster teeth
Deserving us his prey
We stayed out of ditch dirt
And our jeans stayed clean

They all appreciate the simple, fun childhood back then.

Bay City Folks and the Depression

Grandpa and family scoured the railroad tracks where the coal cars traveled. They collected coal pieces that spilled off train cars and took then home to heat the house during the depression.

Farmers were fortunate to have a home and grown food. Some city folks bartered with them for provisions to provide for their families.

Shoes and clothing were passed down through the family. They were altered and repaired from large size to small for children. They replaced insoles with rubber since shoes were necessary to attend to school.

Uncle Ernie had a pet crow and taught it to talk. It flew across the street to a meat market where it asked for a chunk of meat. This was quite a novelty and people increased shopping there. The crow flew back and got half the

166

gift.

A family from the great prairie dust storm stopped at Grandpa's house begging for food. He was kind and willing to share. There was much fish and deer in the area as they fished and hunted often.

The circus came to Bay City and traveled past Grandpa's house north on Euclid to Midland Street, across the Saginaw River Bridge to downtown Bay City. Imagine that!

Front porches were sometimes a get together place for family and friends where they sometimes played musical instruments and socialized, better than texting!

When we parked our car at the curb at his house, we could smell limburg cheese from there. Maybe we should come back later.

Bay City was noted to be a swampland with droves of mosquitoes and Indians along the Saginaw River. The ice business flourished to provide for household iceboxes for food preservation.

The river was thick with huge sturgeon fish and the skies overhead darkened by thick flocks of ducks and waterfowl.

A raft type drawn bridge from east to west first and later was built the Midland Street swing-bridge.

Mail was transported by boats North and south on the Saginaw River from Bay City to Saginaw. Logs floated north on the river and it was a tremendous lumberjack era. There were many bars and bar fights along the riverfront district.

Beautiful mansion style homes dotted Center Avenue. They traveled with trolley cars on rails.

Those were booming times.

Cousin Trouble
By Harold Wright of Kent City, Michigan

I was born on a farm in Newaygo County near the Hardy Dam. When I was four years old, I decided I wanted to be a farmer, so I asked Mother to let Santa know that I would like a farm set. Being a loving mother, she let Santa know and I received a large box of rubber animals. In a sandbox in the front yard, I set up my farm and spent many hours doing farm chores.

Harold and Sally in 1951

One Saturday, a few weeks after Christmas, my uncle dropped my cousin off for Mother to watch while he was taking care of some business. That cousin, who was four years old as well, enjoyed my farm. I played with him there until I had tired of it, so I left him there to play. The following day I went out to play with my farm. I was shocked and horrified. He had bitten all the heads off of all my solid rubber animals. Mother never found an excuse to use when asked to watch this cousin.

When I was five, I started kindergarten in our country school. It was called Oak Grove Country School and was located two miles from home. The first day, after a mile and a half walk, I sat down and told my older brother and sister that I could go no further. They said, "Okay, sit down and wait." Being scared to be alone, I decided to keep up with them. I did the rest of the year.

My cousin the same age also walked with us. He was a troublemaker. Every day on the way home, we passed the local Oak Grove Cemetery. There was a gate on the north side and a gate on the south side. He entered the cemetery from the open gate on the north side and when he reached to the south side, the gate was locked. When he got through, he had to climb over a fence to get out and tore his jeans. When getting home and his mother questioned him about the tear in his jeans, he told his mother that we had locked him in the cemetery and he had to climb over the wires on top of the gate. His angry mother came to our house the following morning with the locked-in story. Mother didn't believe her, but to be sure, she asked the girl next door who was with us what happened. She verified our story.

Another time, the boy became angry because we were walking too fast, so he threw his dinner pail on the ground and stomped on it. When home, he told his mother I had stomped on it. Again, his mother appeared and the neighbor girl confirmed his lie. During the next few years, he did several things to blame on me. His mother never questioned mine, but believed him. To this day, she doesn't like me. One day when alone she said, "You don't look like the rest of the family." She was implying that I am illegitimate child by some bum somewhere.

One year, our teacher, Miss Anderson, asked us to bring in a decorated Easter egg for her to declare a winner. One girl in our class was not real smart and she brought her eggs. At lunchtime, she walked up to the teacher's desk and cracked her lightly boiled eggs on the teachers head. She spent two weeks at her desk at the morning and afternoon rest periods.

This school only went through the sixth grade. We were bussed to Howard City High School for the seventh grade and up. I have never forgotten my first class there. On the stairs, on the way up to our homeroom on the second floor, my principal had a girl on the stair steps giving her a lesson on not skipping school. In the hallway upstairs, a teacher had a very tall man by the ear leading to the principal's office. When I came to my classroom, another student was right behind me. When I passed through the door and he took it, there was a strong wind coming through the hallway from an opened window. The wind blew the door shut before he could do anything. A redheaded, middle-aged teacher jumped up from her desk and grabbed him by the shoulders and shook him hard. When she finished, she told him, "Do not come into my classroom, and slam the door!" I thought what have I gotten into here?

Our English teacher was a well past middle-aged. When she introduced herself, she said, "My name is Eva Lovely." She had a face much like the face of a horse—long and slender. She said, "If I hear one remark out of any of you, you are out of here!" Classes went pretty well throughout the senior year after this.

I dated a girl from the grade below and had become very fond of her. I decided to take her out to dinner and a trip to the local theater, and then to the local dancehall. Returning to the dance hall after two dates, she told me she could go with me on any night except a Saturday night. Saturday night was the only night my father's car was available. I decided Saturday night can have her.

Luckily, my cousin's wife (when she found out I was available) asked me if I would like to take her sister, Sally to the junior prom. I grabbed the date, and what I found of her sister was amazing. She had a nice figure, blue eyes, and light brown hair and a beautiful face. For the following year, we dated every Saturday night and she was in the eleventh grade.

I asked her if she would marry me after her senior graduation. She agreed. Two weeks after she graduated, we were married. I was working in Grand Rapids and had an apartment close to my work. She moved into it. She had no transportation since we had only one car. She didn't obtain a job. However, she didn't like the city so we moved back to our hometown where she worked at

Harold and Sally in 1976

168

several jobs. I obtained a position at Gerber Product Company. I was soon offered a job as a supervisor in the production department; cold storage and office clean up. We raised five boys. One since has died. We are now enjoying our retirement. We have traveled to several parts of the United States, two islands and more. We are ready now to enjoy the rest of our days with our children close and our good old dog, Duke.

Just Use Your Imagination
By Frederick J. Karns of Hersey, Michigan
Born 1931

I grew up in the '30s and '40s in the little Mid-Michigan town of Reed City, and at this time, U.S. Highways 131 and 10 met right in the middle of town. We lived in a big house on a hill in the northwest corner of the city. We needed a big house because our family eventually grew to 12 kids, and I was right in the middle: the third of six boys and the sixth of 12 kids. Since there was such a difference in the ages of my siblings, our house seemed to be a gathering place for the neighborhood kids, especially in the wintertime because our hill made for good sledding.

At this time, most of the roads were just dirt roads, and in this part of town, there was very little traffic. If the kid was clever in his steering of the sled, he could go down

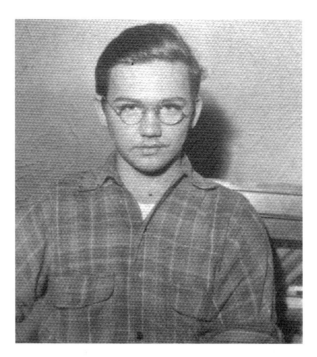

Frederick J. Karns in 1949

the hill, turn onto the road, and go almost a block before he came to a stop. It sounds dangerous, but this was a different time and people didn't drive as fast. Besides, these were neighborhood kids and the parents knew that their children were the ones doing the sledding. Besides, not everyone could afford a car.

It was a free and easy time for kids. There were very few if any TVs and no computer games, so we found our recreation in different ways. Of course, most everyone had radios and there were programs that we would not miss: The Shadow with Lamont Cranston, Jack Armstrong, the All-American Boy, The Lone Ranger and so many more. We never were at a loss for entertainment.

On the other end of town, about a ten minute bike ride away, was the pond. It was manmade by damming up a river, and it was the spot to go to in the real hot weather. As a kid, I never questioned how or why the pond happened to be there; it had just been there all my life and was open to everybody. Every so often, it would be closed so it could be treated for something or other and then it would be open again. There might have been a lifeguard there, but I doubt it. It was usually so crowded that if someone did have some trouble, there would be someone around to help.

The big house on the hill

169

There were so many things to do, games to play, and kids to play with. There were lots of running games like tag, or capture the flag, hide and seek. If the weather was bad, we would go upstairs in our house, or whatever house we happened to be at, and play cards or some board game. Monopoly was popular and we would usually spend a couple of days or more on a game. This would usually be later in the day when it was too dark outside ,so it was hard to finish a game in one setting, but the board would be set up and waiting for the next opportunity.

To the south down the road a bit was a vacant lot that was just perfect for baseball, football or whatever we decided to play. We very seldom chose sides in baseball; we would play workup. We would choose four or five guys to bat first, usually the youngest, and then the rest would arrange themselves around the bases and in the field. Then when an out was made, the one that was out would go to last field and everyone else would move up a position and we would have a new batter. It wasn't very easy to get a hit with a lot of fielders and the only score we kept was how many times at bat we had. This way everyone got to bat at least once and there were very few arguments, just a lot of fun.

Saturdays there was always a movie in the afternoon and for a dime you could get in the theater and another dime would buy a bag of popcorn. Of course, the movie had to be a western, and we knew all the cowboys: Don "Red" Barry, Wild Bill Elliott, Hop-along Cassidy, and of course Gene Autry and Roy Rogers. There was always a serial playing too that would make us want to be there every week to see how they came out. We always had a large garden and unfortunately, Saturdays were also the day that we had to work in the garden if the weeds were coming up. Quite often if there was something that the guys wanted to do, we would have all kinds of help getting the job done.

Our family had a cow, chickens, and sometimes pigs, so there were always chores to do. There was a field west of us down the road probably an eighth of a mile or so where there was a lot of grass. I don't know who owned it, but we would take the cow there every morning before school and tie her to a log so she could drag it around but not go very far. On the way, we had to go past an old mill that had burned down years before, and all that was standing was just four cement walls about ten or twelve feet high with gaping windows and doors. It was quite a frightening place if you had to go past it in the dark, which I had to do many times, but it was quite a place for playing spies or beating the Germans or Japanese. It had "secret" tunnels through the walls, and one of the older neighbor kids had built a small shack beyond the south wall over one of those tunnels. Needless to say, this was used to get away from all kinds of bad guys.

In the northwest corner of the building was another small room about six by six that had the same high walls but the door way was blocked up. There was a big metal contraption that we always called "the boiler," but was probably a part of the circulation system that was leaning against the doorway in such a way that the doorway couldn't be seen. Around this "boiler" was a bunch of bricks and pieces of cement that filled all the places that the boiler didn't. This contraption was round, probably four feet through, and about six feet high. At the bottom it had a square tube about three feet long and about a foot and a half square. The front was open, but where it entered into the boiler was a metal flap that fell down so you couldn't see inside. To get into the center of it, you just had to crawl through the opening, raise the flap, and crawl inside. Once inside, you could go out through the bottom and enter the room. This was the only way in. There was a hole in one of the walls where we kept a deck of playing cards and any other treasures we wanted to keep there where they would be protected from the weather. I have never known an adult to go into this room.

Just outside the walls of the old mill on the East side was a big maple tree that had fell over or had been blown over, but still had enough roots in the ground that it was fully leafed every year. It had a double trunk and both were off the ground, but the top one was about six feet higher than the bottom. We had ropes slung along the branches where we could swing like Tarzan or to get away from an enemy very fast. It was also a good place for an ambush if you were pretending to be a sheriff after some bad guys.

Imagination played a big part in our activities, and we were never bored. Now the pond is gone, the vacant lots are all filled with houses, the theater is gone, and the old mill and the tree have been cleared away to make room for progress. TV and computer games have taken the place of kids getting together to use their imagination to entertain themselves. I am old now, but I still remember those days fondly and I wonder if the new generation will have this kind of happy days to think back on when they get to be my age.

The House, the Grandparents (Andrew and Sophie Little)
Written by Karen Elliott-Grover
Submitted by Raymond A. Elliott of Mount Pleasant, Michigan
Born 1941

It was an old house. For as long as I could remember it was an old house. It was made of stone. It had personality. It changed its face sometimes through the years. I remember sometimes it had red trim around the window and door casings and sometimes white. I remember when the old windmill stood tall and majestic and then when it was no more. The Grandpa Andy, I suspect was fearful of it falling down with age and the grandkids tried a few times to climb the rungs.

I remember when there were many tall oaks and maples, and elms and the yard seemed a forest to a young child and then the shock of seeing the near nakedness when a lot of the old magical masters were cut down. Age, I guess is the reasons, as I recall first branches were trimmed, and little by little, one at a time the trees went. What a violation!

I suspect that grandpa felt as violated. I remember his avid interest in the birds and wee nesting things and vague comments about the "poor birds and nests being disturbed."

The house in 1974

Grandpa Andy was a complex old coot. He lived with his wife, Sophie, the round, and rotund Grandma.

Grandpa claimed to hate the "Old Farm," his inheritance, but could be seen spending awesome hours in the flowerbeds, trimming the lilac hedges, milking the cows, and tending the garden with tender loving care. He would spend hours in his retirement years sitting on the old porch swing or looking out the back stoop watching for the deer that would come out in the before dusk hours. In the years before he retired, he always without fail, "bagged" his buck with the other hunters, but I always suspected it was with a lot of respect and yes, empathy for the critters he so enjoyed watching.

His respect for anything growing and living was a mixture of delight and awe to observe. In his garden, we grandkids were allowed only if we walked in between the rows and were careful not to tread on any living, growing thing. He could be downright strict about some things and we only made a mistake once and learned from it.

He was strict, but always teaching, sometimes firmly, sometimes gently, especially when teaching about plant or animal life. I don't remember ever getting a spanking from Grandpa but his lectures you never forgot. He could shame you until you never wanted to get in his bad graces again.

The most angry I ever saw the Grandpa was the time us kids went to the neighbors, (The Cotter Kids,) and didn't come home on time. I can still see his long, tall frame trotting along beside us with a long, green, willow switch. He never laid a hand on us, he didn't have to. His long, angry stride and the presence of the switch was all we needed to know he meant business!

I remember too, his threats about the dangers of the tomato hornworms and to this day, I'm not sure if it was a sure way for him to get us kids the heck out of his garden or if he truly believed there was some unknown element of danger about the hornworm in those years. (But I have my suspicions.)

I remember too, the "Teaching" experiment when Grandpa decided we ought to learn to use a bow and arrow. Some of it is vague now but I do recall bales of hay and the ever strict, but ever patient way he taught safety first. (And the sore arm after, I suspect he chuckled about in private.)

That is the kind of sense of humor he had. He could tell a fish story like nobody's business, and have you believing every morsel. He liked his beer pretty well and sometimes his trips to town to pay the ole light bill wound up to be an all-day thing. "Town was a little one horse place or should I say a one pub place and everybody there knew Andy as they did everyone else. They knew if your light bull was paid on time, which neighbor got a new bull or how many milking cows you had at that time. The best part about that, "everybody knows everybody's business is when you twisted an ankle or was down with the influenza, sure as heck, there were the Cotters or the Newmans, or some caring neighbor to milk the cows for you.

Grandpa's trips to "town" bring to light memories of Grandma. Some vivid, some now fading, but never will I forget the sometimes mysterious, sometimes comical, loving, little lady who was my dear Grandma. She is the one who taught me how to make mud pies. It was her subtle suggestion to put eggs and vanilla in them, now mind you she never came right out and said, "Put some vanilla and eggs in your mud pies." (But she did suggest they would turn out better.) I do know when my mother caught me at it and I tattled on Grandma, I can still see the silly grin on Grandma's face as my mother chewed her out.

Grandma Sophie had a weird sense of humor, which I know I have inherited, or so my offspring tell me. I recall an incident when we were picking apples and I can still see my Aunt Shirley. She was to shake the limb to bring down apples and the adults and we kids would pick them up. Well, one big, beautiful apple came bounding down and hit my mother right square in the back. Well, you guessed it. Grandma got the giggles, and

guess who didn't think it was so funny. We all had to cover our smirks over that one.

Going forward in time, I remember an incident in my adult life that was a hoot and again involved Grandma and her laughter. My Mother and Grandma had occasion to visit me in my home in West Virginia. I recall two incidents and to this day I associate Limburger Cheese with those "Kodak" moments. On one incident, I remember coming out on the balcony of our upstairs apartment where Grandma was lounging by the railing. She looked a little meditative and I asked her if she was okay. She stated, "Oh, Yes. I just wondered how long I could stand here before I would see one little leaf or twig move." It was so hot and humid and their wasn't the remotest breeze available. I associate that incident with Limburger Cheese because just prior to going out on the balcony, we had feasted on rye bread, onion, and Limburger cheese sandwiches and every time Grandma opened her mouth to say a word, that's all I could smell.

The other laughable situation, well to some, was that when they arrived from Michigan, my mom had a severe case of poison ivy. Well, take poison ivy, hot humid weather, and my poor mother itched all night long and my Grandma, bless her heart, laughed all night long.

Grandma Sophie wasn't all laughs though and she could get downright serious on occasion. I remember at times when someone would get hurt on the farm on in the yard and can still see her standing there with her hands fluttering, chanting, "Oh, Jesus, Mary, and Joseph!"

Sometimes she seemed calm as a rock but quite often she got flustered easily. Usually when she seemed the most calm and serene if you looked close, while she sat in her rocker, she usually had her rosary beads laced through her fingers.

I remember the wonderful smell of cookies and pies baking in her kitchen, her raisin crème pies were out of this world and though I have her recipe, I never could match hers.

I remember her panic when I would be there and she would find out she was getting out of Town Company. She would fret, and stew and wring her hands and them put on the most wonderful meal. She would go out, and kill a chicken and put it in the pressure cooker, quick peel potatoes, (or if someone else was there, they were "entrusted" to that job.) Usually, too, one of us was delegated to go to the basement. God help you if that job was yours and Aunt Shirley went along. She was so afraid of the dark and the basement had all these dark, shadowy corners that could trigger your imagination. Quite often your directions were to get carrots and potatoes from the root cellar, a can of blackberries or peaches, and on special occasions some of Grandmas well known dandelion wine. That was all fine and dandy unless you had Aunt Shirley as "Helper" with you. You'd get halfway up the stairs and she'd take off running as if a giant monster were after her and by that time you were convinced they were going to get you!

Recalling Grandmas sense of humor triggers mine. Growing up I remember her always wearing a housedress, usually an apron, and high heeled shoes. (I never could figure the shoes, either it was an expression to the world that she was always a little bit dressed up, or they were just plain comfy to her.)

The funniest picture I conjure up of her was at my brother's, Mick wedding reception. I will never forget seeing her sitting on the floor of the entryway, trying to put her boots on and giggling. It wasn't dandelion wine but something sure put her in good spirits.

I guess in summary, I remember the heart-to-heart talks we had. How she inadvertently taught me how to cheat at "Rummy," the mud pies, the way she could scowl when she was upset with you, and the amusing complexities in her personality.

I remember how hard she tried to understand the Old Testament and her stating, "All I see is so and so begot so and so and, boy they were busy people!"

I know I was very blessed with my grandparents and the treasure of memories they gave me and all of us.

I remember the old granary and playing in it and eating raw corn and wheat, beehives made in the stone walls and Grandpa finding a huge honeycomb there. Also being scared of going into one of Grandma's upstairs rooms and wouldn't go in there alone. Bedtime snacks when we stayed overnight like apples from the cellar cut into big wedges by Grandpa's jackknife, popcorn, Grandma's homemade

cookies with a glass of good cold, cream rich cow's milk. We'd sit at the kitchen table and have a bowl of home canned stewed tomatoes with a saltshaker available. Other nights it was not uncommon to have homemade bread broken into a cup and again some rich, cold cow's milk poured on to soak into the bread.

Grandma relayed to us about how hard it was during "The Depression" and how Grandpa trudged miles to obtain a few hours work and then walked miles to buy produce on sale for them and to share or trade with the neighbors. Grandpa relating stories about his World War I experiences, and his sense of humor, candor, or downright comical details when he told stories

The Great Depression made a lasting effect on Grandma's life. She remembered the hard times and found it hard to "squander" money.

When Grandma died it felt like the soul went out of the family. Grandpa carried on the best that he could, relying on family, but most especially the kids. Week after week, one grandchild or great grandchild would stay with him. He loved the kids and even the little ones.

The old house still stands as solid and as old as it always seemed. There are new owners to fill it with love and happiness.

Skating Performances
By Dorothy Conrad of Freeland, Michigan
Born 1929

As a child in the 1940s, I remember being on my "vintage metal roller skates" with a key, skating for hours daily. My friend and I would skate up to a business place with a nice circular cement area. That was our pretend stage. The business building was closed on the weekends and it was located away from other homes. No cars or people to bother us. So, we had the whole area to skate and pretend we were outstanding ballerinas, twirling and twirling like we were on stage and in front of a huge audience! Now, if we only had some music from a portable radio, we would have really been in heaven! But, it was in the '40s.

My Mother
By Patricia Alden of Chesaning, Michigan
Born 1933

She was the most wonderful person on earth. She raised ten children after my father died of cancer, when I was nine months old. I was born in 1933.

She had no A.D.C. or help in anyway. She did laundry and sowing for other people to support her family. She raised chickens and had a garden to feed her kids.

I had three brothers who went into the service, two in the Army and one in the Navy.

Those were the days when people took care of themselves.

Winn
By Marjorie Barrett of Mt. Pleasant,
Michigan
Born 1922

I was born and lived 3 1.2 miles south of Winn on Winn Road with dad, Thelo Gifford, mother, two sisters and one brother. It was a forty-acre farm where we raised chickens, had some farm crops and always had a big garden.

We ran a gas station and had a few groceries to sell. Med cut up ice from a small nearby lake (later called "Gifford Lake") which was put in our icehouse so in the summer we made ice cream.

Dad bought and set up large batteries so we were the first place to have electricity in the area.

I lived there until 1941 when I graduated from high school.

My grandpa and grandma had a store in Winn. My son, Wayne Barrett, has an antique store in Winn, Michigan now.

Polio
By Mildred Peterson of Chase, Michigan
Born 1924

When I was 15, we lived in Homer, just outside of Marshall, Michigan. I lived with my dad, three sisters, and one brother. My mother had passed away when I was 10. I arrived home from school one afternoon with a bad headache and weakness in my legs. Dad told me to go to bed and he warmed some blankets in the oven and wrapped them around my legs to help relieve the discomfort. Later the doctor was called. When he arrived, I was so embarrassed because he was young and had to examine me. This was the only way to diagnose polio back then. I was quarantined in the house for six weeks while I recovered. Friends and family came to visit me at my bedroom window. My Aunt Marie came to help with my care. She often did this for women who just gave birth. I was lucky with this experience because I have no crippling effect from the polio like some people did.

My After School Entertainment!
By Robert R. Stroope of Bay City, Michigan

I could hardly wait to get home from school to listen to my radio programs. Our radio was located on top of the refrigerator with instructions not to move. After school, I would put a kitchen chair up next to the refrigerator door so I could stand on it and get my ear close to the radio. My list of programs to listen to were The Lone Ranger, Sergeant Preston, Ski-King, and Ossie and Harriet Nelson. Each series was not too long so I would stay standing on the chair until they were done and then outdoors to play. Somehow, the broadcasts were so real that you swore you were there and on the scene. It was awesome how the voices and sounds could be so real and make you feel that you were part of the story. I loved it!

My Dad's Home Remedies!
I will never forget my dad's cure for all sicknesses, for colds, sore throat, or fever. The very thought of going through this process made staying home from school a hardly never thing to do. I can only remember missing school from being sick maybe twice in my whole high school days.

This was the process. As soon as you mentioned not feeling well it was off to bed immediately. My bedroom was upstairs and I already knew the procedure. First, an extra hard rub down with Ben-Gay until your skin was burning with the heat from the rubdown. Next was the Vicks treatment, both nostrils, lips, and throat. Sometimes he would dip the Vicks on his finger and make you swallow it. Next, the big pile up of blankets, many, many. Then, came the verbal procedure. You never get up only to go to the bathroom. Do nothing, just rest. You always seemed to have the chills at first and then the sweats that was a good sign thing. He would come up and see how things were going. Even if you were not quite up to par you always said you were feeling fine. He said that by sweating you were on your way to getting better.

Way Back When
By Karen Rolley of Hope, Michigan
Born 1939

I grew up on a farm in Michigan with two older brothers, three older sisters, and one younger brother. I, being a girl next to the youngest brother, had lots of instruction. Ha! I am now 75 and a half years of age. I hear the kids nowadays being bored. I loved the farm and was never bored. I met my first sweetheart in the barn—not so boring.

We had milk cows, pigs, and chickens to take care of and we grew crops—corn, hay, wheat, and buckwheat. We had a large vegetable garden and strawberry patch to keep us all busy, along with the barn chores.

Karen and her husband, Jack in 1959

My mother and we girls canned all summer long using one-quart and two-quart jars. When I was nine or ten, it was my job to pack cucumbers in the two-quart jars with a sprig of dill so Mom could make dill pickles. I loved them, so it was a fun job. With nine people around the table at mealtime, canning was necessary.

We had our own meat. Mom canned beef also and we had chicken for Sunday dinner after church.

It was a good life with happy times. I have my oldest sister who is 86 and a brother who is 82 who are both still living. My husband passed on five and half years ago. Living alone is not so much fun. I thank God for being here for me and my family.

Classic Sayings and Cost of Living
By Betty J. Van Alstine of Reed City, Michigan
Born 1923

Enclosed are some old sayings that we used through the years of 85 years or so ago. It seems like every situation that came about, someone had some "old saying" that was appropriate for it. Here are a few that come to mind and still "fit" the subject of today.

My mother was born and raised in Scotland and I've heard her repeat the following many times. "Some have meat, but cannot eat, and some have meat that can eat. And we have meat and we can eat it so let the Lord be thank it."

If you gently touch a nettle, it will sting you for sharp pain, but if you grasp it like a piece of metal, it as soft remains.

Life is like playing cards, you've got to play the ones that are dealt you.

Don't criticize a person until you walk a mile in his shoes.

Red sky in the morning, sailors take warning. Red sky at night is a sailor's delight.

A carpenter's wife usually lives in a shack.

A boy from one of the states in the south saw three men dressed as firemen. He said to his mother, "Look Mom, those men are like the three Wisemen, they just came from a fire."

Equality: What's good for the goose is

good for the gander.

The verse "I give up, I've washed my hands" is found in the Bible Matthew 27 Verse 24.

There is more than one way to skin a cat.

Sometimes I wake up grouchy and then other times I just let him sleep.

The shoe is on the other foot now.

I don't think they have both oars in the water.

Don't jump from the pan into the fire.

There's a screw loose there.

You've made your bed, now lay in it.

The squeaky wheel gets the grease.

Beware of a wolf in sheep's clothing.

Don't bite off more than you can chew.

Their light is on but no one seems to be home.

Can you remember these prices? 1933 Cost of Living:

New House	$5,750
Average Income	$1,555 per year
New Car	$550
Average Rent	$18 per month
Tuition to Harvard University	$410 per year
Movie Ticket	$.25
Gasoline	$.10 per gallon
First Class Postage Stamp	$.03
Granulated Sugar	$.59 for 10lbs
Vitamin D Milk	$.42 per gallon
Ground Coffee	$.35 per pound
Bacon	$.25 per pound
Eggs	$.16 per dozen
Fresh Ground Hamburger	$.11 per pound
Fresh Baked Bread	$.07 per loaf

Chamber Pots and Outhouses
By Lois Laplow of Midland, Michigan
Born 1932

I am now realizing nostalgia. I was born in Midland in 1932, one of four siblings. My ancestors were the Windovers and Wymans.

I married my friend's friend, Ray Laplow, in 1951. Yes, I remember many things that are obsolete now, like the chamber pot and outhouse on the farm on what is now known as Rogers Road. When I was 15 years old, our farmhouse burned to the ground. Dad took the horses out to pull the car through the big snowfall of that year, 1946, I believe. They couldn't pull it through, so I started running

on bare feet, which I froze. But thanks to God, a great aunt brought them back to health again.

Yes, we listened to radio, had party-line phones, record players and teachers, could discipline students, and parents backed the teachers, not the kids. Yes, we took baths in an old washtub on Saturday evenings. And Mom used the old wringer washer, which was in the basement that you had to go outside to get to the basement door.

I hated going to the outdoor toilet because I was terribly afraid of spiders and snakes. I also helped milk cows. And we all ate meals "together."

Trip of a Lifetime
By William A. Jones of Bay City, Michigan
Born 1936

In 1946, my parents took their three kids on the trip of their lives. We travelled out west from early June to late August in a 16 foot travel trailer pulled by a new 1946 Hudson. My folks were both 36, I was 10, my brother was 8, and my sister was 4 years old. My dad had planned the itinerary for months.

Two days before we left, my dad was driving my mother's sister to her wedding in his new Hudson when the car just quit running after smoke came from the dashboard. A tow truck driver found a screwdriver under the dashboard in the radio that had recently been adjusted and shorted out! Our newly ordained cousin/priest awaited patiently at the altar

Bob and Bill in 1946

William's mother, Del, Bill, Sandy, and Bob in 1946

unforgettable memory was one Sunday we were in the middle of nowhere and our mom made us read our prayer books because we couldn't attend mass! My best recollection is meeting and briefly travelling with a family we'd met who had a girl my age and who I had my first "crush" on. Her name was Pat Schoffstall.

We ended up in California at a friend of my dad's. He sold the trailer for about what he'd paid for it and we stayed in motels on the way back home to Michigan. I still have most of the snapshots my mom took. The only double exposure was a picture we took of Gene Autry after seeing his radio show!

After we returned home, in the fall we moved to a larger house and my maternal grandfather died. Yes, 1946 was quite a memorable year for me.

Fun as a Kid
By Janet M. Reis of Saginaw, Michigan
Born 1949

I remember the outhouse we had when I grew up. We had to use it every day. It was far away from the house and in the winter or at night; we had a pan with a lid on top to use.

With the party line, my mom had to wait for someone to get off the phone to use it.

For Saturday night baths, we had a big washtub not a bathtub to get cleaned up in. Each had to wait his turn. My great grandparents had a Banya, a Russian bathhouse, in the backyard where they lived on Burham in Saginaw. We would visit there sometime and would have to use that to clean-up. It had a lot of steam made of wood and we used homemade soap. It stood next to the chicken coup.

My favorite teacher at Shields School was Mrs. Shade in kindergarten. She always gave me a stick of gum and told me to keep quiet and not chew it until I got home. She was really very kind to me. She helped me not to be afraid.

When we moved to the city in Saginaw, we got milk that got delivered to our door and put into an icebox. We would ask the milkman for ice in the summer to suck on. It was cool like a Popsicle. My mom used to make popsicles out of Kool Aid, putting it on

until the bride and my dad arrived a half hour late, in a coal truck.

We left the following Monday after breakfast at a diner my dad owned. He was a self-employed bill collector. This was the first time I'd heard coffee and a donut called a "bellywash and a sinker" and hash referred to as "sweep up the kitchen" by the waitress. Our first stop was the Kellogg factory in Battle Creek, Michigan to watch Rice Krispies being "shot from guns."

Our tour included the National Parks of Yellowstone, Bryce, Zion, the Grand Canyon, Yosemite, and the Petrified Forest. We went to the bottom of Meteor Crater and climbed halfway up the faces on Mount Rushmore. We toured Hoover Dam, swam in the Great Salt Lake in Utah, drove through the Mojave Desert at night, walked through the Redwood Forest, and saw Grauman's Chinese Theater and the Corn Palace in Mitchell, South Dakota.

We were able to camp near the stream in Yellowstone where you now cannot. We didn't know at the time why my dad was extremely cautious driving on mountain roads. He was petrified of heights and I take after him. One a stick and they were really good. We played baseball out in the dirt street in front of our house at Ullvermont. It was two way then.

My mom still lives there. She is eighty-nine years old. I live up the street from her. I visit there every day. I used to go to the old Jerome School. It's gone now and only houses there now. And the pizza place is a vet place now, Sheets Vet. The drug store is a party store now, Iconking and our old church is behind it across the street. It's a Presbyterian church and is over 200 years old.

We played lots of games outside, marbles, cops and robbers, and hide and seek. It was fun with no computers then, just your imagination. We had a bad snowstorm when my brother was in grade school. He is younger than me. There was snow up to our waist and you could not get the backdoor open. Only snowmobiles could move about.

My mom grew up on a farm with cows and pigs. She collected eggs, worked in the field picking raspberries and other stuff. She had lots of chores to do. I had a lot of fun playing as a kid chasing around outside playing in low ditches in Shields after the rain. In the city, we had an ice rink in our backyard that my brother made. It was lots of fun. We made snow forts and stuff. It was more fun when I was little than it is now. You used your mind to think of fun things to do.

The Old Log Cabin in the Woods
By Velma Grey of Hesperia, Michigan
Born 1930

I was one of four children, three sisters, and one brother, born in an old log house in Oceana County, Newfield Township. I was the only child to be born in this house. The old house had only three rooms and my parents' bed was in the living room. All of us kids in the one bedroom.

We only had one kerosene lamp and my mom kept it in the kitchen until the dishes were done and then she would bring it in the living room and read western stories to my dad and us kids. I remember waking up to snow on my pillow.

My dad plowed the fields with our horses; their names were Dan and Ben. One day when my dad was plowing and my brother and I were following behind in the furrow the horses suddenly stopped. So, my dad went in front of them and found my brother Lyle asleep in the furrow.

One night we had an old tramp come to our house and my dad let him sleep in the hay barn. The old tramp's name was Wesley Franklin. We had an old root cellar where we kept our potatoes, carrots, and canned fruit. We had an old hand pump where we got our water.

One day I was in the field picking wild strawberries, I saw a big snake, and when I screamed I saw all its babies run down its throat.

We had an old outside toilet and at night, we had to bring in the slop jar for night potty. Some of our remedies were Fettle, Vermafuge and Castor oil.

A car battery ran our only radio and the only time it was played was at night and only my dad when he listened to Gabriel Heater and he had it on when fights come on, and neighbors came to listen.

My mom scrubbed our clothes on a scrub board and tub. My mom made our toys from old socks, we got new bib overalls for school to start, and that's when we got shoes again.

My favorite teacher was Norma Beckman. We walked to school in very deep snow for about a mile or more.

I was eight years old when we moved from the old log cabin in the woods, and we moved about two miles, and were much closer to school.

It was there I met my husband, but we were just little kids. Later when we got through eighth grade went our separate ways. My brother started running around with what now is my husband.

Quite some time later, we married and had five children, four boys, and one girl. We were able to buy the land where we went to schoolhouse where we now live.

I still own and live where we went to school. Three of our children started school there. My dad who was born in 1895 went to this same schoolhouse I have now.

We were married sixty years and he passed away seven years ago.

I will be eighty-five years old on April 20, 2015.

A Farm on Van Wormer Road
By Richard L. Browne of St. Charles,
Michigan
Born 1924

The only recreation we had was to go dancing and ice-skating. We went to Browne's Dance Hall at the corner of Swan Creek and River Road on Saturday when we could. This one Saturday it was stormy and blowing snow badly. They did not plow the roads back in them times, and we wanted to go dancing. We were not old enough to smoke or drink and we didn't anyway. We told mother we wanted to go dancing and she said, "You better not go, you may not make it home." We said, "We will be alright," and we went. About one o'clock when the dance was over we started for home. It was two miles west on Swan Creek Road to Van Wormer Road. When we turned on Van Wormer Road, we only got a block or two from Swan Creek and we run into three feet drifts of snow. That's when we got out of the car and walked ½-mile home.

When we changed into warm clothes, lit a lantern, went out to the barn, and harnessed one of the horses. We got on the horse and rode a ½ mile to the car. My sister Charlene got off the horse and got into the car and I rode my horse Gyp ½ mile through the drifts home. My sister went into the house, and I went out to the barn to take the harness off Gyp, and ran into the house. After I got warm, I was too glad my mother had put bricks on the stove to be put in my bed that night. I thank the Lord for the wonderful mother, dad, grandmother, brothers, and sisters.

This is a true story of a family on a farm in James Township. It was a farm on Van Wormer Road and the home is still there. Klucks Nursery bought the farm after my grandparents and parents died.

Charles Joe Browne married my mother Bernice Alice Van Wormer, and lived on the Van Wormer Farm. Charles Browne worked for HG Heinz Pickle Company at a substation in St. Charles. He gave pickle contracts to the farmers in the area of Brant. St. Charles.

When they were ready for picking, they brought them in to the station, my dad run for HG Heinz, and they were put in big wooden tanks and when they were filled, they were taken to Saginaw. One day the neighbors noticed that dad did not go home. They went over to see why and found my dad dead at the bottom of one of the tanks. He was overcome with paint fumes, while painting the tank. He left my mother with five children, Morley, Wylie, Robert, Richard, and Charlene a sister. My mother had to go to work in Saginaw, while my grandmother Alice Van Wormer took care of us for five years. My mother remarried a good man by the name of John Wenzel, and they had three boys, Thomas, Earl, and John.

While I was growing up, I worked part time at the Schromke Dairy and other farms. I earned enough to buy a used Model A car. The Saginaw News gave me a route from Van Wormer to Strobel Road and my sister and I delivered papers for eighteen cents a week.

Grateful Experiences
By Dolores Stack of Vestaburg, Michigan
Born 1942

Oh boy, what memories you have stirred up! Where to begin…

The year is around 1946. I was four years old and my sister was six. It was just the two of us, but eight years later we had a baby brother join our family.

There were a lot of kids in the neighborhood. One family had nine children and another family had only one. We played all kinds of games like tag, red rover, Mother May I, Cowboys and Indians, marbles, and iny inie over (not sure how you spell it.) We would toss a ball over a shed and those on the other side had to catch it, not knowing what

Dolores and her sister Darlene

179

direction it was coming from. Occasionally we would get the idea to put on a play, but that was as far as it went.

For a special treat, some of us would go see a Roy Rogers movie. Of course, we walked there, never thought of anyone giving us a ride. The cost, if I remember right, was 20 cents. What a thrill it was to see this movie on such a huge screen. There was no TV yet. Today, many homes have almost as big of a TV in their living room.

The most important memory I have during this part of my childhood was when my mother would call us home from playing to listen to the radio because my dad played saxophone in a group called *The Blues Chasers*. It was on WFDF out of Flint, Michigan. He also would play at New Year's Eve parties and brought us home noisemakers and a hat.

One of the chores we had at this time was pumping water from the well. You had to pour some water in first to prime it, and then start pumping fast and furious. It was hard pushing but you could hear the water coming eventually.

I recall ice being delivered in the neighborhood. The big ice tongs would carry chunks of ice to be put in the icebox.

We can't go without mentioning the … outhouse! No matter the weather, you went outside, unless you had a "pail" inside, which came in handy. There was no squeezing the Charmin either, because there wasn't any. You would use pages from a catalog!

When my grandfather came for a visit, we would usually go for an "enjoy ride" in his 1950 Buick. He would sit in the backseat between my sister and me. Sometimes just the three of us would go get ice cream sodas. He collected pennies in a copper bowl and dumped them on the floor for us to count and we got to keep what we counted. The funny thing about it was I was counting 1, 2, 3, 4, etc. and my sister was counting 2, 4, 6, etc.

We spent a couple Christmas' at my other grandfather's place. We called him Poppa. He had bubble lights on his tree. It was a special time for me because this is where I heard Santa's sleigh bells and knew I'd better get to sleep.

I'm grateful that I experienced these times and others that came later like helping my mother do the wash in a wringer washing machine and hanging it on the clothesline,

playing 45 records, and going to dances and of course listening to the king of rock and roll, Elvis!

Keeping the Faith
By Consepcion V. Buckley of Baldwin, Michigan
Submitted by her husband, William L. Buckley
Born 1967

I remember so much as a little girl that I even shock my own family. We were like the Walton's or Brady Bunch but we were the Villalpando's. As a Baptist Christian family, we read our bible and prayed daily. I believe we prayed morning, noon, and night because of witchcraft in our bloodline. Not anymore since we learned how to pray it away by saying "In the blood of Jesus leave now!" Waking up to Christian music or parents singing. Baths out the way at night so breakfast out the way and so off to wash my face and hands and brush my hair and teeth and put my clothes on that are laid out for me. Looking in our triple mirror dresser, do I look my best? For I am representing my Lord and Savior and my family. All done now to run and use the outhouse. If I should ever fall in, nobody would ever find me I feel. Daytime it was safe to walk anywhere with so many siblings I was never alone nor bored. I watch my family play kick ball and dodge ball but my favorite was marbles, hide and seek and the game called "skipping rocks" where you drop a rock into the water and it just sunk!

I loved playing with the chicken grain, as a chicken would follow the trail of the grain. What a smart chicken! My mother would grab the dumb chickens by the neck and twist it right and left and the head went into a bag as the body went back into the cage. One day my brother decided to let the headless chickens loose so I'm running in circles crying and screaming until he puts them all back in its cage. Naptime waking up so happy seeing my mother always busy. Sad I missed going out with Dad to the river. Everybody returned wet and sad. Daddy said everybody jumped out of the car and into the river swimming and playing in the water with the "Bears" he yelled, "Time to go!"

Consepcion's daddy, Rev. Ignacio Guzman

It's Friday because Mr. Bruheart stops by and hands my daddy cash in his hands. So my brother and I run to collect apples off the ground and handed it to him and we received a shiny quarter. We had so many fruits and vegetables as God promised a table of plenty. Amen! My brother said that sugar cane was the real candy so I'd pull it out of the ground and ate it but I prefer an apple anytime! Oh what fun it is to make mud pies! Rat's I soiled my clothes so off I go to wash up and throw my clothes in our new wringer washer that only adults are allowed to use. They have to pay close attention to it or possibly lose an arm. So nobody is around and I push the big red button on and off. Stick a stick through the arm and I fought to keep it but it won and I ran.

Back to the outhouse I go. I heard my mother yell my name in terror. I came out running trying to pull my pants on and seeing my brother and mother in the middle of the road. It was a hit and run and my mother thought it was me but it was Sheba that died, our dog. Tears just flow from everyone's eyes. Then my other brother was yelling that his dog was having puppies underneath the front steps. As he tried to grab a puppy, his dog almost took his hand off.

Well everybody helped work and clean and cooked. I played in the sink water to help. My daddy had a high IQ. He said the book to read about "our purpose in life" and "how to live" was all in the book called the Bible. With our parents, you were only spoken to once, never spanked! You would hear "Yes," "No," or "Will See" so no broken promises. They could even be so wrong but never disrespected.

We took turns going to a restaurant and sometimes they refused to serve us. So we quietly left. Thanking God for the good, the bad, and the ugly. I feel the good die first and go to Heaven while the ugly stay behind until they get saved to get to Heaven. My turn to go into town. If you're happy and you know it, clap your hands! Keep my hands to myself and don't touch anything. Refuse food and drink until parents says yes or no! At the gas station, one man pumps the gas as another man checks under the hood and clean the windows. As daddy and I walk in he whispers "highway robbery those gas prices!" Daddy buys my bubble gum and says chew it correctly or lose it! I chew with a big smile, thank you.

I will never understand why was it so stressful and tense going grocery shopping with a police officer smiling and laughing. Happy to be home now watching my parents chisel the freezer to make room for the meat. Our parents never discussed anything negative, not bills, not illness, nor death. I guess my brother died at age one and we never talked about him because we knew he was in Heaven with Jesus. That's truly home! We never discussed sex. And don't you dare say you don't feel well because then you see a dark brown bottle with a thick liquid that taste awful! Prefer tea and honey!

We all got excited to have three televisions not in different rooms but one on top of each other. One had a good picture, one with great volume, and one with large buttons to turn the channel. Mickey Mouse was my favorite sing along channel. Disagree on a channel and lose TV for the day.

As far as a telephone, there was private line, three or two lines. Every time I would get bored, I'd pick up the phone and listen to their conversation of other families talking. I'd hang up as soon as I heard my mother coming! Even if there was an emergency people just didn't want to hang up! One night my sister, my brother, and I were home alone and someone tried breaking in the backdoor. Explaining it's an emergency to call the police was hard to get a free line, it took a while. Soon my daddy and all five of my brothers charged the back but he was gone then the police came.

One day everybody was busy and the phone rang off the hook so I decided to answer it. "Hello" I said! What's my name? Concha! Where do I live? Here in a big green house! What am I wearing? My play clothes. All of a sudden, my mother took the phone away from me and announced to everybody that I am never allowed to answer the phone. She explains to me never to talk to strangers alone nor on the phone. Adults go to adults for help not children!

First day of school! My own cubby, change my boots to shoes and crying because I didn't want to leave. Mother said will come back when we have a nickname to call me. My name is Bonnie!

We never missed a day of worship because we worshipped morning, noon, and night every day. Invited to another church we packed-up and moved again. Felt like every year moving. Every sibling born in different cities in Texas and two of us born in Michigan. Men dress their best and women and girls always in dresses was the rule in Texas. Thank God for Michigan who showed us come as you are to church! I get to wear dressy slacks now to church.

Choose your battles, which one is worth fighting for! I'm in sixth grade everybody has a costume and I felt left out. So when I came home I begged for a princess costume for Trick or Treat. And both parents said "No that's the devil's day." I cried until one of my brothers bought me a costume, promised to take me around only one block, and will never worship the devil; it will be for fun. I'd say with excitement "God bless you" but brother said you have to yell "Trick or Treat" and the candy was almost gone before I got home. Thinking candy from strangers might go in the garbage. As much as I love the Lord, I still love that holiday, Halloween.

I ask my daddy to walk me around the carnival please and he did just that! Walked around and left! Watch how you pray and watch what you say! Mother prayed about taking me and my brother to the carnival and after that the fourth of July fireworks. And the next day there was a brown paper bag full of tickets for the rides. Thank you God, we do this every year across from the LC Walker Area on a hill with a blanket.

God doesn't make mistakes. It's up to us our choices in life. Hang around positive people who love you and who bring you up when you're down. Love deep because love forgives! Love is cool, calm, collective not yelling or screaming or in your space. Never hurting or abusing. Words hurt more than a slap in your face. It takes two to make a family both working, cleaning, both cooking, and both caring for a child. Even take turns and take your own time outs with dates alone without your child. Praise each other and saying thank you means a lot. There is no perfect parent nor child. You just do your best and make memories that last forever! Pray for each other! Would you rather be right or happy? The devil is a liar; he puts doubt and fear in you. Don't allow him to steal your joy. He attacks with illness, but keep the faith til the end as God promised.

Family Times
By Virginia (Ginny) Bouchey of Saginaw, Michigan
Born 1930

Our family consisted of mom, dad, four brothers, and two girls.

I was about four years old when we moved from the country to Saginaw to the Dittmar Hotel on Hamilton Street. It is the "The Acorn Press" today. Next, we moved to South Saginaw to a house on Thayer Street between Canbrey Street and Williamson Road. Williamson Road was a dirt road with trees on both sides of the road. After a rain, we kids went there and picked lots of mushrooms. Mom would cook some of them with a dime. If the dime turned a blackish color, Mom said the mushrooms were poisonous. That never happened. I love mushrooms yet today.

All our yards sloped down to a large field, which we called the By U or Bouy'ou. In the winter, some people ice-skated there. In warm weather, my brothers caught garden snakes, sometimes put the snakes around their necks, and chased the other kids on the way to school.

A new owner wanted to move into our house so we had to move again. We liked our neighbors; but we had to keep our poodle inside in the mornings, because our neighbors told us that our poodle was licking the cream off the top of the milk bottles on the porches.

We moved to a very small house at the foot of State Street, east of Michigan Avenue. There were four other houses besides ours. We had no running water on our side of the street, across the road, yes. With our wagon and two very large lard cans from Gase's Bakery, we went onto Michigan Avenue where there were water pumps two blocks apart down the street. We made a lot of trips and in the winter some pumps would be frozen up. We kept on going till we found one that gave water.

We needed water for drinking, cooking, canning, laundry, and bathing. We bathed in a large round galvanized tub. We all bathed in the same water and Mom added hot water from the teakettle on the stove from time to time!

Everyone on our side of the road had outhouses. When we ran out of toilet paper, there were catalogs or newspapers.

Mom and Dad had remedies for us kids to take care of our illnesses. In the winter, around Christmas, we lined up for a short glass of whiskey and menthol crystals, from the drugstore. For chest colds, we had flannel cloths for our chests, soaked with goose grease and turpentine. Sometimes we used Vicks Vapor Rub. We had to take a tablespoon of Cod Liver Oil every day. In the spring, we got a dose of sulfur and molasses to purify our blood. When any of us was grumpy or ornery, Mom gave us two Carters Little Liver Pills. She cooked onions to a mush, strained the juice, added a little sugar, and that was our cough syrup.

Dad bought two large blocks of ice, when needed, for our icebox to keep our food cold for eating.

My brothers went to the local dump to pick up roller skates. They also picked up orange crates from the local grocers. They made scooters and go-carts to play with. My oldest brother used orange crates and a very old car battery to make an electric chair that gave a little jolt for anyone who wanted to try it out.

Sometimes "bums" from the train going by, about a block and a half away, knocked on our backdoor for something to eat, just one at a time though. They would wait so quietly while Mom came back to the door with a sandwich or fruit. They were grateful and we felt sorry for them. I think our house was "marked" for anyone of them.

We kids took grease or oil, when Mom was done with it, to the local meat market and grocer. The clerk told us that it was used in making Nitroglycerin used in the war. We got a little change for it. The boys gathered ragweed and took it to the fire stations. What they did with it I don't know. They paid my brother some change also.

We kids had to learn to make homemade bread about twice a week. We also learned to make other meals. My parents reminded us from time to time that they lived during the Depression Days, so no wasting food whether we liked the food or not.

Mom made newspaper patterns for our clothing, curtains, and slipcovers for our chairs and couch. She was very good cook for what she had to work with. She even cooked for a restaurant for a while.

Gordonville
By Norma Seelye of Midland, Michigan
Born 1941

My name is Norma Bovee Seelye. I was born on August 8, 1941 in a little village called Gordonville, Michigan. Alvah and Ruth Bovee were my dad and mom. I had two brothers and one sister. My brothers, sister, and I went to Gordonville School. We walked about a half-mile one way in snow, rain, and so cold out. I know at one time the Pine River Road was closed because of the snow. In this Gordonville, there was a store, school, church, and a gas station with a garage. Now in Gordonville there is a store with gas, a church, a bar, and a garage. The school is gone. Gordonville Store has the Bigfoot Pizza, the best pizza in Gordonville. We had to go to the outhouse in the winter and summer. We had to get water outside. We had a wood stove for heat in the house. We used a wringer washer to do the clothes and we hung it outside to dry. We had a party line phone. If we wanted to use it, we had to pick it up to hear if someone was using it. Sometimes you could hear four to five people on the phone at one time. If you ask them, how long they were going to be on the phone they would get mad at you.

When I was about ten, some of my friends and I went to the Pine River to go swimming and to play in the water. We had a big ball and

Norma and Larry Seelye

we were playing cather with it. One boy said what is that and we all looked and saw what we didn't know was coming at us. We got out of the water fast, we looked back and it was gone. So back in we went and were playing again when we saw it coming at us again. We all got out to run to my house to tell my mother what we saw. We didn't pick up our clothes or shoes. My mother went back with us to get all of our things. We were surprised to see all the water in the river was about five feet higher than before. We all said we had an angel that day.

I had a pony and her name was Bonnie. If I got into trouble, I would go to the barn. When my ma came to get me, I would go under the pony's belly so my mom couldn't get me. But when she did get me, I got a good spanking for running away. When I was ten years old, I went to school and when school let out, I went to my girlfriend's house to play. I didn't stop at home to let my mom know I was going to my friend's house. About 4 o'clock my mom walked to school for me. I wasn't there and the teacher said I left with the other kids. My mom came to my friend's house. She made me go home. The next time I went in to tell my mom I was going to my friend's.

I got my first car when I was 17. It was a '52 Chevy and gas was 25 to 30 cents per gallon. Lots of things were cheap then so was the paycheck. I was 19 when I met my husband, Larry. My niece, Larry and I were walking to the store to get a pop for us. When this boy stopped and asked me if I would like

to go out with him that weekend. I said no. I would like you to meet my fiancé. After he left, Larry looked at me and said what is a fiancé. I told him I just asked you to marry me. Three months later we got married and have been together for 53 ½ years with five kids, twenty-two grandchildren, and four great-grandchildren. We lived in a house that had no light, an icebox, and an outhouse. We had to get water outdoors and did our washing on a wringer washer outdoors. I have lived in Gordonville all my life. When the kids were all home we had a milkman that left our milk at the door.

Ron, Dale, and dog Pepper in 1980

How My Friends, Siblings and I Survived
By Karen Schoeppach of Bay City, Michigan
Born 1950

When I look back at my younger days, I wonder how my friends, siblings, and I survived! We rode in cars without NASA-worthy car seats, booster seats, seat belts, or air bags! My youngest sister would ride on the "shelf" between the back of our seat and the rear window. When we had a station wagon, my sisters, cousins and I would ride in the "way back" as we called it. We would lie down with our feet propped up in the window, side or rear depending on our size and how many of us. Today, we would never allow our children to ride in such a dangerous fashion!

We lived in one of the very first houses built in our subdivision, Greenbriar Estates on Wilder Road. This meant that every year for most of our elementary school years, we would play on the construction sites. We climbed into the basements and played war or, on occasion, house. During the excavation phase of building there would be large piles of dirt and stone sitting on the lots. One of our favorite pastimes was to walk our bicycles up to the "peak" of the "hill" and then climb on and ride down, usually coasting with our feet flung out to the sides. I pride myself on the fact that I never "crashed." If someone did "kiss the dirt," they kept on going unless there was an actual laceration or broken bone. Scrapes and sprains were just a part of outside play in those days. And, by the way, all our bike rides were taken without helmets or other safety equipment.

We went to school during the coldest weather and played outside at recess. I remember waiting for the bus at the end of our subdivision. There was a large sign at the entrance in those days and we would take turns being on the "inside" where we were shielded from the cold by the other children. At recess, we did the same thing, only using the corner of our school, Bangor West Central, where a short wall extended from the building providing two sides of shelter. Somehow, we always knew when it was time to "shift personnel" and give an "outside" person a chance at warmth. We did not know about wind chill back then, but we did know we were warmer if we could get out of the wind. The adults in charge didn't seem to be concerned about how we would fare our in this subzero weather. All the generations before us had survived; I suppose they expected we would as well. Back then, we girls didn't often wear pants in elementary school. We wore leggings or snow pants to and from school, and at recess. Once you were in junior and senior high, it was skirts and dresses only for girls and we would die before wearing leggings or snow pants. We would freeze our knees, but we were stylish.

One of my fondest memories is of going out to Tony's Park in the summer. It was a small park out by Bay City State Park (it's a recreation area now) with a carousel, bumper cars, kiddie boats, cars, an arcade, and a train ride. I would take the spending money my parents had given me and hit the arcade. I always went to the vending machine that dispensed photo cards of movie stars: Clark Gable, Jimmy Stewart, and Robert Wagner, I didn't collect any female stars. Long after I was "too old," I still enjoyed the carousel and the train ride. It was just as thrilling to sit on the train with younger siblings and friends going through the tunnel and viewing the nursery rhyme characters on the walls, as it had been when I was young.

Deer Acres up in the Pinconning area was another amusement park. It was tradition for many years to take classes of schoolchildren there for an end-of-year excursion. We would purchase corn and deer feed from what resembled a gumball machine. I swear the deer had a Pavlovian-response to the sound of the coins being put in the machine and the turning of the lever. I don't remember being inspected for deer ticks when we left. Do we allow children with food in their hands to wander through herds of deer today? Probably not, I'm sure the insurance premiums for the parks would be sky high.

For several years, I went to the Bay County Fair with a girlfriend. We would spend the day going on the rides and visiting the barns, especially the one with the horses. I liked the Tilt-a-Whirl the best, although I enjoyed all the rides. We would get French fries and a Coke and walk around taking in all the sights and sounds. The two of us went all alone and then walked to her grandparents at the end of the day to have supper and spend the night. No cell phones, we were just two young girls on their own. We didn't have any worries. We just had fun. It isn't that simple today.

Sometimes my sister and I would be allowed to go shopping "downtown." We would always stop at Cunningham's Drugstore on Washington Avenue for a Coke at the counter. It always tasted so much better than the Coke in the bottle. At least, we always thought so. We weren't really allowed to have pop very often. On special occasions, we could have an M&S pop. Dad would buy a case with a variety of flavors from which we could choose.

At the corner of Euclid and Wilder, where K-Mart sits today, was a golf course. In the wintertime, my friend and I would go over there and play. She lived on Wilder Road across from the golf course. In the warm months, we would walk down Euclid (holding our breath as we walked by the huge ditch on the west side of the road) to Arlans, a store much like K-Mart or Target. We would get a powdered donut or a Neapolitan ice cream bar and munch on them as we walked back to her house. Yes, we ate while we walked past the ditch.

When we first moved out to Greenbriar Estates in Bangor Township, Wilder was a gravel road and Euclid was not the 5-lane monster it is today. Huge tractor-trailer trucks did not roar down the road, so walking and bicycling were not the risky adventure they would be today. We would be gone for hours and never give it a thought. We had to be home when the streetlights came on each evening. Other than that, we had some freedom.

There wasn't always the extensive choice for fast food back then. What a day it was when McDonalds opened on Euclid. Just forty-seven cents for a three-course meal was the ad on TV. A treat to be savored, not the routine meal it is today. And you could only get shakes, pop, fries and either a hamburger or cheeseburger. It has changed quite a bit over the years, but McDonalds is still in the same spot.

Another of my girlfriends lived on Allen Court. I would walk to the back of our subdivision and climb down the side of the ditch, jump the water trickling down the center and climb up the other side to her backyard. From there we could walk or bike down Wilder to Two Mile and then down Two Mile to Monitor Pharmacy. We would get a grape pop from the vending machine on the side of the building then start back home. Monitor Pharmacy is still there, but no vending machine is outside.

Life on the Farm
By Keith Van Sickle of Reed City, Michigan
Born 1933

The farm is located four miles west of Reed City, Michigan, one and a half miles north of US 10, on Deer Lake Road. This 80-acre farm produced a good living for my

Keith Van Sickle in 1936

grandparents for over seventy-five years. I was part of this experience, from 1933 until my enlistment in the US Air Force in 1951. In 1941, the "oil boom" hit this area. We never had a "well" on our farm, but several years of oil and gas leases were welcome dollars.

January 1945, a typical Sunday activities went like this, up at 5:30 AM, scrape the ice off the inside of my bedroom window. Then down to the kitchen where my grandmother already had a warm fire going in the 1911 model "Home Comfort Kitchen Range!" Now it's time to take the kerosene lantern to the barn. We didn't get electric service until 1947. In the barn, we fed the animals, and milked the twelve brown Swiss cows. It was fun to squirt milk on the cats and watch the dog lick it off; no this was not animal cruelty. We then ran the milk through a cream separator. Saving the cream for a butter producer in Reed City, now it's time for a warm breakfast, then shovel the snow from the driveway. We would pour water in the radiator of our 1928 Pontiac, then off to church in Reed City.

Now remember, we all took a bath

Time to cut the hay in 1937

Picking apples on the farm in 1937

Saturday night, in a galvanized #3-laundry tub. Back home, after church, for dinner and it was soon time to do all the chores in the barn again.

Monday morning- our one-room Rosenberg Country School was located one-half mile north of the farm. My grandmother was my teacher, and I lived with her. She paid me five dollars a month to be the janitor, now, this may sound a little different, but while everyone walked to school, it was common for many of the guys to bring a shotgun to school and "hunt" on the way home. So did I! In the winter, my first task was to build the fire in the furnace. Then, I pumped water for school use. After the fire was going well, I threw some .22 short ammunition in to hear them "pop!" On the wall was a copy of the Ten Commandments and the Pledge of Allegiance. We repeated the Pledge each morning – one nation under God! We had no fear of repeating that. Most of the desks seated two students, therefore, I sat with the same girl from 1938-1947, and I never dated her. Don't laugh at these kids, they helped win World War II, what did you do?

In reviewing life on the farm, a clevis, eveners, Haynes, and a Whippletree were daily tools for the workhorses and me. The most difficult task I had on the farm was trying to teach our city kid cousins from Jackson, "How to play in the hay!"

Those days we got our news from the Grand Rapids Press, delivered by RFD six days a week. Dick Tracy and Red Ryder caused concerns until the next paper arrived.

On July 28, 1950, I met a girl at a free movie in Chase, Michigan. Over time, and after 600 kisses, we gave up! I joined the Air Force, retiring in 1971. Yes, I went back to the corner of US 10 and 131, my hometown of Reed City, today many memories still linger there.

Dark brown eyes, and long silk hair,
"Now she knows, I still care!"
I don't have the time, and I can't tell it all!
For there's many more things "too close to call."

The Corner of Gaylord and Tinkham
By Elizabeth Hepworth of Ludington, Michigan
Born 1924

I was born in November of 1924, and my mother passed away when I was eighteen months old, May 3, 1926. My Aunt Florence and Uncle Chet took me in and we lived on the corner of Gaylord and Tinkham Avenue.

The circus would come down Gaylord and we'd see the elephants and other animals in cages, go to what is now Oriole Field, they would get water for the animals at my Uncle Pete's home. They were given tickets to the shows, which disappointed me because we didn't get any. Uncle Pete lived at Tinkham and Ferry.

We had a cow, which they pastured, up the hill across from what is now Oriole Field. I'd have to go up the hill past the water tower each night to bring the cow home. Many times, it would get away from me and run down the hill, turn left on Tinkham with me running behind it. I always tell my kids about it and tell them the people on Tinkham probably said, "There goes that Case girl chasing the cow again." I was always afraid the water tower would fall on me.

The real Rolly, Polly, Jolly, Santa came to Lakeview School, and later I found out he was Henry CB or something like that.

It was during the depression and men would go out in the lake, set nets at night to catch fish, and hope they weren't caught.

People made their own whiskey, beer, and root beer, in the basements, because it was during prohibition.

My dad lived in Wisconsin, my sister and I took the boats over and many times sat on the bathroom floor seasick.

My aunt would take me to work with her. She worked at a house on the lakeside of Lakeshore Drive. My uncle worked for the cemetery and would sometimes take me with him when he got sod for the graves, it would be somewhere where there was a stream.

I guess the circus inspired us because my cousins and I would perform in the garage. Ken Case was the director and Harold and I would be the circus people. Ken later worked for the Daily News.

We also would play Eynie Iynie, over the Barn, what it was we'd have a ball with each of us on a side of the barn, we'd throw the ball and yell, "Eynie Iynie, over" and the one on the other side tried to catch it. Sometimes if we didn't have a ball, a stone was used and would fall on us, ouch!

Other times we would stomp cans on our heels of our shoes and when we ran around on hard surfaces they would clamp, clamp and we'd be horses.

In the fall when the chestnut would be falling, the kids in the neighborhood would get up early and see who could get the most. What happened to them after we gathered them I don't remember.

Uncle Pete and Aunt Mary had an outhouse though everyone had an indoor bathroom. This outhouse Aunt Mary kept spotless and I don't remember anyone using it ever, but me. I had to go, and couldn't make it home, so I went in there. I didn't make it and piddled on the floor. Well that was not the thing to do to Aunt Mary's outhouse. I heard about it for a very long time. I left when I was twelve, came back when I was seventeen, and lived with aunt and my sister where the Four Seasons Motel is on Ludington Avenue. We would walk to town almost every night enjoying it, with our friends who lived across where the hospital is now.

We went to movies for ten cents. We would go to a movie, have a hamburger and a Hire's root beer, all for twenty-five cents. We'd roller skate or walk. The bowling alley was where the empty lot is on Ludington Avenue, ten-cent movie house west of James Street on Ludington Avenue. The skating rink was where the putt-putt golf is now. The war was on and boyfriends were gone. It was nice to skate and see the boats come in and go out.

I had gone to a friend's house to feed and let the dog out when they were gone. I turned on the radio on December 7, 1941 and heard the news Pearl Harbor was under attack.

My grandfather Andrew Jackson Case lived on the corner of Decker and Lakeshore Drive when I'd visit there my cousins and I would go to Piney ridge and State Park Road and climb 'ole Baldie, the large dune that was there. It's gone now, I found an arrowhead and gave it to my cousins, I didn't know how rare they were at that time.

I think it was about 1936 when we had a bad winter storm that closed Lakeshore Drive in the area of Jagger Road where there were hills on either side of Lakeshore Drive. It closed in the whole road and they had to get a snow blower truck from the state to plow it out.

The Good Life Our Parents Provided
By Elizabeth J. Gardner of Ludington,
Michigan
Born 1944

When my father returned from serving in the Air Force during World War II, I was 18 months old. He was raised in a large farm family, along with four brothers and three sisters. Three brothers served in the war, too. One brother lost his life. Dad was happy when the war was over and he had a plan for his life. He wanted to buy a farm and raise his family there. Meanwhile, my parents settled in Muskegon in a housing project for GIs returning from the war and their families. Dad took a factory job and saved for the farm.

Elizabeth's father, Clarence Perry in 1944

188

Elizabeth's mother, Martha Perry with Janie

Mom stayed home with the children. In 1954, they found the right farm near Fremont with 80 acres. The buildings weren't much, but there were hayfields and fields for planting.

Dad found a used tractor and equipment for fieldwork. After a day at the factory, he worked on the farm. The days were very long for him. He drove to Muskegon, 30 miles away, every weekday, and sometimes on Saturday. He did lots of overtime, too.

We added a milk cow named Bossy and two dogs, Sparky and Bingo. There was a big vegetable garden that we kids took turns weeding and hoeing. It was a great life for city kids, turned farm kids.

As I wrote, the buildings were not much and the house was small with no indoor plumbing. Dad put water indoors the second year we lived there. The old windmill pumped delicious cold water. We didn't have a water heater and never did in that old house. We heated water on the stove.

My two sisters and I helped Mom on laundry day using an old wringer washing machine. The clothes were hung outside or upstairs in the house. We turned butter by hand, made cottage cheese, baked bread, and canned veggies and fruits. Every night we were thankful for the food on our table, mostly from the farm.

My five brothers worked after school around the farm. They chopped wood, milked and fed the cows, and put water out for the herd of beef stock that Dad was starting to raise.

Some summer days, we walked to friends' houses or went to swim in a nearby lake. We joined a 4-H club and entered our projects in the county fair, often winning ribbons. There was a small country Sunday school that we attended.

Down the road was an 18-hole golf course and the owners gave us summer jobs as teenagers. The spending money was nice and we also could play golf for free. The brothers sold golf balls back to the golfers that ended up in our fields and in ditches.

After the youngest child went off to school, Mom trained for a nurse's aide job at the local nursing home. She and Dad then saved for Building a new house on the farm. It had plenty of room, including two bathrooms and a hot water heater. Mom had lots of windows looking out over the farm.

I'm proud of my parents, of what they achieved over the years and the life they gave their children. Three of my brothers served in the military and all earned college degrees. We girls went on after high school and had careers and families. The folks have passed on now and the family farm is no more. Even the neighborhood is no longer the same. Every time I drive by the old place, I'm flooded with good feelings. My family agrees it was a good life.

Elizabeth's parents, Clarence and Martha Perry

One-room Schools
By Kenneth Warner, Sr. of Clare, Michigan
Born 1939

I started to the Brewer School in September 1944. It was located in Section Two Sheridan Township, Clare County. I wasn't quite five years old yet. I had two older brothers. We walked a mile and a quarter to and from school every day. I remember the first day of school. It was terrible. I had to sit beside a girl. I think I cried most of the morning. I grew up with two older brothers, so I don't believe I was ever around any girls. It must not have hurt me too much; I am still here today and did marry a girl on June 10, 1961. We will celebrate 54 years of marriage this June.

These one-room schools had all eight grades in the same room. There was about 25-30 students total among the eight grades. We didn't have snow days back then. Weather was a way of life. Late one winter, we had an ice storm that covered everything with thick ice. Walking to school that morning was like going through a warzone. The trees in the woods we went by were broken down, and as they broke, it sounded like a bomb going off. When spring did come, the roads were a disaster. They had very little gravel and where there was a water puddle, it soon turned into a sinkhole. The cars and horse and wagons would turn out around the sinkhole. Soon it took up the whole road and into the ditch if there was a ditch.

At recess, we played kick-the-can around the schoolhouse, or in the winter, we played fox-and-geese out in the back of the schoolyard. During the summer, we played softball at noon. This involved the older children. The younger children played on the swings or slide. This was school life in the good old days.

Old Outhouses
Growing up in rural Clare County, Michigan in the '40s, the outhouse wasn't the place you wanted to spend a lot of time in. during the winter, it was just too cold. In the summer, it smelled bad, plus there was lots of flies. We never had the luxury of toilet paper. We had a substitute—the Sears and Roebuck catalog or the Montgomery Ward's catalog to do your wiping with.

Some of the full picture pages were so slipper, they didn't do much good, but they were a step above a corncob by far. It was also quite interesting at times sitting on the throne. You never knew what might come along. Often, a mouse would go scurrying by or a snake might slither across the floor.

I never had the luxury of a bathroom until I was married in the early 1960s. This was a real improvement over the old outhouse, by far!

Hunting Bees
This is an art all of its own. I learned this from my dad, Henry Warner, and a friend of ours, Arkey Watters. To start the process, you pick a nice, sunny day in late October or November. First, you set out honeycomb with some honey on it or put anise oil into a clearing in the woods in about two spots. Then you sit and wait. If there are wild bees around, they will come. When they leave, they will fly straight up, make a circle, and then their GPS will take them straight back to their hive. We don't have any wild bees anymore because of the mites that infect the bees.

I remember one hunt that left a lasting impression in my mind. We had hunted for the bee tree for two weekends before finding it. The tree wasn't hollow. The honeycombs hung about 20 feet up from the ground, hanging from a limb. We decided to go get the honey one night when it started to rain. When we got to the tree, I was elected to climb the tree with a five-gallon bucket on a rope and knife. Things went well until I cut the honeycombs off the limb. They were heavier than I expected and when they went into the pail, there was a jerk, and then the bees came up around my hand and stung me many times. I let the pail down real fast so the ground crew could deal with the bees. Sometimes the best plans go astray as this one did.

The Little Red House on Nine-Mile Road
By Gloria Woodbury of Midland, Michigan
Born 1942

I remember when I was six years old in 1948. We lived in a little red house on Nine-mile Road, Midland County. Whenever we needed potatoes, Mom and us three kids would go to a farm about a mile down the road with our little red wagon to buy potatoes. On the way home, we'd stop at the creek and

Gloria, Susan, Paul and Bob Kirby in 1951

try to find a turtle for supper. Sometimes we got lucky!

We lived about a mile from Olson, which had a little country store, a church, and a one-room school. My little sister and I had to walk to school. I don't remember much about the school or the teacher, but I do remember the store. After school we liked looking in the big window at all the candy until the owners would tell us to go home, that our mother would be worried. One day when I was grown, I stopped in to say hi. They were so happy to see me. We talked for a long time. They were really nice people. Now the school is a house. The store got moved to a museum in Sanford, Michigan. The church is still having services.

In the first grade, we moved a few miles over to West Pine River Road and Nine-mile (Midland County). On the corner was the one-room school, Wayne School. Across the road was the Porter Cemetery. My dad and first brother who started kindergarten there are now buried there, and I will be buried there someday as well.

We lucked out; the school was only a block from the farmhouse that we rented. Being the oldest at eight years old, I had to help Dad paper the whole house. My job was to paste each piece of wallpaper—a big job. We took

care of the Black Angus cattle to help pay the rent. The next summer when I was nine, I had to help Dad pour great big cement corner posts all around the acres of pasture to fasten fence around because the cows kept getting out. After 63 years, all the posts are gone. There's still cattle where the house used to be with an electric fence, now.

In the winter, we played on a big hill in the pasture behind the house. A lot of the neighbor kids came to slide. We enjoyed a lot of hours there, plus ice-skating on the pond. One summer, a few of the neighbor kids and us decided to see if it was true that bulls didn't like red. We found out real fast when the big Angus bull chased us. All the others made it to the fence, but I didn't, so I had to hide under a crabapple bush. After what seemed like hours, the other kids got the bull to move away. Believe me, I never did that again. I was a really tore up from the thorns and a spanking from Dad when he got home. I remember it like it was yesterday.

I remember the old wringer washer. I ruined a lot of Mom's old sticks in the wringer and made Mom really mad. The worse was hanging clothes out in the winter and then bringing them in to drip all over. Mom said it made them softer and smell good. I thought it was crazy then, and I still think it is crazy now.

Mom and Dad never did find out where I spent a lot of my free time; I was sitting in the top of a really big oak tree. The other kids were afraid to climb that high. Now I wonder how I didn't get killed. We never went away much. When my parents went away, I had to take care of the other kids. I got to go to town a couple times a year. Once a year I went to town to buy a set of clothes for school and get them horrible high-top shoes I hated. They were supposed to be good for my ankles. Maybe so.

In 1953, my third brother was born at home. The neighbor woman came to help. She handed him to me and said, "Bathe him." I was only 11 years old and scared. You can probably guess what happened when he hit the water; he peed in my face! I was so upset I started to scream. That gave everyone a good laugh. I was very careful after that. Soon after that, we moved to Muskegon where Dad's job was. I guess it wasn't so bad growing up in the '40s and '50s. We had a lot of work to do, a lot of fresh air because we always spent most of our time outside. We didn't have TVs or games, and most of the time we didn't even have a telephone. But we grew up happy. I now live only five miles from where I grew up.

Boyhood Memories
By Edwin W. Iles of Saginaw, Michigan
Born 1924

I was born and raised on a farm in central Michigan. I had two older sisters, an older brother, and a younger brother. I am now ninety years old and most of this is during the great depression. Saturday night baths were in a copper tub heated on a wooden heated cook stove, one of us at a time with the same water. The two-story house was heated by the cook stove and a round oak stove in the living room. An outdoor outhouse was the toilet. It was real cold going out there in the winter. Maybe that was why I often wet the bed until I was about six years old. Previous year Sears Roebuck and Montgomery Ward catalogs were used for toilet paper. Pages of those catalogs had another use my parents did not know about.

In the late summer, when the corn silk turned brown one of us boys would get some paper from the outhouse and another would snitch some matches. Out to the cornfield we would go gather some corn silk, roll it in the paper, and smoke it. As Mullin leaves turned brown, we often smoked them. To us they looked like tobacco leaves. We also smoked Elm tree roots and Dock (weed) seed.

When there was a township election, the winner would often pass out cigars to the men. When I was about twelve years old, I managed to get my hand in, and grabbed a cigar. About a week later, my parents went to a funeral and while they were gone, I smoked that cigar and got sick. I never smoked again.

When we would get a bad chest cold, we were put to bed with a mustard plaster on our chest. It was hot and messy but usually did the job. If not, about the third night, skunk oil was added. Yes from the animal and it did stink.

When the young chickens first started to lay eggs, the eggs were often a lot smaller. Our older sister and mother made a big deal of finding those eggs for my younger brother, three years old and me, four years old. One afternoon when we were outside playing, we decided to gather those little eggs. I took the ones I got to my mother. That night when our older sister was getting us ready for bed, she said to my brother "What's this mess in your pockets?" He had put his eggs in his pockets. What a mess.

One of my favorite winter activities was when we would need corn from the shocks in the field to feed the animals and chickens. There were always lots of rats and mice in those shocks. Where did they all come from? Us boys and the dog would try to kill them as they ran out from the shock we were loading before they could get in the next shock. Fun!

My favorite Christmas present was when we were about six and seven years old. We got a pair of seven-inch high top shoes with a little pocket on the side with a jack knife in it. We put on the shoes and wore them all winter, except to church on Sunday. In the summer, we went barefoot. In the fall, we put the shoes on again and wore them through the next winter, even though our feet had grown. To this day, my toes curl down as a result.

What did we eat? Wintertime Saturday meals were usually homegrown navy bean soup with potatoes and bread. Sunday meals were baked beans, leftover potatoes, and chicken. Any leftover beans we took to school as bean sandwiches as long as they lasted. In the wintertime, we ate a lot of popcorn in the evening after milking the cows and all other work was done. Sometimes the evening meals were popcorn soaked in milk with just little salt added. Popcorn was homegrown and dried. Wintertime breakfast was usually pancakes with canned fruit that Mom and sister canned; cherries, raspberries, strawberries, peaches, etc. We had four cherry trees and as the cherries started to ripen, the birds would flock in to eat them. My brother and I would take turns shooting at them with a BB gun. Yes, we shot many robins. We knew it was against the law, but hey! They were stealing food from us. The Fourth of July was usually cherry picking day.

One day my brother and I were down by the creek and we saw a snake with a huge lump part way on the back of his body. Why? One of my brothers dropped a rock on the snake's tail and the lump moved forward. One more rock and the snake opened its mouth and out hopped a frog still alive. That snake had swallowed it whole.

We went to a one-room school one and a half miles away. The teacher, usually a woman, was also the janitor. So usually in the wintertime, it was cold in the school until about noon. One student each day was given the task of getting a bucket of water from an outdoor pump. There was one dipper so we all drank from the same dipper. One day a student came down with the measles. One day a couple of weeks later, he and another student who had had measles were the only ones in school.

My Life
By Phyllis Jean Short of Midland, Michigan
Born 1932

My momma is Phyllis Jean Short (Walsh) and I was born December 25, 1932. My parents lived in a barn, made into a living quarter. So when people ask me, "You must have been born in a barn" I could say, "Yes I was." We lived in Sag Township, Frost Road, Freeland. The road is now Dice Road. I lived about one block from River Road near the Tittiwassee River. Yes, we had an outhouse or a pot under our bed. We had a radio and my brother Bill would hog the radio to listen to the Lone Ranger. We didn't have a phone until we moved to Freeland in 1942. The twins, Sharon and Karen, were born in 1942. We moved one mile north of Freeland, then US 10. We did have a wind up record player.

There was no spanking; Dad just gave us that look. One time in school, a teacher hit me with a book on my head, which I deserved.

We had our Saturday night bath all in one tub and each of us hoped to be first.

I was older and helped mom with the washing with a wringer washer. You had to be careful or you would get your finger in the ringers.

My mom had to buy me larger dresses called chubbies from Sears in Sag.

My favorite teacher was Alfreda Swanson who just passed away January 1, 2015 at her residents at Green Acres in Cadillac, Michigan.

We moved to Smithcrossing Road with my husband Milton E. Short, married June 16, 1951. We would go to the neighbor, Ken and Cora Roberson to watch TV. I remember riding in a car that had a rubber seat belonging to Bill Fletcher. Bill lived with us on US 10 for a while when his folks moved. Bill Fletcher and his brother Bill worked at the steering gear in Sag and rode together.

When we lived on Dice, I went to a one-room school that is now a fire station. Back then in the 40s we would have blizzards and the roads were impassable. We always walked to school about one mile and never had a ride, no buses then.

We had pets, hounds and always outside. When we had company, we had to go outside so we would climb trees, ride our bikes, and play leaving the adults to visit. We never went swimming.

I would stay with Dad, sister, Auntie Emerson in a large house on Dice Road which is still there. Auntie was one person I loved. Auntie and Uncle Sam and I spent a lot of time there. I remember they always had a jar of jelly on the kitchen table. She also made butter in the basement. She would slap that butter to get all the juice out. It was so good.

My first kiss was a neighbor. I wouldn't say his name. He was well-liked, good manners, and raised by Christian good parents. I didn't get into trouble. I was not a poplar girl but had a lot of friends. I was a large gal, about 160 pounds in the fifth grade at Freeland High School.

During the winter, we would go ice-skating in a ravine near our house with a gang

2005 Freeland School reunion at the Sky Room

of friends.

We had a milkman, Miles Hetfel. Sometimes we didn't have money for milk but he would always leave the milk because we had the twins who were about two years old. A good guy.

We didn't go to town often but we had a neighbor, Nuenfeldt. They would go to town sometimes three times each day. When we started to school, they would pick us up, Don, Bill and me. I had to sit on top of Joe's lap and I didn't like that. Oh well, got to do what you have to do to get a ride. "No thrill."

Life on the Farm
By Helen Johnson of Midland, Michigan
Born 1936

I'm starting out when I was five. I was born in a house when it didn't rain and didn't leak. But when it rained better grab pails, pots and pans because it leaked bad especially upstairs.

My dad started me out helping on the farm by taking me out in the garden and showing me which was plants and which was weeds. From then on, it was up to me to take care of the garden. I even helped harvest it to take the vegetables in for my mom to can. There were seven of us, five kids, all in the house and my mom canned everything she got her hands on to make sure we ate good all winter. We had a large apple orchard on the left side of the house. We had all kinds of apples form early apples to late ones that we picked after the first snow. We had a root cellar that we kept the canned vegetables in and also off to the right side of the door there was a place where we could bury carrots in the dirt on one side and put potatoes on the other. Then when Mom needed something from the cellar, I'd take a flashlight to see what I was after. We had no electric in the house or anywhere else. We heated the house with a big potbellied stove with wood. We even cooked with wood. It was up to me to bring in wood each night for mom to have enough wood the next day from the woodpile.

Just outside the door, we had a backdoor and front door. We always used the backdoor to go to the barn. We burned kerosene flames

to see at night. I learned to milk cows and shovel manure whenever needed. I worked out in the hay field throwing hay on the wagon; someone would be on the wagon to distribute the hay on the slings. Then when the wagon was full, we would take it over to the barn and we used two hooks, one for each end of the sling. We had a rope coming out from the left side of the barn to hook the horse to in order to pull the sling up into the haymow. We raised corn, hay, rye, pumpkins in the cornfield, and also had a turnip field. I would stop and pull one up when they got big enough to eat. On my way to school, I would peel it with my teeth and eat it on my way home from school. I had to walk a mile and a half to a one-room school. The school ran from first grade to eighth grade. My oldest brother used to walk with me my first year in school because he graduated from the eighth grade.

Yes, we had outhouses at school and at home. The one at school had a board off the back that when you went to the bathroom everybody would gather in the back outside to watch you go to the bathroom. The kids told the teacher I went outside and I didn't. I'm not that dumb but I had to stand in a corner with my nose in a circle for something I didn't do because the kids said I did to the teacher. Yes, we had a radio run by batteries. We listened to the Green Hornet, Roy Rogers and some country music.

I only got one spanking for getting ice on my new snowsuit because I sled down the hill on board at school. I got spanked from a piece from an apple tree.

Saturday night baths were in by the stove kitchen in a big washtub. We had a wringer washer run by a motor started by an engine. My dad bought a farm in 1942 that had electric and we were there two years before we got a colored TV and we even got a refrigerator. I wore hand-me-down clothes when I was in High School.

Talk about blizzards, we used to have enough snow to pile up three cars high on the side of the roads put there by the big plows.

In regards to farm chores, I have done everything, milking cows, carrying out manure, working in hay fields, worked in cornfields, cut corn stalks by hand and put them in shocks for a week or two. I used a corn husker to husk corn later and put in bags to dump in the corncrib. I cut cedar tress down in the winter for fence posts. So I have been there and done that.

Yes we had a swimming hole half mile from the first farm. My brothers drug me thru there and I'm scared of deep water now.

After my dad bought the second farm, he used to go to town and I would go and watch for guys by the car. I was fourteen to fifteen.

We had a rotary phone the second year we were on the second farm. It was a line with several neighbors on it. They always listened in when we got phone calls. It would cause my dad lots of problems.

My mom canned sweet apples. We had a big one in the middle of the orchard. We had lots of bees and had lots of honey, even sold some. We raised pigs, chickens, turkeys on the first farm.

Rollin with his mother, Thelma Yeakle

Hand-milking and Pickle Farming
By Rollin Yeakle of Midland, Michigan
Born 1933

I was born on the farm my grandfather, William Yeakle, bought in 1919 after he moved from Geneva, Indiana to Ingersoll Township Midland County Michigan in 1909. This was a continuation of the Yeakle migration from Switzerland in 1736. My Ancestors came to Philadelphia then to Ohio, Indiana, and Michigan. I was born in 1933 in the same bedroom where my grandfather and father died. We didn't have electricity or inside bathrooms at our farm in 1933. Everyone had an outhouse that sat in their backyard.

Rollin Yeakles' parents, brothers, and sister in 1938

Later, in the 1930s, electricity came to our neighborhood in Midland County. Since my dad was a do-it-yourself guy, he wired our house and most neighbor's houses and barns so they could take advantage of the new electric power. Even though we had an electric water pump, we still had to fill our wringer washer with water using a pail. Our wash water came from a cistern, which stored rainwater that ran off the roof during rainstorms.

On our farm, we had ten cows, which we milked by hand. Some neighbors had electric milkers if they had a larger number of cows to milk, but we continued to milk by hand for several years. My job was to milk two cows each morning before school and every evening before supper. Most of our farm crops like oats, corn, and hay was fed to the cattle, pigs, and chickens, which made it possible to sell cream, eggs, and meat. Most farms were less than 100 acres and farming was done with horses. Our first farm tractor was a 1937 Model "B" John Deere with steel wheels on the front and back. There were only a few farm tractors in our neighborhood with rubber tires.

Milk from the cows was put through a hand cranked cream separator to separate the cream from the milk. The cream would

Rollin and his brother, Richard in "The Scooter" that his dad built in 1944

come out one spout and skim milk would come out the other spout. The cream was sold ten gallons at a time to a receiving station in Midland. The skim milk was fed to the pigs in a trough mixed with grain. Any leftover skim milk was poured into a barrel in the barnyard to make cheese, which was fed to the chickens so they could lay more eggs.

Sundays were special days because we didn't do any farm work and quite often, we would have a chicken dinner. Another one of my jobs was to catch the largest rooster for Sunday dinner. I was always amazed at how the roosters could hide among the hen chickens when I was looking for him. We never would eat a hen chicken because she was laying eggs for us.

When I was about 10 years old, my father planted 5 acres of pickles each year so my brothers, sisters, and I could earn our own money. We had a contract with the Heinz pickle company, which bought all our pickles. They supplied the seed and we did all the work picking. I could earn about $30 a week during July and August. The Heinz Company had a pickle station at a place called Jam, Michigan that was just a crossroads and a store.

The one-room grade school I attended was about one and a half miles from our house. During the winter, we would stop at a neighbor's house to get warm about halfway to school. We didn't have a well for drinking water so the eighth grade boys would walk to a neighbor's house and carry water in a pail for drinking. We also had only one washbasin for 20 kids to wash their hands.

The month of December was muskrat trapping season, so I walked to school through the neighbor's field to check my traps on the

way to school. Any given winter I would catch about 25 muskrats that sold for $3.00-$5.00 each. The muskrats were skinned and their pelts (fur) were nailed to a board for drying. After trapping season, I would send the pelts to Sears Roebuck and Company in Chicago, Illinois and they would send me a check. The pelts would bring less money if they had a hole or a cut from the skinning process.

Our one-room school which I attended from 1938-1947 had a large coal fired furnace at the back of the schoolroom. Some students would put a pint glass jar full of soup near the furnace so they could have hot soup for dinner. The schoolteacher (everyone called her the School Mom) was responsible for keeping the furnace going in addition to all her other duties because she was being paid about $100.00 a month. She would bank the firebox with coal and ashes at night so there would be some hot coals the next morning to start a fire again.

The coal fired kitchen stove at our house had a hot water reservoir at one end, which held about five gallons for our supply of hot water. We used the hot water for Saturday night baths. A large galvanized tub was put by the stove for easy transfer of hot water. There were five kids for baths and the oldest was first. I was fourth of five to get a bath.

Since we lived eight miles from Midland, we only went to town for groceries once a week, usually on Saturday. The cream and eggs were sold and the money was used to buy groceries for the next week. My father always butchered a beef cow each winter so we didn't need to buy meat. When we butchered a beef cow, the meat was cut into small chunks and canned for storage for a year or more. We had to can the meat because there were no freezers. On Saturday evenings, after a day of shopping, my father always liked to listen to a program called "Gang Busters" on the small tabletop radio. We all sat around listening to the cops catch the bad guys; it seemed so real. My grandmother lived in the city and I remember her having an icebox with a pan under it to catch the water as the ice melted. Once or twice a week the iceman would deliver ice. She had a sign to put in the window indicating if she wanted 25 pounds or 50 pounds of ice. The iceman could read the sign from the road.

Most of our entertainment came from

a small tabletop radio or windup Victrola record player. Before electricity came to our neighborhood, the radios operated on batteries. My father played the violin and he sat in the living room and played music for hours in the evenings.

At 19 years old, I got my first job working at the Dow Chemical Company in their plastics department. Plastic had only been made for a few years so it was quite new. We didn't have a telephone at our rural house, so it was difficult for Dow to call me when I was needed to work extra hours. Our neighbor about a half mile away had a phone, so when Dow called their home, a family member would come to our house to tell me I was needed to work extra hours. I worked at Dow for 37 years and have been retired for 25 years.

Now in 2015 it seems impossible to live without a freezer, refrigerator, telephone, electric lights, computers, inside bathrooms, dishwashers TV, DVD, air conditioning, ball point pens and a heater in your car.

On the Shore of Lake Michigan
By Margaret M. Holey of Ludington,
Michigan
Born 1942

I was born on the shore of Lake Michigan in a town called Frankfort Michigan. My mother was a waitress in a little business of Frankfurt. Don't know the name of it. She was the daughter of a farmer in Bear Lake, Michigan. My father was a seaman on the car ferry, Ann Arbor, which sailed out of Frankfurt, Michigan. His parents were from Alpena, Michigan, they were fishermen. I was born in 1942. Having lived on the lakeshore almost all my life, I, two brothers, and two sisters grew up in Ludington, Michigan. At the time and very young, we spent most of our time at the beach. My father was a wheelsman on the car ferry working seven days a week, twenty-four hours a day. Ludington use to have seven car ferries that ran out of Ludington that sailed to three ports in Wisconsin, Milwaukee, Manitowoc, and Kewaunee. They serviced the lake traffic year round; they did rail service, car, and passengers. Only very bad weather stopped the ferry from running. It took approximately seven hours for the longer runs across the lake.

My mother cooked in different restaurants in the area. Gibbs Restaurant at that time was on Ludington Avenue in the 100 block east. Hamlin Café is still in the same spot only bigger and with different owners. The only related Gibbs Restaurant that was on US 10 East highway and across from where Meyers is now. Gibbs Freezer Plant is where House of Flavors Freezer Plant is now on South Pere Marquette Road, the old highway.

In 1942 when I was born, my parents supplemented their income with war bond stamps for ration groceries. I still have some ration stamps that were never used. They are registered to myself and siblings and used for food, fuel, and groceries. People were only allowed so much per person.

I remember the wringer wash machine; used them a long time to do laundry. My parents had an icebox for food and ice was delivered when you needed it. We had a TV, three stations. That was it and it never was on twenty-four hours. TV signed on for morning news and off after night news. The TV had no color, black and white only. We had a radio to listen to. We hung the washed clothes on a close line and hoped the line did not break. Then you started all over again. During the wintertime, we hung them in the basement. Heat for the house we lived in on 115 East Melindy, where I spent most of my time living, was heated by a big coal furnace in the basement. The house had a huge basement with a fruit cellar for home canned food and a coal room. We used to go to the Coal Shack down by the railroad to buy coal. We had a gas meter for natural gas that when you needed more gas you put quarters in it. You would use it and then refill it again. The gasman would come to the house and empty the machine.

My siblings and I would spend our spare time at the beach and on Sunday, my mother would pack a picnic lunch and spend the day with us. We had cane poles that were ten to twelve feet long. We fished mostly for perch, nice big ones. Some days we didn't get any but got to go swimming almost every day.

We went to school at Foster School in the early years. The school was across the street from where the new school is now. I went to Ludington High and met the man I loved. I quit school and had a baby. Seventeen years later,

I graduated from high school, seventeen years later, and the same year as my daughter. She was the youngest and I was the oldest. During the time, I was raising my four children. I drove a school bus for Mason County Center in Scottville, Michigan. The highway was two lanes from Ludington to Scottville, Michigan. Grassa Market was just a little shack the size of a storage shed. Marek junkyard was only about half the size it is now. The Marek boys were no more than toddlers at the time.

The outhouse was the only bathroom you had. You bathed in the round laundry tub for your bath.

Now US 10 and 31 are five lane highways. Back when I drove a school bus in 1964 at the start of the winter, they were heavy with snow and the wind was most of the damage to the roads. One year in approximately 1984, the schools closed for Christmas vacation and did not reopen until February of that year. Snow was over the top of the buses and the roads were one way, like a tunnel. Before the plows got cleared, another storm came along. I quit the school system in 1984, met, and went to work with the second man of my dreams. We drove a semi-truck cross-country and owned our own truck, Holey's Transport. That ceased when we found out he had a terminal sickness. He passed away in 2009. I am still living on the property first purchased by the first husband and the second husband built a new house here in 1989.

I have seen a lot of changes in the area in my lifetime. My children remember a lot of it but my grandchildren look and say "yea," like a story to them. I am seventy-four years old now and expect to still see more changes.

The car ferry, Ann Arbor, is docked in the Manistee, Michigan museum as a museum piece. The tug, Spartan, is docked in Ludington as a barge. The Spartan is one of the car ferries that worked the waterway to the ports in Wisconsin and Michigan.

When I was about ten years old, my parents had a party phone, number 992J. I don't remember how many people the phone line serviced, but quite a few. I still remember the number today. I remember Kings Canyon, which is where the Hydo Plant is today. It was a lover's lane back in the years. Some people know it as Peter Pan Land. We had two movie theaters in town. One was Center Theater on Ludington Avenue in the area of

the center of the block on the south side of the road. The other was Lyric Theater on South James Street. It is now a small church in the building. One of the radio programs was the Green Hornet. It used to be interesting and a lot of action. Stay tuned 'till next week.

That Old Farmhouse
By Marsha A. Klein of Saginaw, Michigan
Born 1937

I remember daily walks to my grandparents' old farmhouse. We had a new home and my grandparents had the old farm. They had an outhouse, which I'd only seen in magazines, and it was only used for Grandpa's outside necessities. There was also a hand pump over a small sink in the back room where Grandpa washed up and Grandma cleaned up her eggs and crated them. She had customers with whom she sold eggs and made her extra money. This back room contained a huge coal furnace and a coal bin in an added-on shed. Grandma used to make the best cakes using 8-12 eggs. Sometimes she would walk over to our house while mixing or beating her egg

Marsha's parents, Jacob and Marcella Kessler with her brother, Jacob and Marsha in 1943

yolks in a bowl. We'd visit for a while then she would go back home and make her Lord Baltimore or Lady Baltimore cakes, which consisted of egg yolks or egg whites.

I learned a lot from my Grandma. We made noodles, crepes (palacsinta), cashe (cottage cheese) strudel, with paper-thin dough stretched over her cloth covered kitchen table, spread with fillings, rolled, and baked. I loved seeing my Grandma in her flower-covered housedress with a zipper down the front and had two big pockets she used sometimes to collect her eggs from the hen house. She always wore an apron.

They had the first telephone lines in the township and had a pedestal phone and later a rotary phone with a seven party line. Boy did we get in trouble from Grandma if we listened in. She made old-fashioned health remedies we still use today such as heated honey, lemon juice, and wine or whisky used for coughs and colds. A bottle was always available in the back of the refrigerator. Vick's Vapo Rub was used as a chest rub and Musterole for sore muscles. Iodine was also used for any abrasions, skin disorders, and for old bones and wow, did it ever sting when applied, but it worked.

We helped on the farm with haying, gathering eggs, feeding chickens, milking the cows by hand with no fancy modern appliances, and we thought we were lucky. Our family always had food as we kept up two gardens with fresh vegetables and fruit trees. We canned peaches, pears, and tomatoes. They were all peeled and sliced by hand and we made butter, ice cream, and cottage cheese with the help of a cream separator. We had beef, pork, and chickens, which we raised and butchered as a family and made lard, steaks, chops, and various kinds of sausages. We used our Maytag wringer washer, twin tubs, and a washboard with Fells Naptha Soap to get the grime out. It was hard work. All clothes were hung outside on a clothesline come winter or summer. I can still see my mother carrying in my Dad's frozen long underwear that was stiff as a board.

We had our favorite pets: my dog Brownie, our calf Snookums, and my quarter horse Lucky. My girlfriend and I would ride down to the river on our horses and swim. My brother and I would fish in the creek behind our farm. There was always something to do. I got into

Marsha and her brother, Jacob in 1943

trouble when my Grandpa found out about me about riding the milk cow. I put my saddle on her and she threw me off. Don't know how he found out. Maybe she gave buttermilk?

As we got older, we went to Hess School out here in the country. It had four grades in a one-room schoolhouse which had a large furnace on the sidewall and our teacher Mrs. Florence Dean kept it stoked. We walked or rode with a neighbor the one mile to school every day. Mom bundled us up well and if I missed my ride, I had to walk. There were no buses back then. Dress codes were different in those days, as I never wore slacks or jeans to school throughout my 12 years of school. I belonged to a 4-H club and made a lot of my dresses, skirts, and blouses which I entered in the Saginaw Fair. I also learned how to cook and bake through many 4-H projects. In school, the naughty boys did get spanked when they misbehaved and then got spanked more at home if parents found out.

We only had one car and Dad used it to drive to his G.M. plant where he worked for 45 years besides working on the farm. Mom would drive Dad to work when we needed the car for our weekly grocery shopping trip to town along with Grandma who loved cowboy movies. We saw one every week at the Mecca, Franklin, Center or Temple theatres and we would have to run to the old Saginaw News building to hail or catch Grandpa for our ride home, as he drove by coming home from work.

Our Grandparents told us many stories growing up in the "old country." They came to America by boat, and I even have my Grandpa's 1906 passport. Grandma told us about the conditions she endured during the long trip crossing the ocean, on the bottom deck of the ship that carried passengers with undo hardships. My mom came from a large Polish family who were all born here and at five feet two inches tall, she took care of her brother's battles by chasing those rascals up to their back doors. No one messed with her. To help their family they picked up coal that had fallen off the railroad cars that passed their home. The times were tough in the 1920s and 1930s. They had to walk everywhere and later my Mom got a job at Sunshine Biscuit Co. and helped support her family.

My mother met my dad through friends at a dance and found they had a lot in common, and they danced at the Armory every week. I think the building is still there. My Dad had a Model T Ford with a rumble seat with "LITTLE JAKE of SAGINAW" painted on the back tire. I have a picture of him standing proudly next to it. They were married during the Depression and later my brother and I came along. We had Saturday night baths, listened to the Lone Ranger on radio and much later, we had a black and white TV. We lived in the country, in Spaulding Township and played outside winter, summer, spring, and fall and on a clear day; I'd lie on the grass and look up at the clouds or look for four-leaf clovers to press in a book for good luck. There was always something to do.

My first kiss was at my birthday party playing "Spin the Bottle." By summertime, I got a job hoeing beans locally and was paid ten cents a row, and later after school, I worked the soda fountain at Luxton's Drug Store. My Dad knew Mr. Luxton personally and he took me to get my working papers at age 14. Gas was 25 cents a gallon and we'd pool 50 cents and put in two gallons and ride to the local drive-ins and have good fun. I earned my spending money from my many jobs and also worked eight years at Michigan Bell Tell Co. and 17 years as an office secretary for the Spaulding Township Office. I loved school,

Elvis, my country life, and what it taught me, along with good work ethics. I look around and see beauty everywhere and became an accomplished artist/painter.

I had parents that I looked up to, who set great family examples. My Dad quit school in the 11th grade to go to work at the G.M. Foundry core room, accounting office and later transferred to tool grinding. My mother, with an eighth grade education, got a job at Jacobson's Department Store and we bought a second car. I married a great guy who worked many jobs even on a stone crusher to make money for his family.

We built our home on the family farm from scratch, starting with one bedroom and later added on two more and a family room and garage. He liked Elvis, too. We watched the moon landings, bowled in leagues, and raised three children. Times have certainly changed a lot since then, but I thank God for a good religious up-bringing, a great family and quality values to pass on to my next generation.

Clare County Park Memories
By William J. White of Clare, Michigan
Born 1936

In the early 1930s my father and mother, Erwin and Mary White built a lunch car from an old streetcar on the west side of US 27 highway, at the time a gravel road.

My father worked on the railroad in previous years and that's where he came up with the idea for a lunch car. From this business, they served lunches to passing motorist.

In 1934 Michigan paved US 27 highway with concrete. In the process they cut the grade of the hill where my parents lunch car was way down, leaving their business far above the roadway not making it practical for motorist to enter from the roadway putting them out of business.

In the process of cutting this grade, the contractors ran into a large spring. They thought they could cover it with large loads of gravel, but after several attempts, the water would flow back through the gravel the next morning. They knew they needed a more drastic plan to stem this flow. They formed a large concrete box over the spring and a pipe was run from the box to the ditch. This solved the problem and the road was paved in that year.

My father loved nature and saw that this piece of land held promise for a nice roadside park. He drew up a plan to build a road around the high ground and to bring the water down from the ditch into the park for a natural fountain. He took his plan to Mr. Parks, who had influence with the State. To Dad's surprise, the state had already made a plan similar to his to build a park there. Because Dad had showed so much interest in the park and maybe because of Mr. Parks' influence and the fact that they had put my parents out of business, they hired my father to help build the park.

The park was built about 1936, year I was born. I was born at the location of the lunch car, which I have no recollection of or pictures of. I have many memories of the park, as you will see when I continue.

After the park was completed, my father was out of work and a man by the name of Spikehorn Meyere had a bear den for tourist about three miles north of the park. He asked my parents if they would like to run his new venture adding a gas station to this site. My parents took on the venture for a couple of years. As with most Spikehorn's promises of staying with him you would get rich, my parents got poorer and Spike got richer.

About 1939 my father obtained permission from Robert Shull, the owner of the land across from the State park to build a roadside stand. My Dad and his brother Adrian began building from poplar logs my Dad cut from his property on Hatton Road. I remember the park well as my older brother, my sister, and I played in the park about every day in the summer as our parents ran the stand across the road.

The park had a great attraction for many people as far south as Detroit, Flint, Saginaw, and Midland. They would come up to spend a summer day in its cooling shade and drink its great tasting water and just enjoy the natural beauty. The State had left the park as natural as it could and added many beautiful shrubs like juniper and dogwood. A regular bridge was over the creek where the road runs at the south end. A rail for the bridge consisted of horizontal logs mounted on short posts either side of the creek and a third pole was bolted to the top of these and stained a deep brown. Short post lined the drive on both sides all around the half circle drive, also stained the same brown. Around the outside perimeters of the park was a fence my father helped build and supplied the poles. As kids, my brother, sister, cousins, and I got where we could walk this fence from one end to the other on top without falling off.

On the west side of the park, stood several large white pines that had escaped the lumberman's ax. The State erected limestone walls around the trunk of these trees to hold back the dirt from the grade of the road. Keeping the dirt from these tree roots and trunk kept them from dying.

The creek, cold as ice, meandered through the center of the southeast corner of the park with several natural logs that had fallen over it and under these were many brown and rainbow trout, some of which the State planted and some native to its water. Over this stream were two split log bridges located in the same places the two present bridges lay. The southernmost bridge was a flat bridge much as it is today. The bridge to the north central part had a nicely constructed handrail of wood. These bridges were varnished in natural wood color. North from the bridge ran a crushed limestone path, through the cedar swamps which covered much of the central part of the park. If you got off this path, you would sink to your ankles and to your knees in some places in muck. This made much of the park unusable, but it was what attracted the city folks. It gave them the sense of being in the wilds. As you walked this trail to the north, you came to the area where dirt had been graded down to make the drive around the park and there you began to see picnic tables constructed by prisoners. Each table had burned into its top a brand M.S.H.D. (Michigan Stated Highway Department.) As you reached this grade to go up to the drive, wooden steps made of treated railroad ties led to the road above. Either side of these steps was again juniper and dogwood. Across the road were more of the same steps leading to more tables on the upper hill. There were stone grills with cast iron grates at many of the table locations.

On the northwest corner of the high ground, a few more wooden steps with low growing juniper on either side led to two toilets that were masterpieces. They were built of split logs in a round snail shell shape. The logs were stood on end in a circle, the rounded side out and stained brown. Then the flat side was varnished in natural wood color. As you entered the four-foot door, you slid a long wooden bar into a slot to lock the door and you were in a circular hallway that led you into the inner part of the shell, and once there you were out of site. The roof was also round and came to a peak with wood shake singles.

Now the real attraction of the park. The things that kept people coming back again and again was the fountain of spring water that was cold, clear, and so pure. This water is brought down to the park from the spring I told you about earlier. A second concrete box was built in the ditch beside the highway a quarter of the way up the hill. From the box, a pipe was run down the hill into the park. About fifty feet in from the south drive on the central path a mound of earth 4 ½ feet high was placed to make a backing for the fountain and again juniper and dogwood were planted to hold the mound from washing away and to add beauty. The front of the mound was stoned up in a partial circle with large slabs of limestone laid flat. From the limestone protruded a pipe that flowed a full stream and from which a person on the path could get a drink of that great water. Two and a half feet away at the top of the limestone wall, a pipe bubbled out a full stream of water that filled a small basin of concrete then flowed down over the front of the limestone facing in a falls and ran off in a small stream to the creek.

To give you an idea of how much water there is in that spring, my father also tapped into that concrete box and ran water over to his stand. He had pipes running two ways for filling jugs, plus a small fountain to get a drink, and ran this cold water into the building to cool soft drinks in a large metal box. These ran constantly.

These were the glory days of the park that were filled on summer weekends with so many people you could hardly find a place to park. The Michigan National Guard had priority on our highways back then and they would fill that park with their vehicles and be backed up for miles on the road. They would buy out all my parent's soft drinks, potato chips, and candy bars.

In the 1950s the State moved again and built the US 27 freeway a mile to the west and old 27 became a secondary road. The State handed the park over to Clare County. Soon nice signs that were up the road that announced you were coming to a park entrance fell to pieces and were not replaced. The County decided to make more area in the park usable and filled in the swamp area killing off most of the cedar and all the tamarack and those nice white pines.

The State had an older gentleman who worked at least five days a week caring for the park. After the county took over the shrubs were out of hand, no one was there to take care of them, and they hid unscrupulous characters in the park so the shrubs were pulled out. The wood steps deteriorated and the stone grills fell apart or were destroyed by vandals.

Sometime in the 1960s a motorcycle gang stayed in the park overnight and when they left both bridges over the creek had been dismantled.

The masterpiece toilets deteriorated and were torn down and replaced with port-a-johns. The great fountain was robbed of its limestone facing for someone's own personal garden until there is no sign of its former glory. The shrubs have been stripped from its back. Many summers its grass has been mowed only two or three times.

Then in the 1990s, the worst thing of all to deface this park happened. A culvert upstream plugged by beavers was dynamited and the whole culvert gave way letting a torrent of water take out other ponds along the creek and washed silt and trees into the park. It also took many trees out of the park, leaving two feet of silt some places as the water receded.

The cable companies damaged the water system to the park by laying cable past the concrete box until there is only a trickle of water the size of my little finger now flowing.

There have been some attempts to improve the park. About fifteen or twenty years ago, new tables were built and new grills constructed, and I want to thank those who put in the time and money. There were those who took on the care of the lawn, thanks again. Now there is a new group of volunteers with the ambition to make this a family park once more. They need help, funding, materials, and many prayers. IF you can help, please do. Much has been done and donated, but it's a long way from a family park.

The park will probably never be what it was in its glory days. But if God gave you the chance to enjoy it in your lifetime and you drank of its clear waters, would it not be nice to be able to pass at least part of it to our children and grandchildren?

Carrying in Water and Working for the Thrashers
By Viola A. Forro of Freeland, Michigan

I believe the first moon landing was in 1960.

Our home remedies was if you were coming down with a cold Mom said heat up some wine and go to bed. I had a stiff neck so Mother put Vicks on it and pinned a towel on.

The radio I remember is *O Henry*. When it came on my brother ran to the radio so fast he broke his toe. Dad sat him down and pulled on his toe to put it in place.

We never had a phone at home. When I got married, I said we're getting a phone. But there was always someone talking on the line. In an emergency, I would ask them to please get off for a few minutes. It was a twelve party line.

My brother got a spanking in the woodshed. I got slapped. The teacher pulled kids' hair. Well, she got fired.

Yes, Saturday afternoon baths meant hauling in pail after pail of water from the pump, which was next to the barnyard so it would pump water for the cows and horses. But we had to put the tub on the stove and then put our water in, and then when it was warm my sister and I took the tub down and hauled it to the bedroom so we could have private room.

We finally got a wringer washer but used the washboard to scrub a lot of stains out.

Late in life there were free movies being shown in Freeland. We sat in the car or set up our lawn chairs. We never knew what was being shown, but it was free.

Yes, my sister and I couldn't wait till Dad brought home chicken feed in printed sacks. Well, we were anxious on which one will get a shirt or top made from it.

Lou Forro in 2000

We walked to school to a one-room school and then home again.

Our farm chores were every night we carried in pails of water so Mother would have it the next day and then we hauled in wood and put it behind the stove. This is what Mom cooked on.

There was a swimming hole the boys only could go to. My brother nearly drowned there. My brother-in-law saved him. Maxine and I went down to the creek to get our feet wet. Then we would go into the rough drinking trough for the cows. But the cows didn't like to drink the dirty water.

Our milkman was in the barnyard. The cows were milked morning and night.

There was a straw stack by the barn from the thrashing that took place. We had to work and set up the table for the thrashers. Happy and Dutch were always there. Dutch would start to sing "Take me out to the ballgame."

An Unusual Fishing Trip for Dad
By Mary Ciszek of Kawkawlin, Michigan
Born 1952

When I was about ten, we used to go up to Houghton Lake most weekends. At first, we only had a shed with an outhouse and a tent, and then the cabin was finished.

One day we went down to the lake swimming, and had a great time until it was time to get dressed again. I grabbed my shorts and t-shirt with my underwear and went into the outhouse to change. Well, someone left the cover open and when I set down my clothes, they fell in the hole! I came out screamin' and yellin' for my dad. Quick thinking on his part – he got a fishing pole and "fished" my clothes out of the hole. Needless to say, I did not wear those clothes till they were washed and deodorized! It was quite the fishin' trip for my dad.

My Grandpa Told Me

From the time I could walk, I always followed my grandpa around. He was a good and patient man and took time to explain things always. But he also was a very good teaser and jokester. One afternoon while out in the yard he explained these funny things I found were "frog stools" (really toadstools).

Well, a few days later while in the yard with my dad I pointed out some "frog stools." Dad said, "No, they are toadstools." I argued with him back and forth, till he finally asked where I'd learned the frog stool theory. Well, when he found out I learned it from Grandpa and I swore that if my grandpa said this I took it as the gospel truth, Dad didn't argue any more. He knew Grandpa was pullin' my leg – again! It happened many times after this, too.

Why I'm Afraid of Snakes!

When I was about four or five, we went to my relatives' house to visit. Well, all us kids would go out back over the bent down wire fence into the three-foot weeds where we had trails. I was lagging behind the others, being smaller. All of a sudden, here's a large blue snake coming right towards me! I took off running and cryin'. By the time I got to the bent down fence, I was petrified. Well, I tripped on the fence and thought I was a goner! By the time I got up to the patio where Mom and my aunt and uncle were I couldn't talk I was crying so hard. When they finally figured out what I was tryin' to say, my uncle went out back with a shovel and rescued me from the giant blue racer snake. I can still run pretty fast if I see a snake!

Ornery Cows and the Weekly Wash
By Susan Granger of Breckenridge,
Michigan
Born 1944

I remember being very young and funerals were in people's houses, and I had to be held up to see my Uncle Charlie. I took my naps with him when I could, so when he died I needed to see him.

The first house I remember was red, and I was four and a half years old. Yes, outhouses were very popular with magazines to read there or newspapers.

The next house was a farm and Dad took care of Black Angus cows for the rent. They can be ornery. The bull had a ring in his nose and he really could throw dirt with his hoofs when we kids upset him. Yes, we had an outhouse there too and no hot water. There was always a teakettle to keep some water warm on the oil stove and it was refilled when used.

We took pans of water to our rooms to bathe as we grew up, and the young ones got the washtub by the heat stove in the kitchen. The two of us older girls had to bathe them four younger brothers. Mom bathed the baby if there was one, which there usually was. I was afraid to go out to the outhouse at night since it was a distance from the house. Mom would wait on the porch for me sometimes or I took a light. I was still scared. I was afraid of the dark. I'm not very good with it yet.

We had a big garden and the weeding, hoeing, and harvesting was no fun for a girl, but I had to do it anyway, and cleaning onions and cucumbers and peppers for meals and tomatoes was hard work when I'd rather play. I had to dig potatoes and haul them up to the basement window, dry them to put in the basement for winter food, carrots, and onions, too. I also had to go with the parents to pick berries for winter, as we got older and not eat what we picked.

We moved again for a couple of years. We had wringer washers. Mom had to heat water. As we got older, my sister and I washed ours by hand and hung them out on the lines because we needed our clothes for school every week and clothes were not washed every week. We had a washboard. That was Sunday's work. It had to be done.

We moved again and there was another outhouse. I was not impressed.

I had to walk to a country school, maybe half a mile, and home again later. I played marbles with the boys sometimes. There was marbles and helped get home quicker.

Sometimes we played baseball at our house or a neighbor's. We swam down the hill or in winter, we went down the hill with our sleds or a piece of tin. We skated on the pond every winter.

Good Neighbors
By Kay Kantola of White Cloud, Michigan
Born 1943

I was born in 1943. Mom and Dad already had a daughter and son. By 1951, we had three more sisters. We lived in a very small house with a kitchen, a living room, two bedrooms, and a path. Later we added two more rooms, one a bedroom, and another, a sun porch where Mom kept her treasured sewing machine. She was self-taught seamstress and years later opened her own upholstery shop.

We lived in the country approximately two miles from town. The town was so small there was no need for a stop light.

We had a lot of good neighbors and a few were African American. One neighbor, Mr. Davis, had an old horse named Dan, which had a very deep swayback. The horse walked real slow but steady and pulled a rickety old, old wagon with iron tires so Mr. Davis could get supplies from town at least once a week. Anytime on his way back from town if us kids were walking along the road he would ask if we wanted a ride, and we never said no thought it was so cool to take a ride in that wagon, no matter how short the distance. Needless to say, we could walk faster than the horse; it was still cool.

Mr. and Mrs. Clark lived north of us down a two-track road. One day after we had gotten our very first television, Mrs. Clark came in and stood there with a puzzled look on her face. She stared at it for a few minutes and then asked, "How did all those people get inside that little box?"

One winter day my sister and I were out playing in the snow. Mrs. Clark told us she had a job for us if we wanted it. She needed some firewood brought in and the mister wasn't feeling very well. We jumped at the chance when she told us she would pay us thirty cents an hour. My sister and I started adding up the money, thinking we could be there three or four hours. We must have done one heck of a good job and fast – after one hour Mrs. Clark said she had enough wood and gave us our thirty cents. We thanked her and walked home thinking we were somewhat rich.

I first heard the name Rosa Parks in 1955. I could not believe what I was hearing. She was in big trouble for not moving to the back of the bus so white people could sit down. We had gone to school with a lot of African American kids and 75% of us had to ride school buses. No one ever had an assigned seat unless they were naughty; then they had to sit directly behind the bus driver. We all drank from the same water fountain, stood together in the same lunch line. Never once did it occur to us that they should be pushed to the back of the line to be served last. There were no riots, no demonstrations, and no looting. They were good, kind, hardworking people and just because their skin was dark, they should not have been treated any different from white folks. If only I could have known Rosa Parks!

I Met My Husband at a Box Social
By Grace Yanke of Howard City, Michigan
Born 1928

My name is Grace. I was born March 1, 1928 in a farmhouse west of Paris, Michigan. My farm was right next to a cemetery, but thank goodness, we never saw any ghosts! We did not have electricity until 1938, and phone service came about the same time. I was an only child and did what I could to occupy myself and help my parents. I had a wagon just my size with rough wooden slat sides, and I hauled a lot of split wood to our woodshed directly attached to our home. This made it so my father didn't have to go outside to access the wood to heat our home during the cold winters.

My mother used to share with me memories from her childhood. She told me about the narrow gage railroad that ran between Paris and Hawkins, Michigan. When in existence, it once crossed our front yard. It hauled harvested logs down to the Muskegon River in Paris. From there the logs floated south to many different markets. Men stood on the logs while they were in the water to keep them moving, so they would not jam up on each other or the shoreline. When the men were working the logs, there was a cook shanty on a raft that floated down the river

Eno and Grace Yanke in 1950

with them. The children would go down to watch the log rollers, and when the cook in the shanty saw the children, he would give them all a cookie. The children also liked to put pennies on the train tracks and then watch and wait for the train to come. Once it passed by, they would recover their pennies and see how flat they had become!

I attended a country school in Paris that still stands there today. It was the same school my mother attended, too. It was an unusual country school because it had two floors. There were ten grades split with the older children upstairs and the younger downstairs. We had two outhouses, too, one for the girls and one for the boys. We loved to sled in the wintertime but couldn't wait until spring when we could play marbles.

After I graduated from high school, I was invited by an aunt to attend a box social in Grant Center with her. It was an event at the school to raise funds for playground equipment. Women decorated baskets or boxes and filled them with a complete meal for two. Gentlemen then bid on them and the highest bidder was entitled to share the meal with the lady who prepared it.

My box had many items, including chicken, rolls, pickles, and banana cake. I

carefully decorated a round hatbox with a pom-pom on top. The gentlemen were not supposed to know which lady prepared the box or basket. Sometimes there was behind the scenes coaxing if someone was attempting to get a particular man and woman together. This is exactly what happened in my case. My aunt had a certain young man that she wanted me to get acquainted with and of course, she knew which box was mine. She eagerly encouraged this gentleman to bid on my box, but in the meantime, there was another man with interest! Bidding went up, up, and my aunt's acquaintance ended up spending $14.50 to buy my box. That was a lot of money back then! Well, we ended up sharing my box meal on what happened to be his 25th birthday on February 25th. My birthday was just one week later, March 1st. Since we enjoyed our box social conversation so much, I decided to invite him to Sunday dinner the following weekend to celebrate my birthday, naturally.

Well, we were married about eighteen months after sharing our box social gathering, and we were married for a total of 57 ½ years before he passed away. I don't think his father ever knew how much he spent at that social

Grace with her cousin Allen

for my box! We raised a family together on a Centennial Farm where I still reside today. It was homesteaded by my husband's family, the Yankes, in 1867. They started out in a little log house and slept on feathered beds.

Grandpa Bill and I Were Close
By Agnes Jason of Middleton, Michigan
Born 1945

I was born near the end of World War II. My mother and I lived with Grandpa Bill, Aunt Mary, Uncle John, his wife, Jay, and their two children. We all lived together so that there was an adult there to watch the children while the others worked.

After my father came home from the war, he became a sharecropper, a farmer who worked for other farm owners who needed their farms and animals taken care of. The pay we got was a share of the crops and animals that were sold and fresh meat. At most of the farms that we lived at, we did not have an indoor bathroom like we have now, we had an outhouse. We all would take baths in the same water that was in a metal tub in the kitchen that my mother heated on the wood stove that we cooked in.

One of the farms that we worked on was Doc McNabb's. We raised his horses, beef cattle, chickens, and hogs for him. We worked this farm for four years. My family took care of all the animals, and my parents took care of all of the crops. My mother also made the butter from the milk. The extra milk, butter, and eggs that we did not use were traded at the grocery store for other goods that we needed. It was a small store just two miles from us.

My Grandpa Bill lived with us also. He took care of me while my parents worked outside. When I was two, I was allowed to go with Grandpa to get the mail that was a half of mile down the road at the crossroads.

We moved by the time I was five to a new place two miles away. It was a new experience for me, moving. The new home had a better outhouse. It was a nice one with three holes to sit on, but still very cold in the winter. We had to clean it every spring and summer. My father would clean the cattle barns and the outhouse and would spread it on the fields.

My mother would milk our cow twice a day. In the summer, she would milk her in the yard and in the barn in the winter.

My grandpa lived with us until he died. He was my sitter while my parents were in the fields working. He and I kept the house and the garden clean and picked. He told me stories about him being young in Poland and how he stowed away on a freighter ship to get to the United States. When he got here, he moved to Chicago and met my Grandma Agnes and married her. They lived there at first then moved to Merrill, Michigan and had a farm. In the Depression of the 1920s, they lost their farm and had to move back to Chicago, Illinois. They ran away one night with a group of migrant workers because Grandma Agnes's brother was trying to recruit him into Al Capone's gang. They worked many different farms. Then he worked at the sugar beet factory in Alma, Michigan and was a bricklayer in Ithaca, Michigan, helping to build the school gym. He was a shoemaker in Ithaca until he retired.

He told me about working in the fields doing sugar beets. The whole family worked all summer in the fields. He also buried large rocks that were in farmers' fields. His wife had died after she had surgery from pneumonia. He had raised his kids alone until they were grown. My mother was only seven years old when her mom died, and the girls took over the cooking and cleaning as well as working in the fields. Grandpa was always a very busy man and helped his kids when they needed help.

Grandpa and I spent a lot of time together as Mom was always busy in the fields. He and I kept the house clean and took care of the chickens and gathered the eggs. I could get all the eggs on the floor and down low, and he got the ones up high. We cleaned the eggs and put away the ones that we needed for our use. The rest were taken to town and sold. Mom did most of the baking and cooking before she went to help Dad. He and I took care of the garden also.

In the summer, my mom went to work for a while at the county farm where people lived that were old and unable to care for them. My aunt and uncle ran it until my uncle died. Grandpa and I used to go there and visit with the people while Mom helped them. It was a cool place, and I loved visiting with all the old people. I loved to hear the stories about the past things they had done during their life. Most of them had no family near enough to take care of them. I always felt that they were like my family and needed someone who cared about them. They were very sad frequently and loved to have someone to talk to.

Our home caught fire from the wood creosote buildup in our chimney. When men came to fix it, they added an indoor bathroom in our new backroom. It was so great to have an indoor bathroom that flushed, and it was warm the year around. It was really cool to have an inside toilet as many didn't then.

I attended a one-room school down the road from our home. There were six kids in my class when I started and 24 in the whole school. They were from kindergarten to eighth grades. We had one teacher, and each class took their turn in their classes up front. I loved school because I had a lot of kids to play with. I felt very safe there and enjoyed school as I had many friends. They all walked to school past my house and I enjoyed it. We walked about a half mile to school all year. I loved riding with the neighbor boy on the back of his bike to school; it was fun. The neighbor boys took turns giving me a ride. Some of the kids walked a couple miles every morning and evening.

I helped with the farming and with the care of the cattle. One year we raised hogs and had a lot of babies running in the feedlot. I was helping move the babies into the barn. I fell and started to cry, and the momma pigs attacked me. My dad lifted me by one arm and beat the pigs as he threw me over the fence. My snowsuit was shredded; I was only bruised and sore, but alive. I wasn't allowed to help again with the babies. I was only six at the time and I was scared of pigs for a long time.

We raised beef cattle on the farm. They were so big.

I learned to hunt there with my dad. He and I hunted pheasants, squirrels, and raccoon, and trapped all winter. We got to have extra things at Christmas. We also fished on weekends, and he fished all winter on the nearby lakes. It gave us a good variety of meats to eat. Dad and I also caught pigeons out of the barns to keep down the diseases they carried to the cattle. Mom would cook them for dinner. We called them squabs. We lived here for another four years, and then we moved to another farm in December.

I was eleven when we moved to the new farm. It was a bigger house and it was really nice there, but there was no indoor bathroom. So we were back to an outhouse again. It had a good outhouse, but it was really cold in the winter. When you wanted to take a bath, Mom had to heat the bath water in a large kettle. They put a big washtub in the middle of the kitchen floor. We took our turn bathing the kids first and then Mom. While we bathed the kettle would heat water again, and then the tub was drained. Fresh water was put into the tub again. My dad and uncle did their baths. It was the way that you did it back then.

I went to city school now on a bus, and there were 38 in my grade and all in one room. This was a big shock as I was used to the teacher helping you to do your work, but not there. I hated the school and had lost all my friends in school. I was scared of everyone and had a hard time coping. I wasn't used to 40 kids in one class. The teacher didn't have time to help anyone like the teacher in country school did.

We had another fire and lost part of our stuff. When they rebuilt the house, it had a new roof and a lot of remodeling but we got our first tub and toilet in the house. We also got an inside dryer for the clothes as Mom had to hang clothes outside on a clothesline to dry winter and summer. It had a great electric stove to cook on and a large living room. Grandpa and I loved it. We had room for the whole family to come for holidays, and we could all sit together at the table. My aunts and uncles and all their kids would come to our house for dinner. We had a lot of fun together. Then Grandpa Bill moved to help my aunt and died shortly thereafter.

This was the first place that really was like a home as we stayed here for eight years. We had made a lot of friends here. We enlarged the farm and fixed it up. We got a new milk house and for the first time we had a bulk tank to keep milk cold. We had cows for the year to milk and were building a good herd. We lived here until I was a senior in high school.

I helped my parents with all parts of the farming and was soon helping Dad do his custom baling of hay and straw. We put in long hours together on many other farms

208

doing the job. I received a penny a bale for every bale I put through the baler. Dad got ten cents a bale so we wanted to push through as many as possible each day. We did the chores in the morning before we left for the field, and Mom did the evening chores.

My father died at the kitchen table one evening of a massive heart attack. Then it was selling most of the things we owned and moving again. I helped do chores after Dad died, as Mom was pregnant. I was halfway through my senior year. I had to do the hogs and the milking with one of the neighbor men. I almost flunked the semester test and ended up taking them all again after a break.

For the first time we lived in town. Mom was so sick and couldn't do a lot so I had to do more plus go to school. We all hated it. My brother, who was ten, was all over town and we had a hard time watching him. After we moved, Mom had my baby brother. He was very ill and had to be in the hospital for his first year.

Mom got a place in the country a year later. We moved to our permanent home that we owned; no more moving every few years. It felt good. I went to work in the nearby hospital as an aide then.

The Farm and All the Memories
By Janet Krzysik DeCatur of Pinconning, Michigan
Born 1951

It all began on April 15, 1951, at Mercy Hospital in Bay City, Michigan, which is now an apartment building. My first recall was kindergarten. One of my neighbors would pick me and several other area kids up in his station wagon and take us to school. The school was the original school before the new school was built. The building was on the main highway M-13. There is a hotel and credit union on that spot now.

When the old school was torn down, I went with my dad to pick up some of the old bricks and in the pile was one of the old wood swing seats. We took it home and hung it in a big tree, and for many years, it was enjoyed by a lot of kids. Now some fifty plus years

The swing recovered from the old school

since we saved it that same swing hangs from my apple tree and is enjoyed every summer.

As country kids most of us grew up on farms. Ours was a dairy farm. We even had an outhouse hidden out behind some buildings facing the backfield along with the old Sears catalog. We did have an indoor bathroom but no hot water for years. Saturday night baths was the thing. Water was heated as everyone took a turn in the tub.

Dairy cows meant a lot of milking, shoveling manure, and tons of hauling hay. Our milkman was the type that came every day with a big truck and a man would lift those heavy milk cans up into the truck. Our milk went to a Kraft processing plant right there in our town.

We also hoed crops and picked pickles, which gave us spending money. There were regular garden chores with a lot of canning and freezing in the fall. The whole family would spend the whole day in the woods picking buckets of blueberries.

Having our own beef and preserving fruits and veggies there wasn't many other shopping trips to town. The big shopping trip was going to the big city, Bay City, for serious shopping at the big store, like Arlans or Yankees. This was maybe a once a month trip unless Dad needed new farm clothes or shoes or school clothes. Mom sewed and she made a lot of her own dresses and nightgowns. She even made some for my sister and me.

Mom was a good cook. She made four pies or a homemade cake every Sunday. She would listen to a radio show, *Listen to the Mrs.*, and jot down a lot of recipes. Sunday morning after church, the radio had the polka station. We are a Polish Catholic home and lived with all the traditional doings and foods. My sister has said to me that my cooking is so much like our mom's was, and that is such a compliment.

Wash day depended on wind and weather. There was no dryer. We had the good ole wringer washer. We did a lot of ironing then. The funniest thing in winter washing was when clothes came back in frozen stiff as boards. You laid them over a drying rack till they dried. There is nothing better than the smell of outdoor fresh laundry.

When we had free time we got together with neighbor kids, boys and girls, and played baseball in the cow pasture. We built tree houses and igloos in the winter. Some snowstorms left drifts big enough to dig into for houses. We went sledding and skating in the local Pinconning River, which was the only water for playing in.

My sister and I played badminton and croquet, made mud pies, rode bikes, and dressed up Barbie. My brother was usually in the field with Dad.

We didn't have a phone until we were in high school. It was a rotary type and on a party line. It was fun to listen to the neighbors' gossip. Dating was done when you planned it while in school. I had to wait till I was sixteen to date. My sister lucked out at fifteen.

The years passed with dating, proms, graduations, marriages, and grandkids. My brother still works the farm, and my sister and I stop by once in a while. The farm is still there and so are all the memories.

No Regrets for This City Girl Turned Country Girl
By Carol L. Salgat of Pinconning, Michigan
Born 1939

My name is Carol and I am 76 years old. My memories of Bay County begin in 1952. My mother and dad and I lived in Dearborn until I was fourteen. My dad was a stonecutter

Carol's dad, Arnold in 1982

who made monuments in Detroit. One day he said he wanted to moved north and start a drive-in restaurant. He had built us a beautiful home, and we had wonderful neighbors, so my mother was not very happy about it. She made great pies, and my dad convinced her that they would make the business. We would drive up north on M-15 through all the neat little towns and end up in Pinconning. There was no expressway. I-75 was made in 1966; I remember my in-laws had to sell the family farmhouse to make way for it.

My dad bought an old, no longer working gas station and auto repair garage. My mother thought it would never be home but it was. I remember the day she freaked out when she saw a live snake curled up under the heat stove. My dad worked to make it a restaurant in the front with living quarters in the back. The first week we were there, we saw a train going down the track through the neighbor's farm field and my dad wrote on the unfinished wall, "Ten to one the train went by."

I remember a great artist in Pinconning, Lee Bowser, who came out and painted a billboard size sign. It was unique, with a cow and a chicken on it and the Farm Diner was born. My dad was quite an artist also. The Farm Diner had red and white stripes painted on the walls outside and a big matching sign on the roof. There was a four-foot grandma out front. He painted signs that said, "We have pop on ice…Mom too."

Lee Bowser's paintings of scenes in the Pinconning area are still displayed in our local funeral home and some other businesses.

We had a grand outhouse in back of the

Carol, holding the rabbit, her mother, Leila and Great-grandmother at one of the umbrella tables

restaurant. It was painted bright colors and on the doors were Mom and Pop. You didn't have to have restrooms in a restaurant back then and some customers used the outhouse, but I remember one nicely dressed woman asking me where the restrooms were. I can still see the picture of her face when I said it was outside as she said, "I'll wait."

The restaurant was ready to open in the spring of 1954. At the age of fourteen, I was their one and only waitress and carhop, Mom was the baker, and Dad ran the restaurant, without any of us having any experience or training. I went from playing jacks with my friends on the front porch and playing baseball in the street to working every day in the restaurant. We later hired help.

In the beginning, we had cute umbrella tables outside. It might have been a good idea, but we didn't know the power of a windy day in the open country. There were tables inside too, and many people ate in their cars.

One Friday evening in the summer of 1955, a tall, dark, and very handsome man drove up in his new Ford. I went out to the car and he said, "I just want a cup of coffee. I will come in." It was a slow evening in the restaurant, and we talked for hours. This man's name was Ted, and he became my one and only love. We were married a year and a half later and as I write this today in 2015, we are going on 59 years together. We raised four children who are such a blessing to us. We also have nine grandchildren and twelve great-grandchildren.

My experience at Old Piny High began in August 1954. I walked up to a two story brown brick building. I went in and did not see anyone so I walked down the hall until I saw an open door. As I looked inside, I saw a man dressed in a plaid shirt and jeans with his feet propped up on the desk. I told him I was looking for the principal, as I wanted to register for the fall classes. He said, "That's me." In Dearborn, the principal always wore a black suit, white shirt, and tie, and you hardly ever saw him unless you were in trouble. Mr. Henry Uhlmann was the principal at Pinconning High School for many years. He was also athletic director, student council director, and involved in many areas with the students and everyone loved him. I made many friends in school and graduated in 1956. To this day, I still meet with some of them for lunch once a month.

When I married Ted, I became a farmer's wife and that was a big change for a "city girl." My dad had a small garden in Dearborn and I sometimes helped him, but I could not imagine a forty-acre field of white navy beans. Ted gave me a hoe and I looked down all the neat rows of green plants that went to the next farm. I said, "You do all of this with a hoe?" I love living here in Fraser Township and having a small garden. It was a great place to raise our children. It helped to made them the successful and wonderful adults that they are today. However, I never did really love farming. It is hard work and a dangerous job.

Ted is 85 now and living with dementia. We still love each other and say so every day. There are still warm hugs, smiles, and kisses. So this city girl turned country girl has no regrets that her dad brought her to Pinconning. It is a full and wonderful life.

Ted and Carol in 1956

Shopping in Downtown Saginaw
By Joan L. Mulder of St. Louis, Michigan
Born 1934

"Come on, Jo, pick up your toys. Your dad just got a phone call. We're going to Saginaw."

The World War II was raging. The family business of plumbing and heating was always short of supplies. The call received was from the Reichle Supply Company on South Jefferson, a supplier for our business. They had had a load of supplies come in. If Dad would come right away, he could buy some needed items. It would be over an hour drive. Top speed between towns and villages was 35 miles an hour. Mom and I would often tag along just for the ride. Of course, I knew there might be a piece of candy waiting for me when we arrived. Walter Leesch, the salesman, would reach into his pocket and find one. The top award would be when Mr. Reichle would also find a piece of candy, a real treat in the war years.

Another trip to the city would be when Dad needed to go "downtown" to Morley Brothers and buy supplies. Mom and I would talk him into an extended trip so we could walk the streets and do some shopping.

As we ventured down the street we would stop at the three dime stores – W.T. Grant, SS Kresge, and Woolworth's – where we would look and look some more. It was the fascination of the elevators and walking steps down into the basement, especially the toy department. The shopping would not be complete without sitting at the counter and having a refresher, a piece of pie or cake or ice cream. Sometimes as we would be walking down the street, a line of women would be forming. "Mom, why are they standing in line?" The answer would be, "Probably the store received a shipment of silk hose." A delightful affair if one could buy even one pair. We would stop and "window shop" along the way, especially the jewelry stores. It was all right to dream a little. We would stop in Montgomery Ward's store and climb the steps to the second floor. They provided a public restroom, which was very much appreciated by all who used it.

The Friday after Thanksgiving, Dad would stay home and Mom and I would travel to Saginaw together for a whole day of shopping. I was amazed at the Christmas wonderland in each store. On Wednesday, it was still fall and Thanksgiving. The store personnel must have worked all night to transform the stores from fall to Christmas. It was the first day of Christmas shopping.

As the war years ended and with Dad retiring from the business, our trips were not as often and usually would be an all-day affair between Mom and daughter. Easter would not be complete without a new spring outfit from J.C. Penney's, Sears, or Montgomery Ward, or some of the other smaller clothing stores along the way. The new hat from the hat store around the corner would complete our new outfit. Lunch would often be eaten at the Home Dairy.

It seemed like a long walk to Wiechmann's, the store for Girl and Boy Scouts. Being able to purchase my Brownie Scout uniform and two Girl Scout uniforms (I outgrew the first one) was worth the walking trip. The uniform was not complete without the belt, scarf, beret, and even anklets. Handbooks were available also. In the same area there was the fur store, Oppermann's, where they not only sold fur coats and other items but they also remade them. Mom's old fur coat turned into a fur cape complete with a fur muff.

As we ended our shopping trip and made our way back to our vehicle, our arms would be full of packages and sacks and full shopping bags. You would have to carefully make your way as you met or passed persons who were also loaded down with their shopping results. A bump from one person to another was fine; you just went your merry way.

As we left downtown or the Reichle Supply Company and turned onto Gratiot Avenue heading west, it wasn't very far until we came to Mooney's Ice Cream store. A trip to Saginaw was not complete without that French vanilla ice cream cone. We would not go faster than the speed limit. A speeding ticket was issued to my father on one trip, and he never forgave the officer and also he never forgot the ticket and would not exceed the speed limit, at least on Gratiot Avenue.

I was growing older. Soon I would graduate from my two-year college course, and I was starting my "hope chest." My present would be complete set of Noritake china from Morley Brothers. There were so many designs to select from.

The day came for shopping for wedding dresses. After shopping here and there, we returned to our first place of looking. The clerk rotated the bolts of material as we purchased yards and yards of material for three bridesmaids, the flower girl, the bride's mom, and the bride. Yes, Mom would make them all. The store was the Diebel Company. The groom was able to find a suit (extra tall) at Heavenrich's.

A collectible item was a cup and saucer set, especially one marked "English bone china," an import from England. Often they were a souvenir brought home when traveling to Canada, where they were lower in price and often the selection from a much larger stock. The collection expanded into adding a matching dessert size plate. Much to my delight, after receiving a beautiful cup and saucer set purchased in Canada, I was shopping at Wiechmann's and found the matching English bone china plate.

A few years passed by with our final shopping trips for downtown having the purpose of buying corrective shoes for our baby daughter at the Dall Shoe Store.

Downtown was changing. The family owned and managed stores were closing. The malls were being built with big department stores, a lot of parking, and the going from one store to the next with protection from the weather. Yes, we transferred our shopping trips to the mall, but it was just not the same as shopping downtown Saginaw.

Washing Bees, Saturday Fun, and Shivers from Radio Shows
By Mary J. Heiskala of Prunedale, California
Born 1938

My cousin, Frank, who is the same age as me, lived across the street. We discovered many wonders of nature together and desired peace and comfort for everything and everyone. We were especially concerned about the hungry giants and hobos, so began to make a pile of chop suey that would be fed to every starving giant and hobo who came along. The chop suey pile was being constructed outside of the wooden fence of my backyard. It consisted of gravel and rocks, grass, dead bugs, sand, dead flowers, weeds, the carrots and peas we would sneak off of our dinner plates, and anything else we could scrounge up. It was a

Mary's cousin, Frank's house

wonderful, productive project that we worked on every day. By the end of the summer, the concoction had a diameter of about four feet and was three feet high. We were confident that amount would be enough chop suey to last through the winter.

When Frank and I were not busy cooking for the giants and hobos, we were catching bumblebees for our roadside bee washing business. A homemade sign with blue print posted on my parents' garage simply read, "Bees washed – five cents a bee." First, we would catch several "buzzers" in one of two ways: either wrapping the petals of a hollyhock around the pretty black and yellow furry body or placing the open mouth of a glass jar around it. When the unsuspecting insect flew into the jar, a lid with air holes punched in it would be screwed on top. Both methods had a drawback. Using the petal method brought many stings to our fingers and bees flew free as we quickly dropped the petal. The other method allowed the bees to escape, especially if there were several in the jar when the lid was removed to catch a new one. But we didn't worry. There were so many tall and beautiful red, pink, and purple hollyhocks in front of both our homes, that there was never a shortage of new recruits.

The next step after trapping an acceptable number of bees was quickly turning the uncovered jar of buzzing victims upside down in a large, wide bowl of water that was previously prepared on our back porch. Using a wooden spoon, we stirred the bees around in the water, insuring all sides were clean. Then the soaked insects were placed under a small, inverted, clay flowerpot to dry. Each bee had its own pot. When an hour or so had passed, the pots would be removed and, using a hoe, the bees were gently prodded. Those that flew

213

Mary J. Heiskala

away were clean and ready to be caught again. Those that just sat or moved slowly were given more drying time. Eventually, it occurred to us that not many folks were concerned about the hygiene of their bees, as our piggy bank till contained no nickels. We didn't mind; it took all our time just keeping the local bees dirt free.

Saturdays were always a special day in my childhood, not because it was the weekend, but because Mom always made spaghetti for supper. The sauce wasn't a combination of homegrown tomatoes, garden herbs, and freshly ground meat, but came from a large can with a red label, black and white print, and a heavily mustached stout chef on the front. Baroni's Spaghetti Sauce, very difficult to obtain because it was manufactured in only one small town in the Midwest, surpassed all of the many homemade versions I've had since.

Sometimes Cousin Frank would come over and eat with us. Since we were the same age, we became partners in crime. The only misdeed we committed on Saturday nights was to slurp the long thin noodles, attempting to get the end of the noodles to slap against the tip of our noses. Of course, this was performed when my parents' back or heads were turned,

but the giggles gave us away. Then, solemnly, we would try to wrap the pasta around our forks – no easy feat for such small hands.

We never invited Frank to dinner when Mom was stretching the budget and using up odds and ends of differently shaped noodles. He didn't like any dissimilar food portions touching each other on his plate, and the frustration of separating the variety of noodles into like piles drove him to tears.

On very warm summer afternoons, we were allowed to go down into the cool basement of my home and play records on the old Victrola. This mahogany piece of furniture was taller than us, and we needed a step stool to place the 78 records on the turntable. The Victrola stood on round metal wheels, and the logo of a white dog peering into a huge megaphone was on the front. First, we would wind the machine up using a large brass handle on the side of the unit. When the correct tautness was reached, one of us would lift the heavy cylindrical head that held a large needle and carefully place it on the record. Frank and I danced around to the staticy music, our movements becoming slower and slower as the machine ran down. The slow motion never failed to amuse us. If the music was vocal, the singer's voice would become lower and lower in range and the words more

Mary's cousin, Frank

and more dragged out until the record came to a grating halt. We could hardly contain our anticipation and giggles as we cranked the wind up handle and the pace of the voices accelerated, words coming faster and faster, higher and higher in pitch, our tummies ached from laughing. These dance sessions worked up appetites and so we were always ready for Mom's spaghetti.

Frank went home shortly after dinner when he ate with us. Then came my special time, my big event of the week, the radio broadcasts of *The Shadow* and *Inner Sanctum*. The entertainment center in those days consisted of a radio and 78 record player. Ours was about 12 square feet in size. The built-in speakers on each side of the front had woven mesh covered by scrolled wood. The record changer and radio were recessed underneath a top-hinged lid. Before listening to the spooky radio programs, I would play my favorite record, "Buttons and Bows" from "Annie Get Your Gun" sung by Betty Garrett. This was my treasure, purchased by saving my ten-cent weekly allowance, earned by doing dishes, dusting, and making my bed. I knew all of the words to "Buttons and Bows." It was my second copy as an out of town uncle with white hairs poking out from his ears and nostrils sat on my first one. Mom and Dad paid for that one, knowing how hard I had struggled to save for it.

Following my duet with Betty Garrett, I prepared for *The Shadow* and *Inner Sanctum* by turning off all the lights except one, grabbing my favorite big green cloth pillow, and laying tummy down on the floor. My head, propped up by my arms, was close to the speakers. The deep, scary voice of Lamont Cranston boomed out "Who knows what evil lurks in the hearts of men? The Shadow knows." The evil laugh that followed sent shivers through my body. In that properly terrified frame of mind, I then listened to *Inner Sanctum*, scared by the squeaking door and what mysteries lay beyond.

After the hour of spine chilling stories, it was time for bed. My parents always allowed me to read later that evening, and the Bobbsey Twins soon had me in a different, kinder world. Before long, I would fall asleep and have pleasant dreams.

The Walk Home from School
By Paul Kruska of Ludington, Michigan
Born 1950

I attended Ludington St. Simons Catholic School from grades three to eight in the late 1950s and early 1960s. As was common then, our family was a "one vehicle" family (besides Mom and Dad there were three younger brothers and one spoiled sister!). Dad was usually away with the car in the afternoon and early evening as he was a traveling (mostly) insurance salesman with an office in our home on Park Street. Mom K was the answering machine for the home office. Dad or a carpool usually got us to school in the morning, but after school, we were on our own to get home. This was before us city kids had busing options. When we got older and the weather was good we had the alternative of our bikes, but most of the time walking was our main mode of transportation.

St. Simons (SS) was about fifteen blocks from our home and was located in the southern end of downtown Ludington while home was one block from Lake Michigan. Alone or with a brother or sister or friend, we made the trek home each school day.

Leaving school down the alley from St. Simons was Bach's Bakery on James Street. After school there were often "day olds" (donuts) for half price. I gorged myself often! Sometimes my friend, Dave Luskin, and I bought more than we could eat and would hide the rest down the alley, but I don't think we ever returned to finish the hidden ones. In the same block as the bakery was the Democratic Party office during election years, and us kids would stop for pins and bumper stickers. Dad would never use the bumper stickers, as he wisely was afraid of alienating potential insurance customers.

After three blocks south of school were the C&O trains and car ferries. We could hear the train and boat whistles all day long. In the same block as the school was Ricker's Pantry, a short order restaurant and candy shop frequented by SS students. The corner across from the Pantry was where I was a safety patrol boy when I was a little older. I was sure proud of that white belt, but that didn't last long as our distance from school and having to be early for patrol duty wasn't possible.

If one wandered the opposite direction

from SS you were in a little rougher area of Ludington near the train and shipyards. As a kid I was fearful of actual black leather jacketed hoods in that area. Piano lessons there kept me alert! Because I didn't practice my piano enough I often distracted my teacher, Mrs. Newell, with talk about the Detroit Tigers, who she liked. The best part of the lessons was all the comic books in the waiting room.

St. Simon's Catholic School

Several alternative street routes were available. One past the Hansen Auto dealership had me drooling over the promo cars in the windows. Our main route, though, was down James Street. Spiegel's catalog store was located there. I remember getting my first transistor radio through them. Catalog ordering was common then as there were no "big box stores" in the area as there are now. Other catalog stores in Ludington included JC Penney's, Sears, and Wards. Wards also had a huge three level store on Ludington Avenue. One block west of James Street was the Star Watchcase Factory, which was an impressive three-story building near the harbor. We walked along an iron pipe fence, which kept us off the nicely manicured grass lawn around the building.

Sometime our route took us down the alleys as we searched for refundable bottles (beer two cents, pop three cents). We usually cashed them in at Bonsers Market at the west end of downtown. They had a gumball/peanut machine that took pennies and also a candy aisle with my cheap favorite, Picnic Bar for three cents.

Back to James Street, we passed the Lyric Theater where we enjoyed Saturday matinees for thirteen cents. I remember lines to get in which wrapped around the corner of the block when a new film was playing. I discovered a mechanical candy machine at the theater was cheaper than the candy counter, but I did get their great popcorn there.

The next block brought us to the impressive Ludington State Bank. I never did much business there, but it was a beautiful building. The next corner was the main intersection of downtown, Ludington Avenue and James Street. The three story National Bank was on the corner. In later years I bugged the tellers there for rolls of coins and then sat there and looked for old dated coins for my coin collection. When I was very young Dad K shared an office with Maurie Tallefson in the building. The neatest store to me was the JJ Newberry dime store, which had entrances on both Ludington Avenue and James Street, basically surrounding the National Bank building. The James Street entrance was the one I used, because the glass cased candy counter, the toy department, and the lunch counter greeted me there. Everything a kid could want! Under the National Bank with a stairwell off the Ludington Avenue sidewalk was a neat barbershop with a white and black tiled floor. As I got older I had a few haircuts there, but usually went to Bob Roach's shop just around the corner from the Lyric. In my early years Dad K "tortured" us with home haircuts in our basement. Across from the bank was Mulligan's Newsstand, a great place for comics, candy, theater quality popcorn, and an impressive array of tobacco products (which I never touched). Outside was a penny weigh scale and a constantly running city water fountain. Lewis Drugstore was across the street. You could get five-cent sherbet cones at their lunch counter and later when I was older the store was a source of chemicals to supplement my chemistry set.

One favorite sighting of ours downtown

was spotting Dad's car outside the Old Hamlin Restaurant where Dad often visited with his friend, the owner Ted Koikas. Spotting the car there meant we might have a chance to get a hot chocolate and a donut if we caught Dad in a good mood and also possibly a ride home. Two doors down (for a short time) Dad's friend George Berdan had an art and gift shop. I used to go to drool over the plastic model kits he sold there.

A block south behind the bowling alley was as repurposed railroad passenger car sitting next to a parking lot. We would go up on the car and look in the door but never did know what group or club met there.

Back to the avenue heading west we came to the A&W Restaurant. In those days it was a drive-in, car parking in back and right off the sidewalk in front were black metal stools by each window ledge, perfect for drinking A&W root beer. It was five cents in a glass mug, and we were shocked later when the price when to ten cents.

Passing Bonsers Market the next block on the way home brought us past the Delicatessen where hamburger and hotdog smells were fanned out to us passersby. The next business that I loved was the Park Dairy. They had seven cent cones, a freezer of frozen treats, and were home of the Pig's Dinner. You got a pin if you finished one. I never did! It is now known as the House of Flavors Restaurant and Dairy Bar. Next-door was another friend of Dad's, Les Blodgett's Hertz car rental and dealership. In later years I got to drive a 1968 white Mustang loaner from there while Dad's car was under repair.

Leaving the business district we now cut diagonally through a block and a half of the city park with a drinking fountain at the corner, a water spraying fountain at the center of the park, and a lot of chestnut trees. We loved when the chestnuts fell. The nuts were beautiful when opened but soon turned hard and ugly with exposure to air.

The last few blocks home were through residential streets. Those running east to west had views down them of Lake Michigan. One problem we faced in these last few blocks was loose dogs. We always took long detours if we spotted any. We passed the old two story Lakeview Public Grade School on Gaylord Avenue with a neat slide fire escape coming down from the second floor. A shortcut through an empty lot on the corner of Fitch and Ferry wore a path through the field from us kids constantly walking there. The lot is still empty but the path has disappeared, as the neighborhood is mostly summer tourists now. Our home on Park Street was just across from Oriole Field, baseball, tennis, track, football, and ice skating in the winter. Park Street in those days was not asphalt, but instead was a liquid oil base overlaid with crushed loose stone. When it was fresh we skinned a lot of knees on it.

Finally we were home at last to Mom K's cookies and/or cake. What great childhood memories of Ludington.

Growing Up in Saginaw
By Robert Gregor Hegler of Saginaw, Michigan
Born 1927

My dad came from Germany on the ship *Washington* at the age of sixteen in 1913. He landed on Ellis Island. I heard he had $25.00 to his name. He made his way to Minnesota where he had a cousin. He went to work in the iron ore mines. When World War I came, Dad went into the Army and was stationed in Mexico. After the war, he married my mother in Minnesota. I had two sisters. My dad and mother moved back and forth from Minnesota to Michigan just to find work. I was born in Saginaw on December 26, 1927 as Robert Gregor Hegler.

The first thing I can remember was my folks renting a house on 10th and Johnson Street. We kids slept upstairs. There was a big potbelly stove in the dining room. We would wait until Dad got it going then run downstairs and get behind the stove. Mom had a wood cooking stove that she cooked on. I remember getting scarlet fever. The visiting nurse made Mom put up a sheet form the front room to the dining room. My sisters would peek their heads into my room. I went to Houghton School in the first and second grades. The teacher passed me, but my mom put me back.

We moved from 10th Street to 9th and Fitzhugh Street. We had a furnace so it was much warmer. I can remember my dad and mom talking about "mustering out" pay for the Army. They got the pay and bought a house on Wilkins Street in the South End. Mom and Dad took the house apart and redid the whole thing. Dad would come home from work and go under the house. He dug a basement by hand so they could have a furnace put in. Then he built an apartment upstairs to rent out. It helped pay for the house.

Bob Robison lived across the street from us. We grew up together. There was a little theater on the South End. On Saturday, Bob and I would put on our guns and holsters and pay five cents to watch cowboy movies all day. The South End was a very busy place. Everything was there – bars and stores of all kinds.

When I was young, we sat by the radio and listened to *Jack Armstrong*, *The Lone Ranger*, and Sergeant Preston and his dog, King. They made you feel you were right there. My dad and mom would listen to the news just like people now watch TV.

Bob's folks moved to Nimons Street right by the Saginaw River. I spent a lot of time over to his house. We would find old boats, tar them up, and put them in the river. We would go across the river and play on Green Point Island and fish the river. Later, we used to hunt on the island. There were a lot of pheasants there. Bob would sleep over at my house a lot. I had a twin bed. My Boston terrier, my large English setter, Bob, and I would all sleep in that bed.

When I was young, I remember men would go up the river and get deadheads out of the river and put them on the shore to dry. They would make nice lumber. That's how they made a living. Deadheads were logs that got stuck in the mud when they were being floated to the sawmills.

After dark, all the kids would be playing under the corner streetlight. At that time, we did not worry about being safe. We did not have the crime we have today. Our doors were never locked. I don't think we even had a key to our doors!

When I was about ten years old, every Saturday my dad would take me over to Washington and Potter Streets. There was a little gas refinery there, and my dad would get ten gallons for one dollar. Then we would go to the coal yard and get two gunnysacks of coal. That would last until the next Saturday.

Most milk was delivered right to homes by a milkman with a horse and buggy. The horse knew the route as well as the milkman. If the milkman took too long at a house, the horse would go to the next stop. A junk man with a horse and wagon would come by once a month to buy iron and rags and paper from us. We would only get a few cents.

In the winter, right after supper, my two sisters and I would go right to the end of Wilkins Street. Then we would cut through the cemetery to get to Hoyt Park, where we would ice skate. We had good ice most of the winter and had a lot of fun. At one point, Saginaw was known to have the biggest ice rink in Michigan. It had good ice for skating, a toboggan run, and a sled slide. We had an old warming house that was replaced by a new, bigger one. There were also lights and music.

There was an airport runway that ran along West Michigan Street up to Center Road. Behind the runway was an old glass works where there was a swimming hole on the Tittabawassee River. We often would swim bare and not worry about Dow at all! Later, they built Anderson Swimming Pool so we did not use the Tittabawassee and Saginaw Rivers to swim any longer.

Later in the 1930s, there was a place called Phoenixville. It was located on the east side of the Saginaw River and on the south side of Rust Street. It was a shantytown. There were also houseboats on the water where people lived. Our parents would not let us go there, but we would sneak out anyway. In the 1940s, the city bulldozed it all down and made the houseboats move.

Back in the 1930s and 1940s, Saginaw had very bad water. You could not drink it. There were corner water pumps with deep wells. We had to carry water to cook and drink.

My dad was in World War I and belonged to the Veterans of Foreign Wars (VFW) Post 1556. I belonged to the Sons of the VFW Drum and Bugle Corps. We were in all of the parades at that time and traveled all over for competitions. At funerals, one of us would hide behind a tree and play "Taps." We really thought we were something!

The state of Michigan had a lot of land up on Higgins Lake. They gave a big piece of that land to the American Legion of Michigan. They would not sell it to you, but you got a 99-year lease on it. Each post had a piece of it. In 1936, my dad got a piece of land and started to build a cabin. It had a front room, a kitchen, two bedrooms, and a big screened-in porch. It took about four to five hours to get to the cabin from Saginaw. We had a lot of fun up there. Dad sold the cabin in 1945 when we moved up to Minnesota.

I quit school in the ninth grade at the age of sixteen. I was a very poor student. I went to work as an iceman for Citizen Ice and Fuel. I had the downtown route, delivering ice for iceboxes, pop coolers, and meat markets. At that time, you could not put ice in your drinks because it tasted bad. The ice was made from city water. Later they put a pipeline in from White Stone Point in Lake Huron. Saginaw had a parade downtown to celebrate the World's Best Water. We put on our trucks the World's Best Ice made from the World's Best Water!

When we were young, Ginny and I ran around in the same bunch but drifted away from each other. One day, I delivered ice to Home Dairy and saw Ginny behind the lunch counter. I sat down for a cup of coffee and asked her out that night. We were married in May 1948 and have been married for 67 years. We had two girls and one boy. Ginny used to go to her mother's house to wash clothes. They had a wringer washer. I was hoping the first night I went to her house that her dad would not remember me. When we were dating, we went to Wenonah Park on the Saginaw Bay. They had a jackrabbit, a merry go round, and a dance hall. Whenever we could borrow a car, we went to Wenonah. It was OUR park.

The first house my wife and I purchased was on Hazelwood near Hess. We paid $3,500.00 for it. Payments were $30.00 a month. We had no water, an outhouse, and chamber pots. I brought water home from the ice plant every day. We sold that house and purchased a house on Miller Road in Shields. That house had water, an inside bathroom, and two bedrooms. We lived like kings! Our daughter, Lori, was born and then our son, Greg. We had to move. We purchased a big old house on Schaefer Street near Weiss. Julie was born. We lived there until the State Department took our house to put in Highway 675. We had a house built in Skyway Subdivision in Carrollton and lived there for 28 years.

When Lori was born in 1955, we started to build a cabin at Higgins Lake near Lyon Manor Township. Ginny and I pounded in every nail. We had a kitchen and front room combined a bathroom, two bedrooms, and a large screened-in porch. We wanted our children to grow up like we did.

My dad sold his White Rose station in Carrollton to us in 1962. We ran it for six years before purchasing a franchise for a Shell Oil station in Zilwaukee. We ran the Shell station until they wanted to make it into a self-serve. Not wanting to run a self-serve station, my son-in-law, Steve, my son, Greg, and I started a mobile truck repair service. We would go where the big rigs broke down and repair them on the spot. I retired from the company 25 years ago and Steve passed away four years ago. My son, Greg, is still in the mobile repair business and my son-in-law, Otto, works as a mechanic for Rohde Brothers.

My daughter, Lori, is a teacher at Bethlehem Lutheran School. My daughter, Julie, is the cook at Immanuel Lutheran School Greg is still fixing trucks with two employees working for him. My wife, Ginny is 85 years old, I am 87 years old, and we have been married for 67 years.

This is the way I grew up and lived my life, and if I had it to do all over, I would not change a thing. Good-bye and good night.

My One-Room Schoolhouse Days
By Roselynn Ederer of Saginaw, Michigan
Born 1942

I attended Liskow School, a one-room standard brick school in Thomas Township from 1947 to 1955. The school was on the dead end of State and Miller Roads. This was the third Liskow School. The first log cabin pioneer school was on North River road near the Owens Cemetery. The second frame school was about one fourth of a mile away from the third school at State and Short Roads. It was converted into a house and the Winslow family lived in it. This was a blue collar working farm community.

My older sister, two years older, was already in the first grade. She told fun stories about her school days when she came home. I wanted to go to school also. I had nobody to play with since my younger sister was just a baby. As soon as I turned five, I begged my mother to let me go to school. Since my father was on the school board and there were only about sixteen kids total in school, the teacher, Clara Hegenauer, let me come. I sat quietly in the seat and watched everyone. Two seventh graders, Lois and Louise, entertained me by showing me how to weave baskets with paper strips and do other art work. I simply loved it. I wanted to go to school every day with my big sister. So in the fall of 1947, at age five, I began my first grade at Liskow School. There were about six pupils in first grade but only twenty total in grades one through eight. I just loved going to school every day. I never missed any time.

One event I remember was the presidential inauguration day of General Dwight Eisenhower about 1952. No one had any television at home. The only one who did was Francis Winslow, because he sold appliances at Godwin's Store. His four daughters also went to Liskow. The teacher, Wanda Munger, arranged for the entire school to go to Winslows to watch the inauguration on television. So we carried our own chairs – wooden ones that didn't fold up – down the road one fourth of a mile away to Winslows, the converted second Liskow School. Anyone who didn't carry his own chair sat on the floor. The small TV was on one end of the large room, and we all sat around it on our wooden chairs watching the inauguration. This was probably the first time I had ever seen a TV program.

My older sister was in a higher grade now and the younger classes, including me, were dismissed early every day. I had to walk home by myself, a distance of two and one fourth miles one way. I walked with my friends, Barbara, Judy, and Rosalie, part of the way. Barbara left at the Short Road intersection; Judy left at North River Road and walked north to her house by the cemetery; Rosalie and I continued a short distance south on North River Road. Sometimes there were days when we played at Barbara's house until my sister got out of school. Sometimes I played at Rosalie's house. She was an only child and had many toys – dolls and stuffed animals. When I went to her house, I could only look at her toys but not touch any. I never knew anyone could have so many toys since I had one doll only.

Then quite often, I walked the entire way home by myself. The farm from Short Road to River Road was still being worked. There was a high hill with a clump of wild rose bushes growing. My mother had said that the original owners were buried there, and I always thought about it when I walked by that farm, saw those bushes, and turned onto North River Road. The owner had beef cattle running on part of the land, but he didn't have good fences to keep them in. So when I walked south down River Road I would see the cattle grazing there. One day as I rounded the bend on River Road there was a bull right out in the middle of the road! We had dairy cattle at home but no bulls. Dad always said they were too dangerous. What was I to do! I couldn't outrun him. I didn't want to be chased either. So I walked up the driveway to the nearest house and waited by their back door. I just waited. No one was home to see me. So I waited out the bull. Maybe it was twenty or thirty minutes. But when I saw cars going down the road I checked and the bull was gone. So I half ran all the way home. I was six or seven years old.

Always at Easter time, Mom would boil eggs in brown and red onionskins. This was an old German custom, and her mother had always done it. Quite often, when we came home from school and walked up the back steps, we would find brown eggs that the Easter bunny had left. It was always exciting even though we had hens ourselves and helped gather the eggs every day. And we raised rabbits and knew they didn't lay eggs.

The woods across from Liskow School had wild flowers. The teacher always checked with the owner and so the Friday before Mother's Day we would all go to the woods and pick flowers. There were many trilliums and violets. Each student would pick a bouquet of flowers to take home to his/her mother that day. The teacher always had us making Christmas presents for our parents every year. One year we actually sawed out wooden doorstoppers and potholder hook items. The teacher helped us but we used the saws. We varnished or painted them. They were somewhat rough looking but usable. Mom saved the ones we made. I still have them today. We also dipped hot wax to make candles.

We always celebrated the holidays. Valentine's Day especially was memorable. Everyone made his own shoebox mailbox.

Everyone wrote out a valentine for every child in the school. On February 14, we put our mailboxes on our own desks. Then everyone went around the room and mailed his own valentines by putting them in each one's box. We had a party in the afternoon. Everyone opened his mailbox and read his valentines. The mothers came with homemade desserts: cakes, cookies, and pop. This is where I first tasted orange pop. We never drank pop at home. Because we had our dairy herd, we always drank milk. I still have my shoebox and all those valentines I received all those years at Liskow School. I always looked forward to these parties and orange pop! We had a Christmas party like this also. We drew names at school and gave each other gifts at our party. The mothers came with food: desserts, sandwiches, and pop. It was always a fun time. We even had a Christmas pageant that we practiced songs and little skits and performed them for our parents.

Ruth, Roselynn, and Mary Lou Ederer in 1952

There were eight grades in the one room school. The teacher called each grade up to the front blackboard and the pupils would sit around her in a circle. She seemed to spend more time with the younger grades. When I reached the higher grades, fifth and higher, it seemed like there were some days when my grade wasn't called. A grade could be called up several times, for English, geography, math, etc. I always had my homework done since I did it at home every night so I had idle time at school. The teacher encouraged us to read books from the library. The library was one large metal cabinet with about three shelves. Parents had donated books, and over the years, the teachers had added books. I would read books from this library. I always said, "I read every book in the library." After a couple of years, I had enough idle time at school where I could read every book. I actually read every book in the cabinet. Mrs. Munger often took some students with her to the city library, Butman Fish, where she selected some books to bring back to Liskow. Sometimes my sister and I went with her. The big library was amazing. She also bought us an ice cream cone before bringing us back home.

When I was in the seventh grade, the Baby Boomers were now in school and actually burst the school. There was not enough room for everyone. So the seventh graders, me included, were bused to North Intermediate School in Saginaw. I never liked that school. The kids were juveniles and city kids. By my eighth grade year, Liskow was now a two-room school. I was glad to return to Liskow for my eighth grade. For the ninth grade, I was sent back to North Intermediate School again. I still didn't like that school.

When I graduated from Liskow School in the eighth grade in 1955, we had to take county tests to measure our achievements. I thought I was really in trouble when the teacher spoke to my mother about my tests. Then it turned out that my reading level was already in the eleventh grade, second semester! I guess reading every book in the school library helped even if I didn't always have class every day.

My eighth grade peers had a class motto: Never put off until tomorrow what you can do today. So often, I have thought about that motto through the years. I have attempted never to put off tasks until tomorrow. When I did put off something, I generally regretted it and remembered that motto.

I always spent my summers working on

our farm, gardening, caring for the animals, and hoeing. We worked from the time we got up until we went to bed. Hoeing occupied most of our day. We got up at 6:00 a.m. so Dad could milk the cows by hand. My older sister usually helped him milk the cows. I helped my mother get the noon dinner ready. She cooked the meat, potatoes, and vegetables. I always made and baked a pie from scratch: raspberry, blueberry, or peach. She had the meal cooked and it just needed a warm up at noon. By 7:00 a.m., all five of us – parents and three sisters - would head out to the corn or bean field to hoe. We made a round, walking between two rows hoeing a row on either side. When we hoed back to the beginning, we had a drink of water. After working in the fields, there were evening chores and milking to do. Then we took care of the garden, harvesting whatever was ready, and preparing it for canning or freezing. There were days when we worked until almost midnight. And of course, we had to hoe the bean field at least twice, if not three times. Spraying fields was unheard of back then. By the end of August, I could hardly wait to go back to school.

About two weeks before school Mom always took us shopping in downtown Saginaw where we were outfitted with new shoes. She bought material and sewed our school dresses also.

The first day of school the teacher always had every student tell what exciting vacation he had taken that summer. Of course, we never had vacations – we had cattle and animals that kept us home. So I always had to tell a story about some of our kitten litters or animals.

When I look back at those one-room school days, I know they are a part of forgotten history that children today cannot understand. Those were simple days – the Good Old Days of our youth! Our country school days and hard work ethic forever shaped us to be productive, patriotic citizens.

Football, Stunt Flying, and Fishing
By Bob Walker of Petoskey, Michigan
Born 1932

Football – I Lasted Three Weeks (1945)
I loved football; that's all there was to it! I wore out footballs and replaced the bladders to avoid buying new ones. I used shoe sole repair kits to seal up the damaged ends after so many place kickings. Our yard gave me a lot of room to kick it all over the place. My grandmother would come outside and scold me when the kicked ball would hit the power wires going over to the house. Somehow, the wires never broke or became unattached.

In seventh grade, I went out for football. What difference did it make if I was only 97 pounds and barely five feet tall? Well, it did make a difference when the varsity team would scrimmage against us to build up their confidence. Jim Faunce was a good friend and one I used to see from time to time. We often played together, but later Jim was busy as he went on to be on the varsity team. It was a miracle, but I did last three weeks before dropping out and feeling very disappointed.

Being in the band for all of my high school years wasn't like playing football, but at least we were at all of the games and had great times together under our band director, Max Smith. Tennis, a non-contact sport, was better suited for me and I came to really enjoy that. I usually won playing our own team members, but I couldn't seem to win any interschool matches. Therefore, our coach, Mr. Dunlevy, dropped me to the number two spot against other schools and my winning increased.

First Plane Ride (1945)
Hitchhiking became the thing to do the summer before starting my job at the sporting goods store. Usually I'd meet another boy downtown in Petoskey, and we'd start out from there. Sometimes at the Par-4 corner of US 31 and M 119, one of us would go over to M 119 while one of us stayed on US 31. Whichever of us got a ride first would determine the direction we both would go. If we ended up in Mackinaw City, we'd take the next boat to Mackinac Island for a quarter and then reverse the process later in the day. No one knew where we were, and later the adults never asked. Probably they were just glad we were out of their hair for the day.

I tried delivering the Grand Rapids Harold for a couple of weeks but did not like it. A friend said, "It's good work caddying over at the Wequetonsing Gold Course in Harbor Springs." Therefore, I quit my job with the paper and became an "expert" caddy, recommending which club a player might use, etc. even though I had never swung a club in my life. Double caddying with two full leather bags was hard work. Caddy code was if a player gives less than a twenty-five cent tip at the end of the round we were to return it and say, "I believe, sir, you probably need this more than I do." Fortunately, I never had to say this.

Hitchhiking toward Petoskey at the end of a caddying day, we got a partial ride only as far as the airport corner. There was a sign, which said something like airplane rides, one dollar for ten minutes. Well, that was for us, with the two of us together on the back seat of a canvas sided Piper Cub. What a trip! What a view for the first time we had ever been in an airplane! The next day we did the same thing, but this time we asked the pilot to do some tricks. He put the plane into a stall, dropping us so fast I thought my cheeks would leave the sides of my head. The pilot looked back at us and said, "You guys don't look so good." Sick? We certainly did not feel good and we never stopped at the airport for any new flight experiences. It was many years later before any adults ever knew about what we had done.

Why in the Dance Band? (1945)

Playing cornet in the band for six years, (only a "senior" band in those days) made it logical for me to also be in the dance band. I really loved being in the dance band. But why? (Don't tell anyone, I would be embarrassed.) It was because while being in the dance band I would not have to face up to being uncomfortable trying to actually dance with a girl.

Now, remember, you promised not to tell...or did you?

May I Use Your Phone? (1944)

My grandma was always in constant motion. Our neighbor across the street, Mr. M, was on the other hand, in constant non-motion. He was of the slower, much more relaxed type. Mr. M didn't have a phone and ours was on a multi-party line, with our number being 190-J. Just like in the olden days, the operator would respond to the phone being picked up by saying, "Number, please." (Hey, I just remembered that *was* the olden days.)

Anyhow, one day I was standing in our dining room when Mr. M came over to our door and gently knocked. My grandmother ran to the door, as she usually did, and our neighbor quietly composed himself. He

then spoke very slowly and deliberately, "Mrs. Monteith, could I use your phone." At that moment there was a pause before he continued, as though his next words might be rejected or at the least that we might feel them an imposition.

He then said very quietly and slowly, "My house is on fire."

Driver's Training in the 1940s (1948)

Mr. Max Smith, our band director, took me under his wing about certain things because that's the sort of helpful person he was, and maybe also because I didn't have a dad. He encouraged me to join the Charlevoix City Band that he directed in the summer, and I really enjoyed being with him during the drive over to Charlevoix.

Starting out for Charlevoix one day, Mr. Smith said, "Bob, why don't you drive." That's how I learned to drive in the '40s, in addition to taking our '35 Buick and going for test drives on the low traffic roads in the Bay View area.

When I was sixteen I went to the police station, which was above the Teen Town Hall on Lake Street and said, "I'd like a driver's license." The policeman said, "How old are you?" and I said, "I'm sixteen." The policeman then simply said, "That will be three dollars." I gave him my three dollars and became a fully licensed driver. That's how we did it in the '40s, at least in regard to getting our genuine, long awaited, adult driver's license.

Taps at the Cemetery (1948)

It was my duty to play Taps for the graveside services of Petoskey servicemen returned for burial. I was glad to do it, but it was stressful for me to so closely experience the reality of the tremendous losses those families endured as a consequence of war. No, I don't have any answers to war, but I do like the comment reportedly made by some mother: "Put a mother in charge of each and every country in the world, and there would be a lot less war" Was this because lack of war requires love, caring, and reverence for life, whereas war can often at least appear to be based on some person's or country's desire for control, dominance, aggression, and lack of reverence for life?

Not a Good Sport? (1953)

Valerie and I had only been married for a few weeks. I was helping with the dishes, took a dab of water on my fingers, and flipped

223

the water drops at Valerie. Without saying anything, she filled a glass of water and poured it down the inside of my shirt. Wow, I thought, this woman I married was definitely going to be a lot of fun to live with. Therefore, I started to fill my own container to douse her with. Suddenly I noticed her shocked and serious facial expression just in time to hear her say, "You're not a good sport!"

Now you may be wanting to ask me what I learned from this experience. My answer would be something like Job said in the Bible when he admitted to God in words something like this, "I just learned there is a whole lot I haven't learned yet and probably never will be able to understand."

Winter "Depression" (1959)

I was seriously depressed. It had been a long winter in Munising, Michigan, up on Lake Superior. We typically had over 200 inches of snow and almost no winter thawing. Therefore, the snow went "layer upon layer' and really got deep in places. On one of our winter snowshoe hikes, I stumbled on something just below the top of the snow. The something was the top of a fence post that was itself at least four feet above the ground. Another time a Scout leader asked my help for winter campout. Everyone feared we'd freeze to death. In reality, we were probably as warm as or warmer than they were in their houses. We dug down through the snow to the ground, then cut saplings and pine branches for our roof. We cut notches in the snow walls of our snug houses for belongings and slept warmly all night long. We were going to go back and see what our campsite looked like in the summer, but we never did.

Sorry, I forgot to tell you why I had been so depressed. You see, it was because I knew there would probably be only one more weekend to enjoy going snowshoeing before the spring thaw would turn all of our wonderful snow to mush!

More Fun than Fishing (1973)

Paul was about eight years old and pestering me almost every day to take him fishing. I had been just too busy with my work. Finally, I told Paul that we were going fishing on the next Saturday no matter what. Saturday came and we drove all over Grand Rapids but finally found a place to buy our worms for bait. I put the aluminum canoe on top of the car and out we went to Cranberry

Lake in the northwest end of Kent County.

The weather was not looking perfect, but we got the canoe in the water and had paddled a few hundred yards into the lake when I noticed in the west some very dark clouds coming at us really fast. In no time it was raining, lightning, and thundering all around us. I knew Paul would be disappointed, but I said, probably with some panic in my voice, "Paul, we've got to get back to the car, fast!" Tall pine trees all around beckoned to the lightning to strike us at any instant.

Paul intently watched through the car window as I struggled to get the canoe back on top of the car. With the canoe half on top, I slipped on the new muddy surface and went crashing to the ground along with the canoe. I was covered with mud all over, including my face from trying to wipe the rain and dirt out of my eyes. With Paul watching from the car window and I'm sure some near lightning strikes, the aluminum canoe was at last on top of the car and the wet and dirty dad was finally in the car. I was sure I knew how disappointed Paul must have felt after not being able to go fishing. As we started home, he spoke up and totally surprised me by saying, "Well Dad, that was a lot more fun than fishing, wasn't it."

Mrs. Beasley Has Her Say
By Thomas M. Boursisseau of Grand Rapids, Michigan
Born 1939

This event took place in a little theater in Hart, Michigan. The year was 1969. Our family was having a quiet day and decided to go to the movies. The movie being shown was *Butch Cassidy and the Sundance Kid*.

At this time, we had three daughters, ages two, three and a half, and five. They always had their favorite doll, and that doll had to go everywhere we went. Well, Mrs. Beasley, a talking doll, was with us, and she was our Holly's favorite doll. Holly was two.

The scene that brought the house down (and newspaper recognitions) was when Butch Cassidy and the Sundance Kid were standing on this hillside waiting for a band of bandoleros who had robbed the bank. All was quiet as the robbers came around the bend,

Holly at age 5

and that is when it happened:

Mrs. Beasley spoke up, "How do you do? I'm Mrs. Beasley."

The whole theater went into a roar. I looked at Holly, and I thought her timing was unbelievable. Her dark brown eyes were shining.

Our daughter, Holly, and only two at that time, still has that doll. It was a never-to-be-forgotten day when Mrs. Beasley went to the show and was the star.

Corn Crib Playhouses and Quart Jar Butter
By Betty Konesko of Saginaw, Michigan
Born 1936

Growing up I always lived on a farm. We raised all our own vegetables and livestock. When a pig had a litter there was always a runt that was pushed aside and didn't get enough to eat, so we bottle fed it. We also bottle fed our lamb, Frisky. My sister and I were very attached to Frisky. We got in trouble because we would go in the house and leave the door open and she would follow us.

We had a building called the corncrib. In the summer, we would make a playhouse in it.

We took old blankets and used them to partition it off into rooms. We were never happy in the fall when Dad filled it with corn and we lost our playhouse. Toys were at a minimum so we took corncobs and wrapped them up for dolls. We also used the hay pulleys in the barn for swings.

We never had a butter churn so Mom would put the cream in a two-quart jar, and we would shake it. Our arms got tired so we took turns. We jumped for joy when we finally got butter. It took us most of the day.

The highlight of the summer was when the crops were ready and the threshers came. The farmer with the threshing machine would take turns going to different farms. All the farmers helped each other. The men did the harvesting, and the wives did the cooking. What a feast. I can still taste all the good food.

Swimming and Celebrating
By Marge Griebel of Bay City, Michigan
Born 1933

I grew up out in the country in Frankenlust Township, Bay City, Michigan. There were four of us in my family, two boys, and two girls, and we all loved the water. That's one of the good things about Michigan. You don't have to drive far before you come across a lake. We have, of course, the Great Lakes, and we lived not far from Saginaw Bay, which is part of Lake Huron. However, the water we were interested in was the Saginaw River.

One of our friends, Christ Appold, had a farm along the banks of this river, and a good swimming hole was not far from his house. His house was one of those great big old farmhouses, two stories, with a huge porch fronting the house. It was just beyond this house that the river ran, and we would beg my mother or father to take us to the swimming hole in the evening of a hot, lazy day. Christ's day wasn't ever lazy, I don't think. His farm kept him busy, as well as the rest of his family. I don't think, though, that Christ was ever too tired to meet us down by the river, and he was oh so willing to get in the water with us. Little by little I found that I could swim because Christ was teaching me, without me knowing it, how to swim.

I remember one evening in August very

well. It had been hot that day, and going swimming was on the agenda for that evening. I couldn't wait. We talked about it all day, and it seemed that evening would never come. However, before we could drive off to the Appold farm, my mother told us we couldn't go. She wanted to drive to downtown Bay City! The news had come over the radio that day that Japan had surrendered. What would the atmosphere be like in town? That's what my mom wanted to know.

We were not happy! She had promised to take us swimming, and swimming we would go. Downtown Bay City didn't interest us. We had been there before, and swimming was so much better. Mom argued and argued with us, but we finally compromised. We would go swimming for a short time, and then we'd go downtown. It was a sacrifice, but we did it and we were glad we did. We had never seen downtown Bay City like this! There were flags flying all over, people dancing on the streets, cameras flashing (unfortunately we had not remembered to take ours), and a general feeling of excitement.

It was one of the most memorable events of my childhood.

Favorite Teacher in the One Room School
By Alice Galster Cook of Big Rapids,
Michigan
Born 1936

In 1941, my twin sister and I entered kindergarten at the Wooster School in Newaygo County. It was a one-room school with grades kindergarten through the eighth grade, and our father, Earl Galster, was the teacher. My sister and I would ride to school with our father and arrive before any of the other students did. Dad would have to get the wood in for the large heating stove which was located in the back left corner of the schoolroom. After the stove was started, Dad would go out and pump the water and bring it in by the pails full to put into the large drinking crock.

At 8:55 a.m., my father went out into the front hall and pulled the rope hung from the ceiling, which rang the "first" bell. That ring told the students that school was about to start. At 9:00 a.m., my father rang the bell once more and school was in session. Every student was seated and would begin their studies for the day. The teacher would call each class independently up to the front of the room for instructions, starting with the kindergarten and ending with the eighth grade. At 10:30 a.m., there was a fifteen-minute recess, and school was back in session at 10:45. Once again, each grade would take its turn up to the front of the room for instruction. Lunch hour was from 12:00 until 1:00. At 12:55, the "first" bell rang and at 1:00 p.m., the "last" bell rang.

The kindergarten students were dismissed at noon and did not have afternoon classes. My sister and I had to stay at school and ride home with Dad, which resulted in us often falling asleep on our desk during the afternoon. School ended at 4:00 p.m. and then my father would sweep the floor, wash the chalkboards, and clean the erasers before leaving for home.

In 1945, my father was hired to teach at the Roottown School, also in Newaygo County, so my parents moved to that district. Roottown was a two-room school. Mrs. Hattie Scott taught kindergarten through fourth grades, and my father taught the upper room, grades fifth through eighth. My sister and I were in the fourth grade, so we had Mrs. Scott. She was a good teacher and we liked her.

However, in 1946 when we were in the fifth grade, we were back in our father's classroom, and I soon realized that Dad was my favorite teacher. He was well known as a strict disciplinarian but was always very calm. My sister and I were never favored, and we had to abide by the same rules as the other students. However, when we were at home Dad was 100% "father," not "teacher."

Learning to Swim on the River
By Bernard "Barney" Barnett of Branch,
Michigan
Born 1925

To call a small brook "shit creek" is probably somewhat insulting, but after all, it was coming to the Pere Marquette River from the very active canning factory up on the hill. Oh, and it did have a slight but distinctive

Barney on the Pere Marquette River in 1937

aroma.

Of course, there were not many places where one could swim privately in the nude. Therefore, we had to determine where would be a suitable location. The beach we located was immediately upstream from the affluent of the Scottville Cannery, and I mean immediately. Like about 40 feet upstream. The ever-present current pushed contaminants downstream and away. We never swam below that spot.

It is not surprising that some parents, if they knew about it, would not condone this activity. Therefore, it was best not to mention river swimming at home.

At this point, I must tell you that in all that time (at least five years) we never had an accident. The older guys protected the younger and taught them how to swim and dive.

There was an admiration of the ability to make it across the river, and if you hadn't done that yet you were jealous of those who were sitting on the other side and diving from the trees. If you were just learning to swim, the current puts a scare into you the first few times you try.

Some of you will remember some of the names Buster Howe, Cubby Howe, Lloyd Stevens, Fred Reader, Ron Howe, Walt Jablonski, Curley Forbes, Slug Howe, Bob Baker, Ollie Dumas, Dunk Sanders, Pid Sanders, and many more.

My family was a river group. My dad, Harry Barnett, had the first livery on the Pere Marquette. He had twelve square-ended flat bottom boats. McDougal also had some of that type. Therefore, when I told my mom, Carrie Barnett, that I knew how to swim, she took it very well.

Our river is very forgiving. In all the years (I'm 89) I have heard of few tragedies. Most of those were labeled "human error" and there were only three of these. I have said that if you are around the river much you are going to get wet, and I have proved that several times.

We have lost our right to naked swimming to the public now, but our river still has much to offer anyone who wants a beautiful experience. Try a midnight float (not paddle) when the moon is bright in July or August. There are no bugs, snakes, or alligators. The bug hatches are earlier in the evening. Ask Patty Smith – she knows.

I guess learning to swim with the wonderful group of guys I was fortunate enough to know is an experience that I treasure.

Growing Up in the Car Culture
By John McMillan of Midland, Michigan
Born 1949

Growing up in the '50s and '60s were great eras with fond memories. In particular is all that I was able to do once I got my driver's license.

Our community was a small town which was a product of the farming era but that was soon to change. The town was small with a general store, a town square, two gas stations, a drug store with a soda fountain where we would treat ourselves to lunch on our noon hour from high school one block away, a bowling alley which had pin boys (not automatic pin setters), and a hardware. I got my first car, a 1953 Ford, free for doing summer work for my dad's boss. I turned sixteen in September and got my license. This was also a time for street racing in many cities and towns in America and drive-ins with burgers and carhops. We were also seeing a crackdown by police in the big cities and larger towns on street racing to discourage the unsafe practice.

The following summer we would notice that the city and big town racers were looking for other places to race, and they found by them coming to the little towns with their racecars, many of them on trailers. The small towns had either no police force or just a town constable. We local boys would find out what night the racers may be coming to our town, and early after nightfall we would drive into town and park along the edges of the town square, which was not lighted. Of course,

227

Main Street had streetlights. Soon a couple of out of town cars, as decoys, would roll in on Main Street and race through our town with our constable in hot pursuit, leading him on a chase. The big boys would pull up on Main Street and unload their drag cars, line them up on a starting line with a flagman, and with the drop of the flag, the race was on. This would go on as long as the town constable was gone or until someone called the county sheriff, and they would show up. Lookouts would alert the racers in plenty of time of them to break up, load up the drag cars, and get away. We were slouched down in our car seats watching and hoping not to be seen. I guess we thought we were doing something wrong, but we were excited to see the race action.

After all quieted down, we were ready to go, primed by the excitement we had just seen. So we decided to drive to some back paved roads to have our own little race fest. After determining the start and finish lines and a couple of race matches, we immediately were run off by the local farmer. He obviously didn't appreciate the noise and let us know by shooting at our cars with his shotgun. Cars back then had thicker steel doors and no one was hurt, just a few BB dents in a couple car doors, thankfully not mine, for how was I going to explain that to my dad. Therefore, we were out of there in a hurry, and we made sure we found a road that had no houses along our race route.

One car in particular I remember was my friend's 1955 "shoebox" Chevy. It had a 348 V8 with tri-power carbs and progressive linkage making all three carburetors always operate. She had so much power "out of the hole" that one night when racing the front mounting bolts for the bench seat pulled out of the floorboard. This made us lean back when the seat went back from the car accelerating so hard, which lifted his foot from the gas pedal. Instead of fixing the seat he said he would leave it that way, figuring it would keep him safe from the wild and dangerous acceleration the car had.

There were not a lot of us that had a car in high school, about a handful of us, so we would double and triple date. I remember we had four couples on a date once. Talk about fun and a great time. It was very tricky driving my stick shift "three on the tree" because with four people in the front bench seat it was crowded, to say the least. To make shifting possible, I would operate the pedals and steering wheel, and my date would operate the shift lever on the column. We made it to the show and a burger after the show. With the others chipping in for gas, my five dollar a week allowance covered the cost for the two of us for the date. It was always a treat to go to the local A&W located in the next town southeast of us. Root beer, a burger, fries, and an attempt to make time with one of the car hops as always a welcome night out. Just cruise the hamburger stand trying to look cool in your car. Simple pleasures for simpler times.

There was a night I came home, of course before 11:00 p.m. curfew, from a date and noticed a noise from the car before I turned it off. I put the car in neutral and revved the engine to listen. All was fine, so I went in the house for the night. My bedroom was next to the kitchen, and I woke up listening to Mom and Dad talking about "I wonder what he did last night and should we ask him why he parked his car there?" Therefore, I got up and went into the kitchen to see what they were talking about. They told me to look out the kitchen window. When I did, I saw my car sitting in the middle of the garden. Some quick recall and I remembered the issue with my car and realized I did not put it back in gear. It rolled into the garden sometime that night, thankfully not hitting anything but a few plants. Thankfully, it didn't hit our two-holer outhouse; that could have been a real mess. However, they accepted the explanation, and I quickly went out and parked the car where it should be.

At times, us guys would chauffeur for the other on his date. However, the rule was you couldn't use the rear view mirror to "check out the action" in the back seat. On snow days when school was called off, we would put tire chains on the cars, on a 1948 Hudson, and run the roads, plowing through snowdrifts. The only way we got stuck was when the car rode up onto a snowdrift. We would then take the shovel out and dig out the snow from under the car and we were again on our way. At times, the snow would collect under the hood, stopping the fan. We knew that because we smelled the fan belt burning. Therefore, we would stop, open the hood on the Hudson, and dig out the snow form around the engine.

Then we were on our way again. This time we had the toboggan on the car and were off to the snow hill for some fast sledding. In the summer, it was off to the beach, up north to a teen nightclub, or wherever we could find some fun and a good time. We were also able to get to our summer jobs or part-time jobs because we had a car.

The cars and trucks for young and old that we were able to own were very liberating, made us very independent, and opened many doors and opportunities for us. The car culture was a big social tool, provided us jobs, or made work easier, and got many into motorsports. A lot of us drag raced or rally raced, and we took great pride in our vehicles because they made a statement of who we were and what we liked. The times they are a changing.

Joyce on the right with her siblings

A Great Time to be a Kid
By Joyce Abler Schumacher of Saginaw, Michigan
Born 1938

I guess I will start by saying I was born during the Depression. Soon after, of course, came World War II. My father and his four brothers were in various branches, as well as my mother's four brothers. There were flags with stars on them to hang in your window. We had one star, and my grandmother had five stars.

We were issued rationing stamps so we could get sugar, coffee, and gas. We smashed all tin cans and aluminum foil. We put them at the edge of the road. I could say curb, but we didn't have one. Someone would pick them up.

Mother had us plant a victory garden to grow veggies, and that kept us busy. We could use the water in the house for the garden but not to drink. Every other block had a water pump for drinking. Off we went with our pail to get filled.

We went to the zoo, and at that time, we could wade in the pool. They didn't have many animals; mostly monkeys.

We didn't have to worry about safety. We could go to Hoyt Park for skating and sledding. They flooded the whole park, the warming house was open all the time, and we could skate under the lights to music. We could

go to Anderson Pool and walk to any theater. There were several downtowns: Temple, Franklin, Center, Mecca, and Michigan. My grandmother had an apartment upstairs above the Michigan Theater. On the west side was Paloma, Wolverine, Marr, and Court theaters. We went to the Court the most. There also was one called Northside and Southside.

We had a wringer washer, and my brother got his arm caught but didn't get hurt. To get warm water for the washer we heated a tubful on the gas stove. We also heated water for baths, because we didn't have a hot water tank.

Our telephone number was only four digits, and several folks were on our line. Most of the time you had to wait to use it and everyone would listen in.

We had a lot of kids our own ages in our neighborhood, and we would play four corners baseball at night under the streetlights. During the day we played baseball in a vacant lot until a pal's grandmother built a new house on it. Marbles and jacks were favorite games. We were outside all day. We went home when we were hungry or heard Mother calling us.

Growing up we had dances at Town Club held on Friday at Masonic Temple and Hoyt Park warming house on Tuesday and Thursday. On Wednesday, we had play night at school.

I am really sad that my own children

229

didn't have the freedom and safety that we had growing up. It was a simpler time. It was great being a kid then.

Crepe Paper Costumes and Doll Buggy Parades
By Viola Shephard of Bay City, Michigan
Born 1932

My earliest years were spent in a medium size home with no basement, no running water, no electricity, and no phone. Our backyard was small with a cherry tree, a pear tree, and an outhouse. Yes, we also used a chamber pail at night, which we procrastinated emptying. The two adjoining lots were all garden, a strawberry patch, a raspberry patch, and two grapevines, plus a small shed. The entire balance was planted with vegetables and fruits each spring. Every item was eaten or canned. That was a *real* job!

Carroll Park was within walking distance, and we got involved in the daily activities, including the maypole dance and the doll buggy parade. Mother sewed crepe paper costumes for each of us with skirts, tops, and hats. She also decorated our doll buggy to match our colors.

Mom sewed all our clothes on a treadle sewing machine. She salvaged an old, worn out coat to make jackets for us. For Easter, she would sew each of us a jacket and a pleated skirt.

I remember the iceman delivering ice. We would put a card in the window showing how much ice we needed. We girls had to empty the pan under the icebox when the ice melted.

We shopped at Buehler's Meat Market. The four or five butchers that were on duty would cut any of your selections of meat that were not in their display case. I remember their floor in front of the counter and behind it being covered with sawdust.

We played games outdoors like kick the can, red light green light, mother may I, hopscotch, tag, marbles, etc.

We saved rainwater for bathing, washing our hair, and laundry. We carried a pail a half a block to our neighbor's to pump water for cooking and drinking. An enameled dipper was used for all drinking.

When weather permitted, we would roller

Viola Shephard in the parade

skate to the public library downtown. It was a lengthy trip. I still have the skate key that we used to attach the skates to our shoes.

The duck pond at Carroll Park was off limits. We were told it was unsafe to put our hands in the water. We were told, and believed, we would get the seven-year duck itch.

On laundry day, it got very busy. We had to bring in the laundry tubs, the stand with the wringer, the scrub board, and the water. There were two or three batches that had to be hung, dried, and taken down, and then we had to remove all of the above from the kitchen.

The Balcer Brothers bus stop was the nearest one, and it was on the corner of Center and Livingston Streets. We would walk to that point to catch a bus to go downtown. The charge was five cents per person. If you were going from the Eastside to the Westside, you were given a transfer ticket to change buses.

We had a wind up Victrola, and many old 78-rpm records purchased from a closed children's home. Our favorite recording was "Down by the Old Apple Tree," and I still remember some of the words.

Saturday night it was bring in the tub, heat water, and take turns getting our baths. On Sunday, we would walk to Immanuel Lutheran Church. While Mother was in church, we girls would go to Sunday school.

During World War II, our mother became a pipe fitter at Defoe Ship Building Company. During this time, Quonset huts were set up in a section of Washington Park for families of service men.

Friday night we would walk to the Tivoli Theater. It was a dish night and a chapter movie. That always ended in suspense until the next Friday. Admission to the movie was twenty-five cents for adults and 12 cents for minors.

The milkman delivered milk. He left us with the amount requested per note left in the returned bottles. In the winter months, the cream would freeze and rise out of the bottles.

Some of the salesmen who would call were the Fuller Brush man, the Watkins man, the Jewel Tea man, and the Prudential Insurance man. He would collect on the five-cent policies.

Some of the radio programs back then were *Jack Armstrong*, *Captain Midnight*, *The Lone Ranger*, *Ghost Stories*, *Terry and the Pirates*, and *Happy Hank*.

Over the years, we did get a phone. It was on a three or four party line. It was a rotary phone and our number was TW20158.

My first car trip was to Saginaw, and it was a bummer. I expected it would be hours of driving and like going on vacation.

Our pets were cats. They kept the house free of mice.

Mom and Grandmother spoke in German when they got together. We always wondered what they were saying.

Mother always made a dishpan full of popcorn when we had playmates over to our house.

Many are the stories and details behind this outline.

One Day in Time
By Merrily Ann Johnson of Saginaw, Michigan
Born 1942

As I was going through the west side of my hometown, I decided to drive by my old neighborhood. I slowly went to the south, turned around, and went north three blocks.

Our house was on the end of a dead end

Jerry, Jay, Merrily, and Jon Tenney

street in the middle of three blocks. It was the only house that was gone. I sat there at the end of the street and memories raced through my head. If only, I think, if only I could go back in time! Just for a little while, a day, an afternoon, an hour, maybe a few minutes. If only!

But when? What day? What year? What season would I pick? All my growing up years with my mommy and my daddy and my four brothers and little sis were there – right at the end of *that street*!

Would I pick spring? It was an old house but still looked pretty with all the trees in blossom. Summer? We had two lots and with us six kids, most neighborhood friends gathered at our home. Something was always going on like playing kick the can, red rover, red rover, hide and seek, statue, and of course, a good game of baseball.

What about fall? We had a lot of fun. Of course, with so many trees we had mountains of leaves to jump in. We also made forts and the layout of our home made for running from room to room.

Winter? Dad would make us an ice skating rink. If not, we would go to Hoyt Park. It was fun skating under the lights to music and warming up in the warming house, meeting school friends (and checking out the boys), and having hot chocolate (and checking out the boys). and meeting school friends (and checking out the boys), I always loved the movie *By the Light of the Silvery Moon* with Doris Day skating with Gordon McCrae, released in 1953.

The street looks so different now with the double duplexes sitting on our large lot and without the eighteen pear trees. I could always envision my outdoor wedding, walking down the row of nine trees on both sides when they were in blossom in the spring.

Golly! It looks to me like it must be a Sunday. Daddy, J.B. Tenney, must have gotten back from the terminal since he is a manager now for the Norwalk Truck Line. He has to make sure all the truck drivers are back form their runs. I always felt so special when it was my turn to go with Dad on Sundays. Mom would dress me up pretty and had used old strips of rags to curl my long hair. I loved going to Dad's office and sitting on his big chair that swiveled around. He taught me how to type on his typewriter using one finger on each hand. He was so smart!

Daddy worked his way up the ladder. He started out on the docks in high school. One night, his dad covered for him for a couple of hours and even lent him his big shoes so he could attend his graduation.

I can see Dad polishing his car now. Boy,

Merrily (Tenney) Johnson in 1947

did he love his cars! I admired his new 1959 Buick convertible with red interior, but that was later in time. I see the boys washing down the hubcaps.

Let's peek in the window. There I am helping Mom with the grinder hooked to the old beat up wooden chair ready to make baloney sandwiches. Mom just took the lemon cake out of the oven and now is getting out the old pickle jar to make Kool-Aid. We just have to add the ice cubes and wrap newspaper around the jar to keep it cold.

It looks like they're ready to pack up. Why am I always stuck in the middle? I can't wait until someday I get to sit by the window like my big brothers. My younger brother gets to sit between my mom and dad in the front seat and the baby is on Mom's lap. They are so lucky! It takes a lot of time and patience growing up as a middle child.

First, we would stop at our corner "mom and pop" neighborhood grocery store. Dad would give us a couple of dollars to buy penny candy and all day suckers (I think to keep us quiet!). We can't forget that he likes licorice squirrels and Bit O'Honeys, and Mom loved her chocolates.

Off we would journey for our Sunday drive. Our radio was always turned on to the Detroit Tigers baseball team. The voice of Ernie Harwell was with us for years. He was like part of our family. My daddy played baseball for the City of Saginaw. We would watch him play in Midland, Sanford, and other towns, but mostly at Hoyt Park in Saginaw. He had been offered to play professionally with the St. Louis Browns team, but he turned it down. He was afraid to give up his job since he had so many mouths to feed.

Sometimes Dad would say, "Which way should we go? North, south, east, or west?" So many times, we would travel to East Tawas. Daddy always said, "You can't get lost in Michigan. If you hit the water you went too far; just turn around." There were times I think we did get lost, but there always seemed to be a lot of roadside parks where we would stop for a picnic and run around and play a little catch.

We didn't have a barrel of money. Maybe we were ragged and funny, but we traveled along singing a song side by side. Daddy always had to sing "White Christmas." Sometimes he would yodel or play his harmonica.

"Ice cream! Ice cream! We all scream for ice cream," we would chant, but that was okay. We didn't dare fight, yell, or scream, or Dad would pull over and then we would be in trouble. Since Dad liked ice cream and if the Detroit Tigers won, sometimes we would be treated on the way home. We just had to remind him, that's all.

We were the third family in our neighborhood to get a seventeen inch black and white TV, so we had to get home in time to watch *The Ed Sullivan Show* at eight o'clock.

If only I could go back in time, just for a little while! A day, an afternoon, an hour, maybe a few minutes. If only!

The Sunrise Side of Michigan
By Lonnie Travis Armstrong of Augres,
Michigan
Born 1947

My name is Lonnie Travis Armstrong and my odyssey began in the late forties in northern Alabama (Roll Tide)! When I was about five or so, my mom coerced me to accompany her to my uncle's wedding. While we were there, my dad and several other men took off for Michigan to look for work in the automotive industry. I guess Dad was tired of working at a gas station recapping tires twelve hours a day for the lofty sum of three dollars. Imagine my surprise when we got home from the wedding only to discover my dad was missing. I was not a happy camper! In retrospect, it was one of the best decisions my parents ever made. I love Michigan and can't imagine living anywhere else!

Fast forward to 1967, I have about fifteen months seniority in (guess what?) the automotive industry, when Uncle Sam tapped me on the shoulder. Apparently, my benevolent uncle has a job waiting for me in Southeast Asia.

So after eight weeks of basic training and nine weeks of advanced individual training (A.I.T.) at Fort Knox, Kentucky and Fort Polk, Louisiana, respectively, I'm on an airplane headed for the jungles of South Vietnam. Yay! About halfway through my twelve-month tour of duty, I received a very nice letter from my girlfriend. She thought this would be a good time to "date other people." To add insult to injury, the letter arrived while I was in a field infirmary receiving treatment for a severe leg infection. What am I going to do now? I did what almost any other guy in my situation would do – I found a teen magazine with a long list of pen pal addresses. I discovered five girls from Michigan and wrote them all the same letter, verbatim. Two of them actually wrote back. One of them has been my wife since June of 1970. In Linda's defense, she didn't put her address in the magazine. Her boyfriend at the time and one of his buddies thought it would be a good joke to pull on her. I guess the joke backfired!

Nowadays, we live on the "sunrise side" of Michigan, about fifteen minutes south of Tawas. We can see Lake Huron from our front lawn and we have woods and wildlife in the back. It's really enjoyable!

Back in 1999, we lost our only child after a ten-year battle with leukemia. She passed away on Linda's birthday. Our precious daughter, Valerie Suzanne Armstrong, was only twenty-five years old. We were devastated! We still are!

Fortunately, for us, Val's boyfriend at the time has stuck with us all these years. Russ calls us "Mom" and "Dad" and he has been a tremendous support for us throughout the years. He's in law enforcement somewhere in Michigan. A few years ago, he married a wonderful girl. Beth is beautiful and an extremely caring person. We think the world of her. They had a little daughter in 2009. We are Ella's godparents. We love her so much! She's a very pretty little girl! Smart, too!

Russ, Beth, and Ella stay overnight with us several times a year and that's always enjoyable. We are truly blessed and fortunate to have them in our lives.

Big Ditch Chickens
By Jerry Pietrzak of Saginaw, Michigan
Born 1940

In the 1940s and 1950s, I was brought up in northeast Saginaw, Michigan, usually called the St. Rita area. It was a small, Catholic community. A place where everybody knew who lived in which house. A place where everybody looked out for each other. We were a very close-knit community.

We have all seen movies of "Our Gang" or "The Little Rascals." There is nothing in those films that we didn't attempt in our little world. There were more homes that did not own an automobile than did. We were lower, middle-class citizens and we did not realize it until later in life. But, in later life, we realized how rich we really were.

When a wedding or church function would take place, it was assumed that all the chicken would be provided by Mr. Wachowicz who lived at the end of Mercer Street. He had a small farm and had hundreds of chickens. This takes me to my story that nearly led my dear mother to an early grave.

One summer morning my friend Carl and I strolled down to the "big ditch" (located on 23rd street) looking to catch some minnows or frogs. Well, we spotted Mr. Wachowicz going to the fenced chicken area with an axe to behead the birds for an up and coming wedding. We asked if we could watch. That would be a cool thing to watch for an eight or 9-year-old boy.

As he started the executions, he would grab an unsuspecting chicken as it walked by, held its body to a wooden stump, and do the dirty deed. Then he would throw the headless body over his shoulder and grab another. Did you ever witness a headless chicken run around you? We thought it was kind of neat to watch these murders.

Carl and I got bored after an hour or so and left. The only time we went back home back then was to eat or sleep and since it was about noon I went home for some food. Mom always had something for me. As I walked in the back door, I said, "Mom, do we have something to eat?" She was standing at the sink doing some dishes. As she turned around, her eyes grew as wide as golf balls and she started screaming at a pitch I have never heard since. The screech sent my aunt Vickie running over from next door in a panic. She too began to harmonize with Mom in the distressing wailing. I thought they had both lost their minds. I knew this was true when they started ripping my clothes off my little 8-year-old body. There I was standing naked as a jaybird and those ladies checking on every part of my body. Finally Mom could talk somewhat and asked where I was injured. I didn't ever think that I was covered in chicken blood from the Wachowicz's "flying" chickens. I can't remember whether Aunt Vickie and my mom cried from relief or from the comical circumstances. They both lived into their late 90s so I guess this little incident didn't hurt them too much.

They were beautiful sisters and ladies.

Life of a Rebel
By Rich Greenfelder of Chesaning, Michigan
Born 1932

I came into this world September 24, 1932. There was trouble just starting out. My mother developed a lung infection that defied all attempts to cure it. The hospital refused to release her x-rays to a hospital in Detroit, so my dad walked into the x-ray department, demanded that they give him the x-rays and when they refused, he walked to a cabinet, grabbed an arm full of x-rays, and started out the door. They said, "You can't have those" and he informed them that if he couldn't have his wife's, they couldn't have these. They gave him her's and he had an ambulance rush her to Harper Hospital in Detroit. She was there for two months before she was well enough to come home.

During the time she was there, I was taken to Bert and Mollie Adelman's to be cared for. She said I cried every night and both of them

Jerry's Dad and Mom with their children

walked the floor most every night trying to quiet me down. My mother told me that when she came home and took me from them, I never cried at night. Mollie said in later years that she wished my folks could have just one night of my crying.

As I grew up, I never got along with my dad. That mutual dislike lasted until he was about 70 years old. He was bipolar and would seem to be normal when all of a sudden he would run off. At first, it would be for a week or two. He would spend the time in the bars.

I remember the first time that I realized he was like that was one evening when I was about 7 years old and my brother Jim and I were helping him mow the grass in a lot behind our home. He was pushing the mower, all of a sudden gave it a shove, and ran off shouting back at us that he was going away and never coming back. Jim and I spent the rest of the night crying until mom said stop (or else). He spent about two weeks drinking, bar fighting, and then came back.

It was over a year before he had another session like that. After that he would have those wild sessions every year or so, and they would stretch out a little longer each time. In between times, he didn't drink much and I don't think he smoked either. With each episode, it would stretch out a little longer. During the Second World War, he worked at a shop in Saginaw for a couple years and had more episodes. These would involve some floozy he worked with. When that ended, he decided he needed to work at the bomber plant in Detroit. That lasted a couple years until he came back home again. Mom and his parents tried many things to see if anything would calm him. One winter my dad and grandfather went to Florida. That didn't seem to help and they jailed him for a while and kicked him out of the state. Another time he was jailed in Saginaw and was going to be sent to Traverse City to get treatment. Somehow, he managed to get one of his buddies that was a lawyer to get him out with the agreement that he would go to Mercy Wood sanitarium in Ann Arbor for treatment. They tried shock treatments and most everything else they had to use. He was a good actor, he had them convinced that he was cured and they let him out. By that time, I was about 14 years old and I drove to Ann Arbor to get him out of jail.

There were many more episodes, each happening with a shorter time in between. Eventually there was no mild time dividing them. About that time, he decided to live in Oklahoma where Jim and his family had moved. He found a small shack in the woods a few miles out of town and worked for the railroad repairing air conditioners on the train cars. He managed to help Elaine Brown care for her husband until he died and then he just stayed on there with her. She was a retired nurse and seemed to be able to calm him down. We went out a few times to visit and I came to appreciate her for what she was able to do for my dad.

That was when he was about 70 years old and one time when he came back, I took him to visit my mom's brother in Saginaw. They got to talking about a pick-up that Dad had and he had taken my uncle Jack with him to Flint. Jack said to him, "I didn't think we were going to live through that trip." Dad said, "Oh, I think you were mistaken." That's when I realized that he didn't think that anything he had ever done was out of the ordinary. He wasn't responsible for all the things he had done. We got along just fine for the rest of his life.

The effects of all that happened between us did harden my attitude about people and I did not trust anyone very far.

When I took over the store I didn't have much patience with the people that worked for me and while many of them said I was a good boss and they learned a great deal working for me, I could have been easier on them.

Army Service
I was drafted into the US Army on March 19, 1953. JoAnn and Mom drove me to the Saginaw bus station where we were put on a bus headed for Fort Wayne in Detroit. That is the only time I remember kissing my mother. I didn't know it at the time but my future wife was in the crowd seeing family off that day. LuAnn was saying goodbye to her brother, Tom Bennett.

We arrived at Ft. Wayne around noon and I had my first taste of Army food. The rest of the day was spent getting a physical and a battery of other tests. We spent quite a lot of time just sitting in old dark brown painted rooms waiting. At the time, I thought it would be okay with me if they just let me sit there for the two years. Later that day we were again loaded on busses and sent to Camp Custer at

Battle Creek. When we arrived there, some "noncom" got on the bus with us and directed the driver to where we were to be unloaded. When the bus stopped and the door opened the guy that got on with us got in a knock down drag out fight with another soldier that was there to meet the bus. We were fed again and assigned to our barracks. They were First World War vintage with coal furnaces that they assigned one to stoke. About every hour, they would come on the bitch box and tell everyone to fall out in to the company street. All they did was a head count and would send us back. As the days went on there would be mail call once a day when they ordered us to assemble. That was the only bright spot of the week.

The mess hall was First War vintage too. They cooked on coal-fired stoves that they started the fire in by throwing in a pound of butter. I was so homesick that food didn't interest me for the two weeks we were there. During one of the meals soon after we arrived one of the guys snapped and came running down the length of the table (they were in long rows end to end). He was stepping in the plates sliding around screaming something I couldn't understand. Someone collared him and they took him off to the mental ward or somewhere. That didn't help the appetite either.

We spent the two weeks taking all sorts of tests, which I liked doing, and getting shots in both arms about every day. We always lined up in the same order so each time they waved a needle at one of the guys that was right ahead of me, I would see him pass out. If he didn't pass out he would tense up and the needle would break off in his arm. When they issued our uniforms and boots to us, one of the guys doing the shoes was a guy with the last name of Rich that I knew a little bit from working at the hardware store.

The only other one that was drafted that day that I knew was Richard Sulen. His dad, Andy, was my barber and Rich and I had started kindergarten together. Rich took his barber tools along and made a little money after a while cutting hair. None of us were enthused about the scalp tight haircuts the army gave. It was funny to watch some guys when they lined us up for our first haircuts. One guy in particular was giving the barber orders on just how he wanted it cut. The barber listened quietly, then took the clipper, and went right over his head skintight.

Andy and Hilda Sulen brought my mom and drove down to Battle Creek to see us. They were a welcome sight. They would stay for a couple hours and that was about the longest we had any relief from being pushed around. One guy that helped lighten the load a bit was from Saginaw. He name was Sam Figaro, he was a Mexican kid, and he spent every waking hour singing "Your Cheatin' Heart" and complaining that they couldn't draft him because he was an American Indian.

After the two weeks there, we were all shipped to different training camps. As it turned out there were several others from the Chesaning area in our group, but most of them were sent to Indiana for Basic and they frequently went home on weekend passes. I was sent to Fort Riley, Kansas and was not to get home for a year. We rode the train from Battle Creek to Fort Riley. It took a couple days to get there. We were assigned to Co. B 85th Inf. for Basic. The first night there, I was awakened at four in the morning to pull KP duty. That was the worst part of army life for me. I was put to work washing trays and the soap was greasy army issue and I didn't get them clean enough to satisfy the sergeant that came in and inspected the rack where they were stored. He tipped the entire storage unit over, dumped them on the floor, and told us to wash them again. Later on, we learned that if we bought hair shampoo and used it the trays were nice and clean. Later I learned that you could hire an off-duty cook to pull your KP duty and I saved enough out of my pay each month to do that after I was transferred to Headquarters Co. One time when I was in Headquarters Co, I had KP and one of the cooks tell me to dump the chicken that they had cooked into the garbage can. I said, "You don't mean that, do you?" and he said, "Do as you are told," so I did. A while later another cook came by and said, "Where is the chicken?" I said, "It's in the garbage and I did it as I was told to do." He went ballistic. We ended up retrieving it and they made chicken salad after washing it off. As my buddies came in line to eat that night, I told them not to eat the chicken salad.

Cotton Candy Cones & White Popcorn Bags
By Louis Gallé of Bay City, Michigan
Born 1945

One of the first memories of my life occurred in 1947 when the train stopped just before the railroad crossing on Fremont Street about a block away from my family's homestead.

I was standing on the porch on the second floor with my sister Cathy and cousin Sally Ann, and from there we could see everything that was going on as the handlers unloaded the animals from the train for the Clyde Beatty Circus.

I remember the sights, the sounds, and the smells of the animals as they were being taken from the train and led to their temporary living quarters. And at the same time that was going on the roust-a-bouts, using big mallets, were driving the stakes in the ground that would eventually become the big top. "Hooray! The circus has come to Bay City!" I was very excited as I watched the circus grow, and it took up much of the forty acres of land before MacGregor School was built in 1950.

It was a hot, sunny, and humid summer day when my mother took my sister, cousin Sally Ann and me to the opening day matinee at the circus. The four of us held hands as she led us across Fremont Street and walked the block to the circus. The closer we got to the circus grounds the more excited I became.

When we entered the main gate on our way to get our tickets we passed other attractions and food stands getting ready for the circus goers to arrive. We walked about half way down the midway where we were joined by other people on their way to the big top for the

Louie's sister, Cathy, Louie and his cousin, Sally Ann

first performance of opening day.

The biggest impression made on me was watching the flow of fresh hot popped corn erupting from the big corn popper inside the glass enclosure. An attendant filled white bags with the hot popcorn, and twisted the ends of each bag to keep the popcorn from spilling out, and she sold them to customers waiting to go into the big top for the matinee performance. The smell of fresh cooked popcorn filled my senses and is still, to this very day, on my five best smells of all-time list.

There were other vendors selling hot dogs, French fries, pop, candy apples, and fresh roasted peanuts. There was a woman in a blue uniform wearing a white apron and her hair net. She was standing behind a big silver kettle with a paper cone in her hand, and she swirled the cone around and around the inside rim of the kettle while it collected this pink fluffy stuff that I learned was called "cotton candy."

We walked over to the ticket booth with my mother to buy tickets for the first performance. She only had to buy one ticket for herself, and because of our ages, we got in free.

The four of us entered the big top and walked over to our seats while listening to the Calliope playing in the background. We carried our popcorn, a paper cone covered with the pink cotton candy and soda pop that we all shared.

I was excited and amazed at all of the acts, especially the trapeze artists, wild animal tamer, horses prancing around the ring with an acrobat on their backs jumping from horse to horse through a hoop.

The clowns were running around everywhere honking their horns and throwing confetti into the audience from water buckets.

They ran all through the crowd passing out suckers and doing silly stuff with each other as part of the show.

That was also the first time I laughed so hard I got a stomachache.

Flashlight Fender & Five Cent Cones
By Floyd W. Schmid of Farwell, Michigan
Born 1926

I am 75 years old, of sound mind and body – until I attempted this autobiography. In the distant future, my children and grandchildren may be interested – who knows! I will try to keep it light and colorful. It wasn't always that way, however I'll leave room between the lines you can add your own interpretation.

I was born July 28, 1926 at the home farm, four miles north of Farwell, Michigan, and the ninth child of Mathias and Clara Schmid. Other siblings were Frieda, Grace, Matt, Lenora, Edna, Carl, Eugene, Louis, myself and the youngest – a sister, Margaret. The soil was quite poor, besides being stony with lots of pine stumps. I guess we never realized we were poor because we always had plenty to eat and a warm, dry house. We milked about six cows and had a few pigs, chickens and a large garden. There was plenty of stuff to can for the winter. We also cut our own firewood and raised our own feed for the livestock. Us boys were always hunting and fishing when we could get away from the farm work. I will state here, that deer were not very plentiful at that time, no turkeys, fox, coyotes or even raccoon, but lots of rabbits, partridge and prairie chickens.

Some of my first memories were about 1930 when I was four years old. About that age, I was my father's favorite. On warm spring and summer days, he would let me ride to Farwell with him on the wagon with a load of ear corn in bags, to be ground at the Farwell Mills. Then we would bring it back home and mix it with oats, mineral and salt to be fed to the horses, cattle, and hogs. It was four miles into town and then four miles back home. While we waited for the corn to be ground, Pa would go grocery shopping to buy kerosene, salt, sugar, flour and sometimes bananas, if Mr. Palmer had some overripe ones – cheap. Every two weeks we'd have a 10 gallon can of

cream and maybe six dozen eggs to sell. Just before we were ready to go home, we'd stop at Burston's Drug Store and Pa would buy me a 5-cent ice cream cone. My favorite was orange-pineapple.

We'd travel west from Vandecar Road to just beyond the Trading Post, then take Mr. Littlefield's "Dinky Line" north to Surrey Road, then continue north on the present day "Finley Lake Road." At that time, the roads weren't named. Of course, US-10 was not built at that time, and Mr. Littlefield had a big sawmill across the road from where the Trading Post is today.

Where the stream goes under the road into the Mill Pond, there was a soft, murky, corduroy road crossing the streams. I remember very vividly one early spring day when the horses sank into the mud and logs to their bellies and just lunged and jumped to pull the wagon through. I hung onto Pa's arm, cried, and begged him not to go back that way. Evidently I had some effect on his judgement because on our return, we went north on Old State Road to VanBuskirk's corner of Surrey Road and then west down to Finley Lake Road. I was afraid of that spot for a long time, until I realized it was only very early in the spring when it was so bad.

Many times while we waited for the corn to be ground Mrs. Seigle would take me upstairs to their living area and give me fresh homemade bread and jelly, and a glass of milk. Pa and Fred Seigle would usually have a bottle of home brew that Fred had made.

Pa was elected Surrey Township Supervisor and he needed a car to get him back and forth to Harrison. So we got our first car in 1933. It was a 1926 Model T Ford. My oldest sister's husband, Emil Briedenbach, from Saginaw, bought it for $20 and brought it up to the farm for Pa, and taught him to drive it. All of us kids and Ma stood on the porch and watched Pa drive about 50 feet, right into a pine stump. Of course, at that time a 5 mph crash on the bumper wasn't given much of a second thought. Everyone knew each bumper could stand at least a 10 mph crash. No damage was done to the old Ford. It jumped back about six feet and stalled. Pa did a better job of steering after that but he never did like to drive, so most of the driving was left up to the kids, especially at night.

Pa got interested in the Farmers Union and

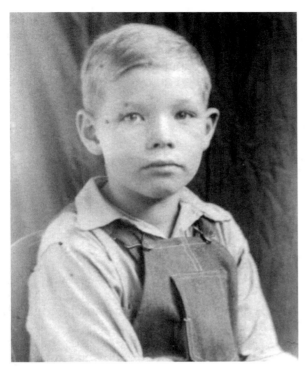

Floyd Schmid in 1934

went all over the county organizing. It was up to brother Carl to drive Pa at night and one of us younger kids had to go along because the lights had a tendency to go out on the rough gravel roads. One of us younger kids had to lay on the fender with a five-cell flashlight to light the way. On rainy nights, we could think of a lot of other places we would rather be.

I started school at five years old in Farwell. Emil Foell, "Emer" as we all knew him, built a school bus on a Model A Ford truck chassis and ran it on our route for many years. About the same time, Ray Wolston and Howard Randall built busses on Chevy frames. One was for the Maple Grove School and one for the Beech School areas. I enjoyed riding the bus. We always saved something from lunch to eat on the bus on the way home. The seats were padded benches along the sides and the only heat came from a manifold heater running from the engine through the firewall. The door didn't fit very tight so most of what little heat there was went back outside. Everyone sat as close to the front as possible anyway.

Brother Louis was two years older than I, but he started school at six, so he was only one year ahead of me. I was worried the first day that I may get lost or the bus would leave without me. Lou said, "I will watch out for

you." He showed me where the bathrooms were and my room, and generally showed me around the school. The first few days I didn't use the bathroom. During recess or at noon some of us boys would go into the marshy area where the middle school is now. It was full of cattails and Elderberry bushes, just like a jungle, and that is where we played. That's where we'd "pee" when we had to also! But one day soon after, I went to the bathroom in the school. They had those urinals of heavy porcelain, about four-foot tall with a tank above that would slowly fill with water, and then flush when it got full. As I was using the urinal, I stood in very close so the kid next to me couldn't see my "thingie." The darn thing flushed and the water caught me in the chest and drenched me all the way to my shoes. I went into the janitor's room and Mr. Masten let me stand by the furnace and dry out some before I went back to the room. He even went with me and explained to my teacher, Mrs. Norton (Thayer) what had happened. It's very funny now, but at the time it was quite embarrassing!

We all took our lunch in peanut butter pails or Karo syrup pails. Mr. Masten always found one or two in the building or playground and would put them on a shelf in the boiler room. Every once in a while I'd go in and look them over and maybe swap for a newer pail. The eraser-cleaning machine was in the boiler room also. It was a large round wheel-brush built like the old pedal grinding wheels. You'd sit on the seat and pedal and hold the felt eraser on the bristles and it would brush the chalk out of the felt. Raymond VanBuskirk and I volunteered many times for that job, just before leaving at four o'clock to go home.

The gymnasium was built in 1933. I was in the second grade and it was built onto the south side of our classroom. Raymond Schofield's dad was the superintendent of construction. The WPA built it. They had a windless stump puller, big steel drum, and cables, and the men walked a large pole around and around to lift the steel beams in place. The teacher, Mrs. Brimmer, let us watch as much as she could. The Ward School on Finley Lake Road was demolished so they could use the lumber for roof boards on the gym. Sports at that time were for the "town" kids. They had very little, or no chores to do and they could practice after school and on Saturdays. We always had chores. Saturday Pa depended on us to help with the harvest and cut the firewood supply for the long winters. Sundays were our days for hunting or fishing.

Seventh grade brings back many memories. Mr. Thomas, "Tommy," was our teacher. Many of the same kids I started Kindergarten with were in the 7th grade together. Raymond Schofield, Raymond VanBuskirk, Mary Sparta, Maribell Weaver, Gerald Coffell, Leo Mills, Ira Welch and Marie Welch. Roddy Raymond joined us that year and stayed through the 8th grade. We developed a close friendship that continues today. The others I mentioned are very good friends also, although I don't see them as often as I do Rod.

One particularly bad day for Mr. Thomas and about ten of us, as I remember it, was a day we insisted on not learning anything, with him insisting that we would! He paddled all of us, one after the other, the girls too! Raymond Schofield was good so he wasn't supposed to get paddled but one of the kids layed on the floor, between the rows of seats and when Mr. Thomas took a swipe at him with the paddle it broke in half and hit Raymond alongside the head. It bent his glasses but did no further harm except for his hurt feelings. A few weeks later Mr. Thomas took the class by bus to the West Grant School for a softball game. We played the agreed seven innings, but at the end of seven, we were behind by one run, so Mr. Thomas talked the lady coach and the teacher at West Grant to play nine innings. Well, needless to say, we won the game! Arlo Barber, Estel Reynolds, and the Clink boys were really mad. The next year in 8th grade, they came to Farwell School. I don't believe they ever got over that game, although we became very good friends afterwards.

About the same time, Esther Reynolds was a sophomore, lived in the West Grant district, and would ride her bike about four miles to school and back, twice a day. She was a beautiful girl and that bike ride kept her in the best physical shape! Bob VanBuskirk claimed her and defended his territory a few times, some quite seriously!

In 1938, Mr. Thomas talked about "Orbital Flight." He said for a vehicle to go into orbit it would have to attain 1700 miles per hour or greater. At that time the fastest planes were going about 200 miles per hour. Jets that travel 600 miles per hour had not been invented yet. He predicted that we would see "Orbital Flights" in our lifetime, and we certainly have. Not only did it happen for us, but he also saw it, because he died about 1998, and I believe he was 85 years old.

Bullfrogs: A Dollar a Dozen
By Margaret Kapuscinski Harris of Saginaw, Michigan
Born 1931

I was born in a little town of Zilwaukee, Michigan. I am now 83 years old. Oh, where did the time go? I was raised with five brothers, Jim and Bernard, and sisters, Mary and Bernadette. The most memorable thing I remember about my childhood was how my brothers and sisters would go frog hunting down by the Consumer's Power Company. We would throw a pillowcase over our shoulder and catch hundreds of bullfrogs. Our cases were half-full on a good day. Not little frogs, but big ones. We would hit them over the head and then cut their legs off and skin the legs. Then Mom would clean the legs and fry them in a pan. Upon frying them, they

Margaret's parents, Ed and Fidelis Kapuscinski

Margaret, Jim, and Mary in 1936

would jump in the pan. This was the nerves in them. We would take orders every week from the neighbors that bought them. We wrapped them in wax paper and sold them for $1.00 a dozen. We were never hard up for orders!

Something we did that was really dangerous was when we went ice-skating. There was a field called the cow pasture where we skated. To think our parents trusted us. We would go out on the ice in the Saginaw River and bounce the red buoys up and down in the water. The Almighty was surely watching over us.

One day our school class (6th grade) was going to take a tour of one of the big ships that docked at Consumer's Power. We were all very excited! When we arrived at the dock, the shipmaster lined us all up to get on it. To our shock, he instructed all the girls to go on first. (Remember in those days we didn't wear slacks?) We really made a big fuss but the captain stuck to his guns!

What a great time we had in the winter! I had a friend who had a sleigh and a beautiful horse. We went out many, many times with the sleigh!

One day in our sewing class, we decided to have some fun. It was in the basement of our school. We decided to lock the door on our teacher when she left the room. So, we sat on the machines and pushed each other all over the room while she went to get the janitor to open the room. Unfortunately, she started blaming me for the rucas. She was yelling and shaking her fingers at me and stuck her hand in my mouth. The crazy thing was, she had a missing finger, and I almost lost my stomach. Yes, I was guilty of closing the door.

A wonderful thing I remember about my parents was we went to Mooney's many nights to get ice cream cones. Even if Dad didn't have much money, we always got ice cream at Mooney's.

Living in Zilwaukee, we were quite a ways from downtown Saginaw. But every weekend or so, we would walk to Saginaw along the railway tracks to the movies. All the things to remember there: Home Dairy, Mecca Theater, Franklin Theater, all the dress shops, Kresge's, etc. Wonderful times we had.

Of course, remember the outhouses? Halloween time only came once a year, thank God. Once my brother tipped one over with a man inside. Boy, did he do some fast running! Also, unrolling the fire hoses.

Boy, and taking baths with seven people was something else! This event was done in a metal tub. The youngest went first and then the last was the oldest. Cold and scummy, yuck! I believe it was a Saturday night event.

All in all, we had a wonderful childhood. We did not have a whole lot but we did have love and great parents. Wonderful memories.

My husband, Jim, and I have been married for 63 years. We have five children and many beautiful grandchildren. God has been very good to us.

Pigs Feet & Ham Hocks
By Mable Johnston of Tucker, Georgia
Born 1936

I was born Mable Zimmerman on April 1, 1936 in a farm house one half mile south off Fillmore Road just east of the Country Sickles Store. The store was owned by Otto Kissane.

My parents were Charles W. Zimmerman and Emma Tester Wiltfong Zimmerman. Doctor Budge in Ithaca came to the house on a snowy morning to deliver me.

241

Mable and her family in 1940

My dad owned a forty-acre farm that he farmed with horses. We had milk cows, pigs, chickens and of course, horses. We had a large garden that supplied our food. Animals were butchered, as we needed meat. My aunt and uncle helped with that job. They didn't waste any of the pig parts. Their intestines were scraped and cleaned in order to stuff them with ground up parts for sausage links. We ate pig's feet called ham hocks now. We had our own eggs and butter, cream, buttermilk, and cottage cheese my mother made in a churn. We also had chicken to eat, and we ate the chicken feet. We were poor and didn't waste anything. I would help my mother gather the chicken eggs.

As a little child, I took my bath in a galvanized tub beside our living room pot-bellied stove. I went bare footed a lot in summer but didn't like it when I would get chicken poop between my toes. Our chickens ran loose in the yard.

My dad had a large wooden rocking chair and sat by his big radio to listen to programs coming from the Grand Old Opera in Nashville. Also other stations that played "The Shadow," "My Gal Sunday" and "Inter-sanctum." The news on December 7, 1941 of the bombing of Pearl Harbor was discussed but I was too young to understand it all.

I had two favorite cousins, Nora and Flora, we visited back and forth. Our toys were a ball we would play catch or ante-I-over the house roof. I had one doll I really loved. Just give me some paper and a pencil and I was content.

My father and mother and myself slept in two beds upstairs in one room. In the winter, I may wake up with snow on my covers.

I started kindergarten in Ithaca, Michigan. I had to walk over a quarter of a mile to Fillmore Road to catch the school bus. I stayed all day in school – no half-day busses. I finished high school in 1954. But before that when I was ten years old my dad sold our farm and we moved to Sickels at the corner of Fillmore and Ransom roads. The Sickels Country School was there and I attended 5th through 8th grades. My favorite teacher was Melba Kostal teaching in a one-room school grades K – 8th.

Going back to an earlier time, we didn't get electricity until 1939. We had outside toilets and a chamber pot in the upstairs bedrooms.

My parents always went to Ithaca for groceries every Saturday. Dad went to watch the men play pool and my mother and I went to a movie. We saw mostly Roy Rogers and Gene Autry. We got in for 12 cents each.

Some considered smoking, drinking, movies, and playing cards sinful. The most embarrassing was a girl having a baby out of wedlock.

After graduation in 1954, I went to work at the Wolverine Shoe Factory in Ithaca. In August, I got married and later had four children. They all graduated from Ithaca High School.

Mable Zimmerman in 1936

As a farmer's wife I helped in the fields driving a tractor, plowing and working up the ground for planting. I also canned a lot of fruits and vegetables. We would also pick wild blueberries and blackberries in the woods.

My husband passed away in 1982 and I became a widow at age 46. In 1986, I remarried and now live in Georgia 6 months and Michigan 6 months after we both retired.

We attend church regularly and enjoy singing in the choir. I now have eight great grandchildren. What a life!

Barbara's parents, Leone and Dale with their children

Pedro Saturday Nights
By Barbara Best of Dewitt, Michigan
Born 1931

Vermontville is a small town in the farming community of Eaton County, Michigan. Men and women from the state of Vermont coming to Michigan in 1836 settled in the area and organized Vermontville. About a mile east of town on Brown Road is where I grew up.

Saturdays, I loved them. The whole day was mine and I took advantage of all the free time. I loved to clean the living room, known as the parlor at my house. I would rearrange the furniture every week while my mother would be busy in the kitchen baking for Sunday dinner. Late afternoon after chores were done and supper was over, we would head for town to get groceries.

In the summer going to town to get groceries was a pretty big deal. While my parents shopped, I would seek out my friends and we would walk up and down the sidewalk.

Some of the older boys who drove cars would cruise past us and let out a whistle as my girlfriends and I sauntered along. We pretended not to pay attention to their whistles, but we would secretly be delighted and giggle amongst ourselves. In our minds, the guys were whistling at just us. Close to dark we joined others walking to the park where we would watch the free movie. We sat on blankets spread out on the ground in front of the big screen that hung between two trees in the corner of the park. This was a social event with all the farm families enjoying a night out to watch a good movie usually a western with Tom Mix or Gene Autry. After the movie I would find my parents and we would go to

the drug store. There with our backs pressed against the harp-shaped chairs we would enjoy delicious butterscotch sundaes. Life was good.

That was in the summer, but what about winter? Saturdays still held their magic, but in a different way. The main thing was, it was not a school day, and I had the whole day to read, play outside, and go to town with my parents.

There was a stretch of time when Saturday nights meant Pedro night. I am surprised when I mention Pedro and people don't seem to know what I am talking about. Pedro was a card game that was embraced by our neighborhood as the thing to do on a Saturday night in the winter.

The neighbors would take turns hosting the evening. Card tables would be set up throughout the house. There would be a head table and a foot table. The winner of a round had a little tally card and sometimes my job would be to punch their tally to show they had won and would be able to proceed to the head table. I never played cards because I was too young and as the night advanced, I would get tired and usually end up on the owner's bed snuggled down amongst all the coats and hats. I would just get to sleep, someone would win an especially good hand, and their yelling and laughter would wake me up.

At 11 o'clock the games stopped. The high winner would receive a gift and the loser received the booby prize. That was fuel for a lot of good-natured teasing and was all taken in good humor.   But the best was yet to come. The ladies would go get their baskets and unload the Jell-O salads, sandwiches, and cakes and everyone would dig in.

Close to midnight, we ventured out into the cold car. As I snuggled down beneath a blanket in the back seat, I would listen to my parents relive the night of card playing and hear what a neighbor had said or did. The party was a success, but it was over for the week.

When the next Saturday night rolled around, the scene was the same. My father tucked a deck of cards in his pocket. The wicker basket set on the end of the cabinet. My mother would carefully put the green glass plates, our party plates, in the basket. The Jell-O dish with whipped cream on top went in next. The lovely little sandwiches cut in half, wrapped in wax paper, and tied with a piece of sugar sack string were placed gently around the edges. Everything fit.

Exciting wasn't a word that I would use to describe my life growing up, but the evenings my parents and I spent at a neighbor's house playing cards and visiting or the nights in town watching the free movie certainly describes excitement for this little farming community on a Saturday night in the forties.

Memory Alley
By Dorothy E. Jones of Bay City, Michigan
Born 1923

Over the passing years, I have experienced many changes in Bay City. You see, I'm a great grandmother at the young age of 92. Sometimes I tend to forget some of the day by day routines I must go through, so I keep notes. Yet at other times, especially when it comes to the distant past, my memories are as colorful and vivid as anything I see today.

In the late 20s, 30s and even into the 40s, a time of bare purses and empty stomachs plagued much of America. In our family, consisting of my grandmother, my mother and my two brothers and myself, the main worry wasn't the plight of the country so much as it was the struggle of survival in our own back yard. But we did survive! I believe it was mainly due to my mother working two low paying jobs and being able to stretch each penny like a tautly pulled rubber band. We may have been wanting for more, but

Dorothy Jones in 1941

we never went hungry. Though nobody was untouched by winter's cruel sting, those of us in the darkest clutches of the depressed years felt it the strongest.

Like most of the people back then, our house was heated by coal. I'm not sure how often we had the coal hauling truck come by for a delivery, but I remember the chunks of black rock rumbling down the coal chute through the basement window onto the floor. We were fairly comfortable on the main floor rooms, but the bedrooms upstairs were a different story. Sleeping on the second floor of a two level house meant waking up to a brisk chill in your room. When bare feet hit the ice cold floor I was instantly awake and it didn't take long to find my slippers! The first order of the day was quickly making my way down to the basement to add fresh coal to the furnace. From the night before, the hot embers were pushed in and banked up against the insides of the cast iron furnace. This usually kept a slow smoldering burn going through the night and had enough heat to rekindle the new coal that was added in the morning.

My uncle Edwin had a rough time of it without a job. He also heated his house with coal, but he used a much smaller potbelly

244

stove in the middle of the house. His method of acquiring coal was neither orthodox nor moral, but it was clever and kept him warm throughout the winter months.

There were several coalmines across the city where miners would shovel coal into train cars, ride atop those cars to the delivery point, and then shovel the coal off again. Uncle Edwin didn't live far from the tracks. When he saw one of these trains going by, he would cuss and swear something fierce at the miners riding the coal cars. Whatever he said angered the miners so much, that they would throw chunks of coal at him. After the train passed by he would gather rocks of coal into a large burlap bag and take it home. Though maybe not the best way to heat your home, he didn't actually steal anything. After all, these gifts were given to him…even if it was in a rather rough manner.

There were no busses in those days to take the kids to school. And let me tell you, walking to school through harsh winds and deep snow was no picnic! Usually we walked in the street and tried to follow any tire tracks we could find. That made walking a little easier. Until several years ago, I insisted that the distance between my house and Central High School was at least five miles. But recently, an odometer on the car proved it to be just over one mile. I guess everything seemed longer and larger when you were a child.

Winter doesn't last forever so with the changing of the seasons gave us the alley once again. The alley behind our house was rarely used by traffic, but was in constant use by us kids. If I wasn't in the house listening to thick 78 speed records of Glenn Miller or Kate Smith on a crank up Victrola Phonograph, I was in the alley behind our house. I spent most of my time outside playing games with other neighborhood children in those days. We didn't have TVs to glue our eyes to and I was only allowed to listen to radio shows like The Shadow or The Lone Ranger on Saturday. After all, "Electricity costs money!" I was constantly reminded of that fact. Some of our favorite alley games were Dock on the Rock, Kick the Can, and if you had enough kids, Baseball. Dock on the Rock and Kick the Can were just extended and more complex versions of Tag. Sometimes we made up our own rules so nothing was for certain. The main purpose of these games was to keep us

running. I loved to run!

On quieter moments, with my girlfriends, I would sit on the porch and trade pictures of the biggest movie stars of the day. The post card sized photos would come from small packs we bought at the store with what few cents we could scrape up. A sheet of bubble gum that came with those snapshots was a real treat. Douglas Fairbanks, Errol Flynn, Mary Pickford, Clara Bow, and other stars from the Silent Films to the early Talkies would pass between us giggling girls. And when grandmother brought out a small tray of her molasses cookies for us to nibble on, nobody refused her kind offering. They don't make molasses cookies that good anymore.

This is just a sampling of my past. Though we lived a poor and simple existence, our memories are rich beyond words. I only hope the young people of today will have half the goodness in their lives as I have had in mine.

Barefoot Days in the Forties
By Elaine L. Onan of Midland, Michigan
Born 1931

In those beautiful days in the early forties, I knew summer was about to start when I could go shoeless. This was about early or mid-May and my country school was out for the summer. The grass always was so green, soft, and cooling to my feet. I don't think we ever had to water it. Another sign that summer was here, was when I could finally eat cold cereal like puffed wheat or puffed rice or the brand new one called Cheerios. In the winter, I had to choke down oatmeal or lumpy cream of wheat every morning. My mother was quite a firm believer about this!

Our old country house was across from a fishing lake with a mucky bottom in which we went swimming alongside a few snakes and lily pads. Many times when I got out of the water I had to race up the hill towards the road chased by a blue racer, a very fast snake, or so it seemed to me. We rented fishing boats to people that drove out from the city. We had two nice fishing boats, both wooden, and we thought beautiful. I rented them for 50 cents for a whole day of fishing. We had some regular customers that returned many times.

245

Something exciting that we loved to do was drive into Lowell and go to the movies. The Strand Theater there was very nice, plush thick red carpeting, and you had to go up some stairs to go to the bathroom. My dad was a big fan of the movies. He especially loved John Wayne. Of course, we saw many war movies at that time. Before we went, the first order of business was to search through the chairs and davenports to see if any loose change had been dropped between the cushions. It was especially good hunting after we had visitors. It didn't take much change in those days, as it was so much cheaper: 50 cents for adults, a quarter for kids or even a dime. That got us one or two movies, a newsreel, a cartoon, a short feature, and coming attractions. I do have a distinct memory of being quite terrified of the movies Wolf Man and Wuthering Heights. My mother had to walk me out of the theater during those two and reassure me that they weren't real and the wolf man was not going to show up and eat me.

Elaine and her brother, Ray in 1942

My father worked for the railroad in Grand Rapids and worked an afternoon to midnight shift. Another favorite thing we loved to do was to ride into the city with him, spend the day, and come home with him when he was done. My mother would pack a lunch: sandwiches, cookies, probably fruit. We had to have fruit, according to Mother. We may have had a thermos filled with milk.

In those days, there were many lovely movie theaters. Some even had live vaudeville shows. Those were great. The theaters showed double features, news and short subjects, also a cartoon. We would scout out really good movies. Sometimes we did two theaters in one day, depending on how much time we had. We ate our lunches in the theaters. We weren't the only ones doing this and it was great fun! I was a big movie and movie star fan so I was in 7th heaven.

Along about 11:30pm we would walk down to the big train depot and train station,

which was a beehive of activity in those days. We watched as trains loaded when troops arrived and trains departed carrying troops to locations where they would be shipped out to fight. There were happy reunions and sad departures to observe. This more than anything brought the war home to us. At midnight, my dad would come and find us and we headed back to the country, often stopping for ice cream cones.

My mother loved to show off our musical abilities. So when we were quite young she would dress us up in our best clothes. For me, I was usually in a fluffy, fancy white or pink dress that she had made. We would be invited around to different functions to sing. Two of our best selections were Billy Boy and Swansea Town. I sang the mother's part in Billy Boy and my brother Ray would sing back the replies to my questions. Swansea Town was a pretty song and I like it to this day and often sing it around the house. I was always pretty sure in later years that Swansea Town is a Welch song. After seeing a map of the UK I actually saw that there is a Swansea in Wales.

Our old house was a little drafty and in some places, there were cracks, especially around the windows. So many mornings I would sit up in bed and see snow that had sifted through and covered the foot of my bed. I can vaguely remember that one winter I was very sick with the flu. I don't remember just how old I was for sure, maybe five or six years old. I ran an extremely high temperature one night. My mother and dad were really scared and decided they should call a doctor. I'm not sure how they got hold of the doctor, as we had no phone at that time. They may have gone over to my grandpa's and used the phone. So a doctor from Freeport came to the house. The doctor was alarmed by my high fever and advised my folks to get me into some cool water at once, which was done right away. I was actually delirious and they had to restrain me and hold me down on the bed. The cold water did the job and actually saved my life and the temperature went down.

Christmases in our little country home were always happy ones but simple. We hung our stockings on the back of a chair. We usually opened our presents when my dad got home from work, which was about 12:30am. In our stockings, we would always find an orange or an apple, some peanuts in the shells, socks, or underwear. Useful things. But Santa always remembered to bring one special gift that we had been hoping for. One Christmas I received a dollhouse and Ray got a whole set of lead soldiers and we would get down on the big piece of carpeting in the living room and play with these for hours.

My mother had this carpet that looked like it came from India. It's design made nice roads for the soldiers and special squares where I put the doll house. One year Ray got a BB gun and I received a big baby doll. I must mention that we always received a Sears catalog in the mail. I know my folks ordered lots of our clothes from this and at Christmas, we got a special Christmas catalog. One year my dad decided he'd order a pail filled with candy, all different kinds of candy. This was kept secret and they hid it in their bedroom. Well they didn't hide it well enough and I found it. Almost every day I would sneak in the room, which was not easy because their bedroom door squeaked when I opened it. Ray caught me several times and told on me. Mother scolded me but that didn't stop me. The sad thing was that by Christmas day I had managed to eat most all the chocolate candy and about all that was left was hard candy. I was forgiven somehow as my dad knew I loved chocolate and I was special to him. He even laughed about it.

Elaine and her dad, George Houghton in 1937

I remember cold winter nights in the house at Morse Lake that we all sat pretty close to our nice warm stove, which was in our dining room. I think it burned coal and wood. If you wanted to really warm up you could lean against the smooth sides of the stove. Or you could sit on the couch near the stove and rub your feet on the sides, if your legs were long enough. In mid-winter, life centered around that great warm stove. We played cards on the dining room table or put up a card table close to the heat. We read lots of books also. I remember reading Little Women and the Five Little Peppers and How They Grew.

On most Saturday nights, it was bath night. We had a big round tin tub and that was placed in back of the stove. My mother had clothes bars, which she would place on either side of the tub. I think towels or blankets were hung over them creating a private bath area. Mother heated water on the kitchen wood stove and my dad carried the hot or warm water by pail-fulls and filled the tub. You kind of had to hurry and get bathed before the water cooled down. We did bathe other days but probably just sponge baths in front of the kitchen sink which I remember was very large.

An exciting event for us was when Thomas Dewey, who ran against Roosevelt in his second term, rode the train and ran on tracks that were down Morse Lake Road from our house. He stood out on the back of the caboose and waved at us as the campaign train went through. The trains on that track were big steam engines that normally went quite fast and always blew their steam whistles. We were cheering for Dewey because my family was strongly Republican at that time. He was Lowell Township Supervisor and a very honest politician. He was a close friend of Gerald Ford and they worked together on getting a new Kent County Airport in Grand Rapids. My grandpa's name is on a plaque in the airport to this day.

I have to tell you about what was a very big source of embarrassment for me and I was thankful we had them. We had no inside bathroom so we had what my mother called potties or Jennies. We each had one in our bedroom to use at night if we needed them. This was a great alternative to running outside to the backhouse in the night and especially in the bad weather. They were white enamel beauties, like fancy pails. My mother, being a very clean person, insisted on making sure they were clean and sanitary. So maybe once a week she would wash and scrub them and set them in a line on one side of our driveway in plain sight. Her idea was to air them off. Four, or five of these white beauties where everyone would see them. It seemed to me that it was usually when they were out there that someone would drive in or a friend would come over on her bike. My mother said not to worry, that this was perfectly alright.

Evenings, both summer and winter, were spent sitting close to our big radio in the living room. Our wonderful Philco radio was most always the focal point of our lives. Many nights we all listened to our favorite radio shows. We could hear Little Orpan Annie, Tom Mix, Tom Armstrong: the All-American Boy, The Shadow, Amos & Andy, Gene Autry, and the Blue Hornet on the weekdays. I remember Saturday nights we listened to The First Nighter, The Great Gildersleeve, Fibber McGee & Molly and The Bob Hope Show. We heard Burns and Allen, Charlie McCarthy and many others, the names I can't remember.

It was a great time in which to be brought up. There were simple pleasures and some serious times. I'm so grateful that I had a chance to live during the 30s and 40s, times I will always remember and cherish.

The Sheep Dip Stage
By Lillian F. Pieniozek of Bay City,
Michigan
Born 1936

As you drive on US-23 heading north, (at that time there was no I-75 and it took over

Lillian's dad and her brother, Clifford

four hours from Detroit to Standish) you pass through Flint continuing north then you would travel through some small towns, Bay City, Linwood, Pinconning and arrive in Standish. At the traffic light in Standish, turn right onto Cedar, which turns into Pine River Road, head east until you come to a four-corner stop. This intersection is located on Old State Road and Pine River Road. This is where our story begins.

The area is referred to as Pine River. Back in the day, Pine River had a large elevator, hotel, homes on each corner, the famous Pine River Tavern, known as the "Stump Pump," and a thriving fishing business. There was also a school down by the curve and close to the river. Next door to the school lived a sheep farmer. At recess the older students would chase the sheep for fun and would sometimes bring back to the playground some sheep do-do and made the younger students eat it. They would also play hide-and-go-seek down in the coal bin, which was under the school. Sometimes at noon recess, the older students would go down to the river for a quick swim. My sister was told time and time again not to go swimming in the river because she was too small. Well she went anyway and almost drowned. When she got home, she received a spanking that she never forgot. She also never went swimming in the river again.

We lived on the southeast corner. My father was the operator of the elevator. My dad knew when the coal train was scheduled and let the area folks know. The people would come with their horses and wagons. They would fill the wagons with the larger chunks of coal leaving the smaller chunks behind. That was good because my brother and sister would pull their little red wagon to the elevator, load it with the smaller chunks of coal, and take it home. We would use it to heat our home. I was born in that house on a snowy February night; the year was 1936. The doctor actually came to our house to deliver me.

We had cows, chickens and some geese. There was one goose that would chase me every time I went outside. Needless to say, I didn't like it either. At lunchtime, my mother would pack a lunch for my brother who was tending the cows down the road in another pasture. I had to walk down there past the cemetery; it gave me the creeps. On really hot days, our parents would take us swimming to an area known as Timber Island. When we got out of the water, my mom would always check between our toes looking for bloodsuckers. It always tickled my toes!

One day I got mad at everyone and decided to run away. I remember walking over to our friend's house and hiding in their old car. My parents found me and I got a scolding. I was lucky.

Lillian and her sister

My brother had a very special dog. His name was Rover. Rover was a Collie and very protective of my brother and the rest of us. He was a good ol' dog!

When I was five we moved into Standish. My parents purchased a house for $500 but we still had the outhouse. There were always catalogs for us to use, as there wasn't any toilet paper available. In the winter, it was always very cold out there. When the remodeling was finally finished we were all happy to have an inside bathroom. This was a big change for all of us. My dad got a new job, my brother and sisters went to school and I went too. Rover came with us but then one day he disappeared and we never saw him again. My mother used to bake bread, eight loaves at a time. That bread was so good! On Sunday morning, she used to cook us a stack of pancakes and brewed a couple pots of coffee. We called it our pancake cake. The first layer had butter, second layer brown sugar and the third layer had real maple syrup! The layers were repeated. They melted in your mouth!

When I was seven, my dad took me to the little hatchery and bought me a baby duck. When we got home, my dad and brother decided that the little duck needed a pool. They took an old lard container, cut it in half and filled it with water. My little duck was a happy pet. One week before Thanksgiving my little duck disappeared! I think my neighbor took him for their Thanksgiving dinner. I was a very sad little girl. So, in the spring my dad and brother bought two old junk bikes, took them apart, and made one for me. They rebuilt and then painted that bike for me! Talk about happy! Wow! My first spin landed me on the metal drain cover; skinned my knee up pretty good. Our parents had five children: my brother, two older sisters, me, and then along came the baby of the family. We were all excited to have a new little one in the family!

When my brother was in high school, a fire broke out at his best friend's house. The boys jumped on one of the school buses and arrived before the fire trucks. The boys were able to save most of the furniture. My brother went upstairs to try to save more furniture but became trapped. He managed to get to a window, broke the glass, and jumped out. He landed on an old dead tree and was impaled on a branch; it stuck into his armpit. He ended up going to the hospital. It was very painful.

The following year, World War II broke out. All of the boys in the senior class wanted to quit school and enlist in the service but the superintendent talked to the students and encouraged them to stay and graduate. They agreed. I remember going to the train station the night they shipped out. There were lots of tears and hugs everywhere.

When I was in high school, this one Halloween a group of about 30 students went to the stockyard and proceeded to move a piece of machinery called a sheep dip. We pushed it from north of town to downtown and parked it under the traffic light. One of the seniors stood on top and was playing his accordion as the rest of us were singing. The police arrived and we scattered in all directions. I crawled into a snow fence roll in the schoolyard. When I tried to get out my sweater caught on the wire. I pulled and tugged, finally getting out!

Many years have gone by. Both of our parents have passed, as have my brother and sister. The elevator and school are gone, as well as our home. A fish store, which is now closed, sets where our home used to be. The only original building left standing is the small gas station party store that stands on the northwest corner.

The Coronation
By Pamela Lillie Newman of Gowen,
Michigan
Born 1944

June 1, 1953 was the day of the Coronation of Elizabeth Alexandra Mary Windsor as Queen of the British Empire…Queen of not only the United Kingdom, but also Queen of Canada, Australia, New Zealand, South Africa, Pakistan, and Ceylon. That was tantamount to Queen of the World, in my 9-year-old eyes.

I was a student at Lincoln Lake Elementary School, a rural school in northeastern Kent County. Television was a rather new contraption. It was becoming common in cities and towns and among professionals, but out in our neighborhood, my family was the only one with a television. The screen resembled an oval, which had been flattened on the top and bottom. The screen measured 11 inches on the diagonal. Most of the time it was covered with what looked like a snowstorm (time

to go outside and turn the antenna by hand for better reception), or covered by quickly moving horizontal lines (the horizontal-hold needed to be adjusted with a pair of pliers.)

There was another wonder making the viewing of the Coronation possible: the film from the Coronation was flown across the ocean by Canberra Jet Bombers so people on this side of the pond could view it on the very same day as the actual event in London (albeit several hours later.) We had the first trans-Atlantic broadcast, although the film did have to be physically flown across the ocean.

A problem to be overcome in this historic accomplishment was the filming itself. Television cameras had never been allowed in Westminster Abbey. "Disrespectful," "sacrilegious," and it would take away from the privilege of the elite who should be the only ones to view the ceremony. Prime Minister Winston Churchill informed Elizabeth of the official decision to not allow the filming, on the pretext that it would be too much strain on the new, young queen. Elizabeth informed Churchill that it was *her* Coronation, and she was having it filmed so all of her subjects could see it…not just the privileged few.

My teacher, Mrs. Florence Rasmussen, wanted our entire group of 3rd – 8th graders to witness "something you will remember your entire lives." So we 25 students were given a few instructions in proper manners, and Mrs. R. led us ½ mile down the dirt road named MacClain to Podunk Road and the place I called home. Mom was happy to play hostess and share that wonderful invention sitting atop our radio cabinet.

Everyone sat quietly on the floor and stared at the grayscale screen, some seeing the wonder of television for the first time. We would all remember how beautiful the new Queen was. The two queens we were most familiar with were both ugly and mean – the Queen of Hearts from Alice in Wonderland and the wicked Queen from the Snow White cartoon movie. No, Elizabeth looked more like a Snow White than a Queen. I found myself a bit jealous of the Canadians…they had Elizabeth, and we had President Eisenhower (who had just replaced President Truman.) Not much glamour for the USA.

To most of us, the service seemed like a fancy wedding. There was a "Cinderella" carriage pulled by white horses. There was

Lincoln Lake Elementary School students and teachers

classical music. There were beautiful clothes.

There were plenty of prayers and scripture readings. Mrs. R. would occasionally interrupt the ceremony with her interesting commentary, since the dialog on television was pretty boring. "There is her husband, Prince Philip Mountbatten, the Duke of Edinburgh. She fell in love with him when she was only 13 years old, and he was 19. He was a foreigner and her mother did not approve, but she married him anyway, 8 years later."

One classmate asked, "Will Philip be the King, then?" "No, because he was not born in the Royal Family," another said.

"But you said Mary was queen and she was the wife of King George V." The King's wife is a Queen because it is a lower position than King. But if Philip were King, it would put him above the Royal Family in position, so this is impossible. A Royal King's wife is a Queen, but a Royal Queen's husband is not a King, he is a Prince.

I asked, "But aren't the children of the Royal Couple the Princes and Princesses?" Yes. It was too much for a 9-year-old to understand.

After warm homemade cookies and Kool-Aid, we walked back to school and talked about why this was an important event. "You will all be grown up and have children of your own before they crown another King or Queen," prophesied Mrs. Rasmussen. Sixty years have passed, and we have yet to see another monarch take the throne. I guess she got that one right – although I am still waiting for my own personal mini-helicopter that she prophesied I would have by the time I was 30.

I can't walk that dirt road anymore – it was paved 30 years ago. My television is 42 inches on the diagonal, full color, and receives live broadcasts from anywhere in the world. We don't have to have an antenna because the picture is received "digitally" (whatever that means.)

Some things haven't changed. 93-year-old Prince Philip and 87-year-old Queen Elizabeth are still a handsome couple and have upheld the dignity of the Throne. Their teen-age infatuation lasted (or else it was too royally unseemly to separate.) And my 95-year-old mom still keeps the cookie jar full of fresh homemade cookies and loves to welcome children into her home on MacClain Road to enjoy them.

Life on Podunk

Those of us who grew up on Podunk Road in northeastern Kent County have sometimes suffered abuse because of our humble beginnings, but most of us would not trade those early days on Podunk for anything.

There actually was a settlement a few miles south on Podunk Road, called – PODUNK. There was a mill there with a waterwheel, and it was always fun for us kids to ride to Podunk with Dad so we could see the old wheel turn in the creek pond. The wheel and mill are long gone. I wish I had a picture.

My research tells me that the first Podunk in the USA was probably in New York, on land purchased from the Podunks, an Algonquin Indian tribe. That Podunk had a mill waterwheel also, and some claimed they kept the name Podunk because of the sound the water made as it fell off the wheel slats: po-dunk, po-dunk, po-dunk. If that is the case it would apply to my Podunk, too.

Over time, Podunk has become a euphemism for a back-woodsy, out-of-touch settlement…something like Dogpatch, Li'l Abner's stomping ground. Now that I'm (sort of) grown up, I'm not sure that is really an insult. Being a former participant in the Rat-Race, and knowing many other people who are currently struggling in that futile sporting event, I know that when we close our eyes at night and seek a place of peace, we long for a back-woodsy, out-of-touch settlement – no cell phones, no internet, no TV. Isn't that what camping is all about?

On the summer days in the early 50s, my cousins, my siblings and I would pick rose bug beetles off the locust tree for Mom. When our baby food jars were full we would count them out, and Mom paid us a penny for every

10 that we had imprisoned. Only 100 bugs each was enough! We would take our dimes and walk ½ mile to A.J.'s country store to buy a Coca Cola to drink on our way home. Pretty back-woodsy.

I spent lots of hot, late summer evenings lying on the grass alongside Podunk Road, staring up at the stars. I learned to find the Big Dipper and Orion. Mom would point out which star was Grandpa Lillie's star, and which was Great-Grandpa's. I don't think those stars are visible from 5th Avenue in Manhatten. With my Mason jar beside me, I would get up from the grass and catch fireflies, trying to fill the jar with enough to actually make a little temporary lamp I could take into my room. Unsophisticated, out-of-touch.

Way out in the boonies of Podunk, we kids would save up the large juice cans. When we had two each, we would string rope through them and make walking stilts. If you grew up sophisticated, I probably could not explain to you how this is done. But if you lived on Podunk, you kept the art, and made them for your own children long after your Podunk days.

I remember when Calvin (an older man who lived on Podunk) married Arlie (an older widow woman.) Late on their wedding night, about 20 adult neighbors plus all of the children made the stealthy hike down Podunk road to surprise them with a "Chiveree." Everyone, even the smallest child, carried a pan and a spoon. We had to be as quiet as mice for the whole trip, then surround the house, and at the signal, bang loudly on our kitchen pans with our kitchen spoons. The dads set off Black Cat firecrackers, shot guns in the air, and we all yelled and screamed. Poor Arlie… we did not know she was in the outhouse all by herself at the time! She was scared to death. But Calvin and Arlie were rewarded with the wedding gifts we brought. We were invited in, but politely declined and walked back down Podunk Road to our homes, laughing and giggling like only unsophisticated hillbillies are inclined to do.

Podunk is mostly paved now – only 1 ½ miles of dirt road remaining to kick up dust storms in the summer, and mud in the spring. I wonder if, when the last section is paved, they will change the name. I hope not!

Still Hanging In
By Venessa I. Rosenfield of Saginaw, Michigan
Born 1922

I was born in Alpena, Michigan on February 3, 1922. My given name was Venessa Isabell Morrison. The family moved to Saginaw, Michigan in 1924. I went to Emerson School and on to Central Junior High and then to Saginaw High and graduated in 1940. I had a job downtown at Kresge and then to Woolworths during my tenth and eleventh grades.

I got married on October 11, 1941 so my name changed to Rosenfield. Then on December 7, 1941, was Pearl Harbor. My husband was drafted in June 19. I moved back home with my parents, Mr. and Mrs. Morrison. Then I went to Missouri to visit my husband and then to Clovis, New Mexico, and I got pregnant. So in 1943, I had a baby girl and named her Sandra Kay. Her father was in Africa when she was born. He came back home in August, and so the first time he saw her she was two years old.

My family was two sisters and two brothers – me and Majorie and Frank and Emery. Marjorie is still living at Shattuch Manor. She had a stroke three years ago and can't talk. I'm living since 1975 in my own home. I go every day to Eleanor Frank's for lunch. I play euchre on Monday and Thursday. I live in Carrollton.

When I was in my eighties, I started

Venessa and Lolly

252

dressing up as a clown and would go to kids' parties at Christmas time. I always had fun. One Christmas day I went downtown to a church and gave out candy canes. I didn't have a very good turnout because we had a snowstorm the night before. My real good friend had a clown suit just like mine, so she would go with me. We would paint each other's faces and laugh while doing it. I don't clown anymore but it was fun while it lasted.

I've survived cancer twice, and I'm 93 years old and still hanging in.

The Post Office Sold Beer and Alcohol!
By Patricia Buckley of Branch, Michigan
Born 1932

I was born and raised in Chicago until the age of fifteen. I was an only child, and my father passed away just before I graduated eighth grade. Mom married my stepdad who had this 120 acres in Mason County since 1934. Mom sold our home in Chicago, and we moved here. Coming to an area that had just gotten electric, REA, in 1938 was a change in lifestyle. There was no indoor bathroom and no kitchen sink. But the good thing to me was the school bus. No more walking to school, then home for lunch, and then back to school. Custer High had 75 students.

The store in Tallman is where we bought gas for their Jeep pickup. I had never seen a non-electric gas pump. We never had an auto in Chicago. I sure wish I had pictures of that store. It sold not only groceries but jeans, gloves, socks, etc.

In Walhalla on US 10 there was also a grocery and gas station owned by Jack and Loyla Pineau. We always wondered why behind the meat counter display was a bookshelf type setup with small slots with what looked like envelops in there. We always bought the *Chicago Sunday Herold American and Tribune*. One had in the comic section the "Believe It or Not." Low and behold, we read about the only post office in the USA that sold beer and alcohol. And it was this store. Later a building was constructed across the highway and was the post office. The building is still there in bad shape, and it has no gas pumps or store anymore.

Growing up in Chicago in the '30s and '40s girls and women never wore slacks. I remember asking my mom if she would buy me slacks like the girls in school were wearing. I tried to explain them to her, but we had never seen females dressed like that. The men and boys who lived on farms were all wearing them. Asking the neighbor ladies got us on track. I am 82 and still wearing jeans.

Custer Grocery has been Bonsers for over 50 years. The Rexal Drug Store across the street was just being built when we came here in 1948, and the roller rink was being built, too. I was so happy because we went to skating rinks in Chicago in winter.

Halloween Night in Riverdale
By Marion Tedhams of St. Louis, Michigan
Born 1925

It was Halloween night in Riverdale, Michigan, a small village fifty miles north of Lansing, Michigan, back in the '30s. I was about ten to twelve years old. My mom said I was old enough to go trick or treat. We had a little barn behind our house, and an alley ran right by it. It had a loft, and we kids would play up there.

Well, that night my sister and I went out to the barn, climbed to the loft, and waited and watched because we knew that a group of bigger boys would be coming down the alley with a manure spreader. Every year they disassembled one and put it on the roof of the high school that was across the road from our house. Sure enough, here they came pulling and pushing it down the alley, and just as they got to our barn the lady that owned it raised up out of it with a sheet over her, arms spread, and said boo boo. Did you ever see those boys scramble! The manure spreader sat in the alley that night. Sis and I laughed and laughed. The barn had a little sliding door in the end overlooking the alley so we had a perfect view. Next day at school, the teacher said that Mrs. Hyde asked if some of the bigger boys would put her manure spreader back up to her sales lot.

I never could figure out how those kids could get one of those big pieces of equipment apart and put clear up on that high roof! Where there's a will there's a way! A lot of folks walked by the high school that morning to see if the manure spreader was up there, but they got a surprise that year.

The Good Old Days were Much Better
By Mary Ann Hale of Elwell, Michigan
Born 1940

I lived in a small college town that had two trailer plants that built house trailers, Alma Trailer and New Moon Trailer, and two hospitals, Memorial and Wilcox. It had three dime stores or five and ten cent stores; two dairies to buy ice cream, milk, butter, etc. that delivered to homes locally; several mom and pop grocery stores around the town; an A&P, Krogers, groceries downtown; two movie theaters, the Strand and a smaller one; women and men's clothing stores; three jeweler stores, Church, Gellers, and Elsea's; a few shoe stores (one even had a special machine to step on and it would x-ray your feet and show how your toes were, etc.); and three grade schools, Republic, Hillcrest, and Lincoln, so the kids walked to school and usually walked home for lunch and very seldom carried their lunches. The kids also had recess periods.

Mostly the men worked at the trailer plants and many walked blocks home for lunchtime. The New Moon Trailer even made the trailer for a movie with Lucille Ball and Ricky Ricardo in the "The Long, Long Trailer."

You could get anything from bulk candy to clothes, hardware, etc., at the five and ten cent stores.

The dairies delivered milk, butter, cheese, cream, etc., to the homes. The people would set wire boxes with glass bottles and leave a note with what they wanted. The milk had about two inches of cream at the top of a quart.

The grocery stores were so people could walk to them and get items, and the main shopping trip was to town on Fridays or Saturdays when people would cash their paychecks. The kids would ride bikes or roller skate on the sidewalks to go to the store for eggs or bread, etc.

The theaters would have showings at 7:00 p.m. and 9:00 p.m. Many times a Saturday matinee could be attended by presenting a can of vegetables, etc. The tickets were ten cents or fifteen cents, and popcorn was ten or fifteen cents. Usually the matinees were cowboys and Indians like Roy Rogers and Dale Evans, Gene Autry, the Lone Ranger and Tonto, or Disney shows, the Three Stooges, Porky Pig, etc. We didn't have a lot of these war shows like they have now. There was only the one show to see. There wasn't these buildings with five to ten different theaters to go in to choose from at the same time. Usually on Saturdays, groups of kids would walk uptown to the movies.

The iceman would come around with a truck full of ice blocks, about a twelve-inch square cube for the iceboxes, which was a three or four door cupboard lined in metal and one door held the ice block to keep it all cold. The iceman had an ice pick to chop the ice into the size people wanted and also a pair of ice tongs to lift it. The kids always watched for the iceman because he'd give us a little chunk of ice to eat.

In the winters, the city would hire a man with a horse and a V shaped plow made of wood to go up and down the sidewalks to clear the snow. Then eventually they had men with small tractors clear the sidewalks.

There were mailboxes on the corners and the mail was delivered into them or also picked up from them, and the mailman walked around the block, etc., delivering the mail to the houses.

The schools had individual grade classrooms with one teacher per class. The kids did their work in class with the teacher there to help them and there weren't aides, etc. The teachers taught the students. If help was needed with a problem, etc., it was worked out in school. There was not all of this homework and heavy backpacks full of homework every night.

We learned how to write and how to read it and not print all the time. We learned how to do math problems, etc., with easy and simple methods and not go around the mountain to figure it out.

There was summer rec programs for the kids. High school or college students were hired to go to the schools and perform physical programs like baseball, badminton, croquet, and arts and crafts with the kids. Two or three times a week a bus trip alternated with the schools to go to Rock Lake for swimming classes.

There was always something for kids to do

and not sit watching TVs, video games, or cell phones all day. There was always something to do. There was riding bikes, roller skating on sidewalks, hopscotch, ballgames, hide and seek, any-I-over, kick the can, or mother may I. Kids didn't seem to be having so many overweight problems and anger management and mental problems like they do now. At least it didn't seem like that. You didn't hear kids saying, "I'm bored." Kids were happier and there were not so many loners like you see now because they aren't happy.

It seemed like there was more families and not so many split up or single parent homes, and kids being on their own to try and find a happy childhood.

Before the streets were paved, the city would brine the dirt roads to keep the dust down. The kids would go along the edges where there wasn't the brine and would gather up the dirt and make a path across the road so not have to walk in the brine to go to friends on the other side. We would take a jar and lid and try to catch bees and sometimes get stung. Kids were kids and had fun.

People didn't carry guns around supposedly to protect themselves. People could leave doors and windows open and not be broken into. Neighbors knew their neighbors and got along. They could leave windows open in cars while in the store and not be broken into. My mother-in-law would take the keys out of the ignition and lay them on the console while in the store and not be afraid her car would be stolen.

People had gardens and raised fruit and vegetables to can and save for winters.

There wasn't so many people on welfare not wanting to work and who thought the world owed them everything and that it was easier and better to have it all given to them and not have to work for it like others.

Not everyone in the neighborhood had the new black and white TV. So the family that did would invite the neighbor kids to watch the puppet show *Kukla, Fran, and Ollie* and would make popcorn for everyone on one night of the week.

Sunday afternoons after church we might get pickle bologna, cheese, and crackers at the local store and ride a few miles up north to Oil City or somewhere to look for mushrooms or blueberries in the woods and hoping we wouldn't see any snakes. Or maybe we would take a ride to visit relatives and see cousins to play with in the country.

Times weren't always easy but people looked forward to being teenagers, to getting their driver's license, and to getting jobs, cars, going to college, or having a career, getting married, having families, grandkids, great-grandkids, and a happy ever after life. Reunions, picnics, etc., homemade ice cream, bonfires and roasting hot dogs and marshmallows, family reunions when grandparents were alive. Then few years went by and there wasn't any.

About eight years ago I took my husband's grandparents photo and wrote up a little note and invited aunts, uncles, sisters, brothers, cousins, nieces, nephews, sons, daughter, etc., to come and get together at our house for a family reunion. I was thinking maybe few people would show up since so many young folks get so busy, etc. There was 70 people. They were so excited and wanted to do it again so now here it is eight reunions later and still going strong. Some of the cousins were friends in school with each other and didn't even know they were related. What started out with Grandpa and Grandma has ended up in 100 plus people. Sweet corn, roasted chicken, hot dogs, burgers, lots and lots of food, games, a raffle, etc., makes a very happy, fun day for all.

When I got married 54 years ago this June, my last name became the same, as my grade school principal's (no relation). My husband plows snow in winters here in the local area. Several years ago, a lady called and wanted to get put on the snowplowing list. Her neighbor recommended my husband. She asked if he was related to Walter and I said yes, Walter was his grandfather. She said she remembered going in a one-horse buggy with her father to Walter's to tell him about a relative's death. So she was a relation, too. She also happened to be my fourth grade teacher in grade school many years before.

Graduating in the class of 1958 from high school kids wore school sweaters and jackets with names, years, etc. Now kids dress all kinds of ways.

Hourly wages were $1.00 per hour at the telephone office and nurse's aides at the local Masonic Home nursing home. So a paycheck would be $40.00 for the 40-hour week. Gas was 25 cents per gallon, and you could fill up a gas tank for a week on almost what a gallon costs today. Car speeds were in the fifties not the sixties and seventies.

There was also an outside drive-in-theater and roller skating rink out of town a mile or so.

People lived on small family farms and could raise families. Some worked a little extra in factories or second jobs. They could raise animals, chickens for milk, meat, and eggs. Now all the little farms are gone, even a lot of the buildings are torn down or falling down. The smell of manure wasn't that bad from the farms. Now the large CAFOs have taken over with hundreds of animals in pens, not even knowing what green grass is. They hardly have room to stand or lay down. The farmers haul animal waste for miles around in semi-truck loads down highways, etc. Some days the odor is smelled for miles in local towns and buildings, etc. You can hardly get out of your car to go into the store.

I am so glad I got to know what the good old days meant and I am so sorry and sad to know that my grandkids and great-grandkids will never have the days memories like these. I hope and pray someday things will change and that they will have good old days with happy, healthy memories in life too for 75 years. This world is so full of changes and problems.

Never Dilly Dally After School
By Awilda Whitehill of Grand Rapids, Michigan
Born 1954

As we had done so many times in the past, my brother Ford and I decided we didn't want to go home from school as soon as it let out. We both attended a one-room school called Randall School with a big bell that we eagerly took turns pulling the rope to make it ring.

The day was beautiful, and we just wanted to be outdoors a little longer before we had to walk home and do chores. We had been told to come straight home that day.

We ran down the little hill in back of the school and down the gravel road to a part of the road that had a huge culvert in it. We usually were lucky and didn't worry about getting wet unless it had rained a lot recently.

We both ran down the side of the hill. I

Awilda Whitehill in 1958

went straight for the culvert while Ford ran a little farther south to mess with some rocks.

Well, it was a very good thing that I was a young, healthy kid because when I ran into the culvert I almost stepped on a huge blue racer snake sunning himself close to the opening. I had never seen a snake in that culvert before.

I screamed at the top of my lungs. Ford came running. He quickly saw why I had screamed.

Needless to say, we never dilly-dallied after school again.

Doing my chores was almost fun that day.

True Friendship Brought My Family to America
By Rula Koutras of Saginaw, Michigan
Born 1944

Can a four-year-old child remember anything? As I am looking out the window on this cold February day with a ten below zero degrees and a mountain of snow that is piled up outside I thought I would doze off and remember the good old days.

It started on a big ship. I remember my mother crying and waving to many people. Where were we going? Lots and lots of people on this big ship. Suddenly the ship was moving, and I remember crying and crying. After many nights, many days, and a big train ride, we arrived in Saginaw, Michigan, on a cold day on December 1, 1947.

What brought us here in a northern small town in the thumb with about 150,000 inhabitants? True friendship – one good friend of my father's named Thomas. They left their families at the age of sixteen from their home in Greece and came to America together. They

256

fought together in the war, worked together, and now were in Saginaw, Michigan, together again after many years of separation. True friendship.

We didn't have a place to live and hardly any money, but this great country of America cared and gave us passage to come. I remember these good old days when true friendship existed, friends for life.

I remember living in an apartment with thirty steps to climb on top of a restaurant on Lapeer Street where two families lived. We were one of them and across a family of twelve lived. Can you imagine ten kids ranging from two and a half to 22? The two and a half year old little girl was my friend for seven years together and still remains my best friend after sixty years and many, many miles away. True friendship existed. These were good old days when neighbors cared for each other. Do we know who lives next door to us today?

I remember not having to play in a nice grass back yard, only on top of a roof from the restaurant and having only pigeons to care for and play with. One day I found the cages and pigeons gone. Did we have them for supper?

I remember falling from the rooftop, and in no time, the doctor was at our apartment making sure I didn't have any broken bones. This was when doctor cared and came to the house. Today we are sitting in their offices, sometimes waiting for hours to see them.

I remember my first grade teacher, Mrs. Muelewis, at Carry Lincoln School, where we walked for several blocks whether it was raining or snowing to get there, and a teacher that cared would button my coat and make sure was warm enough to walk back home.

I remember using God's name in our schools, pictures and crosses, and on Good Friday, everything was closed from noon to 3:00 p.m., respecting our Creator. Now everything is open so we don't lose even one sale. Everything for money! They even want to take God's name away from our money. America was great because we believed in God – God Bless America, in God we trust – does He bless us now?

I remember dressing up for Easter with beautiful outfits and hats. Now we see jeans, tennis shoes, and even shorts on this holy day in church.

I remember working as a waitress my first job at Tony's Restaurant on weekends working from 6:00 p.m. to 3:00 a.m. and not stopping for a few minutes, so busy not having any time to goof off or play around. Today we have some young kids not even moving to wait on you. I remember applying for a bank job not having any experience or knowing anything about banking or operating an adding machine but the personnel manager, Mr. Muscott at Second National Bank, interviewing me gave me a chance only by talking to me and feeling my heart. He gave me a chance and after 39 years and name changing bank, I had given my life to it. Today how many job changes exist? Hard work, loyalty, honesty, does it exist?

Good memories keep us going, and we think of the good old days.

A Sleepover and an Emergency
By Tuesday Summers of Durand, Wisconsin
Born 1952

Being the oldest of eight children can be wondrous and joyful and it prepared you with a lifeboat of tools like multi-tasking, problem solving, first aid, storybooks, and storytelling.

Growing up in a comfy, cozy cabin in northern Michigan with uncompleted plumbing and a wood burning stove meant early to rise to stoke the large stove and then the fireplace in the kitchen where we would bake bread and make our own yogurt from goat's milk.

Flash, our little pygmy was the only one that had not gone dry. We had twenty-seven goats, twenty-five chickens, one turkey, and six dogs.

One day my mother let me have a sleep over. We could stay in one of the cabins at the truck stop my parents managed. All the girls were very excited because we would be alone. I picked cabin 17. It was my favorite because it had many windows. We had to use the outside toilet but no one cared because it was an adventure. When it got late and the sun went down we started telling spooky stories about the cars that came into the station to get gas. The cars would be filled with "dead people" all cut and bloody who would try to pull me into the car, but I would always escape and with tires smoking they would scream out of the driveway and down the highway.

There was a knock at the cabin door and when I opened the door there was my mother with two pizzas she had made, homemade from scratch.

Those were lean years for most people and for us. My mom would get the government surplus food that President Kennedy had released to the people, the flour she used for the pizza crust and canned tomatoes for the sauce and the government cheese that topped it off. My mom was such a great cook. Our little truck stop restaurant was famous because of it.

All the girls owned their own horses or at least a pony, but that night I was one of the richest girls in the group.

My mother told us that she was going to have another baby. I was upset and happy at the same time.

I came home from school and opened the door to the cabin, and there was blood all over the floor. I screamed and yelled for my mom. She answered from her room. I opened the door and she was crying, and there was blood all over her bed and a huge clot that looked like liver. She said, "I need help; call 911."

While we were waiting for whoever 911 would bring, I started cleaning up the blood. I didn't want the small children to see it. Sheets and towels full of blood went into the wringer washer. I washed my mother up as good as possible. Well, it looked much better, and I sat down to calm down. I could hear the sirens and then the knock at the door. There was an ambulance and police. They put her on a stretcher and asked me what had happened. I explained how I found her when I came home from school and showed them the sheets in the washer. I heard the officer gasp. Since no one said anything to help me feel less frightened, I feared the worst, but then I heard someone say, "I hear two heartbeats. She's having twins."

"Praise the Lord," I said in a very weary voice, and that was how I came to find out about Baby A and Baby B.

After five pints of blood and a Caesarian birth, we prepared for the coming home of a mother and two babies. I didn't know much about getting everything ready, only that everything had to be clean and no germs.

I also had to clean the goat's and chicken's pens. Everything went into the garden. My father would say, "We grow clean food – we only use poop." My dad had gotten some horse manure in the spring, and I could tell the strawberries loved it. I was going to see my mother so I made her some yogurt and got a bowl of blackberries from the garden to lie on top – her favorite. I started with goat's milk and brought it to a boil. When it cooled down I put in starter and powdered milk and thickened it to Mother's liking. I put the jars in a water bath in a roaster and voila, in the morning there was yogurt.

Many Surgeries and Running Track
By Michael R. Miller of Ludington,
Michigan
Born 1951

As an infant, I was diagnosed as having cerebral palsy after my mother noticed that I moved my left arm but not my right. As a child, I had periodic appointments with an orthopedist in Muskegon, Michigan, named Douglas Giese. I had two surgeries on my right foot and leg, one in June 1962 and the other in June 1964. They were intended to correct leftward turning of my right foot and to enable me to land on my right heel when I walked. Before these surgeries, I wore orthopedic shoes. A flexible metal cord connected the right shoe to a wide leather belt about my waist.

I've had a number of eye surgeries in Lansing, Michigan. One, in 1968, was intended to correct strabismus, but I still don't have binocular vision.

In medical terminology, what I have is cerebral palsy with right spastic hemiplegia, or spastic cerebral palsy affecting my right limbs. In 2008, I learned that this caused my right leg to be two centimeters shorter than my left. My body had adapted to this, but after age fifty, the adaptation began to break down, resulting in scoliosis, spinal stenosis, and degenerative spondylolisthesis, which is a pain in the back, caused by displacement of a lumbar vertebra, especially the fifth (L5), but sometimes L3 or L4. These conditions led to pain in my left thigh as I walked and numbness in my left foot and leg up to my knee. The numbness spread to my right foot. I opted to have back surgery. On November 9, 2009, back surgery was performed on me at Munson Medical Center by two surgeons, a neurosurgeon, and an orthopedist. Munson Medical Center is in Traverse City, Michigan. The neurosurgeon said I would need to wear a back brace for the rest of my life, though most people have to wear one for three or four months after surgery. On April 19, 2010, the orthopedist said I had fully recuperated. He prescribed physical therapy. I still do the back exercises.

In 1959, my tonsils were removed. Ether was used as an anesthetic. I screamed and put up a fuss, but I was easy to hold down. I was only seven.

I remember swimming at the Sable River outlet at Ludington State Park and swimming in Lake Michigan and sometimes at Hamlin Lake. I remember hiking on the trails in Ludington State Park, playing badminton in the yard, mowing the yard, and getting tiger lily stains on my shirt in August. I remember attending Scout meetings at James Golden Hall by the old St. Simon's Church, Boy Scout camping trips on the weekends, and Gerber Scout camp in northern Muskegon County. When we went winter camping, my feet got very cold one time.

Sometimes we asked Dad to show "pictures on the wall." They were photos Dad had taken that were put on the slide projector.

I also remember the old St. Stan's Parochial School. It had three rooms for grades one through eight. I was there for grades three through eight. It was run by nuns, Felician Sisters. They were very strict with a reputation for being the "marines" of nuns. If a student got on their bad side (the nuns' that is) they tended to stay there. As I recall, I managed to avoid this. Some kids weren't so lucky. A nun might get on a kid's case for mispronunciations, i.e. saying "trespisses" instead of "trespasses." One nun told a story about a family who went riding in their car on Sunday instead of going to mass. Their car had a traffic accident. Everyone in the family was killed and they all were condemned to hell for skipping mass. How the nun knew this, I have no idea. They would have us learn a song in Polish though there were those of us who had no idea what the words meant.

I attended St. Simon's High School as a freshman during 1966-1967, the last year St. Simon's had a high school. Since I was new and different, some of the students treated me as an outsider. For some reason, I decided to try out for the track team. I was accepted, maybe because St. Simon's High School was very small. I remember competing in a race at Oriole Field. When all the other runners had finished, I had just completed three laps, but I was determined to finish. I finished. It must have so impressed a writer for the local paper, the *Ludington Daily News*, that he mentioned it in an article. I think his surname was Danz. I don't remember the date. It was during the spring of 1967.

My Army Time Paid Off in a Family
By Louis H. Witting of Saginaw, Michigan
Born 1933

It was the year 1954. I was a supply sergeant stationed in Alaska during the Korean War and was coming home to Saginaw because my mother had a stroke and was in serious condition. After my time with Mom, I was sent to the Detroit area to an Army AAA outfit.

One of my army buddies was from Marlette, a town in thumb of Michigan. He had dated a girl in high school whose parents were now living not too far from our camp. When he called to say hello to them they

Louis and his wife, Marilyn Witting in 1955

259

invited him over for coffee and I went along. When we got there, we found out his old girlfriend was living with them along with her two little children after a recent divorce.

The two little ones and I hit it off immediately and from then on when I got time off from camp I had a special place to be. My little buddies were waiting. All four of us would go for rides using her car and since gas was so cheap then we would ride and sing. Long story shortened – we became a real family. My army time finished and I moved my family to Saginaw to be near my mom.

We added four more to our family and after 60 years of marriage, I would say my army time was well worth it.

Standish in the Forties and Fifties
By Alex Zawacki of Bentley, Michigan
Born 1939

Standish has changed dramatically in number and kinds of businesses from the mid-forties through the fifties. There were seven car dealers. B.J. Senske sold Hudsons, and Miscisins sold Kaiser and Frazer and in 1955 changed to selling Mercurys. Major Auto sold Pontiacs and Buicks as well as GMC and International trucks. Vics Sales and Service sold Oldsmobiles. Irelands sold Ford cars and trucks, and Pomeroys sold Chevrolet and Cadillac. Where the Chinese restaurant is now a dealer sold Plymouth and Dodge as well as Dodge trucks. Where Richardsons is now was a Chrysler and DeSota dealer. If you wanted a Nash, you could go to Nagys in Sterling. Later on Major Auto sold Ramblers.

There was a wide variety of tractor and farm implement dealers. B.J. Senske sold Fergusons and Olivers. Miscisins sold Allis-Chalmers and Case early on. The Case rep came along one day and told Sam the Allis-Chalmers would have to go if they were going to sell Case. Sam told the Case rep to get lost. Along in the fifties Miscisins picked up Duetz and later Kubota. Major Auto sold Farmalls and International equipment. Al Guisdala sold John Deere and across the street Irelands sold Ford tractors and equipment. If you wanted Case, you could go to Valley Auto sales in Pinconning. If you wanted Minneapolis Moline, Nagys in Sterling would sell you tractors and implements.

There was a wide variety of service stations as well. When Sam Miscisin first went into business, he sold gas from pumps in front of the store. Cavalier gas was available on the south end of town. Sinclair was sold just south of Forwards, Majors sold Total just across the street, and Forwards sold Shell. At the intersection of US 23 and M 61 Rex Allen sold Mobil, Mr. Perrin sold Sunoco, and Fletchers sold Texaco. Wiltes Insurance location was a gas station. Trading Post sold Gulf and just to their north was a Bay station. Art Trombley sold gas and automotive parts on the curve. If I remember right that was twelve places to buy gas and lubricants.

Take your pick on where to buy groceries. The A&P was located just south of the US 23 and M 61 intersection. On Cedar, there was Martin and Reed IGA, across the street was another grocery store. On Forest just north of Cedar was Kutz Groceries. South on Forest was Henry Wajda next to the pool hall, and on down Cedar was John Gwisdala groceries. Back out on US 23 the North Forest Restaurant was a grocery store and across on the west side of 23 was Babas groceries. That makes eight that I remember.

There was four clothing stores within a stone's throw of each other. Sol Marks was on the northwest corner of Cedar and Forest, diagonally across was Harry Blumenthal, Muellers was where Normans finished up and across the street was Peoples Clothing.

There was a Western Auto store run by Elmer Pestrue and his wife, and across on the corner was a Gambles store. There was a Consumers Power Store next to Peoples on Cedar where you could buy electric appliances and pay your electric bill. Consumers also had a utility repair station just east of the fair grounds.

Steve Bernatowicz had a drug store where the Granton is. He had a very nice soda bar in there as well. Across the street was Page Rexall drug store and next to that on the corner was State Bank of Standish. There were two dry cleaners. Blakes was located between Gwisdalas and the Arenac Independent and the other was out on 23 next to Babas Grocery.

There were two creameries that received cream from producers. One was where the bank is now, and the other, a smaller one, was on Forest across from where the bowling alley was before it burned. That creamery also bought eggs. The Michigan Milk Producers receiving station was on US 23. It last served as a tire warehouse for Spartan Tires.

There were two grain receiving elevators, one on each side of the railroad. Baum Bean and Grain was on the west side of the railroad and Mitrzyks on the east side behind the A&P Store. The locker plant was located in what is now Fergie's. Before home freezers became popular, people rented freezer locker space for their frozen foods.

The Lee Haddix and Sons lumberyard was located in what are now the Forward Corporation offices. They also built cabinets, railings, and even small trailer houses.

There were at least five churches, two Catholic, two Methodist, and a Polish National. There were three bars in town, Reds on Cedar, Summer Trail Inn, which was a hotel and North End, both on US 23. The post office later became Dr. Brummer's dentist office. The Y Drive-In was a popular place for us then teenagers to gather. The building is still there just north of the Y. Also on the Y, now Richardson's used cars was the Post House. It served Greyhound travelers. Its downfall was the Trading Post Restaurant retained the ticket franchise, and you couldn't get a bus ticket at the Post House. It later burned down.

The Standish Hospital, which is now apartments I believe, was right across from Sequin Lumber. Ed Kiley's coal yard was trackside where Sequin Warehouse now sits. In the forties, farmers unloaded their sugar beets into railroad cars by hand at this location.

There were five gasoline and petroleum products distributors. Ben Good delivered Texaco, Rex Allen delivered Mobil, Burt Palmer delivered Standard, Forwards delivered Shell, and Trading Post delivered Gulf. Up 23 across from St. Florian's Church was Symborski's Greenhouse and Flower Shop. On up farther was the Standish Livestock Yard where you could sell your livestock. There were two beer and wine distributors. One was located just west of the VFW hall and the other was just across 23.

This was Standish as I remember it from the mid-forties through the fifties. I know I haven't covered all the business. I've tried to cover most of them from sixty to seventy years ago. You could get most everything you wanted or needed right there in Standish.

My Family's Country Store
By Mary McKenna Bremer of Saginaw, Michigan
Born 1929

This is a story of a large family. We had a large country store. It was not like the country stores of today, meaning we sold everything. In addition to groceries, there was clothing, boots, shoes, and dry goods. There was a large bolt rack with bolts of all sizes. The farmers would use those to fix their equipment. There were small barrels of nails of all sizes.

Items such as sugar, brown sugar, oatmeal, flour, etc., did not come prepackaged in those days. It came in very large bags. We would package it in small paper bags of one pound, two pounds, or five pounds. They were tied with string and put on the shelf for sale.

Vinegar was in a large wooden barrel with a pump on top. Customers would bring their own bottle or a jug to be filled by pumping the vinegar out of the barrel. Oil for cars was also pumped out of a barrel.

There was a gasoline pump and a kerosene pump in front of the store. As I remember it, the gas was ten gallons for one dollar. The kerosene was used for lamps to light homes, as there was no electricity in the rural areas then.

At the store, we had our own electricity "plant," which was a large motor in the

McKenna Store in Clare County, MI

261

The McKenna family

basement. Dad would go down there to start it every evening and I suppose in the morning too on the short daylight days. When the store closed at night the lights were shut off, and we used kerosene lamps upstairs.

There were some benches in the store, and the neighbors would gather there to visit.

The farmers would bring their cream to the store. My father would test it in a centrifuge. It was a large, round kettle like appliance. It had small cups around the inside edge. A sample from each can of cream was placed in those cups. A hand crank operated the centrifuge. When it was spun out, it showed the richness of the cream. The farmers would be paid accordingly.

About twice a week, Dad would load up all the cream cans and also eggs that he bought from the farmers. He would take it to the Seidel Creamery Company and sell it to them. He would be paid for it, and he would get fresh butter from them to sell in the store. He would then go to the Lee and Cady Grocery Company and buy groceries to restock the shelves.

We had a large walk-in icebox in the store. In the wintertime, my dad, brothers, and a neighbor or two would go to Budd Lake in Harrison. They would cut large blocks of ice and bring them back to a burned out stone house about a half mile from the store. The ice was stored there under a thick layer of sawdust.

My mother always worked in the store. In between customers, she would make some of our clothes on a treadle sewing machine

Dad had a baseball team made up of him, my brothers, and neighbors. On Sundays, they would play against other teams in the area. When the game was played at our place, my brother Bill would set up a stand to sell homemade ice cream and homemade root beer and candy. We younger kids thought he should give us stuff for free. When he refused, we threw rocks at his makeshift tent!

When we wanted ice cream, we would pull our little red wagon up the road to where the ice was stored. We would get a block of ice, put it in a gunnysack, and pull it back home in the wagon. We had an old-fashioned ice cream maker. First, we had to break up the ice. This was done by smacking the ice inside the bag with a flat side of an axe! Then a mixture of milk, cream, eggs, and sugar went into the container in the center. The ice was packed on the outside, and we took turns turning the crank until it was done. Then we got to get a penny's worth of peanuts to put on top of our dish of ice cream.

Life was Great in Newaygo
By Nancy Carlson of Newaygo, Michigan
Born 1933

Newaygo is on along the Muskegon River, and the downtown main street goes through the valley, across the river, and up the north side. There the road goes north and west.

When we first moved to Newaygo, we lived on the west road next to the Catholic cemetery just inside the city limits. The school was across the river and up the huge hill. I was in third grade and my brother was in second grade. We had to walk to school, and at noontime we had to walk back home for lunch, because we lived inside the city limits. Our cousin Ken went to the school superintendent and raised hob about us not being able to ride the school bus and carry our lunches. After about two or three weeks we were able to do both.

After a year, we moved downtown next to the Matthew Auto Shop. Being downtown was my cup of tea. There were a lot of old ladies on our street and the first day of May, I made Mayday baskets for all the old ladies. I would sneak up to their doors and put the basket on the door, knock, and run and hide in the bushes to see them when they came to answer their door and find their baskets filled with May flowers. They seemed to enjoy their finds.

I got to be friends with most of them. At one home, I helped put together puzzles, and they always had chocolates that I really did not care for. One other lady had her daughter living with her who was a little slow. We just visited, and I did help her rake leaves and pick up her black walnuts in the fall. Another had a daughter who had a mental problem and was fascinated with the local banker and wanted to marry him. She even bought a dress to get married in. There were a couple of others but we usually just visited.

My favorite was Cora. I still call her my best lady friend. I spent hours at their home. I loved the way she dressed: rings on every finger, even her thumbs; two or three necklaces; always a broach; and dangling earrings that hung to her shoulders. Her earlobes were very long. She gave me a beautiful ring, and I was thrilled. I still have it today.

There was one lady on our street who did not like any of us kids when we roller-skated on her side of the street. The reason we did skate there was because the elm tree roots had lifted the sidewalks on our side, and it was impossible to skate there. Well, she always screamed at us and one day I yelled back, "Go paint your face, old lady!" I'm sure she called Mom, and I have to think Mom said something close to what I said.

In the fall, we would rake our neighbors' leaves, and at night make a bonfire and roast apples or potatoes. They were really nice people to put up with us kids.

My mother decided to keep me warmer in the winter and make me some flannel underwear. She did not or would not use a pattern. Those flannel underpants were so wide all my skirts looked like I wore a short hoop under them.

We had a wringer washer like everyone else, and I loved to help putting the clothes through the wringer. I did catch my hand in it, and Mom lost a small chunk of hair. My aunt had her blouse get caught, and one of her breasts got pinched.

We neighbor kids had green apple battles every year, and during World War II, we played army on the hill behind our homes. We fought the Japanese with great gusto and tromped the Germans, too. We fought with heart, and when the war ended, we ran up and down the street for a long time yelling hooray.

Dad rented a cottage at Pickerel Lake when I was going into seventh grade. My dad and my uncle had a roofing business. The second day we were there Dad came to the cottage with his head all swathed in bandages. They had been roofing a building with tar, the tar bucket rope came loose, the bucket fell flat to the ground, and just as Dad looked over the roof edge, the tar came up and caught the right side of his face. He sat up every night we were there just holding his head in his hands. I felt so sorry for him. He died when he was 90, and sometimes he would still get a bit of tar out when cleaning his ears. A couple of days after Dad got hurt, I was swinging on a rope and lost my grip and came face down on a log and put my teeth through my bottom lip. We never rented a cottage again.

My brother and I would swim in the Brooks Creek behind the factory, and I would swim out to the lower bridges pilings. I could not swim on top of the water but could under, so I would swim as far as I could then push up for a breath and go back under until I got out there. Newaygo had a dam at that time, and the water was fast. We never told Mom.

Hess Lake is about three miles from Newaygo and there were three resorts where you could go swimming. Two of them had water slides. Our family went to the North Shore to go swimming. Mom took me with her to ride a sled down. We breezed down way out on the water. The sled went under and so did I. I could hear Mom yelling Nancy but I couldn't come up, because she had her hand on my head. She thought she was holding the sled. My mother never learned to swim.

My brother had gotten a BB gun for his birthday. The neighbor boy and I talked Wayne into letting us shoot an apple off his head. We only got a couple of shots off before we got yelled at.

There was a boy in our neighborhood that thought he was kind of a sissy and we fought a lot. One day I said to him, "Let's kiss and make up." He agreed so I said to him shut your eyes, and when he did I punched him in the nose, and boy did the blood fly. I am still ashamed of doing that.

Dad got a Willy's coupe car for my brother. We were in high school. We had a terrible snowstorm the night before and school was closed. That was the only time school was closed when I was in school. We took the Willy out in the country to an unpaved road and spent a whole afternoon taking turns driving it into huge snowbanks. The passenger had to push the car out and then it was your turn to drive.

I think about times when we were in grade school and in the winter, we spent many an evening tying one another up and then you got to tie up the other. Fun things like that plus books and puzzles kept us busy.

Our home was kiddie corner from the train depot. My parents never had an alarm clock. For us to get to school we ran up a path behind the neighbors behind us and then ran a city block to the school. Mom would wake us up about 8:15 a.m. and we would run, and I was never late for school. We never ate breakfast.

In high school, the waste paper baskets were about three and a half feet high and about twenty inches across. I was five feet one inch tall and weighed ninety pounds. One of the class clowns and upperclassmen would grab me and stuff me in the wastebasket. There was no way I could get out, and someone kind would rescue me. Our lady principal stood about six feet and was nice and slender. Keith would stuff her in the basket but she could pull herself up and get one of her legs out. This guy also locked me in the chemistry room dark room. The superintendent heard me pounding on the door. When he opened it he said, "What were you doing in there?" I replied, "Why would I lock myself in a dark room?"

There was a lot to do in our little town. The movies changed three times a week. In the summer we roller skated at the South Shore Rink at Hess Lake and in summer, my dad and his friend ran dances at North Shore Pavilion and in the winter either at Grand, Ravanna, Baily, and Newaygo. There was always something to do. Life was great.

Middleton – My Hometown
By Ruth Ann Bradley of St. Johns, Michigan
Born 1938

Middleton is a small town or village, but to a young child it was wonderful. There used to be two grocery stores, a church, a hardware, a drug store, a bank, Dr. Ed's office, gas stations, plus the school. The restaurant, now the Middleton Diner, was where I had

Great Grandpa Harley Redman, Grandpa Earl Redman, Bobbie, and Daniel

my first Coke. The band members were given a free Coke after performing at the Saturday evening talent show.

My brother then, Bobbie, raised many white rabbits with pink eyes upstairs in our granary. He sold them at Shady Nook Farms and bought his bicycle. My sister and I worked in the garden and earned a girls bike. That was special.

Our family didn't have much but we were happy. We had an outhouse until after I married and moved east of Maple Rapids. Toilet paper was a luxury. We knew which pages of the Penny's catalog worked best. In the wintertime, our trips to the outhouse were quick.

When Bobbie was little, he had some little patches of dirt, his "farms," where he played with his toy John Deere equipment. When he had his tonsils out, my parents got him a toy manure spreader.

In the summertime, we walked with the neighbor girls to the corner to catch the Bible school bus, but we probably had purple mouths. We enjoyed some mulberries as we passed my grandparents' place.

Since Grandpa and Grandma lived only a fourth of a mile north of us, we walked down there often, but I got poison ivy several times as it was on the east side of the road. Once I had poison ivy blisters on my behind and missed the first week and a half of the second grade. As I got older, I was given shots for poison ivy.

Our little church was very important to us. I remember after I was ready for church I'd swing under the tree until we left in the old Model T. As a preschooler, I remember falling asleep lying in the pew during Sunday evening service. Our junior class had to learn and recite a Bible verse for the congregation. We kids learned pieces, had plays, sang specials, and played the piano. We loved our family church.

We often had the preacher's family over on Sunday for a chicken dinner. Mom could catch, kill, and prepare the large rooster. It would hang headless from the clothesline for a short time.

Speaking of the Model T, we used to pick up an elderly man walking to church. He rode on the running board. I remember after service some of the young boys would go out to the old car and honk the horn, just to hear the sound. I was embarrassed.

My sister and I used to ride bikes the two and a half miles to clean our church. She rode Bobbie's bike. After we graduated, our cousins had the job.

Our cousins lived a half mile away by way of the lane and fields. One time I was going to visit them, and I spotted a dead garter snake and took it to scare them.

Perrinton was a mile away and I attended first, fourth, and fifth grades, and high school there. We walked uptown at noon there, also. All of us kids had Mrs. Sininet, Mrs. Killon, and Mrs. Hinton. We probably had forty students in each class back then. If a person misbehaved, they'd have to stand next to the

Ruth Ann with her husband, Bob and sons, Lynn and Keith in 1962

blackboard with their nose in a circle or sit in the corner. I had a good friend in Perrinton. I'd spend nights with her and go to the basketball tournament games.

My dad was instrumental in starting the Fulton Clippers 4-H Club. We had many different projects to choose from. I took food preparation, sewing, flower gardening, pigs, and then dairy. My cupcakes did poorly as the tops were like little mountains, but I did pretty good with most project exhibits. I still have my 4-H ribbons. 4-H is wonderful. When we went to the fair at Alma, we took a lunch. It was a special treat to buy a giant Nehi orange or grape pop.

I had wonderful 4-H leaders. I've sewed many clothing articles in my lifetime. At our dairy club meeting, we played softball along with learning how to care for our animals. My calf's name was Pansy. The neighbor girls had Daisy and Petunia. Bobbie's calf was named Evelyn. Each night at the fair, we paraded our animals in front of the grandstand. Evelyn being a real young heifer lay down while walking. She was cute. My brother and I had milking short horned heifers. My dad liked them. I did chores morning and evening, fed calves and bedding them with clean straw. I also fed and watered the chickens and gathered eggs.

Back to Middleton, when I learned to drive, Mom would let me drive there for some

Mary Lou and Ruth Ann Redman in 1952

groceries. It was two and a half miles. When I was younger, I even got some new shoes at Glaziers store; one side was groceries and the other side dry goods. Us kids could also walk up town on our noon hour for one-cent bubble gum or a nickel candy bar. School was from nine to four and we rode in red, white, and blue school buses.

I remember when I was a freshman I'd taken a pie to home ec as my home project. Coming home on the bus the glass pie dish broke, and I threw the pieces out the window. How naughty of me!

Now in 2015, my husband and I are still enjoying a good meal at the Middleton Diner along with our three children and their spouses, our eight grandchildren and their spouses, and our three great-grandchildren.

A Hardworking Dad and a Stylish Mom
By Doris Murry of Saginaw, Michigan
Born 1949

I was born in Saginaw, Michigan, on July 3, 1949. My dad, mom, and older brother migrated here from Mississippi in order for my father to find work in the foundries. Times were hard in those days because the plants didn't pay a lot, and they were always on strike.

We lived in a tiny two-bedroom house in the country area that is now called the boondocks. There were six of us in the family – dad, mom, three boys, and one girl (myself). I was the second child. That house was so small but Mother made it into a charming home.

We had an oil heater and inside running water, but we had an outhouse. Most of the time we used a chamber pot inside. We were fortunate; the people next door burned coal and wood for their heat, and they had no running water. They used an outside pump to get water.

I always helped my friend do her chores in exchange for some of the best chili I ever tasted that her mom made.

The winters were cold and brutal and it seems like I never had to use the outhouse until night came. My oldest brother used to have to wake up and stand at the door. Boy, was he ever mad.

Sometimes my stomach would be upset because of the green apples we ate, even though we were warned not to. There was an orchard at the end of our road that was filled with apple, pear, peach, and cherry trees. Once I ate green apples and had to be rushed to the hospital by ambulance. I was unconscious for three days. They thought I was going to die. The green apples had given me diarrhea and then pneumonia. But through prayer, I pulled through. No more green apples for me.

Dad made sure we stayed healthy by giving us big doses of cod liver oil and castor oil.

I was fortunate to have a good hardworking dad who instilled in us good values. I can still feel the wind in my face, as I would run down the dusty road to meet him when he got out of work. After working hard all week, he used to like to go out on Saturday nights. Saginaw was filled with places to go and have a good time.

Mom always stayed home preparing Sunday dinner. She never missed church, and she never missed washing and straightening my hair with a pressing comb. Oh, how I hated it.

Mom was a very stylish woman and dressed beautifully, and she expected the same thing from me. She wore beautiful clothes and fur pieces with eyes and tails on them.

She would be up late listening to Randy's on the radio, a station from Nashville that played the latest rhythm and blues and gospel records.

We had to heat our water and take our baths on Saturday night and be ready for church in the morning. Tabernacle Baptist Church used to be so hot with people falling out and shouting when they caught the Holy Ghost.

We had a wringer washer in which my brother got his arm caught. He was always doing something. One time he almost drowned in a swimming hole that our parents warned us not to go near.

Once, the lady next door told him to go light her cigarette when he was only about five years old. He accidently dropped the paper he was using almost burned their house to the ground. They had to move in with us until their house got rebuilt. Talk about crowded. But it was a fun time.

People in those days cared about one

another. No one locked their doors. It was nothing to borrow sugar or flour from your neighbor. The neighbor lady down the street could whip your behind, and you'd get it again when you got home.

Sometimes we ate Sunday dinner at my aunt's house. She was one of the first women who worked at the malleable iron plant during World War II. She made ammunition and car parts. Her place was small but we all gathered there to feast on some good soul food; fried chicken, dressing, collard greens, and peach cobbler. We topped it off with homemade ice cream that we took turns churning until our arms felt like they would fall off.

Our community was made up of black, Hispanic, Germans, Polish, and Indians. But we all got along. I don't remember any racial tension in those days. Race wasn't discussed in our home, just pride and love.

We went to a little almost one-room schoolhouse. They finally built a newer one that wasn't much larger but we had separate rooms. It was a good school with dedicated teachers.

To get to school we would cut through fields, jump ditches, go through a farmer's field that we called the back tracks. He had a no trespassing sign up but we had to take the chance because we didn't want to be late for school.

My kindergarten teacher was Miss Burt. She would tap your fingers with a big black wooden pencil if you didn't write your ABCs right. Boy, did that hurt. My favorite teacher was my third grade teacher, Mrs. Little. She was a beautiful classy lady who was like a mother to us. She would teach English and math, but she would also tell the older boys about their hygiene, especially when it got warm.

People in those days cared about one another. They took turns taking care of their elderly neighbors. No one went to the nursing home in those days.

We would spend hours on hot summer nights with a fire going with old rags smoking the mosquitos away, telling stories, or running around playing hide and go seek. This was a time when kids really played out of doors. We climbed trees, played marbles, jacks, cowboy and Indians, jumped rope and hula hooped, played baseball, or just raced against each other. We had paper dolls, coloring books, or played house, but we was not going to be in "no" house. You went outdoors!

I remember trips to the Wenonah Beach in the weekends and cookouts on the Bay City Highway. They used to baptize in the Saginaw River.

I will never forget how downtown would be decorated so beautifully at Christmas time.

I remember going to town, passing by the Wickes Building, and seeing the women come out dressed up with their white gloves on and thinking I'm going to work there one day, and one day I did. I was among the first of the minorities to work at Wickes Corporation.

I remember playing with my brothers when I was about six years old, and I heard a voice calling my name. I told my mother and father, and they told me I was going to be a preacher one day, and now I am a preacher some 57 years later. Yes, those were the good old days!

How Dad Got Rid of the Mouse
By James M. Shoup of Custer, Michigan

"I've got to get rid of that vermin," Dad said, sitting in the dining room on that very cold winter night. "We can't let that thing keep getting' our stuff, Louisa. That pest will cost us a fortune, come spring."

We had just finished supper late on a Friday night. The cold wind was rattling the storm windows, but the wood stove in the center of the room kept us warm as a nest of rabbits. Oak and maple were Dad's favorite burning wood, but we also used poplar. Poplar was called go-fer wood because it was said it burned so fast someone was always needing to go-fer more.

"I like burnin' poplar on a night like this," Dad said. "It is so warm. And I enjoy choppin' it when it's so cold. It splits so nice and easy."

"And that's where you should be," Mom said. "You should be out doin' chores and gettin' the wood in."

Dad and Mom usually sat at the table for a last cup of coffee as some of us would clean the table.

"Fill our cups, would ya', Florine?" Dad said to my oldest sister. "And get the cream back out of the icebox."

We had our own cows so anyone drinking

coffee at our house always put thick real cream in it. Often sipping the last cup of steaming coffee Mom and Dad would tell stories of the old days.

This night Dad was telling me some stories of him and his brother Boyd when young and hunting and trapping on their farm near Tallman.

"I didn't know you hunted when you were young," I said to Dad.

"Oh, yes," Dad said, "when I was about your age…"

"You mean eight years old?" I interrupted.

"Yes, about eight years old," Dad said. "I used to go with Grandpa to trap game. We'd go back to the creek. You know, where your Uncle Boyd lives now, and we'd walk the deep snow to get to the Weldon Creek. Grandpa had traps there to catch muskrat and mink. I began to use a gun then and would shoot rabbit, skunk, squirrel, and coon. We'd eat the meat and sell the pelts."

I did not know my dad hunted when he was only my age. I did know when he grew up he hunted deer. Now he would go with family up in Ward Hills to hunt deer. That's where the deer were in burned over forest land. Dad would hunt, but my uncles and aunts would get the deer. Dad never seemed to get any.

"Why don't you ever hunt much anymore?" I asked Dad. "You go hunting with Uncle Bob and Aunt Charity and Uncle James and Uncle Boyd. You're now taking Brother Billy with you. But you only deer hunt."

I asked him why when he was a kid he hunted squirrel, possum, coon, and rabbits, but now he hunted none of these. I looked at Dad sipping steaming coffee. Dad did not answer me, and the steam from the cup circled up past his face. The steam from the hot coffee formed a fog over his head; a head of jet-black hair combed straight back. He sat staring at the table. He didn't speak. I guess he was just thinking.

I broke the silence. "I guess you just ain't got any time now, huh, Dad?" I said.

I used to wish my dad would come home with a big buck on the car fender like we saw on other cars going down the road past our house. I had hoped when he went to Ward Hills to hunt where the deer seemed to be that he would come home with something I could brag about at school to my friends. Their dads were always getting deer, rabbits, raccoons,

and game from trapping mink or muskrat or beaver. Instead, my dad would come home and tell us how the big buck he shot at fell down but got back up and ran over the hill out of sight.

I recalled how dad told me about wounding a big buck, but it ran and another hunter got it. Or dad would see a huge buck, but too far away to shoot. So every year we would watch at dusk in the autumn weather for dad to drive in with a buck. Each year was the same – no deer.

Ma would say to Dad, "How do you expect to get one? You don't practice until the day before hunting season. Our neighbors are target practicing all year. Maybe that's why you don't get a deer. And heaven knows we can sure use the meat."

Dad just looked at Mom and said, "It isn't all that, Louisa. Maybe they're just plain luckier. Besides, I can't afford to shoot up more money in shells than the deer is worth."

Dad stood up from the table pushing his chair back. "As I said a while back, Jimmy, we have to get rid of that vermin. It's coming up through the basement. It comes in the dining room and scoots behind one of the cupboards or the icebox. Then it gets into the cupboard and eats our breakfast oatmeal. Now it's getting into the crackers, and I found some leavings in the bread box and the pile of old papers by the door."

"Can't you get it with a trap?" I asked.

"I've tried that and it is awfully smart," Dad said. "I put good, new cheese on the trap. It nibbles the cheese off and doesn't spring the trap. Or it gets away before the trap springs."

"How many nights have you put traps out?" I wondered.

"Been setting traps every night this week," Dad said. "I take all the precautions. I strike a match and burn all odors off'n it just like my dad taught me when I was your age. I use fresh cheese because they always like fresh cheese. I put the traps right where his path is between the cupboards and icebox. I wouldn't have to do that because I know this one would find the cheese anywhere, but I do it not taking any chances. I even have used those new all metal traps alongside the usual wooden ones. It finds the trap, eats the cheese, and leaves."

"Don't it ever spring the traps?" I asked.

"Oh, yes," Dad said. "It springs the trap

Many times, but it is too smart. It always gets away. And other times it cleans the trap of cheese and never springs the trap."

It was getting later and time for bed. The upstairs in the old farmhouse was unheated. I climbed into bed with younger brother Danny. I heard Dad leave the house. I heard him chopping wood at the woodshed. Two chops on a red oak. Three chops on a white oak. One for a maple. I could tell which kind of wood Dad was splitting by listening to the sound of the axe hitting the wood in the freezing cold night. I looked out the upstairs window at a dark sky, but with some stars. I covered my head with the warm blanket. I fell asleep listening to Dad chopping wood.

Saturday mornings we could sleep late to "catch up on lost sleep" as Mom would say. I awoke early anyway. It was still dark and quiet but I could hear Dad moving around downstairs. I could smell coffee. Going downstairs, I heard Dad fixing breakfast. He was making oatmeal on the kitchen range, which was snapping from a hot fire. Dad and I were the only ones up. Dad took the pan of hot oatmeal and shoved it to the back of the range.

James's Pa

"Help yourself to some hot oatmeal," Dad said, "and here's the milk."

He handed me the quart glass milk bottle filled with our own cow's milk. Thick cream was on top of the milk so I shook the bottle well to mix the cream and milk before pouring it on my hot cereal.

Dad and I took our bowls of cereal and sat at the dining room table. The kitchen was not large enough to house a table. Dad also had the dining room stove going already.

"Guess what I got," Dad said, setting his coffee cup down. "Go ahead and guess what I got after you went to bed."

"I know," I said, swallowing some hot meal, "I bet you got a new calf in the barn. I bet Tinsel had her calf."

Dad laughed a slight laugh. "Naw, it wasn't Tinsel. She's still trying to hold out on us. Go ahead and guess again."

I did not think baby pigs or a new colt were due yet, but I guessed them anyway. I tried to think of what new thing we could have gotten, finally giving up.

"Well, well," Dad said with a grin, "you giving up? Well, you go ahead and finish your breakfast and then I'll show you what I got after you went to sleep."

He did not wait for me to finish breakfast, though. He reached over to the corner behind him by the good dishes cupboard and picked up Billy's new BB gun. He held the gun over the table in front of me.

"You mean you shot a mouse with Billy's BB gun?" I asked, getting up from the chair.

"There it is," said Dad, pointed to the mouse he left lying in back of the stove so he could show it off to us. The mouse no longer would eat our crackers. It would no longer eat the cereal or leave mouse droppings in the bread drawer.

Dad had outsmarted the mouse.

I looked at Dad still holding the gun and looking at the mouse like it was a two hundred pound, fourteen-point buck. Dad stood by me as we both looked at the mouse as if it were a dozen cottontail rabbits or backpack of squirrels.

"See this?" he said.

"Yes, I do," I said.

"Last night I came back in the house after chopping and carrying in the wood for the night and after milking the five cows and after going back out to the barn to check on Tinsel. When I came in for good," Dad said, "I heard the scratching of the mouse.

"I walked into the dining room and sat right there in the chair you're sitting in. I had set the trap earlier, but I knew I had to do something else. I saw Billy's BB gun. I figured I could still shoot pretty good, even though I don't get a deer. I put BBs in the gun. Like I said, I sat in that chair about four steps from the trap. I had the trap between the old dishes cupboard and the icebox. I figured that the mouse would come to the trap to eat the cheese. This time I would try to be the smart one."

It was just a little old field mouse. Yet, I do not know if Dad knew the feeling I had when I knew my dad shot that at four paces with a BB gun. All of a sudden, I did not care how many big bucks my friends' dads had got. I was so proud of Dad, but I did not think I best tell him. Yet, I knew Dad was proud of what he'd done, too. He just was too proud to let me know. He just smiled. I just smiled. Neither Dad nor I picked up the mouse to throw it to the cat out in the entranceway. We both wanted everyone in the house to see it. We both wanted everyone in the house to know – my pa was a hunter again.

He Gave Us Some of His Catch
By Pauline Grant of Fremont, Michigan
Born 1920

When I was a young girl, my mom was left with four little children. I was just one year old. Dad was in the barn working and he caught pneumonia. He died because there was no treatment for the disease then.

After Dad died, Mom lived with us kids for three more years on her own. We lived on a farm and depended solely on our farm produce. Our cattle gave us milk and meat and the chickens gave us eggs. There was nothing like pasteurization then. One day on our lakeside house, a man that had been fishing on the lake stopped by our house. He said he had heard how my mom was alone with four kids and struggling. He gave us some of his catch and asked if he could help clean them. My mom obliged and he did. After he was done, my mom asked if he could stay to eat some of the fish, he had just cleaned. He stayed and we

all had dinner together.

He came back with fish a few other times and he asked if he could become friends with Mom. Mom accepted and after a few months, they were married. He was such a nice man and he quickly stepped into our Dad's shoes. He made sure we were regulars at church because he was a religious man. He and Mom had three more kids and he was a good Dad to all of us children.

He died after fifteen years with Mom. Mom never remarried. At this point Mom's children were excelling and she went back to work at Gerber Products. My farm household has produced all college-educated kids. I got married and have had a beautiful life. I have four beautiful children that love me very much. I am grateful to God for all His love for me. He is my strength and Savior.

Nothing Goes to Waste
By Betty Jacobus of Fremont, Michigan
Born 1931

In the thirties, about when the war started, we had to be careful about the use of almost everything. Nothing goes to waste, to the point of eating every part of the chicken. My clothes were made out of grain sacks from our neighbor's barn.

When I went to school wearing them, people looked at me and complimented me for their bright colors and beauty. In those days, we used to wear nylons on Sundays to church. However, when the war broke out in 1941, we could not afford nylons anymore, so we would get cotton and make them look like our regular nylons. To make it resemble nylon more, we would use eye pencil to draw a line at the back of it.

Pickles
By Helen Van Andel of Fremont, Michigan
Born 1921

I was raised on a farm and believed that my father was the biggest farmer I ever knew, but not the best. We grew pickles and had to harvest them by hand.

On a very hot summer day, we had worked so hard and my Dad had taken a load of pickles to the station outside of town to be sold. Then he came back home with the whole load of pickles as a result of being rejected because they were too big. I remembered when my Dad narrated the story I was so angry that I smashed my bucket on the ground so hard that it was flat and I swore never to pick more pickles unless I was hungry. But a few years later, I had to pick pickles for groceries.

Life Has Been Fair To Me
By John Devries of Fremont, Michigan
Born 1916

I was born in Europe (Netherlands). I came to the USA with my family of six when I was only four years old. My dad's sister was the reason my parents moved to the USA. She was living somewhere around Lansing. My parents were butchers before we moved, but when we got here, they joined my aunt's business in the bakery.

When we kids grew up enough to work, we joined in the bakery shop. In 1944/1945, I joined the military as an airplane mechanic. I was honorably discharged at the end of the war in 1949. Just after my discharge from the military, I was married to my friend and soulmate that I met while at the bakery. Her name was Louise Monny. She had two boys from a previous marriage, Jack and Ron.

We had no children together but her two boys were a blessing. We were married for 44 years. She passed away at 76 years old. Life has been fair to me!

We Would Have Starved To Death
By Jeannette Johnson of Fremont, Michigan
Born 1922

Sod House- Jean remembers visiting her aunt and uncle in Montana. She stated, "I spent some days with them when I was around nine or ten years old." I remember them white washing the inside of the house and walls turning white. It was so dry and very warm. The walls were thick and the wind could not penetrate them. The house had a roof on it and they had an old black stove that you could put wood or coal in it.

Grasshopper Plague- As a little girl, she remembers the sky would darken when the grasshoppers came. They would eat everything in sight, anything green. They would get into everything. The house, food sometimes, they were everywhere. "It reminded me of the Bible when it talks about the locusts. We had to leave or we would have starved to death."

Great Depression- I didn't know we were so poor because everyone was. I remember my mother giving each of us (I had two brothers and a sister) a handful of raisins but only one small handful because we had to ration them out. The raisins came from the government because there was not fruit.

I remember walking three miles to school and I had the best teacher. In the school, we had a big black potbelly stove and a phonograph that we had to crank.

Later on, when I was working in Washington, I remember meeting Eleanor Roosevelt and my impression of her was "drab" because of what she was wearing. I like bright colors.

What a Horrific Event
By Joan S. Pavlick of Essexville, Michigan
Born 1931

I was three months shy of being eleven years old when World War II started.

My dad and uncle went in the army. My sister and I would pick up cigarette and gum wrappers off the ground, peel the silver foil from them, and make balls to be donated for the war effort.

We received thirty-five cents a week allowance and did odd jobs for extra money. We bought a couple of stamps for ten cents each and put them in a booklet toward an $18.75 war bond, which would be worth $25 when it matured.

In the middle of the war and a couple of years older, we would walk to the dairy about five blocks from our house for an ice cream cone. The dairy was on Salizburg Avenue. We passed a tall, brick, nice looking building. There was a tall fence around it, and behind the fence were young men. German POWs.

I could never find out why they were in Bay City.

After high school, I went to nursing school and became an RN. When I was in my 30s, I was talking to a male co-worker who said he and his wife lived on a small farm. He said his parents had had a large farm, and during WWII, all the young men had been drafted so the German POWs were trucked to their farm to work the fields. His mother and other ladies would prepare a noon meal for them. His parents spoke German.

One day one of the POWs asked his mother if he could hold her small blonde daughter. She said yes and the young man picked her up and started to cry. He said he had a wife and a little daughter and did not know if they were still alive.

After so many years, I knew why we had POWs in our city. What a horrific event a war is for both sides.

I also remember my dad's car with the rumble seat, which he called "The mother-in-law seat."

Wheelock Park Midland, Michigan
By Sandra Palmer Zilincik of Sanford, Michigan
Born 1950

Wheelock Park had been built as temporary housing for service men and their dependents. It was located where Cleveland Manor Apartments are now located in Midland.

It was all single level housing with a bachelor or studio apartment, or one and two bedroom apartments.

Most of the men had served in World War II or recently returned from Korea, as my father had done.

One of Dad's friends, in the small village of Newberry, in the Upper Peninsula (UP), helped get him a job at the Dow Chemical Company in Midland. This friend had been best man at Dad's wedding. Another friend from Newberry that lived in Wheelock worked at Neil Lumber.

Mom and Dad also made many new friends. One of them worked in television sales & service. My Dad purchased our first black and white TV set from him. A blond colored cabinet style with a small screen.

When the TV wasn't broadcasting any shows, it had a neat test pattern with a profile view of an Indian Chief! My parents say I would play outside the screen door and if I heard a commercial, I would run in to watch it and then return outside to play! Most commercials back then were cartoons. If any cartoons were on TV, it was usually Saturday mornings only.

It was a great place to live with lots of other children to play with. This was the beginning of the baby boomer growth! Families helped other families to survive and make a living after World War II, and the Korean Conflict.

One family next to us was from the south and my parents said before long I had a southern accent, and were saying 'you all!' This was from a Yooper who was used to her French Canadian roots and all the family members usually ending their sentences in "eh."

The families of Wheelock Park all received our milk in glass bottles from a horse drawn milk cart! The milkman driving the cart always wore a uniform and official looking hat. The horse knew all the stops along the route so the milkman hardly used the runs to direct the horse.

Eventually Wheelock Park was to be demolished and everyone had to move! My parents purchased a house in Midland County on Saginaw Road. Therefore, we moved to Mapleton in 1955 where I started kindergarten.

All the Dads in our neighborhood worked at Dow Chemical Company. We all knew when they were coming home and would need to be cleaned up for supper. They came home down Smith Crossing Road, crossing the Bailey bridge. The bridge platform was constructed of wood planks. When the car wheels drove across the bridge it made a clickety-clackety sound, you could hear for a mile in any direction. Mapleton School was a nice brick country school that use to have grades kindergarten through eighth. As the neighborhood families grew, Mapleton School became too small. After third grade, we were bussed into Midland's Longview School. It was great to make new friends. Our fourth grade teacher Mrs. Arnold would read us a chapter every day from the Laura Ingalls Wilder books. We even wrote a letter from our whole class to Laura's daughter Rose! She responded by writing back to our class.

In 1960, our family of five had outgrown

272

our little two-bedroom home in Mapleton. We moved to a three-bedroom home on Hope Road in Averill in Midland County. There were even more children to play ball with, go sledding and ice-skating, attend Brownies and Cub Scouts, and all the fun mischievous things kids did in the 1960s.

Across the road from our home were a man and his family that Dad grew up with in Newberry! It is a small world!

Two Country Stores
By Frank J. Gotts of Merrill, Michigan
Born 1953

My name is Frank Gotts and I was born in 1953. What I remember from the bygone days is the old country store. Living just in Saginaw County, Gratiot County was across the road. We had access to two country stores.

At Galloway was Henry and Clara's Wenzel's store on the Meridian Road. He also sold fuel oil for your home heat. You could see the meat man in a white coat and on his arm would be several rings of bologna. There was no wrapping on the bologna just the skin. He would take it in the store that way.

The same was true with Ladd's store at Lineport, on the corner of Van Buren and Mason Roads. You could get bubble gum for a penny, and candy bars were five cents, maybe ten cents. However, the best memory of all was this: If you didn't get what you needed by Saturday closing time, you waited until Monday morning when they reopened.

My Big Brothers
By Jack Thornton of Byron Center, Michigan
Born 1937

December 7, 1941 Japan attacked Pearl Harbor, Hawaii, and December 8, the United States declared war on Japan; December 11, the United States declared war on Germany and Italy.

I was only four years old and I did not really understand all the fuss! Family members were arriving for special dinners. Flash bulb pictures were being taken and the attention

Vern Thornton

was focused on my oldest "Big Brother," Lavergne Thornton. His nickname was Vern. He was only twenty years old, when he left Grand Rapids, Michigan. He defended his country in the Army of the United States of America.

Vern served four years. Fort Custer, Michigan; Fort Leonard Wood, Missouri; New Orleans, Louisiana; Southampton, England; at the young age of twenty-one Vern was one of the first waves who invaded the shores of Normandy is our only source of history. Vern participated in the Battle of the Bulge and continued to Cherbourg, France and Kreuzberg, Germany. He became a private first class (PFC). He was discharged October 1945.

January 6, 1943, my second "Big Brother," Robert Thornton age nineteen was inducted into the Army Air Force. Robert served in the Asiatic-Pacific, Fort Sheridan, Illinois; Great Ben, Kansas; Cuba, Salt Lake City, Utah; Tacoma, Washington; Pearl Harbor, Hawaii; and the Island of Guam.

Robert was assigned as a medical corpsman to a B-29 Squadron, being the largest bomber in WWII. I vividly remember an official army staff vehicle coming to our home with tickets and announcing that our local Majestic Theater in Grand Rapids, Michigan will be

Robert Thornton

honoring a newsreel clip of the returning B-29 squadron. We all anxiously went to the local theater and viewed many aircraft crash landings. I saw my Big Brother Robert exiting his plane, and running to help crewmembers escape from their crashed planes. Robert was discharged January 1945.

October 17, 1943 my third "Big Brother," Virgil Thornton, eighteen years old left for active service in the United States Army. Virgil served in Fort Sheridan, Illinois; Camp Grant, Illinois; Camp Reynolds, Pennsylvania; Liverpool, England; Normandy, France; and became a Corporal (CPL) and was discharged April 1, 1946.

After the invasion of France, Virgil became the Captain's personal chauffer and in bold letters below the windshield of the jeep was his mother's name, Flossie.

Soon our home felt empty. Only my parents, Flossie and Albert Thornton and I remained. I can remember three stars were placed in our living room window. Many concerned by-passers would stop and rap on the door to ask about my "Big Brothers."

It was always a fun time when one of my "Big Brothers" would come home for a furlough. I waited anxiously to see what

WWII souvenirs they might bring me. I remember they brought home K-rations and one time they brought me an Army overcoat and hat. They even taught me how to salute. I still have the red silk pillowcase my "Big Brother" sent home to my mother, which reads, "US Army" Fort Leonard Wood, MO.

In France, through the APO, Virgil was able to locate and surprise his brother Vern with weekend visit after a two-year separation. One thing my "Big Brothers" didn't appreciate about me when I was a little boy. They brought home newsreel clips that were shown in the movie theaters as active update news during the WWII era. I sold them on the corners for ten cents apiece. Oh, how I wish I had those news clips today!

I loved to sit and listen to all of my "Big Brothers" reminisce about World War II. It wasn't until just recently that my "Big Brothers" began sharing, what actually went on in the war. I deeply respect and honor each of my "Big Brothers" for their dedication and service to our country of the United States of America.

How fortunate my parents and I were to have all three of my "Big Brothers" return home safely while so many made the ultimate sacrifice, they are the Heroes. All of my "Big Brothers" were honorably discharged with many medals, which are on display in each

Vern and Virgil Thornton

of their homes. I lost my second Big Brother, Robert, November 9, 2009, and my first Big Brother, Vern, December 22, 2010. Each "Big Brother" is registered in the WWII Monument in Washington, DC.

A Small Café in Breckenridge
By Joy McCrory of Breckenridge, Michigan
Born 1935

My folks, Frank and Luella Anschutz, married in 1927 and opened a small café in Breckenridge, Michigan, which my dad bought from his mother and sister in 1919. In the late 1930s, oil was discovered in Porter Township, north of Breckenridge, where people came from all over the country to work, as they hadn't healed from the Great Depression. Business was good and my parents bought a larger building next door where they built their restaurant. They also opened a bunkhouse with food, north of Porter, as the oil workers were working twelve-hour shifts. There were some people at that time who became millionaires!

One story about the restaurant that made it all the way to Texas was when a customer came in at the community table where the singles, widows, and widowers sat. The man ordered liver and onions and found the liver to be tough. He called the waitress over to complain. Another guy got up from the table went out to his truck and brought in a chain saw. Well, he started cutting up the liver on the guy's plate. Pieces of liver were flying all over the other people at the table. Never forget that! Another story, years after my folks had passed was workers claiming they could hear talking and laughing in the basement. They would call another worker to check things out but nobody was ever in the basement. We concluded it was the voices and laughter of Frank and Luella Anschutz.

In the 1940s, Gladys McCrory came to work at the restaurant. Her son Richard came with her to dump baskets, burn papers and keep the floor clean. We married in 1956 until his death in 2006. The days were great but lots of hardships and tears too.

My parents were always helping people, whether having them work at their restaurant, or farm. They had helped a number of people get their businesses started, including Dr. Rotermund, one of the town's first doctors where my dad lent him the money to start his practice. When my mother died in 1993, many of the townspeople came to her estate sale wanting one of her handkerchiefs or teacup, just a little something to remember her for she had been good to them at one point in their lives.

My dad was also famous for keeping $1,000 dollar bills in his wallet. He loved walking up to little kids and showing them! Another tradition my dad was known for was to send a carton of cigarettes off with the boys who were going into service.

My dad liked his high stakes Friday night poker games. One poker game my dad won 20 acres in porter. I remember going there to see the new land he "bought." It was all brush and looked useless, but he managed to turn it into farmland. He didn't always do well in his poker games for there was the missing carat diamond ring, which was a present from my mother. He claimed he lost it shucking corn. He took us into the middle of the barnyard to the big pile of corn and making a big deal of looking for the ring, but we all knew it wouldn't be there. Boy was my mom mad!

My dad also had a colorful past. During prohibition, he and his sisters made moonshine until he was caught in 1927 and served two years in Ionia prison. The night he was arrested, he and my mother had had an argument earlier in the day where she went to her mother's house in Saginaw. My dad went to get her but the Feds had tracked him down-chasing and shooting at him all the way to my grandmothers. That same night, another restaurant worker who was on his way to make the night deposit, was also arrested and kept overnight for questioning at the Ithaca County Jail. They released him the next morning where he walked back to Breckenridge from Ithaca with the restaurant moneybag under his arm to give to my mother. At 20 years old, she was left to run the restaurant. My father died of cancer in 1959, however, my mother stayed active in running the restaurant until her death in 1993 at the age of 87. Anschutz Bar & Café stayed in our family for 94 years until we sold the business in 2010.

The house where I grew up on Chestnut Street was purchased from the McLean's in 1935, the year I was born. My dad also purchased 180 acres in addition to the acre the home still sits on. We had 25 brown Swiss cows, 5 horses used for hauling wagons, 25 pigs including a huge white pig which was daddy's favorite. He would sit in a lawn chair in the back of the barnyard and the pig would sit right next to him like a dog so he could scratch his head. We also had a huge bull. One day when I was three years old, I crawled underneath the fence to see the bull that kept butting me until the hired man rescued me.

In the 40s in Breckenridge, the stockyards were quite a big thing with people coming from all over the state to auction their animals and buy new ones. It caught fire and animals were burning and running wild all over town. I remember many of the elevator fires. One was the farmer's elevator located between Wright and Saginaw Street. It was full of navy beans, which they had to truck north of town-did they ever stink! That elevator never did reopen.

The Breckenridge Elevator (Crawford's Elevator) shelled corn and saved the cobs in a special bin where people with trucks and wagon would pull a rope and fill up corn cobs for free to start their home fires for cooking and heating. East across the street from the elevator was Potter's Lumberyard. It was originally a livery stable for school students and teachers. Teachers took their exams to get their teaching certificate. And there was a drive-thru for people to load their lumber and supplies and kids would walk through too on their way to school. Halfway through the building was a flowing well with the most delicious water you ever tasted. Ice cold! Above the faucet was a brass cup hanging. I don't think there was a person in town who hadn't drank out of that cup! The school was at the end of Eastman Street and held all of the kids from kindergarten to seniors until the new high school was built. All dances, proms, graduation, basketball games, etc. were held in that gymnasium. Lots of memories. On the second floor of the east end of the school was a large tube, which was for students to slide down in case of fire. Glad we didn't have to use that.

Another memory was the telephone office. It was located where Smitty's party store now sits. The telephone operator was Janet Dosson. We could call and ask for someone and she would tell us he or she had gone to Saginaw shopping etc… We could also tell her if we had calls or were at so and so's house. She had a switch she'd pull which would turn on a red light on top of the building. When the town cop drove by, he would go in to see who needed him.

Saturday nights were special. We took our blankets or rugs to watch free movies where the MAC silos now sit. Sometimes we would go to Wheeler for their free shows. Occasionally, my folks would let me go with them to the Merrill theatre for the newsreel to see news on the war. The war was scary. We would have to ration stamps to buy more things such as meat, gas, sugar, stockings and butter. They had a lottery to buy a new car, refrigerator, or other large objects. You could buy meat one day a week at the local meat market west of town, which is now Ryann's Restaurant. I remember seeing a line of people clear down to 3rd street. You couldn't buy many things, nylon stockings, for instance. Some of the women would paint a line on the back of their legs so it would look like the seam.

Most towns had a round wading pond above 12' or 15' in diameter but when the polio scare came in the 60s, the pool was closed and was later filled in with dirt. Many people were crippled for the rest of their lives. Thank goodness for vaccinations!

On the corner of M46 & 2nd Street sat an honor roll board for the men and boys in the military. The town would mourn when a gold star was placed by a name marking he had been killed. The honor roll board was moved to the current location of Auschwitz, which was built in 1947.

Some of the "famous" people from Breckenridge were Earl Peterson and his band Sons of the Golden West who played each weekend at The Pavilion on Bass Lake. His family built a Quonset hut for his band to play during intermission. The theatre is where the library now sits. Another Breckenridge native was Dick Carter, a well-known racecar driver who would have raced in the Indianapolis 500 the year of 1965 but his untimely death in a race at Marne Raceway put that dream away. And our very own Jim Northrup who played for the Detroit Tigers in the 60s with his key role in their winning the 1968 World Series Championship.

Another man we will never forget is Marvin Falor. He donated thousands of dollars to our little town including paying for all of the 4th of July activities and carnival rides for many years. He also bought the entire little league baseball team's uniforms. When Marv passed away, all the teams clad in their uniforms that he had furnished over the years lined the stretch to the gravesite. What a sight to see! He was a good man who helped everyone.

Our little town where "everybody knows everybody" continues to be full of good hearts and helping hands. It was and still is a great place to live!

Erma and Charles

Blue Gill Road
By Erma Ott Kleinhardt of Clare, Michigan
Born 1925

It was Blue Gill Road near Ott Cemetery, Clare County, on the way home from Alpena, Michigan. He, Charles, kissed me. I was ecstatic. He was so nice, and we dated and married May 12, 1945 by his father, Rev. Charles Kleinhardt. It was the first church wedding in Brown Corner U.B. Church. Erma Ott became Mrs. Charles Kleinhardt on May 1, 2012; he passed away after 67 years together. I sure do miss him.

Prior as a child I attended a one-room schoolhouse a half mile from home, across the fields in all kinds of weather. We wore brown bags over our heads to protect us from snow and high winds. The school was named Babsley School and we took turns doing janitorial work. Our teachers were special. I feel sure Mr. Williams had eyes in the back of his head. We never got away with anything unusual.

After our marriage, we farmed on my parents' farm, Wilma and Charles Ott and I worked as a lab x-ray technician for Davis Clinic and CMC hospital (now McLaren Hospital), in Mt. Pleasant, Michigan for seven years, and later devoted my time to raising four children.

Hired help and go-go gal for parts needed on the farm, plus playing taxi for children who were active in sports, piano lessons, etc.

Mother made my clothes for high school from old suits and printed feed sacks from Johnston elevator.

My brother Dr. Arnold Ott, eight years older than me, taught me to drive in a Model A Ford, it was a great experience. I learned shifting and not going into the ditch.

House Remembered
By Lorraine Underwood Wright of Lansing, Michigan
Born 1923

I Pledge
My head to clearer thinking
My heart to greater loyalty
My hands to larger service
My health to better living
For my club, my community,
My country and my world

This special 4-H leader came to our neighborhood area a newlywed, she and her husband George, had met at Michigan State University as college students. George was the adopted son of a large farm owner near us, also Sunday school superintendent. George and Bernice lived in a nice old farmhouse near the farm.

Bernice was a special person to me! She had her degree in Home Economics; this started our 4-H club. Slim and seemed a little tall, to my twelve-year-old height. Not especially attractive looking, dark hair, round face, thick lips, but beautiful white teeth, ruddy complexion, with two or three flat brown moles on her face and neck.

277

My girlfriend, Thelma, up the road, my niece Dorothy and I were among the first to join the 4-H club. As soon as we heard, Bernice was to be the leader of the club.

As I got to know Bernice, I admired her for knowing how to do so much. I wanted to be as good as she was. A seamstress, I never became! I hemmed two linen crash towels one by hand, one by sewing machine that was my first achievement. I still have those two towels!

We made a dress, cut out the pattern, basted, and sewed it by machine. Mine was pink with a nice ruffle over each shoulder. I remember sort of a problem with those ruffles! No ribbons at the 4-H fair for me!

The Underwood and Payne family

In our second year of 4-H, I seemed to really bond with her, she became a special friend. I enjoyed visiting with her. I remember we laughed a lot. She encouraged me to try to do things right even if I was slow in doing them. I always was behind in getting sewing done. My excuse was we didn't have a sewing machine at home.

As we were leaving a 4-H meeting, she said, "Lorraine I'd like you to come over on a certain day, I'll help you catch up!" Of course, I was delighted; it was a special time just for me! I could not wait to tell Mama when I got home.

The special day came. I walked the mile and a half over to her house. Bernice greeted me warmly and we started talking. She had a special lunch prepared for the two of us. My thoughts were how nice of her, yet a little scary when I saw the small table set for two in the kitchen with pretty pink table cloth, cloth napkins, crystal glasses, white with pink edged china, and nice silver. The kitchen was small with the small table on the north side, sink, counter, and cupboards on the south with a built in china hutch near the dining room door. Before we sat down, she explained and showed how the table should be set, the glass, salad plate, bread and butter plate, where silverware and napkin should be. We had a lovely lunch, a casserole served on my plate, a salad, roll, and pudding for

dessert. I did not spill anything or tip over the water glass. I felt as if I had passed a test when we finished eating. This lunch has been remembered for many years, but the next part of that remembered day, was exciting also. Bernice had told us at a club meeting that she was expecting a baby. I was thrilled for her. I watched with awe, as she got bigger, through the winter months.

After our lunch, she asked me if I wanted to see the baby clothes. "Oh yes!" I said, so she took me in the spare bedroom, and opened up a cedar chest. There filled to the top was baby clothes, she kneeled down on her knees and I sat down on the floor. She took out the dainty little dresses with lace and tatting all around the sleeves and hem, one had special little pink rose buds down the front, with the tatting on the sleeves and hem it was so dainty. I oh-ed and ah-ed as she held it up for me to look at and to touch, it was such fine smooth linen, white, with little pink crocheted roses. There were piles of pure white soft diapers, beautiful little pink, yellow, white, and blue sweater sets handmade. I had never seen such beautiful baby clothes.

I think I knew these baby clothes had been a labor of love, from herself, her mother, mother-in-law, and aunt for this new baby to arrive in February.

Early one morning my brother Acil came to the house, cold to the bone, as he stood close to the old round oak stove in our living room, he told us this tragedy. He lived in town, at his house early AM that morning he heard the fire siren, quickly dressed, with coat in hand he ran down the hill as the siren was going north out of town, the fire truck slowed up and he jumped on. The driver telling him the fire was at George Blanks, a neighbor had seen flames through the windows and called the fire department, which was all-volunteer.

Mom, Dad, Bob, and I were all huddled around the warm stove as Acil continues. The fire was controlled, but Bernice had burned to death. She was in her big overstuffed chair, which was burning.

I could hardly believe all this tragic news. I kept remembering her as she was on "our" special day, just a few short days before.

That ole farmhouse has seen a lot of life since. My sister Leda, and her husband, Jack, once lived there.

My brother Oak lived there and raised seven wonderful children. My brother Oak's grandson lives there now.

That small kitchen with a table for two has been enlarged to a big room, a large table, and all modern appliances. The bedroom that held the cedar chest, with the precious baby clothes is a nice bathroom that has seen many scrubbed paddies and little bare feet. The house rings with laughter and sounds of those precious little ones and Mom and Dad.

That house was built in the early 1880s as a schoolhouse. My mother went to school there, finished the 9th and 10th grades in town. She was born in 1880.

I often think of that special bond Bernice and I had, especially when I'm doing some hand sewing and hear her words of wisdom, "Do a good job, even if I'm slow at it." I also wonder at times, whatever happened to all those beautiful baby clothes.

I also enjoy remembering special times under the ole Walnut tree behind the cellar and pitcher pump! Brother Dud was in the Navy during the early 1920s, returning home he was able to bring his hammock that he slept in, on the ship, USS Idaho. He, or one of my brothers, put it up attached to a pole and the walnut tree during summers. It was so much fun and comfort, laying, and swinging in that hammock looking up through the Walnut tree leaves. When it rained, the hammock would fill with rain, so it had to be emptied then dried. It was such a carefree feeling to be swinging in Dud's ole' Navy hammock! I

never knew what happened to that hammock, I've wondered so many times these last 70 years. I'm sure it deteriorated with age! But it was such a pleasure during the 1920s and 30s.

A fascinating memory of the early 1930s for me was watching the raccoons passing back and forth in their cages. I was fascinated watching them at their food, with their front paws. I would sit on the ground under the walnut tree near the cages watching them for hours at a time.

I was also intrigued at this time with the mother cat that had just had a nice litter of kittens they were in a nice big box on the closet floor. There again I would sit on the floor and watch the tiny kittens for hours. One day as I was watching the baby kittens, my older brother who was raising the raccoons called me to him, and handed me a baby raccoon. Just born, apparently the mother coon wouldn't own the baby. My brother Acil, told me to see if the mother cat would let the baby coon nurse with the baby kittens. Very patiently, I handled the little coon; sure enough, the mother cat owned her. I found myself watching the white coon nurse and grow, in about two weeks her eyes opened; they were the prettiest pink eyes you can imagine. With her white fur and pink eyes, I had a beautiful albino pet I called "Coonie."

I loved, petted, and cuddled, that little white "Coonie." She grew and was a constant companion. She loved bread and milk, and cereal sweepings from Kellogg's cereal factory at Battle Creek. She was also potty trained for outdoors. She would sleep at the foot of the bed with me, always under the covers. She would entertain us by using her front paws to get pieces of candy from the pencil pocket of my Dad's and brother's bib overall pockets.

We had a wonderful year or more, growing together and loving each other.

One day I saw her on the kitchen table where mother kept the sugar bowl, pink carnival glass with a cover. Coonie very carefully, with her pure white paws, removed the cover. That sugar tasted so good! I did not want to tell my brother her mischievous trick, but knew I had to; his reply was we better put her in a pen!

After school, I'd go out and talk to her, but she was never able to come back in the house. She never had any babies and Acil eventually sold her. It broke my heart to give up that pink and white pet!

Acil and Dr. Leon F. Whitney from New Orange, Connecticut, wrote and published a book "The Raccoon," which told of raising black wild coons, inbreeding to buff and eventually to pure albino, white with pink eyes. He also was a close friend of Mort Neff, who produced "Michigan Outdoors" on TV. Mort had one of Acil's raccoons called "Goldie" on the TV show. Acil was also on TV with Mort several times. Mort also visited Acil and the Raccoon Ranch in Maple Rapids, during his years on TV's Michigan Outdoors.

Grandmother and the Naked Lady
By Sally Cunningham Kane of Newaygo, Michigan
Born 1947

"Grandmother, why doesn't she have any clothes on?" I asked.

"She's beautiful!" my Grandmother stated, like that explained everything.

I scrutinized the woman in the sepia toned picture with the dark wood frame. Whenever I entered the front foyer of Grandmother's home, my eyes found the picture. It hung next to the window at the rise and curve of her large oak staircase.

"But," I persisted, "she's naked!" My eleventh birthday was near, and with it came a latent boldness with my Grandmother Bessie.

My eyes followed Grandmother's sturdy figure, the dust blue housedress, the low-heeled day shoes, the tilt of her chin, her gray hair secured in a chignon. She watered the African violets on the glass shelves in the foyer window.

"Ye-e-s," Grandmother's tone matter-of-fact. "She's taking a BATH."

In the picture, the lady relaxes beside a lake, cattail rushes at her back. Her body all light and curves. She hugs one knee, a cloth drapes around her thigh. Her lips part in a half smile, and a sweep of wavy blond hair framed her languid eyes. A single leaf wreath weaves her crown.

My eyebrows furrowed. I took a breath, wanting more. Grandmother finished her watering. Her hands stayed busy deadheading the violets. When she spoke, the definitive

tone I knew well edged a new softness. "I really like her."

My eyebrows rose with this naked admission, "Me too," I said, feeling warm inside.

Moving from my perch at the bottom of the foyer stair steps, I felt a quickening, like a germination. That moment marked a confluence between The Naked Lady, my Grandmother Bessie, and me, seeding my life choices.

I only knew Bessie Rippeth Cunningham as a single woman. My father and my Aunt Jane enjoyed telling her history, layering the stories like the bricks of a building. It suggested non-convention, independence, gentry, and economy. Widowed in 1940, seven years before my birth in 1947, she became my Grandfather Arthur's third wife. A stand-alone-light in her own right, Grandmother's single womanhood, and independence, like a prism, refracted the colors of her life with my Grandfather.

My grandparents met during a steamship cruise on The Great Lakes in 1908. Each brought unique backgrounds to the meeting.

Grandmother, born in 1884, grew up in Ohio. She displayed two strong spirits: an expectation to honor tradition with an independent-thinking stream. Both functioned throughout her life. After high school graduation in 1903, Grandmother desired more than "just a housewife role" during a time of limited career options for women. The business world interested her and secretarial training aligned the closest to business. Upon completion of her program, she landed a position as secretary to the president of the Wabash and Erie Railroad. This qualified her for discounts on railroad and affiliated steamship tours, staging another legacy that would continue in our family. Travel. Grandmother gifted her mother and herself to a ten day Great Lakes Cruise. As if cued, in walked the man to become my Grandfather.

Debonair, attentive, a seasoned traveler, Arthur Cunningham initiated conversation with grandmother and her mother. At first, grandmother thought his interest was toward her mother, and then discovered he actually sought her companionship. Already twice a widower, Grandfather was traveling with his eighteen-year-old daughter, Eleanor. His first wife, Eleanor's mother, died of tuberculosis.

His second, from typhoid fever. A cutting edge educator and librarian, Grandfather headed the library at Indiana State Normal School in Terre Haute, Indiana.

I wonder about the consorts of these four people on a Great Lakes steamship in 1908, putting a romantic twist on this event. Displaying proper decorum, I imagine they sought intentional conversations during that cruise, commenting on the lovely fresh water air of the lakes, strolling the decks, perhaps even dining together. For certain, they exchanged addresses.

My grandparents courted by written correspondence. Grandfather requested permission to visit her on his spring break, resulting in their engagement. His daughter, Eleanor, wrote and asked Grandmother to be the "sister she never had." A friendship forged. Eleanor forever became, 'Sister Eleanor.' Their marriage occurred in 1909 and Grandmother moved to Terre

Bessie Rippeth Cunningham in 1965

Haute, Indiana. Grandmother offset her role as a professor's wife by efficient leadership in civic clubs and church guilds. The years 1913 to 1919 added the task of child rearing with the birth of my two aunts and my father. 1913 also ushered in two landmark purchases: their first car, a Black touring Cadillac, and the iconic Victorian house. Situated in a residential neighborhood near the University, it offered the perfect family-raising environment. Grandmother resided in that house until her death in 1977.

While my Grandparents displayed opposite temperaments, he quiet and reserved, she the social one, they fostered their love of travel. They used trains, and boats for greater distances such as Europe or Bermuda, but their first car offered the opportunity for family road trips. Travel by car meant averaging twenty-five miles per hour, muddy roads, ruts, small stretches of bricked highways and frequent stops. A laborious crank started the noisy engine and the small tires gave prone

to blowouts. Relegated to the back seat, their three children kept warm under heavy wool blankets. The family traveled from Indiana to Idaho with that car.

Another level of Grandmother's independence emerged after she and Grandfather purchased a Studebaker sedan in 1923. She wanted to learn to drive. Grandfather opposed this idea and refused to help her. So, Grandmother asked a man at the Studebaker dealer for lessons. He taught her and she continued driving well into her eighties.

A question persisted while growing up: "Where does Grandmother get her money?" Looking at the life events following Grandfather's death shed light on this question. He believed men should manage the money. Grandmother's limited knowledge of their financial matters, coupled with losing her husband, and shortly after, her father and brother, proved daunting. The task of settling two estates loomed before her. She utilized her business sense, combined with fierce "can-do" independence, and sought the help of a financial advisor. Grandmother learned to create financial solvency and a comfortable living for her remaining years.

Twenty years after Grandfather's death in 1940, Indiana State College achieved university status. Grandmother wanted to honor Grandfather's library innovations and his development of the school's first library building. He obtained faculty rank for librarians and department status for the library. Innovations included increasing the pedagogical collections" for different educational department's research, student accessibility, and a children's literature department. Grandmother made a grant to ISU, establishing the "Arthur Cunningham Collection of Monuments in American Education." She donated hundreds of family books, representing numerous genres, archived in his name, each identified with a bookplate from the Cunningham Clan Crest. The library memorialized his legacy in 1973, at a formal dedication, naming it The Cunningham Memorial Library.

I loved my childhood visits to Grandmother's. Father drove mother, my brother and I the four hours from South Bend, Indiana to Terre Haute. He always parked at the front curb. Securing our suitcases, we trouped onto the porch that wrapped the house-front. Even though this had been his boyhood home, dad rang the doorbell. He chuckled, explaining the formality, "It's not a safe neighborhood anymore, so she keeps the door locked." My stomach tightened, a familiar sensation at the onset of our visits. *Many formalities existed here.*

First, we heard her voice calling to us, then her footsteps. The large steel locks turned in her hands. When the huge oak doors opened, familiar aromas wafted out. Old wood, tapestries, furniture polish. Grandmother's glasses reflected the light. "Come in, come in!" Her hand made sweeping motions toward the interior of the house, helping crack the 'formal ice.' "Oh, I was back in the kitchen when I heard the bell." A little hard of hearing, her booming voice belied her small stature. She offered her smooth cheek for rounds of kisses. "Now, get your things upstairs. I got the beds made."

While lugging my suitcase up the staircase, I made the usual pause at the curve to greet the Naked Lady, her sensual beauty illumined by the north window on the staircase, vigiling over the foyer below.

The entire house wove a tapestry with dark paneling, oriental rugs, mission furniture, books, travel collectables, and wood framed pictures. But, the foyer pulsed the heartbeat. An upright player piano nestled under the staircase alcove, and life size, white, marble bust of Homer stood on a pedestal beside the piano. When younger, I gave his unseeing stare a wide berth when passing through the nearby doorway. High on the wall ticked the Cuckoo Clock. The quarter hour bird song sounded throughout the house. At night, from my bedroom upstairs, I listened as Grandmother pulled the long chains over the gears to rewind the clock, the last ritual before retiring to bed.

Grandmother set her dining room table with linen, silver napkin rings and forks: dinner forks for the main course, smaller forks for the salad, a long handled fork and knife for carving the roasted meat. Vegetables steamed under lidded serving dishes. Dinner rolls paired with tiny side plates and curved butter knives. Sherbet or homemade spice cake sweetened the end of the meal. They were the precursor to an even sweeter post-dinner entrée: Grandmother Bessie's Stories.

One of us often prompted her: "Grandmother, tell us about your last trip!" We laid our napkins aside and turned toward her. She sat back in her chair, took a breath, and the opening words hugged our family like the warmth of a fireside.

Grandmother's travel passion continued after Grandfathers' passing and inspired her stories. Commenced by passenger ship and guided tours, she called herself a "Gadbug." Like a bard, her global trips unfolded with word pictures. Travelogues became her modality. As photo technology progressed, she illustrated her talks with slide shows, even dressing in indigenous clothing. Sometimes, she rehearsed her talks with us. Dad set up the screen and we gathered in the Foyer. "Our tour started here…," Grandmother began. The rhythm of her voice secured my attention like the gate to a mystery garden. I smelled pungent outdoor markets heaped with goods, teeming with people speaking unknown languages. I saw purple mountains and minaret-topped towers. Beggars grabbed for coins. Castles loomed upon seaside cliffs. Folk dancers whirled to engaging rhythms.

Grandmother returned with gifts, talismans. My brother and I sat on the foyer steps, the Naked Lady overseeing, opening music boxes, handmade games, and Chinese puzzles. Tissue paper unwrapped, revealing baskets, bracelets, embroidered clothing, tartan hats, and shawls. We could no longer "be seen and not heard."

"Where is this from?" "How do these puzzles work?" "Why are stones on the roof of the music box house?" "When would a kid wear this…?" Grandmother's patient answers beckoned, like the pointer finger of a will-o-the-wisp, pulling me toward a secret passage. At bedtime, as I climbed the staircase carrying a new treasure, passing the Naked Lady, I paused to check on her. She had receded into the evening shadows and her own mystery.

Today, I celebrate Grandmother's influences. Residing on the Little Muskegon River in the Michigan woods with my husband, I live a 21st century version of non-convention, while preserving some traditions. The Naked Lady graces a wall in my living room. Pieces of Grandmother's furniture and artifacts keep her company in our home, as a cat takes to the sun.

Recently, my four-year old granddaughter, Zoe, visited me. In our usual fashion, we played together in the living room, her Beanie Babies piled on the heirloom, marble topped coffee table. She suddenly paused, her eyes beamed on the Naked Lady picture. Her arm rose straight out with her pointer finger extended toward the picture. She turned to me. "Is she naked?" Zoe asked. I smiled, restraining the urge to laugh aloud. "That's almost exactly what I asked my grandmother one time," I said…

A Tree-Climbing, Tunnel-Crawling Little Boy
By Floyd Fox of Shelby, Michigan
Born 1918

Piper Eight Grade School was on 72nd Ave., one mile west of the Village of Shelby Michigan in 1920. In the spring of 1920, Nicholas J. Fox and wife Edith purchased an 80-acre farm on the corner of 72nd Ave. and Woodrow Rd. The farm was an 80-acre fruit and livestock farm. The fruit orchards: apples, tart cherries, sweet cherries, pears, plums and five apricot trees were on the higher elevation of the front 40 acres. The west 40 acres was light sandy soil used for pasturing cattle.

Nick and Edith had one child, a boy named Floyd who was one and a half years old. They moved into the old house on the farm the day they signed the land contract.

I, Floyd Fox reached age five on August 14, 1923. In the afternoon of a spring day in 1924, my dad, carrying a long saw and a neighbor named Grant Cleveland, carrying an axe, walked me to Piper School one-quarter mile north of our home. My Mom thought I should get a little feel for school before starting kindergarten in the fall.

Dad took me into the school and introduced me to the teacher, Mrs. VanderVen. Dad said to me, "I will be nearby; Grant and I will be cutting wood in the woods next to the school playground." I thought nearby meant staying in the school building where I could see him, so I began crying as Dad went out the door.

I cried continuously until my dad returned. I suspect the teacher told Dad. "Floyd is not yet ready for school." When school started in September, I was eager to go to school. I joined older neighborhood kids as they walked past our home on their way to Piper School. We arrived at school with time to play outside before entering the school building.

My memories of Piper Grade School are all pleasant memories. There was a tall maple tree in front of the school. I became the best tree climber in Piper school. I climbed up to the top of the tree as other kids did—limb by limb. But I came down the tree using the outer end of the limbs. I was a showoff; probably because I was a short.

Piper Creek flowed beneath a bridge less than 100 yards from the school. (Creek was pronounced, "Crick.") A creek so close to the Piper School resulted in wet shoes often. The wet shoes were placed on top of the school's heating plant: a large coal-burning stove in the one-room school. The shoes dried slowly because there was little or no fire in the stove in the spring. Many times our shoes dried on our feet or remained wet.

Piper creek merged with Darky Bill creek about two miles downstream. At the junction of the two creeks, the creek's name changed to Stony Creek. Stony Creek flowed into Stony Lake about four miles southwest. Stony Lake channel flowed into Lake Michigan.

In early spring, Steelhead Trout entered Stony Lake Channel on their way upstream to their spawning grounds. It was exciting for us Piper School kids to see those large fish fighting their way up shallow Piper creek to lay their eggs.

Some of us boys made wooden spears. We tried spearing fish during the school noon hour. After many days of trying, I speared a fish. I was so proud of the feat I carried the fish to the school and showed it to our schoolteacher, Mrs. Kelly. Mrs. Kelly admonished me: "Spearing on a trout stream is unlawful." My feelings were hurt. My joy changed to shame. Mrs. Kelly put the fish into a drawer in her desk and said. "You can take the fish home with you after school, but don't do anymore spearing."

One spring morning, I recall looking out a window of our upstairs bedroom. I saw my dad walking across the lawn with a very long fish over his shoulder. I don't know if that occurred before or after my unlawful spearing.

I never saw Dad's big fish again, but I remember having to eat fish frequently. I remember because I didn't like eating fish. Another attraction we kids could reach in about five minutes was the railroad track.

Upper Piper creek flowed under the landfill for the railroad track. The creek flowed into a 36" steel tunnel. There was a smaller second tunnel above and to the right. It was the emergency tunnel, which would take excess water flow during heavy rains or floods.

I don't remember any of the older boys crawling into the tunnel. When I became an older boy, I crawled a few yards into the tunnel several times. My younger brother Ralph remembers crawling into the tunnel, but can't remember if he ever crawled to the end of the tunnel. Ralph remembers crawling into the tunnel when a train passed overhead. The tunnel was over 100 ft. long with a bend near the middle. The bend in the middle prevented us from seeing light at the other end of the tunnel. One of the days we went to the railroad track, I climbed into the tunnel and kept going.

Someone noticed I didn't back out. That inspired all the kids to run up and over the tracks and down to the exit end of the tunnel. The tunnel was completely dark, as I crawled to the bend in the tunnel. At the bend, I saw light at the end of the tunnel and kids looking in. the teacher Mrs. Farr and my Mom and Dad never learned I crawled through the railroad tunnel.

Fun on the Farm
By Donna R. Thiedeman of Belding, Michigan
Born 1935

The Roberts family consisted of 11 children—six boys and five girls located in the small town of Fenwick, Michigan. We had 80 acres and lots of farmland.

My name is Donna and I was born on

Donna Roberts Thiedeman

August 23, 1935 and my sister Marilyn in November of 1936. All of us kids were born on the farm. My brother Stuart was a hunter and loved to get animals and trap some to

Marilyn Roberts Webster

284

sell fur. One day Stuart came home with two badgers, I don't know how old they were. I love animals, so we played with them and took them on as pets. We named them Bum and Bill.

They didn't hurt us or run from us, but were content to play and stay around the farm. Marilyn was about three or four and I was five years old at the time. We have a picture of us together holding them and they were pretty big for our size.

One day Bum went out to the barn on the upper floor and killed all our baby chicks that we got every summer. Daddy was so mad he got rid of Bum! Sometime later, Bill got into a big barrel or pig food (slop we called it) and drowned. After that, we had lots of pups, lambs, squirrels, and a coon named Tootsy.

The Outhouse on the Farm
By Ann K. Tomcho of Akron, Michigan
Born 1940

I was born and raised in Cleveland, Ohio. Mom, Dad, my brother John, and I lived in an average neighborhood where everyone had a telephone, electricity, running water and a real bathroom. In my innocence, I though this simply came with life. All that changed, however, when in 1945 my grandpa purchased a 40-acre plot of land in rural Michigan that was soon to be known simply as 'The Farm."

The next year, the day after school closed for summer vacation, a tradition began that was to last for many years. Early in the morning, Dad would pack the car with a great grumpy growl, as he was positive we were cramming so much into the car an axle was sure to break before we even left Ohio. Axles were minor, however, when compared to the energy needed to keep two small kids from arguing, fussing, poking, and annoying each other on the 9 1/2 hour trip. Two or three days later, he would make the long return trip back to Cleveland in order to return to work. Three months later, he would then drive back and pick us up just in time for the new school year to begin.

Amazingly, we survived the trip and entered a world that was wonderful, free, mosquito-filled, gentle, and loving and which contained the most incredible object I had ever seen. My brother immediately recognized it as a great gift that could keep him busy making my life miserable for a very long time while I just stared as I realized I wasn't going to like this at all. Not at all. For the first time in our lives, we were both right. There it stood – "The Outhouse."

The outhouse was innocent-looking, painted white with a little screen-covered window in the door through which the occasional puff of breeze could be felt. Mom and Grandma kept it extremely clean, but when one is very young and is accustomed to big city creature comforts, this was of little help. There was one hole and a bottle of AirWick was always next to the seat. During the day, it was quite hot in there even though it sat nicely under some wild cherry trees. Lime was dumped down the hole weekly. There was a hook to "lock" the door from the inside and on the outside, a piece of wood was nailed and could be turned to keep the door closed once one escaped.

I learned to pray in that little outhouse. I learned how to pray with all my heart and soul as I opened the door, and whispered the prayer that never varied: "Oh God, PLEASE don't let there be any snakes, spiders or wasps in there while I'm in there!" I had a high success rate with that prayer.

To take one's mind off things there always was a nice pile of comic books and magazines next to the hole. With my prayer firmly established, that's what I was doing when my brother first used the powers of his great gift. I was reading a comic book when John slowly and quietly crept by, ducking low enough so he could not be seen through the little screened window, and very quietly he turned the little piece of wood thereby locking me in.

When I finished my comic book, and whatever else it was that I was doing, I reached for the door, and nothing happened! NOTHING! I yelled and screamed at the top of my lungs. Mom and Grandma finally came running, thinking that something terrible had happened to me (in my opinion that's EXACTLY what happened) and when they found out they were furious at John, which made me feel a little better. John pulled this prank a few more times and then had to promise Mom he'd not do it again. And, he didn't. He did something worse.

I would be working my way through another comic book when suddenly I'd hear a rustling noise and then there would be silence and then the rustling and then I'd hear John saying "Oh gosh!"

"Gosh what?"

"Ann? Are you in there?"

"Yeah. Why?"

"Because I just saw the largest snake I've ever seen slide under the outhouse!"

"WHAT?"

"Oh yes, he was HUGE! Oh, oh—I just saw him again and I think he's going around the corner..."

My heart would pound, I would break out in a cold sweat, and I'd yell and holler. The next time it would be a huge black fuzzy spider. He never ran out of innovative ways to make my life miserable.

The summer drive to the farm lasted eight more years when John finally decided he was far too old to spend another summer where there were no interesting girls around. Also, the outhouse days were over, as indoor plumbing had finally been installed and I was older and wiser. It also was a long time for Mom to be gone and for Dad to fend for himself, but I remained defiant. I loved the farm so much that for a few years I took a bus for at least part of the summer.

Then came college followed by serving as a Peace Corps volunteer in Honduras where once again I had an outhouse and then community development jobs in Cleveland. However, the farm, the trees, the open spaces, and the adventures were all in my blood. One day I looked around my apartment and said, "Okay, that's enough" and I packed my belongings and drove to the farm, where I still live now...with a real bathroom.

Camping With Daddy
By Bamberlee Barnes of Merrill, Michigan
Born 1932

Come, meet a particularly unique man—Daddy. When I came into this world, I was introduced to this old man. Daddy was 59 when I arrived. (Mom was only 33.) Before we venture too far, let's indulge in some background. Daddy was a tall, thin man (about 6 feet tall and weighed in at approximately 135 pounds). Sort of puts you in mind of Ichabod Crane. He was a sweet, gentle man, but a strict German disciplinarian. You could

describe him generous to a fault.

Being an attorney, in those days, it was necessary to go to the source for discussion of a case. In our situation, my dad often defended an old codger by the name of Spikehorn Meyer. He had a tourist trap on the old highway. His added feature was a few bears he kept loose in a pen. You can see the trouble was brewing. He liked the name similarity to ours: Myers-Meyer. He figured added confusion over the names would be an asset in court.

Our home was in Ithaca and Spikehorn lived near Harrison. This was close to Wilson State Park on Budd Lake. How convenient for a vacation for us. We traveled there usually once a year.

Now, let's capture the preparation procedure! At the crack of dawn, five kids sprang out of the sack ready and rearing to roll immediately....wrong. We had to have breakfast. (Daddy was a VERY SLOW eater.) Next, dishes and the ritual teeth brushing routine.

We all pitched in to help Mom pack and fill every cubby in the car and our "honeymoon trailer." There were five kids and two dogs to squeeze into the old '36 Chrysler....mighty tight, but it was fine as long as we could go. The exuberance was almost overwhelming.

Meantime, Daddy had to type one more "brief." He was old school, using the Columbus method, "find a key and land on it." Of course, this antiquated technique consumed the morning. Time for lunch, unpack some of the food, eat, brush teeth and back into his office to complete the needed work to go. Get the picture? My dad did nothing in a hurry.

At last, we were speeding on our way to Wilson State Park. Cheers! Let me elaborate. It usually was between 7 and 9 PM when we would take off. Recall the "nothing in a hurry" remark? Daddy seemed to feel the best way to preserve a car was not to "stress" it by speeding. His definition of speeding was about 45 mph tops. He certainly abided by this belief!

After checking in, Daddy started immediately to put up the tent. We lovingly referred to it as a one-man tent that took ten men to set up. He was struggling in the light of our one flashlight, when invariably one of the kids had to go to the bathroom. Thus, all the work halted while Mom took the only source of light to accompany one of us and

Bamberlee's family in 1950

disappeared into the dark.

Now you may be wondering how Daddy handled this situation—total darkness and four tired, restless kids. He was a great teller of stories. Usually they were of Biblical nature. (At home, each night, he would come to our bedside and listen to us repeat our prayers.) Finally, the battery-operated candle returned and we completed the camp setup.

My folks slept on a three quarters bed. It also proved to be a challenge as it had to be unfolded (it was accordion pleated and to fit in a wooden box) and hooked on each end of a metal frame. He would hook one end and invariably the other end would pop off. It tickled us kids to watch but decided it was best not to laugh out loud.

When the word spread through the camp that the Myers clan had arrived, joy was evident. We vacationed there over many years. My dad played the guitar. Couldn't read a note of music. Many said he "played by ear." It was our part to sing and lead the singing. Did I mention each evening the campers gathered around a large campfire for this fun activity? Never have I felt more warm pleasure than our songfest around the smoky campfire. It was understandable to me at that point, why the people anticipated those evening gatherings.

Dad and Mom were concerned that one of us might get lost so they had unique methods of rounding us up, especially at mealtime. We took along a cowbell. Nice and loud and oh, so embarrassing to be fetched like a bovine.

If that didn't work, when you heard three blasts on the car horn, baby, you better come running. Daddy expected obedience. Hard to keep track of five wanderers!

Never have you seen a week disappear so quickly. It was glorious. Daddy finished his business and it was time to pack up and trek home.

It was a bittersweet time, leaving such fun activities, but there was special compensation. We would sing all the old tunes Daddy had taught us. Made the trip seem much shorter. On top of that, we would stop in Clare for giant ice cream cones. Daddy loved ice cream so this was simply part of the vacation ritual.

There is so much more to relate about this wonderful man. Time and space just won't allow it. Though he has been gone many, many years, he holds a precious place in my heart.

An Adventurous Life
By Tresa Pangborn of Midland, Michigan
Born 1923

It has been a great adventure to have lived between 1923-2015, and to have observed all the tremendous changes. I was born on October 11, 1923 in the tiny town of Hockaday, Gladwin County Michigan, and was the fifth of five children. Hockaday consisted of one schoolhouse, two stores, four houses all of which were surrounded by farms, and supported by one church—the Free Methodist Church. This little white church was a great asset to the community and is where I attended Sunday school, receiving the foundations for many of my beliefs.

In those days, we had no electricity and no running water. We used oil lamps for lighting and a wood burning range for cooking, baking, and heating water. Our weekly baths were taken in the middle of the kitchen floor in a big metal tub. It would take a half hour or so to heat enough water to fill the tub half full. I always tried to beat by older brother to the bath! Our water came from a pump attached to our windmill. It also provided water for a large tank used to water our farm animals. We also collected rainwater from the eaves that was kept in a cistern in the basement. This was "special water" used for bathing and washing your hair. It was very soft and left your hair very shiny! The well and the water was a big part of our chores, although mostly for the boys. My chores consisted of squishing the potato bugs off the back of the potato plant leaves, gathering the eggs from the chicken coop, and assisting my father and siblings in clearing the farm fields of stones.

Our family time each night consisted of gathering in the dining room after dinner. Daddy would read the newspaper, Mother hooked rugs, and we children did our schoolwork or read. During the summer months, we listened to our radio. Daddy especially enjoyed listening to the Detroit Tigers, and I remember the Jimmy Allen show, as well as Amos and Andy. In high school, I liked listening to the Hit Parade, broadcasting popular music.

Every July my family also attended my dad's family reunion. It was a two-day affair. The families went together to purchase a large tent. The children enjoyed swimming in Lake Huron, the men played baseball, and the women sat around, talked, and put good meals on the table. Every family was expected to contribute to the Sunday program before leaving for home. You could sing, recite poetry, or simply share some talent of sorts.

Telephones and automobiles were rare in Hockaday. My family was fortunate enough to have both. In the event of an emergent need of a vet or doctor, our neighbors would come to our home to make a callout. Our phone was on a party line that went into "Central" - at Gladwin, MI. Our number was 2-1 on 120.

My father was a mail carrier. He used our automobile to deliver his mail most of the time. Occasionally a heavy snowstorm or bad weather would prompt the use of the horse pulled mail wagon. During Christmastime, my father made a point to leave oranges at each of his patron's homes, leaving one orange per family member. This was a huge gift, as they would not have had the opportunity to have fresh fruit during the winter.

The men of the community formed a bee in the winter. They would cut ice off the river and store it in a little log hut, in sawdust to be used in the summer for making ice cream. This was called the community icehouse. I can still remember the dark red sawdust!
I have very fond memories of the little one r
The one-room schoolhouse—I can still see it in my mind. It went from kindergarten through the eighth grade. There were four to five students per class. Each class met at the front of the room to the recitation bench to receive their lesson. The rest of the classes remained in their seats studying their lessons. Everyone heard each class's recitation. If you were receptive to learning to any degree you could learn the next years material if you paid attention!

We had a recess period. Most of the kids played softball. If there was a discipline problem, the teacher took the isolation approach. You would be pulled from your class temporarily. The embarrassment of separation was effective. While in class, if we even heard an airplane approaching, we were allowed to go outside to see it! The sight of the plane was a real treat! It was fascinating!

Of all my years in school, my favorite teacher was Margaret Clark. She taught me in the eighth grade. She was responsible for the school district's purchase of a piano, believing music was important in teaching. Another special friend was Grandpa Jewel, a neighbor who loved me and paid special attention. He nicknamed me Midget, and often watched me leave for school. I admired his goodness, and looking back, recognize what a wonderful example he was of living a good life. His wife was also special. She spent time teaching me to knit.

Few students went on in their education beyond the eighth grade. My family believed in going on. All five of us completed high school. I was 13 when I left home and went to live in a rented room in Gladwin. I loved high school. I graduated in 1940. I then went on to business college for a year. Once I graduated that program, I had to wait until I turned 18 and was then hired for work by Dow Chemical Co. They were very involved in the war effort. The war started in 1941.

My sweetheart John went into the Navy in May of '43. He was sent to the South Pacific in December of '43 until December of '45. During this time, we had to use coupons to purchase many items such as: butter, meat, gasoline, tires, nylon hose, etc. The needs of the military came first, as they should have. John was on a refrigerator ship carrying food to the islands for other GIs. Once he was back in the states, he had trouble getting transportation from California to Michigan.

There were so many GIs returning from the South Pacific that he ended up waiting twelve days before he was able to get home.

We were married January 5, 1946. John was discharged in April of '46. We then ran a gas station in Levering, Michigan for five years before leaving for college on the GI bill. We attended college for four years from '51-'55. After receiving degrees from both Albion College and the University of Michigan, John was hired by Dow Chemical Co. and worked 28 years in the power department.

We were blessed with two sons and one daughter. When our children were young, we were privileged to see all 50 states, Canada, and several European countries. It has been a tremendous privilege to have lived all these wonderful years. I am thankful for family, country and give my maker thanks every day.

Patsy Gregg in 1948

Scrap Metal Drives, Victory Celebrations, and Dad's Dance Band
By Patricia Love of Alma, Michigan
Born 1930

When I was young, I attended Foster Elementary School in Lansing, Michigan. During World War II, the school had a scrap metal drive. My father at that time had a hand-printing press in our basement, which he used to make up business cards and flyers advertising his dance band. I can still hear him pulling that handle down in the basement, and it created a lot of scraps from the metal print. I had a red wagon, so I loaded it up with all the scrap iron. It was packed full, and it was heavy. I won first place by a mile. No one else came close.

A favorite place we loved to go as children was out to Lake Lansing, which used to be called Pine Lake, in Haslett, Michigan. There was an amusement park at the lake, with rides and a roller coaster. They had a beautiful musical carousel. We were allowed to go on all the rides but apparently, no one in my family trusted the roller coaster because we never rode on it. Back in the '30s and '40s, there was a big pavilion adjacent to a dock in the amusement park. My father had a dance band and they were regularly hired to play

there on weekends. Lake Lansing remains a very nice family park, but the carousel and the amusement park are long gone.

Since my Dad had the dance band, it was essential for him to stay abreast of the latest hits. He was gone playing on Saturday nights, so it was my job to listen to the Hit Parade on the radio. He relied on me for this, and I made sure I wrote down all the songs in order. I considered this job of the utmost importance and felt proud to do this for my dad. The band brought in steady extra income, so we never suffered for money the way many people did during that time.

When victory was declared at the end of WWII, there was a big celebration in downtown Lansing, as there most likely was in many cities and towns all over America. What stands out in my memory, in addition to the jubilant crowd, was that for some reason my sister and I were allowed to go barefoot to the celebration. My memory has faded as to how or why that came about, but my sister and I felt we were really getting away with something. In those days, you dressed up very nicely to go downtown. My mother had a bit of a fit about it, but perhaps my dad exerted influence and ruled the day...

A Walk Down Memory Lane
By Beverly Barker of Clare, Michigan
Born 1945

My name is Beverly Barker. I have many fond memories of my childhood and growing up. I came from a large family of six brothers and four sisters. Times were hard back then, but neighbors and family seemed closer than they do these days.

My family moved around a lot when I was growing up. My favorite memories are from a farm that we lived on at Oak Grove Michigan. So many memories are coming back as I sit here writing this story. We had all kinds of animals and one that I remember the most was a small little pig that I named Mike. He was the runt of the litter and my dad let me bring him into the house. I fed him and loved him.

Mike started getting to big to stay in the house and my dad said, "I think Mike is big enough now to be put back out with his mother. I didn't want to, but my dad said it would be better because Mike was getting to big. When I got home from school, I found out that Mike was dead. When we put him back in the pen with the other pigs, the mother pig ate him. I was so heartbroken and cried. I never forgot that little pig.

Another memory I have was when I was little I loved to eat tomatoes off the vine. I would like to take the saltshaker off the table, go into the garden, and eat the big, red, ripe tomatoes. One day my mom was looking for me and didn't know where I was. My dad came in and Mom asked if he had seen me. He said, "No, but the salt shaker is missing off the table." They looked in the garden and there I was. They both laughed so hard.

My mom used an old stove that used wood to cook and bake with by adding wood. One day my mom made some Jell-O and put it in the window edge to cool. Me and one of my brothers took some straws, and while standing outside of the window, put the straws into the Jell-O and sucked it all out. Mom was so mad. I can remember it like it was yesterday.

I have so many memories at that farm. We had to walk a mile to school. I remember my favorite teacher's name. Her name was Mrs. Merchant. She took me into her house when our house burnt and it was so nice. She had toys that I wasn't used to and loved living with her. I kind of wanted to stay. My brothers

got so jealous. They still pick on me, saying that I was the teacher's pet. I didn't mind.

When I went to school, I had one of my brothers to walk with me because I was scared and the path I had to walk was through the woods. One day neither one of my brothers could walk me home. They said, "You will be fine; don't be scared." I didn't want to, but I tried to be brave. I started home and then I saw a snake in the road. It was a blue racer, and if you are familiar with this snake, it chases you. I tried to run past it, but it started chasing me! I was so scared. I got home and my mom told my brothers to never let me walk alone again.

I loved going to school. We played a lot of games. We played Red Rover Rover, dodgeball, and King of the Mountain. We learned to entertain ourselves back then. When we weren't in school, we did a lot of things to keep us entertained. We made a hockey puck out of a Cophengan Can. I know times were hard back then but looking back, you just have to smile compared to things these days.

I remember going to Elvis Pressley's first movie when I was 13 years old. It was called Jail House Rock and it only cost 50 cents. You couldn't hardly hear the movie from the girls screaming. He was such a handsome man. You could get a bottle of Coke for only a nickel. If you had a dollar in those days, you were rich.

Another fond memory I have is when we went on hayrides. Those were so much fun. After the hayrides, we would have a bonfire and roast hotdogs. Warms my heart to recall the happiness I felt so many years ago. Time passes so fast that we sometimes don't stop and enjoy the moment, not thinking it will be gone in an instant, and only thing left is a memory.

I remember my mom and dad were such hard workers. My mom worked hard as a cook and a factory worker and my dad was a policeman in Howell, Michigan and Fowlerville, Michigan. Even with the busy schedule that my mom and dad had, we all got together for Sunday dinner. We would get the food from our farm. We would have fried chicken, mashed potatoes, and homemade biscuits with hand churned butter. I can still smell the food cooking and excitement of dinner getting done. We were a close family and enjoyed doing things together. I remember I was nine years old before we got our first television. I was twelve years old before we got our first telephone. You had to take the receiver off the wall and crank this handle and tell the operator what number you wanted.

I guess this is the end of my walk down memory lane for now. I hope you enjoyed it as much as I have. The hardest of times are sometimes the best of times and we don't even know it until later and wish we could go back.

Getting To School With Leg Power
By Evelyn Genson Urban of Fountain,
Michigan
Born 1933

Nordhouse School in Hamlin Township's history goes back to 1847, originally a one-room frame building destroyed by fire in 1893, replaced by a one-room frame building in 1894. After a fire in 1940, the school was replaced with a one-room square brick building with a full basement.

In 1941, this was very special; almost all the one-room country schools were single story frame structure. Indoor plumbing was not yet widely used; the modern entry area contained a closet hiding a deep round pit under a facsimile of a toilet seat called a chemical toilet. The smallest children could have fallen into the pit just doing their duty. The freestanding water cooler was filled everyday with water pumped from a pump outside, and on the walls were coat hooks.

The building was innovative, the desks were new, but the teaching in a one-room country school with one teacher for eight grades was still in place. The children of Warren and Mary Genson attended Nordhouse School from 1944 into the 1950s. I graduated eighth grade in 1948.

My teacher those four years was Mrs. Myrtle Brown of Scottville Michigan. She drove round trip of 28 miles a day and many women in those years didn't drive. She had a nice home in Scottville, a big beautiful car, a husband and two children who went to school in Scottville.

The only school days we missed were when roads were impassable. The students, (about 40) the years I was there, all got to school with their own leg power. They came from all directions and walked up to 2.5 or

more miles one-way The first year we went to Nordhouse, we lived on Beaune road and walked 1.5 miles. There were always other families to join the walking. Along the way, we told stories and created adventures hoping to get to school on time. No one owned a timepiece.

When we moved to our new home on Jebavy Road, We had a one-mile walk, but more interesting. We had two abandoned homes to walk by or explore. They were dilapidated shacks getting more dilapidated every year. They could have fallen in on us at any time in our explorations. One had a burlap sack of potatoes in the corner, a table set for one, like the last person alive died eating supper alone, and no one ever came back.

On the other side of the road was a big white house called the Wigwam. It was a big two-story structure. In my memory, no one ever lived there. Legend has it as an afterhours party place around 1939. After the bars closed, people brought their own bottle, food, was served and the partying continued. One night there was a murder there and the undersheriff was wounded breaking up a party.

The house had the reputation of being haunted. We believed the stories and enriched the legend. We were always glad to get past that place and never explored it. When there were enough kids walking home after school, we would dare each other to run up and touch it. It was way back off the road. Not too many took the dare. I remember one boy did. It was his claim to fame during his career at Nordhouse School.

Mrs. Brown had the freedom to teach and discipline as she saw fit to successfully educate 40 children in at least nine different grades. She had to prepare the lessons for all the classes. This wise teacher had children that were behind for the grade they were in. Most coming from a city schools, when their family moved to the country. Rather than hold them back or bore and discourage the children in her regular classes, she tucked them in between grades. She assigned an older student to tutor the areas they needed help until they caught up. It didn't take long either; I was a tutor.

In one-room classrooms, all the students were exposed to all the teaching, all the other children's wisdom and stories every day, some good, some bad, and many a lesson for Mrs.

Brown to rectify for a teaching moment. If you were bored, you had a library and bookmobile visits to choose reading adventures. You tuned out the classroom. This teacher had complete control of the classroom. Sometimes a child was sent home if they didn't like her discipline or heed her authority. To get home that child had to make the long walk home alone. The school had no telephone and most homes had no telephone. When they got home, they usually got a harsher punishment and had to humble themselves with a sincere apology to Mrs. Brown. It happened to my sister once. Once was usually enough for most students.

We had two recesses and a lunch hour. Spring and fall, the older children had major league baseball games during those time periods. The younger children and the wimps as we called them, (mostly prettily attired girls) played lawn games. If the weather permitted, all students played outside. For Inclement weather, we had the big basement for indoor games. There were

The students of Nordhause School in 1947-1948

no playground aides. We settled our own disputes because we understood Mrs. Brown was not to be bothered during her recess time. It was the responsibility of the citizenship committee to report serious issues. Usually issues were settled by-a committee person saying, "I'm going to tell." No one seemed to want to find out what that meant.

Across the road was a farm field with a good sledding hill. The children had the farmer's permission to enjoy it. As soon as there was enough snow, every child who had anything to slide on brought it to school. Sliding down hills and inclines on their commute. With the right sled, you could take a running start, flop on the sled, and get a good long fast ride without a hill. I lost many coat buttons on that trick. We rarely saw a car on the roads. As cheap as gas was, it wasn't cheap enough. You only used your car if necessary. Most people driving to and from work were off the roads when children were traveling the roads.

We loved Friday afternoon. After last recess, to round out our education, Mrs. Brown made sure she produced Patriotic, responsible citizens of the United States of America. She had citizenship Club. Citizenship Club opened with the Pledge of Allegiance. The meeting following Robert's Rules of Order to the letter. We elected all the officers every month so everyone got to serve. Since schools didn't have janitors, it was the responsibility of students to keep the school maintained daily. There were assignments for everything with time slots to accomplish the chores.

Playground committee had to keep the playground safe and cleaned. Maintenance had the big job. Some chores had to be done every day, pumping water, filling the water cooler, cleaning the toilet closet area, washing blackboards, pounding erasers clean (an outside job on the steps), sweeping the schoolroom, emptying wastebaskets, making sure all the library books were where they belong, and much more. Some jobs were weekly or as needed, like cleaning the basement, snow shoveling, and others. Everything was covered and well maintained. Mrs. Brown had PTA with meetings; parents were assigned for special programs at school.

Every country school in Mason County had an elaborate float in the Scottville Harvest Festival Parade, and a Harvest Festival Queen entry. This was dear to Mrs. Brown's heart because her home and family were in Scottville.

When my brother started school, he got out of school earlier, and was the only one traveling our scary mile, there was a man who walked by the school every day going to work. He hoisted Bob on his shoulders and for that mile, it was a contest of who could tell the tallest tale. We all enjoyed Bob's stories at our dinner table every night.

When we lived on Beaune Road, We had a sledding hill that was the envy of the neighborhood. A well-packed downhill path went from the road, past the house, through the barnyard gate, and across the packed down barnyard that was the playground of Doc and Dolly, our two beautiful workhorses and a cow. The rule to use the sledding hill was that the animals had to be shut in the barn before the gate was opened.

One afternoon, 11-year-old Evelyn, 9-year-old Helen, and 6-year-old Alice came home from school with various neighbor children with sleds. Evelyn went in to get Mother to put the horses in. Someone had opened the gate and Alice, with the judgment of a 6-year-old and anxious to show off her skills, did the run, the stomach flop, flew down the hill, and through the gate, the sharp edge of the steering mechanism catching Dolly's leg. The startled Dolly's hoof caught Alice's head, splitting it wide open, a fraction of an inch from the temple, which would have been fatal.

When Evelyn and Mother got outside, all the children were screaming in shocked horror. Alice was lying in the snow, her blood reddening the snow around her head. Mother screamed to Evelyn, "Get me clean, wet towels fast." Evelyn ran to the house, got towels, and rung them out in the drinking water pail, no plumbing in the house. Mother had put the cleanest snow she could find on Alice's head and covered the wound with towels and light pressure. Mother shifted into "save my child mode."

She quickly examined her options— no car, no telephone, Dad 2.5 miles away working on our new property, no other adult less than half mile away, and a yard full of horrified children. She sent the children home, dispatched hysterical Helen to the nearest neighbor to tell him to come quick with his car, praying the neighbor was home from work, and she sent Evelyn after Dad.

The neighbor arrived home the same time Helen arrived in his yard. He scooped her up and hurried down to our place. He got Mother in the car and placed Alice in her arms. Mother gave Helen orders to take care of 4-year-old Bob until Evelyn and Dad got back. The neighbor drove the agonizing six miles to the Ludington Hospital. Dad brought Evelyn home and left the three children to go to the hospital.

The rescue mission arrived at the small town hospital with no advance warning. An on-duty family doctor took her immediately to surgery. While she was being prepped, he called a colleague, another hometown family doctor. These brave men decided and did what had to be done. It involved cleaning a wound from the hoof of a barnyard animal and installing a steel plate in her head. The surgery took 5 hours; a special nurse was assigned until she stabilized.

She regained consciousness after three weeks. Two weeks later, she wore a helmet home. She wore the helmet a long time. With the help of her mother and sisters, she wasn't held back in school. She is 77 years old (2014), still living an active life with summers in our family home on Jebavy and winters in Florida. She's a pretty good golfer. The only trouble she had with the steel plate is setting off security alarms at airports.

I am so blessed that I lived and experienced a time when parents, teachers, doctors, and neighbors were trusted, respected and had the freedom to make good choices and the courage to do what was best for their children, families and the people they served.

God Bless My America.

Old Days in the Boonies
By Betty-Ann Jolin of Saginaw, Michigan
Born 1944

I am 70 years old. I was born on November 16th, 1944. I was born at Saginaw General Hospital. We lived in Kochville Township, which was then a farming community. My dad (John Bourdow) was deer hunting in the woods. The state police found him and asked him to go to the hospital. I asked my mother (Louise Bourdow) why Daddy was deer hunting when I was born. She told me I wasn't due until December.

I remember the moon landing which was July 20th, 1969. I remember watching it on television and thinking how surreal the thought was. I married Don Jolin from Zilwaukee a short distance from Koehville, on August 9th, 1969, which was only a short time later.

My family grew up on a farm in Kochville. There were my two sisters and I (Mary Lou, Jeanie, BettyAnn) and my two brothers

(Bobby and Danny). There were many memories from growing up on the farm. One of those was having to use an outhouse before there was indoor plumbing. Rather than going outside at night or outside in the wintertime, we would use a metal pot with a cover. I remember when we got an inside toilet. I was about eight years old. It was really something. My sisters and I thought that because our bedrooms were upstairs that we would put the old metal pot that was in our cellar in our closet so that we would not have to walk all the way downstairs. My mother found it in our closet and immediately brought it downstairs and emptied it and put it back in the cellar. I was not supposed to get it again.

I also remember growing up with cows on the farm. We had 12 cows on the farm. My dad would milk all of them. He would sit on a little stool and put the milk in a pail. Then he would pour the milk into milk cans. I remember him squirting the milk in the barn cats' mouths. During the day, the cows went to a pasture down a lane. While they were on the way to the pasture, my sisters and I would hang onto their tails and race to the end of the lane. My younger sisters and I also had calves that we considered our pets. We both had one that we used to walk with chains on their collars like they were dogs. All of a sudden, they were gone.

Besides the cows, I was always bringing home animals and telling my parents that they "followed me home." One time, I brought home a dog, which had nine puppies. When they got old enough, we brought them to Bay City to a pet store, but they would not take them. My sisters and I were so glad.

I also remember when I had won a duck at the church picnic. You had to put a round ring around their neck and then you would get the duck for a prize. I had him in the old chicken coop. I'd feed him and even had a name for him. All of a sudden, he was gone. I found out later that my uncle had taken him and slaughtered him and used its blood to make blood soup. He was Polish.

We had a lot of fun on the farm, but not your normal type of fun. A game we used to play, which my mother didn't know, was called "poop on a stick." My younger sister would stick a stick in the outhouse and then chase my sister and me around with it. We also would play "poke the beehive." We used to have a bumblebee hive in the old pigpen behind the barn. We used to poke it with a stick and then run. If we were to get stung, which we always did, we would go put mud on it and then go right back to poking the hive. We would also climb around in the barn and jump in the straw.

We had a good time living on the farm. We had many friends out by our farm. My older sister, Mary Lou, had girlfriends, Iris Rouech, Shirley Krasinski and others. My good friends were Carol Robinnett and Kaye Anne Leuenberger. My younger sister Jeanie's friends were Juiie Rood and Betty Scharich. The "city" kids at Arthur Hill thought we lived in the "boonies." They never knew how much fun we had.

Family time was much different from what it is today. I remember before there was television. My siblings and I would listen to the radio. We used to listen to "Baby Snooks" and "Gene Autry."

I remember getting our first television. This became a regular family ritual. We used to watch the "Sid Caesar Show." I also remember coming in from outside and watching the "Howdy Doody Show" on TV, which lasted an hour. They used to advertise "Wonder Bread," but instead of commercials, they would advertise right on the show. Sometimes we also used to complete chores as a family. We would all go out as a family and hoe. We would go out from 7 am until 12 noon. We quickly realized that this was not "fun" family time and we kids would quit.

I remember when our winters were much more severe. We had bad storms and blizzards. I remember the snow being very deep. I remember big snowbanks by the garage, which was separate from our house. I remember going down the hill with my sled and hitting the garage. When we would go outside and play, we would wear two pairs of jeans because we did not have any snow pants. We would have to wear our shoes inside of the snow boots.

Our appliances were very different as well. We had rotary phones with party lines. Party lines were where multiple people in the neighborhood could sit and talk to each other at the same time. My mother used to put her hand over the voice and listen to whatever they were saying. I also remember when washers and dryers did not exist. We had a wringer washer and my mother used to hang our clothes outside on the clothesline. If it was raining outside, she hung the clothes inside on clotheslines that she would tie on doors and crisscross. She had to do this in the wintertime as well. Because of this, she did a lot of ironing.

Rather than taking baths every night or every other night, we only took baths on Saturday night because we had church the next day. I also remember when we had an insulated box. When the milkman came, he would put the milk in the box. We would have quart bottles of milk and half cream at the top. We used to get four of them. A "Peter Wheat" guy used to come and my mother would buy bread from him. If we kids were around, he would give us a real little loaf of bread.

I also remember having to make our own butter from milk. We would take turns from the old butter churn. We would have to take the stick and put it inside the churn and put it up and down. Then my mother would put it in a glass jar with paddles. She would then turn it until it was butter. To make cow's milk to drink, she would put a paper strainer in a big metal strainer and pour the milk from the cow in the metal strainer and the pour it into a pitcher and put it in the refrigerator. I loved milk. My older sister did not.

I remember our schools being much different from schools today. We went to a one-room school with 4-5 kids in each grade. Our school was Liberty School and it went from kindergarten to 6th grade. When we were in kindergarten, maybe six weeks, we took a test and if we passed (we all did), then we went to the 1st grade. For school, we each would receive one new pair of jeans and a couple of t-shirts. We never had a phone at school. We always had to go across the road and used the neighbor's (an older couple) phone. We had a basement and a piano.

Our favorite teacher was Mrs. Scharich. She played the piano. Every Friday, we used to go downstairs in the basement and sing songs like "Home On the Range," or "Oh, Where Are You Billy Boy" and "Church in the Valley." We used to have a stage that was chained up. We would have Christmas programs on it. We would have red benches that we used to sit on and then the parents would sit on them too.

There are so many great memories from

growing up in the "old days." I would never want to change anything from my childhood and living in a farm in the "boonies."

Nester School in Ogemaw County
By Marian (Fabera) Neely of Tebbetts, Missouri
Born 1937

This one-room school was a brick building with an entry area where coats and lunches were stored. Above this entry room was a belfry with a heavy iron bell. A thick, strong rope hung through a hole in the ceiling. This rope was pulled to ring the bell. An early bell was rung at 8:30. I suppose this was to remind the pupils (students) to quit dawdling along the road and to hurry on to school. The 9:00 bell was the signal for us to stand, with hand over heart, and recite the Pledge of Allegiance to the United States Flag. In 1942, when I started school, the flag had 48 stars, which were arranged in six straight rows with eight stars in each row.

In our area of Michigan, schools were located two miles apart. Our family property was in a different school district, but a big sinkhole in the road and surrounding area prevented us from attending that school. I

Nester School in 1970

think it took approval of the county officials for us to attend Nester School.

I was allowed to start kindergarten in April after my birthday when I turned five. I walked over two miles each morning and afternoon, with my three older siblings.

Entrance to the school property was at the center of the west side. There was a large gate that opened into a seldom-used parking area. A smaller gate was at the end of a concrete walk. The school building was approximately at the center of the lot. A woodshed was directly behind the school on the east side.

There was a hand pump beside the concrete sidewalk. Water was pumped into a bucket and carried into the school, daily. An enamel dipper was kept in the water. We all drank from this same dipper. Later, the health department got involved and every person had to bring a cup from home.

Inside the school, there were large slate blackboards as part of the wall, on several sides of the room. It seems that the blackboard at the front of the room was used most. Our assignments would be written there. When a pupil misbehaved, that pupil might be required to write, "I will not (whatever the offense was)" up to 500 times. The other blackboards were mostly limited to artwork that stayed for long periods of time.

At the front of the room, there was a recitation bench where the pupils were called to recite their lessons for the teacher. Sometimes the pupils were sent from the bench to the blackboard to write arithmetic problems or spelling words.

Each year Nester School had a Christmas program where the pupils presented plays, songs, poems, etc. The audience (mostly parents) was seated at the school desks. It was not unusual, or a big deal, to see a mother in the audience nursing a baby with a hanky covering her breast and part of the baby's face. At the end of the program, Santa Claus would come in and hand out the gifts from under the tree. These were gifts purchased by families for the name exchange drawing that happened at the school a few weeks earlier. The very last event of the evening was for each pupil to receive a small paper sack with a few pieces of hard candy and usually an orange. The sack was

valued as much as the contents, and was re-used many times.

Another family activity was a picnic at the end of the school year. Each family brought their favorite home cooking (there were no fast food places back then). Eating utensils and plates were provided by, and for, each individual family.

Sometimes during the school year, we might have a box supper where girls and women brought a fancy wrapped box with enough food in it for two people. There would be an auction where men and boys would bid on the boxes. The bringer and buyer would sit together to eat the meal. I was very shy and did not enjoy this activity.

At school, we would have a valentine exchange. Most valentines were homemade. Sometimes a pupil would have a purchased valentine with a frilly fold out skirt. Others might have feet painted on a wheel that rotated and looked like the feet were walking. Fascinating indeed! My parents saved valentines from year to year. When the schoolchildren brought their new valentines home, the box of old valentines would be retrieved from their rafter storage spot so the preschoolers could join the valentine playtime.

We carried our lunches in round metal syrup buckets or small metal lard buckets with a removable lid. Lunch for our family was usually a peanut butter and jelly sandwich on store bought white bread, a cookie or a piece of cake, and sometimes an apple. The sandwich and cookie were always wrapped separately. I don't remember what they were wrapped in. Perhaps it was whatever covered the bread originally. I know the wrappers were always reused.

Nester School pupils with the Teacher in 1942

Typical of one-room schools, Nester School was on one acre. It had a swing set at edge of the parking area. Other schools might have a teeter-totter (seesaw), or even a slide in addition to the swings. Sometimes the children were transported by teacher and/or parents to a neighboring school for a game of softball.

Another competition between schools was the music festival, held each spring. As I recall, this was held at a public building where children from various schools would gather, thanks to transportation provided by parents. One-room schools did not have buses. Back then, buses for the local high school were painted with a combination of colors, always red, white, and blue.

During World War II Nester School would close for one afternoon each autumn and pupils, who had parental consent, would be taken to road ditches where they picked milkweed pods. These were sent to a processing place in Petoskey, Michigan where the fluffy seeds were prepared for use in military life jackets.

What would a school be without some kind of toilet facilities? At Nester School, the girl's outhouse was in the southeast corner of the yard. The boy's outhouse was at the northeast corner of the yard.

There was a concrete walk beside the girl's side of the school. This might have been for easy access to the woodshed. Girls often used this concrete for their games of hopscotch. Another activity enjoyed by the girls was skip or jump rope. They would say rhymes or catchy little phrases as they swung the rope they jumped over. Ball games were played on the boy's side of the school.

I left the area in 1954. The last I knew, Nester School building was still there and being used by a church organization.

Memories along US 27 in Michigan
By Barbara Green Martin of Lakewood,
Colorado
Born 1941

Connections—so important for those of us in small towns. US 27, as it ran through Gratiot County and Ithaca, the county seat, was our link to the rest of the state, opening our eyes to the rest of the world, such as it was in the '50s and '60s. Way before then, Bagley Road became US 27 in 1926. Even though I grew up on a farm in rural Alma, I called Ithaca my hometown, because that's where I attended school, first in the two-story brick Victorian built in 1884. It included grades K-12, and then in 1953 we were moved into the brand new one for our sixth grade in what is now the west wing of the North Elementary School.

US 27 connected us to the first McDonald's south of Ithaca near St. Johns. Five-cent hamburgers were a treat. We all watched for its sign to broadcast how many thousands and then millions of hamburgers had been sold. We had no concept of McDonald's being nationwide.

US 27 was also the final step in our training for our high school drivers-ed class. After driving unmarked, two-lane graveled country roads, making turns, passing other cars on the unmarked tarred Washington Road, we were ready for the heavily traveled but, marked, two-lane highway, US 27. It was scary and I had to pass a large semi. I was doing okay until I started to turn back in to my lane—the instructor yelled and grabbed the steering wheel. I hadn't completely gone by the truck. That's one of those memories that stick—sweaty hands each time I recall it. We passed the driving test if we hadn't turned over the Coke bottle the instructor had placed on the floor to measure our evenness in turning corners.

US 27 connected us with Lansing, the state capital, too. One of our school field trips was there, and those of us in 4-H traveled south for the Michigan State Fair in East Lansing. Also, the school buses that took us to the football and basketball games up and down the state—north to Shepherd, Mt. Pleasant and Clare and south to St. Johns continued to connect us with places away from home.

Our biggest connection to US 27 began when eight Ithaca High School graduates eagerly dipped their toes into the outer world's pond in the summer of 1959.

Four young men headed up north on US 27—to Grayling, the northern terminus of US 27. They worked as part of a laundry service for the Michigan National Guard. They checked in the service men's dirty clothes, labeled them, bagged them, and then loaded them onto a non-military truck, which transported the dirty laundry to Ithaca where they were cleaned. Lots of hands, lots of paperwork. The boys stayed in Grayling, sleeping on cots in the backroom of the retrieving area. They didn't wear uniforms; they were the only non-military in the camp. For years, townspeople had watched the Michigan National Guard convoys pass through Ithaca with its one stoplight on their way from various locations to Grayling, the Guard's summer camp. Depressingly gray, camouflaged military trucks carried supplies, and weekend soldiers to Grayling for their two-week training exercise, which most of us, the non-war-years teens, had no concept. Neither did we question.

At the same time, four young women also found themselves on US 27 heading north, but not as far as Grayling. As one of them, my heart was enfolded in fear of the unknown but also curious and looking forward to an adventure. I was on my way to spend a summer waiting on tables, 80 miles from my isolated farm home. A restaurant owner hired the four of us, sight unseen. He had a connection to a businessman in our town, who somehow found four of us who needed a summer job before heading to college in the fall. The only requirements were that we be willing to work an entire summer, stay on the premises, and wear white nylon uniforms with small powder blue nylon aprons. None of us had waited on tables.

Our parents drove us to the restaurant, leaning against the edges of US 27 on the outskirts of Houghton Lake. We met Robert Schneider, the owner of the R&S Restaurant. He was of German descent with an accent, something I'd never heard. The world was opening up to me.

We slept upstairs, not above the restaurant, but in an attached lean-to with an outside staircase. Thus, room and board were included in our weekly pay. We really worked for the tips. That was the incentive to do a good job—make more money in tips. We were saving money for our first year of college. Work included cleaning the lettuce, celery and carrots when the vegetable truck arrived; an experienced waitress, our mentor, explained this was why waitresses wore colored nail polish (red) to hide the dirt stains that couldn't be removed under the nails. Drinking coffee became a must, too. We didn't wear hairnets or little caps. We wore nurse/waitress white shoes for support.

We worked split shifts. The restaurant opened at 6 a.m. to catch the morning traffic and closed at 10 pm. During the slack periods of the day, only one waitress worked, but two or three were on for the busy shifts of breakfast, lunch, and dinner. I was honored with the breakfast shift as Mr. Schneider said, "You're the fastest one of the bunch. I need fast at breakfast." This early shift cut me out of trips to the Music Box, because that was open until 1 am and I had to be on the floor by 5:30 am.

My parents came to visit once that first summer. Mom had fixed a picnic lunch and we went to a public dock on Houghton Lake to eat. I cried when it was time for them to go home. I was homesick, but I also hated my job. The owner lost his temper frequently, swore at us, but I really needed the money. It would pay for my first year of college ($1000) if I worked the entire summer. As this was the only job I was aware of which would pay for a full year of college, I stuck it out for three more summers.

Eventually, US 27 took me to college in Mt. Pleasant, Central Michigan University. Later, in 1963, I traveled US 27 south to Northville High School for my first teaching job and then to Michigan State University in East Lansing for courses to keep my teaching certificate current.

When I'd meet new people and tell them I was from Ithaca, everyone knew where it was because they had to pass through Ithaca and the one stop light. Town kids always counted the different state license plates, mostly from Ohio. Today, Ithaca is by-passed and the one stop light has become a four-way blinker light. During a recent visit to Ithaca, I realized this when I waited and waited for the light to change to green and the car behind me honked.

Times and names change but the memories of the connections do not. In 1999 the Michigan Department of Transportation changed US 27 to US 127. However, US 27 gained the respect it was due: On August 19, 2010, the Michigan House of Representatives passed a resolution recognizing "Old US 27" as a historic road in the state.

Growing Up in Gunnisonville, Michigan
By Lois Rhynard Baumer of Lansing,
Michigan
Born 1933

"Gunnisonville" no longer appears on maps of the State of Michigan, however from the late 1800s into the early 20th century, a U.S. Post Office was contained in the general store, which was erected in that area, thus "Gunnisonville" is shown on old Michigan maps.

Gunnisonville Community
Gunnisonville is located north of Lansing, Michigan, on the corners of Wood and Clark Roads. It is named for pioneer family of Elihu Gunnison who was born in New York in 1803. His wife Ruth was born in 1815. They and their four sons migrated to this area in 1833. The Elihu Gunnisons now lay buried in the cemetery surrounding the schoolhouse, together with one of their sons and his family.

They built their first home in the middle of a forest. The closest commercial community was DeWitt, which lies about five miles northwest of Gunnisonville. There were no roads in the area and DeWitt was reached by horseback. The forest was dense and trees were marked indicating the route.

Two of their sons were early enrollees at the new Michigan Agricultural College in East Lansing, MI., and they were graduates in that first class from what is now known as Michigan State University.

The community originally contained a general store with its post office, the Episcopal Methodist Church, a one-room schoolhouse which first opened in 1835, a local cemetery, and a community weighing scales for use by local farmers. We were also the proud home of the Gunnisonville Marching Band which had snappy uniforms and played weekly for area events. It was led by a young man from the neighborhood, Reuben Sipley, who later became a member of the famous John Philips Sousa Band.

My Family
My parents Cecil and Gladys (Pilmore) Rhynard were born and raised in the St. Johns, Michigan area some 18 miles north of our home. They moved to Lansing shortly after their marriage in 1922 and originally settled on Comfort Street in Lansing. Four of their children: Lyle Dale, LeRoy Keith, Lois Rae

Lois's parents, Cecil and Gladys Rhynard in 1950

(Me), and Lila Kay were born prior to their later move to Gunnisonville just before my second birthday, in the fall of 1935 some 100 years following the Gunnison Family's entry here.

My father had been raised on a farm and never lost his love for farming. His parents, however, lost their farm during the "Great Depression" of the 1930s. He worked for the Consumer's Power Company for thirteen years and "played" at farming on the 35 acres here in Gunnlsonville, keeping cows, horses, pigs, chickens and raising their feed, etc. Our home cost him $2,500.00, a real bargain due to the depression. We had our own garden, a fruit orchard and lived here quite happily during my growing up years. While here, a third son, Loyal Day (Mike) arrived. I was nine years old at the time and generally treated my baby brother as a toy.

Le(Roy) was my "special" brother. He was just 16 months older than I; due to our closeness in age, we played together a lot. One of my fondest memories relates to our Mom playing "waitress" and taking our luncheon order. Of course, it was only tomato soup and a grilled cheese sandwich, but we loved the playacting involved. I still have a picture of us sitting at our child's table awaiting lunch. Early on, Le became my role model, teaching me to read and print my name before I started school.

Gunnisonville School

I began attending the one-room school here in Gunnisonville in the fall of 1939, just prior to my fifth birthday, together with my two older brothers. Just two years later my baby sister Lila Kay also attended there. This was the beginning of my life-long love affair with Gunnisonville, and I remain here to date, at a different address but still on Boichot Road where I grew up.

During my first four years at Gunnisonville I had three teachers. Commencing with my fourth grade, Irene Davis came and remained with us for the next five years, through my eighth grade. I loved her! She lived in nearby DeWitt with her husband Raymond, and she drove to Gunnisonville in her "new" Oldsmobile each school day. During that early post-depression era, it was unusual for women to drive by themselves, AND for anyone to have a new car was very rare. She was young and pretty and she also loved books. (We all called her "Mrs. Davis" and I continued to until many years later when she gently commented that I, at an advanced fifty years or so, could call her Irene.)

At that time, our school library was somewhat limited and confined to a built-in bookcase of six shelves. One of her first actions was to borrow 25 books from the DeWitt Community Library for our school each month. I devoured as many as possible within that one-month window and she recognized my love of books. Thus, we formed an immediate bond, which continued until her death a few years ago. After completing my study time, I read and read; and it was a common joke that I often didn't hear her call my class to the front for our daily recitations. She often called me to class, saying, "Lois Rae, are you joining us?"

Our teachers at that time were very much a part of community life and they became our friends. They knew our parents, friends, and a great deal about our individual lives. Our Gunnisonville Church lies just across the road from the schoolhouse and we held many school events in the fellowship hall of the church. School P.T.A. meetings were held in the

church each month. Our mothers contributed homemade goodies for these events, and everyone in the community was welcome. Our neighborhood included members of the community who no longer had children of grade school age and they also attended those monthly meetings, their commitment didn't end when their children finished the eighth grade and they continued to attend any event centered around the school.

We also held our annual school Christmas program in the sanctuary of the church each December. We would hang sheets to create the dressing rooms and stage for our Christmas plays. (A few years ago, we renovated the sanctuary of our church and John Headley, Chairman of the Church Trustees, commented on the many holes still appearing in the woodwork, a legacy of those old days when our church and school were partners in the raising of the children.)

After completing our eighth grade, we became tuition students in Lansing's Secondary Schools, attending the Pattengill Junior High and graduating from Eastern High School.

The one-room schoolhouse closed as a kindergarten-eighth School in 1956 and a new school was constructed down the road. However, the building remains standing on the SE corner of Wood and Clark Roads. During the nation's 1976 Bi-Centennial Celebration, a committee of old residents and school officials combined to repair/renovate the building and the Gunnisonville Corners containing both the schoolhouse and church were granted status as a National and State Historic Site. State of Michigan Historic Plaques denoting our historic status are now attached to the two buildings/grounds. And, although it no longer exists as a school, it remains open to host our community events.

Our Gunnisonville United Methodist Church

Commencing in the late 1830s, our pioneer residents met in individual homes and were served by Methodist "Circuit Riders." As the group grew, they began to meet in its (second) log cabin school-house. It was formally organized in January of 1862 as the Gunnisonville Episcopal Methodist Church.

In 1886, Reverend McNutt approached the Ladies Aid Society and asked for their support in making plans to build a church. They

Gunnisonville Community Church in 1937-38

convinced their husbands and the community began plans for building a sanctuary in Gunnisonville. The Philip Krause Family donated an acre of land and the planning began. The church was completed in 1888 with area residents donating most of the materials from their farms. Its pews were built in Adam Rupp's barn using area oak trees donated by residents, sand and gravel for the foundations came from their farms, and the red bricks came from an area brick firing business in nearby Grand Ledge. -Adam and Sara Rupp were the first couple to be married in the new Gunnisonville Methodist Episcopal Church shortly after it opened its doors.

Just before the depression, the church fell on hard times and was closed for a period of ten years. It was re-opened by a retired minister, Reverend Carl Seipp, in the spring of 1937. My family attended that first service and I have been a member ever since.

Our first Sunday school teacher was Mrs. Clark (Jessie) Livermore whose husband operated a large farm about one mile from the church. As we grew older, our teacher was Letha Perry, who died of cancer when I was about ten years old. Our last teacher was Mrs. Herman (Georgia) Gentry. Although our adult church attendance was always small, our

youth fellowship was large and we enjoyed the Sunday evening meetings, hayrides, and parties throughout our teens. Present day attendance is good and we prosper, making those early sacrifices of our parents and community worthwhile.

Another of my special experiences while growing up was membership in Clinton County's 4-H Clubs. Our leader Margaret Stampfly was the wife of one of the Church's pioneer families. She devoted many years teaching us how to sew our own clothing, serve nice teas, and oh so many of the things not previously experienced in our working class background. My life at Gunnisonville continues as I serve as our Church Historian, and as a member of various church committees.

The Best Thing That Ever Happened To Me
By Nellie Mae Everett Turner of Saginaw, Michigan
Born 1933

My name is Nellie Mae Turner. My maiden

Jackie and Nellie

name is Everett. My hometown is Eldorado, Arkansas. My husband's name is Jackie M. Turner. The best thing that ever happened to me is that I chased my husband and finally caught him. He finally slowed down so that I could catch him. I am not ashamed to say I chased him because it paid off. I am the bull and he is the fish. We have been married for 52 years and have been together for 58 years. I have one child, a son. His name is Mark A. Gray. He is 61 years old and I am 81.

My mother passed when I was a year old, they told me. My dad raised two boys and us three girls. I am the baby out of five children.

Feed Sack Bloomers and Maytag Washers
By Doris M. Drake of Barryton, Michigan
Born 1919

I was born in 1919—before the crash of 1929 and our severe depression. We heard about banks closing, people jumping out of windows in suicide when fortunes were lost. When factories shut down for model changes there were serious layoffs. In cities, there were soup lines or bread lines to help cope with the resulting hunger. We often had our city relatives visit us during these times. We usually had potatoes to make soup or other food. Our mother canned all the food she could get her hands on.

We ran milk from our jersey cows through our cream separator daily and sold the cream to Remus. We used the skim milk for our family's consumption, which might include cottage cheese. The pigs got the rest.

Our oleo was white back then. Farmers could not let it look like real butter! I have often put oleo in our wooden butter bowl with a little packet of yellow oil included and mixed it to the desired yellow. This saved us some of the cash we desperately needed. But it's not butter!

Mom baked eleven loaves of bread daily when our family was the largest. We had nine children, our Grandma, our Uncle Lewis, a widower from Ionia, and perhaps a hired man.

Our garden was large. It made lots of work outside and later on at canning time. Grandma dug dandelion greens, both to cook and eat in fresh salad.

Mom ordered baby chicks annually, brought 100 in a box by the mailman. They usually stayed in the house a couple of days until we found a place for them. Later on, Mom had chickens and eggs to sell and eat. This helped when the cows dried up before calving.

Pork butchering time brought us liver on the first day. The other meat was usually put in a barrel of salt brine strong enough to float an egg. The hams made good eating after spending several days in the smokehouse.

We had a cow or maybe a half of one to can periodically. That was a real job in our kitchen on a wood cook stove in a boiler. At some point, our government put a cannery in Barryton. Wonderful! We could take a half a cow, or even a whole butchered cow, there in the morning. In late afternoon, we went home with it all in tin cans. Always we had large cans of meaty broth for making delicious soup or stew in the days ahead.

We slept on straw "ticks," which were bed-sized bags, washed, and filled high with new straw. The straw wore thin and had to be redone about twice a year.

The government set up a place in town to make mattresses out of supplied materials. Mom went and learned to make them. For the first time we laid on mattresses instead of straw "ticks."

Laundry was a big job. Water was heated on the kitchen stove in a boiler. White clothes were boiled in it to keep them white. When I was nine, I scrubbed clothes on the washboard for our family—mostly on Mondays. That was nice for my Mom. She needed some help.

The Maytag washer that we purchased from the salesman who came by our house

One of the early buses for Fork Township Agricultural School

had a "putt-putt" gasoline motor and a long, flexible exhaust hose to be stuck out through an open door, even in frigid winter days, until the motor was turned off. Blessed quietness when that "putt-putt" stopped!

I was the oldest of our family of nine living siblings. One little brother, Robert, lived only a few hours. My oldest brother, Clyde, fourth in the family, built a box to bury him in. He and our father walked four miles to the cemetery to bury him.

We, like our neighbors, had a well-used outhouse. One day the door was closed. I urged a younger sister to run out quickly and shove the door to see if it was occupied. She did, and it was. There sat Uncle Charlie in complete shock. I wanted to go hide!

Our Argue School consolidated with Barryton and five other rural schools when I was in fifth grade. I remember some "raw" feelings in our community, church, and school about that consolidation.

One day when I was in sixth grade, one student said, "My dad works at Barryton co-ops. He gets $25 per week." Another student said, "I wish my dad got $25 a week."

Our school closed two weeks for potato-digging vacation back there. After we had harvested our own potatoes, we looked forward to earning money from other growers, often at $1.00 for all day. The money we received usually bought our clothes, for the next year, out of the Sears, Roebuck or Montgomery Ward sale catalogs. I remember buying a dress for 59 cents.

Some animal feed or other flour or grains were sold in white bags with huge letters or designs on them. Mom bleached some of them white and dyed them bright yellow. They made wonderful, colorful bloomers for her daughters—not expensive either. Our Grandpa called us sunflowers. Some bags came in pretty prints and made attractive aprons, towels, curtains and other things.

When I was in high school, I learned that Montgomery Ward & Co. was helping college students by printing their names on order blanks. They handed the blanks out to people. When they used them to order products, a percentage of the amount was put on the student's scholarship. Most of my first two years at CMU was paid for in this way. How fortunate I was! I could teach for three years. I taught one year at Homestead School,

A school bus driven by Doris's in-laws

southwest of Big Rapids for $75 per month. I paid room and board, paid off a $200 note, and had $40 left to use to get married on.

It is hard to believe the changes that have come in my lifetime. Our country school and church were one-half mile east of us. We walked to both most of the time.

Some people came to church by horse and buggy for years in my childhood. One family drove two horses and a two-seated buggy. Later on when some cars were driven, gas tanks were empty at night when it was time to go home. Some people came to church to get gasoline!

We had a tall windmill that pumped our water. The well pit helped cool our food. We never had an icebox.

One day my three-year-old sister, Tootsie, climbed up the windmill to the rickety broken platform. She stood with her hands behind her and said, "We're going strawberrying, aren't we?" My teenage aunt said, "You stand still!" as she climbed to bring her safely down. Mom could not even look up at her. That night, Grandpa boarded up both sides of the ladder. It could not happen again!

Our house was full. Our Grandma slept in a bedroom with three beds in it. She slept in a bed with one or two children. Her suitcase was a curiosity when she returned from visiting her family. So much for her privacy.

It was my job to keep our lamps and lanterns clean and filled, ready for evening. We also had a gasoline lamp to pump up before lighting. That was not my job. I would get suspicious about another baby coming. Usually we didn't talk about such things. When I finally got courage, I would ask my mother. She would say, "There is always room for one more."

303

Our men needed cash. Michigan needed roads. Roads were built with shovels in those days. Also, our snowplows were not very powerful. In 1933, we had only one day of school in February due to lots of snow. Mom got tired of us all being home—thought it was quite unnecessary. Our road was the last local one to be opened with extra help and some shovels.

We had a car running part of the time. Our car was jacked up sometimes until we had cucumbers or green beans to pick for money for tires. No credit cards then, which was a good thing.

On Sunday, December 7, 1941, my husband and I came home from church to his parents' house. His father had stayed at home. He had a battery radio. As we entered the room, he exclaimed, "We are at war!" Japan had bombed Pearl Harbor! We were in World War II until 1945. We had Germany on the east, Japan on the west. Our defenses were severely down, and our fear was soaring. Our men went to war. Our women went to the factories, and home was never the same as before. My husband was a farmer so he did not go to war.

Our father was a happy, honest, hard worker who taught us how to live and love. He often made us laugh, like grabbing the last piece of pie and running down the road with one of us kids chasing him. He gave us all nicknames and made up funny riddles. His outlook on life was very positive. My mother (called Mamo) sometimes giggled hard, and we all ended up giggling, too. It is a good thing since she had such busy days.

One day Jawdie (my father) backed the car up in the backyard, shocked to find that he had run over our brother's head. There were the tire prints on his forehead! The dense grass had protected him, and he was still all right. Thank God!

Extended families got together for delicious dinners and fellowship. Neighbors sawed ice blocks from the lakes and stored them in old buildings by covering them well with sawdust, which supplied ice way into the summer. The ice and crank freezer made delicious ice cream. Sometimes there was even a little ice cream left the next morning!

We loved singing hymns in church. One of my favorite memories is singing duets with my father. He was a wonderful tenor. When my uncle came to visit, I also enjoyed his rolling bass voice. These are special times.

Little did we realize how soon our wonderful forty-four year old father would be gone. He took a trailer load of grain with our Studebaker to the Barryton Co-ops to be ground. Later on he was coming home, going north on 45th to the comer at Hoover Road to turn left. Two young men came, too fast, over the hill from the west and hit his car in the left side. He was thrown out, unconscious. Neighbors tried to help by getting him to the doctor, in and out of the car several times, and then at home on the bed, not really conscious. My sister spent an anxious night staying up with him. No one knew he must be moved only by trained people. They were trying to help and did the best they knew. Mom was worried in the morning. I still wonder how she got him to the Big Rapids Hospital. He died there in the afternoon.

My future in-laws picked me up in Mt. Pleasant. Someone asked, "Was it bad?" "Yes, it was bad," was the answer. I had no idea how bad until I was home and found him in the bedroom in his casket. You don't accept the worst until you are forced to. My two-year-old sister could not understand what happened to her daddy. My mother was certainly in shock. She couldn't eat, did not cry-was just numb. Our grandma, Dad's mother was just there. Words cannot express grief in such times.

The nine of us have had good lives, enjoyed getting together—never quarreled. We have supported each other in troubling times-and there have been numerous long-lasting situations.

Winter of 1937
By Antonette Groulx of Shepherd, Michigan
Born 1916

It had been snowing all week. This was in the winter of 1937. My baby sister of two months old had just died at home. Therefore, the baby had to be buried from home.

Our neighbors made a casket. It was covered in light blue material. Next morning it was still snowing. The road was not cleared. So, a sleigh pulled by two horses was the way we all rode to the main road. There was a car waiting to take us to the cemetery.

It was in Carson City Cemetery in Michigan. A path had been cleared to the gravesite. The priest went just ahead of us to do the prayers. It was very short as the storm continued.

In Carson City, Michigan Cemetery, there is a small headstone marker with Helen Eva Chomas on it, born January 1937, died January 1937.

I went to a school called a country school. It was a big building of one-room only. A big woodstove set a little of center to heat the whole room. Blackboards up front with chalk and erasers made of some felt cut in shape of the hand.

The teacher kept the stove burning to keep warm during winter and cold days. She taught all eight grades. Some had three or four in each grade. There were desks for two people each.

Only lead pencils were used in those days. Inkwells were there too. Pens were made by sharpening a turkey feather. No ball points were heard of in those days.

We walked up to one or one and a quarter miles to school. It was nine o'clock until four o'clock. No busses were available many of us did chores before going to school. Chores were feeding animals or chickens or milking cows.

We were lucky to get a ride by mom or dad in a pickup truck. We were farmers, small farmers at that.

Devilish Treasure
By John Schwarz of Bay City, Michigan
Born 1948

In the late 1950s, my friend and I would often take a walk into the small town of Bridgeport, Michigan. On the way, we would search around the town dump, and fishing holes for pop bottles. After we had collected five bottles each we would trade them in for two bottles of RC Cola.

We would sit on a telephone pole out in front of the stove. A few feet away there was a stop sign where Williamson Road intersected US 23. We would bet on which cars would squeal their tires when taking off. Quite often,

we couldn't drink all of our "pop," so we would dump the remainder into a crack on the sidewalk. One day, the storeowner yelled at us because the cola was deteriorating the concrete. We soon got even with him by squirting soda all over his new, baby blue Pontiac wagon.

On another trip into town, we stopped into Mr. Alsgaard's new store. When we left, my friend, John, showed me five packs of gum he had stolen. He said, "why don't you go back inside and steal some too?' I didn't know what to say. I had never stolen anything before. Well, maybe I had stolen some of my brother's toys. Anyway, peer pressure won out over morality. I went back in and stole five packs of gum. Then my friend and I went back into the woods to partake in our devilish treasure. We each opened our five packs of gum, and placed all twenty-five sticks of gum into our mouths. That much gum makes a big cud! When we tried to chew, it mushed out onto our chins, which looked hilarious. Laughing with that large a cud did not improve the scenario. It's a wonder we didn't choke to death.

When I got home, I felt horrible. My parents taught me better. They would have been ashamed of me. Being a good Catholic I went to confession. Still I felt guilty about it for years. I often thought of it while in the US Navy.

In 1985, I went into the same store, and chatted with the original owner. I placed a bottle of pop and five packs of gum on the counter then paid for the purchase; I grabbed my pop and headed for the door. The owner said, "Wait, you forgot your gum!" I told him "No, I didn't." and recited my story. He said people had done similar things in the past. However, no one had ever waited twenty-seven years!

He later said he told his family my story over dinner. He said they all had a great laugh. I still think I might go to hell. Did I tell you about the time I...?

The Cat Who Rescued a Bird
By Janet J. Witucki of Bay City, Michigan
Born 1944

Several years ago, the weather was unseasonably cold for the end of October.

It was dark when I returned from church. Walking to the front garage door, I saw our Maine Coon cat, Rusty, looking at something. I held the door open for him but he wouldn't come in. He kept staring at something in the shadows. I turned on the outdoor light and there to my surprise was a beautiful Cockatiel just resting on the driveway. I sort of panicked because we were definitely a cat family and never had any other kind of pets. Cats and birds don't usually mix, however, Rusty wasn't at all aggressive towards the bird. Just the same, I put Rusty indoors.

I quickly called my husband to come outside and see this bird. Clearly, it was someone's pet. My husband bent down to look at this bird and extended his hand to it. It walked right up his arm and rested on his shoulder. We brought him in the garage and gave it some birdseed and water. He took a little of each. Ironically, we put him in a cat carrier for safety sake, since we didn't have anything else to use.

Meanwhile, I called my neighbor from across the street and asked if she knew of anyone in the neighborhood who may have lost a pet bird. She said she knew of a woman a block up our street who had two cockatiels. She called me back and said the lady had her two birds, but would be willing to take this one until we could find its owner. We knew we couldn't keep the bird at our house because of our cats. The woman came over with a birdcage. The Cockatiel went right into the birdcage and went to sleep, quite content. She took the bird home until I could try to find its owner.

The next day, I called our newspaper and put a notice in the Lost and Found section. About two days later, a woman called to say she had lost a Cockatiel. They were in the process of moving and her bird flew out the opened door. I asked her where she lived and by her address, it was about two miles away from us. I gave her the address of the woman who temporarily took her bird. She got in her car and drove to the woman's house and yes, it was her bird. She stopped by our house to thank us again, crying tears of happiness. I told her it was our cat who first noticed her bird. He wasn't trying to hurt the bird and wanted me to see it. How it managed to stay alive for about two months, during some very cold nights was incredible.

Remembering
By Grover Shaw of Ashley, Michigan
Born 1934

Remembering, remembering…that's all I have been doing lately it seems. I am 80 years old and am the baby of the family, a family of thirteen children. This winter I have lost two more siblings bringing the surviving total to the final four. This is a sobering thought and at each funeral, we have gathered to reminisce and talk about "the good old days." In my case there have been good days and bad days, actually bad weeks, bad months, even very bad years but overall my life has been blessed and the remembering of the early years most surely brings joy to my heart and mind. At 80, you have quite a lifeline to examine and looking at it, I feel most of my days have been good. I am one of the lucky ones I would suppose.

Everything moved slower in central Michigan in the 30s and 40s. It was a great time to be a kid. These are some of the memories I have as a child; frankly, I wonder how we all survived. Winter's focus was always keeping warm. Of course, the wood burning stove was the center of activity. We had a typical 1930s wood burning kitchen stove, which had a reservoir on the side. If you kept this full, which also meant you had to take a cup of hot water outside to prime the pump, you would have hot water readily for a cup of coffee or a bath. Baths were less frequent than they are now and of course took more effort to fill the square washtub. Speaking of outside, that was where the outhouse was. I remember wrapping up in my mother's black wool coat, which was always hanging near the back door, to run to the outhouse. There were chamber pots to use if needed but the last person up in the morning had the horrible task of emptying them. The older we got the less we wanted to use the blame things.

Evenings were spent curled up near the wood stove, getting as close as you could without burning your back or socks, depending on which way you faced. Many hours were spent listening to the Victrola. The younger kids would get to wind it up and the older ones would switch the records. We had quite a collection of records for singing and dancing. Dancing would keep us warm. My mom crocheted quite a bit and my dad would play us in checkers. We would play several games and the only time I would win was when he'd "let" me because he was tired. My uncle thrived on this competition and the challenge to beat my dad in checkers. My mom used to say, "Your uncle would run over to play your pa but always walked back home talking to himself." No one could beat my dad in checkers.

Winter brought illnesses and illnesses brought home remedies; castor oil, camphor oil, hot mustard plasters, flax seed poultice and fat meat and turpentine for wounds. I hate to tell you but when modern medicine fails, I still use some of these remedies with success. Unfortunately, my parents lost two children in the winter of 1913 to influenza.

Before electricity, we would also listen to the floor radio. I remember sitting close, trying to hear the Grand Ol' Opry in the evenings. My folks would listen to Gabriel Heatter's "Good evening everyone, there's good news tonight..." for the news, especially during WWII. My mother also liked to listen to the program "Queen for a Day."

Jerry was one of the family with the horses

Another memory before we had electricity is the old icebox. In the winter, we could furnish our own ice by cutting blocks from the ditch. We would place the blocks under sawdust to keep them as long as possible. In the summer, an iceman would deliver ice blocks. Our icebox looked like this: when you were facing it had a short door on the left at the top and bottom. On the right was a long door. The ice blocks went in the upper left door.

Speaking of electricity, I remember when they brought the poles and lines down to our farm. As a child, I thought 'those are the biggest fence posts I have ever seen.' I will never forget how my older brother came over to wire our farmhouse with electricity. When he was done, we had a single hanging lightbulb in each room. That was really something to a kid. A flip of a switch and the room came alive.

I had my share of chores. One was to milk the cows and carry the milk up to the house. In the summer, I also had to pump the cold, cold water to surround the milk pails to keep the milk the right temperature until it was picked up. I also carried wood in for my grandmother. When I did this, she would pay me six cents. Six cents was enough to buy a candy bar and a pop at the Free Show that took place in the nearest town on Monday nights. Summertime was when we had to put up hay for the winter. It was hard work. As I got older, we used bales, which were also very heavy.

Summertime meant many different things but one was the family reunion on my mother's side. Since I was the youngest, my job was to help with the gallons and gallons of lemonade. They would sit me up beside a tub and have me squeeze the lemons. Summer also meant swimming. This is how I learned to swim: my one brother took me by the hands, the other brother took my feet...1, 2, 3, and they threw me into the local gravel pit as far as they could. They told me to float or swim to shore and that was that. I have loved to swim ever since. I guess that could have gone either way.

I suppose that by some standards we were poor. It never felt that way. We didn't have very many clothes, and ma patched the ones that we had. We had farm animals and a favorite dog named Old Pugg. You'd tell him to bring the cows home and that's just what he would do, every one of them. We had music and laughter and would do odd jobs for a little money. I remember one New Year's Eve there was a huge snowstorm. My brother put chains on his tires and then spent most of the day and night pulling other people out of snow banks for a little money. My dad and uncle would also trap muskrats for some extra cash. We always had plenty to eat, well, most days.

Some of the old cars that belonged to Grover's brothers

The same rule applied here…the last one to the table sometimes didn't eat as much. Ma always had a huge garden full of vegetables and, because she loved them so much, row and rows of flowers. The neighbors would stop just to look at her flower garden. I'm the closest to my mother when I'm in my garden. She would put up jars and jars of food for the winter.

My mom believed there were "best" times to plant and harvest. One was planting sweet peas after Good Friday. She told me stories of weird Michigan weather. She remembered one year that it rained so much that the farmers couldn't plant until June 15. After that, it didn't rain again until September 15. Three months without rain is a big deal to a farmer. Another year she had written down that it snowed, sometimes quite briefly, in every month of the calendar. She lived until she was 95 so she saw see a lot of strange weather in Michigan.

Life was good and had some hilarious moments. I can still remember my dad and uncle pitching manure out a barn window. A rat ran by and as my uncle tried to get it, he slipped on the ice, fell through the barn window, and plunged right into the big pile of manure. Pa and I laughed about that for quite a while. Sometimes even now I chuckle to myself when I remember phrases that my ma and pa used to say. If my mom got surprised or pleased with some news or an event she would always say, "Well, Jesus wept while Moses went a fishing'." This was my Dad's favorite quip, "I had to laugh to see the calf go down the path, in an hour and half, to take a bath, in a minute and a half. Now that's a laugh!" My own grandchildren and great grandchildren know this verse now.

As kids, we entertained ourselves with games like Kick the Can, Tag, and Red Rover, which was fun for me since my name is Grover. As I got older, I would ride my bike into town just to get the chance to play softball with the town boys. Finally, one time they needed a catcher. They put me in and I did it! I caught that fast pitched ball and never let it go by me…eventually I discovered a catcher's mitt and started using the baseball glove for what it was built for! After that, sports became a passion for me. They helped make it easier when my brothers and sisters started to leave. Eventually, the youngest one is left alone. My brother Gerald was my best friend while growing up. He taught me how to take care of myself. He taught me how to be strong and to be a good person. Some of my best memories are the walks we would take after we had done chores. Sometimes we would walk until well after dark. We would return to the barn to eventually fall asleep there, between swatting mosquitoes, or course. The calls of the owls, the coons and the whippoorwills… it's something I can still hear whenever I think about it. It was especially hard when my brother Gerald left for Japan.

I remember the moon landing. I'm still waiting for a Mars landing! I remember political highlights and crazy trends. I married and raised four kids in an ever-changing era. In my lifetime, I would be the one to wind the crank on our Victrola and now I listen to my grandkids music on their iPod. I remember sitting next to my dad while he'd steer a team of horses and yet I can travel 70 mph on the interstate. My father and one brother died prematurely due to a heart defect that was prevented in me because of a piece of chicken wire in my heart they call a "stent." I used to wonder…now I can Google and get 40 different answers in less than ten seconds. I wish my older brothers and sisters were here. They would be able to remember even more. To some older people change is scary and intimidating, but not to me. I was the kid that stood in the middle of a room staring at a single hanging lightbulb for the first time wondering 'Well, what will they think of next?'

A Small Farm in the Thumb of Michigan
By Dolores Howell of Essexville, Michigan
Born 1931

I was raised on a small farm in the thumb of Michigan. My parents were very hard workers. My mother had a big garden and canned about one hundred quarts of fruits and vegetables every year. My dad plowed with a one-furrow plow, walking behind it. Sometimes I would ride on the horse. Corn and beans were the main crops.

We usually had eight or nine cows that had to be milked morning and night. No milking machines back then. I use to squirt the cats and they didn't seem to mind.

I spent eight years in a one-room schoolhouse. We had lots to do like playing anti-I-over, playing ball, and sometimes playing against other schools. Box socials were always a lot of fun. Whoever bid the most on your box had to eat with you. They always liked mine because my mother always fixed a good lunch.

My first teacher was my aunt. I colored on a book after she told me not to. No favoritism was shown as she slapped my hand with a ruler.

Delores (Sangster) Howell in 1937 or 1938

Delores (Sangster) Howell in 1949

I had to wear long brown stockings in the winter. I hated them and I would roll them down when I got to school. If I was lucky enough to have a nickel, I could get a bottle of pop or a double dip ice cream cone from the country store across from the school.

Walking a mile to school, we would stop at my aunt's to get warm. She lived halfway to school. She always had something warm for us to drink.

We never had a washing machine. It was hard washing things on a washboard. We also didn't have inside plumbing. We had to prime the pump and carry the water into the house. Going to the outhouse was scary after dark.

When we got our first refrigerator, I was so excited I ran across the field to tell the neighbors.

I worked on the farm in the summer. Forking beans, and topping beets. Picking pickles was a backbreaking job but the money was ours so we could spend a day at the county fair.

I had three best girlfriends in high school. Two have passed away. The other friend and I get together at least twice a year. We always have a lot to talk about.

Having an older sister, I got many hand-me-downs. I got my first new coat in high school. It was ankle length, green and had a hood. It was the style back in the late forties.

Going from county school to high school was a little scary. I had to ride a bus an hour in the morning and an hour at night.

I met my first boyfriend in the ninth grade and had my first kiss. When he broke up with me, I was heartbroken. Memories I will always remember. I graduated from high school in nineteen forty-nine.

Many things I remember like baths in a washtub, party line phones, radio programs like Jack Armstrong and many more.

I was fortunate to have the good life that I had.

A Fond Look Back
By Dave R. Jones of Bay City, Michigan
Born 1954

At the young age of sixty, it's still easy to recall some of the comforting memories of my youth. Growing up in Bay City, Michigan, I have seen some of the fragments of a child's wondering magic vanish to make way for dull money making ventures of the city's fanatically minded men. This is what I'm thinking happened with the Wenona Beach Amusement Park.

That park existed in a time when our TV showed us movies in black and white, and we thought of presidents as being men of honor and high moral standards. Back then, writers of science fiction wrote about talking computers and hand-held phones. "Beam me up Scotty, and set the time machine back to a better time. Try the 50s and 60s. Kirk out!"

At seven years old, my memories of visiting the Wenona Beach Amusement Park were filled with excitement. Upon entering the park, the music of the merry-go-round would occasionally be drowned out by a thundering sound and shrieks of fear and delight to your immediate left. How could a child's eyes not widen in awe at the power and speed of the Jack Rabbit. This modest wooden rollercoaster is tame by today's standards, but managed to pull screams from the throats of all the young girls that rode in it. To my young eyes, it was the largest ride I had ever seen. Adding to the excitement of this ride, were the bumps you

felt, accompanied by complaining moans and creaks that emanated from the acoustically amplified wooden beams as you sailed along. From start to finish of this adventurous ride, it was easy to imagine the boards beneath you collapsing at any moment. The fact that my older brother had told me that people had died on this ride made it even more fearsome. He said that on the first hairpin turn, the cart with all occupants kept going straight and killed all onboard. After giving him a stern look, my father would tell me that nothing like that occurred, but at seven years old, I was ready to believe anything. Therefore, each time the open car would zoom toward the first turn, I would tighten my white knuckled grip on the safety bar and expect the worse. Once that deadly corner was behind me, I found the rest of the swift ride to be exhilarating. Finishing this challenging ride was a relief, yet for some inexplicable reason I wanted to go back and do it all over again.

The penny arcade was also a memorable place. You could buy pictures of movie stars, test your strength, or watch Charlie Chaplin stumble about as you turned a crank that set the pictures in motion. And, if you were fortunate, enough to have a quarter you could sit in a photo booth and receive four pictures of yourself making comical faces. Fifteen pennies in this building was a fortune I parted with easily to purchase the good memories I've never forgotten.

Visiting that park gave me my first taste of cotton candy. Those sticky pink webs of sweet delight wound around a long paper cone were hard to stop eating. And, if a mild stomachache would set in from the nearly poisonous amounts of sugar filling my mouth, I would never tell. Why would I jeopardize my chance at having another happy taste of that unhealthy, yet wondrous treat! My parents had taken me out there three or four times before the park closed in 1964. Now when I drive by a park full of trailers that cover a once joyous spot, I can almost still see the Ferris wheel slowly turning. Each long seat painted a different bright color. Screams of excitement, and constant laughter, whisper to me from a beachfront park full of golden memories.

You know, Hope and Crosby were right, they were thankful for the memories, and sang about it. Even though the Wenona Beach

Amusement Park is only one sparkling gem of a thought from yesterday, and it still remains one of the most important jewels in my life's treasury.

Dangerous Adventures
By Melvin J. Gay of Saginaw, Michigan
Born 1928

I lived on a farm here in Buena Vista Township and went to a one-room school called Leidlein School. It was two and a half miles from our farm to the school and we walked to school each day except when there was bad weather. Then my father or a neighbor would drive my sister and I to school in their cars. I started school at the age of six years, and entered first grade. There was no pre-school.

We had a very nice woman teacher named Viola Strandes, she knew how to lay down the law, and we respected her. There could be no noise in the classroom while we were studying. If there was, she would tap her pencil on the desk and say "no noise or there will be war." Each morning we had to say the pledge of allegiance. She taught all grades from first grade to eighth grade.

We had to memorize Lincoln's Gettysburg address and the preamble to the constitution. In this country school, there were no bullies or unruly students.

If there were an unruly student, our teacher would call on the Saginaw County Truant

Melvin's parents in 1940

officer Mister Bailey. Mr. Bailey would take the unruly student out back of the coal shed and that ended the problem. When he returned later and walked into the schoolroom, you could hear a pin drop and all students sat in their seat in a frozen state.

The school had a coal furnace in the back corner and an older student who lived near the school came early and got the furnace fire going. For the first hour of class, we students kept our jackets on. It took some time for the school to warm up.

In the front of the school was a long table with small chairs. The teacher would call up a grade class such as first grade or fourth grade, they would sit around the table, and the teacher taught lessons for that certain grade while all other students stayed in their regular seats. This worked out very well. If you were in the 7th grade and she was teaching 8th grade you would listen and when you advanced to the 8th grade the following year you already knew some of the lessons.

At the end of the year when we got our report card, it would state that you passed to the higher grade for the next year. If you didn't pass, you stayed in the same grade the following year. You had to take that grade over. That didn't happen very often. Most students always passed to the next upper grade.

On the last day of school each year, our teacher had a party for us. She ordered ice cream from M & B Ice Cream Company and they delivered it to the school in a canvas bag with dry ice packed on top of it. What a treat, we never ever had ice cream at home or anywhere else.

I went to school in the latter part of the Great Depression and Mom and Dad didn't have money for such things. We lived in an old house with no electric so my sister and I did our homework by the light of a kerosene lamp.

In May of 1936, that house burned to the ground and when I came home from school that day I saw nothing but ashes.

I spent all of my grades in the one-room school 1st through 8th grade. World War II started when I was in the 7th grade. Even a little school like this helped to win the war. All the students brought pots, pans, and scrap iron to school for the war effort. We had a big pile back of the school and sometime later, a scrap truck came and picked it up. We also used our index and middle fingers to make a V meant victory of the war.

Sometime around 1933 a coalmine was built across the road from our farm. It only operated to about 1940 and then it closed down. There was a large building called a Tipple, which stood over the mineshaft leading to the bottom of the mine. It was about 80 feet high on one end, and there were coal bins where the coal was dumped and stored. Two sets of cages or elevator cars brought up the coal. As one car went down another car came up. They were side by side. The miners also rode these cages to get to the bottom of the mine and return to the surface.

Several years after the mine closed, my sister and I decided to climb to the top of the tipple. Everything was coal dust and the higher we climbed the more we were covered with black coal dust. When we reached the top, we noticed that the tipple was swaying from the wind and that frightened us and we started down to the ground below all covered with black dust. That was bad enough but now onto another adventure. About 500 feet south of the tipple was another mineshaft leading to the bottom of the mine. It was called the airshaft. A large blower blew air down into the mine for the miners to breathe. The airshaft was all lined with planks on all four sides all the way to the bottom and had a set of stairs that went to the bottom. My sister and I decided to walk to the bottom of the mine using those steps.

As we went down it got darker and darker and when we were halfway down the stairs started to fall apart. They had rotten wood. We went back up to the top in a hurry and got out of there. I have often thought if those stairs had fallen apart, we would have fallen to the bottom of the mine and maybe never been found. To this day, we never told our parents of this adventure.

Before the 1940s, almost all farming was done with horses. My dad had a team of horses and one was a Strawberry Roan mare. He wanted a team with both Strawberry Roan horses. Therefore, he had the mare bred and she produced several Strawberry Roan colts. Her first colt grew up and trained to work alongside her. He named the colt Sally and the mother was Ruby. Now he had the team of horses he wanted. Ruby's last colt had grown up, and was nearly full size. She was not yet

Melvin and his sister, Eleanor

trained to pull a load.

One day when our folks were not home, my sister, and I went to my Grandad's farm next door and found an old buggy harness. We brought the harness home and tied it together with binder twine string, as it was very old and in bad condition.

I held onto the reins and my sister led the colt around the farmyard. We did this for some time and had no problem with the colt. I saw a wooden fence post laying on the ground and I hooked it up to the harness and had the colt drag it around the yard.

Now this was a very dangerous thing to do, it could have frightened the colt, and he could have bolted away. He could have run into a barbed wire fence.

We did tell our Dad about this and he almost fainted. It scared him! Later on, I heard him tell a neighbor "You know what those two kids did? They trained and broke that colt to pull a load." We were not punished for that bad deed.

Sometime in the later part of the Great Depression, electric power was brought to our farm. Up until that time, my mother washed clothes with a scrub board in a big round washtub. It had a hand cranked two-roll wringer fastened to the tub. It was backbreaking work. After many years of having electric power in the house, my mother could still not buy a washing machine. There just wasn't enough money coming in on the farm. She got a job, cleaning house, washing clothes, and ironing them, one day a week at a home in town. Now she had the money, she chose to buy the top of the line washing machine at the time. A Maytag- it cost $59.00. It had all machined gears not like a Sears or Montgomery Ward machines with rough cast iron gears, which were selling for $14.99.

She bought it on what was called "on time." You could pay one dollar a week until it was paid off. I think when she could she would pay two dollars per week.

With this new washing machine, costing this large amount of money my mother took very good care of the machine. Before she started washing, she oiled everything that needed oiling.

When she was done washing, she removed the agitator and rinsed it off with clear water and the inside of the aluminum square tub. She washed clothes in the Maytag for over twenty-five years.

I still have the Maytag Machine and it's in great condition and in working order but has not been used in many years. It seems to be just part of the family and after all how could I get rid of something my mother worked so hard to own.

White Cardboard in a Window
By Mildred Cline of Lewiston, Michigan

I am the third child born to Grover and Ethel. I was born in southern Michigan and had two sisters. I don't recall if we lived with my dad's mom, or if she lived with us. She made a great babysitter and companion. She had a clubfoot so most of her time was spent in a wheelchair.

We didn't have a phone, so the woman that lived kiddy corner from our house would place a 10" X 12" piece of white cardboard in a window that faced our house. That told us that someone wanted us to call them back.

I think I was about twelve or so, that I wanted a perm. After talking to some friends, they suggested I try the beauty school, and it would only cost me a dollar, I said "why not." It turned out good!

My Dad connected the eves to a downspout to collect the rainwater to a cistern. There was a pipe that connected to a hand pump in the basement. The rainwater was used for washing our hair and doing the laundry.

Since we lived in town, we took advantage of the sidewalks. We did a lot of roller-skating and bike riding. When I was growing up us kids could go several blocks from home to play with a friend and your parents didn't have to worry. We always made it home ok.

Dad could do just about anything. We passed away some summer time with the stilts he made and a high trapeze bar.

There was a room, "attic," at the back of the house. It was on the second floor that was never finished; it only had flooring and insulation. If it was bedtime and it was raining, we'd argue over who was going to sleep in the "attic." There was an army cot in there to sleep on and the pitter-patter of the raindrops would put you right to sleep.

I attended Sunday school and sang in the church choir at the Calvary Methodist Church.

I went to the Bennett School in Jackson from kindergarten through the sixth grade. I don't recall how many city blocks to school, but the walk was a long way when you're just starting school.

The 7th, 8th, and 9th grades were a few blocks away at the West Intermediate School.

My parents were hard workers. They worked at different jobs to keep the family going as I recall.

There was a room in the basement that I believe was called a "Michigan" basement. All kinds of home canning were stored on the shelves. Potatoes were on the floor and when they sprouted, that was a job for us kids!

My Dad kept honeybees and he handmade all the equipment that was needed to process the honey and package it. One item was an electric knife to cut the layer of wax off the comb and an extractor to spin the honey out of the comb. My middle sister and I went door to door selling some of the honey.

One experience I had when I was twelve years old, still surprises me. I went ice-skating with my Dad at the Loomis Park skating rink. We hadn't been there long when my Dad fell and broke his arm. "Now what do we do?" I didn't know how to drive. Anyway, Dad said he would tell me what to do. We did make it to the house and my Mom drove him to the hospital.

At least one summer evening was spent admiring the beautiful Cascade Falls in Jackson. The different waterfalls and changing colored lights were spectacular.

When my parents sold their home and moved to a little farm just south of Leslie, I had to change schools. I had just started the 10th grade at Jackson High School. All new teachers and classmates made it hard for this shy little girl.

There was no plumbing in the house at the farm, so I guess you know we had one of those little buildings outside. A chamber pot was put on the floor at the foot of each bed.

I became good friends with a girl that lived on the farm next to ours. We both played violins. When we graduated, the two of us were to play a duet for part of the entertainment. The whole class marched onto the stage. When it was our turn on the program, all you could hear was squeak-squawk. When the class walked on the stage some of the boys loosened the strings on our violins.

We wanted to leave the stage, but the music teacher tuned our violins and we did finish our part of the program.

After graduation, I got a job at the Aeroquip Corporation inspecting airplane parts. I did that for a year. During that time, my girlfriend and her boyfriend set me up for a blind date. The four of us went roller-skating at Hankards Roller Rink. My date must have liked me; we were married the next winter.

In the early years of the 1940s, it was very hard to find a house to rent or buy. In the meantime, I moved my belongings in with my in-laws until we could find a place of our own.

In the summer, we went roller-skating on Wednesday nights and Saturday nights we went across Pleasant Lake to Barletts Provaline and danced to several of the Big Bands that would appear there.

My husband and his dad liked to go deer hunting in the Atlanta, Michigan area. On this deer-hunting trip, they noticed the Shell Gas Station and Restaurant was for sale.

They came home from hunting and told us women that they wanted to buy that business. We sold the farm and moved north. My husband's brother left his job and joined us in Atlanta.

The guys had never worked in a gas station before, nor had my mother-in-law or I worked in a restaurant before. A couple employees that were working for the previous owner stayed on and helped us get the swing of the restaurant business. After closing the business for the night, we'd all meet at the ice cream counter and each of us fixed the ice cream dish they wanted. We went upstairs to the living room and turned out the lights and

ate our treat while watching the drunks come out of Benson Bar.

Four years later, my father-in-law passed away. Since my husband and his brother missed not seeing their father in the station, we all decided to sell that business and move to Lewiston.

Four children and I are the only Oldsters left. There are grandchildren, and great-grandchildren, but that's another story.

The Shack
By Robert K. Robart of Newaygo, Michigan
Born 1940

The summer of 1945 marked the end of World War II. My Dad was transferred from Battle Creek to Grand Rapids at the end of August as he made rubber for the war effort at the plant in Battle Creek and that plant was closing.

By the end of September, we moved to a piece of land on the edge of the city limits of Fremont that my Dad had purchased before the war. He had built a small tarpaper shack

*Robert's parents Elinor Anna and Marvin Carl Robart
with his cousin Margaret*

314

The Robart Family

there and in front of this, he pitched a large army field tent. That was to be our home for the first winter in Fremont.

The shack was converted to a dorm room for us four boys. A section of the tent was curtained off for my sister as well as one for my parents. The rest was used as a living area and kitchen. My mother cooked on a white gas stove, which had a small oven. A coal stove sat in the middle for heat, toasting bread, and heating water for our washtub baths.

We boys were tasked with digging a hole 30 feet or so out in back over which was set a two-hole privy. The left hole was for standing and the right for sitting. In the winter, it was a cold and dark place. In the summer, one had to watch for spiders, bees and other crawly things. When my mother yelled or screamed, we had to remove the occasional snake.

Just five years old, I was the first to have to pee so my first chore of the day was to remove the snow from the path.

I admit there were several yellow spots in the snow along the path and my Dad warned the others against eating yellow snow.

The spring and summer of 1946, my Dad and two uncles constructed a cement block basement and he purchased a pre-fab garage from Sears and Roebuck that he made into a four-room house. The restroom only had room for a commode and sink with a trap door for access to the ladder to enter the basement, which served as a bedroom for us boys, a coal bin and for canned goods that my mother put up. The shack was converted into to a chicken coop and rabbit hutches were built along the east wall. Along with the chickens and rabbits came huge Norway rats, they would dig holes under the coop and birth as many as fifteen little ones every few weeks. Once a week we would plug all but two holes and put a hose in one hole. Then we would place our two rat terriers and ourselves outside the other hole. When we flooded the tunnels, the rats would run out. The dogs would catch them by the neck, bite down and with one shake kill a rat, and then grab another and so on. Any the dogs couldn't get to we clubbed them to death. By late summer, we would have the rats under control and would not have to start our weekly chore until the following spring.

We grew just about every vegetable and berry that would grow in western Michigan. My mother canned and made jams, jellies, and pies of every sort. She spent a great deal of time in the kitchen cooking, baking, canning, and even making candies.

We boys had to dig a huge hole and build a gable roof over it, which we covered with dirt and sod. The soddie was used for storage of fruits and vegetables for winter use. Some called it a Michigan cellar, but we called it a soddie. Almost every day Mom would send one or the other of us out to the soddie for whatever fruit or vegetable she needed that day.

We stored our frozen foods in a rental unit at a frozen food locker downtown and it was an eight-block trip one-way to get a package of burger or a roast.

We hunted and fished when we could and caught snapping turtles and frogs. To this day, two of my favorite foods are frog legs, and turtle stew.

We farmed out to orchards and farms to harvest every fruit, berry, and vegetable grown in Michigan.

The ones I liked the most were cherries and strawberries. However, if I ate one I might as well of gone home.

I used the money to buy my school clothes from the time I was ten years old and bought my first car at age fifteen.

My parents lived in that home until their deaths and willed it to my kid brother who still owns the house today.

My Mother's Trip to See Her Grandfather
By Laurence Gibson of Hudsonville,
Michigan
Born 1937

When my mother was around six or seven (1914–1915), my mother and my grandmother took a trip to visit her grandfather. My mother's grandfather was a French Canadian who ran a logging area in upper Lower Michigan.

My mother and her parents lived near Kent City, Michigan on a farm. They were taken to the train (Union Station) in Grand Rapids, Michigan by horse and buggy. It was an eighteen-mile trip one-way. They boarded a passenger train heading north. My mother told me how much she liked seeing the new countrysides.

They rode on the passenger train as far as it went north. Then they boarded a freight train riding in the caboose with one of the train crew heading north. The freight train took them as far north it went. They next road on a logging train headed to the logging area of her grandfather. They had to ride in the steam locomotive cab with the engineer and firefighter. That train ride took them to the train loading area.

It was winter so they had to ride on a logging sleigh, which took them to the logging camp. The camp had a bunkhouse for the crew, a mess hall, and a house where my mother's grandfather and grandmother lived. They stayed in the house. However, they ate most of their meals in the mess hall with the crew. My mother said she enjoyed her visit with her grandfather, especially eating in the mess hall with the crew.

Laurence's grandmother and her father in 1928

They took the sleigh and trains back to Union Station where my grandfather met them with the horse buggy to take them home.

In 1915 a neighbor took my grandfather and dad (who was 15 years old then) to Howard City, Michigan to buy their first car. My grandfather owned cars but didn't drive. The car salesman drove them around the block to show my dad how to drive the car (a Ford). The Ford had two levers on the steering column, one for spark timing and one for the gas throttle. There were three pedals on the floor. The pedals were for the brake, reverse gear, and two-speed gearshift clutch. Therefore, after the brief driving instructions and finishing the transaction, they were off for home with my dad driving. The car or driver did not have to have a license in 1915. The trip, about twelve miles, went along well until they got home. Grandfather said to pull up to the corncrib, but he got nervous as parents do from time to time. He said, "Stop! Stop!" In response, my dad mistakenly pushed on the wrong pedal and ran into the corncrib. The only damage done was a broken board. Being genteel good-natured my grandfather said it was all right and they went to the house to get the others to come see their first and new car.

While I was in the first grade (1942) at Ensley Center School the U.S., collected milkweed pods for the Armed Forces. The schoolchildren would gather pods for the war effort. I would pick the milkweed pods, put them in a citrus fruit bag, bring them to school, and hang the bags on the fence back of the school. When I would ride with my parents, I would always take bags with me. I would spot some milkweeds, my dad would stop, and I would pick the pods.

The fluff from the pods was used to fill life preservers. I have also learned that the fluff was used to line jackets and underwear. Old vehicle tires were collected also for the rubber. My dad took all his old tires to my school.

My grandmother was out fishing on Hess Lake. She had caught a bass and it was just under the limit. She kept the fish anyway. When she was coming in to shore, she could see Roy Buzzard on the deck of the pavilion having coffee with some other people. Roy was a hunting and fishing game warden. My grandmother put the fish in her large sun hat and put the hat on her head. The fish was not quite dead yet. Of course, everyone talked to Roy. He was a very likeable person and everyone knew him. Therefore, my grandmother stopped and talked to Roy. While she was talking to him, she was worried that the fish might give a last flip at the end of his life. However, as it turned out the fish remained while she had her polite conversation with Roy. She went on up to her cottage. She cooked the fish, and said she never took the chance of keeping an under size fish she caught ever again.

Memories of Growing Up in Midland Michigan
By Anita Barrett of Midland, Michigan
Born 1947

A Midland, Michigan native, born in 1947 during the Baby Boom era is my claim in the annals of history. My parents arrived in Midland in 1946 when my father was hired at the fledgling company of Dow Corning Corporation. He was the first employee that was hired "off the street" after the company was formed. As newcomers to the area, they found that finding a place to live was a great challenge. My mother scoured the town while my Dad was at work and found that there was nothing available to rent. Out of desperation, she even inquired as to whether they could live in someone's barn. One family made room for them in their home and they stayed there for a while. They also shared a home with another young couple for a while. Being in that predicament they quickly realized that the only solution was to build a house for themselves.

Anita with her parents, Wayne and Barbara Barrett

There was an area that had been farmland, and had recently been plotted for single-family homes. My parents were connected with the owner of this land. They had their choice of all the lots and they chose one that would be on the curve of the street, which created more of a pie-shaped lot and would allow for a larger back yard. My mother designed the floor plan and construction began. After the beginning stages, there was a many-month delay. It turned out that there was a shortage of lumber in the state because of the war, and it took a search throughout the state to locate the necessary lumber.

My mother, who was a registered nurse (R.N.), got a job at the Midland Community Hospital. That was back when it was a 35-bed hospital. She used to ride her bike to and from work and during the dark hours she could see men with their flashlights looking for night crawlers on the Midland Country Club Golf Course.

I, the oldest of four girls was born after my parents moved into the house. Construction was still not complete, but enough so that my parents could move in. Back in those days, they did not need an inspection and Certificate of Occupancy before they could take up residence. The street was not yet completed and my parents used the partially paved street behind the house and drove through the field to get to the house. My Dad has told the story of being stuck in the field one time, and the tow truck that came to pull them out got stuck too. It took a second tow truck to pull out both vehicles. Our street eventually was paved. In those early days, I can remember the milkman used a horse to pull his truck. During the summer when we were playing outside, we could hear the clip clop of his horse's shoes on the pavement, which would warn us of his arrival. We would ask him for chips of ice from his big blocks of ice. In addition, we would offer grass pulled from our yards to his horse.

Our first furnace was a coal furnace and I can remember going to the basement with my Dad in the morning and watching him shovel coal from the coal bin into the furnace. A wringer washer was my Mom's first washing machine. There was no dryer so she either would hang the clothes on the clothesline outside during the summer or in the winter would hang them on lines that were strung

Anita with her sisters Becky, Jean, and Elizabeth

in the basement. It was in 2012 that the first dryer was bought for the home.

My elementary school was a bit less than a mile from the house. All through those years I, and my sisters, walked to school in the morning, walked home for lunch, walked back to school for the afternoon and walked home at the end of the day. We walked in the rain, snow, or shine- unless we got lucky and were offered a ride from a neighbor. We walked past a park area, and in the winter it was always fun to stomp on the ice that would cover a wet area. Many times, we would return home with "soakers," which was when water leaked into our boots. My Junior High was also within walking distance, so for three more years I continued to walk to and from school. During those years, we ate our lunch at school, so we didn't have to walk home for lunch. Then for High School, my Mother arranged a car pool with four other girls who were in my class.

My family attended the Memorial Presbyterian Church and I remember that during its construction the bells that are now in the tower sat alongside the street- Allen Street before they were installed. During the late 50s, the two main streets that cross town- Ashman and Rodd were turned into one-way streets. The "Circle" was really a circle. It was a big roundabout. It made a lot more sense to me than the confusing convergence of many streets that it has now become. It was fun and easy to drive.

The Currie-Bennett Park is just around the corner from our house and during the summer, there were frequent softball games that were played there. I could tell when they were being played because I could hear the cheering while I was at home. I enjoyed walking over to watch the games. During the winter, a large area of the park was flooded,

using a big hose, to create a skating rink. We could walk over, carrying our ice skates, to go ice-skating. There is a building that had a wood stove, and it was used as a warming house. It is still there today.

Barstow Woods is just a couple blocks from our house and it provided many hours of activity. I enjoyed walking or riding my bike through the woods and never came home empty-handed. Feathers, acorns, pieces of moss, etc. found their way home with me. One time one of my little sisters decided that she was going to "run away from home" and walked over to Barstow Woods with the family dog and her alarm clock. She returned home for supper.

Back in the '50s and '60s there was not the variety of things to do in Midland that there is today. There was a movie theater on the Circle when I was very young, but by the time, I was in High School it had closed. I was told that it was due to problems with vandalism. It was turned into a bowling alley. Therefore, we went bowling instead of to the movies! The Grace A. Dow Library was built when I was very young, so it provided another place to go, and I learned to enjoy reading at a young age. In the summertime during my high school years, my boyfriend and I enjoyed going bike riding together. Sometimes we borrowed a tandem bike from a family friend. A favorite destination was the hospital where we would go in to see the babies in the nursery. It was open to the public and you could see the babies through large picture windows. That was when all the newborns were taken from their mothers and placed in bassinettes in the nursery and cared for by the nurses. With a limited variety of things to do, we got creative.

For two summers during my High School years, I got a job at Art's Cash and Carry on Ashman St. I would ride my bike over there and in the evening after the store closed there was enough daylight to ride my bike home. We sold mostly milk and ice cream cones, with a few groceries. Those were the days when milk was sold in glass bottles and they were returned when the customer came back to purchase more milk. We had cardboard carriers for the quart-sized bottles and it was most convenient to buy six quarts at a time. A hot summer evening was a popular time for people to come in for ice cream cones. There were a few times when my boss, Art, would let me make an ice cream cone for myself with multiple flavors. We also made malts, and shakes, so I learned what the difference was between them.

I left Midland in 1965 when I graduated from Midland High (the only High School at that time), and went off to college. I moved back to Midland in 2011, back into the house that I grew up in, to help my aging parents. I discovered that Midland has become a wonderful community with lots to do, and a great place to raise a family. I have fallen back in love with Midland. It has everything to offer that a larger metropolis has and you can get anywhere in town in just 10 minutes.

Julia with her brother, Daniel in 1940-41

No Snow Days, No School Buses
By Julia M. Mazurowski of Bay City,
Michigan
Born 1930

In the fall of 1939, our family moved from Bay City's Michigan Avenue to Lafayette Avenue. At this time, Dad worked at the Consumers Gas Plant. Dad thought if he'd go into business for himself, he could better support his wife and five children. Dad did buy the "Old Bar Café" from the Finest Brewing Company. Since we belonged to the Saint Hyacinth's Parish, I'd have twenty-one blocks to walk to its school.

Walking to school in the winter wasn't easy because many of the walks weren't shoveled. A person had to walk in the paths that were made in the snow. This one particular day it was raining, so my mother gave me dad's big black umbrella so I wouldn't get wet. As usual, I left the house with my homemade denim schoolbag filled with my books and bag lunch. I carried that on my left arm, and in my right hand, I held the open umbrella. Now the big Kuhlman field was about halfway to school and had a kitty corner path. About halfway down the path, a gust of wind lifted me up with the umbrella and then came down. I continued but I was cold, tired, and scared. When I reached 34th Street and Michigan, the safety patrol boy gave me the ok to cross the street. As I was crossing the street, again, a strong gust the trapped wind lifted the umbrella and me but this time turned the umbrella inside out. I did land safely and began to cry because the umbrella was broken and looked like a big stick. The safety patrol boy said, "Don't cry, you're ok. I'll take the umbrella home and my dad will fix it." Before school's end, the boy came with the umbrella to Sr. Fulgentia's fourth grade classroom and handed me the fixed umbrella. Boy! That day he was my hero. I never did find out his name but he must have known me. I was nine years at this time. During my grade school years at St. Hyacinth's and St. Stanislaus schools, because there were no school buses I walked to and from school a long distance. There was only one time the lights at the school were out and the doors were closed that I had to go back home in a snowstorm. No snow days, no school buses, and never in all the years did a stranger try to "pick me up."

Fowl Feast
On 27 August 1912 my grandmother, Magdalena Wrona, her four and a half year old daughter, Anna, and grandmother's cousins set sail from Bremen, Germany on the Kronprinzessin Cecille. They landed at New York's port, Ellis Island. They were immigrants from Poland, traveled by train, headed for Bay City, Michigan's south end. At the station they were greeted by grandfather, Jan

(John) Wrona, who came to Michigan earlier. Many of the men found jobs at the "What Cheer" coalmine on Kinney Road in Munger, Michigan. Many of the miners became good friends. On weekends, the miner's families would get together at each other's home. The host would supply the drinks and the woman of the house provided fresh baked bread. Whoever had an instrument would bring it along for entertainment. Because grandmother had chickens, at one of these gatherings, she was told a good feed was malt. The used malt could be gotten at either the Finest Brewery on the east side or the Phoenix Brewery on the west side. Anna now about thirteen years old and her friend were told to take the wooden wagon and go to the Finest Brewery on Water Street. The used malt came out of the brewery through a huge pipe and fell to the ground, picked up with a shovel to load the wagon, and taken back home. Since no one said how much malt to put out, grandmother put the whole load in the chicken yard. After feasting on the malt, the chickens one by one dropped dead. When grandmother saw this, she began to panic and cry. "What is Pa going to say or do when he comes from work and sees that I killed the chickens?" Grandfather came home, grandmother cried, grandfather laughed and said, "Just wait 'til morning." At daybreak the rooster crowed, the chickens sobered up and everyone had a good laugh.

Now in 1983 Mom, Anna and Dad, Leo lived in retirement in Iosco Co. on their 320 acres. Mother loved to sit in her rocker near the double glass doors, watch the wildlife, and view their private lake, which emptied into a

Julia's parents, Anna and Leo

cut, then a pond in front of their home. A daily attraction were the wild turkeys. They would come out of the woods and in a single file walk in front of the pond. They'd stop to pick and the tom would spread out his tail feathers then sway from side to side. Now with Thanksgiving just around the corner Mother is going to get one of those turkeys. Mother's plan, soak cherries in a bottle of brandy. After a couple of weeks, Mother laid out the spiked cherries on the path, went in the house, and waited patiently. As usual there the turkeys appeared. They ate the cherries, the tom spread his tail and swayed from side to side, and then the turkeys in a single file walked into the woods. Mother was disappointed as not one turkey dropped. Darn, I should've had some of that malt from years ago.

Comic Book Plays
By Laurel Richert of Bay City, Michigan
Born 1953

I am a "baby boomer" at the ripe old age of 61, very soon to be 62. I've always said my childhood was one of the happiest times in my life.

In my neighborhood, about 20 of us neighbor kids, all played together, going from house to house. We would get our friends outside to play by melodically calling their names very loudly at the backdoor. One particular instance I recall was when a group of us were gathered around a huge maple tree, watching a squirrel who appeared to be performing acrobatics. My younger sister looked up the tree branch and just at that moment, the squirrel tumbled down and landed on her head. She just stood there, not knowing what to do, while we all yelled hysterically, "Shake your head! Shake your head!" until he finally fell to the ground and ran off. We all enjoyed the show.

One of my more creative cronies would write plays that we were all called upon to participate in. Those who were not lucky enough to be in the show would be charged an admissions fee, usually 10cents, to watch the performance. The cast usually outnumbered the audience. Some of our most memorable performances included, "The Adams Family, A visit from Aunt Finger," and a stint from the

"Richie Rich and Little Dot," comic books. All acted out in the live theater that was actually our neighbor's garage.

I could not conclude my reminiscing without a few words about my dear grandmother. She lived only a few blocks away as I was growing up. At this point, I was already in high school, looking forward, as all my peers were, to obtaining their drivers' licenses. I loved to get behind the wheel whenever the opportunity presented itself. My parents however, were not that eager, even though I've just obtained my permit and would gladly chauffer them anywhere. That's where Grandma came in. I would use her as my accomplice. She was always a willing victim, ready to sprint at a moment's notice. I would get on our telephone with a long 25-foot cord, which reached, up to my bedroom. My parents preferred this, having three teenage girls and one telephone. I would very quietly call Grandma and ask her what she needed from the grocery store. I could always count on her to need something. Then I would hang up and have her call me back with her list so I could tell my dad that Grandma needed "some stuff again," but not to worry, I would be able to take her so "you can stay home and finish your projects."

Is that a great daughter or what?

Fender Rides
By Michael E. Johnson of Custer, Michigan
Born 1944

In the late '50s on Sundays when my father was not working, we would take long rides. There wasn't much traffic on the country roads that we would travel. My mom would cut up some cold meat, salami, and cheese, and bring crackers with us. My father, while driving us, would have a beer or two because he did like Tudor beer.

With three children, it was a challenge as to who gets to sit by the windows. The cars in the '50s had front fenders that us children could sit on as we rode very slowly. We would look for cans and bottles we could sell at the store for 2cents each. These were pop or beer bottles we could trade in for candy. We all had a good time and we took turns riding on the fenders.

In the winter, we would be pulled on skis behind the car on the same roads.

Family Time
By Connie DeLong of Midland, Michigan
Born 1966

One of them was to view the original black and white TV musicals in a festive family foursome.

White Christmas, The Sound of Music, My Fair Lady, Doctor Doolittle, and many more…

The newspaper would tell us they were on and our little, down-home country family would join together, preparing for our festival; making popcorn, then placing potato chips and/or pretzels in Mama's big, brown, clay bowls. We'd grab up the soda pop in the glass bottles from whence it came. As we did so, our dad would prepare us by singing songs from the musical we were to watch together that night and we would guess the singer or the missing words. Then with the night upon us, and the sound of a wind up alarm clock going off, we would prepare our treats and take our seats to laugh, sign along, and stay up past bedtime. We would then go off to bed at the close of the movie. Content, ready for pillows and sweet dreams of love, life, and laughter, as a vital part of a happy family of four.

Summer Jobs and Swimming Holes
By Jack J. Mahar of Belding, Michigan
Born 1923

I was born in Belding in 1923 and I have a good recollection of growing up in the depression years 1929-1941. We lived in a house on N. York Street, which had no electric, no water, no plumbing of any kind and was abandoned. The heat was a potbellied wood burning stove, as was the cook stove.

We walked a mile to school every day, winter, and summer. My underwear was made of cloth from flour and sugar bags, which were homemade. High school Coach Gobel made us take a shower each day after practice. It was very embarrassing because our homemade underwear was stamped with lettering, and everyone knew they were flour sacks.

In 1935, I had a summer job weeding onions south and east of Belding. The pay was $1.00 for 9 hours of hard work, on hands and knees. I saved $15.00 one summer and put it in the local bank, which failed, and I lost all of my hard earned money.

Our swimming hole was in the river at the Arches. No swim suits were allowed. It was interesting to see about 20 bare-bottom boys swimming BARE and several girls hiding in the bushes watching the boys swim.

as many others. We filled our arms full and carried them out to Johnney's little red wagon. We hauled home pound-wise, much more than we brought in. We collected many of the "classics" this way.

In later years, my Aunt Mary borrowed some of these comic book classics because my cousin Keith had a hard time reading and this was how he read his books for his book reports.

Our parents could not afford to buy books and our comic books were read and reread many times. I'm sure that reading those comic books helped me develop my love for reading. I usually read about five books a week.

Bluffton School Paper Drives
By Joan Ransom of Grant, Michigan
Born 1936

As a child of six in 1942, my folks rented a house at 3079 Larkin Street in Muskegon, Michigan. My dad worked at the Continental where he did drafting. My twin brother John and I started kindergarten there. We would walk down Larkin and several other streets until we got to Lake Shore Drive. We had quite a walk before we got to Bluffton School.

I have fond memories of the schools paper drives. Once a year, we would bring in newspapers, magazines, catalogs etc. The school janitor was a small, white haired man who loved children. We were in our glory as we walked through the door leading to the school basement. Stacks of all kinds of paper items greeted us, but we had one special item in mind and that was comic books. From Superman to Blondie and Dagwood, as well

Bluffton School paper drives in 1943

The Lake Raft and Dining Room Dancing
By Clara B. Lozen of Hart, Michigan
Born 1920

When I was little my folks lived near Hesperia, Michigan, but we moved up across the straights of Michigan. We went by train to Frankfort, Michigan. From there we went by boat across Lake Michigan to Manistique, Michigan. Then we had to go about 12 miles to where my great uncle lived and where we lived for a while. My great uncle had written to my folks and said if we'd come up where he lived that my dad and my four older brothers could get work at logging camps. There was a lot of logging going on. They all did get work. Two of my brothers bought log trucks and hauled logs so they made good money.

Of course, us younger children had to go to school. The school was a one-room school with 1st grade through 8th grade. Not a lot of kids in any grade. I believe we had a different teacher each year. One teacher taught all eight grades.

I remember one teacher that we had was named Florence Stanton and was from around Kalamazoo, Michigan. She was very nice. My mother always got acquainted to our teachers. She, sometimes, would have them over for dinner. This one night, she was having Florence over. Florence liked mushrooms, as we all did. In the woods by our place, there were lots of mushrooms, so my mother asked my oldest sister and I to go pick some for dinner that night. We got lots of them and soon had our buckets full. We started home but decided we were lost. We sat down for a while to decide which way to go. We were also looking at our mushrooms and saw little jumping bugs on them. So we decided the mushrooms were not any good and we dumped them all out. Later we found out they were all that way and just had to be washed off. Well, back to deciding which way to go… We decided and came out to our house an entirely different direction than we went in, but that was ok. At least we got home.

My mother was disappointed, no mushrooms for dinner, but she made a good dinner anyway. My mother was a very good cook.

A gentleman found out about her, and asked her if she would run a hotel that he owned. She said she would, so we moved into that hotel. There were two men that lived there all of the time. So of course, they ate there in addition to sleeping there.

This little town was called Gulliver. There were two gas stations, a grocery store, a railroad depot, this hotel, and a post office. My mother made all of her bread, pies, and cakes so she bought little at the store. I do remember bread was 10cents a loaf, and hamburger was 3 pounds for 25cents.

Sometimes the boss of a crew of men, who worked on the railroad, came and asked my mother if they could come to the hotel for their lunch. Of course, she said yes. The extra money was good.

Not far from the hotel was a lake. Gulliver Lake. A younger brother and I would go to the lake and play. A friend of his, a little older boy came too. Also a girlfriend of mine. Now, none of us could swim so we decided it was time to learn. So the boys got some used lumber by his friend's house and made a raft. It was a pretty good one too. We took the raft out on the lake to where we couldn't touch the bottom and we would jump off the raft and make ourselves swim, dog paddle. The rest of the summer, we did this. We learned to swim really good- dog paddle.

In the winter when the lake was froze over, a few men put their fish shanties on this lake. My oldest brother put his shanti out on the lake too. Sometimes my mother and a friend would go out in the shanti and fish. They usually got a few fish. Fish for dinner that night! The boarders always liked that.

There was a room for men to sit in and visit called "The Men's Room." Sometimes, I would sweep this room. Our one boarder was named John. I called him Big John. When I swept by Big John, he didn't get up and move, he just lifted his feet and let me sweep around him.

There was no electric in their hotel. We had gas lanterns in the dining room, kitchen, men's room, and living room. In the bedrooms, there was kerosene lamps. It was my job to keep them filled and to keep the chimneys clean.

On Saturday night, we had dances in the dining room. We had a piano, my one brother played that, and a man played a violin. Someone played a guitar. I learned to dance there. I was 10 years old then, and I've never quit. I'm now 94 and I still like to dance.

We never did tell our mother about the raft. I had six brothers and three sisters. All are gone now except my youngest sister who lives in Virginia. And of course, I'm in Michigan.

The Myers Family
By Madeleine J. Reagan of Branch,
Michigan
Born 1926

In 1908, my grandfather, Frank Myers, from Pawnee City, Nebraska, bought a section of land in Sauble Township, sight unseen. He brought his family, and father-in-law, and a boxcar full of cattle. One of my uncles rode in the cattle car with the cows. They cleared some land and took the logs to a sawmill on Millerton Road to be cut up into lumber. They built a two-story house, barn, smoke house, and icehouse. They cut blocks of ice from two lakes. No electricity or running water in these days. It was a hard life. They mostly lived off the land; hunted, fished, had a huge garden, raised cattle, hogs and chickens.

In 1926, my grandfather died and left 40 acres to each of their surviving children (seven). Five had died at an early age of various illnesses. The rest of the section was left to my grandmother. In the early years, the railroad ran just below their house by the Sauble River. Sometimes the conductor, and if there were any passengers, they would stop and come up to the house and my grandmother would feed them. They were not on a tight schedule in those days. Manister was their last stop.

When I was born, the doctor came from Scottville in a horse and buggy and stayed two days until I was born. When I was six or seven, my folks and I moved into the first floor of the Sauble hall. On Saturday nights, there were dances upstairs. Sometimes some of the men drank too much of their homemade moonshine and would tumble down the stairs and go outside to have fights. No one was ever killed but there were lots of bloody noses and black eyes.

Two of my cousins, two neighbor kids, and I were the last students to go to the Sauble School. In the winter, my mother broke her arm cranking the old Model T. Grandma died in 1937. Later years, the house burnt down and now there is a beautiful log home built by my second cousin.

In 2015, there is still just a dirt road by the homestead. Sauble station has an old house and several of my relatives have lived in it over the years. There is a small log building that once my aunt had a lunchroom in, and on the opposite corner, there was a small grocery store, which is now a cottage. The foundation of the hall is still there but I don't know what happened to the building.

There are grandchildren, great-grandchildren, and great-great-grandchildren that own property on that section. There are great-grandchildren that live nearby and several have homes near and on Bass Lake. We still all like Lake County.

Memory of a Two-Holer Outhouse
By Alan Van Duinen of New Era, Michigan
Born 1946

I grew up on a 60-acre farm one mile south of the little town of New Era, Michigan. I was number four of six kids in the family. We got our first indoor plumbing when I was five. Prior to the installation of indoor facilities, we would have to walk about 60 feet outdoors into the backyard to use the outhouse to relieve ourselves. This outhouse was large enough inside so that the sitting bench had two holes for usage. For a young child, it was a scary experience to walk into a small isolated building with an interior odor and close a tall wooden door, shutting off all light except for the light that came in from a tiny window located high up in each peak. The sound of large horse flies and bees buzzing around in the area below the bench added to the atmosphere of an unpleasant experience.

My mother's wisdom dictated that my four-year-older brother and I would use the facility together. This arrangement alleviated my fear of being alone but also subjected me to the teasing of an older sibling. He would always insist that his place to sit was over the hole on our left as we entered. Every time he would get his way and I would be fully aware of what would follow after we were situated.

The interior of the outhouse was open 2x4 studs and on one stud near where my brother sat was a long, somewhat rusty nail, slightly bent upward to hold a roll of toilet paper. Almost immediately, my brother would remove the toilet paper and set it on the bench. Then he would reach up with his right hand, grab on to the nail, rotate it counter-clockwise a quarter turn, and declare that he was special because he sat on the side that flushed.

Alan's dad, Abie Van Duinen, his brother, John, Alan, and their dog, Tippy in 1950

324

I was always 99% positive that he was wrong but could never win the ensuing argument.

Victory Buns and Milk Can Skates
By Jerry and Emily Slivinski of Saginaw, Michigan
Born 1931 & 1935

Jerry remembers the Victory Buns sold at Anderson Swimming Pool's concession stand. For one nickel, you could purchase a hamburger bun with mustard, ketchup, and pickle relish. No meat!

Empty Pet Milk cans were used for ice skates. You would crush them on your shoes at the arch part of your foot.

Baseball was played with a wooden stick and the ball was taped cloth bounded very tightly.

We also saved foil from gum wrappers and cigarette packages for making balls. We collected these for the War (World War II) effort.

As children, we didn't think we were poor. Everyone was in the same boat.

Red ration chips and stamp books were used for meat, sugar, etc. We purchased groceries at the local meat and grocery store, Mom and Pop stores.

Young boys wore corduroy knickers to school. They would wear one pair all week, got washed on Friday, and would be ready to wear to school on Monday.

At school, if you did something bad, you would have to draw a circle on the black board and put your nose on it with your hands behind your back for 15 minutes. We didn't think anything of it. Simply that if you have been bad, you get punished.

Rock on the Dock, Kick the Can, and Four Corner Tag were some of the favorite games we played in the streets after school.

The water pump on the corner for all the neighbors use was replaced by our very own pump in our backyard. We thought we were rich to have our own pump.

The milkman delivered milk with his horse drawn wagon, Queenie. The horse knew what house to stop at. If we were lucky, we would get a piece of ice to suck on. We had iceboxes, which kept our food cold by blocks of ice from the river. You would put a sign up in the front window when you needed a block of ice.

The Rag Man would walk his wooden car and blow a horn as a signal. He was trying to make a living by picking rags and other junk.

Our first TV was the year we got married, 1955. We thought we really had technology savvy.

As we started to talk about memories, we felt joy and happiness remembering many additional stories but mostly the people in our lives. The many family memories and friends that help mold us. What a great path God steered us on.

The Shower Room and Safety Patrol
By Connie Alvesteffer of Hart, Michigan
Born 1947

As a Baby Boomer, born in 1947, life was full of great adventures, a good time to be a kid. Life was much slower paced than it is now. Soldiers were home, and families were coming back together, and new ones were forming. I grew up in a very small town on the shores of Lake Michigan, close to the Silver Lake Sand Dunes. Kids lived outside every free moment, and our playground was the whole town. We had an inland lake connected to Lake Michigan, sand dunes, woods, creeks, and hills to explore. There was a small theater in town whose admission fee was a whopping 50cents, and a large bag of popcorn was 10cents. My first Disney movie there was Snow White. I never missed a Disney movie after that. After the movie, people would head down to the ice cream store or to the A&W for a root beer or root beer float.

When I was ten, in 1957, our family became one of only eight households in town to have a TV; it was a small screened console. My parents let each of us kids invite our friends over to watch the very first program we saw on our new TV. It was a grand day. Wall to wall kids, lots of popcorn, pillows, and blankets scattered everywhere just so we could watch Peter Pan starring Marion Martin. I was married 23 years before we had a color TV, which we bought in 1980.

In the 1950s, my father was starting his own business, so any extra money went into it, so we didn't have a lot of frills in our household. My mother did laundry with a wringer washer and clothes were hung on the line to dry. In the winter, the wet clothes would freeze like a board.

We didn't have running water but a hand pump at our sink that had to be primped all the time and if we wanted hot water, we had to heat it on the stove. The fuel oil heat stove always had two large tea kettles, filled and hot, sitting on top, ready for use. Bath days were always a big deal. We had no bathroom, so curtains were put up on bath days, by the stove and extra water had to be heated ahead so Mom and Dad could fill the small metal wash tub.

One summer my father converted a shed that was connected to the back of our house into a shower room. He built a slatted floor so water from the shower hose could drain through to stones underneath. On the roof of the house, he placed an old wringer washer tub, which we had to fill each time a shower was taken with cold water from the garden hose. Each time we had to climb a ladder to the roof with tea kettles of hot water. In the winter, we would bundle up and rush out to the heated shed to take a quick shower, dress quickly, and rush back into the house. My friends loved to stay overnight so they could take a shower. They actually thought we were rich because we had a "cool" outdoor shower. Because we had no bathroom, we had to use an outhouse about 100 feet behind the house. It had a candle for light and one did not linger in the winter months.

I remember when we got our first telephone. It was an ugly, black, rotary phone. We shared a "party line" with five other households. Anytime someone dialed out or a call came in, anyone on the party line could listen in or join in on a call. It was a pain if you had nosey neighbors or some that were always talking on the phone.

To keep food fresh, we had an ice box refrigerator. It was electric, but had a large block of ice set in the top and the cold water from the melting ice would filter though a coil to cool the refrigerator. If we wanted ice, we would use an ice pick and chip off what we needed. One fall, my brothers and I picked up potatoes for a local farmer and used our earnings to buy Mom and Dad a new modern electric GE refrigerator that even had a freezer compartment for ice trays. Mom polished that refrigerator every day until 1970, when they bought a new and even more modern refrigerator. That old GE went into the garage to keep pop, veggies, and Dad's fishing worms cold. After 48 years, good old GE gave up the ghost on my father's 90th birthday.

Just outside of the village limits, there was a huge blackberry patch with hired pickers to pick it. My older brother and the neighbor girl talked her brother, sister and I into sneaking into the berry patch to pilfer some tasty fruits while the pickers were busy, thinking no one would notice three extra little kids eating and picking berries. That was until the neighbor's brother came face to face with one huge angry hog nosed snake. He let out a blood curdling scream. A bucket of berries flew into the air, and three terrified little kids were seen running full out from the prickly berry patch. We kept running until we reached the safety of the creek across the road from our house. I say safety because that creek was the best playground in the world. A haven away from rules. In the summer, it was cool and fun to wade and splash in. It had frogs, crayfish, skeeter bugs scooting across the water surface, and at night, we caught lightening bugs in the grass on its banks. Wintertime some parts could be skated on and some parts we took our chances on getting wet feet.

School was like school today, study and homework, but recess was great. The girls would play hop scotch, jump rope and jacks. The boys would shoot marbles and some would flip knives (Mumbley Peg) or bring their wooden homemade or store bought guns so they could play "soldier." Can you imagine the repercussions today if wooden guns or knives for a game were brought to school? In the winter, snow was piled into two huge hills on the baseball field, one for sledding and the other for the braver toughies to play "King of the Hill", a rough and tumble game. On rainy days, we played inside games like "eraser tag" and "hide the thimble." We also did puzzles and colored. No computers. No video games. No tablets or cell phones. Just our imagination.

My 5th and 6th grade years, I served on the school Safety Patrol. We wore thick white belts across our chests that were our "badge of authority." We stood at corners and crosswalks near school, helped with loading and unloading little kids on the bus, and were in charge of bicycle safety. In nice weather, everyone rode bikes. It was a big responsibility that we took very seriously and with much pride because it was not easy to become part of the Safety Patrol.

Our school was a three story building for K-12 grades. It had iron fire escapes on each side of the building but the best fire escape was the tube escape from the third floor assembly room. If you were lucky enough to be in that room during a fire drill, you would get to shoot down the tube at break neck speed. Girl's skirts would fly up into their faces so teachers always made the boys go down last, much to their dismay.

Because all the students in town either walked or rode bikes, and the few country kids rode the bus, the school was never called off because of snow. We just had to bundle up more. Twice we were dismissed for tornado warnings and once because the water pipes broke on the main floor.

My parents were born in 1914. My father attended a two-room country school. In the winter, he stayed with his grandparents because they lived closer to the school but he still had to walk two miles to school, sunshine, rain or snow. Necessity made him quit school during his ninth grade year so he could get a job and help his family financially. He never finished school but a smarter man you couldn't find. My mother was luckier. She lived six blocks from her school and she graduated in 1932. My parents talked about using kerosene lamps for light growing up, and said that when they got married the farmhouse they rented had electric lights but they used them frugally because light bulbs were expensive for them and hard to find. My father worked for Lakey Foundry in Muskegon, and during the Second World War, he worked at Continental in Muskegon, where they made and tested our military tanks. He had to have a special pass to get in, and was told he was not to talk about what they built there. He worked there until the end of the war. My mother, before she met my father, worked in Fremont for Gerber Baby Foods. For her, it was great pay even though she had to stay at an aunt's house.

I watched the first man land on the moon and was in 10th grade at school when they came in and told us that President Kennedy was shot. Teachers and students were crying and they called off school for the rest of the week.

County fairs were big things back then. Families would pack up food, blankets, kids and spent two or three days at the fair. We would sleep in the backs of our trucks or on the ground. Animals, kid's games, rides, horse races, hot dogs, professional tag-team wrestling, and traveling entertainers were all there to enjoy. That is where I first heard Minnie Pearl and her famous "HOWDY" throughout the fairgrounds. It was a long drive to the county fair. Gas was 11cents a gallon, but that horrible price never stopped us from attending the fair.

In 2015, we have so many tools at our disposal to make life easier but I think we are missing out in our personal interactions with each other. Our tools are good and useful but we need to control our use of them and not let them control us. There is something to be said about eating a hot dog at the fair, while drifting off to sleep in a sleeping bag, under the stars, and listening to the animals in the fair barns. Very calming.

With the Class of '59
By Sally L. Kioski of Durand, Michigan
Born 1942

I was born on May 29, 1942 at the Owosso Memorial Hospital. I was named Sally Lee Mead.

When I was 5 years old, I attended a one-room schoolhouse with about 30 other children. Our teacher, Mrs. Allen, became my favorite. She taught kindergarten through 8th grade. I liked school very much and I passed second and third grades in one year. I would cry when I couldn't go to school. I walked to school alone, almost every day, 1 ¼ miles, except when I was given a bicycle at 8 years old.

My brother, Richard, was born in 1945 and so I didn't have to walk alone. We fought a lot, and we had a dog named Brownie.

I graduated from eighth grade and I was the only one in my class, as I had left my classmates behind. At my graduation, I

Sally Kioski with her doll in 1946

recited, by memory, the poem, "The House by the Side of the Road," by Edgar A. Guest.

Then came high school at Ovid High School, which was a two-story building. I had to ask where the 2nd floor was located. I did well in high school and was elected to the National Honor Society and graduated in 1959 with the class of '59 students.

My father was a farmer and my mother was a bookkeeper in a bank until I was born. I liked living on a farm and we certainly kept busy. I had my own cow, which I milked daily. We had a pig and some chickens. My father was very strict, and he said if I got a spanking at school that I would get one when I came home. Why did I need two?

I also had to help pick up stones and ears of corn left in the field. I drove the tractor.

My mom was a Godly lady and very loving. She took me to church every Sunday. I helped her wash with a wringer washer in our kitchen. We hung the clothes on the line both summer and winter. Burrr!

At grade school, we had an outhouse and every Halloween someone would tip it over. My grandparents had an outhouse and used an

Mrs. Allen and students at grade school in 1950

indoor chamber pot.

As for music, we had an old Victrola with 78rpm records. We'd have to crank it to keep it going. I also had a small record player, which played 45rpm records.

I took piano lessons when I was 8 years old for five years. My piano teacher, Mrs. Palen was wonderful.

My Close to Perfect Life
By Donna Jean Faragher Dettloff of West Branch, Michigan
Born 1939

I was born during World War II. We lived in Detroit. The car companies produced war articles (planes, tanks, etc.). Lots of military came to Detroit to manage the production of war items. One stayed in our house. We became good friends with him and later to his family. I don't remember a lot of the war but I do remember when the war ended. My sister and I were already asleep, but our parents woke us up and we drove the streets of Detroit with just about everybody who lived there.

My dad, Dr. Donald Jesse Faragher was a veterinarian doing meat inspections for

Donna's parents, Donald Jesse and Mirabel (Myra) Hitchcock Faragher

Donna and her sister Louise

Detroit. There were two of them, one had to go to war, the other had to stay and inspect meat. My dad inspected meat. He had to take a reduced pay. It went toward the food for soldiers. Awhile after the war ended, my dad got his money refunded all at once. Mom, Dad, my sister, and I, Grandma, and aunts all went on a trip through the USA and Canada. We were gone for about a month. I was 7, my sister, Louise Ann Faragher Padmos was 8. We went to North Dakota. We saw the huge rock formation with the presidents of the United States, Mt. Rushmore. We went to Canada, to a rodeo. We stayed at Banff Springs Park for several days.

Then down the western coast, Washington, Oregon, and California. We went to the Grand Canyon and came home through Wyoming. What a trip! This was an amazing trip. There were no freeways or big motels. We stayed in cabins and private homes. When we filled up with gas, we got a big poster with pictures of that area. We had lots of them and when we got back, we took the murals to school to present to our classes. They loved it.

Mom, Mirabel Hitchcock Faragher

worked for the police department and, for a while, worked at the prison near Pontiac. Because Mom and Dad worked for the City of Detroit, they had to live in the city limits. It was a lot safer back then than it is now.

Because of living in Detroit, Mom and Dad bought a 100 acre farm in Canada, 13 miles from the Blue Water Bridge and right on Lake Huron. We went there almost every weekend all summer, until the snow got deep. It had electricity, but no running water or bathroom. There was an outhouse out in back. The farmer next door could use our barn and outbuilding and he worked all of the fields in exchange for looking after the house, outbuilding, and two horses. They became like family to us. They were very poor and we brought them coffee and other goodies every weekend. They gave us eggs, cream, and garden supplies. They had three kids who were like family to us. One has since died, but we are still in touch. The son now owns their farm. My dad sold our farm in 1959 when my mom died of uterine cancer at 44 years old.

I got married as soon as Mom got cancer and she lived to see 3 of my 4 children.

I spent the last three months with her at our farm in Canada. When we left there, she went to the hospital in Detroit, and died a few weeks later.

In 1966, my husband and I, and our 4 children, moved to Hawaii. I stayed there until I retired. I was a social worker in a mental health clinic. When my last child moved to Maui, I took a job in the mental health department of our local hospital. It was a temporary job because I was alone. Then I loved that job so much, I retired from it. I had started working there 5 years after my primary job, then retired from there 5 years after I retired from my primary job.

When I retired from my second job, I got a motorhome and traveled all over the country. Last year, at 75 years old, I got a home in West Branch, Michigan. My two oldest children who remembered Michigan, both are living there now. The one is still on Maui, he thinks he Hawaiian, and the other lives in Arizona.

I've had a wonderful lie. I'm very grateful for that. It might not have been perfect but it was close.

You Learn and You Pray
By Patricia Hubbert of Saginaw, Michigan
Born 1949

Old school days were the good old days. Some were good and some were bad. Look back at old school days and you see love and understanding and a time to go on.

I lived in a house at that time that was cold and had no running water. We would heat the water on the stove to wash up, and went outside to use the outhouses. It was so cold in the winter; we made it by sitting around the heater and putting blankets around us to keep warm. We pumped water and had to carry it to the house. Our aunt had a pump in the backyard so we got water from there.

I've planted a garden in the summer with flowers.

We walked to school and walked home every day. We went to a school that was a one-room school. When the teacher got on us at school, we got it at home. If we did not understand something, my grandmother would try to help, or she would get us help so we could understand the work.

One day on the walk to school, my brother

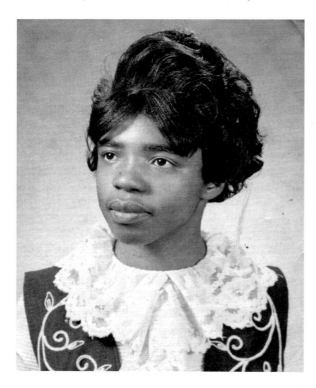

Patricia Hubbert

and I saw snakes on the side of the road. One morning somebody dropped some money. A snake laid beside the money. My brother stopped to pick up the money but I kept on running.

We went to Sunday school. Never missed a Sunday. I liked Sunday school.

We walked to the store in the ice and snow to get food. The milkman came to the house and brought us milk and butter and eggs. There was one time we needed a sofa and the milkman got us one.

Grandmother would make us work for our school clothes. We would clean out people's basements, or rake their gardens. She would have us put the money away for school She was good. She had a pig so we kept him until he got big. Then Grandmother took him to the meat house. That was our meat for the winter.

Grandmother would take us fishing. She would pack a lunch. It was fun. It was like a classroom but at home.

We had a wringer washer to wash clothes and then would hang them on the line to dry.

Grandmother would tell stories about earlier before we had a black and white TV, radio and a bike. Old school back then was good times.

At Christmastime, we had a tree that we put in the middle of the floor. The boy scouts came with a basket of food and sang songs with us now that it was Christmas.

For us, my grandmother came through hard times.

We were always told to keep God in our hearts and we made do with what we had. I think old school was there to teach you what life was. You work to have thing. You learn and you pray.

Memories of the Past
By Katherine Barnes of Ithaca, Michigan
Born 1941

I probably always had ADD but back in the '40s and '50s, it wasn't recognized as anything except an extra active child. I had a great sense of humor. It was just not appreciated by everyone else. I had an older brother, Carl, and sister, Phyllis who often tattled on me. I had a brother, Phillip who was 6 years younger, so my job, much of the

Katherine and her favorite cousin, Barb in 1956

time, was babysitting with him. He and I often played Monopoly. It was a long-lasting game for us, mostly because when he would get far in debt, I felt sorry for him and would lend him money from the bank until he would pass "Go," or I would sell some of my property or houses so he wouldn't go bankrupt.

All my grandparents were special to me. We lived on the farm owned by my mother's parents (D. R. Hill). My dad rented/farmed it. We lived in the big brick house, close to the two big white barns, I often rode my bike the 1 ½ miles to visit my grandparents. I quite often dusted Grandma's furniture for her. Sometimes, she would give me 10cents for doing that. That grandma was also grandma to my favorite cousin, Barb who lived 6 miles away. We often wrote letters back and forth to each other. Stamps cost 2 or 3cents each back then.

In winters, the flu usually hit our home. When I would be pretty much over the flu, my mother would give me a tablespoon of castor oil, then a glass of fresh-squeezed orange juice to wash it down. I loved the orange juice but the castor oil was terrible.

We had indoor plumbing but also had an outhouse, close to the barn that we used now and then. One summer day, my brother, Carl and I were both using it at the same time. We didn't see anything wrong with that, seeing as there were three holes. But my dad didn't think it proper, so that brought on another

licking.

I went to a one-room schoolhouse for all 9 grades. The first two years, I went to Sickles School located a mile south and a mile east of us, on gravel roads. The next 7 years, we went to Zimmerman School located 1 mile north of us.

One warm day, when in the first grade, walking home by myself and about a half mile from home, a car came along. I put up my thumb, so as to hitch a ride. The young man stopped, picked me up, and then dropped me off at my house. I didn't know him, but later found out that he was a neighbor who lived a mile south, across the section from us. He knew me, so he told his dad. Then, his dad told my dad, and they had a good laugh over it.

I liked my kindergarten and first grade teacher, Mrs. Melba Kostal very much. For years later, when I'd see her somewhere, she would say, "I'll never forget the day when you were in kindergarten and I looked back to see you sitting in your chair with your feet up on the desk, eating an apple."

One cold winter night, my parents woke us up to have us look out the upstairs window, to the southeast. The sky was lit up in orange. The oil furnace had blown up in our school and the school burned to the ground. We finished out the school year at Hamilton Township hall located just east of where the school had been.

In the town hall, there were voting booths at the front of the room, behind the teacher's desk. One day, while being punished for whispering, I was sitting on a stool in one of those booths for a period of time. While in that booth, I slipped down off the stool and scooted down below the door of the booth, which was about 2 feet above the floor, to look out at the kids, and make faces at them. When they laughed, of course, the teacher turned around. But, by then, I was back up on the stool.

We used to sit in the living room, relaxing in a soft chair, on Saturday evening, listening to the Beulah Show and other radio programs and laughing. That was our Saturday night entertainment.

My parents were both brought up in loving Christian homes, for which I'm very thankful. I'm thankful for God's forgiveness, or I would not be heading for eternity in Glory Land. My younger brother and I often played church. I would line up 4 or 6 chairs in the kitchen and have an aisle in the middle. I was really a "h&%l and brimstone" preacher. I let the congregation (my brother) know that if he didn't repent, he was going to h&$l. He confessed, repented, and came to the altar many times. In our home, it was just a given that we would go to church every Sunday morning, evening and Thursday nights, for prayer meeting.

My mother raised chickens for many years. The egg money was her grocery money. I helped a lot, but was afraid the chickens would peck at me, so I would throw handfuls of corn way off, so they'd run after it. Then I'd spread more around myself quickly. Many Saturdays my mother killed a chicken or two for Sunday's dinner. Sundays when we didn't have chicken, we'd usually have roast beef with all the trimmings to go with it.

We had a telephone party line of 6 or 8 members. You always knew who was being called, by the number of rings. Ours was 2 longs, and 2 shorts. You knew when someone was listening to your conversations. One day, after I'd called the doctor for my mother, a neighbor on our line, called me to see what was wrong with my mom.

We always had fresh milk, as my dad raised around 10 or 12 cows. We would get a pound of butter from the milkman every week or two. I'd never heard of oleo until at a girlfriend's house. One day she had this plastic bag full of white stuff. After putting some coloring in it, and squeezing it a bit, it turned out to be oleo.

At recess, we played Annie I over, and Red Rover, Red Rover, Let someone Come Over. Those were fun days to remember. One nice fall day, some of us cut come corn out of the cornfield next to the schoolyard to make a playhouse in the cornfield. I don't think it was really large, and I guess the farmer didn't mind. We never heard from him anyway. We had good times back there in the country school.

Once, when in 8th grade, while sitting up front on the recitation seat where we had our class, the teacher asked me how the ear functions. I said, "The sound goes in one eat and comes out the other." I considered it to be funny, but she didn't. She said, "I think that's how it works with you, Kathy."

My Aunt Ruby and Uncle Chet who loved in town were one of the first in the family to have a television. We often went up to their house on Sunday afternoons to watch TV. We'd watch the Lone Ranger or Roy Rogers. That was family fun. While the women and kids watched TV in the living room, the men would be out in the kitchen playing cards. We never had any playing cards in our house back then; only Rook, Authors, Old Maid, or other table games.

Saturday was always cleaning day. Our bedrooms were upstairs and we each had to clean our own. One Saturday after vacuuming his bedroom carpet, my older brother, Carl came down the stairs with the vacuum bag full of dirt and dust. I happened to be at the bottom of the stairs as he hit the bottom step. I quickly threw my hands around the bag and squeezed it. Dust flew in all directions. My mother happened to be there and saw me. Well, you can imagine the rest. It wasn't good for me.

When going to high school, I loved riding the bus. I often rode around the whole route, so I could sit in the back and talk to my girlfriends. One morning I missed the bus. My dad told me to get out there and walk to school (7 miles). So, I went out to the road and started walking towards town. My dad yelled at me and told me to come back home and he'd take me. About that time, my girlfriend's dad, who was the county sheriff, came along and picked me up. So, I wasn't late for school.

I was invited to my girlfriend, Gloria's 16th birthday party, when we were sophomores. We were to have dates, then after the boys left, we had a pajama party. I needed a date, so I invited her boyfriend's friend. Now, over

Katherine, Gloria, and all the girls at the pajama party

50 years later, when anyone asks my husband about our first date, he tells them that our first date was at a pajama party.

The Imagination Reconciliation
By Mary Jane Michael of Merrill, Michigan
Born 1934

Imagine the excitement and anticipation when your dad is bringing home and hooking up your very first television set.

Up to that point, our inside entertainment was games or listening to the radio. My favorite was the radio: "Let's Pretend," "Inner Sanctum" and "The Shadow." We could see every character so vividly. The good guys were so handsome, the ladies so pretty and perfect, and the villains were so easily recognizable.

Our TV is on, and I turned to our first viewing ever. Our eyes are glued to the screen, and we are as quiet as mice. The program ends, and it is time for dinner.

Conversation at the dinner table is all about the first viewing of our new black and white television.

I think we were all happy to have our new entertainment, but a little disappointed to learn that our imagination presented a much better picture than our television ever did.

It took quite a while to reconcile the two, but I guess that's progress.

Building Time
By Bonnie Carroll of Lewiston, Michigan
Born 1942

I was born in Romeo, Michigan, in 1942. In 1947, I moved to a cabin in Lewiston, Michigan with my dad, mom and little sister, Beverly. My folks found property north of town on Olsen Street to build a house. It was in a subdivision that was still part of town but far enough away.

Summer was building time. My folks did a lot of the work themselves. We moved in around the beginning of November 1947. By deer season, we had hunters in our basement. It wasn't finished, but they enjoyed themselves.

In town at that time, there were a couple of gas stations, grocery stores, drug stores, Sacks Hardware, Wellington Shoe Store, a general store, and a couple other businesses. Also, there was a post office, a bank and three churches.

The school was within walking distance from our new house. It was two stories. The first floor held kindergarten, first and second grade in one room. Third and fourth grades were in the other. There was a kitchen and two bathrooms. On the second floor, fifth and sixth grades were held in one room and seventh and eighth grades were in the other room. The second floor also had a fire escape that was fun to play on in the summertime.

In the wintertime, my dad would shovel a path from our house to the school so we didn't have to walk the unplowed roads. In 1950, a new school was built all on one floor. It was nice, but we had to walk to it every day, even in winter. It was only about four blocks from our house. When we entered the ninth grade, we had to ride a bus to Atlanta, Michigan, 17 miles away. High school was ninth to 12th grade. It was fun and a good four years.

Shenanigans in Michigan
By Richard Floyd Lumbert of Mt. Pleasant, Michigan
Born 1938

When I was attending school in the fourth grade, our teacher announced that someone had stolen the milk money out of her desk. After questioning everyone, one girl admitted to taking the money. Shortly thereafter, the principal showed up and took the girl to the front of the class. He sat down in a chair, placed her across his lap, and pulled her dress up exposing her panties. He then spanked her with a rubber hose. His name, believe it or not, was Mr. Hosehawser. I've never forgotten the experience. Imagine this happening in today's world!

We used to have an appliance store downtown. I can remember going there and standing in the street in front of the store with many others to watch Joe Lewis box and wrestling, as we all didn't have or own a TV.

When I was a young man, it was a must to be home on Thursday night to hear "Gang Busters" on the radio. We also listened to

"The Shadow."

When I was young, my father bought a new car: a Model "A" Ford or "T." My brother, who was two years younger, and I would ride in the rear window with our feet toward one another in bad weather. When it was nice, we got to ride in the rumble seat. What a ride! The car only had a front seat in which my mother and dad needed to ride.

My brother and I caught a garter snake and put it in a brown grocery bag. We brought the bag into the kitchen and told our mother she wouldn't believe what we had found. We gave her the paper sack, and she opened it to see what we had found. I can still hear her screaming, as she stuck her head down into the sack to see what treasure we had found. Needless to say, we ran as fast and as far as we could to get away from her.

In the seventh grade, our teacher announced that for our history class we would all learn "The Gettysburg Address" by Abe Lincoln. I questioned her on what good that was, and I wasn't going to do it. After spending three nights after school, I decided maybe I should. I'm now 76 years old and can still recite it by heart. What a teacher! I still don't know what good it did me!

It Wasn't a Rehearsal
By Alberta Leiner of Saginaw, Michigan
Born 1942

I was born in Saginaw, Michigan. In the early years, there were five kids, one dog, Mom and Dad. In the 1940s, there were scary floods. We would go out the front door and get into a boat to go to Otto School. We went from O'Conner Rd up to West Michigan. Sometimes, we went in the duck boat. We had one of the better houses on O'Conner Rd. My dad owned trucks and ran the Center Street dump. He would bring home ice cream for all the kids in the neighborhood. Ice cream stores had a time for ice cream to be sold or taken to the dump, and we were happy to get it.

In the 1950s, we moved from Saginaw to Merrill. The day we moved, we were on the road traveling, and our trailer caught fire, burning a lot of our belongings. Shortly before we moved, my sister, Penny, died

from meningitis. She was 16 months old. My grandma and grandpa both died, and my dad was a drinker and was always full of surprises. When the floodwaters came, and I was lowered into the boat to my dad's reach, he fell over backwards. We both almost went into the water. We also used to play in the boat by the back door. One day, my mom had to rescue my sister and me from the tide that was taking us. I'm a survivor!

After moving to Merrill, my dad didn't work a lot. Consumers would come and turn off the power to our house. Us girls would walk down to the store with a gallon jug with the finger-grip hold handle and carry kerosene back for the kerosene lamps. It was hard for us to clean the globes for these lamps. We would take a wagon down the road to the neighbors' and use a tall milk can to get water. We used wadded up newspaper to clean the globes; we didn't have bathrooms either, so we used newspapers outside in the toilet too.

One night, while walking to the toilet, it was really dark. I felt something grabbed onto my pant lake. The more I ran, the faster I ran, and it wouldn't let go of me. When I finally got back to the house, I discovered what was attached to my leg. It was fly sticker tape that wouldn't come loose. I thought it was a snake! My sister and I still laugh about that night.

We sure learned a lot about life, and I'm glad that was not a rehearsal because I don't want to relive those days. I can tell you, kids these days would never make it. They don't know how to let the pit cock out from under a truck so water drains out, and the truck doesn't freeze up. All in a day's work!

Snowbound
By Diane Lintemuth of Stanwood, Michigan
Born 1946

The winter of 1958 was a memorable one. I was a sixth grader at Weidman School. It was snowing when my two brothers, Roger (a fifth grader) and Rick (a kindergartner), and I boarded the bus that morning. But, that was not unusual for a winter in Michigan!

By 10 am, the wind had picked up, and we had a full-blown "blizzard!" The school decided to feed us lunch and send us home at

12:30 pm.

As we boarded our bus, we noticed we had a sub-driver. Nothing unusual there—we had him as a driver before.

During the trip home, our bus became stuck many times. Our driver was able to get us out until about 5:30 pm we became hopelessly stuck! By this time, it was still snowing and blowing, and there were some pretty big drifts. The five of us left on the bus had no idea where we were, as the driver had taken a road not on the route. We were nearly out of gas. Back then, there were no radios in the bus or pocket phones. Our driver opted to walk to get some help, not realizing the nearest farm was almost a half-mile away! He shut off the bus, told us to behave, and not to leave the bus! As the bus cooled off, we found the iced up aisles made a great skating surface. We were still enjoying our "skating party" when the driver returned. He told us he was able to use the farmer's phone and that our parents would be notified.

Our folks were called by the state police at about 6:30 pm and had no idea where we were or that school had let out at noon!

Needing to get us out of the cold bus, our driver had us put on every bit of extra mittens and scarves left on the bus, and we set out holding hands, a kindergartner in between each older child. It was still blowing and very cold. We were not to let go for any reason, so if one fell, we all fell into the drifts. We were quite the "snow bunnies" when we reached the farmhouse. And hungry!

It just happened the farmer's wife had gotten stuck in town, so all the farmer had to eat was bread and warm milk. I think that's all he knew how to fix. He opened his "parlor," and he had a pool table (wow). As the evening progressed, we all became very tired. We put the kindergartners on top of the pool table to sleep, and the rest of us curled up in chairs.

Later, the driver woke us, and we were surrounded by big lights, big v plows and the police. We were rescued!

My brothers and I rode home in the police car and arrived home very tired and hungry at about 12:30 am.

Later, we found out the bus had gotten stuck about eight miles from the school, and we only lived one mile from the school! And, it took us over 12 hours to get home. What an adventure!

Behind the Barn
By Sandra Dobrowolsky of Saginaw,
Michigan
Born 1938

I grew up in the small town of Hale, Michigan, full of aunts, uncles, and cousins. My dad had a farm a mile south of town. My grandfather and grandmother owned the drugstores, phone company, and soda shop where their home was, also right in Hale. My mother taught school in the country, and when she married my dad, she taught in Hale, first in junior high then kindergarten. She liked it so much; she finished her teaching career in kindergarten the last 13 years in Saginaw.

Living on the farm, my dad used a horse to plow the fields, and then my brother and I would ride her when there were parades downtown or holidays. My brother would ride her, and Dad later got another horse for me to ride. Tops would love to show off; she would know when people were watching her. She would prance around. She was a great horse to have; the other horse would just follow Tops. For a few years, Dad used the horses when he would put loose hay in the barn. He baled hay once he had a tractor.

In the early years, Dad would milk the cows by hand. He got machines to milk them later. I just hated to wash the machine that separated the milk and cream. I had to do it in the summer. My mother had to go to college in the summer and would be gone during the week and home on weekends. She had to take classes to keep on teaching.

We had a vegetable garden where we got most of our food for summer. My mother had to can a lot of it for the winter. We would go to the woods in the area and pick blueberries. They tasted a lot better than what you get in the stores now.

We had a creek in a special spot where my brother, my cousins, and I would go swimming down the hill from the barn. In the winter, there were a lot of spots where the ponds froze for us to ice skate. There was a hill behind the barn where we would sled. One year, my brother got a real good set of skis for Christmas. Before then, we used an old pair my mother had when she was growing up. He would go down, and then I would on the old set.

We had a wood stove to heat the house.

My brother and I had to bring in wood every day when we got home from school.

In the summertime, my brother and I would get together with a group of friends who had horses and go riding together on Saturdays. By then, we had two horses and rode around the Hale area for a few years.

Before TV, we just had a radio and would listen to the shows. In the 1940s, we liked "The Lone Ranger" and "Let's Pretend."

Growing up on A Gas Station
By Linda Hodges of Midland, Michigan
Born 1952

The earliest memories of my childhood began at my parents' independently owned gas station. Mom and Dad owned and operated Reed's Standard Service in North Lansing for 27 years. Their gas station was unique because a large stone house was attached to the little service station and was perfect for my parents' growing family. My dad fixed car motors in the garage. My mom managed the office and the young men who waited on the customers. I thought we were the richest people in the neighborhood because my folks owned the station.

I learned a lot about life, people, and hard work at my mother's side in my growing up years. In the fifties and sixties, many teenage boys' first jobs were to run to a customer's car, fill the tank, wash the window, check the oil or tires or headlights, and do it all with a smile. Even though I was a girl, I learned all those things at a very early age. One of my first lessons was how to sweep the floor in front of the candy counter. Mom said, "You do not throw the dirt with the broom, you push the dirt with the broom." That way, you wouldn't fill a customer's pant cuffs with dust and gum wrappers. Some of my other jobs included filling the pop cooler and candy counter. I also cleaned the bathrooms.

When I was about seven years old, there was a big change in our lives. US-27, which was the major road in front of the station, was going to be widened to four lanes. The change was good for the community but bad for my folks. The extra width of the road would take away the drive where we pumped gas. It was a dilemma, and what made matters worse was the fact that my mom really loved her big old stone house. The only solution to the problem was to move the house and rebuild the station farther back from the highway. It was not a small feat, but it's what they did. On top of it all, my mom was soon to have my baby brother, Patrick. During that busy time, my parents, the new baby, and I lived in a small travel trailer. My three older brothers lived in the big house that would soon be moved to a lot down the street. I was in school when the time came to actually move the two-story stone house two blocks from the place where it had been built. It's quite a shock to get off the school bus and have the only house you have ever lived in not be there!

I've always been very proud of the Herculean feat that my folks took on; especially at the time they did it. I can't even imagine what the cost of doing what they did would be at today's rates. To this day, my mom, who is 93, still lives in her house. The new station my dad built had run down over the years. Just recently, the building was

Reed's Standard Service before and after

336

bought and renovated into a thriving car repair facility.

My brothers and I all went on to our own families and successful careers. I think each of us learned how to live a productive, creative, and courageous life at the sides of our parents at that corner gas station, just north of Lansing, Michigan.

Games in the Depression Days
By Irene Lange of Saginaw, Michigan
Born 1921

My fondest memories were in the thirties. The neighborhood kids would make up their own games as The Depression was in full swing.

Across the street from our house was a bayou. In the wintertime, the owner of the property would cover the drainage tile, do some flooding and that became our ice skating rink. In all, it was at least a block long. A lot of the kids would come in our house to change into their skates. It was a great warming house. One day, one of the kids hid a pair of shoes, but my mother put a stop to that very fast. We'd have as many as 14 kids lining our basement stairs.

Another winter game was to make a "pie" in the snow. It was a big circle, and from the center hub, we'd make spokes. Some of them didn't connect to the rim; so of course, if you got caught in one of them, you were tagged "it."

In the summer, we made up various games. We'd get our swimsuits on after a rain and run around the trees pulling branches and get a nice shower. Thanks to my grandpa for having many trees. Another game was to take tin cans, stomp on them, and then run up and down the sidewalk making sparks fly. Another was "eenie I over." We'd have sides and throw a ball over the house. Whoever caught the ball would run to the other side. Of course, the thrower never knew which way the catcher of the ball was coming. If you got caught, you threw it over. Throwing over a two-story house was quite a feat. We made up a lot of games for our entertainment and had much fun.

We lived one and a half blocks from school, and in the wintertime when we had snow, it always seemed so deep. Our stockings and boys pants would be wet, so we'd go down to the boiler room to dry off. We didn't have ski pants in those days, but we did have long underwear. We never lingered too long, as the janitor was there to send us up to class.

We thought one of our teachers had eyes in the back of his head. When he'd be at the blackboard, we'd get a bit noisy; he'd call the student's name out to sit down and be quiet. It was a mystery until he told us years later when asked.

A rule at our house was if you got a spanking at school, you'd get one at home also. My grandpa was my first grade teacher. One day, he hit me with the pointer he was using. I don't remember why, but I sure wasn't going to tell my mother. Well, my grandpa told her, so of course, lean over the chair! My third and fourth grade teacher used to have us make a fist, and then she'd hit our knuckles with a ruler. That really hurt.

Some of the radio programs we listened to were "Amos and Andy," "Roy Rogers," "The Lone Ranger and Tonto" and "Stella Dallas." We all sat around the radio so as not to miss a thing. I used to sit in front of the radio and listen to the opera because I hated to dust... anything to prolong the ordeal. I still had to do the dusting. I guess I didn't learn very well; I still don't like to dust.

A Bittersweet Christmas
By Genevieve Morell Gracey of Bad Axe, Michigan
Born 1929

My most memorable Christmas was when I was seven years old. That Christmas Eve at our house was like many before and many to follow, except that year would be a little different because my oldest sister had just given birth to a baby boy. We had a new baby in our lives. He was my parents' first grandchild and my first nephew. Every Christmas Eve after our family supper, my older brothers would light the lantern and go to the barn to milk the cows. It had grown dark and we knew it wouldn't be long before Santa would come. It seemed every year, mother knew exactly when to expect him. She would go outside to feed the dog, and when she came in, she would say, "I think I see a little light coming down the road."

We ran to the window to see, and sure enough, he was coming. We waited to see if he would turn into our driveway, and he did, walking up to our house carrying a lantern and ringing his string of bells. He got closer and closer, the bells grew louder and louder. The excitement we felt soon grew into fright. Now, he was on our front porch, knocking very loud on the door. My brother Floyd, who was two years older than me, opened the door and invited him in.

When I saw him, I remember running and jumping into my dad's lap as he sat in his big rocking chair. I felt secure now. Santa had a rosy red face and big black eyes; his long fur coat almost touched the floor. Surprisingly, he was about the same size as my oldest brother. My brother Floyd then invited him into the living room to see our tree. We all followed him. He asked each of us if we had been good all year and what we would like for Christmas. Then, we had to kneel down and say our prayers. By that time, we were so excited and scared. We didn't remember anything. When he was ready to leave, he would say, "I will be back tonight when you are asleep. Be good, and go to bed early."

All of us younger children when to bed early, but Mom and Dad and some of the older brothers and sisters stayed up and went to midnight mass.

That Christmas morning, my younger sister, my older brother, and I ran downstairs to see if Santa came back and what he gave us. To our surprise, the French door to the living room was locked and a quilt hung on the inside over the door. My brother Floyd soon noticed one corner of the quilt on top had fallen down a little, so he got a chair to stand on and climbed up to look.

He said, "I see a doll in a bed, a doll in a rocking chair and a sled." He pushed me up to have a look. We all ran back upstairs to our parents' bedroom to tell them the good news, that Santa had come and that we saw.

I remember Dad telling Mom to go down and unlock the door. She thought maybe it would be a good idea for us younger children to go to church (mass) first. But, we convinced her otherwise. When she unlocked those doors, I remember taking the doll and rocking chair, and my sister Bernice got the doll and

Genevieve's Christmas doll

bed. My brother Floyd got the sled. I held my doll and rocked her, thinking I was just like my older sister, Sophie who had the new baby. I had one too.

All of a sudden, my grandmother came out of our guest bedroom. She was so confused; she didn't know where she was and who we were. My mother tried to comfort her and said everything will be fine. She was still very confused until my sister Sophie, her husband Cass and baby Elmer came for dinner. I was confused because I didn't know how she got to our house or when she came. Mother explained they brought her home with them from midnight mass.

The sad part about that Christmas is my grandmother, who was so confused. My mother who comforted her, my father whose arms I felt so secure in, and my sister Sophie, her husband Cass and her baby Elmer have all passed on. My little rocking chair that I spent so many hours in over the years is gone. I still have my doll. Her body is limp, and she has a few dark spots on her face, but that comes when you get old. Come Christmas, I will make her a new dress, and the bonnet she will wear was made by a handicapped girl for my baby daughter Marlene. She will take her place under my tree, as our granddaughters will come Christmas Day. They probably won't make much fuss over her; but to me, she is precious. The memories of that Christmas will last a lifetime.

Before the Tech Era
By Marlene Rood of St. Johns, Michigan
Born 1950

Progress is a great thing unless it has gone too far, like it has the past couple decades.

I remember when winter came. As kids, you were always out in the yard playing. Some of those times, you were shoveling a driveway, but winter was fun. Every once in a while, the older brothers of my friends and mine would get our parents car, go out on a back road and tie a toboggan to the rear of the car. Then, three of us girls would get on the toboggan, and the car would take off. After a good distance, we would switch places with some of the boys. Of course, you were not allowed to do this, but all we cared about was how much fun it was. When we were finished, we would go back to our friend's house where their mom would make us hot chocolate from scratch, not from a packet where you just add water.

During the winter, if you were within a mile you walked to school. For girls going to school back then, you had to wear skirts or dresses. To keep warm, you could wear slacks under the skirt/dress but had to take them off once you got to your classroom.

When Christmas came, it would also bring out carolers. We would all get together at our church, get our songbooks, and head out to sing our hearts out. Afterwards, we'd go back to the church for hot chocolate, which was greatly needed. By that time, you were froze from the walk.

It was rare when you would get a store-bought Halloween costume, as they were really limited. The mothers would help us make them. One year, my oldest brother was a mummy. Mom took toilet paper and wrapped him from head to toe. There was this one house at the end of our road where the people would give you candy if you did a trick. A trick to them was anything from a joke to a dance. Those were the days when

you left mom and dad at home, and you walked the neighborhood by yourself. This only happened if you were in a neighborhood with lots of homes. Once you were done trick or treating, you headed for the grade school for a party.

Long before all this wonderful tech era, kids would use their imagination when it was playtime. After supper, we would usually go outside until bedtime and play. During the day, you never knew what you would be doing, from climbing trees, playing hide and seek, football and badminton. I even had a mud pie stand where you would make mud pies or cakes and dry them in the sun.

My mother was a good one for using turpentine on a cut. Once, I accidentally stepped on a rusty spike that went through the bottom of my shoe up through the top. I pulled it out and went to the house where Mom removed my shoe and sock and poured turpentine on it. Another time, I fell off the back steps and scraped my leg from the knee to almost my ankle. Again, the turpentine came out. Let me tell you, that hurt worse than the actual injury.

When it rained, you put on a bathing suit, went out, and played. Mud puddles were a good place to play. Rain was a good time for

Marlene with her brothers, Lyle, Bruce, and Dennis

the car to get washed because you didn't need that extra water to rinse the car. The rain took care of that for you.

Babysitting was a good way to get money. For an hour, you were paid 25 to 50 cents, and there was no fear to babysit for people you didn't know.

As we became old enough to push a lawn mower, you mowed the yard. It was with a manual, people-powered lawn mower. Dad would keep the blades sharp enough. In a family of four, we all took our turn. During the fall, the rakes would come out, and all the leaves would be raked to the road and burned.

When I was about eight or nine, we moved to our new house. The house was built completely by my father and a couple of his friends. Even the closets and drawers were built by hand in knotty pine. There were seven of us in a three-bedroom, one-bath home. There was no dining room, but a big table was in the kitchen. The kitchen was so small; we sat around three sides because one side was up against the wall. My three brothers shared a room, Mom and Dad were in one, and I shared a small bedroom with my grandmother. There was no heat in each room, so it was great sharing a room with Grandma. During the winter, she always kept me warm by snuggling up to me and putting one arm over me.

Since we had no heat in the bedrooms, Mom would come and get our clothes and take them to the living room to get them warm by putting them around a potbelly stove. When you came from playing outside, you would take your scarves, hats, and gloves and put them by the stove. At the bottom of the stove, there were these two pullouts, so you could put your feet up and get warm. Occasionally, we would take our gloves, crusted in snow/ice and snap them on the stove just to hear the sizzle it would make on impact. Oh, the days before the 70s.

Imagine Life Today
By Shirley E. Stoddard of Caro, Michigan
Born 1934

We had a Christmas tree but no electricity, cell phone, TV, microwave, McDonald's or Walmart; there were just dime stores, little grocery stores, and gas stations located every few miles on well-traveled roads. There were larger stores in surrounding towns. There were no Pampers, just cloth diapers. Imagine life today without a handheld remote.

I was born at home, in Denmark Township, Tuscola County, Reese, Michigan, in 1934. My parents were middle class farmers on an 80-acre farm. My maternal grandparents lived with us since the farm was passed down from generation to generation. My great grandparents homesteaded there in 1862, so that makes the farm a centennial farm and is still in the family today.

I feel blessed to have had my grandparents in my early life. I remember sitting on my grandfather's lap when I was three years old and reciting the ABCs that he taught me. I grew up in a home where we were provided the basic needs of love, food, and shelter.

I was the second child of four. I had an older sister Betty Spencer, younger brother Glenn Dinsmore and a younger sister Norma Rickwalt. Kerosene lamps were used for light until our house was wired for electricity in 1939.

Horses were used to till the farmland since my parents did not have a tractor until 1946. There were many Indian artifacts found on a small knoll there. I remember a small orchard where fruit was grown. We always had a large garden, and food was preserved from that. During World War II, gardens were called "Victory Gardens" because other food was sent to feed the soldiers. Some foods were rationed and each person was given a ration book with stamps to purchase some foods. Sugar, coffee, meat, and some canned goods were rationed. I have my ration book with very few stamps used since we were self-sufficient with our own meat, fruit, and vegetables. Very few bananas were ever in the grocery stores. Soap and coffee was hard to get. Silk and nylon were scarce since they were used in life jackets. Gas was also rationed. I believe it was about 10 cents a gallon then.

I remember being very frightened during the latter part of the 1930s. We listened to the news on a battery-powered radio. I remember listening to the radio and conversations of the adults and knew that the US was a target for attack by the Japanese. When they did attack Pearl Harbor on December 7, 1941, the horror magnified.

When the US did become involved in the war, the car factories were turned into defense plants where war materials were made. Ford Motor Co. in Ypsilanti's Willow Run Plant produced 400 bombers a month. The Chrysler Plant in River Rouge made tanks. We visited an uncle in St. Clair Shores and when we went by the Chrysler Plant on M-53, I remember seeing tanks being tested on their grounds. Women took the place of men in the plants. They were called "Rosie the Riveters."

All men 18 years of age or older were classified for the war. My father was deferred because he had four children and was a farmer. I have a German medal taken from a dead German soldier and brought back by an uncle.

I attended the Van Petten School (kindergarten through eighth grade), a one-room country school that was two miles from home. The schools were situated only a few miles apart so the children wouldn't have more than two miles to walk. A huge stove in a back corner of the school heated the school. We carried wood and coal into the school from a small building used to store it. A lot of the time, we walked to school if the weather was nice.

I remember my parents having to come get us from school in the middle of a snowstorm. I believe it was 1947. The roads were impassable by car so they used the tractor and trailer to transport others and us home. The snow was so deep that when a car drove on the roads, the snow banks on the side of the road (when the roads were finally cleared) were higher than the cars. We were snowed in for days without electricity. My father attached a crank to the wheel on the water tank in the basement, and we turned it by hand to get pressure enough to get water. It seemed like the winters were much more severe then, and there was always a lot of snow to play in and ponds to skate on.

There was always a lot to do on the farm. We had work to do in the fields like hoeing, cutting weeds out of the crops, picking corn, putting hay up in the barn for the animals to eat in the winter and straw for their bedding (this was done by hand before bailers came into existence). We had cattle so we had our own milk. My parents had a separator that separated the milk from the cream. They sold the cream to a creamery to be made into butter.

We had chickens; my job was to feed, water and gather eggs that were also sold. At times, the chickens didn't like being disturbed, so when anyone reached in to get the eggs, they would peck the hand. I used a corncob to keep their heads away from my hand. We also had pigs that were sold to a slaughterhouse in Bay City.

Pelts from muskrats and mink were very valuable during the 1940s. My dad trapped in the Quanicasee River, and I remember helping him skin the rats. The pelts were sold to furriers in Bay City. My parents bought a 1942 Hudson from some of the money they received from trapping. It was one of the last cars made before the war. They never did get the spare tire since tires were also scarce and rationed during the war. No cars were manufactured between 1942 and 1946 due to the war.

During the war, we had air raid practices. We were not to have any lights on at night. People went around to check if everyone was following instructions. It was frightening, especially to a child. Thankfully, we never had to go through a real attack.

Air raid shelters were set up in towns. There were signs and arrows to show the designated shelters. I imagine we would have had to use our basement, as is with a storm warning today.

During the second war, there were German prisoners housed at the fairgrounds in Caro, the town in which I now reside. I remember seeing them work in the fields and guards watching them.

While attending grade school and during the war, the students gathered paper, tin cans and milkweed pods. The plants' floss was used as the all-important filler for floatation devices. Prior to the war, the material used for life preservers was Kapok, a fiber cultivated in the rain forests in Asia. Access to that had been cut off. A little more than a pound of milkweed floss could keep a 150-pound man afloat for more than 40 hours. The processing plant for the silky material was located in Petoskey, Michigan. I remember going out into the fields with a burlap bag to pick the pods. We sold them to the US Government, as well as paper and tin. We used the money for special lunches at school. How ironic that we have gone back to recycling paper, metal and plastic. We should have been doing it all along.

Christmas was a lot of fun. We didn't get as many gifts then as kids do now. We always had a Christmas program at school. There was a stage set up, and we spent a lot of time learning lines, etc. Of course, Santa always made an appearance with candy and gifts. We drew names to exchange gifts. We also had a rhythm band. It consisted of blocks, tambourines, sticks, bells or anything to make noise.

I remember going to my paternal grandparents for Christmas. My grandpa would hitch his horses to a sleigh and take all the kids for a ride. I had thirty-two cousins on that side of the family, so we had a lot of fun.

I attended a small country church in the small town of Gilford, which was a mile from home. We had Sunday school and church every week. We also attended Bible School in the summer. I helped with those activities when I got older. I also sang in the choir. I went to high school in Fairgrove, Michigan, and I graduated in 1952. We had a lot of field trips. One that stands out was a football game between Michigan State and the University of Michigan in Ann Arbor. Another standout was our senior trip by train to Washington, D.C. We went by way of "Chessie High School Tours." There were 32 students and two chaperones (teachers). The total cost for the whole trip was $2,177.10. It figures out to be $64.03 per person. Unbelievable! I was senior class treasurer and still have the records.

We did a lot of family activities like a movie if there was an interesting or good one. We went to the Saginaw Zoo a lot, and I remember going to the Barnum Bailey Ringling Brothers three-ring circus at the fairgrounds in Bay City, Michigan. It was in the early 1940s. I remember a clown walking around the ring that circled the performers, and he had a broom in his hand and was sweeping the midway. This probably was Emmett Kelly, since he was with the circus at the time. I have a plaster head of Emmett Kelly, and it is signed by Emmett Kelly, Jr.

There wasn't a lot of time to get into much trouble while I was growing up. I remember having lots of pets (cats and dogs) and the sadness when we would lose one. My older sister was allergic to cow's milk, so we had a goat to supply her with milk. They say goats can eat everything even tin cans. Well, ours didn't eat tin cans but she would chew on the clothes that were hung out to dry. We taught that goat to go from one end of the trailer to the other and watch it go up and down. We also would coax her into the house.

I got married in 1953 and, unfortunately, I lost my husband, Dwain, in 1997. I have six children, three girls, and three boys. I have fourteen grandchildren and five great grandchildren.

My husband was a veteran of the Korean War and belonged to the 17th Regiment, 7th Division Association, and I was able to join as an associate member. There is an annual reunion each year, so I have been able to visit many states, including Alaska and Hawaii. I have seen two presidents in person and watched television as another was assassinated. I have been at a football game when the goal post was torn down after an unexpected victory.

Most of the events of my life would give me much pleasure to re-live, but to face the loss of loved ones again would be painful, "like crossing a bridge over troubled water".

In 1934, the Dione Quints were born. Shirley Temple starred in three movies that year, the average cost of a movie ticket was 23 cents, and a bottle of Pepsi cost 10 cents. The federal prison at Alcatraz Island opened and Al Capone, known as "Scar Face," was locked up there. I had the privilege of visiting there in 2004. "Blue Moon" was a popular song then and is still heard today. Bonnie and Clyde, notorious bank robbers, were killed in a police ambush, Hank Aaron, baseball great, was born. The Civil Works Administration provided employment for millions.

Shirley's family in 1973

342

Shelby, a Compassionate Community
By Linda Benedict Schultz of Muskegon,
Michigan
Born 1948

I was born in Shelby, Michigan in 1948 to Alice Ohlyne Wall Benedict and Howard Thurlow Benedict. My father worked at Rankin Hardware in downtown Shelby for nearly 50 years, and my mother was a stay-at-home wife and mother, later in life working at the Shelby Library.

I attended elementary school in a two-story, four-classroom building between Fifth and Sixth Streets in Shelby. Mrs. Mae Sanford was my kindergarten teacher, and I remember a long, tall sandbox that my classmates and I stood around to play as part of our sharing and socialization time. My first grade teacher was Mrs. Gladys Vanzanten. She was the wife of the school's superintendent. In second grade, I had Mrs. Letha Powers, and Miss Bernice Smith taught my third grade class. Second and third grades were on the second floor of the building. Each morning, two of the children that were assigned, would climb down what seemed like hundreds of stairs to pick up the metal container of small glass milk bottles and carry them back up the stairs to our classroom. Mr. Walter Abbott, the milkman, delivered milk to the school each day. This milk was used during our snack time each morning. Since we were now on the top floor of the building, we had the "fun" of sliding down the inside/outside tube fire escapes during occasional fire drills. Boys would occasionally get in trouble for climbing up the fire escapes during recess!

The girls all wore dresses or skirts and blouses/sweaters to school. When it was cold,

Linda Benedict around 1957 to 1958

we could wear pants under our skirts if we didn't have snow pants. However, girls were not allowed to wear the pants in class. The boys could not wear jeans. Every class had a cloakroom where we hung our coats and left our boots during class time.

In the fourth grade, we moved to the new Thomas Reed Elementary, just behind the two-story building facing Sixth Street. I had Miss Esther Doolittle as my teacher. She was married during the school year, then becoming Mrs. Wiard. Fifth grade was Mrs. Wiard again, and sixth grade I had Mrs. Hazel Balkema.

In the seventh grade, we attended class in the three-story high school building. My teacher was Mr. James Burton. In the eighth grade, we began switching some classes, as the high school students did. We had our own lunch period, which was different from the high school lunchtime. There was no hot lunch program at our school, so everyone brought a sack lunch. After eating, we were allowed to clear the floor of desks in our homeroom and turn music on to dance during the remainder of lunchtime.

My parents were always very active in the Methodist church. They both sang in the choir and were a part of many committees. My mother taught Sunday school and Bible School during the summer months. She also was a part of the Child Evangelism Program of Oceana County and voluntarily went to many area churches telling stories with her felt board of biblical characters. During the summer months, the migrant workers came to Oceana County to pick fruit crops; she would gather her props and head to the migrant camps. I remember sitting on the ground with so many little Spanish children listening to the Bible stories she told.

Another memory with my mother was hiking to Piper Creek, which was located in a wooded area near my home. We spent many days walking the trail together, climbing atop fallen tree trunks, and jumping over those that blocked the path. It was fun picking wildflowers and observing the habits of small wild life and hearing the sounds of the beautiful birds. Once we arrived at the creek, we followed it for a while, looking for little fish, pretty leaves, and unusual stones.

At a young age, I joined a group of children for swimming lessons. There were no pools outside of homes or in our school, so we were bussed to Stony Lake for these lessons several times a week during the summer months.

When I was a little older, I remember picking cherries for local fruit farmers in the summer. It was sometimes very uncomfortable picking all day in the heat, but it was a way of making some extra money. The Mexican migrant workers and their families were very hard workers and picked very fast and long hours, as this was their only income. Most migrant workers would come from Texas in the summer and then head back south before school started to harvest the crops in the southern states during the winter months.

The Shelby Pavilion was a great way to spend Saturday mornings. As I grew older, I went to the Saturday night skates. Burdette and Estella McClouth owned and operated the rink during my first years there, but Nick and Dottie Elliott took over the reigns and had a lot of different activities there for all aged kids. There was a teen dance there on Friday nights where everyone gathered after football and basketball games during the school year and as an evening of fun in the summer.

When I entered high school, I made many new friends, as kids from the surrounding country elementary schools (Benona, Blooming Valley, Ferry, New Era, Shelby Center, and Piper schools) joined our class.

I played clarinet in the band and enjoyed marching for parades and football halftime shows. Mr. Richard Granger produced some excellent bands while there.

In July 1965, my senior year in high school, we hosted a foreign exchange student from Northern Ireland for the year. Her name was Alison Bain. She and I became very close throughout the year and have remained in touch with each other, each visiting the other on occasion. Her brother, Fergus, traveled to the USA for her high school graduation.

I remember being able to go to the gas station and put $0.50 worth of gas so my Dad wouldn't realize I had driven his car as far as I had! Unfortunately, living in a small town, everyone knew my dad, and the gas station owner was happy to let him know his daughter had been in to see him!

Shelby was such a friendly, caring, and compassionate community. Kids were always put first, supported, and protected by everyone in the town. I can't imagine my life having a better beginning than this wholesome, American lifestyle filled with so many wonderful people.

Howard, Alice Ohlyne, and Linda Benedict

My Memories

My Memories

Index A
Hometown

Alice Galster Cook	Big Rapids	Michigan	226
D. L. Farnham	Big Rapids	Michigan	25
Bernie Kelsch	Big Rapids	Michigan	107
Florence Pemberton	Big Rapids	Michigan	37
Mirdza S. Randall	Big Rapids	Michigan	53
Bertha Cross	Blanchard	Michigan	130
Bernard "Barney" Barnett	Branch	Michigan	122
Patricia Buckley	Branch	Michigan	253
Madeleine J. Reagan	Branch	Michigan	323
Susan Granger	Breckenridge	Michigan	204
Joy McCrory	Breckenridge	Michigan	275
Jack Thornton	Byron Center	Michigan	273
Robert A. Bellomo	Canadian Lakes	Michigan	86
Kent Graf	Caro	Michigan	204
Shirley E. Stoddard	Caro	Michigan	340
Thomas Haradine	Carson City	Michigan	94
Mildred Peterson	Chase	Michigan	174
Patricia Alden	Chesaning	Michigan	174
Rich Greenfelder	Chesaning	Michigan	234
Beverly Barker	Clare	Michigan	286
Patricia A. Haring	Clare	Michigan	163
Erma Ott Kleinhardt	Clare	Michigan	277
Kenneth Warner, Sr.	Clare	Michigan	190
William J. White	Clare	Michigan	200
Jerry J. Konopnicki	Coleman	Michigan	137
Michael E. Johnson	Custer	Michigan	321
James M. Shoup	Custer	Michigan	267
Barbara Best	Dewitt	Michigan	90
Sally L. Kioski	Durand	Michigan	327
Tuesday Summers	Durand	Michigan	257
Mabel B. Crooks	Edmore	Michigan	45
Ronald Hoodak	Elmira	New York	122
Mary Ann Hale	Elwell	Michigan	254
Dolores Howell	Essexville	Michigan	309
Joan S. Pavlick	Essexville	Michigan	271
Janet Coleman	Evart	Michigan	58
Floyd W. Schmid	Farwell	Michigan	238
Evelyn Genson Urban	Fountain	Michigan	291
Dorothy Conrad	Freeland	Michigan	173
Viola A. Forro	Freeland	Michigan	203
Richard "Dick" Guttowsky	Freeland	Michigan	49
Carolyn Lawmaster	Freeland	Michigan	103
Richard Redifer	Freeland	Michigan	79
Clyde Shaffner	Freeland	Michigan	52
Doris Barnhard	Fremont	Michigan	317
John Devries	Fremont	Michigan	271
Pauline Grant	Fremont	Michigan	331
Betty Jacobus	Fremont	Michigan	270
Jeannette Johnson	Fremont	Michigan	271
Cora Longstreet	Fremont	Michigan	110
Helen Van Andel	Fremont	Michigan	270
Barbara J. Langley	Gladwin	Michigan	69
Wanda Ogg	Gladwin	Michigan	41
Lola Wright Steele	Gladwin	Michigan	147

Florence M. Martin	Gowen	Michigan	24
Pamela Lillie Newman	Gowen	Michigan	250
Timothy L. Perry	Grand Ledge	Michigan	84
Reva Swanson	Grand Ledge	Michigan	128
Thomas M. Boursisseau	Grand Rapids	Michigan	72
Awilda Whitehill	Grand Rapids	Michigan	256
Joan Ransom	Grant	Michigan	322
Patti Gustin	Green Valley	Arizona	74
Linda Collins	Greenville	Michigan	28
Joanne Lee Durham	Greenville	Michigan	140
Judy Laux	Greenville	Michigan	44
Gerald Meade	Greenville	Michigan	35
Loretta R. Merritt	Greenville	Michigan	67
Martha Schoolcraft	Greenville	Michigan	129
George Fabera	Hale	Michigan	54
Connie Alvesteffer	Hart	Michigan	325
Joseph H. Fishel	Hart	Michigan	160
Clara B. Lozen	Hart	Michigan	323
Carol Jurek	Hemlock	Michigan	31
Patricia Murphy	Hemlock	Michigan	138
Frederick J. Karnes	Hersey	Michigan	169
Velma Grey	Hesperia	Michigan	178
Winnona Evanauski	Holton	Michigan	136
Karen Rolley	Hope	Michigan	175
Grace Yanke	Howard City	Michigan	205
Laurence Gibson	Hudsonville	Michigan	316
Katherine Barnes	Ithaca	Michigan	266
Waneta Bender	Ithaca	Michigan	114
Mary Ciszek	Kawkawlin	Michigan	203
Keith Hardy	Kawkawlin	Michigan	112
Harold Wright	Kent City	Michigan	167
Charlene Laper	Lakeview	Michigan	76
Barbara Green Martin	Lakewood	Colorado	297
Lois Baumer	Lansing	Michigan	33
Ruby Klanecky	Lansing	Michigan	88
Alta Reed	Lansing	Michigan	117
Lorraine Underwood Wright	Lansing	Michigan	277
Dorothy Baer Wolf	Lapeer	Michigan	72
Bonnie Carroll	Lewiston	Michigan	333
Mildred Cline	Lewiston	Michigan	313
Thomas A. Coleman	Ludington	Michigan	143
Elizabeth J. Gardner	Ludington	Michigan	188
Elizabeth Hepworth	Ludington	Michigan	187
Sharon Hilyard	Ludington	Michigan	111
Margaret M. Holey	Ludington	Michigan	197
Paul Kruska	Ludington	Michigan	215
Michael R. Miller	Ludington	Michigan	258
Carl Patterson	Marion	Michigan	22
Bamber Barnes	Merrill	Michigan	330
Frank J. Gotts	Merrill	Michigan	273
Mary Jane Michael	Merrill	Michigan	333
Luann L. Ludwick	Mesa	Arizona	131
Agnes Jason	Middleton	Michigan	207
Anita Barrett	Midland	Michigan	174

Barbara Boyer	Midland	Michigan	290
Marilyn F. Clink	Midland	Michigan	138
Connie DeLong	Midland	Michigan	321
Betty Gaffee	Midland	Michigan	99
Robert Gofton	Midland	Michigan	83
Linda Hodges	Midland	Michigan	336
Keith A. Humbert	Midland	Michigan	137
Helen Johnson	Midland	Michigan	194
Lois Laplow	Midland	Michigan	176
Shirley Larson	Midland	Michigan	26
Jean S. Mathieu	Midland	Michigan	25
John McMillan	Midland	Michigan	227
Elaine L. Onan	Midland	Michigan	245
Tresa Pangborn	Midland	Michigan	287
Jean Parkinson	Midland	Michigan	100
Norma Seelye	Midland	Michigan	183
Phyllis Jean Short	Midland	Michigan	193
Gloria Woodbury	Midland	Michigan	190
Rollin Yeakle	Midland	Michigan	195
Lloyd David Ball	Morley	Michigan	30
Marjorie Barrett	Mt. Pleasant	Michigan	299
Raymond A. Elliott	Mt. Pleasant	Michigan	171
Karen Elliott-Grover	Mt. Pleasant	Michigan	171
Richard E. Hartlep	Mt. Pleasant	Michigan	91
Joanne Hetherington	Mt. Pleasant	Michigan	73
Evald Kruut	Mt. Pleasant	Michigan	73
Richard Floyd Lumbert	Mt. Pleasant	Michigan	333
Virginia Showalter	Mt. Pleasant	Michigan	134
Norma Aebig Halverson	Muskegon	Michigan	52
Linda Benedict Schultz	Muskegon	Michigan	343
Dennette McDermott	Natchitoches	Louisiana	40
Judy Pranger	New Era	Michigan	54
Alan Van Duinen	New Era	Michigan	324
Nancy Carlson	Newaygo	Michigan	262
Donna Carpenter	Newaygo	Michigan	17
Susan Cunningham Kane	Newaygo	Michigan	280
Robert K. Robart	Newaygo	Michigan	314
Bob Walker	Petoskey	Michigan	222
Ronald Sampson	Pigeon	Michigan	40
Janet Krzysik DeCatur	Pinconning	Michigan	209
Helen Rice	Pinconning	Michigan	142
Carol L. Salgat	Pinconning	Michigan	210
Edwin W. Jablonski	Prescott	Michigan	113
Mary J. Heiskala	Prunedale	California	213
Joshua Clark	Reed City	Michigan	72
Lynn Holmquist	Reed City	Michigan	46
Creal Hoover	Reed City	Michigan	119
Richard K. Karns	Reed City	Michigan	60
Betty J. Van Alstine	Reed City	Michigan	175
Keith Van Sickle	Reed City	Michigan	186
Shirley A. Weber	Richville	Michigan	61
Sharon Kathleen Smith	Rincon	Michigan	159
Wayne George Aebig	Rothbury	Michigan	27
Barbara L. Orlando	Rothbury	Michigan	43

David J. Banaszek	Saginaw	Michigan	150
Bruce A. Beckert	Saginaw	Michigan	137
Barbara Ann Bell	Saginaw	Michigan	135
Elizabeth L. Berg	Saginaw	Michigan	243
Rosalie Bierlein	Saginaw	Michigan	182
Virginia (Ginny) Bouchey	Saginaw	Michigan	224
Donald Brady	Saginaw	Michigan	93
Edward Breitkreitz	Saginaw	Michigan	93
Mary Bremer	Saginaw	Michigan	261
William Denzer	Saginaw	Michigan	42
Paul R. Desander	Saginaw	Michigan	161
Sandra Dobrowolsky	Saginaw	Michigan	334
Lois Doran	Saginaw	Michigan	66
Roselynn Ederer	Saginaw	Michigan	219
Donald E. Elliott	Saginaw	Michigan	135
Thomas M. Evon	Saginaw	Michigan	68
Carolyn Fleming	Saginaw	Michigan	43
William Fleming	Saginaw	Michigan	66
Melvin J. Gay	Saginaw	Michigan	311
Margaret Harris	Saginaw	Michigan	240
Sandra L. Hecht	Saginaw	Michigan	165
Robert Gregor Hegler	Saginaw	Michigan	217
Patricia Hubbert	Saginaw	Michigan	303
Edwin W. Iles	Saginaw	Michigan	192
Bille D. Jex	Saginaw	Michigan	23
Merrily Ann Johnson	Saginaw	Michigan	231
Betty-Ann Jolin	Saginaw	Michigan	293
Karl H. Klein	Saginaw	Michigan	57
Marsha A. Klein	Saginaw	Michigan	198
Betty Konesko	Saginaw	Michigan	225
Rula Koutras	Saginaw	Michigan	256
Irene Lange	Saginaw	Michigan	337
Louraine T. Latty	Saginaw	Michigan	126
Alberta Leiner	Saginaw	Michigan	334
Bruce Kenneth Lennox	Saginaw	Michigan	46
Jack L. Long	Saginaw	Michigan	47
Esther A. Mack	Saginaw	Michigan	136
Hayes J. Mack	Saginaw	Michigan	135
Dorothy Clark McKandes	Saginaw	Michigan	48
DeVere Mosher	Saginaw	Michigan	44
Doris Murray	Saginaw	Michigan	266
Eugene Olivares	Saginaw	Michigan	104
Alice Piechotte	Saginaw	Michigan	50
Laura Sue Piechowiak	Saginaw	Michigan	20
Jerry Pietrzak	Saginaw	Michigan	233
Janet M. Reis	Saginaw	Michigan	177
Marian K. Rodriquez	Saginaw	Michigan	110
Venessa I. Rosenfield	Saginaw	Michigan	252
Delores F. Schmidt	Saginaw	Michigan	147
Jerry Schmolitz	Saginaw	Michigan	73
Joyce Abler Schumacher	Saginaw	Michigan	229
Emily Slivinski	Saginaw	Michigan	325
Jerry Slivinski	Saginaw	Michigan	325
Katherine Smekar	Saginaw	Michigan	35

Lillian M. Smokoska	Saginaw	Michigan	24
Ann M. Stueber	Saginaw	Michigan	34
Marion Frahm Tincknell	Saginaw	Michigan	152
Nellie Mae Everett Turner	Saginaw	Michigan	301
Louis H. Witting	Saginaw	Michigan	259
Marilyn Witting	Saginaw	Michigan	98
Wayne E. Diveley	Sanford	Michigan	16
Oliver "Ollie" Leigeb	Sanford	Michigan	120
Charles Robinson	Sanford	Michigan	123
Nancy Wrathell	Sanford	Michigan	53
Sandra Palmer Zilincik	Sanford	Michigan	272
Edwin M. Koziol	Scottville	Michigan	156
Floyd Fox	Shelby	Michigan	283
Joyce Griffin	Shelby	Michigan	73
Richard Lound	Shelby	Michigan	89
Debby Mitteer	Shelby	Michigan	77
Mary Morningstar	Shelby	Michigan	82
Theodore G. Zoulek	Shelby	Michigan	144
Antonette Groulx	Shepherd	Michigan	304
Richard Langin	Sheridan	Michigan	23
Ilene R. Thomsen	Sidney	Michigan	148
Richard L. Browne	St. Charles	Michigan	179
Ruth Ann Bradley	St. Johns	Michigan	264
Marlene Rood	St. Johns	Michigan	339
Rita Morgan	St. Louis	Michigan	56
Alma Moyes	St. Louis	Michigan	36
Joan L. Mulder	St. Louis	Michigan	212
Michael O. Patterson	St. Louis	Michigan	18
Sharon Reavis	St. Louis	Michigan	88
Marion Tedhams	St. Louis	Michigan	253
Mary Lou Ely	Stanton	Michigan	111
Donna Hart	Stanton	Michigan	80
Sharon Ritter	Stanton	Michigan	97
Nicholas S. Green	Stanwood	Michigan	23
Diane Lintemuth	Stanwood	Michigan	334
Jack Hitchcock	Stoughton	Wisconsin	124
Marian (Fabera) Neely	Tebbetts	Missouri	295
Mable Johnston	Tucker	Georgia	241
Clayton Brauher	Vestaburg	Michigan	47
Thelma Brauher	Vestaburg	Michigan	112
Dolores Stack	Vestaburg	Michigan	179
Donna Jean Faragher Dettloff	West Branch	Michigan	328
Mary L. Cotton	White Cloud	Michigan	63
Kay Kantola	White Cloud	Michigan	205